mbia

The McGraw·Hill Companies

SPORT PSYCHOLOGY: CONCEPTS AND APPLICATIONS, SEVENTH EDITION
International Edition 2012

10 09 08 07 06 05 04 03 02 01
20 15 14 13 12 11
CTP   ANL

When ordering this title, use ISBN: 978-007-108622-6 or MHID: 007-108622-6

Printed in Singapore

www.mhhe.com

Contents

Chapter 19
Negative Aspects of Sport and Exercise   462

Preface

In recent years, interest in applied sport and exercise psychology has soared. *Sport Psychology: Concepts and Applications* is written for students who are interested in learning about sport and exercise psychology as an academic discipline *and* in using that knowledge in applied settings. The book is designed primarily for upper-level undergraduate students, but instructors can easily adapt the book as a foundation text for graduate students by supplementing the text with current articles from sport psychology journals.

The focus of the book is reflected both in the subtitle and in the "Concept and Application" boxes that appear throughout the chapters. The concepts and applications presented are all supported by scientific research. Where research has led to inconsistent conclusions, concepts and applications have been derived based on the preponderance of the evidence.

As in all earlier editions, the title *Sport Psychology* has been retained as opposed to the longer term *Sport and Exercise Psychology*. This usage reflects the view that that *sport psychology* is a broad and readily recognized term used by educators and psychologists worldwide. The text is divided into six major parts. The first four parts are devoted specifically to sport psychology topics, while parts 5 and 6 are devoted to social psychology of sport and psychobiology of sport and exercise respectively. If an instructor wishes to focus exclusively on sport psychology topics, then parts 1 through 4 would suffice. However, if a broader perspective is desired, then parts 5 and 6 could be included.

New to the Seventh Edition

The seventh edition of this textbook includes three new chapters: Chapter 5, "Youth Sports" discusses the goals and outcomes and the relationships among participants of youth sports programs; Chapter 8, "Alternatives to Inverted-U Theory" discusses alternative theories regarding athlete emotions; and Chapter 19, "Negative Aspects of Sport and Exercise" covers drug abuse, eating disorders, exercise dependence, muscle dysmorphia, and burnout in sport. In addition to the new chapters listed above, the book's content has been updated throughout with the latest research findings. Approximately 800 new references have been cited in the seventh edition. Some of the important changes and additions to the text are as follows:

Part 1: Foundations of Sport Psychology

Part 1 includes two chapters. Chapter 1, "Sport Psychology: A Discipline and Profession," focuses on introductory material, such as history, professional issues, certification, ethics, accreditation, and multicultural issues dealing with race and gender. Of note, the history section has been expanded to include noteworthy contributions from Europe and the United Kingdom. Chapter 2, "Personality as the Core Characteristic of the Individual," discusses relatively permanent dispositions of the athlete. New material on emotional intelligence and mental resilience are treated in this focused chapter.

Part 2: Motivation in Sport and Exercise

Part 2 includes three chapters. Chapter 3, "Self-Confidence and Intrinsic Motivation," contains new research that supports the integrated model of intrinsic and extrinsic motivation. Several new inventories were introduced that measure self-determined motivation. In addition, the "hot hand" phenomenon in psychological momentum was revisited and the concepts obsessive and harmonious passion was introduced. Chapter 4, "Goal Perspective Theory," introduces dispositional goal orientations and situation-specific motivational climates. A new inventory titled the Achievement Goals Questionnaire for Sports (AGQ-S) was introduced and its theoretical importance discussed. Sportspersonship was discussed as it relates to prosocial and antisocial behavior. New material on the matching hypothesis and antecedents and outcomes of goal orientation were introduced and discussed. Chapter 5, "Youth Sports," is a new chapter that expands on material that was previously a subsection to Chapter 3 in the sixth edition of *Sport Psychology*. New material discusses the coach, parent, and peer relationships; goal perspective and motivational climate; and issues associated with developing a youth sport program. These topics should be especially relevant to students who will be entering the workforce as physical education teachers or coaches.

Part 3: Effects of Attention, Emotion, and Mood on Performance

Part 3 includes three chapters. Chapter 6, "Attention and Concentration in Sport and Exercise," explains the important role that quality attention plays in the execution of skilled motor performance. New to this chapter is a discussion of the mechanisms that bring together the relationship between attention and performance. Chapter 7, "Anxiety, Stress, and Mood Relationships," describes the interactive relationships and meaning of the terms *anxiety, stress*, and *mood*; as well as explaining how each influences athletic performance. New to this chapter is a discussion of the role of perfectionism in sport and how perfectionism influences performance as well as how perfectionism is measured. Also new to this chapter is the treatment of mood states and how they also influence athletic performance. The new Chapter 8, "Alternatives to Inverted-U Theory," is devoted to alternative theories. This chapter builds on the sixth edition by expanding coverage of Hanin's zone of optimal functioning to include information on emotions generally, and to introduce and explain the probabilistic model for determining an

individual affect-related performance zone (IAPZ). Each of the presented alternatives to inverted-U theory have also been updated.

Part 4: Cognitive and Behavioral Interventions

Part 4 includes four chapters. Chapter 9, "Coping and Intervention Strategies in Sport," analyzes coping, self-talk, relaxation strategies, and arousal energizing strategies. New to this chapter are topics related to sources of stress and coping responses, the measurement of self-talk, and integrative mind-body training. Chapter 10, "Goal Setting in Sport," explains the mechanics of goal setting and how goals can be energizing and motivational. New to this chapter is a discussion on goal setting and goal perspective relationships. Chapter 11, "Imagery and Hypnosis in Sport," describes imagery and hypnosis as interventions that influence both cognition and motivation. New to this chapter is a discussion of the functional equivalence hypothesis as it relates to imagery and to PETTLEP based imagery. Chapter 12, "Psychological Skills Training," outlines psychological methods designed to develop psychological skill in sport. New to this chapter are discussions on mental toughness, spirituality, superstitious behavior, and a mindfulness-acceptance-commitment approach to psychological skill training.

Part 5: Social Psychology of Sport

Part 5 includes four chapters. Chapter 13, "Aggression and Violence in Sport," contains examples, theories, and explanations of aggression by athletes in sport. New to this chapter is a discussion of perceived legitimacy of aggression in sport, and an expanded explanation of moral development as it relates to aggression. Chapter 14, "Audience and Self-Presentation Effects in Sport," describes the effect that an audience of one or more has upon athletic performance, as well as a consideration of self-presentation and self-handicapping. Chapter 15, "Team Cohesion in Sport," discusses factors that determine team cohesion and consequences of team cohesion with an emphasis on performance and individual satisfaction. Chapter 16, "Leadership and Communication in Sport," goes over major theories of leadership with a specific focus on situation-specific sport models of leadership. New to this chapter are discussions of Smith's sport personality contingency model of leadership, a coaching competency model of predicting outcome, and Jowett's 3 + 1 Cs model of coach-athlete relationships.

Part 6: Psychobiology of Sport and Exercise

Part 6 includes three chapters. Chapter 17, "Exercise Psychology," outlines selected topics that make up the sport psychology subdiscipline of exercise psychology. New to this chapter are expanded treatments of the important topics of exercise intensity (dual-mode hypothesis, circumplex model), the effects of exercise on cognitive function, applied self-determination theory, and the drive for muscularity. Chapter 18, "The Psychology of Athletic Injuries and Career Termination," discusses psychological antecedents and rehabilitation from athletic injuries. New to this chapter are an expansion of the section on emotional response to injury, the use of writing to reduce emotional trauma, the use of music to reduce pain, the psychology of returning to competition following rehabilitation, and a discussion of career termination due to injury and other causes. The new Chapter 19, "Negative Aspects of Sport and Exercise," brings together a discussion of negative effects of drug abuse, exercise dependence, eating disorders, muscle dysmorphia, and burnout on athlete behavior. This chapter consolidates the content on these negative aspects of exercise and competition so that students can better analyze their interrelationships.

Pedagogical Aids

Several pedagogical aids are included in the text for the benefit of the students, instructors, and coaches. Most significantly, many sports-related examples are included to illustrate chapter topics. In addition, "Concept & Application" boxes appear throughout the chapters, following the introduction of major themes and topics. The concepts are derived from pertinent scientific literature, and the applications are designed to assist practitioners in making practical use of research findings in their day-to-day teaching and coaching activities.

Also included in each chapter are a list of key terms, a chapter summary, critical thought questions, and a glossary of terms. The key terms are listed at the beginning of the chapter to focus students' attention on the important concepts they will encounter in the chapter. These same key terms appear in boldface type when they are introduced in the text and are defined in the chapter ending glossary.

Supplements

Available with Sport Psychology is an Online Learning Center at www.mhhe.com/cox7e. The student side of the Online Learning Center includes a recommended reading list and review questions for each chapter. The instructor side of the Online Learning Center includes sample course syllabi and PowerPoint slide presentations for each chapter. Instructors should contact their McGraw-Hill sales representative for a username and password for this site.

Organizations Associated with Sport Psychology

For additional information on topics in sport and - exercise psychology, instructors and students may wish to consult any of the following Web sites. Please note, however, that while these Websites were correct at time of publications, they are subject to change.

Sport Psychology Organizations

- Association for Applied Sport Psychology (AASP). www.appliedsportpsych.org/

- Division 47 of the American Psychological Association (APA). www.apa47.org/

- North American Society for the Psychology of Sport and Physical Activity (NASPSPA). www.naspspa.org/

- Canadian Society for Psychomotor Learning and Sport Psychology (SCAPPS). www.scapps.org/

- European Federation of Sport Psychology (EFSP/FEPAC). www.fepsac.org/

USA National Organizations with a Sport Psychology Sub-focus

- American Alliance for Health, Physical Education, Recreation and Dance (AAHPERD). www.aahperd.org/

- American College of Sports Medicine (ACSM). www.acsm.org/

CourseSmart eTextbooks

This text is available as an eTextbook from CourseSmart, a new way for faculty to find and review eTextbooks. It's also a great option for students who are interested in accessing their course materials digitally and saving money. CourseSmart offers thousands of the most commonly adopted textbooks across hundreds of courses from a wide variety of higher education publishers. It is the only place for faculty to review and compare the full text of a textbook online, providing immediate access without the environmental impact of requesting a print exam copy. At CourseSmart, students can save up to 50% off the cost of a print book, reduce their impact on the environment, and gain access to powerful web tools for learning including full text search, notes and highlighting, and email tools for sharing notes between classmates. For further details contact your sales representative or go to www.coursesmart.com.

McGraw-Hill Create
www.mcgrawhillcreate.com

Craft your teaching resources to match the way you teach! With McGraw-Hill Create you can easily rearrange chapters, combine material from other content sources, and quickly upload content you have written like your course syllabus or teaching notes. Find the content you need in Create by searching through thousands of leading McGraw-Hill textbooks. Arrange your book to fit your teaching style. Create even allows you to personalize your book's appearance by selecting the cover and adding your name, school, and course information. Order a Create book and you'll receive a complimentary print review copy in 3–5 business days or a complimentary electronic review copy (eComp) via email in about one hour. Go to www.mcgrawhillcreate.com today and register. Experience how McGraw-Hill Create empowers you to teach *your* students *your* way.

Acknowledgments

I am indebted to a host of people who have contributed to the completion of this work. First, I am grateful to my wife, Linda, for her patience and support. Second, I am appreciative of the terrific work of the Interlibrary Loan Department at Ellis Library on the University of Missouri-Columbia campus. They have been truly wonderful. Third, I am grateful for all of the assistance I have received from McGraw-Hill editors as I have worked through the seventh edition of this textbook. Fourth, I am grateful to all those instructors in North America and throughout the world who have adopted my textbook for use in their university courses. Finally, I am indebted to the following reviewers who contributed excellent suggestions and feedback to ensure that the book is a success:

Rick Albrecht
Grand Valley State University

Doug Berry
Paradise Valley Community College

Robert Brustad
University of Northern Colorado

Teresa Marino Carper
University of Central Florida

Lindsay Edwards
University of Houston

Martha E. Ewing
Michigan State University

Russell Medbery
Colby-Sawyer College

Ron Mulson
Hudson Valley Community College

Richard K. Stratton
Virginia Tech

Brad Vickers
Mississippi State University

Foundations of Sport Psychology

Part 1 of this text is composed of two distinct chapters. The first chapter, "Sport Psychology: A Discipline and Profession," provides a framework for understanding, among other things, what sport psychology is; where it came from (a brief history); what professional organizations are involved; how one becomes a sport psychologist; the role of multicultural education; and gender issues that impact the lives of athletes, coaches, and everyone interested in the sport and exercise psychology culture. The second foundation chapter deals with personality of the athlete and is entitled "Personality as a Core Characteristic of the Individual." In this chapter we define personality, introduce theories of personality, discuss ways that personality is measured, and discuss how personality affects sport performance.

The following historical event provides an example of why sport is so exciting, and why sport psychologists are interested in understanding everything they can about the personality and psychology of athletes at all levels, from youth sport to professional sport. In the 1999 National League Professional Baseball Championship Series, the Atlanta Braves were pitted against the New York Mets. Atlanta won the first two games in Atlanta and won the third game in New York. The Mets won game four in New York. The Braves led the series 3–1 before game number five at New York's Shea Stadium. Game number five was to become one of the most exciting baseball games ever played in Major League Baseball history. As described by Bamberger (1999), "On Sunday night at half past nine on the East Coast, time stopped." The New York Mets were at bat and the Atlanta Braves were in the field. The lead-off hitter was Shawon Dunston, with his team trailing 2 to 3 in the bottom of the fifteenth inning.

Dunston fouled off pitch after pitch and finally stroked a single to center field. Dunston stole second and later walked home to tie the score at 3 to 3. Now it was Robin Ventura's turn to bat. Bases were loaded and Ventura was facing rookie right-hander Kevin McGlinchy. Ventura was 1 for 18 thus far in the series. With two strikes against him, he made the swing that a ballplayer dreams about. He hit a two-strike pitch into the rain and through the night over the right center field wall. It was a grand slam! After reaching first base Robin was mobbed by players and fans, so he never made it to home plate—or second base, for that matter. The official score was 4–3, and Ventura was credited with a single to end the longest postseason game ever, five hours and forty-five minutes. During the game 126 batters came to the plate, but only seven scored (officially). ∽

CHAPTER 1

Sport Psychology: A Discipline and Profession

KEY TERMS

Accreditation
Acculturation
Clinical/counseling sport
  psychologist
Coubertin, Pierre de
Cultural compatibility model
Cultural competence
Diversity
Educational sport psychologist
Enculturation
Evidence-based practice
Feminism
Gay
Griffith, Coleman
Heterosexist behavior
Heterosexual
Homophobia
Homophobic behavior
Homosexual
Hostile environment
  harassment
Inclusiveness
Lesbian
Martens, Rainer
Multicultural training
Ogilvie, Bruce
Positive psychology
Puni, Avksenty Cezarevich
Quid pro quo harassment

Race thinking
Racist thinking
Research sport psychologist
Roudik, Piotr Antonovich
Sexism
Sexual orientation

Sport Psychology Registry
Triplett, Norman
Universalistic model
USOC
White privilege

Hardly a subject associated with sport is more intriguing than the subject of sport psychology. Perhaps this is so because it is a subject coaches, athletes, and fans feel comfortable discussing. The average spectator does not usually venture to offer a biomechanical explanation for an athlete's achievement of a near-superhuman feat, yet the same spectator is often willing to give a psychological explanation (e.g., mental toughness, motivation, strength of character). Every four years, sport fans from all over the world become transfixed by the spectacle of the Summer or Winter Olympic Games. Throughout the television broadcasts of these games, viewers are exposed to frequent references to athletes who train with the aid of professional sport psychologists. Many times the sport psychologist will be identified as the camera zooms in on the individual athlete. It is also becoming somewhat common for television crews to identify professional golfers who employ the services of sport psychologists. Somewhat recently, a sport psychologist was given credit for the Indianapolis Colts' decision to select Peyton Manning over Ryan Leaf in the 1998 professional football draft (Carey, 1999). Manning went on to stardom in Indianapolis, while Leaf continued to struggle for several years with the San Diego Chargers and other teams. Over the years, selected professional baseball teams have acquired the services of applied sport psychologists. At the present time there are many young people seeking to earn a living providing sport psychology services to professional, Olympic, or even collegiate sports teams. Hopefully, these young people will acquire the knowledge, experience, and certification/licensure that will allow them to realize their dreams.

One wonders, however, who will provide sport psychology services to the coaches and players of millions of youth and high school sports teams that do not have the financial resources to employ a full- or even part-time sport psychologist. The goal of providing sport psychology services to every coach and athlete is unrealistic. A better goal might be to train coaches and athletes to serve as their own sport psychology consultants and to train one another. The ultimate goal of a sport psychology consultant should be to teach clients to teach or counsel themselves.

Think of the marvelous example of coaching that was provided by UCLA's legendary John Wooden, and contrast that with the intimidation style of former Indiana and Texas Tech coach Bob Knight. Either John Wooden was a great applied sport psychologist, or he had someone on his staff who was. Knight, on the other hand, has been an example of a coach in desperate need of a sport psychologist to help him relate in a positive way with his athletes and fellow coaches. Bill Walton said it best:

> With Coach Wooden, an Indiana native, life was always fun, always upbeat, always positive, always about the team, always about the greatness of the game. Sadly you don't get any sense of that from Knight. There's no joy. Even worse, there's no happiness on the faces of his players (Walton, 2000, p. 96).

As a student of sport psychology, you may not go on to become a consultant to a professional team, but hopefully you will be able to apply what you have learned from this book and to share it with others.

As we begin our discussion of sport psychology, it is important to introduce two relatively new emphases within psychology generally and sport psychology specifically. These are the concepts of positive psychology and evidence-based practice. **Positive psychology** is an approach to human behavior that focuses upon wellness and not merely absence of disease. A focus upon quality of life and the positive aspects of psychology will have the effect of preventing mental illness before it can start (Gordon, 2008; Seligman & Csikszentmihalyi, 2000). This is the approach to sport psychology that we will focus upon throughout the text. In many ways, sport psychology has always focused upon a wellness or positive approach to psychology. **Evidence-based practice** underscores the notion that sound application and practice must be based upon good science (Gill, 2009; Moore, 2007). Sport psychology must continue to develop as a scientific discipline in such a manner that an evidence-based body of knowledge is developed. In an important review article, Gardner (2009) addressed the issue of evidence-based practice and asked three fundamental questions about the discipline of sport psychology: (1) can sport psychology claim to be a scientific discipline? (2) Why has there not been more emphasis upon professional advancement and scientific development? (3) Various interventions have been proposed to bring about psychological change in athletes, but why has there not been more emphasis upon identifying the mechanisms that allow meaningful change? Relative to this third question, if it is believed that one variable causes or has an effect on a second variable, can a third variable be identified that mediates or moderates (modifies) this effect? This would be an example of a mechanism of change. These and other questions need to be asked about the development of sport psychology as a discipline. If the discipline is not based upon good science, then applied sport psychology cannot be evidence-based. To this end, the focus of this textbook is upon concepts and applications of sport psychology that are evidence-based. Smith (2006) described the ideal student-scholar view of the relationship between research, theory, and applied practice (intervention) as follows:

> Theories inspire research, and scientific research tests and sometimes leads to expansion and revisions in theory. Theories and research also inspire interventions, and intervention research is one way to assess the adequacy of the intervention, but also of the underlying theory.

This text offers the prospective coach and scholar the opportunity to learn correct concepts and applications of sport psychology, even though sport psychology is not a perfect science. We have a great deal to learn about mental preparation for sport competition. We will always have a need for the scientist who is interested in discovering new knowledge. As you read this text, keep an open mind and become interested in sport psychology as a science.

In the paragraphs that follow, a number of peripheral issues will be discussed that provide background information for the study of sport and exercise psychology. Specifically, this chapter provides a definition of sport psychology; sketches a brief history of sport psychology, including development of professional organizations; discusses the issue of certification; reviews various roles of the sport psychologist; discusses ethics associated with applied sport psychology; broaches the issue of accreditation; and concludes with a discussion of multicultural issues that relate to race and gender.

Sport and Exercise Psychology Defined

Sport psychology is a science in which the principles of psychology are applied in a sport or exercise setting. These principles are often applied to enhance performance. However, the true sport psychologist is interested in much more than performance enhancement and sees sport as a vehicle for human enrichment. A win-at-all-costs attitude is inconsistent with the goals and aspirations of the best sport psychologist. The sport psychologist is interested in helping every sport participant reach his or her potential as an athlete. If helping a young athlete develop self-control and confidence results in superior athletic performance, this is good. However, it is also possible that a quality sport experience can enhance an athlete's intrinsic motivation without the athlete's necessarily winning. Taken as a whole, sport psychology is an exciting subject dedicated to the enhancement of both athletic performance and the social-psychological aspects of human enrichment.

Stated more simply, sport and exercise psychology is the study of the effect of psychological and emotional factors on sport and exercise performance, and the effect of sport and exercise involvement on psychological and emotional factors.

This is an easy-to-understand definition that shows clearly the interactive relationship between sport and exercise involvement and psychological and emotional factors. It is upon this basic construct that this book is based. Athletic performance is influenced by psychological and emotional factors that can be fine-tuned and learned. Conversely, involvement in sport and exercise activities can have a positive effect upon an individual's psychological and emotional makeup.

History of Sport Psychology in North America

Sport psychology as a distinct field of study is extremely young and is evolving. Perhaps the first clear historical example of research being conducted in the area of sport psychology was reported by **Norman Triplett** in 1897. Drawing upon field observations and secondary data, Triplett analyzed the performance of cyclists under conditions of social facilitation. He concluded from this "milestone" research that the presence of other competitors was capable of facilitating better cycling performance (Davis, Huss, & Becker, 1995).

While Triplett provided an example of one of the earliest recorded sport psychology research investigations, he was not the first person to systematically carry out sport psychology research over an extended period of time. This distinction is attributed to **Coleman Griffith,** often referred to as the "father of sport psychology in North America" (Gould & Pick, 1995). Griffith is credited with establishing the first sport psychology laboratory at the University of Illinois in 1925. Griffith, a psychologist, was selected by George Huff, head of the Department of Physical Education at the University of Illinois, to develop this new laboratory based on Huff's vision. Dr. Griffith's laboratory was devoted to solving psychological and physiological problems associated with sport and athletic performance. Over an extended period of time, Griffith studied the nature of psychomotor skills, motor learning, and the relationship between personality variables and physical performance. Thus, the historical trend for the next sixty years was established in this early event. Physical Education, a cross-disciplinary entity, would provide the academic home for the application of psychology to sport and athletics.

Along with developing the first sport psychology laboratory at the University of Illinois, Griffith was also the first psychologist hired by a professional sports team in the United States. In 1938, P. K. Wrigley, owner of the Chicago Cubs, hired him to be the team sport psychologist and to improve performance. Resisted by the team manager, Charlie Grimm, Griffith did not enjoy great success with the Chicago Cubs, but his scientific approach to the psychology of coaching has emerged as the current model for sport psychologists working with professional teams (Green, 2003).

While Coleman Griffith was credited with the development of the first sport psychology research laboratory, others would follow his lead. Following World War II, such notables as Franklin M. Henry at the University of California, John Lawther at Pennsylvania State University, and Arthur Slater-Hammel at Indiana University pioneered graduate-level courses and developed research laboratories of their own.

Many women were also instrumental in the early development of sport psychology in North America. Such notables as Dorothy Harris, Eleanor Metheny, Camille Brown, Celeste Ulrich, and Aileen Lockhart could all be considered the "mothers of sport psychology," with Dorothy Harris also being the "mother of applied sport psychology" (Gill, 1995; Granito, 2002; Oglesby, 2001). Women such as Joan Duda, Deb Feltz, Diane Gill, Penny McCullagh, Carole Oglesby, Tara Scanlan, Maureen weiss, and Jean Williams not only made significant contributions to the development of modern sport psychology, but remain to this day leaders in the field (Krane & Whaley, 2010).

Dan Landers (1995) referred to the period of time from 1950 to 1980 as the "formative years"

Baseball is an excellent game in which to observe sport psychology in action. Courtesy Ball State University Sports Information.

for sport psychology. During this time, sport psychology began to emerge as a discipline somewhat distinct from exercise physiology and motor learning. This is especially true of "applied" sport psychology. Prior to the emergence of applied sport psychology, most research related to sport psychology was conducted within a laboratory setting and was referred to as motor learning research. During the formative years, a number of important research initiatives and textbooks were published. These early sporadic initiatives paved the way for the emergence of sport psychology as an academic subdiscipline within physical education and psychology. Some of the early textbooks included *Psychology of Coaching,* by John D. Lawther (1951); *Problem Athletes and How to Handle Them,* by Bruce Ogilvie and Tom Tutko (1966); *Motor Learning and Human Performance,* by Robert

Singer (1968); *Psychology of Motor Learning,* by Joseph B. Oxendine (1968); *Psychology and the Superior Athlete,* by Miroslaw Vanek and Bryant Cratty (1970); *Social Psychology and Physical Activity,* by Rainer Martens (1975); and *Social Psychology of Sport,* by Albert Carron (1980).

As mentioned earlier, the book titled *Problem Athletes and How to Handle Them* was authored in 1966 by Thomas Tutko and Bruce Ogilvie. This book and the authors' personality inventory for athletes—the Athletic Motivation Inventory (AMI)—caught on with coaches and athletes. Notwithstanding the popularity of the book and the inventory with the athletic community, Tutko and Ogilvie's work was not well received by the sport psychology community of scholars at the time. For reasons to be discussed in detail in the chapter on personality, the AMI and the book on how to handle problem athletes were deemed by the scientific community to be overly simplistic and not based on good science. Interestingly, Bruce Ogilvie's work as an applied sport psychologist is much better received by the scientific community today than it was in the 1960s. Because of his pioneering work with personality and applied sport psychology, **Bruce Ogilvie** is referred to as the father of applied sport psychology in North America.

If Coleman Griffith is the father of sport psychology in North America and Bruce Ogilvie the father of applied sport psychology, then the title "father of modern sport psychology" should go to **Rainer Martens,** former professor of sport psychology at the University of Illinois and founder of Human Kinetics Publishers. In modern times, Rainer Martens has done more for the development of sport psychology in North America than any other single individual. This assessment is based upon his research initiatives while a professor at Illinois, and on the fact that the students that he mentored are now leaders in the field throughout the world.

History of Sport Psychology in Europe

Conventional wisdom would suggest that the discipline of sport psychology emerged in North America with students from Europe and the United Kingdom coming to North America to study under professors at North American universities. These students then took their knowledge back to Europe and began their own programs. While much of this can be documented, it can also be argued that to some degree the discipline of sport psychology in Europe emerged independent of the discipline in North America (Seiler & Wylleman, 2009). While a comprehensive review of the development of sport psychology in Europe is beyond the scope of this textbook, a brief review of the contributions of three early European pioneers in sport psychology is instructive.

Pierre de Coubertin, a French educator and president of the International Olympic Committee (IOC) from 1896 to 1925, is credited with being the first person to introduce the term *sport psychology.* While Coubertin may not have influenced the development of sport psychology in North America, he did have an influence on members of the IOC relative to sport psychology (Kornspan, 2007). As president of the IOC, Coubertin was instrumental in organizing two Olympic Congresses in which a focus on sport psychology was included. The first was the Le Havre, France Congress in 1897, and the second in Lausanne, Switzerland in 1913. It was at the Lausanne Congress that the discipline of sport psychology was formerly introduced as a new branch of sport science. Two papers presented at the Lausanne Congress included one by Paul Rousseau on "The State of Mind of a Champion Athlete," and another by J. Phillipe on "The Study of Sport in the Psychology Laboratory." According to Müller (1997), Coubertin often stated that the 1913 Lausanne Congress represented the birth of sport psychology. This would make Pierre de Coubertin the father of sport psychology in Europe, if not in the world.

The sometimes "disputed" father of sport psychology in the Soviet Union (Russia) was **Avksenty Cezarevich Puni.** Puni completed his undergraduate and graduate degrees at the Lesgaft Institute of Physical Culture in Leningrad and served on the faculty until his death at age 87 (1898–1986). He established the new discipline of Sport psychology, while in Leningrad, by creating the Department of Sport Psychology. While Puni was developing the new Soviet discipline of sport psychology in Leningrad, his colleague and competitor, **Piotr Antonovich Roudik,** was doing the same thing in the psychology department at the State Central Institute of Physical Culture in Moscow. In 1925, Roudik founded the first sport psychology laboratory in the Soviet Union at the same time that Coleman Griffith was establishing one at the University of Illinois. Though some research interests overlapped between Puni and Roudik, it is generally reported that Roudik's orientation was more ideological and less applied than Puni's (Ryba, Stambulova, & Wrisberg, 2005). As a testament to his work as an applied sport psychologist, Puni developed and published his model of "Psychological Preparation for Competition" in the late 1960s and early 1970s at a time when North American Sport Psychologists were focusing upon the sport sciences and not upon applied sport psychology. It may be argued that Puni's applied model of sport psychology was instrumental in bringing about the athletic successes that the Soviet Union (USSR) enjoyed during this period (Stambulova, Wrisberg, & Ryba, 2006).

Development of Professional Organizations

A number of professional sport psychology organizations have evolved since the 1960s. In 1965 the *International Society of Sport Psychology* (ISSP) was formed. Organized in Rome, ISSP was created to promote and disseminate information about the practice of sport psychology throughout the world. In North America a small group of sport psychologists from Canada and the United States met in Dallas, Texas, to discuss the feasibility of forming a professional organization distinct from the American Alliance for Health, Physical Education, Recreation, and Dance (AAHPERD). The efforts of this small group came to fruition in 1966 when it was recognized by ISSP. The name of this new organization was the *North American Society for the Psychology of Sport and Physical Activity* (NASPSPA). The first annual meeting of NASPSPA was held prior to the 1967 AAHPERD National Convention in Las Vegas. Since that time, NASPSPA has evolved into an influential academic society focusing on sport psychology in the broadest sense. NASPSPA provides a forum for researchers in the areas of sport psychology, sport sociology, motor learning, motor control, and motor development to meet and exchange ideas and research. Shortly after the emergence of NASPSPA in the United States, another significant professional organization came into existence in Canada in 1969. This organization was named the *Canadian Society for Psychomotor Learning*

and Sport Psychology (CSPLSP). CSPLSP was originally organized under the auspices of the Canadian Association for Health, Physical Education, and Recreation (CAHPER), but became an independent society in 1977. Somewhat concurrent with the emergence of the Canadian society, the *Sports Psychology Academy* (SPA) emerged in the United States as one of six academies within the National Association for Sport and Physical Education (NASPE). NASPE is an association within AAHPERD. Also in 1969, the European Federation of Sport Psychology (EFSP) was founded at the second European Congress of Sport Psychology held in Vittel, France (Fédération Européenne de Psychologie des Sports et des Activities Corporelles [FEPSAC]). The idea for the EFSP originated in 1968 in Varna, Bulgaria at the First European Congress of Sport Psychology. The establishment of the EFSP in 1969, only four years after the establishment of the ISSP in 1965, begs the question as to why a second European organization dedicated to sport psychology was needed. While many different reasons may be posited, the development of the EFSP may be seen as a needed step to bridge the gap between two political socioeconomic systems existing at the time in greater Europe (Seiler & Wylleman, 2009). In order to better address the interests and needs of sport psychologists interested in applying the principles of psychology to sport and exercise, the *Association for the Advancement of Applied Sport Psychology* (AAASP) was formed in the fall of 1985 (Silva, 1989). AAASP emerged in the 1990s as the dominant association for the advancement of applied sport psychology as well as research in North America, and perhaps in the world. The name of AAASP was officially changed to the Association of Applied Sport Psychology (AASP) at the AAASP business meeting on September 29, 2006, in Miami, Florida. Most recently, the International Society for Sport Psychiatry (ISSP) was formed in 1992.

In addition to the specialized organizations mentioned above, two significant North American–based associations created interest areas dedicated to sport psychology within their organizations. These include the American Psychological Association (APA) with its Division 47 (formed in 1986), and the American College of Sports Medicine (ACSM). Paralleling the emergence of professional sport psychology organizations are journals that provide an outlet and forum for research generated by members of these organizations.

As a summary, table 1.1 lists professional organizations partially or completely dedicated to sport and exercise psychology. This table also indicates the year each organization was formed. Table 1.2 provides an incomplete list of research journals that are partially or completely dedicated to sport and exercise psychology.

Issue of Certification

Historically, sport psychology emerged as a discipline from physical education. In recent years, however, a significant interest in the discipline has developed among individuals prepared in psychology and counseling. This has raised the issue among practicing sport psychologists as to which people are qualified to call themselves "sport psychologists" and to provide services to athletes.

TABLE 1.1 | Summary of Major Professional Societies That Are Dedicated or Partially Dedicated to the Discipline/Profession of Sport Psychology

Genesis	Name of Association or Society
1954	American College of Sports Medicine (ACSM)
1965	International Society of Sport Psychology (ISSP)
1967	North American Society for the Psychology of Sport and Physical Activity (NASPSPA)
1969	European Federation of Sport Psychology (EFSP)*
1977	Canadian Society for Psychomotor Learning and Sport Psychology (CSPLSP)
1977	Sport Psychology Academy (SPA) (Division within AAHPERD)
1985	Association for the Advancement of Applied Sport Psychology (AAASP)
1986	Division 47 of the American Psychological Association (APA)
1992	International Society for Sport Psychiatry (ISSP)

*Fédération Européenne de Psychologie des Sports et des Activities Corporelles (FEPSAC)

TABLE 1.2 | Incomplete List of Journals Completely or Partially Dedicated to the Advancement/Application of Knowledge in Sport and Exercise Psychology

Journal Name	Affiliation
International Journal of Sport Psychology (IJSP)	ISSP
Journal of Applied Sport Psychology (JASP)	AASP
Journal of Clinical Sport Psychiatry	None
Journal of Sport Behavior (JSB)	None
Journal of Sport & Exercise Psychology (JS&EP)	NASPSPA
Medicine and Science in Sports and Exercise (MSSE)	ACSM
Psychology of Sport and Exercise	EFSP
Research Quarterly for Exercise and Sport (RQES)	AAHPERD
The Sport Psychologist (TSP)	None

Some have gone so far as to argue that only licensed psychologists should be allowed to call themselves sport psychologists (Morse, 2009), and suggest that the appropriate title for a nonlicensed "sport psychologist" would be "mental training consultant." Most agree, however, that even licensed psychologists should have significant academic training in the exercise and sport sciences before practicing applied sport psychology (Taylor, 1994).

A partial solution to the issue of professionalization of sport psychology was presented by the **United States Olympic Committee (USOC)** (1983) and clarified by May (1986). The USOC developed the **Sport Psychology Registry** to identify three categories in which a person can demonstrate competence. These categories correspond to three types of sport psychologists: the clinical/counseling sport psychologist, the educational sport psychologist, and the research sport psychologist. The purpose of the Sport Psychology Registry was to identify individuals in the area of sport psychology who could work with specific national teams within the Olympic movement. The registry was not meant to be a licensing or authorizing committee.

The AASP took the issue of who is qualified to deliver sport psychology services one step further. It adopted a certification document outlining the process an individual must take to be given the title "Certified Consultant, Association of Applied Sport Psychology." As one of the certification criteria, the applicant is required to hold a doctorate in an area related to sport psychology (e.g., psychology, sport science, or physical education). In addition, numerous specific courses and experiences are identified. While this certification process adopted by the AASP may not be the final one, it is a good beginning, since it recognizes that an individual needs specialized training in psychology and physical education (sport and exercise science) to be certified as a practicing sport psychologist.

The issue of what sport psychology is and who is qualified to practice applied sport psychology was addressed by the European Federation of Sport Psychology (EFSP, 1996). This body took the position that the term *sport psychology* was properly used in a broad sense, and included all qualified persons, independent of their specific academic fields. It did, however, acknowledge that different countries and different states within the U.S. may have restrictions on the use of the term *psychologist*.

What Does the Sport Psychologist Do?

In an effort to promote the virtues of sport psychology to coaches, athletes, and prospective students, many thoughtful professionals have suggested contributions that sport psychologists can make to sport. In the paragraphs that follow, different roles and functions of the sport psychologist are outlined. Generally, these roles and functions describe the sport psychologist in the categories of clinician, educator, and researcher. The practicing sport psychologist often fits into more than one category.

The Clinical/Counseling Sport Psychologist

The **clinical/counseling sport psychologist** is a person trained in clinical or counseling psychology and may be a licensed psychologist. Generally, the clinical/counseling sport psychologist also has a deep interest in and understanding of the athletic experience. Training may also include coursework and experience in sport psychology from programs in physical education. Clinical/counseling sport psychologists are individuals who are prepared to deal with emotional and personality disorder problems that affect some athletes. The athletic experience can be very stressful to some athletes, and can negatively affect their performance or their ability to function as healthy human beings. In these cases, sport psychologists trained in counseling psychology or clinical psychology are needed.

The Educational Sport Psychologist

Most sport psychologists who received their academic training through departments of physical education (i.e., sport and exercise science) consider themselves to be **educational sport psychologists.** These individuals have mastered the knowledge base of sport psychology and serve as practitioners. They use the medium of education to teach correct principles of sport and exercise psychology to athletes and coaches. In general, their mission and role is to help athletes develop psychological skills for performance enhancement. They also help athletes, young and old, to enjoy sport and use it as a vehicle for improving their quality of life.

The Research Sport Psychologist

For sport and exercise psychology to be a recognized and respected science, the knowledge base must continue to grow. It is the **research sport psychologist** who serves this important role. For the practicing sport psychologist to enjoy professional credibility, there must exist a credible scientific body of knowledge.

Given the different roles that sport psychologists can play, it is of interest to note the kinds of jobs that recent graduates are placed in and their job satisfaction. For the years 1994 to 1999, a study reported that 73 percent of individuals who graduated with a doctoral degree in a sport psychology–related field found employment in academia. Almost half of the students with a master's degree found jobs in sport psychology–related fields. A large portion of the remainder found jobs related to their academic training. Students who graduated during the indicated timeframe also reported improved job satisfaction and success in achieving career goals, as compared to those who graduated between the years 1989 and 1994 (Anderson, Williams, Aldridge, & Taylor, 1997; Williams & Scherzer, 2003).

Ethics in Sport Psychology

While the ethical application of sport psychology principles is discussed throughout this text, and more specifically in the chapter on psychological skills training, it is important to emphasize the topic at the outset. In recent years it has become clear that theories and techniques derived from the study of sport psychology can provide the winning edge for athletes and athletic teams. In this text, you will learn many of the psychological theories and techniques that can make you a more effective teacher and/or coach. This does not mean, however, that you will be qualified to provide psychological services to coaches and athletes. It takes much more than one or two courses in sport psychology to become a consulting sport psychologist. This is true despite the fact that at the present time there are limited licensing procedures in sport psychology; almost anyone can claim to be a sport psychologist. However, without certain minimal qualifications this would be unethical. When one considers the dangers involved in the inappropriate application of psychological theory, personality assessment, and intervention strategies, it is no wonder that many professionals are concerned.

The practice of sport psychology, whether by a coach or by a licensed psychologist, involves two diverse components. The first has to do with teaching, while the second is clinical in nature. For example, the sport psychologist uses teaching principles to help an athlete learn how to use imagery and/or relaxation techniques effectively. A well-trained and informed coach or teacher should be able to give such service. However, when the sport psychologist is called upon to provide clinical services such as crisis counseling, psychotherapy, or psychological testing, it is important that that person be specifically trained and licensed. To do otherwise would be unethical and irresponsible.

Accreditation Issues in Sport Psychology

The issue of who is qualified to deliver sport psychology services has been addressed to some degree by AASP with its certification program and by the USOC with its classification of three different kinds of sports psychologists. The issue still remains, however, as to who is qualified to prepare or train sport and exercise psychologists. Silva, Conroy, and Zizzi (1999) have argued that AASP should provide leadership for a movement to accredit university sport psychology programs. They argue that **accreditation** is the only way to ensure quality and consistency of academic training. Students graduating from accredited programs would be prepared to become certified AASP consultants. Arguments in favor of accreditation are bolstered by research that shows that of programs listed in the *Directory of Graduate Programs in Applied Sport Psychology* (see the AASP website), only about 25 percent offer coursework in all of the 12 different content areas mandated by AASP for certification.

In response to arguments in favor of accreditation, critics suggest that the issue of accreditation is premature and naive relative to the complex issues involved. They point out that unless an academic program is viewed as "critical" to the mission of a university, the university will be reluctant to pay the cost of accreditation. Second, they point out that accreditation would certainly raise the issue of who is qualified to call himself or herself a "psychologist." The APA and departments of psychology would resist accreditation of programs that produce sport psychologists who are not licensable as psychologists. Third, the debate over accreditation standards within AASP would be costly, from both a monetary and an emotional perspective. Finally, they argue that the impact of accreditation upon university programs would be to reduce academic freedom and program flexibility. While it is true that most programs in sport psychology continue to be in departments of physical education (e.g., kinesiology, exercise and sport science, etc.), the trend is moving slowly toward having departments of psychology, and particularly counseling psychology, provide training in sport psychology. It would be difficult for faculty from such diverse program areas to agree upon accreditation standards that they could take back and sell to their university deans and department chairs.

Multicultural Issues that Relate to Race

In this section we talk first about why race is an issue in sport psychology, and then about different multicultural training models that can be developed. In a subsequent section we will address multicultural issues related to gender, but in this section the focus is upon racial issues. In the broad sense, multicultural issues go well beyond race to include the concepts of **diversity** and **inclusiveness** (Sue & Sue, 1999). Diversity implies that people from diverse cultural backgrounds are represented in any group; inclusiveness implies that individuals are not excluded from a group because of their race, ethnic background, gender, sexual orientation, or religion. Sport psychology clients include individuals of different races, different cultures, and different sexual orientations, and they have different ways of thinking about sport and the world we live in.

The Issue of Race in Applied Sport Psychology

An important goal of applied sport psychology should be to attract into the field more individuals from different races. This is important because the vast majority of sport psychologists are Caucasians from a European background, while many college and professional athletes are African American blacks (Kontos & Breland-Noble, 2002). This not to say, however, that a white sport psychologist cannot provide excellent services to black or non-white athletes. Until more African Americans and members of other ethnic groups enter the discipline of sport psychology, those who are Caucasian must focus upon understanding and accepting cultural differences. Butryn (2002) addresses this difficult issue by reporting on a life history interview with a white male sport psychologist consultant and a male African American athlete, in which they discussed racial awareness and the notion of **white privilege** in North America, and particularly in the United States. Butryn argues that it is not enough to be "color blind." The white sport psychologist must also come to recognize the fact that he is privileged simply by having been born white. Butryn insists, "White people carry with them a host of unearned, largely unconscious privileges, which are conferred upon them simply because they were born with a white skin" (2002, p. 318). He goes on: ". . . white people may not recognize that the way whiteness is represented in the consciousness of many black people are [is] profoundly negative and intimately connected with the systematic and destructive oppression of African-Americans by white people throughout history" (p. 318).

What is the white sport psychologist to do? One cannot stop being white, but one can come to recognize why resentment and distrust may exist between a white consultant and black athlete. Furthermore, it is important to recognize the difference between **race thinking,** which is not racist, and **racist thinking,** which is. For a white sport psychologist to work with a black athlete, she must engage in race thinking. A failure to engage in race thinking is illustrated in a study reported by Ram, Stareck, and Johnson (2004). In this study, the researchers reviewed 982 articles published in *The Sport Psychologist, Journal of Applied Sport Psychology,* and the *Journal of Sport & Exercise Psychology* from 1987 to 2000 inclusive, relative to reference to race/ethnicity or sexual orientation. Results of the study showed that only 20 percent made reference in any way to race/ethnicity, while only 2 percent made substantive reference to sexual orientation.

In a thoughtful article, Kontos and Breland-Noble (2002) discuss the meaning of **cultural competence** and the ways a person becomes culturally competent. Cultural competence means that the coach or sport psychologist understands his client's racial identity, his own racial identity, and the role that race and cultural ethnicity play in the athlete/consultant relationship. The distinction between acculturation and enculturation is made. An individual is encultured, or experiences **enculturation,** simply by being born and raised in a particular group or culture. Conversely, **acculturation** implies learning to look at the world through a multicultural lens. It involves assimilation, truly understanding the culture of other ethnic groups, developing a world view of multiculturalism, and focusing upon the individual and not the group.

Multicultural Training in Sport Psychology

An accreditation issue that must be addressed, either formally or informally, is the issue of **multicultural training.** Graduates of sport psychology programs should be adequately trained in issues that relate to culture and race. According to Martens, Mobley, and Zizzi (2000), multicultural counseling is defined as counseling that takes place among individuals from different cultural/racial backgrounds.

Multicultural training of sport psychology students should be provided in four domains. First, students should experience a heightened awareness of and sensitivity to cultural groups different from their own. Second, they should gain knowledge about people who belong to cultures different from their own. Third, students should learn helping and intervention skills through the process of role playing and simulated interaction. Finally, each prospective graduate should experience a supervised practicum to gain hands-on experience working with members of a different culture or race.

According to census reports, approximately 30 percent of all people in the United States belong to racial and/or ethnic minorities. Yet, in some National Collegiate Athletic Association sports, the proportion of racial minorities is much greater than 30 percent. For example, in men's basketball, it is estimated to be as high as 68 percent; in football, 57 percent; and in women's basketball, 43 percent. Contrast this to the fact that most sport psychologists are white, and you see a clear need for multicultural training. Martens et al. identified two basic strategies for addressing the cultural disparity between athletes and applied sport psychologists. The **universalistic model**

Sports competition brings out the best in athletes, regardless of racial background. Courtesy University of Missouri–Columbia Sports Information.

endorses the concept of teaching prospective sport psychologists cultural sensitivity and how to be culturally competent. In the absence of more minority sport psychologists, this is the model that must be aggressively promoted. The **cultural compatibility model** proposes to address multicultural issues by matching the background of the counseling sport psychologist with that of the athlete. Given an increase in the number of minority sport psychologists, a combination of the two models would seem to be most appropriate. If sport psychologists are truly sensitive and educated relative to racial/cultural issues, it should not matter what race or culture the athlete and psychologist belong to.

A number of different multicultural training designs may be implemented. Four different designs are listed in table 1.3. They range from the least preferred design (workshop) to the most preferred (integrated model). Where there is no formal course or concentration for teaching multicultural issues, then workshops may be organized and provided. While a workshop is better than no training at all, this method of delivery does not assure that participants gain a desired level of knowledge and sensitivity to issues. A separate semester-long course dedicated to multicultural

issues would be much more likely to successfully enhance cultural sensitivity. An even better approach would be to provide students with an area of concentration that focuses upon different aspects of multicultural issues. Finally, the integrated model endorses the concept that multicultural issues be addressed in all courses within the sport psychology curriculum. In addition, the integrated model would use workshops, dedicated courses, and the area of concentration concept to make sure that all sport psychology students were thoroughly immersed in multicultural issues.

Multicultural Issues that Relate to Gender

In the previous section of this chapter, we talked about multicultural issues in sport psychology that relate to race. In this section we turn our attention to multicultural issues in sport that relate to gender and to sexual orientation within gender.

Gender and Feminist Issues in Sport Psychology

As pointed out by Oglesby (2001), women have been largely overlooked and unrecognized in any

CONCEPT   It is the responsibility of the coach and team leaders to foster multiculturalism in sport teams with respect to accepting diversity and being inclusive when it comes to individuals from different racial and ethnic backgrounds.

APPLICATION   Acculturation must take place among the athletes and between athletes and coaches. This means that team members learn to look at the world through a multicultural lens. They do this by understanding themselves first, and then taking the time to learn and understand the cultures that other teammates belong to.

TABLE 1.3 | Multicultural Training Designs in Sport Psychology

Design	Design Characteristics
1. Workshop Model	One- or two-day workshops are provided as needed.
2. Separate Course Model	Free-standing semester-long course on multicultural issues is provided.
3. Area of Concentration	Several free-standing courses and experiences are provided as part of a program concentration.
4. Integrated Model	Multicultural training is provided through all of the above, as well as integrated within each course in the curriculum.

historical discussion of the development of sport psychology in North America. As defined by hooks (2000), **feminism** is "a movement to end sexism, sexist exploitation, and oppression" (p. viii). Leaving the contribution of women out of a historical description of the development of sport psychology in North America would be an example of unintentional **sexism.** Volume 15 (issue 4) of the 2001 edition of *The Sport Psychologist* is edited by Diane Gill and is dedicated to feminism in sport psychology. Gill (2001) identifies four themes drawn from feminist theory and sport psychologist scholarship:

1. Gender is relational rather than categorical.
2. Gender is inextricably linked with race/ethnicity, class, and other social identities.
3. Gender and cultural relations involve power and privilege.
4. Feminism demands action.

Consistent with Diane Gill's item number two, Hall (2001) makes the inextricable connection between gender and race in this way:

> When we discuss women or feminism, the focus is on white women. Conversely, when we discuss athletes of color, the focus is on males, especially African-American males. As a result, women of color frequently feel isolated and are treated as if their race and/or gender are non-issues, or at the very least have little relevance to these respective groups. Consequently, women of color frequently feel alienated in the sport arena and in the sport psychology literature. (p. 391)

Past research and practice in sport psychology focused almost exclusively on a masculine perspective and utilized male participants to a large degree. This has changed a great deal in recent years, as university human subject committees require justification for excluding either male or female participants. The feminist movement has served as an effective reminder to researchers and practitioners to avoid sexist practices or sexist language in all aspects of sport psychology. When conducting research, sport psychologists can

(a) include males and females, people of color, and people with diverse sexual orientations as participants; (b) include gender and race as categorical variables; (c) include references that address race and gender; and (d) include substantive discussions related to race and gender (Ram et al., 2004). We will return to this important topic throughout the text, as gender issues are woven into the fabric of every chapter in the book.

Sexual Orientation in Sport Psychology

The multicultural concepts of diversity and inclusiveness extend to the inclusion of individuals who have a **sexual orientation** that may be different from the traditional heterosexual one. By definition, males who embrace a homosexual sexual orientation describe themselves as **gay,** while women who embrace a homosexual sexual orientation describe themselves as **lesbian.** For an individual to describe him or herself as gay or lesbian is to indicate sexual attraction to members of his or her own sex. Thus, to be **heterosexual** is to be sexually attracted to members of the opposite sex, while to be **homosexual** is to be sexually attracted to members of the same sex. To be inclusive is to accept both heterosexual and homosexual individuals into a group.

Homophobic behavior is defined as harmful behavior directed at individuals who are believed to be gay or lesbian, or such behavior directed at organizations or groups that support gay and lesbian people (Morrow & Gill, 2003). Examples of homophobic behavior include, but are not limited to, name calling, physical assaults, and destruction of property. As it relates to gay and lesbian people, inclusive behavior is behavior that is accepting and non-prejudiced. **Homophobia** is defined as irrational fear and intolerance of homosexual individuals or organizations (Roper, 2002). While not as directly harmful as homophobic behavior, **heterosexist behavior** is more insidious. Heterosexist behavior is behavior that implies that everyone in a group is heterosexual, or that everyone lives in a traditional family or is attracted to someone of the opposite sex. In many ways, this is more damaging than homophobic behavior, because it marginalizes people and forces them into thinking of themselves as "other" (Krane, 2001).

In a study involving a sample of high school physical education teachers and college students asked to reflect on the high school experience, Morrow and Gill (2003) reported that (a) homophobic behavior is as common in physical education classes as in the wider school population; (b) homophobic and heterosexist behavior is a regular part of the secondary school experience; and (c) despite the high level of homophobic and heterosexist behavior that exists, few teachers or students regularly confront the behaviors. The researchers reported that the most dramatic finding of the study was the great disparity between teachers' perception and students' perception of the creation of a psychologically "safe environment" for the students by the teachers.

Research also shows that the media treat men and women differently when it comes to athletic accomplishments and athletic prowess (Knight & Giuliano, 2003). Male athletes are perceived and assumed by the media to be heterosexual. Consequently, the media don't focus upon sexual orientation, but move on immediately to the athletic achievements of the male athletes. However, with female athletes, the media has a tendency to "heterosexualize" women by emphasizing their relationships with men. An emphasis on a woman's athletic prowess is secondary to an emphasis on her sexual orientation. This occurs because the media is anxious to overcome the image of homosexuality among women athletes. This research further showed that male and female athletes described as clearly heterosexual were perceived more favorably than athletes with an ambiguous sexual orientation.

Finally, we conclude this section by discussing the difficult issue of lesbian college coaches who coach female athletes. The basis of this discussion is a study reported by Krane and Barber (2005) in which they interviewed 13 lesbian college coaches about their experiences and

CONCEPT It is the responsibility of the coach and team leaders to foster multiculturalism in sports teams with respect to being accepting of homosexual individuals and being inclusive when it comes to sexual orientation.

APPLICATION Coaches and team leaders can cultivate multiculturalism with respect to different sexual orientations by educating athletes about homophobic behavior and about what it means to practice heterosexist behavior. Once this is accomplished, the focus should be upon treating every athlete with respect and dignity and upon valuing the athletic abilities of each athlete, regardless of sexual orientation.

---

the daily identity tensions they are confronted with. The study revealed that lesbian coaches are constantly negotiating with themselves about their social identities associated with being lesbian and coaching young women. On one hand they want to confront homophobia, but on the other hand they need to protect their professional careers (e.g., remain silent about their sexual orientation). The results of this particular study indicated that this sample of lesbian coaches did not choose to passively accept their fate, but rather fought against the prevailing heterosexist atmosphere and worked to create positive social change.

Sexual Exploitation in Coach-Athlete Relationships

While the primary focus of this section is upon sexual exploitation of female athletes by male authority figures (usually coaches), it should be understood that this is not the only type of sexual exploitation that takes place. In a large sample of elite female Norwegian athletes, as many as 45 percent indicated that they had been either sexually harassed or assaulted by a male authority figure, but another 15 percent indicated that they had been harassed or otherwise assaulted by a female coach or female peer (Fasting, Brackenridge, & Sundgot-Borgen, 2003). Even though our focus will be upon the more prevalent male authority figure harassment/assault of a female athlete, it is important to remember that harassment can also come from other females.

There are two types of sexual harassment mentioned in the literature (Fasting, Brackenridge, & Walseth, 2007). These include the quid pro quo and hostile environment varieties. In **quid pro quo harassment,** there is a bargaining of privileges for sexual favors that goes from the male authority figure toward the female athlete. In **hostile environment harassment,** a negative and debilitating atmosphere is created by the male authority figure that is both hostile and unwelcoming. Research reported by Fasting, Brackenridge, and Walseth (2007), involving elite world-class female athletes who experienced male authority sexual harassment, reveals both emotional and behavioral responses to unwanted sexual harassment. Emotional responses to sexual harassment include feelings of disgust, fear, irritation, and anger. Behavioral responses to sexual harassment include passivity, avoidance, direct confrontation, and confrontation with humor. These are all methods of effective or ineffective coping. Internally focused strategies for coping with sexual harassment (e.g. detachment, denial, endurance, relabeling, self-blame) are largely ineffective as they do not stop the unwanted behavior. Externally focused strategies for coping with sexual harassment are required if the harassment is to end. These include, but are not limited to, avoidance, confrontation, seeking organizational relief, social support, and appeasement. Conclusions from the Fasting, Brackenridge, and Walseth (2007) study indicate that many female athletes do nothing to stop the harassment or resort to ineffective internally focused coping methods.

CHAPTER 2

Personality as a Core Characteristic of the Individual

KEY TERMS

Athletic Motivation Inventory
Athletic pyramid
Big five personality traits
Cattell 16 PF
Cognitive-affective
  processing system
Disposition
Emotional intelligence
Global personality traits
Gravitational hypothesis
Interactional model
MMPI
Multivariate approach
Myers-Briggs Type
  Indicator
Personality
Personality paradox
Personality profile
Personality trait
Resilience

Troutwine Athletic Profile
Winning Profile Athletic
  Instrument

Sport psychologists have long been intrigued with the question of whether or not successful athletic performance can be accurately predicted on the basis of personality assessment. Personality assessment was apparently a factor in the Indianapolis Colts professional football team's decision to select Peyton Manning over Ryan Leaf to be its first-round draft pick in 1998 (Carey, 1999; Rand, 2000). History records that Manning went on to stardom with the Colts, while Ryan Leaf continued to struggle with the San Diego Chargers and later was traded. Ryan Leaf retired in the year 2002 after a lack-luster career (King, 2002). This single event is built up in the press as evidence of the

Athletes also exhibit interesting personality styles. Courtesy Kansas State University Sports Information.

effectiveness of personality testing in predicting athletic success. Apparently, a large percentage of professional teams use personality testing to assist them in making personnel decisions. Not everyone, however, agrees with this practice.

In the 1960s and 1970s, research involving the athlete and personality assessment was very popular. Ruffer (1975, 1976a, 1976b), for example, cited 572 sources of original research in a compilation of references on the relationship between personality and athletic performance. In recent years, however, interest in this kind of research has waned because of a lack of consistent correlation between personality factors and athletic prowess. However, in view of the current practice of many teams in the National Football League to include personality assessment in decision making, it behooves the sport psychology student to be knowledgeable about personality and personality assessment in sport.

Concepts to be introduced and studied in this section include (a) a definition of personality, (b) theories of personality, (c) measurement of personality, and (d) personality and sport performance. As we shall learn, personality assessment involves measuring relatively stable personality traits, and not unstable mood and emotion.

Personality Defined

As defined by Kalat (1999, p. 477), **personality** is "all the consistent ways in which the behavior of one person differs from that of others, especially in social situations." The key words in this definition are the words "consistent" and "differs." An individual's personality defines the person in unique ways that remain stable and consistent over time. If an athlete consistently exhibits the characteristics of being assertive on and off the athletic field, we might say that he is an assertive person.

One of the difficulties scientists have in determining the personality characteristics of an individual is that the individual may purposely or inadvertently "mask" her true personality. Hollander (1976) wrote about this problem when he said that *typical responses* and *role-related behaviors* don't always reflect a person's true personality, or *psychological core*. A typical response is indicative of how an individual usually behaves in a social setting, while a role-related behavior is indicative of how the person behaves in various specific situations. Consider the example of the athlete who is being recruited to play football at a major university. The university representative asks the high school football coach about the athlete's personality. The coach responds that he is very quiet, but hard-working. When this same question is asked of the athlete's girlfriend, she replies that he is actually very sociable and outgoing.

Theories of Personality

In this section we will consider five major theoretical approaches to the study of personality: psychodynamic theory, social learning theory, humanistic theory, trait theory, and Jung's theory of personality types. Each will be briefly discussed.

Psychodynamic Theory

Sigmund Freud's psychodynamic theory (1933) and his method of treating personality disturbances were based primarily upon self-analysis and extensive clinical observation of neurotics. Two distinguishing characteristics of the psychodynamic approach to personality have been its emphasis upon in-depth examination of the *whole* person, and its emphasis upon unconscious motives.

In Freud's view, the id, ego, and superego form the tripartite structure of personality. The id represents the unconscious instinctual core of personality; in a sense, the id is the pleasure-seeking mechanism. In contrast, the ego represents the conscious, logical, reality-oriented aspect of the personality. The superego represents the conscience of the individual. Essentially, Freud advocated a conflict theory of personality. In this respect, the three parts of the psychic structure are always in conflict. The individual's personality is the sum total of the dynamic conflicts

between the impulse to seek release and the inhibition against these impulses.

Social Learning Theory

From the viewpoint of social learning theory, behavior is not simply a function of unconscious motives (as in psychoanalytic theory) or underlying predispositions. Rather, human behavior is a function of social learning and the strength of the situation. An individual behaves according to how she has learned to behave, as this is consistent with environmental constraints. If the environmental situation is prominent, the effect of personality traits or unconscious motives upon behavior should be minimal.

The origin of social learning theory can be traced to Clark Hull's (1943) theory of learning and to B. F. Skinner's (1953) behaviorism. Hull's stimulus-response theory of learning was based on laboratory experimentation with animals. According to stimulus-response theory, an individual's behavior in any given situation is a function of his learned experiences. Other researchers, such as Miller and Dollard (Miller, 1941), Mischel (1986), and Bandura (1977, 1986), extended the Hullian notions of complex human behavior.

Humanistic Theory

The major proponents of the humanistic theory of personality are Carl Rogers and Abraham Maslow. Unlike the pessimistic Freud, Rogers and Maslow argued that human nature is inherently healthy and constructive. At the center of the humanistic theory of personality is the concept of *self-actualization.* The human organism possesses an innate drive or tendency to enhance itself, to realize capacities, and to act to become a better and more self-fulfilled person. In the developing personality, openness to experiences that then shape the individual is of critical importance. It is not necessarily the experience that shapes the individual, but the individual's perception of that experience. Self-actualization is an ongoing process of seeking congruence between one's experiences and one's self-concept. Rogers's

CONCEPT   Five basic approaches for explaining the phenomenon of personality include psychodynamic theory, social learning theory, humanistic theory, trait theory, and Jung's theory of personality.

APPLICATION   In attempting to explain behavior on the basis of personality, it is important to recognize the ramifications of adopting one theoretical approach over another. The teacher's or coach's belief system will influence athlete-coach interactions.

influence on the development of the humanistic theory of personality is largely due to his method of psychotherapy, which is nondirective and client-centered. Maslow's contribution to the humanistic theory is in the development of his hierarchical motive system based on the notion of hierarchical needs.

Trait Theory

The basic position of trait, or factor, theory is that personality can be described in terms of traits possessed by individuals. These **personality traits** are considered synonymous with **dispositions** to act in a certain way. Traits are considered to be stable, enduring, and consistent across a variety of differing situations. Those who exhibit the trait of a need to achieve success, for example, can be expected to have a disposition toward competitiveness and assertiveness in many situations. A disposition toward a certain trait means not that the individual will *always* respond in this manner, but that a certain likelihood exists.

Among the most ardent advocates of trait psychology are psychologists such as Gordon Allport, Raymond Cattell, and Hans Eysenck. Cattell (1965, 1973) identified 35 different traits that he believed describe a personality. Using a similar approach, British psychologists (Eysenck & Eysenck, 1968) concentrated on the dimensional traits of neuroticism-stability and introversion-extraversion.

Jung's Theory of Personality

Up to this point, reliance on trait theory has overshadowed Jung's theory of personality types in the sport psychology literature. As articulated by

Jacobi (1973) and more recently by Beauchamp, Maclachlan, and Lothian (2005), the foundation of Carl Jung's theory of personality is the notion that an individual's personality is based on two personality attitudes (introversion and extraversion) and four functions or mental processes (thinking, feeling, sensing, and intuition). The two functions of thinking and feeling are classified as being rational or judging, while the two functions of sensing and intuition are classified as being irrational or perceiving. The combination of the two attitudes and the four functions allows for the categorization of individuals into eight personality types. Because each of these eight personality types can be either primary (dominant) or inferior (auxillary) you have a total of 16 possible personality types. Jung, however, argued against simply classifying individuals into genetically determined personality typologies. While Jung recognized the influence of genetic factors in shaping personality, he also believed that individuals are active agents in shaping their own personalities as they interact with the environment and other people. The Myers-Briggs Type Indicator, to be discussed in the measurement section of this chapter, is based on Carl Jung's theory of personality.

The Measurement of Personality

This section will identify and briefly discuss various techniques used for assessing personality. It should be pointed out that the various methods of assessing personality correspond closely to the basic personality theories we have just discussed. For example, projective tests such as the Rorschach test are closely linked to the psychoanalytic theory of personality. Conversely, the various paper-and-pencil inventories are linked to trait theory. In this brief overview of personality measurement techniques, the reader should be aware that many issues regarding personality assessment remain unresolved. The methods outlined here are not perfect; nor do psychologists agree on the meaning of the results of any particular test.

Three basic classes of measurement techniques may be identified. These are (1) rating scales, (2) unstructured projective tests, and (3) questionnaires. Each of these three categories will now be discussed, with particular emphasis upon the questionnaire method. The questionnaire method is highlighted because it is the measurement technique most commonly used by sport psychologists today.

Rating Scales

Characteristically, *rating scales* involve the use of a judge or judges who are asked to observe an individual in some situation. The judges employ the use of a checklist or scale that has been predesigned for maximum objectivity. Usually, if the checklist is used properly and the judges are well trained, the results can be fairly reliable and objective.

Typically, two types of situations are involved in personality assessment using rating scales. These are the *interview* and the *observation of performance.* In the interview, the judge asks the subject numerous open-ended and specific questions designed to ascertain personality traits and general impressions. Observation of a participant during some type of performance situation is the second kind of rating system used for ascertaining personality. As with the interview, observations can be effective if the checklist being used is well-designed and planned, and if the observer is highly trained.

Unstructured Projective Procedures

The foregoing rating methods are generally used for ascertaining data on traits of personality, although in many instances inferences may be made concerning underlying motives. Projective procedures may also be used to identify traits, but they are commonly used to determine information about underlying motives. Projective techniques allow subjects to reveal their inner feelings and motives through unstructured tasks. These unstructured techniques are used primarily in clinical psychology and are somewhat synonymous with the psychoanalytic and humanistic approaches to explaining personality. The underlying assumption in the unstructured test situation is that if subjects perceive that there are no right or wrong responses, they will likely be open and honest in their responses.

Several kinds of unstructured tests have been developed. Among them are the Rorschach Test (Sarason, 1954), the Thematic Apperception Test (Tompkins, 1947), the Sentence Completion Test (Holsopple & Miale, 1954), and the House-Tree-Person Test (Buck, 1948). For our purposes, only the Rorschach (also known as the "inkblot") and Thematic Apperception Tests (TAT) will be discussed. The inkblot and the TAT are by far the most commonly used projective tests.

The Rorschach Test   Herman Rorschach, a Swiss psychiatrist, was the first to apply the inkblot to the study of personality (Kalat, 1999). The Rorschach test was introduced in 1921, and remains the most famous of all the projective testing devices. The test material consists of ten cards. Each card has an inkblot on it, which is symmetrical and intricate. Some of the cards are entirely in black and white, while others have a splash of color or are nearly all in color. The cards are presented to the subject one at a time and in a prescribed order. As the cards are presented, the subject is encouraged to tell what he sees. The tester keeps a verbatim record of the subject's responses to each, and notes any spontaneous remarks, emotional reactions, or other incidental behaviors. After all the cards have been viewed, the examiner questions the subject in a systematic manner regarding associations made with each card.

The Thematic Apperception Test   The Thematic Apperception Test, developed by Henry Murray and his associates in 1943 at the Harvard

University Psychological Clinic, has been used almost as extensively as the Rorschach test. The TAT is composed of nineteen cards containing pictures depicting vague situations, and one blank card. The subject is encouraged to make up a story about each picture. In contrast to the vague blots in the Rorschach test, pictures in the TAT are rather clear and vivid. It is believed that subjects reveal or project important aspects of their personalities as they weave the characters and objects in the pictures into either an oral or a written story.

Structured Questionnaires

The structured questionnaire is a paper-and-pencil test in which the subject answers specific true-false or Likert scale–type statements. A typical Likert scale–type statement is illustrated in the following example:

In athletic situations, I find myself getting very uptight and anxious as the contest progresses.

DEFINITELY FALSE				DEFINITELY TRUE
1	2	3	4	5

There are many different kinds of questionnaire-type personality inventories. Certain specific personality types or traits are believed to be identified through the administration of these questionnaires. For our purposes we will focus our discussion on the four most commonly used personality inventories. One of these inventories was developed to be used with individuals suffering from personality disorders, while the other three were developed for normal populations. All of these inventories are of interest, because both have been used in sport-related research involving athletes. Following the discussion of these four general inventories, we will briefly discuss the personality inventories designed specifically for athletes. In addition, we will discuss inventories designed to measure emotional intelligence and resilience as they relate to sport performers.

Minnesota Multiphasic Personality Inventory

The Minnesota Multiphasic Personality Inventory (**MMPI**) is the most widely used of all personality inventories. The MMPI consists of a series of true-false questions designed to measure certain personality traits and clinical conditions such as depression. The original version of the MMPI, composed of 550 items, was developed in the 1940s and is still in use (Hathaway & McKinley, 1940). A revised version of the inventory, composed of 567 items, was developed in 1990 and named the MMPI-2 (Butcher, Graham, Williams, & Ben-Porath, 1990). These authors also developed a new form of the inventory to be used with adolescents (MMPI-A). Traits measured by the MMPI-2 include the following: hypochondria, depression, hysteria, psychopathic deviation, masculinity-feminity, paranoia, obsessive-compulsive behavior, schizophrenia, hypomania, and social introversion.

Cattell's Sixteen Factor Personality Inventory

Developed by Robert Cattell (1965), the Sixteen Factor Personality Inventory (**Cattell 16 PF**) is based upon 35 personality traits originally identified by Cattell. Through a statistical process known as factor analysis, Cattell reduced the 35 specific traits to 16 broader traits or factors. The 16 factors measured by the 16 PF are believed to be personality traits exhibited by normal individuals. The current edition of the 16 PF is titled the 16 PF Fifth Edition (Russell & Karol, 1994), and is composed of 185 items.

Cattell believed that the 16 traits measured by the 16 PF could be further condensed down to five secondary or **global personality traits.** Cattell's global traits and the big five traits are presented in table 2.1 along with Cattell's 16 primary traits. In comparing the descriptions of the Cattell global traits with those of the big five traits, it is clear that they are not exactly the same. However, extraversion appears on both lists, and neuroticism and anxiety are essentially the same.

From Cattell's perspective, it is interesting to look at table 2.1 to see what factors constitute

TABLE 2.1 | Primary and Global Personality Traits Associated with the 16 PF, as Well as Personality Traits Associated with the "Big Five"

16 PF Primary Traits	16 PF Global Traits	Big Five Traits
1. Warmth	1. Extraversion	1. Extraversion
2. Reasoning	2. Anxiety	2. Neuroticism
3. Emotional Stability	3. Tough-Mindedness	3. Conscientiousness
4. Dominance	4. Independence	4. Openness
5. Liveliness	5. Self-Control	5. Agreeableness
6. Rule-Consciousness		
7. Social Boldness		
8. Sensitivity		
9. Vigilance		
10. Abstractedness		
11. Privateness		
12. Apprehension		
13. Openness to Change		
14. Self-Reliance		
15. Perfectionism		
16. Tension		

what we call personality. Of even greater interest is the plotting of the an individual's standardized scores for each of the 16 personality traits on a line graph. Plotted standardized scores produce what sport psychologists call a **personality profile.** A hypothetical personality profile is illustrated in figure 2.1.

NEO–Five Factor Personality Inventory

The NEO–Five Factor Personality Inventory (NEO-FFI) is a 60-item personality inventory designed to measure the **big five personality traits** of extraversion, neuroticism, conscientiousness, openness, and agreeableness. The 60-item NEO-FFI is extracted from the more comprehensive NEO Personality Inventory-R (Costa & McCrae, 1992). For ease of administration and when time is important, Gosling, Rentfrow, and Swann (2009), reported on the development and testing of both a 5- and 10-item version of the NEO-FFI. Of the two brief versions, their data supported the use of the 10-item version over the 5-item.

Myers-Briggs Type Indicator The **Myers-Briggs Type Indicator** (MBTI; Myers, 1962; Myers, McCaulley, Quenk, & Hammer, 1998) is based on Jung's theory of personality types, previously introduced. While the MBTI has not been used very often with athlete populations, it has been used extensively in business and in other professions where organizational leadership and behavior are important (e.g., industry, corporations, armed forces). The MBTI is composed of 93 forced choice questions that represent word pairs that the participant must decide between. Based on the choices that are made, the participant is assigned one of 16 personality types. Scores on other types are not necessarily dismissed, as a participant may score relatively high on more than one typology. As explained by Beauchamp et al. (2005), the results of the MBTI provide the athlete and coach with a theoretical framework for interacting with each other and other members of a team. If everyone on an athletic team completes the MBTI, then the results provide a framework

FIGURE 2.1 | Personality profile showing how an athlete's scores compare to the population mean (zero).

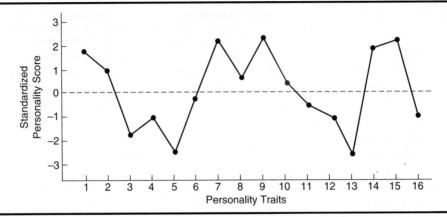

for athletes to learn more about themselves as well as about other members of the team.

Structured Questionnaires Designed for Athletes

In addition to the specific personality inventories identified in the previous paragraphs, sport psychologists have developed personality inventories designed to measure personality traits in athletes. These inventories have generally been developed for the purpose of studying the relationship between personality and athletic performance. A few of these inventories will be introduced here.

Before we begin this discussion, you should know that *no scientific study to date has shown a strong statistical relationship between personality variables and athletic ability.* We will look at the evidence on this matter later in the chapter, but for now it is important for you to understand this fact about personality testing. This statement casts doubt on the practices of professional teams that use personality testing for the purposes of team selection, especially if they give significant weight to results of the testing. Personality testing can play an important role in player development, but no evidence exists to justify its use in making

personnel decisions. If a test developer believes that he has developed an inventory that can accurately predict athletic success, he has the responsibility to put it to the test and make the data available to scientists. Three personality/psychological inventories will be mentioned in this section, along with a brief discussion of two inventories designed to measure a single personality trait.

Athletic Motivation Inventory   The **Athletic Motivation Inventory** (AMI) was developed by Thomas Tutko, Bruce Ogilvie, and Leland Lyon at the Institute for the Study of Athletic Motivation at San Jose State College (Tutko & Richards, 1971, 1972). According to its authors, the AMI measures a number of personality traits related to high athletic achievement: drive, aggression, determination, responsibility, leadership, self-confidence, emotional control, mental toughness, coachability, conscience development, and trust.

The reliability and validity of the instrument have been questioned by Rushall (1973), Corbin (1977), and Martens (1975). However, Tutko and Richards (1972) say that thousands of athletes have been tested and that the AMI was originally based upon the 16 PF and the Jackson Personality Research Form (Ogilvie, Johnsgard, & Tutko, 1971).

CONCEPT   Many structured personality inventories are available for measuring the personality traits of athletes. Each of these inventories or tests was designed for a specific purpose and with a particular participant in mind. Tests should be selected with care.

APPLICATION   In terms of reliability and validity, the Cattell 16 PF is a good test to be used for measuring the personality of athletes. When using this test, consult your team sport psychologist, your school psychologist, or other trained professionals regarding the correct administration of the test and interpretation of results.

Perhaps the real concern of sport psychologists is not that the test is more or less reliable than other personality inventories, but that the developers implied that it could predict athletic success. No other organization, researcher, or promoter has made similar claims about other more distinguished personality inventories. The unsubstantiated claims of the developers of the AMI hurt the field of sport psychology in terms of legitimacy.

A study by Davis (1991) supports this position. Davis studied the relationship between AMI subscales and psychological strength in 649 ice hockey players who were eligible for the National Hockey League (NHL) entry draft. The criterion measure of psychological strength was based on an evaluation of on-ice play by NHL scouts. The results showed that less than 4 percent of the variance in scout ratings was accounted for by AMI scores ($r = .20$). This outcome suggests that the AMI is a poor predictor of psychological strength of ice hockey players.

Winning Profile Athletic Instrument   The **Winning Profile Athletic Instrument** (WPAI) was developed by Jesse Llobet of PsyMetrics. The WPAI is a fifty-item inventory that measures conscientiousness and mental toughness. Llobet (1999) reported internal reliability coefficients of .83 and .87 for these two factors respectively. When completing the instrument, athletes are asked to use their own sport as a frame of reference for answering questions. In one investigation, Llobet (1999) reported correlations of between .30 and .43 between WPAI scores and coaches' ratings for

conscientiousness and mental toughness. In a second study, Paa, Sime, and Llobet (1999) administered the WPAI to high school, collegiate, semiprofessional, and professional athletes. Results showed significant differences between the mean total WPAI scores for high school athletes and all other groups, and between collegiate athletes and professional athletes.

Troutwine Athletic Profile   The **Troutwine Athletic Profile** (TAP) was developed by Bob Troutwine, a professor of psychology at William Jewell College (Carey, 1999; Rand, 2000). According to news reports, the TAP was used by the Indianapolis Colts to help them make their decision to select Peyton Manning over Ryan Leaf in the 1998 professional football draft. Psychometric properties of the TAP have not been published in any of the mainline sport psychology journals; nor has anything scientific been published about the validity of the test in terms of predicting athletic success.

Emotional Intelligence   Depending on how it is measured, **emotional intelligence** may be conceptualized as either a personality trait or as a mental ability to be learned. The two approaches to conceptualize emotional intelligence are captured within the two emotional intelligence inventories described below. Regardless of which approach is used to measure emotional intelligence, it is expected that emotional intelligence is associated with the ability to regulate emotions and with increased positive mood and self-esteem (Schutte, Malouff, Simunek, McKenley, & Hollander, 2002).

Emotional Intelligence Scale The Emotional Intelligence Scale (EIS; Schutte, Malouff, Hall, et al., 1998; Schutte, Malouff, Simunek, et al., 2002) is a 32-item inventory designed to measure emotional intelligence as a relatively stable personality disposition or trait. As originally conceptualized, the EIS measured emotional intelligence as a unidimensional construct (single score). However, based on a factor analysis study, it was suggested that emotional intelligence, as measured by the EIS, was actually multidimensional in nature and composed of four relatively independent subscales (Petrides & Furnham, 2000). These four subscales were (a) perception of emotions, (b) managing emotions in the self, (c) social skills or managing others' emotions, and (d) utilizing emotions. In an applied study involving baseball players, Zizzi, Deaner, and Hirschhorn (2003) observed that emotional intelligence, as measured by the EIS, was correlated with pitching but not hitting performance.

Mayer-Salovey-Caruso Emotional Intelligence Test The Mayer-Salovey-Caruso Emotional Intelligence Test (MSCEIT; Mayer, Salovey, & Caruso, 2002) is a 141-item scale designed to measure specific emotional intelligence skills that may be learned over time. As originally conceptualized by Mayer and Salovey (1997), emotional intelligence is composed of the following four skills or branches: (a) ability to perceive and express emotion, (b) ability to assimilate emotion in thought, (c) ability to understand and analyze emotion, and (d) ability to regulate emotions. The advantage of the learned ability approach to conceptualizing emotional intelligence is that it is optimistic in nature, as it implies that one can learn to be emotionally intelligent. Meyer and Fletcher (2007) provide an excellent contrast between the trait and learned ability approach to conceptualizing emotional intelligence. In the final analysis, Meyer and Fletcher argue in favor of the learned ability approach to conceptualizing emotional intelligence.

Resilience The importance of resilience in sport is addressed by Galli and Vealey (2008). In their research, they asked athletes how they overcome their most difficult and challenging examples of adversity (e.g., injury, slump, burnout, college transition, illness). Four general themes emerged from this research, including dealing with agitation and adversity through coping strategies, positive outcomes from the agitation and coping process, identification of personal resources to support coping efforts, and sociocultural influences that also support coping efforts. Taken together these four themes formed the basis of their conceptual model of how sport resilience is developed. In addressing the notion of resilience theory, Richardson (2002) identified three levels or waves of resiliency inquiry. The first wave involves the identification of the qualities possessed by resilient individuals. The second wave involves a description of the disruptive process by which resilient qualities are integrated or learned by individuals. The Galli and Vealey investigation is an example of this kind of research. The third wave involves the process by which individual athletes discover the innate and learned forces within themselves that allow them to possess personal resilience. As explained by Richardson (2002), personal **resilience** is the force within the individual that drives a person to confront and overcome adversity. This force may be described as an innate righting mechanism and as the human capacity to confront and overcome adversity.

As conceptualized by Bartone, Ursano, Wright, and Ingraham (1989), the Dispositional Resilience Scale (DRS) is a 45-item inventory that measures dispositional resilience or hardiness. The inventory measures the three dimensions of control, commitment, and challenge. An abbreviated version of the DRS was also suggested by the developers of the DRS. The abbreviated version is composed of 30 items also rated on a 4-point Likert scale. High scores on the three dimensions indicate high resilience, while low scores indicate low resilience.

Personality and Sport Performance

Since 1960, several comprehensive literature reviews have been completed in an attempt to clarify the relationship between personality and

John McEnroe dominated men's professional tennis in
the 1980s though superior skill and a volatile personality.
Courtesy Kansas State University Sports Information.

sport performance (Cofer & Johnson, 1960; Cooper, 1969; Hardman, 1973; Ogilvie, 1968, 1976; Morgan, 1980b). Of these, the review by Morgan (1980b) provided the most comprehensive treatment of the subject. While not fully endorsing the position that personality profiles can accurately predict sport performance, Morgan argued that the literature shows a consistent relationship between personality and sport performance when (a) response distortion is removed, and (b) data are analyzed using a multivariate approach. A **multivariate approach** is used when multiple measures of personality are analyzed simultaneously, as opposed to separately. Since personality is multifaceted and complex, it is appropriate that statistics used to analyze personality measures also be complex. While it is good to remember that the relationship between sport performance and personality is far from crystal clear, it seems equally true that certain general conclusions can be drawn.

In the paragraphs that follow, sport personality research will be synthesized and general conclusions drawn on several topics of interest.

Athletes Versus Nonathletes

Athletes differ from nonathletes on many personality traits (Gat & McWhirter, 1998). It is often a matter of conjecture whether these differences favor the athletes or the nonathletes. Schurr, Ashley, and Joy (1977) clearly showed that athletes who participate in team and individual sports are more independent, more objective, and less anxious than nonathletes. From Hardman's (1973) review it is also clear that the athlete is often more intelligent than average. Additionally, Cooper (1969) describes the athlete as being more self-confident, competitive, and socially outgoing than the nonathlete. This is supportive of Morgan's (1980b) conclusions that the athlete is basically an extravert and low in anxiety.

In several investigations, a number of comparisons have been made between an athlete's score on various personality and psychological inventories and scores associated with norm groups. For example, compared to published normative data, the scores of professional cowboys indicate that they tend to be alert, enthusiastic, forthright, self-sufficient, reality based, and practical (McGill, Hall, Ratliff, & Moss, 1986). Compared to norm groups, elite rock climbers exhibit low anxiety, emotional detachment, low superegos, and high levels of sensation seeking (Robinson, 1985).

While the evidence favors the conclusion that the athlete differs from the nonathlete in many personality traits, the problem arises in the definition of what constitutes an athlete. In the Schurr et al. (1977) research, an athlete was defined as a person who participated in the university intercollegiate athletic program. This would seem to be a viable criterion. However, this classification system has not been universally adopted by researchers. Some studies, for example, have classified intramural and club sports participants as athletes. Other studies have required that participants earn

CONCEPT   Generally speaking, athletes differ from nonathletes in many personality traits. For example, it can be demonstrated that athletes are generally more independent, objective, and extraverted than nonathletes, but less anxious.

APPLICATION   As a coach, expect your athletes to be generally higher in such traits as independence, extraversion, and self-confidence, and lower in anxiety, than nonathletes. One cannot, however, rank athletes on the basis of these traits or make team roster decisions based on them. A statistical relationship (often low) does not suggest a cause-and-effect relationship.

CONCEPT   Athletes tend to be more extraverted, independent, and self-confident than nonathletes because of a process of "natural selection," and not necessarily due to learning. Individuals who exhibit certain personality traits may tend to gravitate toward athletics. An important exception to this principle occurs in the formative years before the young athlete reaches maturity. During the early maturing years, the youth sport experience is critical in forming positive personality traits such as independence and low trait anxiety.

APPLICATION   Coaches and teachers who work with young boys and girls must be very careful that the athletic experience is a positive one in the lives of young people. Athletic programs designed for youth should place a premium on the development of feelings of self-worth, confidence, and independence, and relegate winning to a position of secondary importance. Winning must not be more important than the needs of the boys and girls.

awards, such as letters, in order to be considered athletes. Until some unifying system is adopted, it will always be difficult to compare results from one study with those from another.

Developmental Effects of Athletic Participation upon Personality

Given that athletes and nonathletes differ on the personality dimensions of extraversion and stability, is this due to the athletic experience (learning), or to a natural selection process in which individuals possessing certain personality traits gravitate toward athletics? Perhaps an unequivocal answer to this question will never be known; however, the evidence typically supports the **gravitational hypothesis.** Individuals who possess stable, extraverted personalities tend to gravitate toward the athletic experience. As the competitive process weeds out all but the keenest of competitors, those who remain are those having the greatest levels of extraversion and stability. This could be described as sort of an athletic Darwinism (survival of the fittest). Some of the studies that support the gravitational model are those by Kane (1970) and Rushall (1970).

CONCEPT Generally speaking, it can be demonstrated that differences exist in the personalities of athletes who engage in different types of sports. Perhaps the clearest distinction occurs between athletes involved in team sports and those involved in individual sports. For example, team sport athletes are more extraverted, dependent, and anxious than individual sport athletes. Certainly, one might expect some differences to emerge between football players and tennis players in terms of personality traits.

APPLICATION Personality profiles may be used by trained sport psychologists to help athletes decide which sports to devote their energies to, but they should never be used to coerce the athletes into making such decisions. If a young athlete with a tennis player's personality wants to be a golfer, so be it. Occasionally, an athlete reaches a juncture in her athletic career when she must decide between two sports in order to devote adequate time to academic work. Perhaps consideration of the athlete's personality profile would be useful at this point.

The viability of the gravitational model, however, does not preclude the possibility that sport participation can enhance personality development. In this respect, Tattersfield (1971) has provided longitudinal evidence that athletic participation before maturity has a developmental effect upon personality. Specifically, Tattersfield monitored the personality profiles of boys participating in an age-group swimming program across a five-year training period. Significant changes toward greater extraversion, stability, and dependence were observed in the boys during this period. From an educational perspective, all but the factor of dependence would be considered positive in nature.

Personality Sport Type

Can personality profiles of athletes in one sport be reliably differentiated from those of athletes in another sport? Perhaps the first real attempts to answer this question were made with bodybuilders. Research by Henry (1941), Thune (1949), and Harlow (1951), for example, suggested that bodybuilders suffer from feelings of masculine inadequacy, and are overly concerned with health, body build, and manliness. A study by Thirer and Greer (1981), however, would tend to cast doubt on these earlier stereotypes. In a well-conceived and controlled study, the authors concluded that intermediate and competitive

bodybuilders were high in achievement motivation and resistance to change, but relatively normal in all other traits measured. They found no support for the previous generalities and negative stereotyping sometimes applied to bodybuilders.

Kroll and Crenshaw (1970) reported a study in which highly skilled football, wrestling, gymnastic, and karate athletes were compared on the basis of Cattell's 16 PF. The results showed that when the football players and wrestlers were contrasted with the gymnasts and karate participants, significantly different personality profiles emerged. The wrestlers and football players had similar profiles, while the gymnasts and karate athletes differed from each other, as well as from the wrestlers and football players.

Similarly, Singer (1969) observed that collegiate baseball players (a team sport) differed significantly from tennis players (an individual sport) in several personality variables. Specifically, tennis players scored higher than baseball players on the desire to do one's best, desire to lead, and ability to analyze others, but were less willing to accept blame.

Schurr et al. (1977), in their signal research, clearly demonstrated that personality profile differences exist between players of team and individual sports, and between players of direct and parallel sports. Team sport athletes were observed to be more anxious, dependent, extraverted,

CONCEPT In many cases, athletes playing different positions on the same team can be differentiated as a function of personality characteristics. This is especially pronounced in sports in which athletes are required to do very different kinds of things. Point guards in basketball, setters in volleyball, quarterbacks in American football, and goalies in soccer and/or ice hockey can be expected to exhibit personality characteristics decidedly different from those of some other position players.

APPLICATION Personality characteristics of athletes can be considered in the selection of players for certain specialized positions. Results of personality tests and the like may be helpful in identifying a self-confident, energetic, and outgoing extravert to run your multiple offense in volleyball or your motion offense in basketball. You may also ascertain that an individual has these same important characteristics by simply observing athletes in competitive situations. It may not take a pencil-and-paper test to tell you that Mary excels at taking charge of the team when she is on the court. One should not forget, however, that physical characteristics such as speed, power, and quickness are also critically important.

and alert-objective, but less sensitive-imaginative, than individual sport athletes. Direct sport athletes (basketball, football, soccer, etc.) were observed to be more independent and to have less ego strength than parallel sport athletes (volleyball, baseball, etc.).

Clingman and Hilliard (1987) examined the personality characteristics of super-adherers and found them to differ significantly from the population norm in the personality traits of achievement, aggression, autonomy, dominance, endurance, harm avoidance, and play. Super-adherers are runners, swimmers, cyclists, and triathletes who are dedicated to endurance activities. While data were not provided, the expectation is that the super-adherer would also differ from athletes in other sports in certain personality traits.

The literature shows that athletes in one sport often differ in personality type and profile from athletes in other sports (Franken, Hill, & Kierstead, 1994). It seems reasonable, for example, to expect a football player to be more aggressive, anxious, and tolerant of pain than a golfer or a tennis player. However, the point still needs to be made that the state of the art (or science) is still not so refined that one could feel justified in arbitrarily categorizing young athletes based on their personality profiles.

Player Position and Personality Profile

In the previous section, the notion of personality types among athletes of differing sports was discussed. It was concluded that in many circumstances, differences exist between the personality profiles of athletes from different sports. The same concept can be applied to whether athletes of a certain sport exhibit different personality profiles based on player position.

In recent years we have experienced an age of superspecialization in team sports. In baseball, outfielders are inserted based on whether they hit left- or right-handed. In football, the offense and defense of the same team rarely come in contact with each other. In volleyball, hitters and setters have specialized roles that dictate the sorts of defensive and offensive assignments they fulfill. Similar kinds of specializations can be observed with most other team sports.

While this area of research would seem to be of interest to coaches and athletes, very little has been reported on it. Cox (1987) asked the following question relative to the sport of volleyball. Do center blockers, strong-side hitters, and setters display different psychological profiles due to their different assignments? The participants were

157 female volleyball players who participated in an invitational volleyball tournament. The results indicated that the three groups of athletes were very similar in terms of their psychological profiles, with the exception of certain attentional focus variables. Compared to middle blockers and strong-side hitters, setters were observed to have a broad internal focus and be able to think about several things at one time. The setter on a volleyball team is like the point guard on a basketball team or the quarterback on a football team. She must be cognizant at all times of what plays to call and of the strengths and weaknesses of front-line attackers, as well as the strengths and weaknesses of the opposing team's blockers and defensive alignment.

In a similar study reported by Schurr, Ruble, Nisbet, and Wallace (1984), a comparison was made between player position in football and personality traits. Using the Myers-Briggs Type Inventory (MBTI), the authors concluded that linesmen differ significantly from backfield players in terms of judging and perceiving traits. Linesmen tend to be more organized and practical, while defensive and offensive backs are more flexible and adaptable. Interestingly, no reliable differences were noted between offensive and defensive linesmen, while offensive backs tended to be more extraverted and defensive backs more introverted.

Personality Profiles of Athletes Differing in Skill Level

The ability to distinguish between successful and unsuccessful athletes in any particular sport using personality traits has never been particularly successful (Davis & Mogk, 1994; Morgan, 1980b). For example, Kroll (1967), using collegiate wrestlers, and Kroll and Carlson (1967), using karate participants, could not successfully distinguish between the successful and unsuccessful performers. Rushall (1972), using football players, and Singer (1969), using tennis and baseball players, likewise could not distinguish between the successful and unsuccessful players. In addition,

Craighead, Privette, and Byrkit (1986) were unable to distinguish between starters and nonstarters in high school boys' basketball.

A study by Williams and Parkin (1980) provides clarity to this line of reasoning. Specifically, they compared the personality profiles (Cattell's 16 PF) of 18 international-level male hockey players with those of 34 national-level and 33 club players. Their results showed that the international players had significantly different profiles from the club players, but that the national-level players could not be distinguished from players in either of the other two groups.

Thus, one exception to the general rule that skill level cannot be differentiated as a function of personality may occur when *elite athletes* are compared with athletes of lesser ability. Notice that in the Williams and Parkin (1980) study cited above, international-level hockey players exhibited personality profiles that differed from those of club-level players, but not national-level players. Silva (1984) provided a plausible explanation for this phenomenon. As illustrated in figure 2.2, as aspiring elite athletes move up the **athletic pyramid,** they become more alike in their personality and psychological traits. At the base or entrance level of sport, athletes are very heterogeneous, or have different personalities. However, certain personality traits will enhance an athlete's likelihood of advancing to a higher level, while other traits will undermine it. Through a process of "natural selection," at each higher level of the athletic personality pyramid, the athletes become more alike, or more homogeneous, in their personality traits. When trying to differentiate between athletes of varying skill levels in the middle and lower parts of the pyramid, we meet with failure. Elite athletes, however, will exhibit similar profiles and will differ as a group from less-skilled groups.

The Female Athlete

The conclusions and generalizations that have been drawn from the previous comparison areas have come primarily through research conducted

FIGURE 2.2 | The personality-performance athletic pyramid.

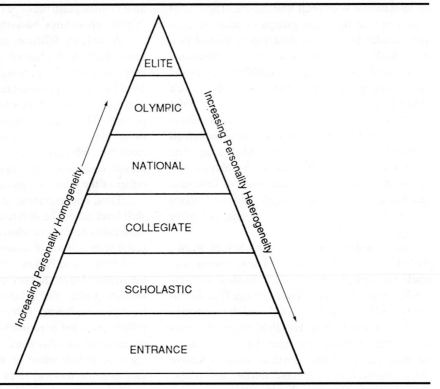

Source: From Personality and sport performance: Controversy and challenge by Silva, J. M., III. (1984). In J. M., Silva, III and R. S. Weinberg (Eds.), *Psychological foundations of sport,* Human Kinetics Publishers, Inc. Reproduced by permission of publisher.

on male rather than female participants. This is not to say that the conclusions would have been any different if female participants had been used. Indeed, we should expect the results to be essentially the same. However, after a thorough review of the available literature, Morgan (1980a) drew this conclusion: "Comparisons of college athletes and nonathletes, or athletes from different sport groups, did not appear to be consistent in the literature dealing with females" (p. 60). Morgan blames methodological and design problems for the inconsistent results. He points out that this inconsistency seems to disappear when the successful or elite female athlete is compared with the "normative" female.

After reviewing much of the available literature on the female athlete and personality, Williams (1980) cautiously concluded that the "normative" female differs in personality profile from the successful female athlete. Specifically, the female athlete is found to exhibit personality traits much like those of both the normative male and the male athlete (i.e., assertive, achievement-oriented, dominant, self-sufficient, independent, aggressive, intelligent, and reserved). For example, in comparison with available norms, female bodybuilders were observed to be more extraverted, more vigorous, less anxious, less neurotic, less depressed, less angry, and less confused (Freedson, Mihevic, Loucks, & Girandola, 1983).

CONCEPT As they move up the athletic pyramid, as illustrated in figure 2.2, athletes become more alike, or homogeneous, in terms of both their personalities and their skill levels. Correlations between athletic ability and personality traits are either nonexistent or trivial for athletes within the same hierarchical level.

APPLICATION Results of personality testing should not be used to decide who should be first- or second-string players on an athletic team. Similarly, results of personality testing should not be used to decide whether an athlete is selected

for a team at any level of competition. Results of personality testing are somewhat effective in distinguishing players on an elite level from players on a lower level, but this provides little new information. Results of personality testing may provide some useful diagnostic information to help an athlete make needed personal adjustments, but they provide only a small amount of athletic ability information. Organizations that insist on using personality or psychological testing to make personnel decisions will make some good decisions, but they will also make a lot of bad decisions.

The Interactional Model

In the previous sections, we learned that personality alone is a weak predictor of athletic behavior (performance). The individual, however, does not normally function in isolation. The athlete, possessed with a distinct set of personality traits, performs alongside other individuals and in changing environmental conditions (situation). It is believed, therefore, that the sum of the two plus their interaction would be a stronger predictor of athletic behavior. The notion that the personality interacts with situation to predict performance is known as the **interactional model.** Situational factors include stressful situations and perceived intensity of the situations. Information about personality plus information about the situation plus the interaction between the two is a better predictor of athlete behavior than personality or the situation alone. This relationship is represented in the following formula:

$$\text{Behavior} = \text{Personality} + \text{Situation} + \text{P} \times \text{S} + \text{Error}$$

The error in the formula represents all of the *unmeasured* factors that may contribute to athletic behavior.

The relationship between the personality of the individual and the situation is illustrated in figure 2.3. In this figure, the total pie represents all the factors that can contribute to athletic behavior or performance. Only a small part of the total pie is due to factors associated with the athlete's personality. Another small portion is due to factors directly related to the situation and independent of or unrelated to the person. Next, a certain part of the pie is represented by the interaction between the personality and the situation. When factors associated with the athlete's personality, the environmental situation, and the interaction between these three are summed, approximately 30 percent of the athlete's behavior is accounted for. If we were to consider only the athlete's personality, then we could explain only about 10 to 15 percent of the athlete's performance or behavior.

While the interaction concept illustrated in figure 2.3 is conceptually accurate, the reality is that in many situations the strength of the environmental conditions is so strong that it essentially dwarfs the influence of personality on performance. For example, consider the situation in which a basketball player is sent to the foul line to shoot two free throws with his team trailing by one point and there is no time left on the clock. The athlete shooting the

39

FIGURE 2.3 | Illustration showing the contribution of personality and situation to total athlete behavior.

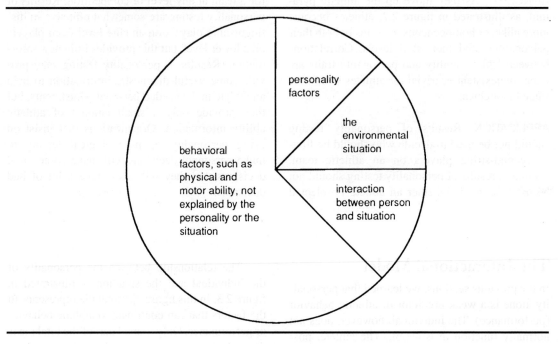

free throw may have a disposition to be low in anxiety, but it is unlikely that anyone could approach this situation without feeling anxious. In this particular situation, the athlete who normally hits 85 percent of his free throws might hit both shots or uncharacteristically miss one or both. It is also conceivable that an athlete who normally hits 65 percent of her free throws might hit both shots and win the game. In both situations, the athlete's personality remains the same because it is relatively stable, yet actual athlete behavior (performance) may be inconsistent. Smith (2006) referred to this inconsistency between behavior and personality as the **personality paradox.**

Based on earlier work by Mischel and Shoda (1995) Smith proposed the **cognitive affective processing system** (CAPS) (Figure 2.4) as a way to explain the personality paradox. According to CAPS, an individual's personality interacts with

the environment (situation) to determine a behavioral response (performance). The actual response (shooting the free throws), however, is filtered through the five elements of the CAPS system. The resultant behavioral response will be the end result of the filtering. Because every situation is different, the behavioral responses will also be different and inconsistent from one occasion to the next. This is true despite the fact that the athlete's basic personality has not changed from one situation to the next. As illustrated in figure 2.4, the five elements of the CAPS system are as follows:

1. Stimuli are *encoded* and are mentally represented in memory.

2. Predetermined *expectations* and *beliefs* confer meaning on events.

3. *Affects* and *emotions* influence behavior.

4. Personal *goals* and *values* influence behavior.

CONCEPT   The combined and interactive effects of personality and the environment constitute a stronger predictor of athletic performance than personality alone.

APPLICATION   The fact that Linda is an anxious person may not be predictive of athletic performance, but the fact that Linda is an anxious person *and* that she gets very anxious in competitive situations might be. These two factors together, and the interaction between them, may create a situation that will not be conducive to consistent ground stroking in competitive tennis. The coach needs to know more about Linda than that she is generally an anxious person. The coach also needs to know how she responds in a specific competitive situation.

FIGURE 2.4 | The Cognative-Affective Processing System (CAPS) applied to athlete behaviour (based on Mischel & Shoda, 1995; Smith, 2006).

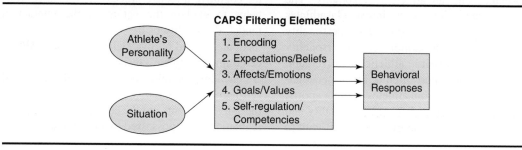

5. *Competencies* and *self-regulation skills* interact with the other four elements to determine behavior.

The fifth element of the filter interacts with the other four elements to determine how the environmental situation interacts with personality to determine the behavioral response. Behavioral responses are inconsistent and vary from situation to situation because of the changing environmental situation and the influence of the elements of the filter.

Summary

Personality is defined as all the consistent ways in which the behavior of one person differs from that of others, especially in social situations. An individual's personality defines the person in unique ways that remain stable and consistent over time. A person's typical responses and role-related behaviors don't always reflect that person's true personality.

Five theories or approaches to studying personality were reviewed. These were (1) the psychodynamic approach, (2) social learning theory, (3) humanistic theory, (4) the trait theory approach, and (5) Jung's theory of personality types. A number of different approaches to measuring personality were also discussed. These included rating scales, projective procedures, and pencil-and-paper inventories. A number of different personality inventories were described, including the Minnesota Multiphasic Personality Inventory, Cattell's 16 PF, the NEO–Five Factor Personality Inventory, the Myers-Briggs Type Indicator, the Athletic Motivation Inventory, the Winning Profile Athletic Instrument, and the Troutwine Athletic Profile. In addition, inventories that measure emotional intelligence and resilience were discussed.

Several factors were considered concerning whether a relationship exists between athletic performance and an athlete's personality. The following conclusions were drawn: (1) athletes differ from nonathletes on many personality traits; (2) athletes who exhibit certain personality traits gravitate toward athletic involvement; (3) athletes in one sport often differ in personality, type, and profile from athletes in other sports; (4) an association exists between personality and player position in some sports; (5) it is difficult to discriminate between players of differing skill level based purely upon personality variables; (6) elite athletes can be discriminated from athletes of low ability based on personality variables; and (7) female athletes are very similar to male athletes in the general conclusions that have been drawn.

Personality by itself is an important but relatively weak predictor of athletic performance and behavior. In conjunction with the situation or environment, however, the influence of personality on behavior is enhanced (the interaction model). The interaction model is described in mathematical terms as follows: Behavior = Personality (P) + Situation (S) + P × S + error. The application of the cognitive-affective processing system (CAPS) helps to explain the nature of the interaction model. Personality of the athlete and the environment are filtered by five elements of the CAPS to determine the athlete's response. The five elements are encoding, beliefs, affect, goal and values, and self-regulation skills. The most important of these five elements are the competencies and self-regulation skills possessed by the athlete.

Critical Thought Questions

1. Why do you think the big five personality traits do not agree exactly with Cattell's five global traits?

2. Now that you have studied the various ways that sport psychologists measure personality, which inventory would you recommend for use? Why?

3. Given that research does not support the use of personality profiles for making athlete personnel decisions, why do you think the practice persists?

4. Provide a summary statement about the existence and strength of the relationship between personality and athletic performance.

5. Why would the interactional model improve the prediction of athletic performance? Do you think it improves it enough to make the model useful for personnel decisions about athletes?

6. Discuss the cognitive-affective processing system (CAPS) as a way of understanding the interaction model.

Glossary

Athletic Motivation Inventory A personality inventory designed to predict athletic success (Institute for the Study of Athletic Motivation).

athletic pyramid A pyramid showing less-skilled players at the base and more highly skilled players at the top. Athletes at the bottom are more heterogeneous in terms of personality characteristics, while those at the top are more homogeneous.

big five personality traits Trait psychologists identified the five major personality traits to be neuroticism, extraversion, agreeableness, conscientiousness, and openness.

Cattell 16 PF Cattell's Personality Factor Questionnaire, measuring the 16 source traits of personality.

Cognitive-affective processing system (CAPS) Model of leadership and personality that explains how personality interacts with the environment to produce a behavioral response.

disposition A tendency to behave in a certain manner. Also called a personality trait.

Emotional intelligence The innate or learned ability to regulate emotions, typically associated with positive mood and self-esteem.

global personality traits Cattell's version of the big five personality traits: extraversion, anxiety, tough-mindedness, independence, and self-control.

gravitational hypothesis The notion that athletes possessing stable, extraverted personalities gravitate toward athletics.

interactional model An approach to sport personality based on the notion that both personality traits and situational states should be used in any prediction equation.

MMPI Minnesota Multiphasic Personality Inventory; a 12-scale test designed for clinical populations.

multivariate approach The practice of measuring and analyzing correlated dependent variables simultaneously, as opposed to separately, as in the univariate approach.

Myers-Briggs Type Indicator A personality inventory, based on Jung's theory of personality types, that categorizes individuals according to personality type.

personality All the consistent ways in which the behavior of one person differs from that of others, especially in social situations.

Personality paradox The seeming contradiction that although personality traits within an individual are considered to be stable and consistent, the individual's behavioral responses in varied situations are not consistent.

personality profile The plotting of an athlete's standardized personality scores on a line or bar graph.

personality trait A disposition to exhibit certain personality characteristics.

Resilience The force within the individual that drives a person to confront and overcome adversity.

Troutwine Athletic Profile A personality inventory designed to predict athletic success (Troutwine).

Winning Profile Athletic Instrument A personality inventory designed to predict athletic success (PsyMetrics).

PART 2

Motivation in Sport and Exercise

I t is difficult to imagine anything being more important to success in sport than motivation. Sometimes we assume that great sport performances are based upon innate natural ability. Some might think, for example, that Tiger Woods' recent domination of the professional golf tour is somehow due to physical abilities that he was born with. Or we might believe that Michael Jordan's stature as perhaps the greatest basketball player in the history of the game was somehow based on innate physical abilities. However, close scrutiny of the training and preparation habits of all great performers can be traced to a combination of physical ability and *a drive to be the very best*. When Michael Jordan finished his college career at North Carolina, he possessed only an average outside jump shot. Through thousands of hours of practice and working on technique, he became a complete player. Defensive players feared his fall-away jump shot as much as they feared his explosive drive to the basket.

The athletic literature and folk history are full of examples of athletes who have excelled because of an internal desire, as opposed to physical attributes such as size, strength, power, and quickness. Former Boston Celtic great Larry Bird may be a case in point. Bird was never accused of possessing great quickness, speed, or vertical jumping ability, yet he remains one of the greatest basketball players of all time. Much of his greatness can be attributed to an intense internal desire to work hard and to achieve success. Examples of motivation are not restricted to sport. An admirer once remarked to a highly accomplished concert pianist, "I would give half my life to play as you do." The pianist responded, "That's exactly what I did." What is it that motivates an individual to give much of her life to accomplish a goal? For some reason (or reasons), the individual comes to believe that the goal is worth spending a lifetime and large amounts of money to achieve.

Motivation comes in many forms. Sometimes it is internal in nature and comes from a personal desire to find success independent of external rewards and enticements. Sometimes it is external in nature and comes from a desire to gain notoriety, fame, or financial rewards. Evidence exists to suggest that external rewards are often only fleeting motivators, and can in the end actually undermine intrinsic, or internal, motivation. In the chapters that follow, we will examine the literature and unravel many of the mysteries surrounding the sometimes elusive concept of motivation.

Insight into the deeper meaning of motivation comes from the early work of psychologists such as Hull (1943, 1951) and Spence (1956), who demonstrated that animals will go to extraordinary lengths to reduce an internal drive such as hunger or thirst. Drive theory, as proposed by these psychologists, is a theory of motivation based upon the notion of drive reduction. Drive theory states that motivation is related to a desire to reduce or satisfy an internal drive. In the case of sport, the drive may be to become an All-American track star or to make a high school basketball or football team. Motivation to achieve success in sport, however, is not simply an innate drive, such as the drive to satisfy hunger or thirst, but one that is developed and learned. The root of the word *motivation* is the word *motive*. The Latin form of this word is *movere,* meaning "to move." The desire to move, as opposed to remaining stationary, is the essence of motivation.

Another insight into the basic concept of motivation comes from the classic work of Abraham Maslow (1970, 1987). Maslow's concept of motivation is based upon a needs hierarchy. A person must first satisfy lower-level needs before he can turn his attention to satisfying higher-level needs. Lower-level needs include the basic need to feel safe and the needs to satisfy the cravings of hunger and thirst. Once these fundamental needs have been satisfied, the individual can turn his attention to satisfying higher-level human needs, such as the needs to be loved, to feel worthy, to feel competent, and to realize self-fulfillment. Maslow's higher-level needs are the ones that can be achieved through involvement in sport and exercise. Maslow's hierarchy of needs is helpful, however, as it demonstrates that it is difficult to focus upon a higher need such as competence and self-fulfillment if you are hungry, thirsty, or fearing for your personal safety.

Building upon the theories of Hull (1943, 1951) and Spence (1956), Atkinson (1964) and

McClelland (McClelland, Atkinson, Clark, & Lowell, 1953) developed what was to be called the McClelland-Atkinson model of motivation. This model was based upon two basic psychological constructs that remain important in understanding motivation to this day. The first is the construct of intrinsic motivation, or what McClelland and Atkinson called the motive to achieve success; and the second was anxiety, or what they called fear of failure. The theory was an approach-avoidance model in the sense that an individual makes a decision to either engage in (approach) or withdraw from (avoid) an achievement situation based upon the magnitude or strength of the two psychological constructs. If the individual's intrinsic motivation to take part in an achievement situation were greater than her fear of failing at it, she would take part. Conversely, if the individual's fear of failure were stronger than her intrinsic motivation to take part, she would withdraw from the situation. In its simplest form, the model is represented by the following equation:

Participation = intrinsic motivation − fear of failure

As the McClelland-Atkinson model evolved, it took on added features, referred to as elaborations. While thoroughly studied between 1950 and 1970, the theory has been largely abandoned by most psychologists and sport psychologists in favor of more situation-specific theories. One reason the theory was abandoned was its complexity and the difficulty of measuring its psychological constructs. The one redeeming characteristic of the theory, however, was that the specific psychological constructs were systematically identified and studied in an attempt to explain the phenomenon of human motivation.

In this part of the book, motivation in sport will be thoroughly investigated and explained through three important chapters. The three chapters will cover the important topics of self-confidence and intrinsic motivation, goal perspective theory, and youth sports. Each of these chapters will explain motivation from the perspective of sport and exercise involvement. We seek to understand what motivation is and how it can be developed in sport and exercise. ∞

Self-Confidence and Intrinsic Motivation

KEY TERMS

Achievement situation
Additive principle
Amotivation
Attribution theory
Attribution training
Autonomous extrinsic motivation
Autonomy
Cognitive evaluation theory
Competence motivation
Controlled extrinsic motivation
Controlling aspect of external motivation
Efficacious pawn
External regulation
Extrinsic motivation
Gender stereotyping
Global self-confidence
Harmonious passion
Hot hand phenomenon
Identified regulation
Informational aspect of external motivation
Integrated regulation
Internalization
Intrinsic motivation
Introjected regulation
Mediator variable
Moderator variable
Multiplicative principle

Observational learning
Obsessive passion
Participatory modeling
Precipitating event
Psychological momentum
Reflected appraisal process
Relatedness
Self-determination

Self-determination and autonomy continuum
Self-determination theory
Self-efficacy
Situation-specific self-confidence
Social comparison
Sport-confidence
Stereotype threat theory

Self-confidence and motivation are not synonymous concepts, but they are very closely related. Athletes who are highly motivated tend to be very self-confident about their abilities. Yet, a distinction must be made between **global self-confidence** and **situation-specific self-confidence.** Global self-confidence is more of a personality trait or disposition. One can exhibit a great deal of global self-confidence and not be successful at a specific sport or physical activity. Global self-confidence is an important personality characteristic that facilitates daily living. It can be instrumental in encouraging a young person to try new things, but it is not the same as believing that you can succeed at a specific task. The basketball player who enjoys situation-specific self-confidence truly believes that she can make her free throws when the game is on the line. In the closing moments of a close competition between two teams, the coach wants the ball in the hands of the individual who believes completely in his ability to succeed. This is situation-specific self-confidence.

In this chapter we will (a) provide an in-depth discussion of self-confidence and the role it plays in the development of intrinsic motivation, (b) discuss sport psychology topics related to sport psychology, (c) introduce the integrated theory of motivation in sport, and (d) conclude with a discussion of cognitive evaluation theory. It is often thought that self-confidence is something that the skilled athlete exhibits, but in reality self-confidence is a fundamental building block in the development of motivation. Athletes are motivated to practice and to perform because they possess confidence that they can eventually succeed and excel at their sport. It is critical that athletes develop both situation-specific self-confidence and global self-confidence. A historical example of an athlete who possessed overwhelming skill as well as extreme self-confidence is Jack Morris. Morris was the winning pitcher in game 7 of the 1991 World Series between the Minnesota Twins and the Atlanta Braves. "In perhaps the best World Series game ever played, the Twins' Jack Morris gave us one final glimpse of a dying breed: a pitcher who was determined to finish whatever he started" (Verducci, 2003, p. 71). Following the game which the Twins won 1–0 in the tenth inning, Jack Morris made the following statement in a post-game interview: "I never had as much will to win a game as I did on that day. I was in trouble many times during the game but didn't realize it because I never once had a negative thought" (Jack Morris, Minnesota Twins pitcher, in Verducci, 2003, p. 71). Another example of an athlete who exhibited great self-confidence and motivation was Karch Kiraly (kirai). Karch Kiraly was the only male volleyball player to win Olympic Gold Medals in both the indoor game (1984, 1988) and in beach volleyball (1996). Karch was only 6'2", short for most front line attackers, but he had a rare blend of skill and motivation that put him in a class of his own. When he retired from the professional beach volleyball circuit at 46, no one could pass better, defend tougher, last longer, or win more than Karch Kiraly. He will go down in history as the Michael Jordan of men's volleyball (Anderson, 2007).

Models of Self-Confidence

In this section a number of cognitive models will be introduced that use terms essentially equivalent to the concept of situation-specific self-confidence. These include Bandura's *self-efficacy,* Harter's *competence motivation,* and Vealey's *sport-confidence.* Each reflects the notion of situation-specific self-confidence, as opposed to a global personality trait.

Bandura's Theory of Self-Efficacy

Bandura (1997) defined **self-efficacy** as "beliefs in one's capabilities to organize and execute the courses of action required to produce given attainments" (p. 3). As such, self-efficacy is a form of situation-specific self-confidence (Feltz & Chase, 1998). Self-efficacy is the critical component of what Bandura refers to as *social cognitive theory.* Other important components of social cognitive theory are agency and personal control. In order for self-efficacy to develop, the individual must believe that she is in control and that acts she

FIGURE 3.1 | Relationship between factors leading to self-efficacy beliefs and athletic performance.

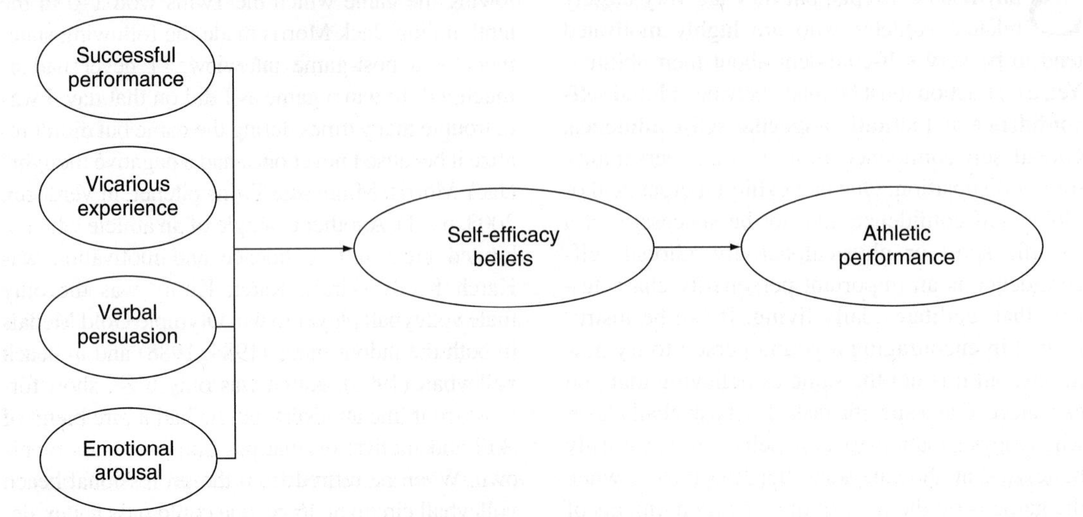

performed were performed intentionally. If an athlete perceives or believes that she can influence for good the outcome of a contest, she will eagerly enter into the competition. Thus, an efficacious athlete is a motivated athlete. The athlete is motivated to work hard to ensure success because she believes that she can succeed.

Bandura (1977, 1982, 1986, 1997) proposed four fundamental elements effective in developing self-efficacy (see fig. 3.1). Each of these elements is critical in understanding how an athlete can develop self-efficacy and self-confidence:

1. *Successful Performance*   The athlete must experience success in order for self-efficacy to develop. With a difficult task, this is an unrealistic expectation, so the coach or teacher must ensure success by initially reducing the difficulty of the task. An example of how this can be accomplished is found in tennis and volleyball instruction. A beginner may not be able to successfully serve a volleyball across the net on a regulation court, but when the coach encourages the athlete to step into the court several meters, it can be accomplished.

2. *Vicarious Experience*   Beginning athletes can experience success through the use of models. This is also referred to as **observational learning.** In learning a new skill, the learner needs a template or model to copy. This can be provided by the instructor, a skilled teammate, or a film or video of a skilled performer. An important component of Bandura's theory is the concept of participatory modeling. In **participatory modeling,** the learner first observes a model perform a task. Then the model or instructor assists the subject in successfully performing the task. Observational learning may be measured with the Functions of Observational Learning Questionnaire (FOLQ; Cumming, Clark, Ste-Marie, McCullagh, & Hall, 2005). The FOLQ measures three functions of observational learning including skill, strategy, and performance. Research suggests that the skill development function of observational learning is higher for younger golfers compared to older golfers, especially when the skill level of the older golfers is low. The strategy and performance development functions of

observational learning are both facilitated by decreased age and increased skill level (Law & Hall, 2009). This suggests that age and skill level of the athlete influence the effectiveness of observational learning.

3. *Verbal Persuasion* Verbal persuasion usually comes in the form of encouragement from the coach, parents, or peers. Helpful verbal statements that suggest that the athlete is competent and can succeed are most desirable. Negative comments should always be avoided. Coaching tips can be given in such a way that they do not convey negativism. For example, the coach could say, "Good swing, Mary; now remember to keep your eyes on the ball." Verbal persuasion can also take the form of self-persuasion. This is referred to as self-talk, and will be discussed in greater detail in chapter 9.

4. *Emotional Arousal* Emotional and physiological arousal are factors that can influence readiness for learning. Details as to exactly how this can happen will be discussed in a subsequent chapter. For now, it is important to understand that we must be emotionally ready and optimally aroused in order to be attentive. Proper attention is important in helping the athlete to master a particular skill and develop a feeling of efficacy.

The efficacy of Bandura's model in the sport setting is well documented. Perceived self-efficacy is a strong and consistent predictor of individual athletic performance (Feltz, Chow, & Hepler, 2008; Gao, Kosmo, & Harrison, 2009; Gau, Xiang, Lee, & Harrison, 2008; Moritz, Feltz, Fahrbach, & Mack, 2000). As a general rule, compared with persons who doubt their capabilities, those exhibiting high self-efficacy work harder, persist in the task longer, and achieve at a higher level. Furthermore, logic and some evidence suggest that situation-specific self-confidence can generalize to other situations and to global self- confidence (Zinsser, Bunker, & Williams, 2010). Every child should become competent in at least one sport or activity. This will provide the foundation for the development of self-efficacy in other areas, as well as increasing global self-confidence.

Sport-related research continues to inform our understanding of the relationship between self-efficacy and athletic performance. Research shows that self-efficacy beliefs are influenced by perceived outcome. Experimentally manipulated success results in increased self-efficacy beliefs, but manipulated failure results in decreased self-efficacy (Gernigon & Delloye, 2003). In an earlier investigation by Feltz (1982), it was concluded that past diving performance was a stronger predictor of subsequent diving performance than was self-efficacy. However, Feltz et al. (2008) later reported that when the effect of self-efficacy to the past performance was statistically removed, self-efficacy to the subsequent performance was actually a stronger predictor than was past performance. Thus, self-efficacy is a stronger predictor of subsequent performance than even past performance.

Given that self-efficacy is important for athletic success, what are some of the strategies that coaches say they find most effective for enhancing self-efficacy? Male and female Division I and II collegiate coaches from the sports of baseball, basketball, softball, and soccer believe that the most effective strategies for enhancing self-efficacy are (a) instruction drilling, (b) acting confident themselves, and (c) encouraging positive self-talk (Vargas-Tonsing, Myers, & Feltz, 2004).

In a study involving self-efficacy for performing physically challenging outdoor recreational tasks (e.g., jogging three miles, mountain biking) it was observed that personal characteristics associated with a task determine whether or not self-efficacy will develop. Strong self-efficacy for a task was associated with high performance when the participant believed she or he possessed the personal characteristics considered to facilitate performance. Conversely, weak self-efficacy for a task was associated with low performance when the participant believed she or he did not possess the personal characteristics required to facilitate performance (Wise, 2007).

CONCEPT Development of perceived self-efficacy and self-confidence is closely associated with the level of success experienced by the athlete.

APPLICATION Find ways to help the athlete experience success. You can accomplish this by reducing the initial difficulty of the task, or through participatory modeling, in which the instructor or model assists the athlete in learning the skill.

The benefits of perceived self-efficacy are not limited to the individual. Groups that collectively exhibit high self-efficacy also tend to perform at a higher level than groups exhibiting low collective self-efficacy (George & Feltz, 1995; Magyar, Feltz, & Simpson, 2004). This confidence in the team is referred to as *collective self-efficacy*. Just as it is important to develop self-efficacy in individual athletes, it is also important to develop a sense of collective self-efficacy in a team. In later chapters we will introduce and develop the related concepts of team building and team cohesion.

Harter's Competence Motivation Theory

Patterned after White's (1959) theory of effectance motivation, Harter (1978) proposed a theory of achievement motivation that is based on an athlete's feeling of personal competence. According to Harter, individuals are innately motivated to be competent in all areas of human achievement. To satisfy the urge to be competent in an achievement area such as sport, the person attempts mastery. An individual's self-perception of success at these mastery attempts develops feelings of positive or negative affect. As illustrated in figure 3.2, successful attempts at mastery promote self-efficacy and feelings of personal competence, which in turn foster high competence motivation. As **competence motivation** increases, the athlete is encouraged to make further mastery attempts.

Conversely, if a young athlete's attempts at mastery result in perceived social rejection and failure, then low competence motivation and negative

affect will be the end product. It is hypothesized that low competence motivation will result in a youth sport dropout.

An investigation by Weiss and Horn (1990) underscores the importance of accurately assessing personal competence. Boys and girls who underestimate their own competence tend to be candidates for dropping out of sports. Girls who underestimate their own competence tend to drop

FIGURE 3.2 | Harter's competence motivation theory.

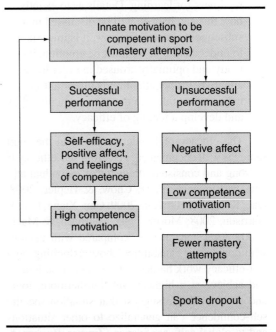

Source: From Harter, S. (1978). Effectance motivation reconsidered. *Human Development, 21,* 34–64. Adapted by permission of S. Karger AG, Basel.

CONCEPT Competence motivation may be enhanced in children through repeated successful mastery attempts.

APPLICATION Redefining success to include positive outcomes other than winning will allow more children to succeed. Success may come in the form of skill improvement, trying, or having fun.

out of sport involvement, suffer from high trait anxiety, prefer unchallenging activities, and be controlled by external forces. The effect of underestimation on boys seems to be less damaging. Generally, children who accurately assess their own ability feel more in control and seek involvement in challenging activities.

In a related investigation (Weiss & Amorose, 2005), youth sport participants were assessed relative to perceived physical competence, actual physical competence, and perceived sources of competence information. Participants were grouped as a function of age, perceived competence, actual competence, and a difference score between the two measures of competence (under, accurate, or over estimates of competence). The five emerging clusters were then contrasted on perceived sources of competence. Based on a cluster analysis (statistical grouping), two healthy profiles emerged. These were the "contenders" and "rising stars," who differed only in age but were similar in terms of high perceived competence, high actual competence, and accurate estimation of perceived competence. The contenders and the rising stars tended to score higher in sources of competence than other groups (e.g., performance, improvement, peer evaluation, enjoyment, and effort).

In Harter's model, high competence motivation leads to successful task performance, much as high self-efficacy leads to successful performance. Factors that enhance the development of high competence motivation include intrinsic motivation, years of sport experience, perceived control, praise and technical information, friendship, and peer group acceptance (Allen & Howe, 1998; Smith, 1999; Weigand & Broadhurst, 1998). Interestingly, Allen and Howe noted that praise

and technical information are effective in enhancing competence motivation in response to a good performance, but counter-productive when given in response to a poor performance. They suggested that "supportive silence" might be the best response to a poor performance.

Amorose (2003) provided specific evidence relative to the notion that social support from

The balance beam requires high level of confidences.
Courtesy University of Missouri-Columbia Sports Information.

significant others is important for developing and maintaining competence motivation. The process by which an individual comes to see himself as competent is referred to as the *reflected appraisal process*. The **reflected appraisal process** is a function of the actual appraisal of others, one's own appraisal of self, and one's perception of how others appraise you. The reflected appraisal of parents, coaches, and significant others is predictive of an athlete's perceived competence. As a result of an eight-week Girls on Track (GOT) program, Waldron (2007) noted improvements in five aspects of perceived competence, some of which relate directly to social support. These included perceived social competence and perceived close friendship competence.

Vealey's Multidimensional Model of Sport-Confidence

The multidimensional model of **sport-confidence** is a revision of Vealey's (1986, 1988) model of sport-confidence. The original model conceptualized trait sport-confidence, state sport-confidence, and competitive orientation as predictors of satisfaction and performance success. Limitations of the original model included inability of state sport-confidence (as measured by the State Sport-Confidence Inventory) to predict performance, and failure of the model to conceptualize measures of sport-confidence as being multidimensional in nature. To address these shortcomings in the original model, Vealey, Knight, and Pappas (2002) developed the Multidimensional Model of Sport-Confidence. The *Multidimensional Model of Sport-Confidence (MMSC)* is a model in which multidimensional sport-confidence is conceptualized as being more dispositional (trait) or state-like across a continuum of time.

As illustrated in figure 3.3, the rectangle at the top shows three source domains of sport-confidence (Vealey, Hayashi, Garner-Holman, & Giacobbi, 1998), as well as three types of sport-confidence. Together, the sport-confidence source domains and sport-confidence types are referred to as the *sport-confidence rectangle*. Constructs within the sport-confidence rectangle influence and are influenced by *characteristics of the athlete* (personality traits, attitudes, values), *demographic characteristics* (age, sex, ethnicity, culture), and *organizational culture* (competitive level, motivational climate, program goals). The three source domains of sport-confidence are identified in the figure as *achievement* (mastery and demonstration of ability), *self-regulation* (physical/mental preparation, physical self-presentation), and *social climate* (social support, coaches' leadership, vicarious experience, environmental comfort, situational favorableness). In the model, the sources of sport-confidence both influence and are influenced by the three types of sport-confidence. The three types of sport-confidence (SC) are *SC–cognitive efficiency* (decision making, thought management, maintaining focus), *SC–physical skills/training* (skill execution and training), and *SC-resilience* (overcoming obstacles, overcoming setbacks, overcoming doubts, refocusing after errors).

As also illustrated in figure 3.3, the self-confidence rectangle and, specifically, multidimensional sport-confidence determine how athlete and demographic characteristics and organizational culture influence the affect, behavior, and cognitions of the athlete (triangle). Affect, behavior, and cognition in turn influence athlete performance, which is also influenced by uncontrollable external factors and the physical skill and characteristics of the athlete. The utility and elegance of the model are that it shows how different types of sport-confidence are developed and how sport-confidence influences athletic performance.

In order to measure multidimensional sport-confidence and to test various aspects of the sport-confidence model, it was necessary to develop a sport-confidence inventory. The development of the Sport-Confidence Inventory (SCI) is chronicled in Vealey, Knight, et al. (2002). The resultant SCI is composed of 14 items anchored to a 7-point Likert scale that ranges from "Totally Certain" to "Can't Do It At All." The stem for all 14 item is "How certain are you that. . . ," and a sample item might

FIGURE 3.3 | Vealey's multidimensional model of sport-confidence.

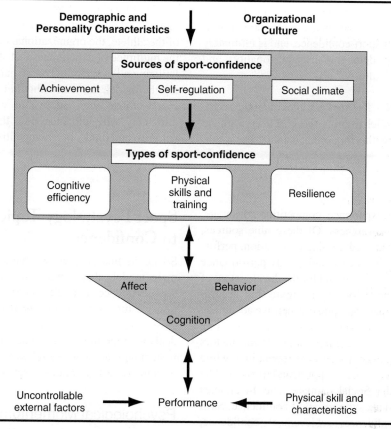

Source: Reproduced with permission from Vealey, R. S., Knight, B.J., & Pappas, G. (2002, November 2). *Self-confidence in sport: Conceptual and psychological advancement.* Paper presented at the annual convention of the Association for the Advancement of Applied Sport Psychology, Tucson, AZ.

be ". . . you can successfully perform the physical skills required in your sport?"

In support of the model, a number of recent investigations have shown a consistent relationship between an athlete's self-confidence and athletic performance (Beattie, Hardy, & Woodman, 2004; Craft, Magyar, Becker, & Feltz, 2003; Marsh & Perry, 2005; Sheldon & Eccles, 2005; Woodman & Hardy, 2003). Using slalom canoeists as participants, Beattie et al. (2004) showed that it is not just self-confidence that is related to performance, but also the discrepancy between an athlete's perception of ideal self-confidence and actual measured

self-confidence. A small discrepancy is correlated with athletic performance. In other words, best performance occurs when ideal self-confidence is the same as actual self-confidence.

Consistent with Vealey's model of sport confidence, Hays, Maynard, Thomas, and Bawden (2007) reported on an investigation that identified sources and types of sport confidence in 14 successful world-class elite athletes. These athletes identified the following nine sources of sport confidence as being important in their competitive careers: training preparation, performance accomplishments, quality coaching, social support,

CONCEPT Sport-confidence is multidimensional in nature, is developed as a function of multiple sources of sport-confidence, and is ultimately influenced by demographics, personality, and organizational culture.

APPLICATION The very complexity of the sport-confidence model informs the coach and athlete that something this important cannot be left to chance. In seeking to develop confidence in young athletes, attention must be given to the personality of the athlete, the organizational environment, and the multitude of experiences that shape the athlete. Utilizing all of the information gained from studying the model, the coach should patiently provide every athlete with successful experiences that ultimately will influence how the athlete feels, behaves, and thinks in a competitive situation.

innate factors, experience, competitive advantage, trust, and self-awareness. Of these nine sources, the athletes identified training preparation, performance accomplishments, and quality performance as being the most important for the development of sport confidence. Looking at figure 3.3, accomplishments, experience, and competitive advantage could be classified under Achievement; training preparation, self-awareness, and innate factors could be classified under Self-regulation; while quality coaching, social support, and trust could be classified under Social Climate. The 14 athletes also identified six types of sport confidence. Skill execution confidence, achievement confidence, physical confidence, and psychological confidence were identified by both the male and female athletes. Superiority to opposition and tactical awareness were two types of sport confidence identified by the male athletes only. Again, looking at figure 3.3, psychological confidence and superiority to opponents could be classified under SC-Cognitive Efficiency; skill execution, physical attributes, and tactical awareness could be classified under SC-Physical Skills and Training; while achievement could be classified under SC-Resilience. Thus, the Hays, Maynard, et al. (2007) study seems to provide supporting evidence for Vealey's multidimensional model of sport-confidence. In addition, an investigation reported by Kingston, Lane, and Thomas (2010) provides support for the Vealey model relative to sport confidence sources.

Sport Psychology Topics Related to Confidence

So far in this chapter, we have discussed three main models that explain how athletes develop self-confidence and self-efficacy. In this subsection we turn our attention to two topics that are closely related to confidence in sport. The first deals with the important concept of psychological momentum, and the second with the development of confidence as it relates to sex and gender.

Psychological Momentum in Sport

Among other things, athletes report a feeling of increased confidence during periods of perceived psychological momentum. For this reason, we are going to consider psychological momentum as a self-confidence topic. It is hard to escape experiencing the phenomenon of momentum as either a performing athlete or a spectator. Television announcers frequently use the term to describe an apparent shift in good fortune for an athlete or an athletic team. Athletic teams often seem to behave like giant boulders rolling down a mountain, gaining speed and momentum as they move downward. As the boulder picks up speed and is assisted by gravity, it seems unstoppable. Often, however, the boulder crashes into other large boulders or trees that slow its momentum and, in many cases, stop its downward plunge altogether.

CONCEPT   It is critical to the development of intrinsic motivation that the athlete develops a sense of psychological autonomy or agency. Social factors such as success, cooperation, and coaching behavior can facilitate the development of autonomy, but autonomy supportive coaching behavior is the best way to accomplish this.

APPLICATION   The coach should apply autonomy supportive coaching behaviors and strategies calculated to enhance autonomy in the athlete. Suggested strategies include providing choices and boundaries and explanations for training regimens, showing respect for athletes' perspectives, providing opportunities for taking the initiative, providing constructive feedback, not engaging in bullying, and encouraging a mastery approach. Measure autonomy supportive coaching behaviors using PASSES or some other scale designed to measure perceived autonomy supportive coaching.

The perception of autonomy on the part of the athlete is critical to the development of intrinsic motivation. Mageau and Vallerand (2003) and Mallett (2005) identified and tested specific strategies for developing the psychological need of autonomy. An incomplete list of strategies for developing autonomy in athletes includes the following:

1. Provide the athlete with boundaries and choices.

2. Provide a rationale for training tasks and regimen.

3. Acknowledge and respect athletes' perspectives and feelings.

4. Provide opportunities for independent work and for taking the initiative.

5. Provide feedback about competence that does not control or constrain behavior.

6. Avoid conscious bullying (a common coaching behavior).

7. Encourage a mastery approach to learning and discourage social comparison (e.g., I am better than you because I won the game).

A coach or teacher can promote the perception of autonomy in the athlete by applying these strategies. When the coach does this, she is exhibiting autonomy supportive coaching behavior. The Perceived Autonomy Support Scale for Exercise Settings (PASSES; Hagger, Chatzisarantis, Hein, et al., 2007) and the Autonomy-Supportive Coaching Questionnaire (ASCQ; Conroy & Coatsworth, 2007) allow the sport psychologist or coach to determine the degree to which the athlete perceives that the coach, parent, or peers exhibit autonomy supportive behavior. If the coach exhibits autonomy supportive behavior, it is predicted that the athlete will develop autonomy, a critical antecedent for intrinsic motivation (Gillet, Vallerand, Amoura, & Baldes, 2010; Mouratidis, Lens, & Vansteenkiste, 2010).

Relatedness   The third innate psychological need is the need for relatedness. Along with competence and autonomy, relatedness is necessary for a person to be self-actualized, or to realize his full potential as an athlete and as a human being. **Relatedness** has to do with the basic need to relate to other people, to care for others and have others care for you. Humans are social animals and have a basic need to interact in positive ways with other humans. In sport it is interesting to see how athletes support each other on the playing field. To a large extent, an athlete's enjoyment in sport is associated with how she relates to other athletes on her team, as well as to the coaches and support personnel. In the case of youth sports, relationships with parents and peers are also critical to children's satisfaction with the sport experience.

FIGURE 3.6 | The self-determination and autonomy continuum and the different types of motivation.

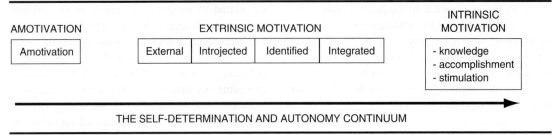

Source: Adapted from Vallerand, R. J., & Losier, G. F. (1999). An integrative analysis of intrinsic and extrinsic motivation in sport. *Journal of Applied Sport Psychology, 11,* 142–169. With permission of publisher.

Motivation

Looking at figure 3.5, we understand that social factors and psychological mediators are determinants of motivation. We should understand that competence, autonomy, and relatedness are psychological needs that mediate the relationship between social factors and the manifestation of motivation.

We should further understand that the degree to which an athlete feels competent, autonomous, and related depends on the quality of the social experiences that she has had. These social experiences come in the form of perceptions of success and failure, competition and cooperation, and coaching behaviors. This explains why the motivational climate created by the coaches is so critical to the development of motivation in athletes.

Looking again at figure 3.5, we can see that social factors and psychological mediators lead to motivation, but we can see also that there are different kinds of motivation. It is now time to discuss and define each type of motivation and explain how they relate to self-determination and to each other.

Motivation as it relates to self-determination is best conceptualized as a continuum. This is illustrated in figure 3.6 as the **self-determination and autonomy continuum.** What this figure illustrates is that the less self-determining forms of motivation are found to the far left of the continuum (amotivation), while the most self-determining forms of motivation are found to the far right of the

continuum (intrinsic motivation). At various stages along the middle of the continuum you have different kinds of extrinsic motivation. Some kinds of extrinsic motivation are associated with more self-determination, while others are associated with less self-determination.

Amotivation   The least self-determining kind of motivation is no motivation at all. This is referred to as amotivation. **Amotivation** refers to behaviors that are neither internally nor externally based. It is the relative absence of motivation. Relative to playing tennis, an amotivated athlete might say that he doesn't know why he plays tennis and that he doesn't see any particular benefit associated with it. In practice this seems to be a relatively rare form of motivation. Amotivated individuals usually will not even bother to become involved in sport.

Intrinsic Motivation   The kind of motivation that exhibits the highest level of self-determination, autonomy, and agency is referred to as being intrinsic or internal in nature. **Intrinsic motivation** is motivation that comes from within. Intrinsically motivated individuals engage in activities that interest them, and they engage in them freely, with a full sense of volition and personal control. There is no sense of engaging in the activity for a material reward or for any other kind of external reward or motivation. Intrinsic motivation is believed to be multidimensional in nature, or composed of more

CONCEPT Motivation that comes from within is intrinsic in nature. Tasks that are intrinsically motivating are tasks that are interesting and that are performed by the athlete because they are interesting. Personal volition and control are critical components of intrinsic motivation. An athlete spontaneously engages in an activity that is intrinsically motivating. There is no need for rewards or any sort of external control to motivate an athlete to engage in an intrinsically motivating behavior.

APPLICATION People readily participate in activities that they perceive to be interesting and unthreatening. Most young athletes start this way. A child wants to play baseball because it looks like a lot of fun and it is very interesting. The single most important goal of youth sport programs should be to retain a young person's intrinsic motivation and love for sport. Coaches and youth leaders should study the sport experience and focus on those activities and experiences that would cause a child to retain his intrinsic motivation.

than one dimension. The three aspects or manifestations of intrinsic motivation are motivation toward knowledge, toward accomplishment, and toward experiencing stimulation.

Intrinsic motivation *toward knowledge* reflects an athlete's desire to learn new skills and ways of accomplishing a task. Intrinsic motivation *toward accomplishment* reflects an athlete's desire to gain mastery over a particular skill and the pleasure that comes from reaching a personal goal for mastery. Intrinsic motivation *toward experiencing stimulation* reflects the feeling that an athlete gets from physically experiencing a sensation innate to a specific task.

Embedded within intrinsic motivation is the recently identified concept of passion. According to Vallerand, Blanchard, et al. (2003, p. 756), passion is defined as "a strong inclination toward an activity that people like, that they find important, and in which they invest time and energy." Passion is composed of two subscales and is measured in sport using the 14-item Passion Scale (Vallerand, Blanchard, et al., 2003). The two aspects of sport passion are obsessive and harmonious passion. **Obsessive passion** is controlling in nature and drives a person to engage in an activity they like. Conversely, **harmonious passion** is autonomous in nature and leads the person to choose to engage in an activity that they like. In obsessive passion a person feels compelled to engage in the activity even

though it conflicts with other aspects of their life and conflict is experienced. With harmonious passion the individual's passion for a sport or activity is in harmony with other aspects of their life and they are not conflicted. Research shows that sport valuation (sport importance) and an autonomous personality orientation lead to harmonious passion. Conversely, sport valuation and a controlled personality orientation lead to obsessive passion. Furthermore, harmonious passion leads to an increase in subjective well-being whereas obsessive passion leads to a decrease in subjective well-being. Clearly, harmonious as opposed to obsessive passion is preferred (Vallerand, Rousseau, et al., 2006).

Extrinsic Motivation While amotivation and intrinsic motivation lie at the two extremes of the self-determination continuum, extrinsic motivation falls in the large middle area. By definition, **extrinsic motivation** refers to motivation that comes from an external as opposed to an internal source. Extrinsic motivation comes in many forms, but common examples include awards, trophies, money, praise, social approval, and fear of punishment. As you will notice in figure 3.6, intrinsic and extrinsic motivation are not dichotomous concepts, as they were once believed to be. There are many degrees of extrinsic motivation. As one moves closer to the far right on the self-determination continuum, extrinsic motivation and

CONCEPT A skilled athlete who performs a behavior purely for external reasons is an efficacious pawn. Externally regulated behavior is behavior that is controlled by external sources.

APPLICATION Locus of causality shifts from an internal to an external cause when an athlete performs a behavior for purely external reasons. This shift may result in the athlete's losing a sense of personal control over her environment. Before engaging in a system of external rewards or punishment,

the coach should always ask the following question: "If I quit rewarding the athlete or quit threatening punishment, will this athlete perform the desired behavior?" If the answer to that question is "no" or "probably not," then the coach is engaging in coaching behaviors that are undermining the athlete's intrinsic motivation for the activity. Once an athlete's intrinsic motivation has been severely diminished, it is only a matter of time before the athlete either gives up the activity or performs it without passion. It is difficult to say which outcome is worse.

intrinsic motivation become more alike in terms of self-determinism. Deci and Ryan (1991) identified four different types of extrinsic motivation. These four different types of extrinsic motivation are titled external regulation, introjected regulation, identified regulation, and integrated regulation. The term *regulation* refers to the perception that a behavior is either internally or externally regulated. External regulation is believed to be the furthest removed from intrinsic motivation, while integrated regulation is believed to be the most closely associated with intrinsic motivation in terms of self-determinism. With this concept clearly in mind, the notion that intrinsic and extrinsic motivation are dichotomous in nature loses meaning.

External regulation describes the least self-determined form of extrinsic motivation. A behavior that is performed only to obtain an external reward or to avoid punishment is said to be externally regulated. For example, an externally regulated runner takes part in a weekend 10-kilometer race because of the promise of a trophy and a cash reward. An externally regulated basketball player carefully avoids the appearance of "slacking off" to avoid the punishment of running extra exhausting sprints after practice. Neither of these behaviors leads to self-determination and the perception of being in personal control. The athletes in these

two examples are pawns in terms of exercising personal control of their behavior.

Together, the last three types of extrinsic motivation (introjected, identified, integrated) represent various levels of internalization. **Internalization** is a natural outcome of integration that comes as people obtain meaningful relationships with others. Rewards and other forms of extrinsic motivation become less external and more internal through the process of internalization. The process of internalization involves assimilation. External motives become assimilated as they are accepted as one's own and become part of the person.

Extrinsic motivation that has undergone **introjected regulation** is only partially internalized. It evokes a greater degree of self-determination than an externally regulated motive, but it is still not completely assimilated. In this state of assimilation, the athlete still struggles with the notion of causality. He has partially internalized a motive, but he still perceives the motivation as controlling. An example might be the degree to which an athlete feels that he practices daily to please his coach, as opposed to practicing to become a better player because he wants to become a better player. The motive has become partially internalized or regulated.

When an athlete comes to "identify" with an extrinsic motivation to the degree that it is perceived as being her own, it is referred to as being an

CONCEPT   Through a process of assimilation, motives originally perceived as being externally controlling and uninteresting may become internalized. Once internalized, extrinsic motivations become associated with higher levels of self-determination.

APPLICATION   Asking an athlete to conceptualize the reasons that she participates in sport is a worthwhile exercise. Perhaps of greater importance is to determine to what degree extrinsic motives are internalized. Steps should be taken by the coach to remove or restructure motivations that are perceived by the athlete as being externally controlling. The athlete should feel as if she is participating in sport and practicing long hours for reasons that she has chosen or internalized, and not reasons that others have imposed on her.

---

identified regulation. Identified regulation is present when an athlete engages in an activity that she does not perceive as being particularly interesting, but does so because she sees the activity as being instrumental for her to obtain another goal that is interesting to her. An example might be a soccer player who lifts weight in the off-season to improve her kicking power. She participates in soccer because it is an interesting activity. She wants to excel in soccer, so she engages in what she perceives to be an uninteresting activity to obtain her goal.

The most internalized form of regulation is referred to as **integrated regulation.** When regulatory mechanisms are well integrated, they become personally valued and freely done. At this level of integration, a behavior previously considered to be externally controlled becomes fully assimilated and internally controlled. From the perspective of self-determination, the fully integrated extrinsic motivation can hardly be distinguished from intrinsic motivation. At this stage the athlete perceives a coach's controlling behaviors as being completely consistent with his own aspirations and goals and no longer perceives them as being externally controlling.

Consequences of Motivation

Referring back to figure 3.5, we see that there are hypothesized consequences associated with motivation. High levels of intrinsic motivation and internalized extrinsic motivation should lead to positive affect, positive behavioral outcomes, and improved cognition. Research shows (Vallerand & Losier, 1999) that athletes who engage in sport for self-determined reasons experience more positive and less negative affect, have greater persistence, and exhibit higher levels of sportspersonship (why you play determines how you play).

Measuring Self-determined Motivation

Pelletier et al. (1995) reported on the development of the Sport Motivation Scale (SMS), designed to measure the different aspects of motivation that are illustrated in figure 3.6. The SMS measures amotivation, external regulation, introjected regulation, identified regulation, and three aspects of intrinsic motivation. As noted, the SMS does not measure integrated regulation. The authors explained that integrated regulation was not included because of the difficulty of measuring the construct. While the SMS has been largely embraced by researchers seeking to measure motivation within the self-determination model, its failure to measure integrated regulation along with problems associated with its hypothesized factor structure (Martens & Webber, 2002) have raised questions about the inventory. Because of the large number of constructs measured by the SMS, researchers have sometimes tended to group or combine different elements of the inventory in meaningful ways. For example, the three aspects of intrinsic motivation are often averaged, and in many cases a single relative autonomy index (RAI) or self-determination index (SDI) is calculated. Vallerand and Losier (1999) recommended that the SDI be calculated as follows:

$$SDI = [(2)(Intrinsic\ Motivation)] \\ + [Identified\ Regulation] - [(External \\ + Introjected)/2] - [(2)(Amotivation)]$$

In the SDI formula, the three aspects of intrinsic motivation are first summed and then divided by three to yield a single value for intrinsic motivation. In practice, Ullrich-French and Cox (2009) utilized a slightly different version of the formula.

Because of criticisms of the SMS, Mallett, Kawabata, Newcombe, Otero-Forero, and Jackson (2007) developed the Sport Motivation Scale-6 (SMS-6) which included an integrated regulation scale and a single intrinsic motivation scale. Thus, the 24-item SMS-6 measures amotivation, external regulation, introjected regulation, identified regulation, integrated regulation, and intrinsic motivation (Mallett, Kawabata, & Newcombe, 2007; Pelletier, Vallerand, & Sarrazin, 2007). As such, the SMS-6 was developed as a revision and not an alternative to the original SMS. As an alternative to the SMS, Lonsdale, Hodge, and Rose (2008) reported on the development of the Behavioral Regulation in Sport Questionnaire (BRSQ). The BRSQ is a 24-item 6-factor inventory that measures the same motivational constructs as the SMS-6. In developing the BRSQ, the authors clarify that together, external and introjected regulation represent **controlled extrinsic motivation,** while identified regulation and integrated regulation represent **autonomous extrinsic motivation.** Other inventories that have been developed to measure the self-determination motivation constructs include the Perceived Locus of Causality scale (PLOC; Goudas, Biddle, & Fox, 1994; Wang, Hagger & Liu, 2009) and the Global Motivation Scale (GMS; Guay, Mageau, & Vallerand, 2003).

Research Support for the Integrated Model of Motivation

To a large extent, research support for the integrated model (figure 3.5) is a study in meditational analysis. The majority of researchers have focused on testing the hypothesis that psychological need satisfaction mediates the relationship between social factors and motivation, while a smaller number have focused upon testing the hypothesis that motivation (in all of its forms) mediates the relationship between psychological needs and consequences. Two ambitious investigations focused upon the full model in a single investigation. In the first investigation, Standage, Duda, and Ntoumanis (2006) provided evidence that coaching behavior (autonomous support) predicted all three aspects of psychological needs (autonomy, competence, relatedness), and that psychological need in turn predicted self-determined motivation, which in turn predicted motivational behavior (consequence). Thus, psychological need satisfaction mediated the relationship between autonomy support from coaches and self-determined motivation. In addition, self-determined motivation mediated the relationship between psychological needs and behavioral consequence. In the second investigation, Taylor, Ntoumanis, and Standage (2008) studied the integrated model of intrinsic motivation using physical education teachers as study participants. The results of their investigation showed that autonomous causality orientation and job pressure predicted psychological need which in turn predicted teachers' self-determined motivation which in turn predicted teachers' perceived use of student instructional support. Tests confirmed that psychological need and self-determined motivation were either partial or full mediators in model relationships.

Several studies can be cited that focused only upon testing the hypothesis that psychological need satisfaction mediates the relationship between social factors and motivation. Kowal and Fortier (2000) demonstrated that psychological need mediates the relationship between perceptions of success and motivational climate with motivation in master's level swimmers. Hollembeak and Amorose (2005) reported that, using college athletes, psychological need mediates the relationship between coaching behavior and intrinsic motivation. Importantly, Amorose and Anderson-Butcher (2007) observed that, using high school athletes, psychological need satisfaction mediates the relationship between perceived autonomy-supportive coaching and motivational orientation. Finally, research using physical education students showed that psychological need satisfaction mediates the relationship between teaching behavior (e.g., positive feedback) and self-determined motivation (Koka & Hagger, 2010).

One investigation reported by McDonough and Crocker (2007) focused on testing whether or not self-determined motivation mediates the relationship between psychological need satisfaction (autonomy, competence, relatedness) and outcome/consequence measures (positive and negative affect, physical self-worth, physical activity). Results showed that self-determined motivation is a partial mediator between psychological need and outcome, as in many cases psychological need predicts outcome directly.

Three additional investigations provide support for the integrated model of intrinsic and extrinsic motivation, but in different ways. A study reported by Reed and Cox (2007) showed that intrinsic motivation, identified regulation, and external regulation were all strongly associated with motives for seniors to participate in the Missouri State Senior Games. Using sixth-, seventh-, and eighth-grade physical education students, Ullrich-French and Cox (2009) used a cluster analysis to assign students to five different groups based on self-determined motivation scores. Using analysis of variance procedures, they demonstrated that the five groups differed as a function of an overall self-determination index, measures of psychological need satisfaction, and consequences of motivation (enjoyment, value, worry, effort, physical activity). The group highest in self-determined (autonomous) forms of motivation scored best in terms of overall motivation, psychological need satisfaction (autonomy, competence, relatedness), and positive

outcomes. Finally, Radel, Sarrazin, and Pelletier (2009) demonstrated that college undergraduates could be primed for autonomous or controlling motivation orientations using subliminal presentations of autonomous words (desire, willing, freedom, choice) or controlling words (constrained, obligation, duty, obey). Students primed for autonomous motivation performed better than those students primed for controlling words in terms of a motor task, persistence, and effort. Thus, it would appear that simply suggesting an autonomous motivational orientation to students may have the effect of enhancing various outcome measures.

Cognitive Evaluation Theory

Cognitive evaluation theory is a subtheory to the integrated theory of intrinsic and extrinsic motivation. Notions of cognitive evaluation theory were developed in the 1980s by Deci and Ryan (1985), but were later assimilated into the broader theory of self-determination (Deci & Ryan, 1991) that is the centerpiece for the integrated theory of motivation presented in this chapter. To give the reader a sense of the importance and influence of cognitive evaluation theory, consider that Vallerand reported in 1997 that over eight hundred studies had been published on this psychological topic alone. Research support for cognitive evaluation theory is strong, as evidenced by a meta-analysis and other investigations (Deci, Koestner, & Ryan, 1999; Ryan, 2000).

When someone engages in an interesting activity for its own sake and not for any other reason, we may conclude that she engages in the activity with an intrinsic motivation. On the other hand, if someone has an external reason for engaging in the activity, we would agree that she is externally motivated. If the external motivation is a reward, then it can be assumed that the reward may be part of the reason the person is participating.

It is appealing to assume that external rewards can enhance motivation. But what happens to an athlete's motivation if the rewards are withdrawn? Can external rewards actually damage rather than enhance motivation?

Can trophies such as this one contribute to a decrease in intrinsic motivation?
Courtesy Kansas State University Sports Information.

According to the **additive principle,** a young athlete who is low in intrinsic motivation will participate in an achievement situation if there is sufficient reward or external motivation for doing so. Yet a great deal of research evidence seems to cast doubt on the additive principle. Specifically, it has been argued that the relationship between intrinsic and external motivation is *multiplicative,* not additive. That is, external rewards can either add to or detract from intrinsic motivation. This principle is illustrated in the story of a retired psychologist who wanted to chase away some noisy children who liked to play near his home (Siedentop & Ramey, 1977). The man tried several strategies to get the boys to play elsewhere, but to no avail. Finally, he came up with a new and interesting strategy. He decided to pay the boys to play near his house! He offered them 25 cents apiece to return the next day. Naturally, the boys returned the next day to receive their pay, at which time the man offered them 20 cents to come the following day. When they returned again he offered them

only 15 cents to come the next day, and he added that for the next few days he would give them only a nickel for their efforts. The boys became very agitated, since they felt their efforts were worth more than a nickel, and they told the man that they would not return!

The boys in this story came to believe that the reason they were playing near the man's house was for pay and not for fun. Therefore, their perceived sense of control shifted from an internal to an external source. When this happens, an activity can lose its intrinsic value. Is it possible that this is happening today in professional sports? There are no doubt many highly paid athletes who have shifted their sense of control from an internal source—love of the game—to an external source. If the high salaries were reduced, how many would continue playing the game?

A similar thing could be happening to our young athletes as they receive trophies, money, pins, and awards for athletic participation. Is the relationship between intrinsic and external

CONCEPT An external reward that encourages athletes to attribute their participation to external causes can reduce intrinsic motivation.

APPLICATION Coaches should discourage any form of external reward that athletes may perceive to be more important than athletic participation itself.

rewards additive, or is it multiplicative? The **multiplicative principle** suggests that the interaction between intrinsic and external rewards could either add to or detract from intrinsic motivation.

While not discussed in detail in this book, **attribution theory** is a theory of motivation based on the kinds of attributions or causes that individuals give for successful or unsuccessful outcomes. For example, an athlete might simultaneously attribute an outcome (perceived success/failure) to an external or internal cause, a stable or unstable cause, and to a controllable or uncontrollable cause. Research shows that the successful athlete typically attributes successful outcomes to an internal, stable, and controllable cause. This is a very functional attribution strategy, as it suggests to the mind that future success is anticipated and expected. Conversely, the individual who chronically experiences failure typically attributes their failures to internal, stable, but uncontrollable causes. This suggests to the mind that future failure is anticipated and expected. Through **attribution training,** chronically unsuccessful participants may be taught to attribute unsuccessful performance to causes that are unstable but within their control. For example, attributing an unsuccessful performance to lack of effort empowers the athlete to accept responsibility for their performance (internal cause) while at the same time recognizing that the outcome can change (unstable) and that they have some control over the outcome (controllability).

Embedded within attribution theory are the principles of *overjustification* and *discounting.* These concepts suggest that adding external rewards to an otherwise interesting activity may represent an overjustification for participation, which may lead to discounting the intrinsic value

of the activity (Cox, 2007). Perhaps the single most important contribution to our understanding of the relationship between intrinsic motivation and external rewards comes from cognitive evaluation theory. As proposed by Deci and Ryan (1985), **cognitive evaluation theory** posits that external rewards can affect intrinsic motivation in one of two ways. The first is to produce a decrement in intrinsic motivation; this occurs as people perceive a change in sense of control from an internal to an external one. That is, when people come to perceive that their behavior is controlled by external forces, they respond with decreased levels of intrinsic motivation. This is referred to as the **controlling aspect of external motivation,** and serves to place an athlete in the position of a pawn who is acted upon. The second effect of external rewards is informational in nature, and results in an increase in intrinsic motivation. If an external award provides feedback to the person and enhances that person's sense of competence and self-determination, increased intrinsic motivation will be the end result. This is referred to as the **informational aspect of external motivation,** and it places an athlete in the position of an originator who does the acting.

Consider the following situation: A 10-year-old boy agrees to run in a five-mile road race with his father. As further incentive to train and finish the race, the father promises the boy 10 dollars. Later on, the boy passes up a second opportunity to run in a race with his father because, as he puts it, "Why, what's in it for me?" This may seem like an extreme example, yet situations like this occur every day. Why did this boy lose interest in this intrinsically interesting activity? Because he came to perceive that the primary reason for his running in the race was money. The money, not the intrinsic

CONCEPT External rewards (such as praise, awards, ribbons, and trophies) that athletes view as rewards for competent performance and encouragement for further participation will enhance intrinsic motivation.

APPLICATION Coaches and teachers should carefully consider the perceptions that young athletes have about external rewards. If the rewards are perceived to represent excellence, they can be valuable. However, if they become more important than the sport itself, they can be damaging.

CONCEPT The development of an athlete's intrinsic motivation and self-confidence is the ultimate goal of youth sport programs.

APPLICATION Coaches and administrators should define program goals in terms of the intrinsic values the participants will gain.

fun of running, became the source of his motivation. Once the shift in locus of causality was made from the internal cause to the external cause, the boy came to feel controlled by the external reward. He was running for the money and not for the intrinsic value of the experience; consequently, when the salient external motivation was withdrawn, intrinsic motivation was insufficient.

Conversely, consider the example of Ricky Henderson, who was inducted into the Major League Baseball (MLB) Hall of Fame on August 2, 2009 (Patrick, 2009). Upon first entering the major leagues with the Oakland Athletics, he received a cash million-dollar signing bonus check that he framed and placed on his wall instead of cashing. He explained later that the money was not important and that the check was merely recognition of accomplishments that he had achieved. In this case the cash reward did not undermine his intrinsic motivation to play baseball but rather enhanced it.

In addition to external rewards, competition may lead to a reduction in intrinsic motivation because of its controlling nature. When athletes compete only for the purpose of winning and

demonstrating superiority over others, the main reason for their participation is an external reward (winning), and not the joy of participation. Fortier, Vallerand, Briere, and Provencher (1995) reported that French Canadian recreational athletes enjoy higher levels of intrinsic motivation for their sport involvement than do competitive collegiate athletes. Ryan (1980) reported that scholarship football players exhibit lower intrinsic motivation than nonscholarship wrestlers and female athletes.

These two studies by Fortier et al. (1995) and Ryan (1980), and an earlier study by Ryan (1977), seem to suggest that collegiate scholarship athletes suffer a loss of intrinsic motivation due to the controlling nature of being paid to play sports. Receiving financial support to play collegiate sports, however, should also provide information to the athlete that would be suggestive of competence and self-determination. Consequently, it does not follow that scholarship athletes should necessarily exhibit lower levels of intrinsic motivation than nonscholarship athletes.

An important study reported by Amorose and Horn (2000) seems to provide important insight into the relationship between intrinsic motivation and rewards in the form of an athletic scholarship. Participants for this research were 386 Division I collegiate athletes participating in the sports of football, field hockey, gymnastics, swimming, and wrestling. Results of the investigation revealed that male athletes exhibit higher levels of intrinsic motivation than female athletes, and that scholarship athletes exhibit higher levels of intrinsic motivation than nonscholarship athletes. The authors concluded that scholarships may actually serve to enhance intrinsic motivation by conveying positive information suggesting a higher level of competence. In a follow-up investigation involving collegiate male and female gymnasts, Amorose and Horn (2001) reported that there was no difference between scholarship and nonscholarship athletes on five aspects of intrinsic motivation.

Most recently, Aoyagi and Cox (2009) reported on research that is consistent with the findings reported by Amorose and Horn (2000, 2001). Student athletes were asked to rate the extent to which they perceived their athletic scholarships to be more or less informational or more or less controlling. Results showed that an athletes' perception of a scholarship providing competence feedback was predictive of intrinsic motivation, while perception of a scholarship being controlling did not predict intrinsic motivation. While it is certainly possible that a scholarship athlete could view a scholarship as being controlling and perhaps destructive of intrinsic motivation, it appears from the research that just the opposite is more likely. The athlete is appreciative of the scholarship and believes that the financial support provides information suggesting personal accomplishment, competence, and hard work.

Summary

Three models of self-confidence were discussed. They included Bandura's theory of self-efficacy, Harter's competence motivation theory, and Vealey's multidimensional model of sport-confidence. Self-efficacy is the belief an individual holds that he can accomplish a specific task, and as such, is a form of situation-specific self-confidence. Factors required to develop self-efficacy include successful performance, vicarious experience, verbal persuasion, and emotional arousal. Harter's competence motivation theory is based upon mastery attempts and an individual's innate desire to be competent. Vealey's sport-confidence model shows how sources of sport-confidence lead to sport-confidence, which leads to enhanced performance.

Psychological momentum was defined as "a positive or negative change in cognition, affect, physiology, and behavior caused by an event or series of events that will result in a commensurate shift in performance and competitive outcome." Three different models for explaining psychological momentum were discussed. The three models were the antecedents-consequences model, the multidimensional model, and the projected performance model. Research supports the antecedents-consequences and multidimensional models over the projected performance model. The "hot hand" phenomenon in basketball shooting was introduced and discussed as being consistent with positive psychological momentum.

Notwithstanding the passage of Title IX, girls and women still lag behind men in the development of self-confidence relative to sport and exercise participation. Factors that contribute to this phenomenon include nature of the task, ambiguity of feedback information, and social comparison cues. In conjunction with the gender aspect of self-confidence, gender stereotyping and stereotype threat theory were discussed as factors that may influence a woman's self-confidence.

Vallerand and Losier's integrated model of intrinsic and extrinsic motivation is presented in this chapter as a unifying theory of motivation that includes the concepts of self-confidence, goal perspective, and attribution, with self-determination at its core. In the integrated theory, social factors and psychological need satisfaction are conceptualized as determinants of motivation. Motivation in turn is predictive of outcomes or consequences of integrated intrinsic and extrinsic motivation. In the model, psychological need satisfaction is hypothesized to mediate the relationship between social factors such as coaching behavior and motivation, while motivation is hypothesized to mediate the relationship between psychological need and outcomes. These predictions and relationships are largely supported by research.

Self-determination and choice are best conceptualized as being on a continuum relative to motivation. The most self-determining or autonomous kind of motivation is intrinsic motivation. Extrinsic motivation may be conceptualized as being completely external in nature and therefore low in self-determination, or it may be conceptualized as being internalized and having increasingly greater levels of self-determination. Embedded within intrinsic motivation is the concept of passion. Two kinds of passion are identified: obsessive and harmonious. Obsessive passion is controlling in nature, while harmonious passion is autonomous in nature.

Self-determined motivation has been largely measured with the Sport Motivation Scale (SMS). However, concerns about the factor structure of the SMS has led to the development of the Sport Motivation Scale-6 (SMS-6) and the Behavioral Regulation in Sport Questionnaire (BRSQ). Other inventories designed to measure self-determined motivational regulation include the Perceived Locus of Causality (PLOC) scale and the Global Motivation Scale (GMS).

Cognitive evaluation theory is a subtheory to Vallerand and Losier's integrated theory of motivation. Cognitive evaluation theory posits that extrinsic motivation has the potential of diminishing an individual's intrinsic motivation. There are two components to the theory. The controlling aspect of the theory predicts that intrinsic motivation will be reduced if extrinsic motivation is perceived as being controlling. The informational aspect of the theory predicts that extrinsic motivation will actually enhance intrinsic motivation if an external reward is perceived as being suggestive of personal competence.

Critical Thought Questions

1. How do you think situation-specific self-confidence can be best developed in athletes? Provide a model and a theory.

2. Do you think that situation-specific self-confidence developed in one sport situation can be transferred to another situation or even to global self-confidence? Explain and defend your response.

3. Is psychological momentum fact or fiction? How do you feel about the projected performance model of psychological momentum?

4. Do you think the effects of Title IX on sport have completely eliminated the disparity in self-confidence sometimes exhibited by men and women? Explain and defend your answer.

5. What is gender stereotyping and how does it relate to stereotype threat theory? Relate these concepts to the different kinds of sports that women participate in and their effect upon self-confidence.

6. Using the integrated theory of motivation as your knowledge base, describe the steps you would follow in making sure that your own child is motivated to succeed in some particular sport or activity.

7. What can coaches do to make sure that their athletes develop the characteristic and perception of being autonomous in the way they interact with their environment?

8. From a practical perspective, discuss steps you as a coach or parent can take to make sure that extrinsic motivation does not have the undesirable effect of reducing an athlete's intrinsic motivation.

9. Discuss and explain the mediational effects of psychological need satisfaction and motivation in the integrated model. Based on research, what, if any, modifications would you recommend in the model?

Glossary

achievement situation A condition of expectation that one's performance will be subject to evaluation.

additive principle The notion that an athlete low in intrinsic motivation will participate in a competitive situation if there is an extrinsic reward or motivation.

amotivation The complete lack of any kind of motivation.

attribution theory A cognitive approach to motivation in which perceived causation plays an important role in explaining behavior.

attribution training A process by which attributions given for chronic failure are manipulated in order to overcome feelings of future failure.

autonomous extrinsic motivation The combined effects of identified and integrated regulation, which are more autonomous and more closely associated with intrinsic motivation than controlled extrinsic motivation.

autonomy The belief a person has that she is in control of her destiny and her own actions and choices.

cognitive evaluation theory A theory that proposes that external rewards may have either a controlling or an informational effect upon the person receiving the reward.

competence motivation An individual's belief that he is competent, which leads to the motivation to try to learn new tasks.

controlled extrinsic motivation The combined effects of external and introjected regulation, which are more controlling and less closely

associated with intrinsic motivation than autonomous extrinsic motivation.

controlling aspect of external motivation A term describing the tendency of people who come to perceive that their behavior is controlled by external forces to respond with decreased levels of intrinsic motivation.

efficacious pawn A competent individual who performs a task for an external reason or cause.

external regulation The least self-determined form of extrinsic motivation.

extrinsic motivation Motivation that comes from an external as opposed to an internal source.

gender stereotyping The notion that certain sports, such as gymnastics and aerobic exercise, are only appropriate for girls, while certain sports, such as football and wrestling, are only appropriate for boys.

global self-confidence A personality trait or disposition to be a self-confident person.

harmonious passion Passion that is autonomous in nature and leads a person to choose to engage in an activity that they like.

hot hand phenomenon The belief that performance of an athlete temporarily improves following a string of successes.

identified regulation The process by which an athlete engages in an activity that he doesn't perceive as being particularly interesting, but does so because he sees the activity as being instrumental to obtaining another goal that is interesting to him.

informational aspect of external motivation
A term describing the tendency of people who come to perceive that extrinsic motivation provides them with information that suggests personal competence to respond with increased levels of intrinsic motivation.

integrated regulation The process by which an extrinsic motivation has been fully integrated or internalized by the individual. In terms of self-determination, it is very similar to intrinsic motivation.

internalization The process by which rewards and other forms of extrinsic motivation become less external and more internal.

intrinsic motivation Motivation that comes from within the individual.

introjected regulation Extrinsic motivation that has undergone only partial internalization.

mediator variable A variable that determines how a previous variable affects a subsequent variable.

moderator variable An independent variable that modifies or determines the effect that a second independent variable has upon a dependent variable.

multiplicative principle The notion that extrinsic motivation interacts with intrinsic motivation to either add to or detract from it.

observational learning Vicarious learning in which the learner benefits from watching other people perform or by watching themselves perform in a video clip.

obsessive passion Passion that is controlling in nature and drives a person to engage in an activity they like.

participatory modeling The learner first observes a model perform a task, then the model or instructor assists the athlete in successfully performing the task.

precipitating event An important event in an athletic contest that precipitates psychological momentum.

psychological momentum A positive or negative change in cognition, affect, physiology, and behavior that will result in a shift in performance and outcome.

reflected appraisal process An appraisal process that is a function of the actual appraisal of others, one's own appraisal of self, and one's perception of how others appraise one.

relatedness The basic need to relate to other people, to care for others and have others care for you.

self-determination A unifying concept that brings meaning to the overall concept of motivation. It refers to a person's having autonomy and agency to act for herself and to make her own decisions.

self-determination and autonomy continuum
The notion that extrinsic motivation lies on a continuum relative to self-determination and to the degree that extrinsic motivation has been internalized.

self-determination theory A theory of motivation that is based on the writings of Deci and Ryan and describes how motivation is developed and how it relates to the concept of autonomy or agency.

self-efficacy A person's belief that she is competent and can succeed in a particular task.

situation-specific self-confidence The sense of sureness a person has that he can be successful at a specific task or sport.

social comparison Comparing one's own performance with another person's performance.

sport-confidence The perception of confidence in a sport-related achievement situation.

stereotype threat theory The theory that framing a task as a measure of athletic ability is masculine in nature, while framing a task as a measure of technical skill is feminine in nature.

CHAPTER 4

Goal Perspective Theory

KEY TERMS

Achievement motivation
Adaptive motivational pattern
Antisocial behavior
Cluster analysis
Cognitive restructuring
Competitive climate
Competitive goal orientation
Deliberate practice
Differentiated goal perspective
Ego involvement
Ego goal orientation
Entity ability beliefs
Goal involvement
Goal orientation
Incremental ability beliefs
Maladaptive motivational
   pattern
Mastery climate
Mastery goal orientation
Matching hypothesis
Moral functioning
Motivational climate
Perceived ability

Prosocial behavior
Social approval goal
   orientation
Sportspersonship

Task involvement
Task goal orientation
Undifferentiated goal
   perspective

I n this chapter we will introduce a theory of motivation that focuses upon the different ways children and adults think about their own competence and about the different ways they conceptualize ability. The phrase *goal perspective theory* was introduced by researchers to describe this approach to theorizing about motivation. The word "goal" in the phrase is a little confusing because goal perspective theory is not about setting goals; it is about the different ways that athletes approach and think about achievement situations. By way of example, consider the goal perspective orientations of two hypothetical athletes. Joe is 16 years old and has been playing tennis competitively for four years. His friends describe him as being a highly competitive person because he becomes very distraught if he loses a match. Winning seems to mean everything to him. For example, he once commented to a friend that he didn't care how he played the game, just as long as he was victorious. Contrast this orientation with that of Mary, a 16-year-old gymnast who has been competing for eight years but approaches every tournament from the perspective of having fun and doing her very best. Because of her work ethic and desire to excel, she puts in many hours of practice, but never seems to get overly upset when she does not win a competition. Her friends describe her as a person who strives for perfection but does not seem to be caught up in defeating her opponent. Her focus always seems to be on self-improvement and working hard. With this lay introduction to goal perspective theory, let us now turn our attention to a more theoretical discussion of goal perspective theory.

Nicholls's (1984, 1989) theory of motivation provides a framework for considering individuals' motivational perspectives across the lifespan. Nicholls's developmentally based theory of **achievement motivation** is a logical extension of both Bandura's theory of self-efficacy and Harter's theory of competence motivation. According to Nicholls (1984) and Duda (1989), the defining feature of achievement motivation is the way children come to view their own **perceived ability.** In goal perspective theory, the nature of perceived ability changes initially as a function of developmental level of the child, and later as a function of learning and **cognitive restructuring.** The sections of this chapter are logically developed to assure a systematic and clear understanding of the important concepts that make up Nicholls's goal perspective theory. Important concepts to be discussed in this chapter include (a) achievement goal orientation, (b) developmental nature of goal orientation, (c) measuring goal orientation, (d) goal involvement, (e) motivational climate, (f) goal orientation and moral functioning, (g) characteristics of task and ego

orientation, (h) the matching hypothesis, and (i) goal orientation antecedents and outcomes.

Achievement Goal Orientation

There are two **goal orientations** mentioned by Nicholls. They are task orientation and ego orientation. These two orientations are referred to as goal orientations because they differ as a function of the individual's achievement goal. In the case of **task goal orientation,** the goal is mastery of a particular skill. Perceived ability for the task-oriented individual is a function of perceived improvement from one point in time to the next. The task-oriented athlete perceives herself to be of high ability if she can perform a task better today than she could one week ago. The task-oriented individual continues to work for mastery of the skill she is working on, and enjoys feelings of self-efficacy and confidence in so doing.

At this point, you are probably thinking that everyone must be task oriented, because everyone enjoys mastering a task. Not necessarily. At some point in our lives we become aware of the consequences of social comparison. When we start to make social comparisons, we adopt a different sort of goal orientation. It is no longer enough simply to gain mastery over a skill and make personal improvements. We must also demonstrate that we can outperform another individual or other individuals. For the person with an **ego goal orientation,** perceived ability is measured as a function of outperforming others, as opposed to self-improvement. The ego-oriented individual's perceived ability and self-confidence is tied to how he compares with others as opposed to objective improvement in skill.

Traditionalists such as Treasure, Duda, Hall, Roberts, Ames, and Maehr (2001) argue persuasively that there are only two basic goal orientations (task and ego goal orientation), while researchers such as Harwood, Hardy, and Swain (2000) have argued that a third or even fourth goal orientation might exist. For example, Gernigon, d'Arripe-Longueville, Delignieres, and Ninot

(2004) conducted a qualitative study on judo competitors who they claimed revealed a third perspective for conceptualizing goal orientation. They described this third goal orientation to be ego involved in nature, but with a focus on avoiding embarrassment or defeat, as opposed to wanting to outperform the opponent. Two other groups of researchers identified **social approval goal orientation** to be a third goal perspective (Schilling & Hayashi, 2001; Stuntz & Weiss, 2003). Social goal orientation emphasizes the desire for social acceptance through conformity to norms while displaying maximum effort.

Developmental Nature of Goal Orientation

According to Nicholls (1984, 1989), a child two to six years old views perceived ability in terms of how well she performed the task the last time. If the child notices an improvement in performance from time one to time two, she naturally assumes that ability has increased and that she is competent at performing the task. High amounts of effort in mastering the task are perceived by the child as evidence of high ability and competence. Competence is perceived by the child as a function of hard work and absolute capacity. At this early age, the child is said to be task oriented, as opposed to ego oriented.

At the age of six or seven, the child begins to view perceived ability in terms of how other children perform. The child becomes ego oriented, as opposed to task oriented. No longer is it enough to perform the task better than she performed it the last time; the child must now perform the task better than other children do. Perceived ability is now a function of one's own capacity as it is relative to that of others, as opposed to being a function of absolute ability. High ability and competence are only perceived as such if they are better than the performance of others.

After age 11 or 12, the child may exhibit either a task- or an ego-involved disposition, depending upon the situation at hand. Environmental factors causing a person to focus upon social comparisons will result in an ego-oriented disposition, while situations causing a person to focus upon personal mastery and improved performance will foster a task-oriented disposition.

From a developmental perspective, children mature with respect to how well they are able to differentiate between the concepts of effort, ability, and outcome. According to Nicholls, children pass developmentally through four levels as they come to fully understand these three concepts, as well as the concepts of luck and task difficulty.

Level 1   At this early level, the child views effort, ability, and outcome as the same thing. At this level of development, the child is said to have an **undifferentiated goal perspective.** To the child at this age level, effort, or trying hard, is the same as ability or having a successful outcome. Furthermore, the child has no concept of how luck differs from ability or how one task can be more difficult than another.

Level 2   At Level 2, the child is beginning to recognize that there is a difference between effort and ability, but the child believes that effort is the major determinant of achieving success. If you try hard and expend lots of effort, you will find success.

Level 3   The third level is transitional, in the sense that the child is beginning to differentiate between ability and effort. Sometimes the child will recognize that effort is not the same as ability, but at other times he will revert back to an undifferentiated conceptualization of the two.

Level 4   Children and adults in Level 4 have a **differentiated goal perspective.** At around age 12, the child can clearly distinguish among the concepts of ability, effort, luck, and outcome. She also clearly understands the ramifications of task difficulty and recognizes that some tasks

CONCEPT   Children pass through four developmental levels in terms of their understanding of the concepts of effort, ability, and outcome. In Level 1 they cannot differentiate among concepts of effort, ability, and outcome; by Level 4, they can.

APPLICATION   Knowing where a child is in the developmental hierarchy will help the adult leader to plan activities for children. Keeping score with children in Level 1 makes no theoretical sense. If all the children try equally hard, they should exhibit the same ability and have the same score. That is how children in the first level see things, and forcing them to think in terms of winning and losing is only confusing.

(opponents) will be more difficult than others. For example, the child understands that effort enhances performance of tasks requiring high ability (skill), but not that of tasks requiring luck. Furthermore, the child understands that low effort coupled with strong performance is probably indicative of high ability.

Research by Fry (2000) and Fry and Duda (1997) shows support for Nicholls' developmental theory of achievement motivation in the physical or sport and exercise domain. Children do in fact pass through these four developmental levels. Children in Level 1 exhibit a task goal orientation, but this is not by choice. The child simply cannot differentiate between effort and ability, so he thinks only in terms of mastery and trying hard. Children and adults in Level 4 have a mature concept of the meaning of effort and ability, and can therefore learn to exhibit either a task or an ego orientation toward achievement or competitive situations.

As a child matures, he will go from being task goal oriented to being more ego goal oriented. After the age of around 12, however, goal orientations fluctuate as a function of life's experiences as well as personality characteristics. Of interest is the effect that significant others may have on goal orientation in children. Carr and Weigand (2002) showed that task-oriented children perceive significant others and sport heroes to favor a task-oriented learning environment.

Young children cannot differentiate between ability and effort, perceiving that trying hard is the same as ability. Conversely, older children can differentiate between effort and ability, recognizing that great effort may not mean success if ability is lacking (Chase, 2001).

Measuring Goal Orientation

Two main inventories were originally developed for measuring the two primary aspects of goal orientation in sport and exercise. These include the Task and Ego Orientation in Sport Questionnaire (TEOSQ; Duda, 1989; Lane, Nevill, Bowes, & Fox, 2005; White & Duda, 1994), and the Perceptions of Success Questionnaire (POSQ; Roberts, 1993; Roberts & Treasure, 1995; Roberts, Treasure, & Balague, 1998). Both the TEOSQ and the POSQ were designed to measure task and ego goal achievement orientation in sport. The POSQ, however, adopted the terms **mastery goal orientation** and **competitive goal orientation** to represent task and ego goal orientation respectively. The use of different terms to represent the same cognitive constructs has caused some confusion in the literature, but it does appear that the mastery and competitive goal orientation labels are more descriptive of the concepts being measured. While the TEOSQ and POSQ were developed for measuring goal orientation in sport, two parallel inventories were developed for measuring the same constructs in the exercise environment. These include the Goal Orientation in Exercise Scale (GOES; Kilpatrick, Bartholomew, & Reimer, 2003) and

Athletes may be both mastery and performance goal oriented. PhotoLink/Getty Images.

the Perceptions of Success Questionnaire for Exercise (POSQ-E; Zizi, Keeler, & Watson, 2006).

According to goal orientation theory, task and ego goal orientations are hypothesized to be independent or orthogonal to each other. An athlete who has a high score in task goal orientation will not necessarily have a low score in ego goal orientation. This means that an athlete can be task and ego goal oriented at the same time. The orthogonal relationship between the two goal orientations is supported by the literature (Gernigon et al., 2004; Harwood & Hardy, 2001; Harwood & Swain, 2001). This concept is illustrated in figure 4.1.

For many years, the TEOSQ and POSQ were the "gold standard" for measuring the two orthogonal goal orientations in sport. However, ambiguous findings emerging from the conventional two-goal model led to a new way of conceptualizing the measurement of goal orientation. Elliot and McGregor (2001) conceptualized a 2 × 2 achievement goal framework in which achievement goals (task/ego) were crossed with the classic approach-avoidance conflict seen in the early McClelland-Atkinson model of achievement motivation (McClelland et al., 1953). The 2 × 2 model is illustrated in figure 4.2. Based on this theoretical model,

FIGURE 4.1 | Task and goal orientation are independent or orthogonal to each other.

	High
High task/ low ego	High task/ high ego
Ego goal orientation Low	High
Low task/ low ego	Low task/ high ego
	Low

Task goal orientation

FIGURE 4.2 | The Achievement Goals Questionnaire for Sport (AGS-S; Conroy et al., 2003) is based on Elliot and McGregor's (2001) 2 × 2 conceptual framework.

	Mastery (Task)	***Performance (Ego)**
Approach (Valence)	**Mastery/ Approach** (desire for mastery)	**Performance/ Approach** (desire to be competent relative to others)
Avoidance (Valence)	**Mastery/Avoidance** (desire to avoid seeming incompetent in mastering task)	**Performance/ Avoidance** (desire to avoid performing worse than others)

* Performance and competitive goal orientations are the same.

Conroy, Elliot, and Hofner (2003) developed the Achievement Goals Questionnaire for Sport (AGQ-S). The AGQ-S is composed of 12 items that result in a mastery/approach score, a mastery/avoidance score, a performance/approach score, and a performance/avoidance score. The 2 × 2 achievement goal framework was supported through a confirmatory factor analysis reported by Wang, Biddle, and Elliot (2007). Since its conception in 2003, goal orientation research utilizing the AGQ-S has become very common (Adie, Duda, & Ntoumanis, 2010; Ciani & Sheldon, 2010; Wang, Liu, Chatzisarantis, & Lim, 2010.)

In addition to the TEOSQ, the POSQ, and the AGQ-S, a plethora of inventories have been developed for measuring different aspects of goal orientation. Four will be mentioned here. The Achievement Goal Scale (AGS) was developed by Papaioannou, Milosis, Kosmidou, and Tsigilis (2007) to measure four achievement goal orientations (mastery, performance/approach, performance/avoidance, and social approval). The Social Motivational Orientation Scale for Sport (SMOSS) was developed by Allen (2003) to measure three aspects of social goal orientation (affiliation, recognition,

status). The Achievement Goal Scale for Youth Sport (AGSYS) was developed by Cumming, Smith, Smoll, Standage, and Grossland (2008) to measure two aspects of goal orientation in youth sport athletes (mastery/approach, performance/approach). Finally, the Global Goal Orientation Instrument (GGOI) was developed by Papaioannou, Simou, Kosmidou, Milosi, and Tsigilis (2009) to measure three global or nonspecific goal orientations in life (personal improvement goal, ego-enhancing goal, ego-protection goal).

Goal Involvement

Related to the measurement issue is the observation by Nicholls (1989) and L. Williams (1998) that there are really two types of goal perspective. One is referred to as goal orientation as described above, and the other is called goal involvement. Instruments such as the TEOSQ and POSQ measure goal orientation (i.e., task and ego orientation) and represent dispositional or personality traits relative to the two orientations. Conversely, **goal involvement** is a situation-specific state measure of how an individual relates to an achievement situation at a specific point in time.

According to Nicholls (1989), situations that heighten awareness of social evaluation induce a state of **ego involvement,** accompanied by feelings of increased anxiety. Conversely, situations that do not heighten an awareness of social evaluation evoke a state of **task involvement,** accompanied by feelings of low anxiety. To be ego involved is to display characteristics of an ego-oriented person in a specific situation. To be task involved is to display characteristics of a task-oriented person in a specific situation. As might be surmised, goal involvement is greatly influenced by the motivational climate or environment, a topic we will discuss in the next section.

L. Williams (1998) reported an investigation in which the concept of goal involvement was measured and studied in a sport-related environment. In this investigation, goal involvement was measured using the Goal Involvement in Sport

Children enjoying a mastery motivational climate. Digital Vision/PunchStock.

Questionnaire (GISQ), which is nothing more than the TEOSQ with situation-specific instructions. Instead of asking an athlete how she generally felt relative to an item on the TEOSQ, Williams asked the athlete to indicate how she felt "right now" on the same item relative to a current situation. In the Williams study, the "current situation" was either a team practice or a team competition. The results of the investigation confirmed that athletes exhibit higher levels of task involvement and lower levels of anxiety prior to a practice than prior to an actual game.

Motivational Climate

We don't really look at 8–0, we look at each match. We try to prepare for each match that we are going to play, and our focus is what we're doing out on the court. Regardless of the opponent we've got to prepare to play and we've got to take care of business. And if we work hard hopefully good things will happen (Susan Kreklow, Volleyball Coach, University of Missouri–Columbia, Hopp, 2000).

Perhaps of greater import than whether an individual is task or ego oriented is the **motivational climate** that the individual is placed in. Just as individuals can be task or ego oriented, learning environments can also be task or ego oriented. An ego-oriented environment, with its emphasis upon social comparison, can be particularly harmful to low-ability youth. Conversely, high-ability children seem to thrive in either environment. The effects of a mastery-, or task-oriented, learning environment can reverse the negative effects of an ego orientation.

The Perceived Motivational Climate in Sport Questionnaire (PMCSQ; Seifriz, Duda, & Chi, 1992) and the PMCSQ–2 (Newton, 1994; Newton, Duda & Yin, 2000) were developed to assess an athlete's perception of whether a motivational climate emphasized mastery-based (task orientation) or competitive-based (ego orientation) goals. Other inventories developed to measure motivational climate include the Perception of Motivational Climate Scale (PMCS; Papaioannou et al., 2007), the Motivational Climate Scale for Youth Sports

(MCSYS; Smith, Cummings, & Smoll, 2008), and the Peer Motivational Climate in Youth Sport Questionnaire (PeerMCYSQ; Ntoumanis & Vazou, 2005).

A **mastery climate** is one in which athletes receive positive reinforcement from the coach when they (a) work hard, (b) demonstrate improvement, (c) help others learn through cooperation, and (d) believe that each player's contribution is important. A **competitive climate** is one in which athletes perceive that (a) poor performance and mistakes will be punished, (b) high-ability athletes will receive the most attention and recognition, and (c) competition between team members is encouraged by the coach. For purposes of clarification, it should be noted that in the literature "competitive climate" is often referred to as "performance climate."

In explaining goal perspective theory, we have introduced and explained two different kinds of goal orientation, two different kinds of goal involvement, and two different kinds of motivational climate. These several concepts are summarized in table 4.1.

Epstein (1989) and Treasure and Roberts (1995) have proposed that a mastery-oriented climate can be created by the coach or teacher that will be instrumental in developing and fostering self-confidence and intrinsic motivation in youth sport participants. As originally coined by Epstein, the acronym TARGET has come to represent the manipulation of environmental conditions that will lead to a mastery climate conducive to the devel-

opment of intrinsic motivation. It is proposed that coaches address each of these conditions in order to create a mastery environment. The conditions are as follows:

1. *Tasks*—Tasks involving variety and diversity facilitate an interest in learning and task involvement.

2. *Authority*—Students should be given opportunities to participate actively in the learning process by being involved in decision making and monitoring their own personal progress.

3. *Reward*—Rewards for participation should focus upon individual gains and improvement, and away from social comparisons.

4. *Grouping*—Students should be placed in groups so that they can work on individual skills in a cooperative learning climate.

5. *Evaluation*—Evaluation should involve numerous self-tests that focus upon effort and personal improvement.

6. *Timing*—Timing is critical to the interaction of all of these conditions.

Motivational climate is important because it can influence both goal orientation (disposition) and goal involvement (state). Over time, an emphasis on a mastery or task goal climate can cause an athlete to have more of a mastery goal orientation (Gano-Overway & Ewing, 2004; Harwood & Swain, 2002; Weigand & Burton, 2002). With this in mind, it is useful to examine the positive

TABLE 4.1 | Characteristics of Different Types of Goal Orientation, Goal Involvement, and Motivational Climate

Goal Orientation (Personality Trait)	Goal Involvement (Psychological State)	Motivational Climate (Environment)

1. Task or Mastery Orientation
  a. Effort important
  b. Mastery important
	1. Task or Mastery Involvement
	  a. Athlete works hard
	  b. Athlete strives for mastery
		1. Mastery Climate
		  a. Effort rewarded
		  b. Cooperation emphasized

2. Ego or Competitive Orientation
  a. Social comparisons important
  b. Winning important
	2. Ego or Competitive Involvement
	  a. Athlete defines ability as winning
	  b. Athlete strives to win
		2. Competitive Climate
		  a. Mistakes punished
		  b. Competition encouraged

CONCEPT The climate and environment created by the coach or teacher can be a powerful determinant as to whether a young athlete will increase in intrinsic motivation and self-confidence.

APPLICATION TARGET structures provide specific suggestions as to how the coach can create an atmosphere conducive to the development of self-confidence and the motive to achieve success.

Factors such as making practices interesting, involving athletes in decision making, basing rewards on individual gains, and creating an atmosphere of cooperation are all important TARGET structures. Other strategies used by coaches to enhance self-confidence include (a) instruction/drilling, (b) encouraging positive self-talk, (c) acting self-confident, (d) liberal use of praise, and (e) physical conditioning sessions.

CONCEPT Perceived ability moderates the effect that a high competition motivational climate will have on self-esteem. Those most vulnerable to a loss of self-esteem associated with an ego-involved competitive environment are the low-ability athletes.

APPLICATION Coaches must be mindful that a planned competitive environment affects each member of a team differently. High-ability athletes will probably not be negatively affected by

an ego-involved climate, but they can benefit from a mastery climate. Because a mastery climate promises beneficial outcomes for all athletes, the focus of practice situations should be upon teamwork, skill mastery, and cooperative behavior that will be beneficial to the whole team. Competitive game-like situations can be beneficial to all athletes if they are organized in a way that does not always result in the low-ability athletes' losing or coming up second best.

benefits of creating a mastery-focused motivational climate for athletes. Some of the benefits associated with a mastery motivational climate include enhanced perception of competence, increased satisfaction, reduced boredom, perceived ability, reduced rough play, heightened effort, greater enjoyment, increased self-esteem, increased collective efficacy, reduced performance anxiety, and increased mastery goal orientation (Abrahamsen, Roberts, & Pensgaard, 2008; Boixados, Cruz, Torregrosa, & Valiente, 2004; Halliburton & Weiss, 2002; Magyar et al., 2004; Papaioannou, Marsh, & Theordorakis, 2004; Weigand & Burton, 2002). An investigation reported by Reinboth

and Duda (2004) is of particular interest, as it shows how motivational climate can interact with perceived ability to affect self-esteem. A motivational climate that is highly ego involved (competitive environment) can have a deleterious effect upon self-esteem, but only when associated with perceived low ability. This means that in the presence of an ego-involved environment, self-esteem is protected if the athlete enjoys the perception of high personal ability. As illustrated in figure 4.3, this also means that the low-ability athlete is particularly vulnerable to a decline in self-esteem in the presence of a competitive environment.

FIGURE 4.3 | The deleterious effects of an ego-involved competitive climate on a perceived low-ability athlete's self-esteem.

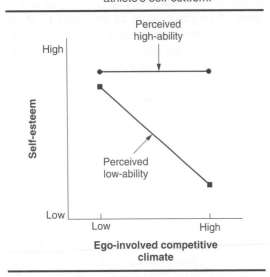

Source: Reinboth, M., & Duda, J. L. (2004). The motivational climate, perceived ability, and athletes' psychological and physical well-being. *The Sport Psychologist, 18,* 237–251.

In the previous paragraphs we discussed outcomes associated with a designed mastery motivational climate. Some researchers, however, have been interested in identifying antecedents or factors that lead to a mastery climate in an athletic setting. Smith, Fry, Ethington, and Li (2005), for example, demonstrated that when coaches provide athletes with positive encouraging feedback and do not ignore performance mistakes, the athletes are likely to perceive a mastery involved motivational climate on their team. Conversely, when athletes perceive that their coaches respond to mistakes with punishment and do not provide positive or encouraging feedback, the athletes are more likely to perceive a competitive motivational climate on their team. Taking a different approach, Chian and Wang (2008) utilized cluster analysis to divide college athletes into four meaningful clusters based on such factors as task and ego goal orientation, ability beliefs, sport competence, and self-determined motivation. **Cluster analysis**

magnifies differences between athletes in different clusters while at the same time minimizing differences between athletes that are within the same cluster or group. The four emerging groups or clusters were titled (a) high motivation, (b) maladaptive motivation, (c) low competence, and (d) amotivation. Univariate and multivariate variance analysis was then used to determine if differences existed between the four clusters based on selected criterion or dependent variables. Results showed that the highly motivated athletes scored highest, compared to other groups, on mastery climate, enjoyment, and effort. Thus high motivation is predictive of a mastery but not a competitive motivational climate. Research also suggests that identifying factors that influence perceptions of coach-generated motivational climate may be important in strengthening task involving practices (Vazou, 2010).

Goal Orientation and Moral Functioning

In this section we relate the concept of moral functioning with the concept of good or bad **sportspersonship.** Athletes who perform with a high level of **moral functioning** are said to exhibit good sportspersonship, while those exhibiting a low level of moral functioning are said to exhibit unsportspersonlike behavior. Low moral functioning is linked to an ego goal orientation; because "the ego-oriented athlete's perceptions of competence are dependent on outdoing others, he or she may be more likely to break the rules and behave in an unsportspersonlike fashion when winning is at stake" (Kavussanu & Ntoumanis, 2003, p. 503). Conversely, task goal orientation is linked to sportspersonlike behavior because the athlete's focus is upon the task at hand and whether or not she performs up to her potential.

Research by Kavussanu and Ntoumanis (2003) showed that participation in contact sports is predictive of an ego goal orientation, which in turn is predictive of lower levels of moral functioning in terms of judgments, intentions, and actual behaviors (more willingness to break rules, risk injury, and deliberately hurt opponents). This research showed a strong relationship between an ego goal orientation and reported low levels of moral functioning, while task orientation had the opposite effect. After reviewing the related literature, Kavussanu, Roberts, and Ntoumanis (2002) observed that unbridled competition reduces *prosocial behavior,* whereas cooperation enhances *prosocial behavior.*

Two measurable aspects of moral functioning are prosocial and antisocial behavior, and as previously mentioned, moral functioning is the core of sportspersonship. **Prosocial behavior** is defined as voluntary behavior designed to benefit another person, while **antisocial behavior** is voluntary behavior designed to disadvantage and perhaps harm another person (Kavussanu & Boardley, 2009). In a study reported by Sage and Kavussanu (2007a), participants assigned to an ego or competitive motivational climate condition exhibited higher levels of observed antisocial behavior than those assigned to a mastery climate condition. In a similar study reported by Sage and Kavussanu (2007b), prosocial behavior was predicted by task goal orientation, social affiliation goal orientation, and low levels of social status orientation; while antisocial behavior was predicted by ego goal orientation, low task goal orientation, and social status. Thus, prosocial behavior is linked to a mastery goal orientation and certain aspects of social goal orientation; while antisocial behavior is linked to a competitive goal orientation and certain aspects of social goal orientation. Recognizing the importance of measuring prosocial and antisocial behavior in research related to moral behavior, Kavussanu and Boardley (2009) reported on the development of the Prosocial and Antisocial Behavior in Sport Scale (PABSS). The PABSS is composed of 20 items that measure prosocial behavior directed toward teammates, prosocial behavior directed toward opponents, antisocial behavior directed toward teammates, and antisocial behavior toward opponents. Relatedly, goal orientation has been shown to have both a direct and indirect effect upon antisocial behavior

towards opponents through moral disengagement (Boardley & Kavussanu, 2010).

Lemyre, Roberts, and Ommundsen (2002) measured dispositional goal orientation, perceived ability, and moral functioning in 511 male youth soccer players. Moral functioning was measured as a function of respect for social conventions, respect for rules and officials, respect for one's full commitment toward sport, and true respect and concern for the opponent. Results showed that (a) ego goal orientation has a negative effect on all four measures of sportspersonship, (b) perceived ability has a positive significant effect on all four measures of moral reasoning, and (c) perceived ability moderates (determines) the relationship between ego goal orientation and respect for rules and officials. The highest respect for rules and officials occurs with low ego goal orientation and high perceived ability, whereas the lowest respect occurs with high ego goal orientation and low perceived ability. Research by Fry and Newton (2003), Kavussanu and Roberts (2001), and Stuntz and Weiss (2003) reported similar findings in their investigations.

Characteristics of Task and Ego Goal Orientations

A task or mastery goal orientation is associated with the belief that success is a function of effort and mastery. Mastery-oriented individuals feel most successful when they experience personal improvement that they believe is due to their hard work and effort. They gain a sense of accomplishment through learning and mastering a difficult task. Task-oriented individuals, regardless of their perception of personal ability, tend to exhibit **adaptive motivational patterns.** This means that they choose to participate in challenging tasks that allow them to demonstrate persistence and sustained effort. Mastery-oriented persons focus on developing skill, exerting effort, and self-improvement (Carpenter & Yates, 1997; Fry & Duda, 1997; Williams, 1998).

An ego or competitive goal orientation is associated with the belief that success is a function of

CONCEPT An ego goal orientation and focus upon a competitive environment are related to low moral functioning and low sportspersonship. This relationship is due to the focus upon outperforming or defeating the opposition that is present in ego goal oriented/involved achievement situations.

APPLICATION If as a coach or teacher you are concerned about the unsportspersonlike behavior of your athletes you must turn your attention to the kind of social environment that is fostered during practices and games. If the social norm is to win at all costs, then the seeds of unsportspersonship are embedded within the fabric of the team. This can only be reversed by changing the motivational climate of the team from being focused on competition and winning at all costs to one of cooperation and a focus upon effort, teamwork, and skill improvement.

how well a person performs relative to other people. Ability is independent of effort. If a person performs well against other competitors, yet does not expend much effort, this is evidence of great ability. Thus, for the ego-oriented athlete, success is outperforming an opponent using superior ability as opposed to high effort or personal improvement. An ego-oriented individual who has high perception of ability should exhibit adaptive motivational patterns (engage willingly in challenging tasks). However, an ego-oriented individual who has low perception of ability should exhibit a **maladaptive motivational pattern.** Because his motivation is to win and he does not believe he can win, he will not likely take part in a challenging activity. The obvious disadvantage of an ego orientation is that it discourages participation simply for the fun of it unless one is certain of experiencing success. In summary, ego-oriented individuals focus on beating others with minimal effort in order to enhance their social status (Carpenter & Yates, 1997; Fry & Duda, 1997; Williams, 1998).

Research on goal orientation has revealed that individuals who are high in task orientation can also be high in ego orientation; other combinations of the two orientations are also possible. In other words, the two orientations are independent of each other. The best combination is for a young athlete to be high in both orientations (Dunn, Dunn, & Syrotuik, 2002). Individuals with high task and ego orientations exhibit the highest levels of motivation and perceived competence. The worst combination in terms of motivation and perceived competence is to be low in both task and ego orientations.

Several studies point to the superiority of a task orientation over an ego orientation in athletes. King and Williams (1997), utilizing martial arts students as participants, demonstrated that task but not ego orientation was related to martial arts performance. Furthermore, they observed that task orientation but not ego orientation was related to students' perceptions of satisfaction and enjoyment. Similarly, Vlachopoulos and Biddle (1999) reported a large-scale study in which goal orientation was measured in over one thousand British physical education students. The results of the investigation led investigators to conclude that a task orientation should be promoted for physical education students and athletes.

While it sometimes appears from the literature that an ego goal orientation is usually undesirable, this conclusion is oversimplified and could be misleading. An ego goal orientation in the presence of a very low task goal orientation is undesirable, but in combination with a high level of task orientation, this is not necessarily the case. Using a statistical procedure called cluster analysis, Hodge and Petlichkoff (2000) grouped 257 rugby players into distinct goal orientation group combinations. The results showed that high levels of perceived rugby ability are associated with a high degree of

CONCEPT In terms of satisfaction, enjoyment, and performance, it is desirable for an athlete to exhibit a high as opposed to a low task orientation. This is true regardless of the athlete's perception of ability.

APPLICATION Regardless of perceived ability, highly task-oriented individuals believe that suc-

cess, satisfaction, and enjoyment are a function of the effort that they expend striving for mastery. Because task and ego goal orientations are believed to be independent of each other, it is desirable to encourage an athlete to exhibit mastery behaviors and beliefs regardless of her ego orientation. This can be accomplished through cognitive restructuring or by exposing the athlete to a mastery climate.

CONCEPT It is not desirable for an athlete to be highly ego oriented if he harbors feelings of low ability. However, if an athlete perceives that he is highly skilled, then to be ego oriented is not entirely undesirable, especially if the athlete is also highly mastery oriented.

APPLICATION It is always important to remember that the two types of goal orientation are independent of each other. Research has shown that in

terms of performance, satisfaction, and enjoyment, it is best to be high in both task and ego orientation. The athlete's perception of his own ability is of critical importance. An athlete who is ego oriented and has low perception of ability is at risk of avoiding competitive challenges for fear of failing. For this reason, it is important for the coach or sport psychologist to be aware of an athlete's goal orientation and perception of ability.

ego orientation when coupled with high or moderately high levels of task orientation. Thus, in terms of perceived ability and competence, high levels of ego orientation are not necessarily bad.

The observation that an ego goal orientation is not always bad was further clarified in a study reported by Wang and Biddle (2001). The focus of this investigation was upon goal orientation in combination with conceptions of ability and self-determination theory. Using cluster analysis procedures, the researchers were able to differentiate five distinct cluster profiles ranging from highly motivated to amotivated. The two highest motivational clusters were characterized as being high

in task goal orientation, able to view ability as changeable, high in self-determination, and high in perceived competence. The next-to-highest motivational cluster, however, was also high in ego goal orientation, making it clear that an ego goal orientation in combination with a high task orientation is associated with high levels of motivation.

The Matching Hypothesis

In our previous discussion about personality in chapter 2, we understand that the strength of the environment or situation can overwhelm any

FIGURE 4.4 | This illustration shows the interaction between goal orientation (mastery/competitive) and motivational climate (separately for mastery and competitive climate). The matching hypothesis suggests that performance, satisfaction, and enjoyment (outcomes) should be best when the athlete's goal orientation matches the motivational climate created by the coach. For the mastery climate, best outcomes should occur at cell 1, while for the competitive climate they should occur at cell 3.

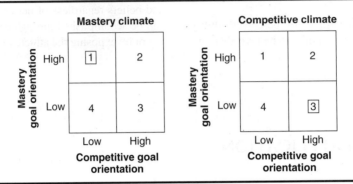

personality disposition. Goal orientation is a personality disposition, while motivational climate is representative of the environment or the situation. Consequently, we might expect that a strong mastery climate might overwhelm or override a disposition toward an ego goal orientation. Nevertheless, we might logically expect that best outcomes in terms of intrinsic motivation, satisfaction, and performance might be associated with a match between goal orientation and motivational climate. Thus, the **matching hypothesis** suggests that a high mastery (task) goal orientation in combination with a high mastery (task) environmental climate should yield better outcomes than a mismatch between the two (i.e., high mastery goal orientation and low mastery climate). Similarly, we would expect that a high competitive (ego) goal orientation in combination with a high competitive (task) motivational climate should yield better outcomes than a mismatch between the two. While this hypothesis would seem to be easy to test, it is actually very complex because of the orthogonal relationship between the mastery and competitive goal orientation. We can experimentally manipulate the motivational climate that athletes are placed in, but in terms of personality disposition, they may be high in mastery and competitive goal orientation, low in both, or high in one and low in the other. This complexity is illustrated in figure 4.4. On the left we have the different combinations of goal orientation under a mastery climate and on the right the different combinations of goal orientation under a competitive climate. Consistent with the matching hypothesis we would expect best outcomes in the mastery climate situation to occur with individuals high in a mastery goal orientation. Yet, we see that due to the hypothesis of independence of goal orientations, two cells are associated with high mastery goal orientation: one for low competitive goal orientation and one for high (cells 1 and 2). The same paradox can be observed on the right relative to a competitive goal orientation.

Notwithstanding these complexities, a number of investigations have been reported relative to the matching hypothesis. Generally speaking, a focused interaction between motivational climate and goal orientation would provide statistical

CONCEPT It is hypothesized that a matching relationship exists between goal orientation and motivational climate relative to desired outcomes. This is referred to as the *matching hypothesis*. This hypothesis suggests that outcomes such as high performance, satisfaction, or intrinsic motivation will be highest if an athlete's goal orientation and motivational climate, that she is placed in, will be complimentary (e.g., mastery goal orientation and mastery climate).

APPLICATION It is important for the coach or sports psychologist to be aware of the goal orienta-

tion of the athlete, but also to be aware of the motivational climate that is being created for the athlete. A competitive (task) goal-oriented athlete should do better in a competitive climate than a mastery-oriented athlete. Ideally, a coach or teacher should try to create a mastery climate for his students or athletes. Once the nature of the climate is well established, it will be much easier for the coach to work with individual athletes relative to compatibility issues. Serious outcome problems can be expected if the coach does not provide a consistent motivational climate and/or is not aware of the goal orientations of her athletes.

evidence for the matching hypothesis. We will now review a few of the investigations that have attempted to test the matching hypothesis for goal orientation and motivational climate.

Treasure and Roberts (1998) measured perceived motivational climate and goal orientations of adolescent female basketball players. In terms of predicting ability beliefs, they observed a significant interaction between a competitive goal orientation and competitive climate. Specifically, competitive goal orientation was observed to moderate (determine) the nature of the relationship between a competitive climate and ability beliefs. If competitive goal orientation was low, a competitive climate did not predict ability belief. Conversely, if competitive goal orientation was high, a competitive climate did predict ability belief. Furthermore, in terms of predicting the belief that mastery experiences were important for success, they observed a significant interaction between mastery goal orientation and mastery climate. Specifically, mastery goal orientation was observed to moderate the nature of the relationship between mastery climate and importance of mastery experiences. The perception that mastery experiences were important increased as the per-

ception of mastery climate increased for both high and low mastery oriented females, but at a faster rate for high mastery oriented individuals.

In an investigation reported by Newton and Duda (1999), the interaction between motivational climate and goal orientation was studied using junior female volleyball players. The dependent variables in the study were tension, intrinsic motivation, belief that effort leads to success, and belief that ability leads to success. A significant interaction was observed between goal orientation and motivational climate relative to predicting the belief that effort leads to success, but no other interaction was significant. Specifically, it was observed that mastery goal orientation moderates the relationship between mastery climate and effort beliefs. As the perception of mastery climate increases, so does the perception that effort is important. But the strength of this relationship increases as mastery orientation increases from low to high. A high level of mastery environment in combination with a high level of mastery goal orientation yields the highest level of effort belief.

In an investigation involving physical education students, Papaioannou et al. (2004) did not find support for the compatibility component of the matching hypothesis, but they did find support for the incompatibility component of the hypothesis. The compatibility component is that high mastery goal orientation and high mastery climate or high competitive goal orientation and high competitive climate should yield the best outcome results (e.g., performance, effort, satisfaction). The incompatibility component of the matching hypothesis is that a mismatch between goal orientation and motivational climate will yield poor outcomes. In this specific case it was observed that placing a high mastery goal-oriented person in an incompatible high competitive climate situation results in reduced mastery goal orientation (not a desired outcome). This result provides indirect but not direct support for the matching hypothesis.

Goal Orientation Antecedents and Outcomes

In this section we turn our attention to research that has considered (a) goal orientation antecedents, (b) goal orientation outcomes, and/or (c) goal orientation as a mediator between antecedents and outcomes. In this case, an antecedent is a variable that proceeds or goes before a goal orientation variable. In some cases, an antecedent variable can be considered to have a cause-and-effect relationship on goal orientation. Variables that are believed to follow or be caused by goal orientation are referred to as outcome variables. In this case we may say that goal orientation causes or predicts a subsequent outcome variable. Some researchers have studied goal orientation as a mediator between antecedents and outcome variables.

In an investigation involving university athletes, Morris and Kavussanu (2008) studied the effect that selected antecedents have upon mastery-approach, mastery-avoidance, performance-approach, and performance-avoidance goal orientations. Results showed that (a) athlete gender (men higher than women), perceived competence, a mastery motivational team cli-

mate, and a learning/enjoyment parental climate all lead to an increase in a mastery-approach goal orientation; (b) athlete gender (women higher than men) and a learning/enjoyment parental climate both lead to an increase in a mastery-avoidance goal orientation; (c) perceived competence and a performance motivational team climate both lead to an increase in performance-approach goal orientation; and (d) a worry conducive parental climate leads to an increase in performance-avoidance goal orientation. This set of findings show clearly that motivational climate and perceived competence can influence an athlete's goal orientation.

Three recent investigations focused upon the effects that goal orientations have upon subsequent outcomes. Papaioannou et al. (2004) showed that a mastery goal orientation increased effort, attitude, and exercise behavior; while a performance goal orientation increased attitude and physical self-concept over a school year for physical education students. Adie, Duda, and Ntoumanis (2008) tested a model in which the goal orientations of adult team sport participants were hypothesized to predict cognitive appraisals (challenge/threat) which in turn were hypothesized to predict self-esteem, positive affect, and negative affect. In this study, cognitive appraisals of competitive situations believed to be positive and challenging were named challenge appraisals, while those appraised to be threatening were named threat appraisals. Results revealed a partial mediation model in which (a) mastery-approach, performance-approach, and performance-avoidance (negative effect) goal orientations predicts challenge appraisals, which in turn positively influence self-esteem and positive affect; and (b) mastery-approach (negative effect), mastery-avoidance, and performance-approach goal orientations predict threat appraisal, which in turn positively influence negative affect but negatively influence self-esteem. Finally, Stuntz and Weiss (2009) demonstrated that social goal orientation is important in predicting perceived competence, enjoyment, and intrinsic motivation in middle school students. These studies show clearly the

CONCEPT   Such things as perceived competence, mastery team climate, learning/enjoyment parental climate, harmonious passion, and an incremental (changeable) ability belief all facilitate the development of a mastery goal orientation. In turn, a mastery goal orientation leads to increased effort, improved attitude, exercise behavior, challenge cognitive appraisal, self-esteem, positive affect, intrinsic motivation, deliberate practice, and increased performance.

APPLICATION   Even though mastery goal orientation is conceptualized as a dispositional construct, there is evidence to suggest that it can be developed and enhanced through many of the antecedents mentioned above (perceived competence, mastery climate, harmonious passion, etc.). Because of the multitude of positive outcomes associated with a mastery goal orientation, it is important for the coach, teacher, and parent, to go to extraordinary lengths to develop the construct in athletes, students, and children. Much of this can be accomplished through the type of climate that is developed in the home, the classroom, and the athletic field.

positive effect that a mastery goal orientation has upon subsequent cognitive, emotional, and physical outcomes.

Three recent investigations will be reviewed that tested whether goal orientation mediates the relationship between selected goal orientation antecedents and outcomes. In the first study, Nien and Duda (2008) tested a model in which goal orientations were hypothesized to mediate the relationship between selected antecedents (perceived competence, fear of failure) and motivational regulation (intrinsic motivation, extrinsic motivation, amotivation) in British adult athletes. Results showed that (a) perceived competence predicts mastery approach goal orientation, which in turn positively predicts intrinsic motivation and negatively predicts amotivation; (b) perceived competence also predicts performance-approach goal orientation, which in turn predicts extrinsic motivation; (c) fear of failure predicts mastery-avoidance goal orientation, which in turn predicts amotivation; (d) fear of failure also predicts performance-approach goal orientation, which in turn predicts extrinsic motivation; and (e) fear of failure also predicts performance-avoidance goal orientation, which in turn predicts amotivation. In summary, competence motivation has a positive influence upon mastery-approach and performance-approach goal orientations which in turn enhance motivational regulation. Also in summary, fear of failure operates through three of four forms of goal orientation (all but mastery approach) to increase extrinsic motivation and in particular amotivation. Clearly, perceived competence and a mastery-approach goal orientation are to be encouraged in terms of enhancing intrinsic motivation, while fear of failure (anxiety) is to be avoided.

In a second meditational investigation, Vallerand et al. (2008) tested a model in which goal orientation was hypothesized to mediate the relationship between passion and deliberate practice and performance in synchronized swimmers and water polo athletes. Results showed that harmonious passion predicts a mastery goal orientation, which in turn predicts deliberate practice, which in turn predicts performance. Results also showed that obsessive passion predicts all measured forms of goal orientation, but that only performance-avoidance goal orientation mediates the relationship between obsessive compassion and performance (negatively). As opposed to practice for fun, **deliberate practice** was defined in this study as practice designed to enhance performance (de Bruin, Rikers, & Schmidt, 2007). In summary, this study shows that a mastery goal orientation mediates the relationship between harmonious passion and increased deliberate practice as well as improved performance. In a similar, but negative fashion, obsessive passion operates through a performance-avoidance goal orientation to inhibit performance.

Finally, in an investigation reported by Wang, Liu, Lochbaum, and Stevenson (2009), it was hypothesized that goal orientation mediates the relationship between sport ability beliefs and intrinsic motivation. **Entity ability beliefs** are those in which the athlete believes that ability is a fixed and unchangeable capacity. Conversely, **incremental ability beliefs** are those in which ability is conceptualized as something that can be changed through effort and practice. Results of the investigation showed that mastery-approach and mastery-avoidance goal orientations mediate the relationship between incremental ability and intrinsic motivation. Conversely, it was shown that entity beliefs about ability predicts both performance-approach and performance-avoidance goal orientation, but performance goal orientation does not predict an increase or change in intrinsic motivation. In summary, an incremental belief (changeable) about ability increases mastery goal orientation, which in turn increases intrinsic motivation (this is particularly true in the case of a mastery-approach goal orientation). Conversely, an entity (unchanging) belief about ability increases performance goal orientation, but performance goal orientation does not have any effect upon intrinsic motivation.

Summary

Goal perspective theory is a developmentally based theory of achievement motivation. Children pass through four developmental levels as they move from not being able to differentiate between ability and effort to being able to differentiate between the two at about 12 years of age. Three psychological constructs are important in understanding goal perspective theory. These three constructs are goal orientation, goal involvement, and motivational climate.

Two dispositional goal orientations are mentioned by Nicholls. These two are task orientation and ego orientation. The goal orientation that an athlete has determines how she will evaluate her own ability. Task-oriented children perceive ability as being a function of effort and mastery. Ego-oriented children perceive ability as being a function of social comparison. The terms *task* and *ego orientation* are used interchangeably with the terms *mastery* and *competitive orientation*. Additional goal orientations are suggested by some researchers.

Early on, the Task and Ego Goal Orientation in Sport and Exercise (TEOSQ) and the Perceptions of Success Questionnaire (POSQ) were developed to measure the two orthogonal goal orientations (task/mastery and ego/competitive). In recent years, the Achievement Goals Questionnaire for Sport (AGQ-S) was developed as an alternative to the TEOSQ and POSQ. The AGQ-S is based on Elliot and McGregor's 2×2 achievement goal framework (mastery/competitive by approach/avoidance). A plethora of other inventories has also been introduced by researchers to measure achievement goal orientation in sport.

Goal orientation is a personality disposition, whereas goal involvement is a situation-specific state, or way of responding to an achievement situation at a specific point in time. There are two kinds of goal orientations. They are task or mastery goal orientation and ego or competitive goal orientation.

Just as individuals can be task or ego oriented, motivational climates can be task or ego oriented. A task-oriented environment is referred to as a mastery climate, while an ego-oriented environment is referred to as a competitive climate. A mastery climate is one in which effort, mastery, and cooperation are emphasized. A competitive or performance climate is one in which social comparison and competition are emphasized. Research supports the efficacy of providing a mastery climate for enhancing learning, self-confidence, and perceived ability.

New research relating the concept of moral functioning to sportspersonship was discussed. Two measurable aspects of moral functioning are prosocial and antisocial behavior. These two constructs are measured with the Prosocial and Antisocial Behavior in Sport Scale (PABSS). Research suggests a link between sportspersonship and task and ego goal orientation. Contact sports are linked to an ego goal orientation, which is predictive of lower levels of moral functioning in terms of judgments, intentions, and actual behaviors.

An important area of needed research is to study the interaction between goal orientation and motivational climate. Theory suggests that certain goal orientation dispositions should do best in certain motivational climates relative to success,

satisfaction, and enjoyment. This is the matching hypothesis, which suggests that a high mastery goal orientation in combination with a high mastery environmental climate should yield better outcomes than a mismatch between the two. Although some research has been conducted relative to the matching hypothesis, additional research is needed.

The final section of this chapter on goal perspective theory focuses on goal orientation antecedents and outcomes. Such things as perceived competence, mastery team climate, learning/ enjoyment parental climate, harmonious passion, and an incremental ability belief all facilitate the development of a mastery goal orientation (antecedents). In turn, a mastery goal orientation leads to increased effort, improved attitude, exercise behavior, challenge cognitive appraisal, self-esteem, positive affect, intrinsic motivation, deliberate practice, and increased performance (outcomes).

Critical Thought Questions

1. Goal orientations are described as being relatively stable personality dispositions. Yet, research suggests that a person's disposition to be ego involved can be changed over time to be more mastery oriented through long-term exposure to a mastery climate. Critically discuss this paradoxical issue.

2. It seems as though a child moves developmentally from having a task orientation relative to perceived ability to having an ego orientation at about age 12. Yet, a task orientation is often described as being more desirable than an ego orientation in terms of developing self-confidence and experiencing satisfaction and enjoyment in sport. Are we saying that moving backwards developmentally is desirable? Explain.

3. In terms of measuring goal orientation, contrast the Task and Ego Orientation in Sport Questionnaire (TEOSQ) and the Perceptions of Success Questionnaire (POSQ) with the Achievement Goals Questionnaire for Sport (AGQ-S). How do these inventories differ theoretically? Do you think the AGQ-S is an important advancement in goal orientation research, or an unnecessary complexity? Explain and justify your answer.

4. What do you think is the most desirable motivational climate for developing self-confidence and motivation in children and young athletes? Explain why you think this is so. Provide a detailed description of your ideal motivational climate.

5. Why would an ego goal orientation or competitive orientation be more associated with poor sportspersonship than a mastery goal

orientation? What is there about the ego orientation that causes an athlete to be more willing to break rules and perhaps inflict harm on another athlete?

6. Discuss the matching hypothesis relative to goal orientation and motivational climate. Does current research support this hypothesis? Explain. Discuss how an interaction between goal orientation and motivational climate can provide evidence of the matching hypothesis. Why is testing the matching hypothesis more complicated than it looks?

7. Discuss antecedents and outcomes of goal orientation. How can you utilize this information to help you understand your athletes (students) better and to get the most from them in terms of motivation? Does it really matter if your athletes are task or ego goal oriented? Explain.

Glossary

achievement motivation An athlete's predisposition to approach or avoid a competitive situation.

adaptive motivational pattern Motivation to participate in challenging activities.

antisocial behavior Voluntary behavior designed to disadvantage or perhaps harm another person.

cluster analysis Statistical procedure that magnifies differences between athletes in different groups or clusters while at the same time minimizing differences between athletes that are within the same group or cluster.

cognitive restructuring The use of cognitive or mental skills to restructure or change the way one views certain situations.

competitive climate An environment in which athletes perceive that mistakes will be punished and competition between teammates will be encouraged.

competitive goal orientation Goal disposition that perceives ability as a function of outperforming others as opposed to self-improvement (see ego orientation).

deliberate practice Practice designed to enhance performance as opposed to practicing for fun.

differentiated goal perspective Ability of a child to clearly distinguish or differentiate among the concepts of ability, effort, luck, and outcome.

ego involvement A situation-specific manifestation of being ego or competition oriented. Similar to ego orientation.

ego goal orientation Goal disposition that perceives ability as being a function of outperforming others as opposed to self-improvement (see competitive orientation).

entity ability beliefs Ability is conceptualized as a fixed and unchangeable capacity.

goal involvement A situation-specific state measure of how an individual relates to an achievement situation at a specific point in time.

goal orientation A person's disposition to be task goal oriented and/or ego goal oriented.

incremental ability beliefs Ability is conceptualized as something that can change with effort and practice.

maladaptive motivational pattern Lack of motivation to participate in challenging activities.

mastery climate Environment in which athletes receive positive reinforcement from the coach when they work hard, cooperate, and demonstrate improvement.

mastery goal orientation Goal disposition to view perceived ability as a function of effort and improvement (see task orientation).

matching hypothesis As used in this chapter, the term relates to matching a person's goal orientation with a person's motivational climate to bring about maximum achievement benefits.

moral functioning Relative to sport, moral functioning represents respect for social conventions, respect for rules and officials, respect for one's full commitment toward sport, and true respect and concern for the teammates and opponents.

motivational climate The motivational environment a person is placed in relative to factors that relate to mastery or competition.

perceived ability A conceptualization of ability that is based upon how a person views the relationships between ability, effort, mastery, and social comparison.

prosocial behavior Voluntary behavior designed to benefit another person.

social approval goal orientation The desire for social acceptance through conformity to norms while displaying maximum effort.

sportspersonship Performance of athletic tasks with a high level of moral functioning. Those exhibiting a low level of moral functioning are said to exhibit unsportspersonlike behavior.

task involvement A situation-specific manifestation of being task- or mastery-oriented; similar to task orientation.

task goal orientation Goal disposition to view perceived ability as a function of effort and improvement (see mastery goal orientation).

undifferentiated goal perspective Point of view in which a child cannot distinguish or differentiate among the concepts of ability, effort, luck, and outcome.

Youth Sports

KEY TERMS

Developmental model of sport
  participation
Five Cs
General-sport dropout
Investment years
Motives for particpation
Parents' code of conduct
Professional sports model
Reversed-dependency trap
Sampling years
Sources of Sport Enjoyment
Specialization years
Specific-sport dropout
Sport commitment model
Sport Friendship Quality Scale
Surface reasons for withdrawal
  from sport
Underlying psychological
  reasons for withdrawal
  from sport
Youth sports
Youth sports model

"If you want to teach kids to hit, you tell them, 'Wait for a good pitch to hit.' If you want to win, you tell them, 'I want you to take [don't swing] until you get two strikes,' but in the end, what have you got? You haven't taught them how to hit, only how to draw a walk and run the bases" (Cal Ripken, Jr., in Menez, 2003, p. 65).

Most people, when they think of applied sport psychology, think of elite athletes and how to improve athletic performance. This is certainly the focus of sport psychology during the winter and summer Olympic Games that so captivate the nation and the world. However, when you consider that approximately 41 million children between the ages of 6 and 18 participate in agency-sponsored youth sport programs each year, and another 7 million 14- to 18-year-old youth participate in school-sponsored programs (Smoll & Smith, 2010), you see the tremendous potential for human enrichment and development. If every child who participated in sport emerged with increased self-confidence, greater perceived ability, increased intrinsic motivation, and greater self-esteem, the world and society would certainly be better for it. Unfortunately, this is not always the case, as the following true story reveals.

> This is the story of a child named Johnny who had not yet succeeded in hitting a baseball off a tee (T-ball). One day, after several attempts, the boy, for the first time in his young life, succeeded in hitting the ball. Overcome with happiness and joy, the boy jumped up and down with glee as his parents and other fans cheered his success. In his excitement, however, he forgot that he was supposed to run to first base. In anger, his volunteer coach grabbed him and said "Johnny, you dummy, you can't even run to first. You will never get another chance to bat on my team." Needless to say, Johnny became a sports dropout. Johnny's experience could have been one of the greatest in his life, but an untrained, insensitive volunteer coach turned it into one of his worst (K. Dimick, Personal Communication, September 1990).

Historically, youth sport originated in the United States free from adult surveillance, in settings as diverse as New York City, southern slave communities, and western frontier towns (Wiggins, 1996). Children enjoyed unsupervised marbles, crack-the-whip, capture-the-flag, soccer, and all sorts of variations of baseball and other sports. "The essential wonderment of the games we played is that we played them blessedly free from adults. There were no soccer moms or Little League dads. For better and for worse, we defined and lived in our own world." (Maraniss, 2001, p. 86).

Over time, adults saw the need to provide organized and supervised sport programs for youth. Adults were motivated then, as now, along various lines of thinking. Sometimes they promoted sports for educational and moral development reasons, but at other times competition itself was their goal. Interestingly, highly competitive youth sport programs emerged in the United States as early as the 1920s and 1930s, prompting educators to warn against the dangers of highly competitive sport. The Youth Sport Institute at Michigan State University set the stage for programs designed to study ways in which youth sport could be developed for the maximum personal benefit of the youth participants. This program emerged in 1978 under the leadership of Vern Seefeldt (Wiggins, 1996).

There are two types of youth sport programs. One is sponsored by the schools, and the other is sponsored by agencies and city recreation departments. *School-sponsored programs* generally have the luxury of dedicated facilities and qualified coaches, although this is not always the case. State high school athletic associations mandate a certain level in the qualifications of coaches. Requirements for coaches of school-sponsored teams vary from state to state. The standard for a head coach of a major sport is usually a teaching certificate, with some coaching experience and training desired. In some states the requirements are even higher, but hardship exceptions are routinely given, as school administrators are hard pressed to find coaches for all the sports. Theoretically, the higher coaching standards in the school-sponsored programs result in better, more educationally sound programs, but this is not always true. Because school administrators can hire and fire coaches, they have a level of control that is not often available in nonschool youth sports programs. However, stipends for coaching are often so low that they offer little encouragement to coaches to meet desired coaching standards.

Nonschool youth sports programs operate in quite a different way. These programs use volunteers as coaches, and it is often difficult for teams to find places to practice. The primary focus of this chapter on youth sports is upon nonschool youth sports programs, so we will simply refer to them as

youth sports throughout the rest of the chapter. The very nature of youth sports is very dynamic, as it brings together all aspects of society. The only paid participants in the youth sports experience are the organizers (e.g., city recreation department staff) and the referees and officials. The participants, coaches, parents, and other interested adults are all volunteers with various levels of expertise. What typically happens in a youth sports program, such as a basketball program, is that a call goes out from the organizers for youth participants and coaches. Coaches are selected and the youth are assigned or drafted into teams (this process varies greatly from program to program). The organizers have an important voice in determining who will be selected for coaches, but if they have a shortage of volunteers their options are limited. Typically, an adult volunteer is assigned to coach a team that includes the coach's own son or daughter. This, of course, is the primary motivation of the adult to volunteer to spend hundreds of hours of his free time coaching children. Coaching is an opportunity to be with his child, as well as an opportunity to have a major voice in how much playing time his child gets. It is a very interesting cultural experience. While the youth participants are playing, some of the parents are coaching, and other parents are in the stands either supporting or not supporting the decisions of the volunteer coach on the field.

With the scenario just described, there is tremendous opportunity for human development and enrichment to take place as children, parents, coaches, and officials interact to provide a learning experience for the children. Overall, the experience is a positive one and a marvel to behold, but there are many opportunities for and examples of abuse. In this chapter we will learn about the youth sport experience by discussing (a) benefits of youth sports and reasons children participate, (b) potential negative factors associated with the youth sport experience, (c) why youth withdraw from sport, (d) coach, parent, and peer relationships, (e) goal perspective and motivational climate, and (f) issues associated with developing a youth sport program.

Benefits of Youth Sports and Reasons Children Participate

Being a part of sport should enhance people's lives. Kids weren't put on earth to become tools of entertainment for adults. Kids are on earth to grow into happy, healthy, contributing, fulfilled, satisfied adults and parents. That's what it is. That's why I'm a teacher. That's what education is about. (Rick McGuire, Head Track Coach, University of Missouri-Columbia, May 28, 2006; Walljasper, 2006)

Numerous investigations have been reported in which youth sport participants were asked to give or identify reasons why they participate in sport (Ewing & Seefeldt, 1996; Lee, Whitehead, & Balchin, 2000; Sit & Lindner, 2006; White, Duda,

Children who participate in sports have fun and learn new skills. © Royalty-Free Corbis.

CONCEPT The motives that young athletes have for participating in youth sports programs are the same motives that lead to the development of intrinsic motivation and self-confidence.

APPLICATION Youth sport promises an exciting and challenging environment in which participants can realize enhanced self-esteem and motivation.

Some youth sports programs may be based on participation motives of organizers and parents that are not consistent with the motives of the participants themselves. In order to assist participants in the development of intrinsic love for sport and increased self-confidence relative to sport participation, the participant's motives for participation must be of primary concern.

& Keller, 1998). While the studies do not yield identical reasons for participation, there are common themes. The number one reason children give for participating in youth sports is "to have fun." When it isn't fun anymore, the young athletes will find something else to do. Based on numerous investigations, the following **motives for participation** have been identified repeatedly by youth sports participants:

1. To have fun and to enjoy participating in sport

2. To learn new skills and to improve on existing sports skills

3. To become physically fit and to enjoy good health

4. To enjoy the challenge and excitement of sports participation and competition

5. To enjoy a team atmosphere and to be with friends

In addition to representing motives for participation, the above list represents some of the perceived benefits of youth sports participation. The benefits of youth sports participation include having fun, learning new sports skills, getting physically fit, experiencing the excitement of competition, and making new friends. This is, however, an incomplete list of the potential benefits of youth sport participation. The intangibles that children do not list include things like learning to cooperate with teammates and coaches, learning what it means to be a good sport, and developing a sense

of perceived competence and self-efficacy. A positive youth sports experience will enhance intrinsic motivation, which will in turn lead to continued participation in sports throughout a lifetime. Interestingly, "winning" or "to win" is seldom at the top of any child's list of reasons for participating (Lee, Whitehead, & Balchin, 2000).

Potential Negative Factors Associated with the Youth Sports Experience

If youth sports programs are properly organized and supervised by responsible adults, there is no reason why there should be any negative outcomes associated with the experience. To avoid negative experiences in the youth sports experience, organizers should host two mandatory educational sessions. One training session would be held for youth sports coaches and the other for all parents of youth participants. The focus of these two sessions should be, first, how to make the youth sports experience a positive one for the participants, and second, how to avoid negative consequences associated with youth sports.

What are the potential negative consequences of youth sports participation? We will focus upon three negative consequences here. They are (a) too much competition and focus upon winning, (b) too much distress and anxiety in the minds and bodies of the participants, and (c) violence involving adults.

Competition and Focus upon Winning

If kept within the appropriate bounds, competition satisfies one of the motives of youth sports participation, which is to enjoy challenging and exciting competition. Competition gives the youth sports participants an opportunity to put all of their practice and hard work to the test. A loss should mean not that a player has low ability, but that through hard work she can improve. This is where attribution training comes into play. The problem arises when winning becomes so important that it becomes the sole purpose of competition. When winning becomes that important, it forces an external locus of causality, and the athlete's sense of self-determination and autonomy is diminished, as is intrinsic motivation.

Who decides that winning is the only reason that a team plays a basketball game against an opponent? How do the youth sports participants come to believe that winning is the primary reason that they are involved in youth sports? These are good questions that have fairly complex answers. We should look first of all to the organizers of the youth sports league to see how important winning is to such things as the format for postseason play, selection to all-star teams, and efforts made to equalize teams on the basis of skill and maturity. Organizers can deemphasize the importance of winning by allowing all teams to go into a playoff round and to equalize skill level among teams so that no one team has an unfair advantage to begin with.

Next, we can look to the coaches of the youth sports teams to see what their motivations are. Why should a coach believe that winning is so important that only the most skilled players get to play most of the time? What effect does sitting on the bench and watching his peers play most of the game have on the perceived confidence of a young athlete? There is a clear message here, and it is not lost on the young athlete—or his parents. The athlete suffers a loss of perceived ability, and he comes to fear competition for fear of failing. Some organizers of youth sports programs will require that every athlete get a chance to play in every game, but they need to take that policy a little further and require that every youth has an equal opportunity to play. Still, even with all the safeguards against unequal opportunity, an overemphasis on the importance of winning ruins the experience for many of the participants.

Just as athletes can be competition or "win" oriented as opposed to mastery oriented, so can coaches be win oriented. To the competition-oriented coach, coaching ability is associated with defeating another team or another coach. It has nothing to do with improving the skill level of an entire group of young people, including those with very little skill. The mastery-oriented coach is going to look at competition and winning from a totally different perspective from that of the competition-oriented coach. She will take satisfaction in seeing a group of youngsters learn to work together and improve their individual and team skills, independent of the final game score. Winning the contest is a secondary goal to the mastery-oriented coach.

> Thanks to a remarkable woman (Luma), young war refugees from three continents found a new home on a soccer field in Georgia. They called their team the Fugees. The driving force was this young Moslem, the daughter of a steel magnate from Amman, Jordan. She found herself in America helping these poor refugees of war torn countries. . . . It occurred to her one day: Why not turn these refugee kids into a team. . . and become their coach? She had just resigned after four years as a coach of a girls' YMCA team, weary of players and parents so fixated on playing time, winning and scholarships that she barely recognized her childhood game. . . None had ever been coached. They'd learned the game on streets and in refugee camps. Luma didn't know whether to laugh or whoop or cover her eyes, but damn, the game was fun again. (Smith, 2008)

Distress and Anxiety

Too much emphasis upon competition and winning leads to increased levels of distress and anxiety. A detailed explanation of the meaning of distress and

CONCEPT An inordinate focus upon winning leads to a negative experience for youth sports participants.

APPLICATION The number one reason children give for participating in sports is to have fun. This number one reason for participating in youth sports is sacrificed when coaches and adults overemphasize the importance of winning. The adults set the tone, from the organizers down to the coaches and the parents. Adult training sessions for parents and coaches are ways to teach adults how to make the sports experience a joyful one for their children.

anxiety will be given in a later chapter, but for now it is sufficient to understand that these terms are related to a child's fear of failure and worry about disappointing others. The primary reason that youth sports participants give for involvement in sport is to have fun; distress and anxiety are certainly not fun. You simply cannot enjoy playing a baseball or softball game if you are fearful every time it is your turn to bat, or are worrying that the ball might be hit to you when you are in the field.

Over time, with the proper coaching and experience, young athletes can learn to appreciate and enjoy the excitement of competition as an end in itself. Everyone enjoys the euphoria and thrill of victory, but in reality it cannot be fully appreciated unless one has experienced defeat. More important than the actual winning or losing of an athletic contest is the pure joy of being part of the experience.

Violence Involving Adults

The whole topic of sport aggression among players and fans will be discussed in detail in a later chapter of the text, but for now our focus is upon violence in youth sports. Violence among adults in youth sports is truly reprehensible and must be stopped. Unfortunately, according to the national news media, it is something that is increasing rather than decreasing.

- Albany, Georgia: Ray Knight, former Cincinnati Reds third baseman and manager, and father of a 12-year-old girl, punched the father of a girl belonging to an opposing softball team following a heated exchange.

- Swiftwater, Pennsylvania: Police were called in to stop a brawl between parents and players following a football game between 11- to 13-year-olds.

- Staten Island, New York: Following a hockey game for 11- and 12-year-old boys, a father struck his son's coach in the face with two hockey sticks.

- Sacramento, California: Following a Little League game, a father who was coaching his son's team beat up the manager of the opposing team.

- Eastlake, Ohio: A soccer dad punched a 14-year-old boy who had scuffled for the ball with the man's 14-year-old son.

- La Vista, Nebraska: A former corrections officer assaulted a 16-year-old referee at a flag football game for 6- and 7-year-old boys.

- Philadelphia, Pennsylvania: The father of a 6-year-old pee-wee football player got into a scuffle with his boy's coach over playing time. Before the fracus ended, 6–7-year-old kids had seen an angry dad punch his son's coach and brandish a .357 magnum. The referee punched the dad's angry brother and two men were arrested.

These are just some of the examples of adult violence associated with youth sport. Perhaps the most outrageous and flagrant example of adult violence took place in July 5, 2000 at the Burbank Ice Arena in Reading, Massachusetts. The altercation, involving two fathers, occurred in front of the victim's three sons. The altercation began on the ice, when the

CONCEPT Distress and anxiety, when associated with the youth sports experience, are almost always caused by an overemphasis upon competition and winning.

APPLICATION Rather than trying to reduce distress through some sort of psychological intervention, why not go right to the heart of the problem and reduce the emphasis placed upon winning? Ask yourself why it is so important to win this game, match, or contest. This question should not be asked repeatedly before each competition, because then it is too late. This question needs to be asked early on, when team and individual goals are being set and when organizers are planning postseason tournaments and determining what the purposes of youth sports should be. If organizers decide that the youth sports experience is for the purpose of identifying the best players and winning postseason tournaments, then the participants should be informed early on of this fact.

assailant accused the victim of not controlling rough play among the boys during an ice hockey team practice. Hard feelings and words continued outside of the arena at the pop machine following the practice. The assailant knocked the smaller man down, pinned him to the floor with his knee, and beat him to death with his fists while the victim's boys watched in horror. History records that Thomas Junta was convicted of involuntary manslaughter for his role in this event.

As may be noted, all of these examples but one involved parents of youth sports participants. Somewhat tongue-in-cheek, Rick Reilly (2000) wrote an editorial titled "Bringing Parents Up to Code," in which he wrote a code of conduct for parents of youth sports participants. His fourth code of conduct goes like this: "I'll realize that the guy behind the umpire's mask, whom I've been calling 'Jose Feliciano' and 'Coco, the talking ape,' is probably just a 15-year-old kid with a tube of Oxy 10 in his pocket, making $12 the hard way. I'll shut up" (Reilly, 2000, p. 88). In this same editorial, Reilly mentions the fact that the athletic association of the town of Jupiter, Florida, requires parents of all youth sports participants to view a film on sportspersonship and to sign a code of conduct.

Taking it one step further, the New Brunswick, New Jersey Recreation Department has designed and built unique raised baseball fields. The fields at their new parks are raised 10 feet above the ground. Anyone standing behind the backstop can't see the action. The design places the bleachers well down the foul line into the outfield, separating parents from the dugouts (Bach, 2002).

Why Do Youth Withdraw from Sport?

The answer to this question is partly the reverse of all the motives that children give for wanting to be involved in youth sport. Children's **surface reasons for withdrawal from sport** are as follows:

1. Participating in sport not being fun anymore
2. Failure to learn new skills or to improve on existing skills
3. Lack of physical activity
4. Lack of thrills, challenges, and excitement
5. Poor team atmosphere, not making friends

In addition to surface reasons for why young people withdraw from sports are the **underlying psychological reasons for withdrawal from sport.** First, you have the distress and worry associated with too much emphasis upon winning and competition. These factors undermine a child's intrinsic motivation or love for an activity. There is no longer an intrinsic reason to continue sports participation, and the external rewards are insufficient motivators.

Another surface reason youth sports participants give for dropping out is described by

CONCEPT Incidents of sport violence in youth sports usually involve fathers of the youth participants.

APPLICATION There are really only two potential solutions to this dilemma. One is to ban parents from youth sports involvement altogether, and the second is to require in-service training of parents, similar to that in the Jupiter, Florida, experiment. Most parents are wonderful, well-behaved supporters of the youth sports experience, but it is the volatile exception that causes all of the problems. Parents must be firmly taught that if they cannot control their emotions, tempers, and egos, they are not welcome on the field, on the floor, or at any other place their son or daughter is performing.

---

age-group swimmers as simply "change of interest" or "other things to do" (Butcher, Linder & Jones, 2002). An athlete's decision to drop out of swimming, however, does not mean that he is a dropout from all youth sport activities. Swimming is a very demanding activity involving little social interaction. Consequently, it is important to determine if a youth sport dropout is a **specific-sport dropout** or a **general-sport dropout.** Withdrawing from one sport to participate in another is less of a concern to sport psychologists than dropping out of sports altogether.

Fraser-Thomas, Côté, and Deakin (2008a, 2008b) reported on two investigations in which adolescent age group swimmers who dropped out of competition were contrasted with a comparable group of swimmers who remained engaged and committed to their sport. Some of the findings were as follows:

- Compared to engaged swimmers, dropouts participated in less extracurricular activities.

- Dropout swimmers participated in less unstructured play swim time.

- Engaged and dropout swimmers did not differ in terms of swim practice time, swim competition time, or swim dry land practice.

- Dropouts started training camps and dry land training at an earlier age.

- Dropouts became "top" swimmers at a younger age and took less time off from swimming, and switched clubs less often compared to engaged swimmers.

- Dropouts experienced less one-on-one coaching time.

- Compared to engaged athletes, more parents of dropout swimmers had parents who excelled as youth athletes.

- Dropouts reported that their best friend was another swimmer less often than fully engaged swimmers.

- Dropouts reported being the youngest in training camps more often than engaged swimmers.

- Dropouts spoke more often of demanding parents, early peak performances, and lack of swimming friends; whereas, engaged swimmers spoke more often of open communication with parents, school friend support, and sibling support.

In summary, it would appear that dropouts experience too early and too much specialization, and experience too much parental pressure and high expectations at an early age. While age group swimming is a very demanding youth sport, many of the findings of these two studies will generalize to other sports as well.

Children who succeed in sports gain the admiration of their friends and peers. This opens up tremendous social opportunities for them, and has considerable influence on their psychological development. Conversely, if a child is perceived by herself and her peers as having low skill, she may suffer a loss of friends, a loss of self-confidence, and an increase in anxiety about competition. Adults associated with youth sport programs must make every effort to make them meaningful,

CONCEPT   Youth withdraw from the sport experience for surface as well as underlying psychological reasons.

APPLICATION   Research shows that the dropout rate for organized youth sport programs is 35 percent for any given year. Youth sports leaders should consider a complete dropout from sport for any reason other than "change of interest" or "other things to do" to be of major concern.

Dropping out for surface reasons such as "not having fun" or "not learning new skills" suggests weaknesses in the program, while dropping out for underlying psychological reasons suggests insensitivity to the psychological needs of children. When young people drop out of sports, a systematic follow-up should be made to determine why they have dropped out. A simple, confidential questionnaire could be developed for this purpose.

positive experiences for each participant. Withdrawal from sport for underlying psychological reasons is more serious than withdrawal out of simply losing interest or finding other things to do.

Whether or not young athletes continue to participate in sport or withdraw (dropout) is related to the concepts of *sport commitment* and *persistence*. The **sport commitment model** was simultaneously developed by Weiss and Weiss (2007) and Scanlan, Russell, Magyar, and Scanlan (2009). The sport commitment model describes and identifies factors (antecedents) believed to determine an athlete's level of sport commitment. As illustrated in figure 5.1, sport enjoyment, valuable opportunities, other priorities (attractive alternatives), personal investments, social constraints, and social support all lead to and determine the athlete's sport commitment. Also illustrated in figure 5.1 is an arrow leading from sport commitment to the behavioral consequence of persistence. If the athlete remains committed to her sport, she will persist in it and not become a sport dropout. While each of the antecedents leading to sport commitment are important, the most critical one is *sport enjoyment*. The athlete will not remain committed to his sport if he does not find enjoyment in continuing his involvement. As measured by the Sources of Enjoyment in Youth Sport Questionnaire (SEYSQ: Wiersma, 2001), antecedents or **sources of sport enjoyment** include:

- Self-referenced competency
- Other referenced competency

- Effort expenditure
- Competitive excitement
- Affiliation with peers
- Positive parental involvement

Research reported by McCarthy, Jones, and Clark-Carter (2008) demonstrated that sources of enjoyment do lead to sport enjoyment. To feel sport enjoyment, the athlete must feel competent, engage in effortful activity, experience the excitement of competition, make friends, and benefit from positive parental support.

Coach, Parent, and Peer Relationships

Youth sport interactions are very complex, because the three critical players in the phenomenon all interact and influence each other in very important ways. Part of this complexity is due to the fact that in youth sports, the coach is often also a parent of one or more of the youth participants. This affects the social dynamics of the youth sport experience in very complex ways. In this section we will learn about these complex issues by discussing (a) training volunteer coaches, (b) coach–parent relationships, (c) parental influences, and (d) peer friendship influences.

Training Volunteer Coaches

The best way to assure a quality youth sport program is to provide quality training and supervision

CONCEPT   Although other antecedents are in-volved, sport enjoyment leads to sport commit-ment which, in turn, leads to persistence or the desire to continue sport participation.

APPLICATION   In order to encourage continued sport involvement and avoid sport withdrawal (dropout), it is critical that youth sport participation is fun and enjoyable. Many factors or antecedents determine whether or not the sport experience is

enjoyable. The coach and teacher must be aware of the sources of enjoyment and provide the motiva-tional climate to ensure that they are present in the youth sport experience. Critical antecedents of sport enjoyment include competence, friendship, positive parental support, competitive excitement, and effortful participation. While no one can guar-antee that the youth sport experience is joyful, knowing what leads to fun and enjoyment should make the leader's task more certain.

FIGURE 5.1 | The sport commitment model showing the antecedents of sport commitment and persistence. In the model, sport enjoyment is the most critical and important of the antecedents.

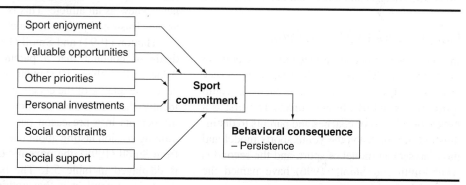

Source: Adapted with permission from Scanlan, T. K., Russell, D. G., Magyar, T. M. & Scanlan, L. A. 2009. Project on elite athlete commitment (PEAK): III. An examination of the external validity across gender, and the expansion and clarification of the sport commitment model. *Journal of Sport & Exercise Psychology, 31* (6), 685–705.

of volunteer coaches. A number of formal coach training programs have been developed in the United States to assist youth coaches in creating a positive and enjoyable athletic experience. Exam-ples include these:

1. American Sport Education Program (ASEP; Martens, 1987).

2. Program for Athletic Coaches' Education (PACE; Seefeldt & Brown, 1992).

3. Coach Effectiveness Training (CET; Smith & Smoll, 1997b).

Research has demonstrated the effectiveness of these coach training programs in teaching volunteers to be more effective and knowledgeable youth sport coaches (Malete & Feltz, 2000). The Coach Effectiveness Training (CET) program, along with the Coaches Behavioral Assessment System (CBAS) will be discussed in greater detail in a later chapter on leadership. While the above-mentioned coach training programs are available to the organizers of youth sport programs, research documents that youth sport coaches gain their knowledge and experience in many different ways

(Lemyre, Trudel, & Durand-Bush, 2007; Wiersma & Sherman, 2005). To begin with, most youth sport head coaches had both playing experience and/or coaching experience prior to becoming a head coach. What they generally lack is experience in working with children and with parents of children. Building upon previous chapters, they also lack knowledge and experience in developing a mastery or task-oriented learning environment and in promoting prosocial behavior in young people. During the first three years of being a head coach, volunteer youth coaches typically gain their knowledge and experience through (a) coach training courses, (b) written resource material, (c) interaction with assistant coaches and other head coaches, (d) discussions with athletes and parents, and (e) discussions with friends and family members.

Coach-Parent Relationships

In youth sports, coaches are also often parents, so the relationship between coach and parent is a very sensitive one. To a large extent, problems in youth sport come from two basic sources. The first is a failure on the part of coaches and parents to distinguish clearly between the youth sports model and the professional model of sport, and the second is what Smith and Smoll (1996) have named the "reversed-dependency trap."

The **youth sports model** provides an educational setting for the development of desirable physical and psychosocial characteristics in young athletes. Conversely, the **professional sports model** is a commercial enterprise in which the stated goals are to entertain and to make money. Sometimes parents and coaches fail to see the distinction between the two and act as if they are one and the same.

The **reversed-dependency trap** describes a situation in youth sport in which the child becomes an extension of the parent. A parent comes to define his own sense of self-worth in terms of the success and failure of his son or daughter. When this happens, the parent becomes a "winner" or a "loser" through his young athlete. A parent may seek to experience through his child the success he never knew as an athlete. This is often referred to as the "frustrated jock syndrome".

Hanlon (1994) and Smoll (1998) list 10 standards of conduct that a parent should follow. Adherence to these 10 standards will greatly enhance the quality of the coach–parent relationship. Ideally, these 10 standards should be presented to the parents in a preseason parents' and coaches' training session lasting about one hour. As adapted from Smoll (1998), the **parents' code of conduct** is displayed in table 5.1. The basic premise of the code of conduct is that nothing in a parent's

---

TABLE 5.1 | Parents' Code of Conduct

1. I will remain in the spectator area during games.
2. I will not advise the coach on how to coach.
3. I will not direct derogatory comments toward coaches, officials, or players of either team.
4. I will not try to coach my child during the course of a contest.
5. I will not drink alcohol at contests or come to a contest having drunk too much.
6. I will cheer for my child's team and give them my support.
7. I will show interest, enthusiasm, and support for my child.
8. I will be in control of my emotions at all times.
9. I will help when asked by coaches or officials.
10. I will thank coaches, officials, and other volunteers who conducted the event.

Source: Smoll, F. L. (1998). Improving the quality of coach-parent relationships in youth sports. In J. M. Williams (Ed.), *Applied sport psychology: Personal growth to peak performance* (p. 67). Mountain View, CA: Mayfield.

CONCEPT   The key to a good coach–parent relationship is effective and open communication. The lines of communication must be kept open and encouraged by the coach. Parents must be informed about when it is inappropriate to enter into a dialogue with the coach.

APPLICATION   The coach should call a coach-parent meeting before the season begins. At this meeting the parents' code of conduct, as outlined in table 5.1, should be reviewed. In addition, the coach should use this time to encourage two-way communication with the parents and to clarify the purpose of the youth sports program. Parents should be employed as valuable resources to assist the coach in achieving the objectives of the youth sports program.

TABLE 5.2 | Common Types of "Problem Parents" and How to Handle Them

Problem Type	How to Handle Them
1. Disinterested	1. Try to find out what the problem is and encourage their involvement.
2. Overcritical	2. Explain damaging effect of criticism on their child.
3. Scream from behind bench	3. During break in action tactfully explain that loud behavior is distracting.
4. Sideline coaches	4. Privately explain to parent how confusing it is to child to have two coaches.
5. Overprotective	5. Reassure parent that the event is fairly safe as long as child is attentive.
6. Abusive	6. With the assistance of a program supervisor, privately assure parent that their behavior will not be tolerated. If not curtailed, they will be given a police escort off the premises.

Source: Smoll, F. L., & Cumming, S. P. (192–204). Enhancing coach-parent relationships in youth sports: Increasing harmony and minimizing hassle. In J. M. Williams (Ed.), *Applied sport psychology: Personal growth to peak performance* (pp. 197–198). Boston, MA: McGraw-Hill.

behavior should detract from or interfere with any child's enjoyment of sport.

The guiding principle for a coach–parent relationship is that communication should take place, and that it is a *two-way street*. Coaches must take the initiative to encourage communication, but at the same time they must identify the parameters for when the communication should take place. Discussions between coach and parent should never take place in front of a child, should never take place during a game, and should rarely take place during practice. The one topic about which coaches and parents will often disagree is a given athlete's ability. Coaches must learn to listen patiently, thank the parents for their thoughts, and assure them that their input will be given every consideration. Parents will often present some very challenging problems for coaches. Some common types of "problem parents" and suggestions on how to handle them are identified in table 5.2.

Parental Influences

Notwithstanding the challenges that overinvolved parents give to youth sport teams, organized youth sport programs could not survive in the absence of parental support. This support comes in the form of such things as transportation, fundraising, and volunteer coaches. Parent involvement and support also permeate every aspect of the social fabric of the youth sport experience. Parent and family socialization of the youth sport experience can be organized around the three components of (a) parents as role models, (b) parents as interpreters of experience, and (c) parents as providers of experience (Fredricks & Eccles, 2004). Current

TABLE 5.3 | Synthesis of Knowledge Associated with How Parent Socialization Affects the Youth Sport Experience

PARENTS AS ROLE MODELS

1. Active parents have active children.
2. Parent participation in athletics is particularly important for girls.
3. Female athletes are more likely to have parents who participate in athletics than are female nonathletes.

PARENTS AS INTERPRETERS OF EXPERIENCE

1. Higher parental pressure is related to negative child outcomes.
2. Low to moderate levels of parental pressure is related to children's higher enjoyment of athletics.
3. Parental beliefs are positively related to children's own competency beliefs, interests, and participation.
4. Parents hold gender-stereotyped beliefs, believing that athletics is more important for boys than for girls and that boys have more athletic talent than girls.
5. Children's perceptions of parents' beliefs are more strongly related to children's self-perceptions than are parent-reported beliefs.

PARENTS AS PROVIDERS OF EXPERIENCE

1. Parents support and encourage children's athletic involvement in a variety of ways, from time involvement to monetary support.
2. Parental encouragement is positively related to children's sports involvement.
3. Parents are gender-typed in their behaviors. They encourage their sons to be physically active more than they encourage their daughters.
4. Over-involvement by parents can contribute to children's negative emotional reactions to sports and ultimately to athlete burnout.

Source: Fredricks, J. A. & Eccles, J. (2004). Parental influences on youth involvement in sports. In M. R. Weiss (Ed.), *Developmental sport and exercise psychology: A lifespan perspective* (pp. 145–164). Morgantown, WV: Fitness Information Technology. Reproduced with permission of the publisher.

knowledge of the effects of parental socialization in the youth sport experience is summarized in table 5.3.

Of particular interest to parents and children alike is athletic success. Children's primary motivation for sport and exercise participation is fun and enjoyment, but they have more fun if they can experience some success. For example, it is fun to shoot baskets in a game of basketball, but it is even more fun if some of those shots actually go into the basket.

In addition to the information displayed in table 5.3, recent research shows that parental influences are mostly positive and focused on supporting the coach and enhancing the child's sport development. However, there is a minority group of parents who have a negative influence on the youth sport program. According to coaches, these parents are demanding overbearing, and exhibit an outcome goal orientation to the youth sport experience (Gould, Lauer, Rolo, Jannes, & Pennise, 2008). Parental verbal reactions to their child's sport performance range from very supportive (praise/encouragement) to very controlling and derogatory (Holt, Tamminen, Black, Sehn, & Wall, 2008). Parent's bad behavior in the youth sport environment encourages bad behavior on the part of their children (Arthur-Banning, Wells, Baker, & Hegreness, 2009). The amount of pressure that youth sport parents place upon their child is directly related to how the child feels about his or her youth sport participation. From the child's perspective, participation in the youth sport experience comes with both benefits and costs. Benefits include personal perks, praise from parents and coach, technical instruction, awareness of ability level, decision making, personal attention, quality time with parent and coach, and motivation. Costs may include negative pressure and expectations, conflict, criticism, and unfair behavior (Weiss & Fretwell, 2005).

Lauer, Gould, Roman, and Pierce (2010) retrospectively interviewed nine professional tennis players, their parents, and coaches about their pathways to elite status. Three pathways to elite status were identified as they related to parental pressure and expectations. These included smooth, difficult, and turbulent pathways. In the *smooth pathway,* parents were supportive and maintained a healthy relationship with the athlete. In the *difficult* and *turbulent pathways,* parents created psychological pressure and tension as they pushed for tennis excellence. With *turbulent pathways,* conflicts between parents and athletes often remained unresolved.

Setting elite status aside, some youth sport participants develop a strong *fear of failure* that can be attributed to misguided socialization practices of their parents (Sager & Lavallee, 2010). Fear of failure is a motivational construct that is associated with high levels of state anxiety. Parents mean well, but in an effort to motivate their child they may resort to three kinds of behavior in response to perceived failure on the part of their child. These three socialization practices include punitive behavior, controlling behavior, and excessively high expectations. When a child fails to perform up to the parent's expectations, the parent responds with these three behaviors. The parent's response to the child's failure is perceived by the child to be an aversive consequence of failure and therefore fears failure. Thus, we have one explanation for the developmental origin of the fear of failure construct.

Most research involving parents and the youth sport experience focuses on parental influences on their child, the coach, and the youth sport phenomenon generally. A few studies, however, have focused on how the youth sport experience affects the parent. According to Dorsch, Smith, and McDonough (2009), parents are socialized by the youth sport experience in terms of their behavior, their thought processes (cognition), how they feel (affect), and personal relationships. As a result of the youth sport experience, parents find themselves behaving in very interesting and new ways. They find themselves actively participating with their child, other parents, and coaches in a common cause that requires support and sacrifice. They become cognitively aware of their child's goals and aspirations as well as becoming knowledgeable about the sport their child is participating in. Parents finds themselves getting emotionally involved in how the youth sport program is managed, how their child responds to the sporting experience, and how other adults and children feel about their involvement. Finally, parents learn to communicate with their child, their child's friends, the coach, and other parents.

Peer Friendship Influences

While parental influences are important to the overall psychological development of the youth sport participant, the influence of peers and friendships within sport cannot be overestimated. Peer acceptance and peer friendships are associated with the athletes' perceived ability, perceived competence, perceived self-worth, and positive affect. Thus, studying peer relationships in youth sport is easily as important as the more commonly studied parent–coach relationship (Holt, Black, Tamminen, Fox, & Mandigo, 2008).

The quality of peer friendship relationships are typically measured using the **Sport Friendship Quality Scale** (SFQS), originally developed by Weiss and Smith (1999) but more recently refined and tested by McDonough and Crocker (2005). The SFQS measures six positive and one

CONCEPT Peer friendships are important predictors of important motivational variables such as perceived competence, perceived enjoyment, and self-determined motivation of the athlete. Possession of these important motivational characteristics will enhance the possibility that the athlete will enjoy a long-term youth sport experience.

APPLICATION This concept makes it clear that the youth sport coaches' responsibility goes far beyond teaching sport skills and winning games.

It is their responsibility to create the motivational climate that encourages and facilitates the development of strong friendships among youth sport participants. The coach cannot pick a child's friend for him, but she can create a cooperative mastery-oriented motivational climate that will facilitate kids wanting to come to practice and enjoy playing together. Parents can help with this process as well as they come to recognize the important role they play in friendship development.

---

negative aspect of youth sport friendship. The positive aspects include (a) self-esteem enhancement and supportiveness, (b) loyalty, (c) intimacy, (d) things in common, (e) companionship and pleasant play, and (f) conflict resolution. The single negative aspect measured by the SFQS is conflict. In completing the 22-item SFQS, the athlete is asked to write the first name or initials of their best friend in their current sport involvement and to answer questions while thinking about their relationship with this person.

In a study reported by Smith, Ullrich-French, Walker, and Hurley (2006), youth sport participants were grouped into five clusters (cluster analysis) based on their scores on perceived friendship quality, perceived peer acceptance, and friendship conflict. The resultant clusters were as follows:

- Thrive—high on friend quality and peer acceptance, but low on friend conflict.
- Alpha—high on all three measures of friendship (including high conflict).
- Survive—average on friend quality and conflict, but quite low on peer acceptance.
- Isolate—below average on conflict and peer acceptance but very low on positive friend quality.
- Reject—below average on friend quality and peer acceptance, but very high on friend conflict.

The group named "thrive" was characterized as an *adaptive cluster* profile, while the group labeled "reject" was characterized as a *maladaptive cluster* profile. The remaining three clusters (alpha, survive, and isolate) were all characterized as being mixed profiles in that they each possessed at least one adaptive peer relationship. Statistical contrasts (tests) were then conducted to see if these disparate clusters differed as a function of five measured motivational variables (perceived competence, enjoyment, anxiety, self-presentional concerns, self-determined motivation). Results showed that the mixed clusters were all very similar to each other relative to all motivational variables, but inferior to the thrive adaptive cluster in all but anxiety. The thrive cluster was also superior to the alpha cluster on anxiety (lower) and self-presentational concerns (lower). These findings make it clear that adaptive friendship characteristics are associated with higher levels of perceived competence, enjoyment, and self-determined motivation compared to groups possessing maladaptive friendship characteristics.

Finally, research suggests that the quality of the parent–adolescent relationship is predictive of more positive sporting friendships (Carr, 2009). There is something about a secure and positive relationship between parent and child that facilitates the child being able to negotiate friendships with her peers on sport teams. These positive peer relationships then lead to positive motivational perceptions.

Goal Perspective and Motivational Climate

The nature of the motivational climate created by the coach has profound effects upon the youth sport participant in terms of perceived coach behaviors and outcomes as well as dispositional goal structure. Motivational climate is a situational specific state variable while goal orientation is a dispositional personality variable. Never-the-less, research demonstrates that the motivational climate created by the coach may result in a change in the athletes' goal orientation structure (Boyce, Gano-Overway, & Campbell, 2009; Conroy, Kaye, & Coatsworth, 2006; Smoll, Smith, & Cumming, 2007).

Boyce et al. (2009) utilized middle-school-age student athletes to study the effect that motivational climate measured across their seasons has upon goal orientation, perceived competence, and practice strategies (goal setting, attentional focus, effort regulation, etc.). In terms of goal orientation, results showed that when perceived motivational climate was incompatible with goal orientation, there was a shift, over time, in goal orientation to match the motivational climate. For example, an athlete categorized initially as being low in task goal orientation but who perceives the presence of a mastery or task motivational climate experienced an increase in task (mastery) goal orientation over time. Results also showed that a mastery motivational climate was predictive of perceived high levels of competence and the use of practice strategies.

In the Smoll, Smith, et al. (2007) investigation, youth sport participants completed inventories to measure season changes in motivational climate and goal orientation. Some of the participants played basketball for coaches who completed a coach training workshop designed to foster a mastery motivational climate in which success was defined in terms of self-improvement and maximum effort, while others did not (control group). At the end of the sport season, the experimental group subjects reported significantly higher levels of mastery climate coaching and lower levels of ego

or performance climate coaching compared to the control group. In addition, the experimental group athletes reported an increase in mastery goal orientation from preseason to post season, while the control athletes actually decreased their mastery goal orientation. Relative to ego (performance) goal orientation, both the experimental and control athletes experienced a decrease, but the rate of decrease or change was much more rapid for the experimental participants.

In the Conroy, Kaye, et al. (2006) investigation, young swim athletes' dispositional goal orientation was assessed three times across a six week period of time. Perceived coaching climate was assessed at the end of the season. Results demonstrated that an avoidance (mastery or competitive) coaching climate was predictive of a more avoidance oriented goal structure across the six week season. Youths' perception of an avoidance-oriented coaching climate leads to the athlete adopting a more avoidance oriented goal structure across the swim season. In another related investigation, Cumming, Smoll, Smith, and Grossbard (2007) demonstrated that perceived motivational climate has a stronger and more consistent predictive relationship to coach outcome variables (e.g., enjoyment, parents like coach, attraction to coach) than do team won/loss records in youth basketball. Specifically, mastery climate scores positively predict coach outcome variables whereas ego or performance motivational climate scores negatively predict these same outcome variables. Again, research underscores the importance of the coach creating a mastery motivational climate. Athletes of all ages like to experience success, yet this study showed that win/loss percentage was a weaker predictor of positive coach outcomes than motivational climate.

In a related investigation, Lee, Whitehead, Ntoumanis, and Hatzigeorgiadis (2008) demonstrated that an athlete's goal orientation may serve as a mediator between sport moral values and sportspersonship attitudes (pro and antisocial). In particular, this study suggested that task goal orientation partially mediates the effect that competence values have upon prosocial attitudes; while ego goal orientation partially mediates the effect that status values (I am better than others) have upon antisocial attitudes. This says that positive competence values may directly increase prosocial sportpersonship attitudes directly, but they also may accomplish this through the presence of a high mastery goal orientation. Similarly, negative status values may directly increase antisocial attitudes directly, but they may also accomplish this through the presence of a high ego goal orientation.

Issues Associated with Developing a Youth Sports Program

In this section we discuss issues that influence or determine the quality of a youth sport program. Without question, organizers of youth sport programs intend positive things for participants. Evidence suggests, however, that youth sport participation does not always yield positive outcomes. For example, sometimes it appears that the outcomes are associated with poor sportspersonship, withdrawal from sport, and sometimes poor behavior on the part of players, coaches, and parents. Here we consider some of the issues that one should be particularly aware of in order to realize positive outcomes and avoid negative outcomes in youth sports. We look at these issues in terms of (a) stages of sport involvement, (b) developmental assets lead to positive outcomes, (c) promoting sportspersonship and prosocial behavior, and (d) program development considerations.

Stages of Sport Involvement

Parents are becoming concerned about two troubling trends in youth sport participation. These include the trend toward early participation in competitive sport and the trend toward yearlong involvement in a single sport. Many parents worry that if they don't start their children when

Youth sports are enjoyed by all involved.
Ryan McVay/Getty Images.

they are young, they will not be competitive in high school and beyond. Consequently, children start playing at a very young age, often at the expense of school and other social activities. The trend toward yearlong involvement in a single sport is particularly stressful on parents and children. In many cases different sports or other activities compete for a child's time, with parents running frantically to get the children to practice or to games. Too much sport involvement can lead to burnout in sport, a topic we will address in detail in chapter 19.

To address the problem of too early involvement in sport and too early sport specialization, Côté and Fraser-Thomas (2007) proposed the adoption of the **developmental model of sport participation** that is built upon the premise of early sport diversification as opposed to specialization. The model proposes that the youth sport participant should pass through three stages of sport development as follows:

- Sampling years (ages 6–12)
- Specialization years (ages 13–15)
- Investment years (ages 16+)

The model proposes that during the **sampling years**, parents encourage their child to sample several different sports without specialization in any single sport. During the **specialization years**, athletes focus their time and energy on a minimum of two or three sports with none of them overlapping significantly with the others in terms of season of the year. Finally, during the **investment years** athletes invest their time and talents on a single sport of their choosing. Not every youth sport athlete will want to enter into this third stage of single sport specialization. Those athletes that enter into this third stage of development are often on an elite sport athlete trajectory.

In a partial test of the sport stage developmental model, Strachan, Côté, and Deakin (2009a) contrasted two groups of young athletes (ages 12–16) who were on an elite sport trajectory. The two groups differed, however, in terms of specialization. The sampling group were involved in at least three sports and invested at least 15 hours per week on the sports collectively. The specialization group focused on a single sport and invested 15 hours per week as well. Sports involved included swimming, artistic gymnastics, rhythmic gymnastics, and diving. Analyses revealed that the two groups did not differ from each other as a function of enjoyment or developmental assets such as positive identity, empowerment, and social support; but did differ in terms of potential burnout and youth experiences. Specifically, the specializers scored higher than samplers on emotional and physical exhaustion (burnout); and lower than samplers on family integration and linkages to the community (but higher on diverse peer relationships). The model was supported in that some differences emerged between the two groups of athletes.

In a second investigation, parents who had children from the three stages of the developmental model were interviewed (Harwood & Knight, 2009). The results of the interviews revealed that parents experience three dimensions of parental stressors. These include organizational stressors (time management, finances, coaching and training, governing body guidelines); competitive stressors (performance, training, behavior of others, and ethics); and developmental stressors (education, uncertainty of child's skill progress and transition, and future decisions related to child's continued involvement in sport at an advanced level). Parents who had children in the sampling stage experienced less developmental stress compared to later stages, a wide variety of competitive stress, but little organizational stress. Parents who had children in the specialization and investment stages experienced high levels of all three categories of stressors.

Focusing upon the specialization years, Keegan, Spray, Harwood, and Lavallee (2010) asked athletes ages of 9–19 to provide information and to discuss ways that coaches, parents, and peers could best motivate them to work hard and to enjoy their youth sport experience. Results were somewhat predictable as coach, parent, and peer influences reflected their respective roles: (a) instruction/assessment from coaches; (b) support/facilitation from parents; and (c) competition, collaboration, evaluation, and social relationships from peers.

Developmental Assets Lead to Positive Outcomes

Early on, Benson (1997) proposed 40 developmental assets that children need for positive psychological development. Building on Benson's early work, the Search Institute (2004) developed the Developmental Assets Profile (DAP) for measuring four external and four internal assets. These eight developmental assets are as follows:

External Assets

- Support
- Empowerment

- Boundaries and expectations
- Constructive use of time

Internal Assets

- Commitment to learning
- Positive values
- Social competencies
- Positive identity

Lerner, Fisher, and Weinberg (2000) further proposed that possession of both external and internal developmental assets should lead to the possession of the five Cs of youth development, including youth sport development. The **five Cs** or outcomes of youth development, are competence, character, connection, confidence, and caring/compassion. Theoretically, if the athlete possesses the necessary assets for quality youth development, then the outcome should be the five Cs of youth sport development. In arguing for the development of youth sport programs that create a mastery climate over a performance/competitive climate, Petitpas, Cornelius, Van Raalte, and Jones (2005) include an emphasis upon developing self-determined motivation, a mastery climate, external assets, and internal assets. Partial support for a youth sport model based on the development or possession of psychological assets was reported by Strachan, Côté, and Deakin (2009b). In this study, the external asset of empowerment and the internal assets of positive identity and social competence were predictive of enjoyment.

Promoting Sportspersonship and Prosocial Behavior

Sportspersonship (prosocial behavior) will be more fully discussed in chapter 4 relative to a discussion on goal perspective theory. We revisit the topic here because of its critical role in the development of positive youth development in youth sports (Weiss, 2008). Youth sports participation does not automatically produce prosocial behavior. In fact, evidence suggests that programs based on a competitive environment or upon controlling motivational regulation can just as easily produce antisocial behavior or poor sportspersonship (Arthur-Banning et al., 2009).

Relative to self-determination theory, Ntoumanis and Standage (2009) demonstrated quite clearly that autonomous motivation leads to sportspersonship, whereas controlling motivational regulation leads to antisocial attitudes and behavior. This study also provides excellent research support for the integrated theory of intrinsic and extrinsic motivation as applied to youth sport participants and as previously illustrated in figure 3.5 of chapter 3. Results of an investigation by Gano-Overway, Newton, Magyar, Fry, and Guivernau (2009) also supports the notion that prosocial behavior in youth sports can be facilitated by developing a caring mastery climate, ability to regulate positive emotions, and empathetic self-efficacy (recognize emotions and support needs of others). Additionally, the ability to regulate positive emotions can inhibit antisocial behavior.

A very enlightening investigation by Shields, LaVoi, Bredemeier, and Power (2007) looked at sportspersonship by identifying the factors that predict poor sport behavior in youth sport participants. If we can identify the factors that lead to poor sport behavior, this will tell us a lot about developing good sport behavior (prosocial behavior). *After* taking into account the effect of all other independent variables, the following factors (in descending order of importance) predict poor sport behavior in youth sport participants:

1. Coach's poor sport behavior increases poor sport behavior in athlete
2. Spectators' poor sport behavior increases poor sport behavior in athlete
3. Teammates' poor sport behavior increases poor sport behavior in athlete
4. Parental disappointment in child's poor sport behavior *decreases* poor sport behavior
5. Coach disappointment in athlete's poor sport behavior *decreases* poor sport behavior
6. Athlete's poor sport attitude increases poor sport behavior

CONCEPT   Placing a child in a youth sport program does not necessarily develop good character and prosocial behavior (good sportspersonship). To enhance the probability of positive outcomes associated with youth sport involvement, organizers must put research into practice.

APPLICATION   To develop a youth sport program that actually develops prosocial behavior organizers, coaches, and parents must create a mastery motivational climate in every youth sport experience (practice, competition, training events). The motivational climate that develops must not be left up to chance or the whim of any particular leadership group. A motivational climate that focuses on mastery as opposed to competition must be encouraged. In addition, a motivational climate that focuses upon the development of autonomous motivational regulation as opposed to a controlling one is critical. Without these basic understandings and goals, the development of prosocial behavior is not at all assured.

Interestingly, in this study the researchers expected that the athlete's poor sport attitude would be the strongest predictor of poor sport behavior, but it was actually the weakest of the six. At the top of the list were coach's poor sport behavior, spectators' poor sport behavior, and teammates' poor sport behavior.

Program Development Considerations

In developing a youth sport program of any type, what should be the overarching goal or goals? We should attend to two main goals. The first is to create a program that is fun and that participants will find enjoyable (i.e., sport enjoyment), and the second is to create a program that promotes the development of prosocial and not antisocial sport behavior (Coatsworth & Conroy, 2009; Fraser-Thomas, & Côté, 2009; Henley, Schweizer, de Gara, & Vetter, 2007; McCarthy & Jones, 2007; Petitpas et al., 2005).

Many factors determine and make up *enjoyment* in sport. According to McCarthy and Jones (2007), enjoyment is a function of the following factors:

- Perceived competence
- Social involvement and friendship
- Psychosocial support from parents
- Mastery learning environment (effort, skill improvement, autonomy, etc.)
- Excitement and challenge of practice and competition without a competitive orientation (i.e., social comparison)
- Movement sensation
- Social recognition of effort and competence
- Encouragement from coach, parents, and peers

There are many levels of youth sport experiences running from low organization (e.g., neighborhood pick-up games) to high organization (leagues, clubs, etc.). Organized youth sport programs (e.g., summer baseball) all have one thing in common, and that is a head coach or group leader. In order to promote a youth sport program based on enjoyment (as previously defined) and the development of prosocial behavior, adult leaders, parents, and participants must be educated on how to develop this kind of program (Petitpas et al., 2005). Based on the research literature, figure 5.2 provides a framework for how to develop a quality youth sport program.

FIGURE 5.2 | Factors involved in developing a youth sport program that promotes enjoyment and prosocial behavior

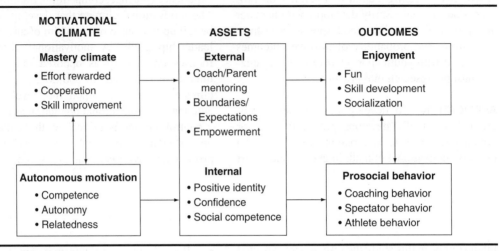

Summary

There are two types of youth sport programs. One is sponsored by the schools, and the other is sponsored by agencies and city recreation programs. The primary focus of this chapter is on the non-school youth sport programs. These programs use volunteers as coaches, and it is often difficult for teams to find places to practice. Main topics covered in this chapter included (a) benefits of youth sports and reasons children participate, (b) potential negative factors associated with the youth sport experience, (c) why do youth withdraw from sport, (d) coach, parent, and peer relationships, (e) goal perspective and motivational climate, and (f) issues associated with developing a youth sport program.

Benefits and reasons why youth participate in youth sport are referred to as motives for participation and include to have fun, learn new skills, become physically fit, enjoy the challenge and excitement of competition, and enjoy making friends. Potential negative factors associated with youth sport participation include an overemphasis on winning, distress and anxiety, and violence involving adults. Reasons that youth give for withdrawing from sport are basically the opposite of their reasons for participating in youth sport. These are generally referred to as surface reasons for withdrawal from sport, but there are also psychological reasons for withdrawal. Psychological reasons for withdrawal are more serious because they may involve a loss of intrinsic motivation for sport. The sport commitment model was introduced as a way to describe how antecedents such as sport enjoyment lead to sport commitment and to persistence. Clearly, sport enjoyment is the most critical and important of all of the antecedents of sport commitment. Sources of enjoyment were also identified and discussed.

Topics discussed under the heading of coach, parent, and peer relationships included (a) training volunteer coaches, (b) coach–parent relationships, (c) parental influences, and (d) peer friendship influences. Programs such as the Coach Effectiveness Training program were identified as ways to provide coach training. Parents sometimes get confused about the differences between the youth sport model and the professional sport model. A parents' code of conduct was suggested as a way to help parents respect the youth sport model. While misguided parents can create problems for coaches and athletes, their involvement is critical in order for youth sport programs to succeed. Parents make positive athlete socialization contributions as role models, interpreters of experience, and providers of experience. While parental influences are important, the importance of peers and friendship influences cannot be overestimated. Peer acceptance and peer friendships are associated with the athletes' perceived ability, perceived competence, perceived self-worth, and positive affect.

The nature of the motivational climate created by the coach has profound effects upon the youth sport participant in terms of perceived coach behaviors and outcomes as well as dispositional goal structure. Motivational climate is a situational-specific state variable, while goal orientation is a dispositional personality variable. Nevertheless, research demonstrates that the motivational climate created by the coach may result in a change in the athletes' goal orientation structure.

Issues associated with developing a youth sport program include (a) stages of sport involvement, (b) developmental assets lead to positive outcomes, (c) promoting sportspersonship and prosocial behavior, and (d) program development considerations. The developmental model of sport participation suggests that the youth sport participant should pass through three stages of sport development, including the sampling years, the specialization years, and the investment years. External assets and internal assets possessed by the youth sport participant determine whether or not desirable outcomes such as competence, character, connection, confidence, and compassion will be the end result. Youth sports participation does not automatically produce prosocial behavior. In fact, evidence suggests that programs based on a competitive environment or upon controlling motivational regulation can just as easily produce antisocial behavior or poor sportspersonship. In developing a quality youth sport program, two overarching goals should be achieved. The first is to create a program that is fun and that participants will find enjoyable, and the second is to create a program that promotes the development of prosocial and not antisocial antisocial behavior. There are, however, many factors that determine whether or not a youth sport experience is enjoyable, including perceived competence, social involvement, parental support, mastery learning environment, social recognition of effort and competence, and encouragement from coach, parents, and peers.

Critical Thought Questions

1. Discuss the sport commitment model as a way to develop sport commitment and persistence and to counter sport withdrawal. What is the most critical aspect of this model and how can it be developed?

2. Some people believe that the only way to have a good nonschool-sponsored youth sports program is to deny parents access to it. What do you think about this argument? Does it make sense? Can there be a volunteer youth sports program without parents?

3. Discuss ways in which youth sports programs can feature healthy, stimulating competition without focusing upon winning. Is this possible?

4. Other than banning parents, how do you solve the problem of adult violence in youth sports?

5. What would you include in a training session for volunteer coaches if you were in charge and why?

6. What is the reverse-dependency trap? Why is it a problem associated with parent involvement in youth sports? What steps could you as a program organizer take to minimize the negative effects of this trap?

7. How can the motivational climate created by the coach affect athletes' goal orientation? In what ways could this be a good thing, and in

what ways could it be detrimental to the youth sport participant?

8. What is the developmental model of youth sport participation? What stages should the youth sport participant pass through before they invest all of their sport time on a single sport? What are the potential dangers associated with too early sport specialization? What are the dangers associated with extending sport specialization across the entire year?

9. How do external and internal assets determine youth sport outcomes such as competence, character, connection, confidence, and compassion? What can be done to facilitate positive youth sport outcomes?

10. What are the two overarching goals of a youth sport program, and how can each be best realized? Describe your ideal youth sport program for accomplishing this.

Glossary

developmental model of sport participation A youth sport model that is based upon early diversification as opposed to specialization.

five Cs Desired outcomes of a youth sport program, including but not limited to, the development of competence, character, connection, confidence, and compassion.

general-sport dropout A child who withdraws from sport participation altogether.

investment years The time when athletes invest their time and talents on a single sport of their choosing.

motives for participation Reasons children give for why they participate in sport. They may also be considered benefits of sports participation.

parents' code of conduct Ten standards of conduct that a parent of a youth in sports agrees to respect.

professional sports model Model of a commercial sports enterprise in which the stated goals are to entertain and to make money.

reversed-dependency trap A situation in which a parent comes to define his own sense of self-worth in terms of the success and failure of his son or daughter.

sampling years The period when parents encourage their child to sample several different sports without specializing in a single sport.

sources of sport enjoyment Factors that lead to the development of sport enjoyment include such things as perceived competency, effort,

competitive excitement, friendships, and positive parental involvement.

specialization years The period when athletes focus their time and energy on a minimum of two or three sports with none of them overlapping significantly with the others in terms of season of the year.

specific-sport dropout A child who withdraws from participation in one specific sport, but not from participation in all sports.

sport commitment model A model that describes and identifies factors (antecedents) believed to determine an athlete's level of sport commitment and persistence.

Sport Friendship Quality Scale A pencil-and-paper scale that measures six positive and one negative aspect of youth sport friendship.

surface reasons for withdrawal from sports The reasons that children give for withdrawing from sport, which seldom reflect deeper psychological reasons.

underlying psychological reasons for withdrawal for sport "Deeper" reasons children drop out of sports, including stress, fear of failure, loss of self-esteem, and loss of confidence.

youth sports Nonschool youth sports programs, designed to develop desirable physical and psychological characteristics in young athletes.

youth sports model Sports model dedicated to the development of desirable physical and psychosocial characteristics in young athletes.

Effects of Attention, Emotion and Mood on Performance

Part 3 of this text is composed of three chapters titled (a) attention and concentration in sport and exercise, (b) anxiety, stress, and mood relationships, and (c) alternatives to inverted-U theory. Chapter 6, on attention and concentration in sport and exercise, serves as the foundation chapter for part 3 of the text. The very act of focusing one's attention on an object is associated with a neurophysiological response. This response is commonly referred to as arousal or activation. Imagine that you are sitting at your computer writing a term paper when suddenly you hear a loud explosion outside your window. At the same time that your attention is diverted from your computer to the loud explosion, you experience a sudden increase in a number of physiological indicators of arousal (e.g., heart rate, blood pressure). In chapter 7 we build upon our understanding of attention and concentration to discuss the related concepts of anxiety, stress, and mood as they relate to each other and to athletic performance. Most research involving arousal and performance observe an inverted-U relationship between increased activation and performance. While critically important to understanding the relationship between increased arousal and performance, the inverted-U is not the only description of the relationship. In chapter 8 we build upon our understanding of anxiety, stress, and mood, discussed in chapter 7 to consider a number of alternative theories for explaining the arousal-performance relationship. Over the last 10 years, the number and complexity of these alternative explanations have increased dramatically, thus the need for a separate chapter on alternative explanations to the inverted-U hypothesis. ∾

Attention and Concentration in Sport and Exercise

KEY TERMS

Anticipatory skill
Associators
Attentional control theory
Attention control training
Attentional flexibility
Attentional focus
Attentional narrowing
Attentional style
Attentional threshold model
Automatic processing
Bit of information
Capacity model
Centering
Centering breath
Choking
Chunking
Clutch performance
Cognitive interference
Conscious processing
  hypothesis
Constrained action hypothesis
Controlled processing
Cue utilization
Direction of attention
Dissociators
Distractibility
Effort-related model
Explicit processing hypothesis

Gate out
Inattentional blindness
Individual differences
Information conveyed
Information processing
  model
Ironic effect
Long-term memory
Mechanism

Memory storage
Monitoring process
Motor schema
Operating process
Perceptual cognitive
  skill
Peripheral scanning
Playing in the zone
Processing capacity

Processing efficacy
  theory
Quiet eye period
Retrieval
Selective attention
Sensory register
Short-term memory
Thought stopping
Width of attention

We open this chapter on attention and concentration with a real-life example of applied attention in major league baseball (MLB). This example took place in the top half of the ninth inning of the fourth game of the 2009 World Series between the New York Yankees and the Philadelphia Phillies. The score was tied at four runs apiece with two outs and Johnny Damon of the Yankees facing the Phillies closer and left-handed sinker-ball pitcher Brad Lidge. There were no base runners. After running the pitch count to three balls and two strikes, Damon stroked Lidge's 10th pitch for a single. The next batter to face Lidge was Yankee switch-hitting first baseman Mark Teixeira. The Phillies infield played Teixeira as a straight pull hitter to the right side, which placed the third baseman almost behind second base leaving third base uncovered. Early in the count, Damon stole second base and then stole third base when he could see that no one was covering third base. Lidge hit Teixeira with the next pitch placing Teixeira on first base with Damon on third. The Yankees now had base runners on first and third base with two outs and Alex Rodriguez coming to the plate. Rodriguez, a good fastball hitter was now facing Lidge, a good sinker-ball pitcher, but Lidge could not throw Rodriguez a sinker because Damon was on third base and there was too much chance of the sinker getting past the catcher. Having no other choice, Lidge threw a fastball, which Rodriguez stroked for a double. The next batter, Jorge Posada, hit a single scoring two runs and the Yankees went on to win game four 7–4 and the series 4–1. This example illustrates several concentration-related concepts we will introduce in this chapter including attentional control, attentional focus, arousal regulation, and information reduction.

The concept of concentration, or what may be referred to as applied attention, epitomizes the accomplishments of Tiger Woods during the year 2000 professional golf tour. Tiger started his incredible year by winning the U.S. Open at Pebble Beach by 15 strokes over his nearest competitor. Thirty-five days later he won the British Open by eight strokes. In so doing, he accomplished a career grand slam at age 24, two years younger than Jack Nicklaus was when he accomplished it. In golf, the Grand Slam includes the Masters, the U.S. Open, the British Open, and the PGA Championship. Within one month Tiger won the PGA Championship for the second time in two years, making him the only other golfer besides Ben Hogan to win three majors in a single year. Besides being incredibly talented, Tiger accomplished this task by being completely focused and single-minded on each hole, and even each stroke. Notwithstanding Tiger's recent off-course marital and personal challenges, he remains one of the best examples of applied attentional focus in sport.

According to William James (1890), attention is "the taking possession by the mind, in clear and vivid form, of one out of what seem several simultaneously possible objects or trains of thought. . . . It implies withdrawal from some things in order to deal effectively with others" (pp. 403–4). In sport, nothing can be more important than paying attention to the object at hand. On the surface, the idea of paying attention seems simple enough, but psychologists have long recognized that the attention process can be very complex. In discussing the complex nature of attention, this section is divided into several related sub-sections. Each section builds upon the previous section and helps explain why attention is important in sport. Important concepts to be introduced include (a) information processing, (b) memory systems, (c) measuring information, (d) selective attention, (e) limited information processing capacity, (f) attentional narrowing, (g) when athletes are in the zone, (h) mechanisms that explain the relationship between attention and performance, (i) measuring attentional focus, (j) attention control training, and (k) associative versus dissociative style.

Information Processing

Perhaps the most critical difference between the modern game of volleyball and the same game many years ago is in the complexity of the offense.

Many years ago, volleyball was a relatively predictable game in which the spiker attacked from one of two positions on the court. These two positions were the left and right sides of the court near the sidelines. The ball was always set high and there was never any deviation from this pattern. This changed in the late 1960s and early 1970s, when the Japanese revolutionized the game with their version of the multiple offense. In this remarkable offense, attackers spiked the ball from numerous positions at the net. In so doing, the spikers often switched attack positions and called for sets of varying heights and speeds. The result was predictable. Defensive net players were jumping at the wrong time, responding to the wrong attackers, crashing into their own players, and generally falling all over themselves. From an information processing point of view, they were simply overwhelmed. Up to this point, the blockers had only been required to attend to one or two spikers at a time. But now they had to deal with three or four times as much information. Later on, when opposing teams were able to study the multiple offense, defensive players were taught to ignore irrelevant movement and fakes and to concentrate on the important elements of the attack.

In a very general way, there are two basic approaches to explaining behavior. The first and probably better understood is the behavioral, or stimulus-response, approach. In this way of looking at things, the world is explained through a series of stimulus-response (S-R) connections. In fact, psychologists such as B. F. Skinner (1938) would have us believe that all behavior can be reduced to a mathematical model in which specific stimuli go in and predicted responses come out. With animals, this approach has been extremely successful. However, for human beings this approach seems too simplistic. There seems to be more to human behavior than the simple act of strengthening the bond between a stimulus and a response. Certainly, a great deal goes on in the brain between the time that a stimulus is given and the time that a response is initiated. This notion is well accepted by cognitive psychologists, and is

illustrated below. It is referred to as the **information processing model** of behavior. The information processing model contains a stimulus and a response, but a large number of mental operations occur between the two.

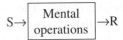

For a person to experience a stimulus and respond to it at a later time, there must be a **memory storage** capability. That is, the person must have a memory, or place to save important information. Once the information has been saved, the person must be able to reactivate or retrieve it. **Retrieval** enables us to use the information to make decisions about forthcoming responses. A football quarterback stores thousands of pieces of information about offenses and defenses. As he approaches the line of scrimmage after calling one play in the huddle, he may observe the defensive alignment and change the play prior to the snap (this is termed "calling an audible"). What has happened here? The answer is simple. Previously stored information about the opposing team was retrieved from memory and used to initiate a different but appropriate response. This is information processing in action, and it takes place constantly on the athletic field or court. The concept is based on the notion of a storage or memory system, which we will discuss next.

Memory Systems

One basic question we may ask about memory is whether there is one memory system, or are there several? While many researchers have tried to show that the different types of memory are clearly distinct from one another, the current thinking is that the distinction among memory systems is for convenience and should not be interpreted to mean that they reside in different parts of the brain. With this in mind, the three basic memory systems will be described.

CONCEPT The working capacity of short-term memory can be effectively enhanced through the process of "chunking."

APPLICATION Grouping separate words, thoughts, ideas, and motor movements into meaningful wholes is a skill that can be learned. The wholes, or "chunks," can be memorized, rehearsed, and practiced much more efficiently in this way. Athletes should be taught how to utilize this skill when trying to learn and manage large amounts of verbal or motor information.

Sensory Information Store

The first stage in the human memory system is the sensory information store, sometimes called the **sensory register.** This storage system is capable of holding large amounts of sensory information for a very brief amount of time before most of it is lost. Information is thought to remain in the sensory register for up to one-half second before it is either lost or transferred to a more permanent storage system. The limitations of the sensory register are illustrated in a volleyball officiating situation. Events often occur so rapidly in a play at the net that it is hard for the referee to make an immediate decision. However, if the decision is not immediate, the referee will discover that the image is no longer available.

Short-Term Memory (STM)

Often referred to as working memory, **short-term memory** (STM) is the center, or crossroads, of activity in the information processing system. Information comes into STM for rehearsal from both the sensory store and permanent memory. Information that comes into STM from the sensory store is often new or original information. If we do not rehearse and memorize it quickly, we will likely forget it. Generally, if a person can rehearse new information for 20 to 30 seconds in STM, it will be sufficiently learned to be passed on to long-term memory for permanent storage. Quality of rehearsal will determine whether or not information in STM will be passed on to long-term memory. Short-term memory is often referred to as "working memory," to emphasize the dynamic nature of this memory system.

The absolute capacity of short-term memory is relatively limited. It would be very difficult, for example, for the average person to retain more than seven separate words or numbers in STM at one time. However, through the process of chunking, it is possible for an individual to retain far more than this. **Chunking** is the process of combining several separate pieces of information into larger ones. The larger chunks are combined in such a way that they can be rehearsed as a unit. Key words or phrases are then used to represent and recall the larger chunks.

Long-Term Memory (LTM)

Whereas information in short-term memory is present for only a brief period of time, information in **long-term memory** (LTM) is relatively permanent. The purpose of the memory system is to store information in LTM. Once information is stored in LTM, it is theoretically permanent. This may seem difficult to understand, since we all have occasionally had trouble remembering things we thought were permanently learned. In conjunction with STM, information in long-term memory can be continually updated, reorganized, and strengthened. New information can also be added to LTM. The relationship between the three basic memory systems is illustrated in figure 6.1.

FIGURE 6.1 | The three stages of memory, showing rehearsal in STM and retrieval in LTM.

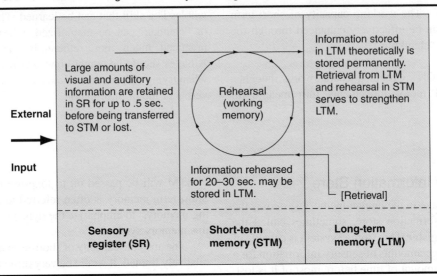

External

Input

| Large amounts of visual and auditory information are retained in SR for up to .5 sec. before being transferred to STM or lost. | Rehearsal (working memory)

Information rehearsed for 20–30 sec. may be stored in LTM. | Information stored in LTM theoretically is stored permanently. Retrieval from LTM and rehearsal in STM serves to strengthen LTM.

[Retrieval] |
| --- | --- | --- |
| **Sensory register (SR)** | **Short-term memory (STM)** | **Long-term memory (LTM)** |

FIGURE 6.2 | Pitcher A has four pitches at his command. The probability of his throwing any one of the pitches is 25 percent. What is the average amount of information conveyed?

Pitcher A

Changeup 25%	Slider 25%
Curve 25%	Fastball 25%

Measuring Information

Psychologists can measure the amount of information that is conveyed by a particular problem or task. The amount of **information conveyed** or transmitted by a particular problem is measured in **bits** of information, (short for "binary digit"). Intuitively, bits of information conveyed is equal to the number of questions that would have to be systematically asked to solve the problem.

Illustrated in figure 6.2 is a rectangle divided into four quadrants. Each quadrant shows the probability that a particular major league pitcher throws each of four pitches. From this diagram we know that the pitcher has command of four pitches that he uses with equal probability. If the balls and strikes count is 3 and 2 and you guess that he is going to throw you a fastball, you have a 75 percent chance of being wrong.

CONCEPT An athletic response can be made more difficult to interpret in terms of information conveyed.

APPLICATION Let's use the baseball pitching example. Your pitcher's difficulty in terms of information conveyed can be increased in three ways.

First, the pitcher must master as many different pitches as possible. Second, the pitcher must throw each pitch with equal probability.

Finally, the delivery should provide no cues to the batter as to which pitch is coming. A combination of these three factors maximizes the amount of information conveyed.

This is a difficult problem that conveys or transmits two bits of information. How do we know that this problem conveys two bits of information? Because it would take two "planned" questions to correctly solve the problem. Now, understand, this is not how you determine which pitch he is going to throw, but how you determine *the number of bits of information conveyed by the problem.* Okay, so what are the two questions? Question one might be, "Are you going to throw either a slider or a fastball?" If his answer to that question is no, then *one column* is eliminated and we can focus on the other column. The second question might be, "Are you going to throw a changeup?" If he answers yes, we know he is going to throw a changeup. If he answers no, we know he is going to throw a curve ball, and no further questions are required. How much information would be conveyed by a pitcher who only had one pitch, say, a fastball? No questions would have to be asked, so if you said zero, you would have been correct. A major league pitcher who had only one pitch would certainly be in trouble after just a few innings (Hopkins & Magel, 2008). This is the situation that Alex Rodriguez was presented with in the opening paragraph of this chapter.

The more bits of information conveyed, the more difficult the problem being presented. We have illustrated this concept using a pitcher in baseball, but you could apply the same principle to other sports. The defensive player in basketball looks at the point guard and wonders if she is going to drive right, drive left, or pull up and shoot

a jump shot. The defensive back in football looks at the wide receiver and wonders if he is going to execute any number of inside/outside moves, or if he will go long, or if he will execute a button hook. The more quality moves an offensive player has, the more information is conveyed, and the more difficult it will be to defend. For an illustration and discussion involving more complex situations involving unequal response probabilities, see Cox (1985).

This discussion was not presented so that you could calculate information conveyed, but so that you can clearly understand the relationship between an athlete's skill and information conveyed. As skill increases, information conveyed increases. The more information conveyed by an offensive player, the more difficult it is going to be for the defensive player to respond.

Selective Attention

Humans' ability to **gate out,** or ignore, irrelevant sensory information, and to pay **selective attention** to relevant information, is of incalculable value. Perhaps the best way to dramatize this point is to consider the schizophrenic patient who may suffer an impaired capacity to sustain attention. At one extreme, the patient may attend to some internal thought to such an extent that she becomes catatonic. At the other extreme, the patient may be incapable of selectively attending to anything. Although young schizophrenic patients describe their difficulties in different ways, the following extract is considered typical (McGhie & Chapman, 1961):

> I can't concentrate. It's diversion of attention that troubles me . . . the sounds are coming through to me but I feel my mind cannot cope with everything. It is difficult to concentrate on any one sound . . . it's like trying to do two or three different things at one time. . . . Everything seems to grip my attention although I am not particularly interested in anything. I'm speaking to you just now but I can hear noises going on next door and in the corridor (p. 104).

Each of us has experienced the feeling of overstimulation that can result in an inability to concentrate, but can you imagine experiencing this problem every waking hour? If it were not for our ability to concentrate on one or two relevant items at a time, we simply could not function. While you are reading this page, you are selectively attending to one thing at the expense of several others.

The ability to selectively attend to the appropriate stimuli is critical in most athletic situations. In basketball, the athlete must concentrate on the basket while shooting a free throw rather than being distracted by the noise from the crowd. In volleyball, the athlete must selectively attend to the server instead of being distracted by thoughts of a previous play. In baseball, the base runner must attend to the pitcher, and not to the jabbering of the second baseman. In football, the quarterback must selectively attend to his receivers, while gating out the sights and sounds of the huge defensive linesmen who are lunging at him. Of course, some athletes are better than others at selectively attending to important cues. This is one difference between the good athlete and the outstanding athlete.

As we watch sport on television and in person, many times we can observe athletes engaging in various psychological ploys to gain an advantage. Usually these ploys are manifested in some sort of verbal dialogue, such as commenting on things unrelated to the contest. In baseball, base runners have been picked off first or second base while engaging in innocent chatting with infielders.

When and if these ploys (intentional or otherwise) are successful, this is usually related to inappropriate selective attention. The athlete simply is not attending to the appropriate stimuli. This, as well as information overload, will cause a delay in responding.

A number of complex models have been proposed to explain the phenomenon of selective attention. These models include the Broadbent Model (1957, 1958), Norman's Pertinence Model (1968), and Treisman's Attenuation Model (1965). Each of these models propose mechanisms that allow us to selectively attend to one item at the expense of several others, while at the same time allowing for a shift in attention from one important item to an even more important item. A concrete sports-related example of this would be the defensive basketball player intent upon cutting off the passing lane to the person she is guarding, only to be beaten by the back-door play. In this example, the shift from selectively attending to cutting off the passing lane to anticipating the back-door play was too slow.

For highly trained and skilled athletes, the process of selective attention is very efficient. When skilled basketball players step up to the free throw line, they refuse to allow anyone or anything besides the task at hand to capture their attention. Coaches refer to this process as "concentration." However, some athletes never do learn how to cope with distraction. Every little event distracts them, or they concentrate on the wrong things (e.g., dribbling), and miss relevant cues.

One concluding comment about selective attention is in order. Our ability to selectively attend to stimuli is based on the correct distribution of neurochemicals in the brain. A disruption in the balanced distribution of dopamine and norepinephrine is associated with an inability to selectively attend to stimuli, and with mental disorders such as schizophrenia, depression, and attentional deficit disorder. Various prescription drugs have been developed to control symptoms associated with attentional disruption, but sometimes even these drugs have unfortunate movement disorder

CONCEPT Selective attention is perhaps the single most important cognitive characteristic of the successful athlete.

APPLICATION All sporting events contain critical "keys," or cues, that must be selectively attended to. In volleyball, blocking is one of the most decisive offensive weapon in scoring points. To take advantage of this situation, the blockers must selectively attend to the assigned attacker and must not be distracted by actions of the setter, by fakes by other spikers, or even by the ball.

---

side effects (Posner & Raichle, 1997). We mention this so that the sport psychologist is aware of the critical importance of selective attention, and is aware that the inability to selectively attend to instructions is not always due to a lack of effort on the part of the athlete.

Limited Information Processing Capacity

An alternative approach to studying attention is to view it in terms of information **processing capacity,** or *space*. In the previous section we discussed attention in terms of our ability to selectively gate out irrelevant information. In this section, we are concerned with the capacity to attend to more than one thing at a time. In view of our discussion of selective attention, this may seem paradoxical. However, we can readily see that human beings seem to be able to attend to more than one thing at a time. For example, a skilled basketball player can dribble a basketball, hold up one hand to signal a play, and respond to a teammate who is cutting to the basket. A person driving a car can carry on a conversation with a passenger, steer the car, and shift gears all at the same time. How can this be? Didn't we just conclude that the human mind can attend to only one piece of information at a time? Not necessarily; we concluded only that the human mind is *capable* of selectively attending to one thing at a time. Several possibilities exist. An athlete might (a) be compelled to selectively attend to only one action at one time because it consumes all of his attention, (b) choose to selectively attend to

Digging a hard-driven spike is a complex information problem that requires the athlete's undivided attention. Courtesy Kansas State University Sports Information.

CONCEPT   Selective attention is a skill that can be learned.

APPLICATION   There is no doubt that some athletes are better at selective attention than others. However, there is no reason to believe that this skill cannot be learned. The secret is for the coach to identify the important cues and then to provide drills that require the athlete to selectively attend to them. A good example might be shooting free throws in basketball. The key, of course, is to concentrate on the basket. However, few athletes learn to do this during practice, since there are rarely any distractions to cause their attention to wander. A gamelike situation with fans and opponents would help the athlete to learn selective attention.

one action or thought to avoid distraction, or (c) simultaneously attend to more than one thought or action because he is able to.

Keele (1973) was one of the first psychologists to introduce the notion that individuals may be limited by the amount of processing space available to them. In this way of looking at attention, we think in terms of different mental and motor tasks requiring a finite amount of information processing space. If a specific task requires all of the information processing space, then that specific task is selectively attended to at the expense of all others. If a specific task does not require all of the available information processing space, then more than one task can be attended to at one time, depending upon the attentional demands of the second task. This is referred to as the **capacity model** of selective attention. The great Boston Celtics basketball star Bill Russell used different words to describe it, but he had a similar concept in mind when he said this:

> Remember, each of us has a finite amount of energy, and things you do well don't require as much. Things you don't do well take more concentration. And if you're fatigued by that, then the things you do best are going to be affected. (Deford, 1999, p. 110)

In the capacity model of attention, more than one piece of input can be attended to at one time and more than one response can be made at one time, if the demands on available space are not too severe. If any particular task requires all available space, then only that task will be attended to, and all others will suffer a performance decrement.

The significant difference between a beginning basketball player and a skilled one appears in the demands placed on information processing space. In a game, dribbling requires nearly all of the available processing space of the beginner. She cannot hear the coach, see the basket, see other players, or do anything except attend to the task of dribbling. On the other hand, the skilled player has reduced the attentional demands of dribbling to such a degree that she can see and hear all kinds of relevant cues while dribbling. The important concept of processing space is illustrated in figure 6.3.

The capacity model of attention takes into consideration the notion that the information processing requirements of tasks are modified by learning. That is, information processing demands of a specific task (e.g., dribbling in basketball) may be reduced over time. Another factor that should be considered when conceptualizing the capacity model of attention is the notion of **individual differences.** No two individuals are alike in terms of the amount of attention required to deal with more than one task at a time. Therefore, you should not assume that two athletes possessing an equal amount of playing experience will perform the same when confronted with a multiple-task problem. One person may experience task interference in attempting tasks A and B together, but experience no difficulty with tasks A and C together. Conversely, a second athlete may experience an

CONCEPT   Each athlete's information processing capacity, or space, is limited.

APPLICATION   If, as a coach, you require athletes
to attend to more information than they have processing space to handle, you are inviting failure.
Processing space is not the same as intelligence.

FIGURE 6.3 | Relative amounts of available information processing space for a beginning basketball
player and a skilled player.

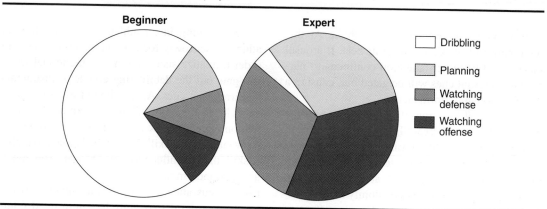

entirely different set of problems relative to the
same tasks. Coaches must be particularly sensitive
and aware of individual differences when teaching
athletes how to manage multiple-task athletic situations. Basketball and soccer are sports that are
very similar in this respect: an athlete must be able
to control a ball while at the same time planning
and taking into consideration offensive and defensive players around her.

Attentional Narrowing

An athlete's ability to attend to appropriate stimuli
during competition has been termed **attentional
focus.** The concept of attentional focus includes
the ability of an athlete to both narrow and broaden
her attention when necessary. For example, in basketball, the guard who initiates a fast break must
be able to broaden her attentional focus in order to

see teammates on either side as they break toward
the basket. This same player must be able to narrow attentional focus while shooting free throws in
order to gate out distractions from the crowd.

The notion of **attentional narrowing** is best
understood in terms of **cue utilization.** As explained by Easterbrook (1959), attentional narrowing is a function of available cues. Environmental
cues provide the athlete with needed information
for a skilled performance. In any sport task, many
cues are available to the athlete. Some are relevant
and necessary for quality performance; others are
irrelevant and can damage performance. Under
conditions of low arousal, the athlete picks up both
relevant and irrelevant cues. The presence of irrelevant cues should result in a decrement in performance. As arousal increases, the athlete's attention
begins to narrow. At some optimal point, attentional narrowing gates out all of the irrelevant cues

CONCEPT The information content of various skills and processes can be reduced so that available information processing space seems to increase.

APPLICATION For a beginning soccer player, the mere act of dribbling the ball will require so much information processing space that there is room for nothing else. The athlete will not be able to pass to the open player, see plays develop, or even avoid an opponent. However, once the player has mastered the skill of dribbling, he will be able to do all of this and more. It is not that information processing space has increased, but that the information content of dribbling has been reduced to nearly zero.

---

and allows the relevant cues to remain. At this point performance should be at its best. If arousal increases still further, attention continues to narrow and relevant cues will be gated out, causing a deterioration in performance.

High levels of arousal may also lead to the phenomenon of **distractibility.** In addition to gating out potentially relevant cues, high arousal may also decrease an athlete's ability to selectively attend to one stimulus at a time. Rather, the athlete's attention shifts randomly from stimulus to stimulus. Distractibility has the effect of decreasing the athlete's ability to discriminate between relevant and irrelevant cues, and to focus upon relevant cues. The athlete who is suffering from distractibility tends to experience sudden and significant decrements in performance. The phenomenon of attentional narrowing is illustrated in figure 6.4.

When a quarterback drops back for a pass, he needs a relatively wide band of attentional focus in order to pick up his receivers. However, if the band is too wide, he will pick up such irrelevant cues as the noisy crowd and the cheerleaders. This will cause a decrement in performance (arousal level is too low). As arousal level increases, attention narrows and irrelevant cues are eliminated. However, in a very intense game situation, arousal may be very high. Consequently, further narrowing of attention may cause the quarterback to gate out such relevant cues as the secondary receivers, the position of defensive backs, and the possible outlet pass.

Performing in an athletic event requires an athlete to narrowly focus upon the task at hand in order to realize success. Quality attentional focus can gate out the debilitating effects of distractors and irrelevant cues. As the time to execute a skill gets closer, the requirement to narrowly focus attention increases. The ability to focus narrowly on relevant cues is a skill that can be learned, but also a skill that is influenced by arousal. Too much arousal undermines the athlete's ability to narrowly focus attention in a quality manner, while too little arousal may introduce unwanted competition between irrelevant and relevant cues. (Janelle, Singer & Williams, 1999; Williams & Elliot, 1999).

A number of interesting studies have been reported and new terms introduced that relate to the concepts of attentional narrowing and cue utilization. In an investigation reported by Williams and Elliot (1999), it was observed that under conditions of heightened arousal karate performers focused their eyes on the chests of their opponents, but also used **peripheral scanning** to see the hands and feet of the opponents. In the sports of basketball and football, the situation often occurs where the out-of-bounds passer fails to see an open cutter right in front of her, or the quarterback fails to see an open receiver right in front of him. In both situations, this is phenomenon is referred to as **inattentional blindness** (Memmert & Furley, 2007). Inattentional blindness typically occurs in situations where the primary task consumes most of the available information-processing space. For

FIGURE 6.4 | Cue utilization and the arousal-performance relationship.

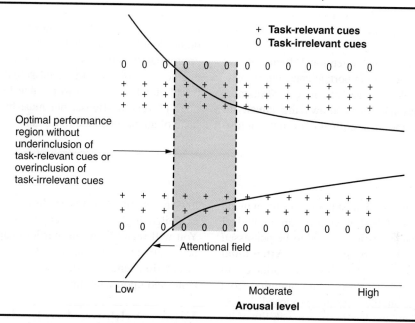

Source: Landers, D. M. (1980). The arousal-performance relationship revisited. *Research Quarterly for Exercise and Sport, 51,* 77–90. Reproduced by permission of the publisher, the American Alliance for Health, Physical Education. Recreation and Dance, 1900 Association Dr., Reston, VA 22091.

example, in the football example, the quarterback may be focusing on the first option of the pass play and fails to see an obvious option right in the middle of his field of view. Several investigations suggest that various perceptual skills related to attention and concentration may be enhanced or improved through training. For example, Hagemann, Strauss, and Canal-Bruland (2006) demonstrated that **anticipatory skill** can be enhanced by teaching badminton players to orient their visual attention to predetermined informative cues on the opponents body (e.g., arm position at specific points of time). In a study involving senior tennis players (Caserta, Young, & Janelle, 2007) and another involving senior orienteering participants (Pesce, Cereatti, Casella, Baldari, & Capranica, 2007), a sport that requires aerobic training and extensive map and compass-reading skills, it was reported that **perceptual cognitive skill** (reduced response time, increased accuracy, improved decision making) can be enhanced with training. Mann, Williams, Ward, and Janelle (2007) reported on a meta-analysis that looked at 42 studies and 388 effect sizes relative to identifying perceptual-cognitive abilities that differentiate expert from nonexpert athletes. Results confirmed the expectation that the expert athlete would exhibit greater response accuracy, faster response time, fewer but longer visual fixations, and a longer quiet eye period compared to nonexpert athletes. The **quiet eye period** is calculated as the time elapse between the last eye fixation and the initiation of a motor response, and is believed to be the time when relevant cues are processed and motor programs or plans are coordinated. In summary, it would appear that the skilled athlete maintains a perceptual advantage over less-skilled counterparts.

CONCEPT   Attentional narrowing has the effect of reducing cue utilization.

APPLICATION   Broad attentional focus allows the athlete to attend to important cues, but the distraction of irrelevant cues can hurt performance. Narrow attentional focus allows the athlete to attend to only the most critical cues, but can also hurt performance, because many relevant cues can be eliminated. Successful athletes are often required to adjust their attentional focus so that it is appropriately narrow in one situation, yet broad in another. A point guard in basketball must have broad attentional focus to be able to pass to the open player on offense, but must have a narrow band of attention on the foul line.

In recent years, interest has been shown in the concept of attentional flexibility, an individual difference characteristic believed to be possessed in different amounts by individuals. **Attentional flexibility** refers to the ability of athletes to quickly and effectively shift their attention from one location to another. Another proposed characteristic of attentional flexibility is the ability of individuals to shift from a very narrow attentional focus to a very broad focus. It is believed that athletes who are high in this characteristic should have an advantage in certain athletic contests and tasks.

Finally, Hatzigeorgiadis and Biddle (1999) reported an interesting connection between cognitive interference and goal orientation. **Cognitive interference** was defined as "thoughts of escape" and "task-irrelevant thoughts." Any random thought or event that would tend to break an athlete's concentration could be considered cognitive interference. A case in point is an incident related by Schmid and Peper (1998) in which a 16-year-old U.S. rhythmic gymnast lost her poise and concentration when a loud teenage voice yelled a lewd comment as she walked toward the mat in an international meet. In the Hatzigeorgiadis and Biddle investigation, snooker and tennis players who were high in task orientation exhibited low levels of cognitive interference. That is, they were less likely to be negatively influenced by random cognitive thoughts. Conversely, individuals who were high in ego orientation and low in perceived ability (a deadly combination) exhibited high levels of cognitive interference. You will recall from our earlier chapter on goal perspective in sport that an individual high in ego orientation tends to focus upon social comparisons and upon winning.

When Athletes Are in the Zone

> When the body is brought to peak condition and the mind is completely focused, even unaware of what it's doing, an individual can achieve the extraordinary. (Tolson, 2000, p. 38)

The above statement was made by the author of a popular news magazine article following Tiger Woods' extraordinary performance at the U.S. Open Golf Tournament at Pebble Beach. Tiger won this tournament by 15 strokes over his nearest competitor. In that same tournament, John Daly, another golfing great, dropped out of the tournament on the first day, after posting 14 strokes on the 18th hole. The title of Tolson's article was "Into the Zone." A question you might ask relative to Tolson's quote is, "Is an athlete ever unaware of what his body is doing?" An athlete's mind may not be consciously thinking about what his left arm is doing during a golf swing, but it is highly likely that the brain is always aware, on some level, of what the body is doing. The brain is continually receiving sensory information from muscles, joints, and ligaments about body movement.

Tolson is not the first person to use the phrase **playing in the zone** to refer to extraordinary performance of an athlete. The concept of a zone of optimal functioning may have been first introduced by Russian psychologist Yuri Hanin (1980) when he presented his theory of optimal functioning relative to state anxiety. This is a topic that we will discuss in greater detail in chapter 8.

In an article written in *The New York Times,* Gould (2000) takes particular issue with the notion that skilled athletic performance is somehow wholly associated with "bodily intelligence." He argues that skilled athletic performance reflects close coordination between mind and body, and that it is demeaning to the intelligence of athletes to suggest that it is just a physical thing. Supporting Gould's contentions, Gladwell (1999) wrote a highly insightful article titled "The Physical Genius." In his article, Gladwell provides a very intelligent research-based discussion of exactly what great athletes, great surgeons, and great musicians have in common. He suggests that there are three things that go into making the physical genius. First are the raw physical and mental abilities that the athlete or surgeon is born with. Second is the time spent in practicing to become the best in the world. Tiger Woods got to be a "physical genius" by physically and mentally practicing golf for thousands and thousands of hours, and after that he practiced another thousand hours. It is no accident that an elite athlete plays in the "zone," because he is potentially in the zone every time she performs. Third is what Gladwell calls "imagination." The great athlete has imagined every possible situation that could occur in a game. There are no surprises to the elite athlete. In describing the mindset of the great athlete, Gladwell quotes Wayne Gretzky, one of the greatest ice hockey players ever to have set foot on the ice:

> People talk about skating, puck-handling, and shooting, but the whole sport is angles and caroms, forgetting the straight direction the puck is going, calculating where it will be diverted, factoring in all the interruptions. (p. 59)

Regarding this last area of imagination, Gladwell makes an insightful comparison between the great basketball player, Karl Malone, and the greatest basketball player of all time, Michael Jordan. Malone had raw ability and work ethic equal to those of Michael Jordan, but he never had an imagination to equal Jordan's. Gladwell points to the sixth game of the 1998 World Championships in Salt Lake City. The game came down to a few seconds in which the Utah Jazz and Karl Malone had both the ball and the lead. Malone, unaware of where Jordan (Chicago Bulls) was on the court, jockeyed for position in the low post with Dennis Rodman. Using the imagination that he had, Michael came up on Malone's blind side and stripped the ball from him. Malone never saw it coming—but he should have. This is what is meant by imagination. Jordan went on to make the final shot of the game and sealed the victory and championship for Chicago. Being a "physical genius" is not just being in the "zone"; it is perfecting your game mentally and physically, so that you are in the "zone" when you need to be. For the accomplished surgeon, it means being in the "zone" all of the time.

What about the notion of "automaticity," the idea that while in the "zone" the athlete is somehow disconnected from interference of conscious thought? After an amazing play by Michael Jordan, the announcer comments that he is playing "unconscious." After an errant throw by an otherwise steady second baseman, the announcer implies that the conscious brain interfered. These statements are best understood within the framework of the information processing model and allocated attention. While not an expert in human movement, Bandura (1997), a social psychologist, made the following insightful observation:

> Partial disengagement of thought from proficient action has considerable functional value. Having to think about the details of every skilled activity before carrying it out in recurrent situations would consume most of one's precious attentional and cognitive resources and create a monotonously dull inner life. After people develop adequate

ways of managing situations that recur regularly, they act on their perceived efficacy without requiring continuing directive or reflective thought. (p. 34)

As explained by Smith (1996), cognitive psychologists distinguish between controlled and automatic processing of information. In learning a new sports skill, an athlete must focus upon **controlled processing** of information. This means that the athlete must attend to the details of executing the skill to be learned. This is what is happening to the beginning basketball player in figure 6.3. Almost all of the athlete's attention is focused on learning how to dribble a basketball, to the exclusion of other important cues. Controlled processing is relatively slow and effortful, consuming most of the available information processing capacity of the individual.

Once a sport skill is mastered, it comes under **automatic processing.** The execution of the skill is still being monitored by the brain, but because it is well learned it requires little conscious attention. Again, as illustrated in figure 6.3, the skilled basketball player may now focus most of the available information processing space upon other relevant basketball-related cues. One of the vulnerabilities of automatic processing is that if the smooth operation of the task is interfered with, it is susceptible to error. It is a little like reciting a poem. If you make an error and forget where you are in the poem, you often have to start over to get back on track. So it is with completing a double play in baseball or softball. You don't want to hesitate or entertain a negative thought about the throw to first base, because if you do you may upset the automatic execution of the skill.

None of this discussion about automatic processing of a skilled movement implies that the brain of an individual is not involved; it only clarifies the nature and level of conscious involvement. The perfect execution of a sports skill is best thought of as an elegant interaction between mind and body. Describing a peak performance as simply being in the "zone," as if there is a separation of the mind from the body, diminishes the immense preparation that goes into training to become an elite athlete, at any level of competition.

Having established that the brain is not disengaged during skilled athletic performance, it is also important to note that the brain is essentially in a "do not interfere" mode. This is why superior performers typically indicate an absence of conscious regulation during an outstanding performance. This concept was experimentally observed in a laboratory investigation by Deeny, Hillman, Janelle, and Hatfield (2003). In this study, EEG recordings were monitored in expert and less skilled rifle marksmen during competitive shooting. Results showed less intercortical communication in the expert shooters compared to the less skilled, which implies decreased cognition during highly skilled motor processes.

Gladwell (2000) also makes some interesting observations regarding the difference between *choking* and *panicking*. Gladwell links the common occurrence of choking with the shifting of attention from the automatic mode (implicit learning) to the controlled process mode (explicit learning) when the athlete starts to think too much. This can occur with the pitcher who, in an effort to throw a perfect strike, goes into a control mode and tries to guide the pitch to its target with disastrous results. Thus, choking is associated with thinking too much, while panicking is associated with thinking too little. In a panic attack, the athlete reverts to instinct and quits thinking logically. In sport the difference between choking and panicking might not matter much; you lose the point or miss the shot in either case. However, in flying an airplane or in SCUBA diving, the difference between choking and panicking is a life-and-death matter. If her equipment fails in SCUBA diving, the diver can go back to a controlled processing mode and fall back on a checklist to save his life. However, if the SCUBA diver or pilot panics and reverts to instinct, the outcome could be death. For example, the airplane pilot must not revert to instinct when he experiences vertigo in a storm.

Mechanisms that Explain the Relationship between Attention and Performance

If there is a cause-and-effect relationship between concentration and how well an athlete learns or performs an athletic skill, what is the psychological or physiological **mechanism** that explains this relationship? It is one thing to say that increased arousal causes a narrowing of attention, but what is the mechanism to explain this? In this section we will discuss different mechanisms or theories that purport to explain cause-and-effect relationships. To accomplish this, we will divide this section into three related subsections titled (a) ironic effects, (b) internal versus external attentional focus, and (c) competing mechanisms that explain the detrimental effect of psychological pressure on learning and performance.

Ironic Effects

Has this ever happened to you? The golfer hits his fairway drive so that the ball settles in front of a large pond that separates his ball from the putting green 100 yards away. It is a fairly routine pitching wedge shot to place the ball on or near the green. Your mind, however, looks at the intervening pond and thinks, "I better not miss this shot or I'll be in the pond." You can guess what happens next, the golfer misses his pitch shot, and the ball lands in the pond. This phenomenon is referred to as an ironic effect. The **ironic effect** is that people, when under mental load, tend to do the very thing that they are trying not to do. In that sense, the very act is ironic indeed (Beilock, Afremow, Rabe, & Carr, 2001; Binsch, Oudejans, Bakker, & Savelsbergh, 2009; Wegner, 1994; Wegner, Ansfield, & Pilloff, 1998; Woodman & Davis, 2008).

While the effect itself is fairly easy to understand and is experienced from time to time by all athletes, understanding the mechanism that brings it about is more complex. As explained by Woodman and Davis (2008), the ironic effect process is based upon dual control systems comprising an operating process and monitoring process. The **operating process** is believed to be intentional, effortful, and under conscious control; while the **monitoring process** is believed to be generally unconscious. Under conditions of mental load (e.g., pressure, anxiety, high cognitive demand) the conscious operating system is overloaded and superseded by the monitoring process. Consequently, and ironically, when mental capacity is undermined or overwhelmed, the monitoring system creates the mental state that corresponds to control failure. Basically, the role of the operating process is to replace a negative thought with a correct thought and action. However, when the operating system is overwhelmed due to mental load, the unwanted thought or action prevails.

All unwanted thoughts and actions, however, are not due to ironic effects. Some unwanted actions are due to *overcompensation*. Ironic effects are not intention driven, while overcompensation effects are. To illustrate this point, Binsch et al. (2009) reported on an investigation in which golfers were instructed to putt a ball to a target, but to be careful not to "overshoot" or "undershoot" the hole. Visual gaze behavior was monitored so that the researchers could tell where the gaze was directed prior to the shot. Based on gaze behavior, instructions given, and results of each putt, the researchers were able to classify the putt results as being due to overcompensation or to ironic effects.

Internal versus External Attentional Focus

In learning or performing a motor task it is possible to focus one's attention on the step-by-step internal actions of skill execution or to focus one's attention on the external effects of skill execution on the environment. Common examples of an internal attentional focus include conscious attempts to (a) keep the lead elbow straight in executing a golf swing, (b) keep the wrist firm and elbow pointed down in executing a backstroke in tennis, and (c) keep the elbow pointed down and extend the wrist and elbow in executing a basketball free throw. Common examples of an external

Decision making requires practiced attentional focus.
Eyewire/Getty Images.

attentional focus include (a) focus on the catcher's target in pitching a baseball to the plate, (b) stroke through the ball and follow its trajectory in hitting a baseline tennis stroke, and (c) keep your eye on the back of the rim in shooting a basketball free throw. As you can see from these examples, in an internal focus the athlete is instructed to attend to internal actions of the body, while in the external focus the athlete is instructed to attend to the goal and external effects (outcome) of skill execution. As a general rule, research has supported the position that an external focus is preferred and that an internal focus is harmful to efficient skill execution (Beilock, Carr, MacMahon, & Starkes, 2002; Beilock, Bertenthal, McCoy, & Carr, 2004; Bell & Hardy, 2009; Castaneda & Gray, 2007; Cottyn, de Clercq, Crombez, & Lenoir, 2008; Poolton,

Maxwell, Masters, & Raab, 2006; Wulf, 2008; Wulf & Prinz, 2001;Wulf & Su, 2007; Wulf, Tollner, & Shea, 2007; Zentgraf & Munzert, 2009).

Given the overwhelming research support for avoiding an internal focus of attention in favor of and external focus of attention, two important questions remain. First, what are the hypothesized mechanisms for the detrimental effects of an internal focus, and second, are there exceptions to this general finding? Let's begin with the first question dealing with hypothesized mechanisms. Two mechanisms or theoretical explanations for the debilitating effects of an internal focus have been hypothesized (Bell & Hardy, 2009; Poolton et al., 2006). These include the constrained action hypothesis and the explicit processing hypothesis. According to the **constrained action hypothesis**, conscious attempts to control movement interferes with automatic motor control processes (internal focus), whereas, focusing on movement effects (external focus) leaves the motor system unconstrained by conscious control. According to the **explicit processing hypothesis**, focusing internally on the execution of a movement elevates the level of conscious control and demands for working memory (processing space). A decrement in performance is due to greater demands placed on the information processing system. Consensus of thought would seem to favor the constrained action hypothesis, but it is likely that both mechanisms are involved in explaining the detrimental effects of an internal focus on performance.

Regarding the second question, research reported by Beilock, Bertenthal, et al. (2004) and Castaneda and Gray (2007) indicates that focusing upon internal cues applies to expert performers, but not necessarily for beginners or less skilled athletes. The Beilock, Bertenthal, et al. (2004) investigation involved novice and expert golfers participating in putting experiments. Results showed in two separate experiments that beginners performed best in internally focused conditions, while expert performers performed best in conditions that did not include internal focusing of attention. The Castaneda and Gray (2007) investigation involved less-skilled

CONCEPT In a situation in which mental pressure is not a factor, skilled athletes should utilize an external focus of attention, while the beginner should use both an internal and external focus of attention. The beginner has not yet developed a motor schema for executing a skill whereas the expert has. An internal focus of attention has the effect of disrupting the smooth automatic execution of a motor skill.

APPLICATION Once an athlete has mastered a sport skill such as hitting a backhand in tennis, she should be encouraged to focus upon external aspects of skill execution such as the follow-through or the flight of the ball and not upon where the elbow is or if the wrist is firm. Focusing upon internal cues will only disrupt the smooth execution of the skill. If an athlete needs to go "back to the basics," this should be done during controlled practices and not during competition. Beginners may use both an internal and external focus of attention until the skill has been well learned.

and highly skilled college baseball players participating in laboratory experiments that asked the participants to direct their attention to internal skill cues (hands), external skill cues (bat movement), or to external environmental cues (e.g., flight of the ball). Results of the investigation suggested that for highly skilled players it was best to focus upon external skill or external environmental cues as opposed to internal skill cues. For the less skilled players, the results failed to show any advantage between using an internal or external skill focus. Intuitively, the results of these two investigations make sense. Focusing upon external cues instead of internal cues would be superior for highly skilled performers because the **motor schema** for executing a sport skill would be well established. Reverting back to an internal, step-by-step execution of the skill would only disrupt the smooth automatic execution of the skill. However, for the beginner or less-skilled athlete, the motor schema for executing a motor skill would not be well established and may even be nonexistent. In this case, utilizing both an internal focus of attention and an external focus would be best because the beginner does not have a well-established motor schema or program. For anyone who has taught beginners how to hit a backhand in tennis, this will make intuitive sense. With the beginner you have to continually remind them to use proper form in executing a skill that is completely foreign to them.

A number of terms have been used to describe or to denote self-focused or internal attention focus. These include the following: conscious control, explicit learning, controlled processing, declarative knowledge, and reinvestment. Conversely, a number of different terms have been used in the literature to describe external attentional focus. These include the following: implicit learning, automatic processing, procedural knowledge, and analogy learning (Jackson, Ashford, & Norsworthy, 2006). Authors typically use these terms when they are discussing internal and external control of attention.

Competing Mechanisms That Explain the Detrimental Effects of Psychological Pressure on Learning and Performance

From the literature, it is abundantly clear that psychological pressure, stress, and anxiety can have debilitating effects on both cognitive and motor performance. The literature associated with these relationships will be discussed extensively in chapters 7 and 8 of this text. Given that psychological pressure can cause a decrement in skilled athletic performance (i.e., choking), the question that we address in this section is, why this is the case? Gladwell (2000) linked choking to the shift of attention from the automatic mode to the controlled process mode, which we will see is a viable explanation for choking, but there may be other explanations. Consequently, in this section we define **choking** more broadly as "a critical deterioration in the execution of habitual processes as a result of an elevation in anxiety levels under perceived pressure, leading to substandard performance" (Mesagno, Marchant, & Morris, 2009, p. 131). Conversely, we will define a **clutch performance** as an above-standard performance under conditions of significant pressure. The 2008 NCAA men's basketball championship game between the University of Kansas and the University of Memphis provides an excellent example of choking under pressure. Memphis was leading 60-51 with only 2 minutes and 12 seconds remaining in the game. Over the next 2 minutes and 12 seconds, Memphis missed 4 of 5 free throws and allowed Kansas time for one last shot. Kansas won the game 75 to 68 in overtime. Interventions such as focus upon process goals, cognitive restructuring, simulation training, imagery, and preperformance routines have been suggested as ways to prevent choking (Hill, Hanton, Matthews, & Fleming, 2010).

In this section, we will first identify and describe three main theories or mechanisms that purport to explain why mental pressure hampers performance and causes the athlete to choke. Second, we will provide a brief review of the literature that supports the different proposed explanations.

As we begin this discussion, it is important for the student to understand the difference between theories that *describe the nature of the relationship* between psychological pressure and performance, and those that *explain why* psychological pressure causes a performance decrement. The inverted-U theory (figure 7.4), which we will discuss in chapter 7 is a theory that describes the relationship, while Easterbrook's cue utilization theory, shown in figure 6.4, is a theory that attempts to explain why psychological pressure causes a decrement in performance.

A number of different authors have provided descriptions of three different theories that describe mechanisms that explain why pressure causes a decrement in performance (Lam, Maxwell, & Masters, 2009; Wilson, Chattington, Marple-Horvat, & Smith, 2007; Wilson, Smith, & Holmes, 2007; Wilson, Vine, & Wood, 2009; Wilson, Wood, & Vine, 2009). These three theories include processing efficacy theory, attentional control theory, and the conscious processing hypothesis.

Processing efficacy theory (PET) is a theory that posits that mental pressure and stress reduces the processing and storage capacity of the information processing system. Worry and psychological pressure cause a diversion of attention from task-relevant cues. Pressure places an overload on the information processing system that initially reduces the efficiency of the system. However, in addition to diverting attention from task relevant cues, worry stimulates increased effort which partially compensates for reduced performance effectiveness. The negative effect of worry and pressure on the information processing system would be worse if it were not for this compensating feature of the system.

Attentional control theory (ACT) is not proposed as an alternative to PET, but as an extension. Consequently, it still proposes that psychological pressure hinders the efficiency of the information processing system. However, ACT further hypothesizes that stress and pressure disrupts the balance between two attentional systems: a top-down *goal directed system,* and a bottom-up *stimulus-driven system.* In the stimulus-driven system, pressure causes the individual to respond to salient or conspicuous stimuli as opposed to focusing on current goals and expectations. Anxiety and stress impairs processing efficiency by increasing the influence of the stimulus-driven system at the expense of the goal-directed system. For example, in a soccer penalty kick situation, pressure may cause the kicker to visually fixate on the goalie, as a conspicuous stimulus, instead of the corner of the goal (Wilson, Wood, et al., 2009). ACT incorporates elements of inhibition, irrelevant information, and shifting attention. Both PET and ACT are believed to be distraction theories in that attention is distracted by irrelevant stimuli, or by a reduced ability to focus on relevant stimuli. East-erbrook's cue utilization theory, as illustrated in figure 6.4, is an example of a distraction theory.

Conscious processing hypothesis (CPH) is different from both PET and ACT in that it is hypothesized that reduced performance due to pressure is caused by heightened self-consciousness, which causes the athlete to attempt to consciously control previously automated motor skills and motor schema. In so doing, the individual turns to an internal focus of attention and adopts self-focusing behaviors. As we learned previously, self-focusing internal behavior is used in learning a motor skill, but becomes dormant when the skill becomes well-learned and automated. Reinvesting in conscious control disrupts the automatic execution of a previously well-learned skill, causing a decrement in performance. In the literature, CPH is also referred to as the *explicit monitoring hypothesis*. Related to the CPH and the explicit monitoring hypothesis, the Reinvestment Scale (RS; Masters, Polman, & Hammond, 1993) was developed to measure the personality dimension to "use explicit rules to consciously control normally automatic motor output."

Here we briefly review research that contrasts these three theories in terms of how well they explain a decrement in performance due to increased mental pressure (e.g., anxiety, stress, psychological pressure). Generally, most of the research has attempted to contrast CPH with either PET or ACT. Rarely is PET contrasted with ACT, as they are both distraction theories. In a sense, the research question that is typically asked is whether a reduction in performance, associated with mental pressure, is due to attentional distraction or to an attempt to explicitly monitor skill execution. While results vary as a function of design of the experiment, skill of participants, and sport skill involved, several investigations generally showed that attentional distraction theories such as PET and ACT provide the best explanation for choking under

pressure (Nieuwenhuys, Pijpers, Oudejans, & Bakker, 2008; Otten, 2009; Wilson, Chattington, et al., 2007; Wilson, Smith, et al., 2007; Wilson, Wood, et al., 2009). Conversely, several studies show that the conscious processing hypothesis (CPH) provides the best explanation for choking under pressure (Beilock & Carr, 2001; Gucciardi & Dimmock, 2008; Jackson, et al., 2006; Lam et al., 2009; Maxwell, Masters, & Poolton, 2006).

Based on this brief review of studies, it is apparent that none of the three explanations for choking under pressure received unequivocal research support as the single best explanation. However, the very likely probability exists that an eclectic or combination theory might provide the best explanation. If significant decline in skilled performance occurs as a result of mental pressure (choking) it is likely due to attentional distraction, conscious processing, or perhaps a combination of both. Mullen, Hardy, and Tattersall (2005) and Mesagno, Marchant, and Morris (2009) found experimental support for an eclectic model they call the attentional threshold model. The **attentional threshold model** is a combination of the self-focus and distraction models. According to this model, distractions from worry and self-focus (explicit instructions) do not individually cause a performance decrement, but together they exceed a threshold of attentional capacity. While not theoretical in nature, a recent study by Gucciardi, Longbottom, Jackson, and Dimmock (2010) provide important practical information about the choking phenomenon from the perspective of experienced golfers. They concluded that the choking phenomenon is a "complex process involving the interplay of several cognitive, attentional, emotional, and situational factors." (p. 61)

Measuring Attentional Focus

Landers (1988) identified three primary ways in which attention may be measured by sport psychologists. In method one, a *behavioral* assessment of attention is made using the reaction time probe

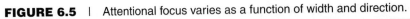

FIGURE 6.5 | Attentional focus varies as a function of width and direction.

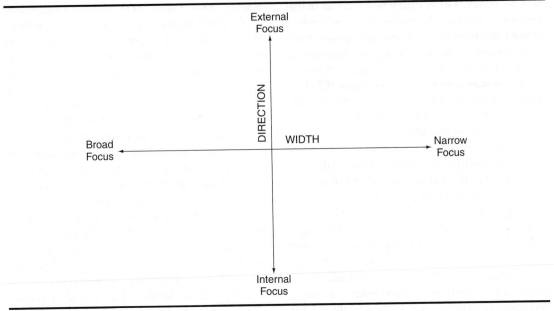

technique. In this procedure, attention demands of a primary task are estimated based on a subject's performance on a secondary reaction time task.

The second method used by sport psychologists for assessing attention is the use of *physiological indicators*. As illustrated in figure 6.4, physiological arousal and attentional focus are closely related. As the level of arousal increases, an individual's attentional focus tends to narrow.

The third method identified by Landers for assessing attention is the use of the *self-report*. While behavioral and physiological indicators of attention tend to measure attentional abilities at a specific point in time, the self-report method has tended to be more of an indicator of attentional focus as a personality trait or disposition. The primary originator of the self-report method for assessing attentional focus is Robert Nideffer (1976). Nideffer called his self-report inventory the Test of Attentional and Interpersonal Style (TAIS). Nideffer reasoned that an athlete's attentional processes could be represented as a function of two independent dimensions. The first he called

width and the second he called *direction*. The width dimension of the athlete's attentional focus ranges from narrow to broad, while the direction dimension varies from internal to external.

The width and direction dimensions of attentional focus are illustrated in figure 6.5. We were previously introduced to the notion of **width of attention** in figure 6.4. This dimension implies that an athlete's attentional focus can range from broad to narrow, and that it is closely associated with arousal. The **direction of attention** dimension, however, is new, and implies that an athlete can be internally or externally focused. In internal focus, the athlete's thoughts and feelings are directed inward; in external focus, the athlete's attention is directed to external cues such as the ball and the opponents.

Nideffer's TAIS was developed, in part, to measure an athlete's disposition to be narrowly or broadly focused and to be internally or externally focused. The TAIS is composed of 144 items which purport to measure seventeen subscales, six of which are attentional subscales. The six attentional subscales are identified in table 6.1, along

TABLE 6.1 | Description and Classification of Attentional Subscales as Measured by the Test of Attentional and Interpersonal Style

Scale	Name	Type	Dimension Measured	Scale Description
BET	Broad-External	Positive	Dir/Width	Environmental awareness
BIT	Broad-Internal	Positive	Dir/Width	Analytical planning skill
NAR	Narrow-Focused	Positive	Width	Avoid distractions and ability to stay focused
OET	External-Overload	Negative	Direction	Inappropriate attention to external stimuli
OIT	Internal-Overload	Negative	Direction	Inappropriate attention to internal stimuli
RED	Reduced Attention	Negative	Direction	Inability to shift direction (internal/external)

Source: Nideffer, R. N., & Sagal, M. (2006). Concentration and attentional control training. In J. M. Williams (Ed.), *Applied sport psychology: Personal growth to peak performance* (pp. 382–403). St. Louis, MO: McGraw-Hill.

with identifying characteristics. Three of the attentional subscales measure positive aspects of attentional focus (BET, BIT, NAR), while three measure negative aspects (OET, OIT, RED). In addition, table 6.1 provides a brief description of each scale, including dimension measured. Except for the BET and BIT, the six dimensions do not allow for a clear categorization into the four quadrants of attentional focus illustrated in figure 6.5.

Perhaps more important than an athlete's disposition toward a particular attentional profile is that athlete's ability to adopt an effective attentional focus for specific situations. In dynamic team sports such as basketball and football, an athlete's ideal attentional focus may change from moment to moment, as well as situation to situation. From an attentional perspective, the challenge faced by the quarterback in American football is particularly intriguing. In a pass play, the quarterback must simultaneously disregard the sights and sounds of charging defensive linesmen, and expand his field of vision so that he can see all of his receivers either directly or peripherally. We will discuss this problem further in the next section, on attention control training.

Attention Control Training

Sport psychologists have written extensively about attention control training (Williams, Nideffer, & Wilson, 2010). The primary component of

attention control training (ACT) is the process of narrowing or widening attention through arousal management strategies. As illustrated in figure 6.4, attention narrows as arousal increases. Also illustrated in this figure is the very clear concept that best performance occurs at an optimal level of arousal. The different interventions used to achieve optimal arousal are discussed in detail in part 4 of this book.

Focusing Attention

Let us return briefly to figure 6.5 and consider the challenges that confront the quarterback in American football. When the quarterback drops back for a pass play, he must gate out the sights and sounds of the attacking defensive line, while at the same time maintaining a broad external focus so that he will be able to see all of his potential receivers. If the quarterback fails to gate out the sights and sounds of the charging linemen, an incomplete pass, an interception, or a sack is a high probability. If the quarterback maintains an external focus that is too narrow due to high arousal, he will likely stare at a single receiver and be intercepted. The primary intent of attention control training for the quarterback should be to (a) teach him to have confidence in his offensive line so that he can gate out the sights and sounds of charging defensive linemen, and (b) teach him to control his emotions and arousal so that he can create an optimal width of

CONCEPT Thought-stopping and centering skills help an athlete avoid errors caused by negative thoughts and diverted attention.

APPLICATION Thought-stopping and centering skills practiced and developed prior to competition can be used when they are needed. Specific positive thoughts, relevant cues, and task-oriented suggestions should be practiced and readied for competition.

attention focus. Due to individual differences, the optimal band of attention will vary from athlete to athlete and from situation to situation. The concepts introduced in figure 6.5 about attention can be applied to any sport or performance situation.

Thought Stopping and Centering

In addition to arousal management, attention training must teach the athlete how to eliminate negative thoughts. It is critically important that the athlete learn to use attention to stop negative thoughts and to focus on positive thoughts. This is a problem that confronts athletes regularly. To overcome feelings of self-doubt, it is necessary to apply the principles of selective attention as discussed in this chapter. In other words, the athlete must develop a high degree of attentional control. As defined by Williams et al. (2010), attention control is a technique designed to keep the athlete from slipping into a cycle of anxiety and self-doubt.

It is important that the athlete approach every sport situation with a positive attitude and belief that she will succeed. When negative thoughts come into consciousness, they must be removed or displaced with positive thoughts. The process of stopping a negative thought and replacing it with a positive one is referred to as **thought stopping.** It is a basic principle of psychology that an athlete cannot give quality attention to more than one attention-demanding task at a time. In this case, it is the mental task of thinking a positive as opposed to a negative thought. Once the negative thought has been displaced, the athlete centers her attention internally. The process of **centering** involves directing thoughts internally. It is during the internal process of centering that the athlete makes conscious adjustments in attention and arousal. An important component of centering is the **centering breath,** designed to gain internal physical balance and to focus on the task mentally. The centering breath technique involves a deep breath, beginning at the diaphragm, followed by strong exhalation and muscle relaxation (Haddad & Tremayne, 2009). Immediately following the centering process, the athlete narrowly focuses her attention on a task-relevant external cue. It is at this point that she takes skilled action. Any delay between directing attention externally and skill execution will only invite distractions in the form of negative thoughts or unwanted environmental stimuli.

Let's take a specific example. Say you are standing at the foul line and are about to shoot a game-winning (or game-losing) foul shot. The thought goes through your mind, "I'm going to miss, I can feel it. The basket is too small, it's a mile away, and I'm scared!" You are losing control. To successfully use the thought-stopping and centering procedure, you must first use the principle of selective attention to drive out the negative thought with a positive thought. You might say to yourself, "No, I'm an excellent shooter; I'm the best person on the team to be shooting in this situation." At this point you center your attention internally as you make minor adjustments in your level of arousal. Take a deep centering breath and exhale strongly but not forcefully. Then you turn your attention to the basketball hoop and focus upon an external cue such as the back of the basket rim (Maxwell et al., 2006). By using the thought-stopping and centering procedure correctly and practicing it in many different situations, you will have an instant weapon to use against the occasional loss of attentional control.

The following basic steps are used in the thought-stopping and centering procedure:

1. Displace any negative thought that comes into your mind with a positive thought.

2. Center your attention with a centering breath while making minor adjustments in arousal.

3. Focus your attention on an external cue such as the back of the basket rim.

4. Execute the sport skill as soon as you have achieved a feeling of attentional control.

Learning the thought-stopping and centering procedure takes practice. The critical point to understand is that negative thoughts can be displaced, and that through the process of centering, the thoughts that capture attention can be controlled. The conscious process of thought stopping and centering will divert the athlete's attention away from threatening thoughts and anxiety- producing stimuli. Selective attention will effectively gate out the unwanted thoughts if the correct thoughts are pertinent and meaningful to the athlete (Singer, 2002).

Associative versus Dissociative Attentional Style

Morgan (1978) hypothesized that marathon runners adopt one of two **attentional styles** to assist them in training and competition. He defined **associators** as those runners who *internalize* the direction dimension of attention and focus on the body's sensory feedback signals. Conversely, he defined **dissociators** as those runners who *externalize* the direction dimension of attention and gate out or block out sensory information from the body. It was Morgan's basic hypothesis that elite marathon runners tend to be associators, while less elite runners tend to be dissociators. He

further hypothesized that associators would be less prone to injury due to their monitoring of sensory feedback. Morgan's basic theory has generated a great deal of interest on the part of sport psychologists and runners.

Terminology and Classification

Since 1978, the basic concept of associators versus dissociators has persisted, but there has been concern expressed about terminology. Masters and Ogles (1998a) point out that the term "dissociative" is confusing, because it is so similar to the term "dissociative disorder" in clinical psychology. In response, Stevinson and Biddle (1999) suggested that the term "dissociation" be replaced with the term "distraction," and that both association and distraction be divided into internal and external components. In this regard, Couture, Jerome, and Tihanyi (1999) noted that working on a math problem or reciting poetry would be examples of internal distraction, while attending to scenery, trees, and the environment would be examples of external distraction.

Consistent with suggestions made by Masters and Ogles (1998b) and Stevinson and Biddle (1999), figure 6.6 illustrates the two-dimensional model of attentional strategy. In this model, the term "distraction" replaces the controversial term "dissociative"; and both "associative" and "distraction" are conceptualized as having internal and external direction components. Prior to the introduction of the two-dimensional model, everything that was previously labeled associative would fit into the single cell labeled associative-internal, while everything else would be considered dissociative (the other three cells). Not-with-standing the utility of the associative versus dissociative dicotomy, a literature review by Salmon, Hannenman, and Harwood (2010) called for a shift toward a "mindfulness" approach to understanding the moment-by-moment attentional demands of sustained activity. The mindfulness approach to addressing cognitive psychology issues will be discussed in some detail in chapter 12.

CONCEPT The proportion of associative (internal) attentional focus is directly related to perceived exertion in skilled marathoners and long-distance runners. Consequently, the proportion of internal focus increases during competition, but decreases during training runs.

APPLICATION In order to be an effective long-distance runner, it is important that the athlete be able to internally focus a large proportion of the time. Through careful coaching, the athlete can learn to use an associative attentional strategy. It would be a mistake, however, to insist that an athlete associate all of the time. Dissociating is more relaxing, and provides a needed psychological break for the marathoner.

FIGURE 6.6 | Stevinson and Biddle's (1999) two-dimensional classification system for conceptualizing attentional strategy.

	Direction of attention	
	Internal	External
Associative	Associative–Internal	Associative–External
	Focus on form, how muscles feel, and breathing	Focus on time splits, distance completed, and strategy
Distraction	Distraction–Internal	Distraction–External
	Daydreaming, fantasizing, and problem solving in the mind	Focus on external or environmental stimuli, such as scenery and wildlife

(left axis label: **Task Relevance**)

Source: Stevinson, C.D., & Biddle, S.J.H. (1999). Cognitive strategies in running: A response to Masters and Ogles. *The Sport Psychologist, 13:* 236, figure 1. Adapted with permission from Human Kinetics (Champaign, IL)

Measurement of Attentional Style

Researchers have utilized at least six different methods of measuring attentional style. Methods of measurement include pencil-and-paper inventories, structured interviews, tape recordings during running, objective data, subjective data, and experimenter rating. Pencil-and-paper inventories include the Running Style Questionnaire (RSQ; Silva & Appelbaum, 1989), the Attentional Focus Questionnaire (AFQ; Brewer, Van Raalte, & Linder, 1996), and the Thoughts During Running Scale (TDRS; Goode & Roth, 1993).

Research Findings

In the following paragraphs, research findings related to attentional style will be discussed as a function of attentional preferences, effort and attentional style, and link to injuries.

Attentional Preferences Marathon runners and other long-distance runners use both associative and dissociative styles of attention. During competition, the vast majority of running time is linked to the associative attentional style. Conversely, during training runs, the vast majority of running time is linked to the dissociative style. Runners prefer the associative style for competition and the dissociative style for practice runs (Masters & Ogles, 1998a). It is believed that the greater intensity needed for competition can be best obtained by internally associating with sensory feedback from the body (Nietfeld, 2003). The dissociative style is believed to be more relaxing and preferred during training and recreation runs. The dissociative style allows the body to either disregard sensory feedback or simply drift off to more pleasant and distracting thoughts.

Effort and Attentional Style Beginning with Schomer's (1990) initial ground-breaking research, it has been demonstrated that (independent of preference or physical activity) as physiological and muscular effort increases, utilization of an associative strategy also increases. Relative to this observation, Tenenbaum (2001, 2002) proposed the effort-related model as it relates to attentional style. The **effort-related model** posits that there is a tight relationship between effort and attentional style. Specifically, as effort increases athletes' attentional style shifts from being dissociative to being more associative (Hutchinson & Tenenbaum, 2007; Stanley, Pargman, & Tenenbaum, 2007; Tenenbaum & Connolly, 2008). Relative to an investigation that involved both handgrip strength and stationary cycling, Hutchinson and Tenenbaum (2007) stated "During conditions of high workload and prolonged duration, attention is focused on overwhelming physiological sensations, which dominate focal awareness. At this point an associative attention focus is almost unavoidable" (p. 233).

Link to Injuries Morgan (1978) hypothesized that the greater incidence of injuries would be linked to the dissociative style of running, because the athlete is not attending to his body signals. Research, however, has failed to support this hypothesis. Research and literature reviews by Masters and Ogles (1998a, 1998b) provide strong evidence that the associative strategy has a stronger link to physical injuries than the dissociative strategy. It is believed that athletes engaging in a dissociative style of attentional focusing are running with less intensity in a more relaxed mode, and therefore are less susceptible to injury. Conversely, the associator is running with great intensity, and is therefore more susceptible to athletic injury, even though she is attending to body signals.

Summary

The focus of this chapter was upon attention and concentration in sport. The information processing model of attention recognizes the presence of many variables and processes between a stimulus and a response. Memory plays an important role in information processing. The three types, or stages, of memory are the sensory register, short-term memory, and long-term memory. Information is measured in bits. The amount of information conveyed by a particular problem can be quantified in terms of questions asked, or in terms of a mathematical formula.

The ability to gate out irrelevant information and attend to important information is called selective attention. A number of structural models of selective attention have been proposed. Three models mentioned in this chapter were the Broadbent model, Norman's pertinence model, and the Triesman model.

The notion of limited information processing capacity helps explain the difference between skilled and unskilled athletes. If a particular task requires all of a person's information processing space, then none will be left over for attending to other tasks that also require attention.

Easterbrook's cue utilization theory deals with the phenomenon of attentional narrowing. As an athlete's arousal increases, the athlete's attentional focus narrows. The narrowing process tends to gate out irrelevant cues, and sometimes relevant ones as well.

The perfect execution of a sports skill is best thought of as an elegant interaction between mind and body. Describing a peak performance as simply being in the "zone," as if there is a separation of the mind from the body, diminishes the immense preparation that goes into training to become an elite athlete, at any level of competition.

Mechanisms and theories were discussed which explain the relationship between attention and arousal. This was accomplished through a discussion of ironic effects, internal versus external attentional control, and competing mechanisms that explain the detrimental effect of psychological pressure on learning and performance. The ironic effect is that people, when under mental load, tend to do the very thing they are trying not to do. For skilled performers it is best to adopt an external focus as opposed to an internal focus when executing a well-learned skill. Focusing on the internal actions of a motor skill has the effect of disrupting the smooth automatic operation of the skill. For beginners, both an internal and external focus is recommended during learning. Three theories were introduced that explain why mental pressure can cause a decrement in performance (choking). These include processing efficacy theory (PET), attentional control theory (ACT), and the conscious processing hypothesis. The first two theories are distraction theories.

Attentional focus is measured through behavioral assessment (e.g., reaction time probe), physiological indicators, and pencil-and-paper self-report. The most common self-report method is Nideffer's Test of Attentional and Interpersonal Style (TAIS). The TAIS continues to be a popular inventory for assessing width and direction of attention.

The primary component of attention control training (ACT) is the process of narrowing or widening attention through arousal management strategies. Every sport situation requires an optimal level of arousal to create an optimal width of attention focus. In addition to arousal management, attention training teaches the athlete how to eliminate negative thoughts. This is accomplished through thought stopping and centering.

Marathon runners tend to both internalize (associate) and externalize (dissociate) in terms of attentional focus. Marathoners prefer the associative style for competition and the dissociative style for practice runs and training. Because marathoners prefer the associative style during competition, it can be inferred that this style yields superior running times. Research supports the effort-related model in that an associative attentional style is linked to greater physiological and muscular effort. Athletes engaging in a dissociative style of attentional focusing are running with less intensity, in a more relaxed mode, and therefore are less susceptible to injury. The chapter concluded with a discussion of the two-dimensional classification system for conceptualizing attentional strategy.

Critical Thought Questions

1. What does knowing how to calculate bits of information conveyed in a sports situation have to do with athletic performance? Provide examples to support your arguments.

2. Can an athlete gate out distracting information while at the same time maintain a broad external focus of attention? If so, give examples in sport where this occurs.

3. What does it mean to you when a sports announcer says that an athlete is in the "zone"? Do you think this term represents an oversimplification of a complex interaction between mind and body? What is an athlete's mind doing when the athlete is in the "zone"?

4. Distinguish between effects, causes, and mechanisms associated with "choking" and "panicking" in human performance. Give examples.

5. What is the ironic effect in sport? Give some examples of the effect. Explain, in your own words, what causes the ironic effect. Are all unwanted actions ironic effects? Explain.

6. What is the difference between an internal attentional focus and an external focus when executing a well-learned motor skill? Give some examples of each. When is it prudent for a skilled performer to focus his attention on the step-by-step internal actions of skill execution? How about the beginner?

7. Contrast the constrained action hypothesis with the explicit processing hypothesis as explanations for the debilitating effects of using an internal focus during the execution of a skilled action.

8. Identify and explain the three theories or mechanisms that purport to explain why mental pressure causes a decrement in performance of a well-learned motor skill. Which one do you think provides the best explanation and why?

9. What are your feelings about using the TAIS to evaluate an athlete's attentional abilities?

10. Develop thought-stopping and centering scenarios for five different sporting situations. Assume you are the coach and you are doing this for your athletes.

11. Why is the research on attentional style important to the coach and the athlete?

12. Discuss the two dimensional classification system for conceptualizing attentional strategy as it relates to performance, effort, and environmental application.

Glossary

anticipatory skill The cognitive and perceptual skill to anticipate stimuli that have not appeared.

associators Endurance athletes who internalize, or adopt an internal attentional focus.

attentional control theory An extension of processing efficacy theory that further posits that performance decrement in the presence of mental pressure is due to an imbalance between a goal-directed information processing system and the stimulus-driven system.

attention control training The process of teaching athletes how to narrow and widen their attentional focus and to control their thoughts

attentional flexibility The ability of athletes to shift their attention quickly and effectively from one location to another.

attentional focus In sports, an athlete's ability to focus on relevant information during competition.

attentional narrowing The narrowing of an athlete's attentional focus due to an increase in arousal.

attentional style An athlete's particular style of attending to stimuli.

attentional threshold model Distractions from worry and self-focus do not individually cause a performance decrement, but together they exceed a threshold of attentional capacity.

automatic processing The execution of a skill that, although it is being monitored by the brain, requires little conscious attention because it is well learned.

bit of information A term that stands for binary digit, a unit of information measurement. The number of bits corresponds to the number of questions needed to accurately predict the occurrence of an event.

capacity model A model of attention based on limited information processing space.

centering The process whereby an athlete's attention is brought to focus on an important task-oriented suggestion.

centering breath A technique that involves a deep breath, beginning at the diaphragm, followed by strong but not forceful exhalation and muscle relaxation.

choking Below-standard execution of a well-learned sports skill due to mental pressure.

chunking The cognitive process of combining several pieces of information into larger ones.

clutch performance Above-standard performance under conditions of significant pressure.

cognitive interference Random thought or distraction that breaks an athlete's concentration.

conscious processing hypothesis Reduced pressure due to mental pressure is due to heightened self-consciousness, which causes the athlete to attempt to control previously automated motor skills and motor schema.

constrained action hypothesis Conscious attempts to control movement interferes with automatic motor processes, which results in performance deterioration.

controlled processing An athlete's necessary attentional focus on the details of executing a skill that is being learned.

cue utilization According to Easterbrook, the process of narrowing attention to gate out environmental cues.

direction of attention An athlete's attentional focus, categorized as being internal or external.

dissociators Endurance athletes who externalize, or adopt an external attentional focus.

distractibility An athlete's inability to selectively attend to relevant stimuli due to very high levels of arousal.

effort-related model Posits a tight relationship between effort and attentional style. Specifically, as effort increases the athlete's attentional style shifts from dissociative to more associative.

explicit processing hypothesis Focusing internally on the execution of a movement elevates the level of conscious control and demands for working memory, resulting in performance decrement.

gate out Exclude or ignore irrelevant sensory information.

inattentional blindness Inability to see an object or stimulus that is in plain view due to attentional overload.

individual differences Relative to information processing, the differences between individual athletes in the amount of processing capacity they have available, as well as in how they utilize the capacity they have.

information conveyed The amount of information, in bits, contained in a particular problem. For example, a reaction-time problem containing four lights conveys two bits of information if all four lights are equally likely to flash.

information processing model A model based on the theory that human beings process information rather than merely respond to stimuli. Many cognitive processes are involved. For example, information must be stored, retrieved, and rehearsed.

ironic effect The ironic event of making the error that you consciously are trying to avoid.

long-term memory Long-term or permanent memory.

mechanism The explanation of why a cause-and-effect event occurs.

memory storage Capacity to store all information reaching memory for future recall.

monitoring process As a companion to the operating process, it is the unconscious component of information processing responsible for detecting errors.

motor schema Controls the development and execution of a smooth skilled action or motor program.

operating process The cognitive process responsible for intentional, effortful, and conscious control of motor responses.

perceptual cognitive skill Skills such as response time, increased accuracy, improved decision making.

peripheral scanning Instead of seeing objects peripherally while focusing on a central task, the athlete repeatedly scans peripheral objects and then quickly returns to the central task.

playing in the zone A nondescriptive term that refers to extraordinary performance of an athlete.

processing capacity The limited amount of space people have available for the processing of information.

processing efficacy theory A theory that posits that mental pressure and stress reduces the processing capacity of the information processing system.

quiet eye period Lapsed time between the last eye fixation and the initiation of a motor response. A longer quiet eye period is indicative of greater planning and coordinating of motor programs.

retrieval The mental process of retrieving information to make decisions about forthcoming responses.

selective attention The capability to attend to one stimulus to the exclusion of others.

sensory register A short-term sensory store that effectively retains information for about one-half second before it is lost or transferred to a more permanent storage system.

short-term memory Working memory, or the center of activity in the information processing system.

thought stopping In sport, the process of replacing a negative thought with a success-oriented, positive thought.

width of attention An athlete's attentional focus, ranging from broad to narrow.

Anxiety, Stress, and Mood Relationships

KEY TERMS

Affect
Alexithymia
Antecedent
Anxiety
Cognitive anxiety
Competitive situation
Competitive state
  anxiety
Conceptual model
  of mood
Distress
Drive
Drive theory
Dysfunctional
  perfectionism
Effect size
Emotion
Eustress
Functional
  perfectionism
Iceberg profile
Inverted-U theory
Mental health model
Meta-analysis
Mood
Mood profile
Mood state
Multidimensional

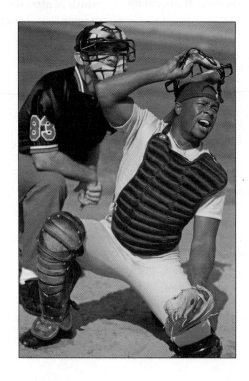

Organizational stress
Precompetitive mood
Precompetitive state
  anxiety
Primary appraisal
Profile of Mood States (POMS)
Secondary appraisal

Signal detection theory
Somatic anxiety
State anxiety
Stress
Stress process
Trait anxiety
Yerkes-Dodson law

The following story about a young athlete illustrates the potentially debilitating effects of anxiety on athletic performance. Ryan is a physically gifted 16-year-old athlete. He participates in several sports for his high school during the academic year and plays summer baseball as well. Some of the team sports he excels in are football, basketball, and baseball. However, his favorite sport is track and field, which is primarily an individual sport.

Ryan is a highly anxious young man with a tendency toward perfectionism. In Ryan's particular case, these traits had very little negative effect on his performance in the team sports he played. He would often get uptight about a big game, but he could always rely upon his teammates to help him out. The fact that team games involved other players seemed to help control the negative impact his anxiety could have had on his performance. Ryan occasionally "clutched" during baseball games, but the outcome of the game was rarely affected. Usually, only Ryan and Ryan's parents were aware of the anxiety and tension that were boiling within.

However, track and field was a different matter. Ryan was a sprinter and hurdler. His physical power and mesomorphic build made him especially well equipped for running and jumping events that required speed and leg power. Unfortunately, his basic anxiety and worry about failing had a serious effect on his performance during competition. During practice, Ryan always did well. In fact, during three years of high school Ryan had never lost a race to a teammate during practice. In actual competition, things were different. Ryan began preparing mentally for his races days in advance of the actual competition. During the days and hours preceding competition, his anxiety would rise to fearful levels. By the time actual competition came, Ryan could hardly walk, let alone run or jump. Several times he had to vomit before important races. His coach talked to him a great deal about learning to relax and not worry about the race, but didn't give him specific suggestions on how to accomplish this. Finally, the coach decided to remove Ryan from his favorite events because he was actually a detriment to the team. This was more than Ryan could take. He approached the coach one day and announced that he was going to give up athletics altogether and concentrate on his studies. This story has a successful conclusion, but it will be shared later, at the beginning of the cognitive and behavioral intervention section of the book (part 4).

In explaining the relationships among anxiety, stress, and mood, and their relationship to athletic performance, it is important to be introduced to a number of concepts and their relationships to each other. To accomplish this, this chapter is divided into the following eight sections: (a) differentiating among the terms *affect, emotion, anxiety, mood,* and *stress,* (b) multidimensional nature of anxiety, (c) stress process and antecedents of the state anxiety response, (d) measurement of anxiety, (e) time to event nature of precompetitive anxiety, (f) perfectionism in sport, (g) relationship between anxiety and performance, and (h) relationship between mood and performance.

Differentiating Among the Terms Affect, Emotion, Anxiety, Mood, and Stress

To begin with, **affect** is a generic term used to describe emotions, feelings, and moods. **Emotion** is a situation-specific affective response to the environment. Lazarus (2000a) defined emotion as "an organized psychophysiological reaction to ongoing relationships with the environment, most often, but not always interpersonal or social" (p. 230). Lazarus further identified 15 specific emotions and core themes associated with each emotion. The primary focus of this chapter is on just one of these emotions, specifically the emotion of **anxiety,** which he defined as "facing uncertain, existential threat" (p. 234). Other example emotions that might influence athletic performance include anger, guilt, shame, relief, happiness, and pride. Anxiety is the emotion that has been most studied and is believed

CONCEPT Anxiety is one of many emotions that may arise in response to a competitive situation. An emotion is associated with a physiological change, a subjective experience, and an action tendency. Conversely, a mood is more diffuse, longer lasting, and associated with life generally.

APPLICATION Athletes who experience the emotion of anxiety or anger do so in response to

an environmental experience. The emotion will be associated with an increase in physiological arousal and with the tendency to take action of some sort. How the athlete responds to increased emotion is the topic of discussion in much of sections 3 and 4 of this book. For now, it is important to understand the difference between an emotion and a mood and that there are many different emotions.

---

to have the most influence upon athletic performance. This does not mean that powerful emotions such as anger, happiness, and hope do not influence performance, only that anxiety is the main focus of this chapter (Seve, Ria, Poizat, Saury, & Durand, 2007; Williams & Desteno, 2008; Woodman et al., 2009). To aid researchers in studying the effect of emotions on athletic performance, Jones, Lane, Bray, Uphill, and Catlin (2005) developed the Sport Emotion Questionnaire (2005). The study of emotion relative to the zone of optimal function (ZOF) in sport will be discussed as an alternative to inverted-U theory in chapter 8. In chapter 8 we will elaborate more on the influence of emotions generally on athletic performance. The balance of this chapter will focus on the emotion of anxiety and the effects of mood on performance. While emotions are instantaneous discrete responses to the environment that last only seconds, minutes, or perhaps hours, **moods** are more diffuse, and may last for weeks or even months (Jones, 2003; Vallerand & Blanchard, 2000). Furthermore, emotions are directed toward something associated with the environment (e.g., inside pitch in baseball), whereas moods are more diffuse, relate more to how we are doing in life and not easily associated with anything specific (Uphill & Jones, 2007). Jones (2003) further clarified that an emotion is composed of three main elements including a physiological change, a subjective experience, and an action tendency. Moods are generally referred to as mood states and are

often measured by sport psychologists using the Profile of Mood States (POMS), to be discussed later in this chapter.

The emotion of anxiety is closely related to Han Selye's concept of stress (pronounced "sale-ye"). Selye (1983, p. 2) defined **stress** as the "nonspecific response to the body to any demand made upon it." When aroused, the body is under stress regardless of whether the cause is something negative like anger or something positive like joy. Exercising at a high intensity would be classified as stressful to the body, because the heart is pumping faster and blood pressure is increased in the arteries and the veins. It can be argued, however, that anger and anxiety are much more stressful to the body than are joy and happiness. To take these factors into consideration, Selye allowed that there must be two different kinds of stress. He labeled the "good stress" **eustress** and the "bad stress" he labeled **distress.** In this chapter distress will be considered to be synonymous with the emotion of anxiety or what we will later refer to as situation-specific state anxiety.

The Multidimensional Nature of Anxiety

Anxiety is **multidimensional** in two different ways. Like all other emotions, anxiety has both a trait component and a state component. The trait component is like a personality disposition, whereas the state

FIGURE 7.1 | Both trait and state anxiety exhibit cognitive and somatic anxiety components.

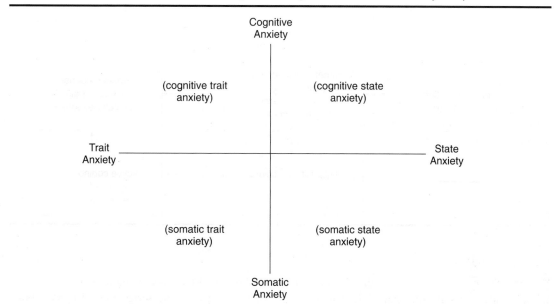

component is a situation-specific response. **State anxiety** is an immediate emotional state that is characterized by apprehension, fear, tension, and an increase in physiological arousal. Conversely, **trait anxiety** is a *predisposition* to perceive certain environmental situations as threatening and to respond to these situations with increased state anxiety (Spielberger, 1971). If an athlete has a high level of competitive trait anxiety, she is likely to respond to an actual competitive situation with a high level of competitive state anxiety.

Anxiety is also multidimensional in the sense that it is believed that there are both cognitive and somatic components to anxiety (Endler, Parker, Bagby, & Cox, 1991). **Cognitive anxiety** is the mental component of anxiety caused by such things as fear of negative social evaluation, fear of failure, and loss of self-esteem. **Somatic anxiety** is the physical component of anxiety and reflects the *perception* of such physiological responses as increased heart rate, respiration, and muscular tension. Both state and trait anxiety are believed to have cognitive and somatic components. In the

sport psychology literature, the notion that anxiety has both cognitive and somatic components is referred to as *multidimensional anxiety theory* (Martens, Vealey, & Burton, 1990). The bipolar, multidimensional nature of anxiety is illustrated in figure 7.1.

The Stress Process and Antecedents of the State Anxiety Response

The best way to understand stress is to conceptualize it as a process, as opposed to an outcome. The **stress process,** as illustrated in figure 7.2, is really the information processing model in action. The stress process begins with the stimulus (competitive situation) on the left and results in the response (stress response) on the right. In between the stimulus and the response is cognition, or thought processes. Cognition determines how the athlete will respond (Lazarus, 2000a, 2000b; Lazarus & Folkman, 1984).

FIGURE 7.2 | The stress process and not the competitive situation determines the extent of the stress response.

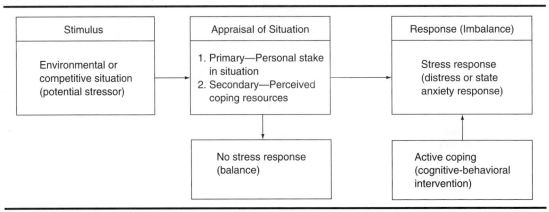

The stress process begins with the environmental or competitive situation on the left. This is the stimulus. The **competitive situation** is not by itself stressful. It is how the athlete interprets the situation that determines whether or not the situation is stressful. Consider the situation in which an athlete finds himself on the foul line in a basketball game with the outcome of the game resting upon his performance. To most people this would be an extremely stressful situation. However, to many basketball players this is exactly the kind of situation that they seek. The situation is not intimidating because they have supreme confidence in their skill and the thought of failure does not enter their minds.

In October of 2004, the Boston Red Sox made history by defeating the New York Yankees in seven games to get into baseball's World Series. There were many heroes in that series, but none greater than David Ortiz. What Ortiz accomplished in the face of potential extreme anxiety and tension speaks to his ability to manage the stress process. In game four of the American League Championship Series (ALCS), and down three games to none, David Ortiz hit a walk-off home run in the 12th inning to win the game and stave off what seemed to be a sure four-game sweep by the Yankees. Then, in game five, Ortiz hit a single in

the bottom of the 14th inning to win the game and keep the seven-game series alive (Kepner, 2004).

Consider a nonathletic situation. Suppose you walk into an old abandoned home and notice that right on the ceiling above you is a very large spider. Does this evoke the stress response in your body? For most people it would, but not for all. Some individuals are not afraid of spiders because of their experiences with them. They know that most spiders are harmless and that this one is big and harmless. The difference is in perception. To understand this we look at the middle panel of figure 7.2.

Upon being confronted with a *potentially* stressful situation, the individual conducts an instantaneous appraisal or evaluation of the situation. Appraisal of the situation occurs on two levels. The first is referred to as primary appraisal, and the second as secondary appraisal. In **primary appraisal,** the athlete determines if she has a personal stake in the outcome. If the athlete determines that the outcome is very important to her, then secondary appraisal becomes important. In **secondary appraisal,** the athlete evaluates her personal coping resources to deal with the competitive situation. The outcomes of the primary and secondary appraisals determine whether the stress response will or will not occur.

CONCEPT   Whether or not an athlete responds to a threatening situation with high levels of state anxiety will depend entirely on the athlete's perception of the situation.

APPLICATION   Each athlete is unique and should be treated as an individual. Do not attempt to predict an athlete's anxiety response to a competitive situation based on your own perception of the same situation. The athlete's own perception of the situation will determine the level of anxiety response, if any.

If an athlete determines either that it makes no difference to him personally if he makes a play, or that he is perfectly capable of coping with the situation, then the stress response does not occur. In this case, we say that there is a *balance* between the stressful nature of the competitive situation and the athlete's perceived ability to cope with the situation. If, however, the athlete determines that he does not have the resources (skill, confidence, experience) to cope with the situation, the stress response will occur. In this case we say that there is an *imbalance* between the stressful nature of the competitive situation and the athlete's perceived ability to cope. The stress response is equated with Selye's concept of distress, or what we defined as state anxiety.

Also shown in figure 7.2 is a box labeled "active coping." If the state anxiety response proves to be detrimental to performance, it may become necessary to intervene in some way to reduce debilitating anxiety. We will discuss active coping, or cognitive-behavioral interventions, in part 4 of the text.

An anecdote related by Fisher (1976) serves to clarify the relationships illustrated in figure 7.2. Two researchers were studying the effects of fear of drowning on the physiological responses of a participant. The participant was strapped to the side of a swimming tank with the water steadily rising. For some reason the researchers left the test area and forgot about their participant. When they remembered, they were aghast and numb with fear. Dropping everything, they raced to the test area to find the water level dangerously high. Quickly, they unstrapped the participant and pulled him from the water. Safe on the pool deck, they asked the participant if he was frightened. The participant responded that he wasn't at all worried, because it was just an experiment and he knew that the researchers wouldn't let any harm come to him! The participant perceived the test situation to be nonthreatening, and therefore the state anxiety reaction was not evoked.

To this point, all of our discussion on the stress process has focused on the individual athlete relative to figure 7.2, but there is another kind of stress that we have not talked about, and that is the stress placed on the athlete by the organizing body. **Organizational stress** is the stress placed on the athlete by the competitive sport environment, not just the coaches or a specific competitive event (Fletcher & Hanton, 2003). Fletcher and Hanton (2003) identified four sources of potential organizational stress: (a) environmental issues (selection, travel, accommodations, competitive environment, etc.), (b) personal issues (nutrition, injury, goals, expectations, etc.), (c) leadership issues (coaches and coaching style, etc.), and (d) team issues (team atmosphere, support network, roles, communication, etc.). Taken together, issues associated with organizational stress can take their toll on the athlete.

Competitive state anxiety that occurs prior to a competitive situation is referred to as **precompetitive state anxiety.** According to Endler (1983), there are five specific **antecedents,** or factors that lead to an increase in anxiety in anticipation of an achievement (competitive) situation. These five factors include fear of performance failure, fear of negative social evaluation, fear of physical harm,

CONCEPT   The primary cause or antecedent of competitive state anxiety in athletes relates to fear of failure and fear of negative social evaluation. Fear of harm, ambiguity, and disruption of routine are weaker predictors of anxiety in athletes.

APPLICATION   Knowing the factors that are most likely to cause a state anxiety response in an athlete should assist the coach in helping the athlete overcome these fears. Fear of physical harm can be of major concern in certain sports and by certain athletes. For example, fear of physical injury in football by an athlete who has already sustained a season-ending injury could be of major concern. Situation ambiguity and disruption of routine are antecedents of anxiety that ought to be easily managed and controlled if the athlete and coach are aware of them.

situation ambiguity, and disruption of a well-learned routine. Thatcher and Day (2008) identified eight antecedents, but they are largely redundant to the five identified by Endler. It is these sources of stress and others that are appraised, as in figure 7.2, to determine if an imbalance exists between the stimulus and the athletes' perceived ability to deal with the stress.

Sport psychology researchers have been particularly interested in studying antecedents or sources of stress and anxiety in various sports and situations. For example, Dunn (1999) reported that fear of failure and negative social evaluation were sources of distress in ice hockey. High school basketball players experience high levels of anxiety relative to the perceived skill level of their opponents (Thuot, Kavouras, & Kenefick, 1998). In addition to perceived threat, perceived lack of control and coping resources are sources of stress (Hammereister & Burton, 2001). Personal sources of strain and stress experienced by British senior elite track-and-field athletes include lack of confidence, injury concerns, social evaluation, lack of social support, underperforming, and pressure to perform (McKay, Niven, Lavallee, & White, 2008). Personal appraisals of goal relevance, ego involvement, blame/credit, coping potential, and future expectations are associated with a wide range of emotions (including anxiety) in international athletes from various sports (Uphill & Jones, 2007).

Measurement of Anxiety

In recent years, the preferred method of measuring trait and state anxiety has been through the use of pencil-and-paper inventories. For your perusal a number of the most common anxiety inventories as used or developed by sport psychologists are listed in table 7.1.

While pencil-and-paper inventories are the most common measures of anxiety, behavioral and physiological assessment can be very effective. One category of behavioral measurement is direct observation, where the experimenter looks for objective signs of arousal in the subject and records them. Such things as nervous fidgeting, licking the lips, rubbing palms on pants or shirt, and change in respiration could all be interpreted as behavioral signs of activation. Such a system was developed and used by Lowe (1973) for ascertaining arousal through "on-deck activity" of batters in Little League baseball.

Along these lines, table 7.2 displays a list of overt behavioral responses that can be used by the athlete to identify indicators of distress, or state anxiety. The list is arranged in alphabetical order and may be used by the athlete as a checklist to monitor state anxiety response during practice, immediately before competition, and during competition.

From the perspective of applied (nonlaboratory) field research, pencil-and-paper inventories

TABLE 7.1 | Common Anxiety Inventories Utilized or Developed by Sport Psychologists

Trait/State	Dimension	Inventory	Reference
TRAIT	*Unidimensional*	Spielberger's Trait Anxiety Inventory (TAI) Sport Competition Anxiety Test (SCAT)	Spielberger (1983) Martens, Vealey, et al. (1990)
	Multidimensional	Cognitive Somatic Anxiety Questionnaire (CSAQ) Sport Anxiety Scale-2 (SAS-2)	Schwartz, Davidson, and Goleman (1978) Smith, Smoll, Cumming, and Grossbard (2006)
STATE	*Unidimensional*	Spielberger's State Anxiety Inventory (SAI) Competitive State Anxiety Inventory (CSAI)	Spielberger (1983) Martens (1977, 1982)
	Multidimensional	Activation-Deactivation Checklist (AD-ACL) Competitive State Anxiety Inventory-2 (CSAI-2) Revised Competitive State Anxiety Inventory-2 (CSAI-2R)	Thayer (1986) Martens, Vealey, et al. (1990) Cox, Martens, and Russell (2003)

TABLE 7.2 | Incomplete Checklist for Monitoring Distress-Related Behavioral Responses of the Athlete

_____ Clammy Hands		_____ Nausea	
_____ Diarrhea		_____ Need to Urinate	
_____ Dry Mouth		_____ Physical Fatigue	
_____ Fidgeting		_____ Rapid Heart Rate	
_____ Increased Respiration		_____ Scattered Attention	
_____ Irritability		_____ Tense Muscles	
_____ Jitters		_____ Tense Stomach	
_____ Licking of Lips		_____ Trembling Legs	
_____ Mental Confusion		_____ Unsettled Stomach	
_____ Mental Fatigue		_____ Voice Distortion	

and behavioral assessment techniques seem most feasible. This will remain true as long as electrophysiological indicators require expensive instruments. Advances in the field of applied psychophysiology, however, may change this perspective. Improvements in the use of telemetry will make it possible to monitor an athlete's heart rate, blood pressure, and muscular tension while he is competing in such dynamic activities as swimming, batting in baseball, and sprinting in track. It has long been argued that both physiological and psychological assessments of anxiety should be taken to measure anxiety and arousal. In this regard, however, it is important to point out

that the correlation between physiological and psychological measures of state anxiety is quite low (Karteroliotis & Gill, 1987). Consequently, if both physiological and psychological measures of state anxiety are recorded simultaneously, it is possible that conflicting results may be obtained (Tenenbaum, 1984).

Multidimensional anxiety theory has precipitated the development of anxiety inventories that measure both trait and state anxiety, as well as cognitive and somatic anxiety. Referring again to table 7.1, we can note that several of the inventories are identified as being multidimensional in nature, as opposed to unidimensional. A multidimensional

CONCEPT   The state anxiety response to stressful situations can be observed and recorded through the use of a behavioral checklist.

APPLICATION   The athlete should systematically chronicle anxiety-related behavioral responses. Once these are recorded, the coach will be able to help an athlete identify and control competitive stress.

---

measure of trait or state anxiety partitions the construct into at least two components: cognitive and somatic. A *unidimensional* measure of trait or state anxiety makes no attempt to partition the construct into multiple parts. Among the trait inventories, those that measure anxiety as a multidimensional construct include the Cognitive Somatic Anxiety Questionnaire (CSAQ) and the Sport Anxiety Scale-2 (SAS-2). Among the state inventories, those that measure anxiety as a multidimensional construct include the Activation-Deactivation Checklist (AD-ACL), the Competitive State Anxiety Inventory-2 (CSAI-2), and the Revised Competitive State Anxiety Inventory-2 (CSAI-2R).

Since 1990, the CSAI-2 has been the instrument of choice for measuring multidimensional competitive state anxiety. The CSAI-2 is composed of 27 items that measure cognitive state anxiety, somatic state anxiety, and self-confidence. Recent research with the CSAI-2, however, failed to confirm the hypothesized three-factor structure of the inventory (Cox, 2000; Lane, Sewell, Terry, Bertram, & Nesti, 1999). Consequently, the Revised Competitive State Anxiety Inventory–2 (CSAI-2R) was developed by Cox, Martens, et al. (2003). The CSAI-2R is composed of 17 items that measure the constructs of cognitive anxiety (5 items), somatic anxiety (7 items), and self-confidence (5 items). Items that were removed were items that tended to be highly correlated with more than one construct or subscale. A French version of the CSAI-2R was tested by Martinent, Ferrand, Guillet, and Gautheur (2010). While the three-factor structure of the CSAI-2R was confirmed, they suggested that the somatic factor could be improved by dropping the first somatic item in the inventory (i.e., "I feel jittery"), reducing the CSAI-2R to 16 instead of 17 items.

Both the CSAI-2 and the CSAI-2R take several minutes to administer, so they can be a distraction to athletes who are preparing for competition. To address this shortcoming, several very short versions of the CSAI-2 have been developed. They include the Mental Readiness Form (Murphy, Greenspan, Jowdy, & Tammen, 1989); the Anxiety Rating Scale (Cox, Robb, & Russell, 2000, 2001); the Immediate Anxiety Measurement Scale (Thomas, Hanton, & Jones, 2002); the Sport Grid (Raedeke & Stein, 1994; Ward & Cox, 2004), and the Affect Grid (Russell, 2003; Russell, Weiss, & Mendelsohn, 1989).

A 15-item version of the CSAI-2 (CSAI-2C) has also been developed for children (Stadulis, Eidson, & MacCracken, 1994). Finally, the CSAI-2R can be modified to provide a multidimensional measure of competitive trait anxiety. This is accomplished through a simple modification of premeasurement instructions (Albrecht & Feltz, 1987). Instead of being asked to respond as to how she feels "at this moment" relative to a competition, the athlete is asked to respond to how she "usually feels" about competition in general.

Time-to-Event Nature of Precompetitive Anxiety

Our ability to obtain independent measures of cognitive and somatic state anxiety has greatly enhanced our knowledge about the athletic situation. One of the factors that is believed to significantly influence the quality of the athletic experience is the level of state anxiety during the time leading up to competition. We have already referred to this as precompetitive anxiety. We now know quite a bit

CONCEPT   Pencil-and-paper inventories, behavioral checklists, and electrophysiological measures all provide somewhat independent measures of state anxiety.

APPLICATION   Notwithstanding the lack of correlation among the various measures, it is useful to measure state anxiety from at least two perspectives. A pencil-and-paper inventory provides an easily administered assessment of state anxiety *prior* to the event, while the other two techniques theoretically assess state anxiety *during* the event.

CONCEPT   Cognitive and somatic state anxiety are differentially manifested as the time to the competitive event approaches.

APPLICATION   Bodily perceptions of increased sympathetic nervous system activity (somatic anxiety) are normal and healthy indicators of an approaching athletic contest. If allowed to dissipate, they should be viewed as indicators of physiological readiness. Conversely, cognitive state anxiety has the potential of causing a decrement in athletic performance if it is not controlled.

about the temporal changes in anxiety during the period of time leading up to and immediately following the beginning of the event. Precompetitive cognitive anxiety starts relatively high and remains high and stable as the time of the event approaches. Conversely, somatic anxiety remains relatively low until approximately 24 hours before the event, and then increases rapidly as the event approaches. Once performance begins, somatic anxiety dissipates rapidly, whereas cognitive state anxiety fluctuates throughout the contest as the probability of success/failure changes (Fenz, 1975; Hardy & Parfitt, 1991; Jones & Cale, 1989; Jones, Swain & Cale, 1991; Martens, Vealey, et al., 1990; Parfitt, Hardy, & Pates, 1995; Schedlowski & Tewes, 1992; Swain & Jones, 1992; Wiggins, 1998). The relationship between competitive state anxiety and time-to-event is graphically illustrated in figure 7.3.

In a related investigation (Woodman, Cazenave, & Le Scanff, 2008), the unidimensional state anxiety of two groups of female skydivers was ascertained 30 minutes before, 10 minutes after, and 70 minutes after their jump from their airplane. Results showed no time difference in state anxiety for the group of nonalexithymic skydivers, while time differences were significant for the group of alexithymic skydivers. For the alexithymic skydivers, state anxiety was high to begin with, dropped significantly right after the dive, but rose again 70–90 minutes after their jump. **Alexithymia** is defined as a difficulty in acknowledging one's own emotions and feelings along with the inability to express them to others. For this high-risk sport, alexithymic women's ability to express their emotions was facilitated.

FIGURE 7.3 | Changes in competitive state anxiety prior to competition (decline in cognitive anxiety fluctuates with probability of success/failure).

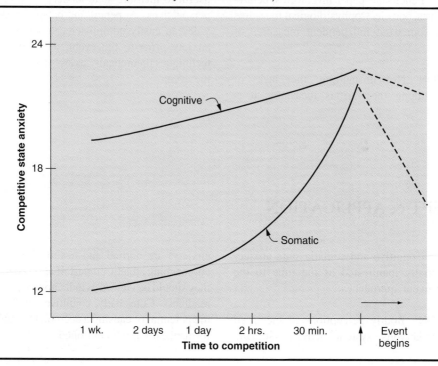

Perfectionism in Sport

Perfectionism and anxiety are not the same, but because they are sometimes strongly associated with each other, perfectionism in sport is discussed in this chapter (Hall, Kerr, & Matthews, 1998; Stoeber, Otto, Pescheck, Becker, & Stoll, 2007). Studies show that perfectionism is multidimensional and that the various factors attributed to perfectionism can be reduced down to two overarching factors (Sager & Stoeber, 2009). The first is functional perfectionism and the second is dysfunctional perfectionism. **Functional perfectionism** is positive in nature and considered to be adaptive. Functional perfectionism is characterized by perfectionistic strivings, high personal standards, desire for organization, self-oriented striving, and other oriented striving. Conversely, **dysfunctional perfectionism** is negative in nature and considered

to be maladaptive. Dysfunctional perfectionism includes such things as perfectionistic concerns, concern over mistakes, parental expectations, parental criticism, self-doubts about actions, and socially prescribed expectations (Anshel & Sutarso, 2010). Finally, research reported by Appleton, Hall, and Hill (2010) suggests that perfectionism in children is predicted by parental perfectionism.

Measuring Perfectionism

In the literature, four different but related inventories have been developed or utilized to measure perfectionism in athletes. We will discuss these briefly to help the student to understand the multidimensional nature of perfectionism. The *Frost Multidimensional Perfectionism Scale* (FMPS; Frost, Marten, Lahart, & Rosenblate, 1990) was composed of 35 items that measured six subscales

FIGURE 7.6 | Application of the Yerkes-Dodson law in athletic events.

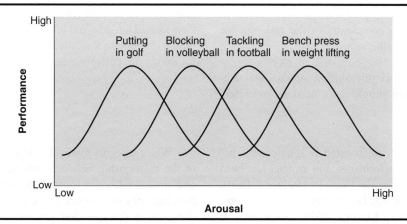

FIGURE 7.7 | Application of the Yerkes-Dodson law to tennis players at various skill levels.

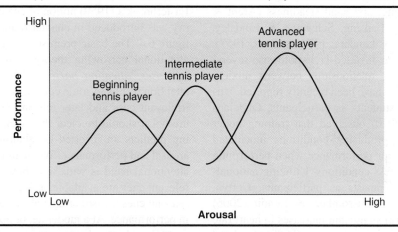

As can be observed in figure 7.6, a high level of arousal is necessary for the best performance in gross motor activities such as weight lifting. Conversely, a lower level of arousal is best for a fine motor task such as putting in golf. Each sport skill has its theoretical optimal level of arousal for best performance. Regardless of which type of skill is being performed, they all conform to the inverted-U principle. Specifically, performance is lowest when arousal is very high or very low, and highest when arousal is moderate, or optimum.

Another important consideration relating to the Yerkes-Dodson law is skill level. Just as putting in golf is a complex activity compared to weight lifting, learning to dribble a basketball is more difficult for a beginner than for someone performing the same task as an expert. The optimal level of arousal for a beginner should be considerably lower than the optimal level for an expert performing the same task. As illustrated in figure 7.7, this concept explains why highly skilled athletes often perform better in competitive situations than do novices.

CONCEPT   The optimal level of arousal varies as a function of the complexity of the task and the skill level of the athlete.

APPLICATION   Highly skilled athletes and athletes performing simple tasks need a moderately high level of arousal for maximum performance. Less skilled athletes and athletes performing complex tasks require a relatively low level of arousal for maximum performance.

Evidence of an inverted-U relationship between athletic performance and arousal has been well documented in the literature (Beuter & Duda, 1985; Burton, 1988; Gould, Petlichkoff, Simons, & Vevera, 1987; Klavora, 1978; Sonstroem & Bernado, 1982). The inverted-U relationship has also been documented between arousal and performance on laboratory tasks such as reaction time, auditory tracking, and hand steadiness (Arent & Landers, 2003; Lansing, Schwartz, & Lindsley, 1956; Martens & Landers, 1970; Stennet, 1957). Unrelated to the inverted-U hypothesis, several other interesting relationships between anxiety and performance have been recently reported. Utilizing college students as participants, Oudejans and Pijpers (2010) observed that training under mildly anxiety-producing conditions inoculated them against poor performance when performing later in high-stress conditions. Utilizing national-level female gymnasts as participants, Cottyn, de Clercq, Pannier, Crombez, & Lenoir (2006) observed that (a) significant increases in heart rate (HR) during training and competition is associated with reduced performance, (b) HR is higher during competition compared to training, and (c) falls and foibles are associated with significant increases in HR during training and competition. Finally, utilizing novice skiers as participants, Kunzell and Muller (2008) observed that early training with short and wide "bigfoot" skis results in lower anxiety toward skiing later in their instruction compared to a control group. Taken together, these studies all illustrate the critical relationship between anxiety and arousal with athletic performance.

While it seems relatively clear that the nature of the relationship between athletic performance and arousal takes the form of the inverted U, it is not clear why this occurs. In the following subsections, three theories that predict the inverted-U relationship will be briefly reviewed.

Easterbrook's Cue Utilization Theory

Easterbrook's (1959) notion of cue utilization theory was introduced in chapter 6 and illustrated in figure 6.4. The basic premise of cue utilization or attentional narrowing theory is that *as arousal increases, attention narrows*. The narrowing of attention results in some cues being gated out, first irrelevant cues and later relevant cues. From figure 6.4 it should be clear that attentional narrowing predicts an inverted-U relationship between arousal and performance. When arousal is low, the attentional band is wide, and both irrelevant and relevant cues are available. The presence of the irrelevant cues is distracting and causes a decrement in performance. At a moderate, or optimal, level of arousal, only the irrelevant cues are eliminated, and therefore performance is high. Finally, when arousal is high, attentional focus is narrow, and both relevant and irrelevant cues are gated out. This results in a decrement in performance, as predicted by the inverted-U theory.

Cue utilization theory also addresses the problem of task complexity and learning. With a complex or unlearned motor skill, there are a greater number of task-relevant cues to manage. Consequently, with increased arousal, the probability of error increases at a faster rate than it would for a simple motor skill. Because there are

CONCEPT   Increased arousal has the effect of narrowing an athlete's attention.

APPLICATION   Athletes who participate in a sport that requires broad attentional awareness need lower levels of arousal for best performance. The setter in volleyball must be particularly aware of all aspects of the game. Narrow vision would seem to be particularly damaging to the setter's play selection.

CONCEPT   Decreased arousal has the effect of broadening an athlete's attentional focus.

APPLICATION   Athletes who participate in a sport that requires narrow attentional focus need appropriately increased levels of arousal for optimal performance. An athlete attempting a single feat of power and force will need a narrowed focus of attention.

so many task-relevant cues to manage, the relevant as well as irrelevant cues get gated out as arousal increases and attention narrows.

Signal Detection Theory   Another theory that predicts a curvilinear relationship between arousal and performance is signal detection theory (SDT). **Signal detection theory** is a theory of perception that predicts that increased decision errors will occur when an individual is either insensitive to a physical stimulus (stringent response criterion) or supersensitive to a physical stimulus (lenient response criterion). The lowest number of decision errors should occur with an optimal, or balanced, sensitivity to stimuli.

According to signal detection theory, the response criterion, or sensitivity to a physical stimulus, changes as a function of physiological arousal. At a very low level of arousal, the individual exhibits a stringent response criterion and is insensitive to signals from the environment (errors of omission). At a very high level of arousal, the individual exhibits a lenient response criterion and is very sensitive to signals from the environment (errors of commission). At a moderate level of arousal, the individual exhibits an optimal, or balanced, response criterion (fewer errors). Thus, low and high levels of arousal are associated with a large number of signal detection errors, while an optimal or moderate level of arousal is associated with fewer signal detection errors. This pattern of errors is consistent with inverted-U theory.

Consider an example in American football. The defensive lineman is interested in exploding out of his ready position and across the line of scrimmage when he detects the ball has been snapped. There is considerable advantage to be gained from exploding across the line of scrimmage before the offensive line can block movement. If the linesman is underaroused, he will not get across the line as quickly as he should; this represents an error of omission. If the linesman is overaroused, he will explode across the line of scrimmage too quickly and be called for being offside. This would be an error of commission. If the linesman is optimally aroused with a moderate

171

CONCEPT Athletes in sports that require instant decisions require a moderate level of arousal to avoid errors of commission or omission.

APPLICATION An overly aroused batter in baseball will tend to swing at bad pitches (error of commission), while an underaroused hitter will allow called strikes (error of omission). A moderate level of arousal will tend to balance out the two kinds of decision errors.

level of arousal, he will move with the snap of the ball and make fewer errors of either commission or omission. For a detailed review of signal detection theory applied to sport, see Cox (1998).

Information Processing Theory The basic predictions of information processing theory for the arousal/performance relationship are identical to those of signal detection theory. Both theories predict the inverted-U relationship between performance and arousal, and both support the Yerkes-Dodson law. Welford (1962, 1965) gives a basic outline of the theory's predictions.

According to Welford (1962, 1973), brain cells become active with increased levels of arousal, and they begin to fire. As this happens, the information processing system becomes noisy, and its channel capacity is reduced. At low levels of arousal, the system is relatively inert and performance is low. At high levels of arousal, a performance decrement occurs because of the reduced information processing capacity of the channels. At some optimal level of arousal, the information processing capacity of the system is at its maximum, and performance is at its best.

Drive Theory

Perhaps the great contribution of drive theory is that it helps to explain the relationships between learning and arousal, and between performance and arousal. Many young athletes are just beginning the process of becoming skilled performers. The effect of arousal upon a beginner may be different from its effect upon a skilled performer. The basic relationship between arousal and an athlete's performance at any skill level is given in the following formula:

$$\text{Performance} = \text{Arousal} \times \text{Skill Level}$$

As developed by Hull (1943, 1951) and Spence (1956), drive theory is a complex stimulus-response theory of motivation and learning. It is a theory of competing responses, in which increased **drive** (arousal) facilitates the elicitation of the dominant response. The basic tenets of drive theory are as follows:

1. Increased arousal (drive) will elicit the dominant response.

2. The response associated with the strongest potential to respond is the dominant response.

3. Early in learning or for complex tasks, the dominant response is the incorrect response.

4. Late in learning or for simple tasks, the dominant response is the correct response.

We can make several practical applications of these drive theory tenets. First, heightened levels of arousal should benefit the skilled performer, but hamper the beginner. The coach with a relatively young team should strive to create an atmosphere relatively low in anxiety and arousal. Low levels of arousal should increase the beginner's chances of a successful performance. In turn, the experience of success should strengthen self-confidence. Skilled athletes, on the other hand, will benefit from an

CONCEPT & APPLICATION

CONCEPT The effect of increased arousal on an athlete performing a complex task or learning a novel task will be to elicit an incorrect response, which is the dominant response.

APPLICATION With beginners it is important that the environment be one of low arousal and stress. Young athletes tend to make more mistakes if they become excited and overly activated.

CONCEPT & APPLICATION

CONCEPT The effect of increased arousal on an athlete performing a simple or well-learned task will be to elicit a correct response, which is the dominant response.

APPLICATION Highly skilled athletes will often benefit from increased arousal. Psyching up a basketball star like Michael Jordan, Kobe Bryant, or Le Bron James could have grave consequences for the opposing team.

increase in arousal. Similar applications can be made to the performance of simple and complex tasks. For example, a complex task, such as throwing a knuckleball in baseball, will always require a low level of arousal. Conversely, a very simple task, such as doing a high number of push-ups, would seem to benefit from arousal. A case in point is a study reported by Davis and Harvey (1992). Utilizing drive theory predictions, the researchers hypothesized that increased arousal caused by major league baseball pressure situations would cause a decrement in batting (a complex task). Four late-game pressure situations were compared with nonpressure situations relative to batting performance. Results showed a decrement in batting performance associated with increased arousal, as predicted by drive theory.

Drive theory received tremendous amounts of attention from researchers between 1943 and 1970. However, since then, interest in the theory has diminished significantly. The theory was extremely difficult to test, and the tests that were conducted often yielded conflicting results. For an in-depth review of research associated with drive theory, the reader is referred to Cox (1990).

Mood State and Athletic Performance

As introduced in the beginning of this chapter, a **mood state** differs from an emotion in that it is more diffuse and may last for weeks or even months. Emotions are instantaneous discrete responses to the environment and last for only seconds, minutes, or perhaps hours. While a mood state is more stable than an emotion, both differ from a personality disposition in that they are not enduring traits. Mellalieu (2003) differentiated between emotions and moods as follows:

> Emotions are suggested to be relatively brief but intense experiences activated by cognitive appraisal of situation factors, while moods are deemed less intense, more prolonged experiences that relate to the individual rather than the situation. (Mellalier, 2003, p. 100)

As we learned in chapter 2, there has been a great deal of interest in discovering if a relationship exists between personality and athletic performance. Similarly, researchers have been interested in discovering if a predictive relationship exists between mood states and athletic performance. In the pages that follow, we will discuss (a) measurement of mood state, (b) Morgan's mental health model, and (c) mood state relationships in sport.

Measurement of Mood State

While other inventories have been developed for measuring mood states, the inventory most commonly used by sport psychologists is the **Profile of Mood States** (POMS; McNair, Lorr, & Droppleman, 1992). The POMS is published by the Educational and Industrial Testing Service (EDITS). LeUnes and Burger (1998) noted that the POMS was first used in 1975 by sport psychologists, and was used with 257 published articles between 1975 and 1998. More recently, McNair, Heuchert, and Shilony (2003) documented the use of the POMS in more than 5,000 educational and industrial studies between 1964 and 2002.

The most commonly used version of the POMS is the original 65-item version that measures the following six mood states: tension, depression, anger, vigor, fatigue, and confusion. Five of these mood states are negative in nature, while one is positive (vigor). Since the original development of the 65-item version of POMS, two additional EDITS versions have been developed. One of them was a bipolar 72-item version, and the other a short 30-item version. Recent psychometric analyses of the POMS reveal that compared to the 65-item version, the 30-item short version of the POMS is the superior instrument. The factorial

Does this highly successful collegiate athlete exhibit the mood state "iceberg profile" of the elite athlete? Courtesy University of Missouri–Columbia Sports Information.

integrity of the 65-item POMS was called into question because of failure of the confusion factor to fit the data as hypothesized (Bourgeois, LeUnes, & Myers, 2010).

In addition to the three authorized versions of the POMS mentioned above, independent researchers have developed four other shortened

TABLE 7.3 | Authorized and Independently Developed Versions of the Profile of Mood States (POMS)

Category	Items	POMS Version
Authorized	65	Profile of Mood States (McNair et al., 1971, 1981, 1992)
	72	Profile of Mood States—Bipolar (Lorr & McNair, 1988)
	30	Profile of Mood States—Short version (McNair et al., 1992)
Independent	37	Shortened Version of POMS (Shacham, 1983)
	40	Abbreviated POMS (Grove & Prapavessis, 1992)
	27	Short POMS for Young Athletes (Terry, Keohane, & Lane, 1996)
	06	Brief Assessment of Mood (Whelan & Meyers, 1998)

versions (LeUnes & Burger, 2000; Terry, 1995). These four versions, along with the three authorized versions of the POMS are listed in table 7.3. Research has shown that all of the shortened versions are correlated with the 65-item POMS (Bourgeois, LeUnes, & Myers, 2010).

The Profile of Mood States and Morgan's Mental Health Model

It appears that Morgan (1979) was one of the first to utilize the Profile of Mood States (POMS) in sport- and exercise-related research. Morgan plotted standardized POMS scores for elite athletes and noted that (a) elite athletes exhibited a **mood profile** that was lower in negative moods and higher in vigor than a normative sample, and (b) elite athletes also exhibited a more mentally healthy mood profile than less successful athletes. Morgan referred to the notion that the successful athlete exhibits a more healthy mood profile than less successful athletes or a normative population as the **mental health model.** According to this model, the successful athlete is viewed as a mentally healthy individual relative to psychological mood. When the standardized POMS scores of the elite athlete are plotted as in figure 7.8, they take the form of an iceberg, with all of the negative moods falling below the population norm and the vigor

score falling well above the norm. This mood profile has come to be referred to as the **iceberg profile.**

Research has been very supportive of the notion that the successful athlete exhibits an iceberg profile relative to the population norm (average of the population), but not so supportive in terms of discriminating between successful and less successful athletes. We will discuss the issue of discriminating among athletes in the next section.

Terry and Lane (2000), however, found strong support for the notion that the athlete exhibits a mood profile that is superior to that of the population norm. They administered the POMS to 2,086 athletes and found differences between the athletic sample and the existing population norm for all mood subscales. Consistent with the mental health model, athletes exhibit lower negative mood states and a higher vigor score compared to a POMS normative sample of a similar age group.

Mood State Relationships in Sport

As with personality research, investigators have been interested in studying the relationship between **precompetitive mood** and athletic performance. One approach has been to determine if athletes belonging to different achievement levels can be differentiated based on mood state measures. A

FIGURE 7.8 | Illustration of the iceberg profile of the elite athlete.

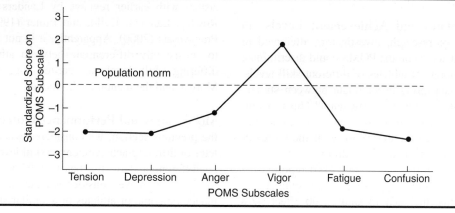

7.15 CONCEPT & APPLICATION

CONCEPT Researchers cannot consistently and effectively discriminate between athletes of differing skill level on the basis of mood state scores alone.

APPLICATION You will note that we observed a similar outcome when we tried to discriminate between athletes of different skill level based on

personality. While the mental health model does discriminate between athletes and nonathletes, it is not a reliable predictor of whether an athlete belongs to a high achievement group or a low achievement group. As with personality, coaches should not use POMS scores to make personnel decisions.

7.16 CONCEPT & APPLICATION

CONCEPT A weak to moderate relationship exists between precompetitive mood and performance outcome. This relationship is enhanced when performance is measured subjectively as opposed to objectively.

APPLICATION An athlete's mood prior to an athletic contest is related to athletic performance. The

less negative mood and the more positive mood the athlete experiences, the better he is likely to perform. This relationship is not so strong, however, that the coach should use it to predict objective performance outcome.

---

second approach has been to determine if performance outcome can be predicted based on precompetitive mood. In this section, we will consider both of these approaches. In addition, a conceptual model for studying the relationship between mood and performance will be considered.

Mood States and Achievement Levels In this line of research, investigators attempted to show that scores on the POMS could discriminate among groups of athletes of different skill levels. That is, can mood differentiate between starters and nonstarters on an athletic team? This is a situation in which athletes of clearly different skill levels are given the POMS to see if the scores of the differently skilled groups differ.

Beedie, Terry, and Lane (2000) reported the results of a **meta-analysis** (statistical summary of studies) that included 13 studies, 90 effect sizes

(mean comparisons), and 2,285 participants. The overall **effect size** for this investigation was .10, which is considered to be very low (Cohen, 1992). Except for a small difference in vigor scores, athletes at different levels of achievement report essentially the same moods. These results are consistent with earlier reviews by Landers (1991); Rowley, Landers, Kyllo, and Etnier (1995); and Prapavessis (2000). Apparently, it is not possible to consistently differentiate between athletes of differing skill level, as earlier suggested by Morgan and the mental health model.

Mood States and Performance Outcome In the previous section, we considered whether athletes of differing achievement or skill levels could be differentiated on the basis of POMS scores. In this section we consider whether the performance outcome of athletes of a similar skill level

CONCEPT Depression moderates the relationship between the other mood states and athletic performance. In the presence of depression, the increased levels of negative mood will have a debilitating effect on performance. Increased depression is also associated with reduced vigor, which results in a reduced facilitative effect.

APPLICATION Coaches and athletes must be concerned about the debilitating levels of depression. Depression can negatively influence the other moods, as well as performance. If high levels of depression are suspected, the athlete may need to seek professional help from a counseling or clinical sport psychologist.

---

can be predicted based on POMS scores. If I know an athlete's precompetitive mood profile, can I use it to predict how she will do in the competition?

Beedie et al. (2000) reported the results of a second meta-analysis that included 16 studies, 102 effect sizes, and 1,126 participants. The overall effect size for this investigation was .35, which is considered to be small to medium. In addition, some moderating variables were identified. A moderating variable is a variable that determines the relationship between two other variables. Moderating variables to be considered here included type of sport and how performance was measured.

Type of Sport Performance was predicted a little better in open skills as opposed to closed skills. Closed skills are believed to be closed to the environment (e.g., bowling, clean-and-jerk), while open skills are believed to be open to the environment (e.g., tennis, soccer). Effects were slightly larger for individual sports compared to team sports, and effects were larger for short-duration sports (rowing, wrestling) compared to long-duration sports (e.g., basketball, volleyball).

Measurement of Performance Effects were larger when performance outcome was conceptualized as subjective and self-referenced, as opposed to objective. An objective outcome would be whether you won or lost a contest, or whether you recorded a better time than another athlete in a contest. Examples of subjective self-referenced outcomes include (a) a post-event self-rating of performance, (b) percentage of a personal best, and (c) comparison to expectations. In post-event self-rating, an athlete has an opportunity to subjectively indicate how she feels she performed independent of objective outcome (win/loss). In the percentage of personal best method, performance is measured as a percentage of how the athlete did compared to her personal best. If she lost a race, but performed at 95 percent of her personal best, this may be a better performance outcome than the 90 percent of personal best displayed by the winner. Finally, in the comparison to expectations method, the athlete compares her performance with how she expected to perform. For example, an athlete's expected performance in golf is her golf handicap. If she normally shoots seven over par and she shoots four over par today, she has had a good performance, regardless of objective outcome.

A stronger relationship exists between mood and performance when performance is measured subjectively than when it is measured objectively. If you are simply trying to predict whether an athlete wins or loses a contest or finishes higher than another runner in a race, mood is a relatively weak predictor of performance (effect size = .28). If you are trying to predict if an athlete will perform up to personal expectations and past performance, then the relationship between mood and performance is a little stronger (effect size = .37). Cohen (1992) has indicated that effect sizes of .20, .50, and .80 are considered to be small, medium, and large, respectively.

A Conceptual Model for Predicting Performance Based on the literature, Lane and

Terry (2000) proposed a **conceptual model of mood** for explaining the relationship between precompetitive mood and performance. At the present time the model should be considered to be theoretical in nature. A theory allows investigators to test various aspects of a model to either modify it, verify it, or reject it. For this reason, a testable theory is very important to the advancement of science.

Lane and Terry propose that depression is a moderator between other manifestations of mood and athletic performance. As can be observed in figure 7.9, *high levels of depression are associated with increased anger, tension, confusion, and fatigue, but with reduced vigor.* The increased levels of negative mood have a debilitative effect upon performance, while

FIGURE 7.9 | Lane and Terry's (2000) conceptual model to predict performance from precompetitive mood.

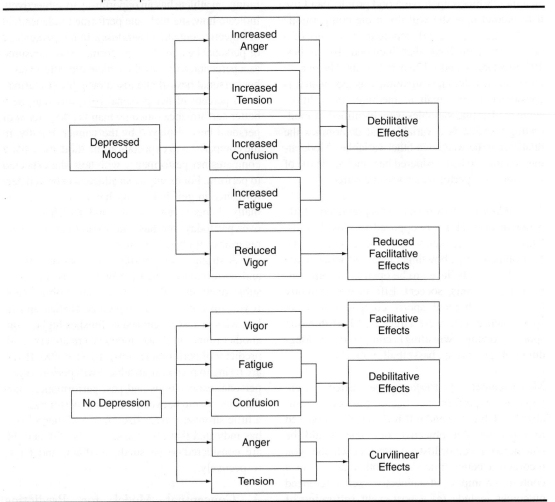

reduced vigor has a reduced facilitative effect upon performance.

In the *absence of depression,* vigor will have a facilitative effect on performance, fatigue and confusion will have a debilitative effect upon performance, and anger and tension will have a curvilinear effect upon performance. Note that fatigue and confusion are predicted to have a debilitative effect upon performance regardless of whether the athlete is depressed or not. Anger and tension, in the absence of depression, can actually facilitate performance up to a point, but when they get too high they will cause a decrement in performance.

Some of the tenets of the conceptual model were tested by Lane, Terry, Beedie, Curry, and Clark (2002) utilizing a large sample (N = 451) of school-age children. Mood was assessed, using an adolescent version of the POMS, 10 minutes prior to a running competition in which participants completed a self-referenced race for distance or time. Consistent with the conceptual model, participants categorized as depressed scored higher on anger, confusion, fatigue and tension, but lower in vigor compared to the nondepressed group. Also

consistent with the conceptual model, larger correlations were observed among the moods of anger, tension, confusion, fatigue, and vigor for the depressed mood group compared to the nondepressed group. As predicted, vigor significantly predicted increased performance regardless of level of depression; however, confusion and fatigue did not lead to a reduction in performance as expected. Finally, in the depressed group, anger predicted reduced performance as expected, but anger in the no-depression group and tension in both groups failed to influence performance as expected. Overall, this study provided support for some aspects of the Lane and Terry (2000) conceptual model, partial support for others, and no support for the notion that a curvilinear relationship would exist between anger and tension with performance in the no-depression group. Finally, it is important to note that while many predicted relationships were significant, due to a large sample size, many of the significant effects were very weak. Clearly, the model needs further testing before we can conclude that depression acts as a moderator of the relationship between mood state and athletic performance.

Summary

Affect is a generic term used to describe emotions, feelings, and moods. Emotion is a situation specific affective response to the environment. Anxiety is one example of 15 specific emotions identified by Lazarus. While emotions are instantaneous discrete responses to the environment, moods are more diffuse and may last for weeks or months. Selye defined stress as the "nonspecific response to the body to any demand placed upon it." Distress and eustress are two manifestations of stress; distress is equated with state anxiety.

Anxiety is multidimensional in two different ways. First, anxiety can be conceptualized as a

personality disposition (trait anxiety) or as situation-specific emotional response to an environmental stimulus (state anxiety). Secondly, both trait and state anxiety can be conceptualized as being cognitive (cognitive anxiety) or somatic (somatic anxiety) in nature. A number of unidimensional and multidimensional inventories have been developed for measuring state and trait anxiety prior to and during competition.

The best way to understand stress is to conceptualize it as a process, as opposed to an outcome. The stress process begins with a stimulus and ends with the potential of a response. Distress and state anxiety (stress response) only occurs if an imbalance is perceived between the stimulus and the individual's perceived ability to cope with the stimulus threat. Competitive state anxiety that occurs prior to a competitive situation is referred to as precompetitive state anxiety. Antecedents that precede the competitive state anxiety response include such things as fear of performance failure, fear of negative social evaluation, fear of physical harm, situation ambiguity, and disruption of a well-learned routine.

Precompetitive cognitive anxiety starts relatively high and remains high and stable as the time-to-event approaches. Conversely, somatic anxiety remains relatively low until approximately 24 hours before the event, and then increases rapidly as the event approaches. Once performance begins, somatic anxiety dissipates rapidly, whereas cognitive state anxiety fluctuates throughout the contest as the probability of success/failure changes.

Perfectionism is multidimensional in nature and can be reduced to two overarching factors named functional perfectionism and dysfunctional perfectionism. Four inventories are identified that measure multidimensional perfectionism. These include the Frost Multidimensional Perfectionism Scale (FMPS), the Hewitt Multidimensional Perfectionism Scale (HMPS), the Sport Multidimensional Perfectionism Scale (Sport-MPS), and the Multidimensional Inventory of Perfectionism in Sport. Overall striving for perfection is associated with elevated cognitive and somatic state anxiety, but when functional and dysfunctional perfectionism are considered separately, a different result is obtained. Functional perfectionism predicts lower levels of state anxiety and higher levels of self-confidence, whereas dysfunctional perfectionism predicts elevated levels of somatic and cognitive state anxiety.

The relationship between arousal/anxiety and athletic performance is represented best by the inverted-U curve. The foundation of inverted-U theory is the classic work of Yerkes and Dodson (1908). Three theories that predict a curvilinear relationship between performance and arousal are cue utilization, signal detection theory, and information processing theory. Conversely, drive theory posits a linear relationship between arousal and performance. Perhaps the greatest contribution of drive theory is that it helps to explain the relationship between arousal and learning as well as arousal and performance.

As introduced in the beginning of the chapter, a mood state differs from an emotion in that it is more diffuse and may last for weeks or even months. While other inventories have been developed for measuring mood states, the most commonly used inventory used in sport is the Profile of Mood States (POMS). The POMS measure the moods of tension, depression, anger, vigor, fatigue, and confusion. The mental health model and the iceberg profile of the elite athlete all describe a mood profile in which negative moods are low and positive mood is high. It is not recommended that any attempt be made to distinguish between athletes' differing skill levels based on POMS scores. However, it may be possible to make a modest prediction of performance outcome based on precompetitive POMS scores if sport type and method of defining success are taken into consideration. Lane and Terry (2000) proposed a conceptual model of mood as a theoretical approach to predicting mood effects on performance outcome. The theory identifies the mood of depression as a moderator variable in the model.

Critical Thought Questions

1. Differentiate among the terms *emotion*, *anxiety*, *stress*, and *mood*. Provide examples of each showing differences and why they are different.

2. Discuss and clarify Selye's notion of stress relative to your answer to question number one.

3. Discuss the stress process, and give examples of each stage of the process. What is the importance of appraisal and coping in the model? What is meant by a balance between the stressful nature of a competitive situation and the athlete's perceived ability to cope with the situation?

4. Provide some practical application suggestions about research associated with the time to event nature of precompetitive anxiety.

5. Differentiate between functional and dysfunctional perfectionism and relate perfectionism to anxiety and motivation (e.g., autonomous motivation, goal orientation, attribution).

6. How is mood state measured and how does mood relate to athletic performance?

Glossary

affect A generic term used to describe emotions, feelings, and moods.

alexithymia Difficulty in acknowledging ones' own emotions and feelings along with inability to express them to others.

antecedent A preceding event or predictor of a later event.

anxiety Facing uncertain, existential threat.

cognitive anxiety The mental component of anxiety, caused by such things as fear of negative social evaluation, fear of failure, and loss of self-esteem.

competitive situation Situation-specific achievement environment that involves competition.

competitive state anxiety State anxiety associated with a competitive situation.

conceptual model of mood Theoretical model that explains how mood predicts performance, and one in which depression is a moderator variable that determines how the other moods affect performance.

distress According to Selye, bad stress, as represented by such things as anger and anxiety.

drive Represented by arousal and anxiety within the drive theory model.

drive theory A complex theory of learning that predicts a linear relationship between drive (arousal) and learning or performance.

dysfunctional perfectionism Perfectionism that is negative in nature and considered to be maladaptive.

effect size The number of times that a pooled standard deviation can be divided into the difference between two means.

emotion Instantaneous discrete response to the environment that lasts only seconds, minutes, or perhaps hours.

eustress According to Selye, good stress, as represented by such things as joy and happiness.

functional perfectionism Perfectionism that is positive in nature and considered to be adaptive.

iceberg profile A profile of the elite athlete on the six mood states measured by the POMS. Vigor is the only mood state for which elite athletes score well above the population mean, causing the profile to resemble an iceberg when charted on a graph.

inverted-U theory A model describing the hypothesized curvilinear relationship between arousal and performance. The term originates from the shape of the curve that results when this relationship is plotted on a graph.

mental health model Developed by Morgan, a model that proposes that the elite athlete is a mentally healthy individual.

meta-analysis Based on effect sizes, a statistical summary and comparison of independent samples associated with a literature review.

mood While emotions are directed toward something associated with the environment, moods are more diffuse and relate to how we are doing in our life.

mood profile Plotting of standardized mood state scores on a graph.

mood state Differs from an emotion in that it is more diffuse and may last for weeks or even months.

multidimensional The notion that a particular concept or psychological construct is composed of several different dimensions as opposed to just one.

organizational stress Stress placed on an athlete by the competitive sport environment, not just the coaches or a specific competitive event.

precompetitive mood An athlete's mood immediately before a competitive event.

precompetitive state anxiety Competitive state anxiety that occurs prior to or in anticipation of competition.

primary appraisal The first state of appraisal in the stress process, in which the individual determines the personal importance of the outcome of a situation.

profile of Mood States (POMS) A 65-item inventory designed to measure a person's mood state on six subscales.

secondary appraisal The second stage of appraisal in the stress process which involves appraisal of the individual's coping resources.

signal detection theory A theory of perception that predicts that increased decision errors will occur when an individual is either insensitive or supersensitive to a physical stimulus.

somatic anxiety The physical component of anxiety that reflects the perception of such physiological responses as increased heart rate, respiration, and muscular tension.

state anxiety An immediate emotional state that is characterized by apprehension, fear, tension, and an increase in physiological arousal.

stress The nonspecific response of the body to any demand made upon it.

stress process The process by which a potential stressful event elicits a stress response following an unfavorable appraisal of coping resources.

trait anxiety A predisposition to perceive certain environmental situations as threatening and to respond to these situations with increased state anxiety.

Yerkes-Dodson law A principle based on the classic work by Yerkes and Dodson (1908) that predicts an inverted-U relationship between arousal and performance.

CHAPTER 8

Alternatives to Inverted-U Theory

KEY TERMS

Athlete engagement
Autotelic experience
Butterfly catastrophe model
Catastrophe theory
Core flow
Cusp catastrophe model
Direction component of
  anxiety
Flow
Frequency component of
  anxiety
Hysteresis
Individual affect-related
  performance zone
Individual zone of optimal
  functioning
Intensity component of anxiety
Intraindividualized scores
Ipsative z-score
Metamotivational
Mindfulness
Multidimensional anxiety
  theory
Multiple baseline single
  subject design
Orthogonal model of flow

Paratelic-dominant individual
Pleasant dysfunctional
  emotions
Pleasant functional emotions
Prestart state anxiety
Probabilistic model
Protective frame
Psychological reversal
Recall method

Reversal theory
Standard deviation
Telic-dominant individual
Unpleasant dysfunctional
  emotions
Unpleasant functional
  emotions
z-score

In the previous chapter we learned that the primary theory sport psychologists have used to explain the relationship between anxiety and performance is inverted-U theory. For a number of reasons, however, sport psychologists have turned to other more complex theories to explain this relationship. It is believed by many that the inverted-U theory is a simple theory that does not capture or explain the complexities of the anxiety-performance relationship.

As you look back to figure 7.4, relative to inverted-U theory, you will note that the hypothesized relationship between anxiety and performance is smooth, suggesting that smooth and measured changes in performance occur in conjunction with gradual and measured increases in anxiety/arousal. We can think of many examples that would suggest that changes in performance associated with changes in anxiety are anything but smooth. A case in point is the real-life experience (or rather, nightmare) of professional golfer Greg Norman (Reilly, 1996). After the third round of the 1996 Masters golf tournament, Greg Norman held a six-shot lead over his nearest competitor, with just one round (18 holes) to go. On Sunday, during the final and fourth round, came the most "catastrophic" four holes in Greg's professional career. On the ninth through the twelfth holes, he surrendered his six-stroke lead to Nick Faldo. He then went on to lose the Masters by five strokes.

Whether the theories that we will discuss in this chapter are really alternatives to inverted-U theory or just modifications is a matter of discussion by sport psychologists. Clearly, you will see some aspects of inverted-U theory in all of the theories that we will discuss. The six anxiety performance theories we will discuss in this chapter include (a) Martens' multidimensional anxiety theory, (b) Fazey and Hardy's catastrophe theory, (c) Hanin's individual zone of optimal functioning theory, (d) Csikszentmihalyi's concept of flow, (e) Jones's directionality theory, and (f) Apter's reversal theory.

Martens's Multidimensional Anxiety Theory

Multidimensional anxiety theory (Martens, Vealey, et al., 1990) is based on the notion that anxiety is multidimensional in nature, composed of a cognitive anxiety component and a somatic anxiety component. As you will recall, multidimensional anxiety theory and the multidimensional nature of anxiety were introduced in chapter 7. At that time, however, we did not discuss the specific anxiety-performance relationship that is hypothesized by multidimensional anxiety theory. Relative to anxiety, multidimensional theory specifically hypothesizes these things:

1. A negative linear relationship exists between cognitive state anxiety and athletic performance.

2. An inverted-U relationship exists between somatic anxiety and performance.

The two basic principles of multidimensional anxiety theory are illustrated in figure 8.1. The relationships displayed in this figure are consistent with research conducted by Burton (1988) using swimmers and by Gould, Petlichkoff, et al. (1987) using pistol shooting. While this relationship is very appealing and seems to make practical sense, many investigators have failed to confirm multidimensional anxiety theory as illustrated in figure 8.1 (Jerome & Williams, 2000).

Because **intraindividualized scores** or ipsative z-scores are routinely mentioned in the sport psychology literature (Burton, 1988; Gould Petlichkoff, et al., 1987; Sonstroem & Bernando, 1982), it is useful for the beginning sport psychology student to be familiar with how these scores are computed. As you are probably aware, a **z-score** is a standardized score formed by subtracting the mean (m) of a group of scores from a single subject's score (x) and dividing by the group **standard deviation** (z = x − m ÷ sd).

In the case of the **ipsative z-score,** you do the same thing as with a regular z-score, but you use

FIGURE 8.1 | Multidimensional theory relationship between athletic performance and state anxiety.

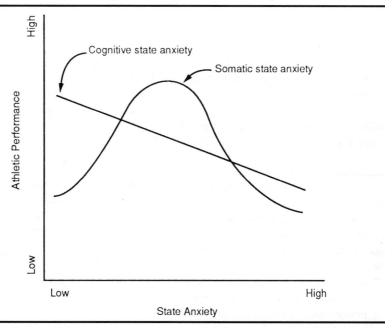

the mean and standard deviation associated with a specific individual's multiple observations. By way of illustration, assume that an athlete completed an anxiety inventory 25 times over a three-week period. This would yield 25 separate anxiety scores for this one athlete. Assume that the mean and standard deviation for the 25 observations were 30 and 5, respectively, and that the athlete's anxiety score for the 10th observation was 25. The ipsative z-score for this specific observation would be -1.00 ($25 - 30 \div 5 = -1.00$). You could then calculate the ipsative z-scores for all 25 observations. In any subsequent data analysis, it would be the ipsatized or intraindividualized scores that would enter into the analysis.

Fazey and Hardy's Catastrophe Theory

A fundamental weakness of Martens' multidimensional theory is the notion that cognitive anxiety and somatic anxiety have independent effects upon athletic performance. Looking at figure 8.1, consider the case in which an athlete exhibits a high level of cognitive anxiety and a moderate level of somatic anxiety. What would be the predicted level of performance in this case? If you looked at the prediction line for cognitive anxiety, you would predict poor performance. Conversely, if you looked at the prediction line for somatic anxiety, you would predict high performance. Can you have it both ways? Not likely. Cognitive and somatic anxiety must work together in some interactive way to affect performance. What is needed is a theory that can consider the independent effects of anxiety and physiological arousal in the same model. Fazey and Hardy's catastrophe theory is just such a model.

As illustrated in figure 7.4, inverted-U theory predicts a smooth bell-shaped (inverted U) curve relationship between physiological arousal and athletic performance. The basic assumptions of the theory are that (a) small incremental increases in arousal result in small incremental increases or decreases in performance, and that (b) moderate

CONCEPT According to multidimensional anxiety theory, an inverted-U relationship should exist between athletic performance and somatic state anxiety. Conversely, a negative linear relationship should exist between cognitive state anxiety and athletic performance.

APPLICATION Consistent with predictions of multidimensional anxiety theory, an athlete should seek to obtain a moderate level of somatic anxiety or perceived arousal (heart rate, tension, jitters, etc.), and a low level of cognitive state anxiety (fear of failure, fear of performing poorly, etc.). Ideally, a low level of cognitive state anxiety should also be associated with a high level of self-efficacy and confidence.

arousal results in optimal performance. **Catastrophe theory** questions both of these basic assumptions, but more specifically, the notion that small incremental increases in arousal result in small changes in performance. At critical points in the performance curve, quite the opposite may be observed. When faced with debilitating stress and arousal, athletes do not experience small incremental decreases in performance; they suffer large and dramatic decrements that may be described as catastrophic in nature. In addition, once the athlete suffers a catastrophic decrement in performance, small incremental reductions in arousal rarely bring performance back to the pre-catastrophic level (Fazey & Hardy, 1988). Inverted-U theory cannot account for these sudden and extreme reductions in performance. A case in point is the Greg Norman golf example that we discussed at the beginning of this chapter. Greg Norman's golf performance did not decline in small measured amounts; instead, he suffered a catastrophic drop-off in performance.

Unfortunately, the complexity of the catastrophe model is so high that students are typically "discouraged" before they come to appreciate the elegant predictions of the theory. Before we begin a more detailed discussion of the model, it is well that we look at it in a more simplified fashion. In figure 8.2 (a, b, c), the model is represented as a function of level of cognitive anxiety. The basic variables of the model include cognitive anxiety, physiological arousal (not somatic anxiety), and performance.

FIGURE 8.2 | Simplified illustration of the catastrophe model at different levels of cognitive anxiety.

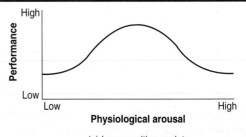

(a) Low cognitive anxiety

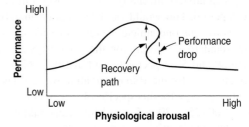

(b) Moderate cognitive anxiety

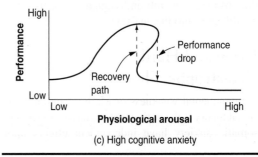

(c) High cognitive anxiety

At the top, figure 8.2 (a) shows that under conditions of *low cognitive anxiety,* the relationship between physiological arousal and athletic performance takes the form of a well-proportioned bell-shaped curve. When cognitive anxiety is very low, the model predicts a smooth inverted-U relationship between performance and arousal. This is the performance situation in which the athlete is not worried about performance outcome or negative social evaluation, yet arousal is free to fluctuate from low to high.

In the middle of figure 8.2, illustration (b) shows that under conditions of *moderate cognitive anxiety,* the relationship between physiological arousal and athletic performance takes the form of a somewhat distorted bell-shaped curve. At a moderate level of cognitive anxiety, the model predicts an increase in performance with increased arousal, but then a fairly significant drop-off in performance as arousal gets too high. As the figure shows, arousal will have to return to a level below

that where the drop-off occurred in order for the athlete to get back to a high level of performance (recovery path).

At the bottom of figure 8.2, section (c) indicates that under conditions of *high cognitive anxiety,* the relationship between physiological arousal and athletic performance takes the form of a very distorted inverted U. At a high level of cognitive anxiety, the model predicts an increase in performance with increased arousal, but then a *catastrophic* drop in performance as arousal gets too high. Again, as the figure shows, arousal will have to return to a level well below that where the drop-off occurred for the athlete to get back to a high level of performance (recovery path).

Fazey and Hardy's catastrophe model is illustrated in figure 8.3. In this model, physiological arousal is represented on the back horizontal edge of the floor of the three-dimensional model (X). Cognitive anxiety is represented as being at a right angle to arousal and on the left edge of the floor of

FIGURE 8.3 | Fazey and Hardy's (1988) catastrophe model of the relationship between anxiety and performance.

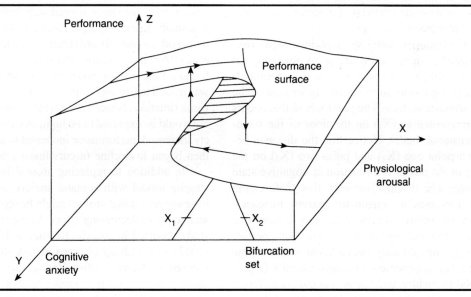

Source: From Fazey, J., & Hardy, L. (1988). The inverted-U hypothesis: A catastrophe for sport psychology? *Bass Monograph No. 1.* Leeds, UK: British Association of Sports Sciences and National Coaching Foundation. Reprinted with permission.

the model (Y). Performance is represented as being the height of the performance surface (Z). For every (X, Y) coordinate on the floor of the model, a point exists on the performance surface directly above it.

If cognitive anxiety is very low, the relationship between arousal and performance is predicted to take the form of the traditional inverted U, as represented by the back edge of the performance surface. Cognitive anxiety is represented in the model as the decisive factor for determining whether performance changes will be smooth and small, abrupt and large, or somewhere in between. With increasing physiological arousal, a catastrophe is predicted to occur at point (X_2), when cognitive anxiety is high. At this point, performance drops over the edge of the upper fold's performance surface down to a very low point on the same surface. Thus, with a very small increase in physiological arousal, a very large and abrupt decrease in performance occurs. Notice that the severity of the catastrophic decrease in performance depends on the level of cognitive anxiety. A small decrease in physiological arousal will not result in performance returning to its former lofty height, even though a small incremental increase in physiological arousal resulted in the performance catastrophe in the first place.

If cognitive anxiety remains high (unchanged), a significant decrease in physiological arousal will be necessary to return performance back to a position on top of the upper fold of the performance surface. The point where this occurs is represented as (X_1) on the floor of the three-dimensional model. Notice that the distance between point one (X_1) and point two (X_2) on the floor of the model is a function of cognitive state anxiety. The distance between this "bifurcation set" increases as cognitive anxiety increases. When physiological arousal recedes to point one (X_1), with no change in cognitive anxiety, performance jumps abruptly back to its pre-catastrophic level. The requirement that discontinuity (represented by sudden large jumps) occurs at different points along the normal factor (physiological arousal) is known as **hysteresis.**

The basic tenets of Fazey and Hardy's catastrophe model were tested by Hardy and Parfitt (1991) and Hardy, Parfitt, and Pates (1994). In both of these studies, cognitive anxiety and physiological arousal were manipulated. Setting cognitive anxiety at a high level and systematically increasing physiological arousal resulted in catastrophic decrements in basketball and bowling performance. Minimal changes in performance were observed when cognitive anxiety was low and physiological arousal was systematically increased. Both of these studies provided strong support for the basic tenets of catastrophe theory. A more recent investigation by Cohen, Pargman, and Tenenbaum (2003), however, failed to obtain experimental support for the model. In the Cohen et al. investigation, arousal was manipulated via treadmill walking while cognitive anxiety was manipulated using threat of random electrical shock. It was difficult to be convinced, however, that cognitive anxiety was effectively manipulated.

Several investigators have replaced physiological arousal with somatic anxiety and tested the revised catastrophe model in competitive situations. In these investigations, cognitive and somatic state anxiety were measured immediately before batting in softball (Krane, Joyce, & Rafeld, 1994), or before diving off a 3-meter board (Durr, 1996). In the Krane et al. (1994) investigation, very minimal support was found for the revised model, in that somatic anxiety was related to batting performance in certain critical game situations (situations in which cognitive anxiety would be expected to be high). As somatic anxiety increased, performance increased to a point, but then began to decline (a curvilinear relationship).

In addition to replacing arousal in the catastrophe model with somatic anxiety, researchers have suggested that arousal might be replaced with increasing or decreasing effort. A case in point is a study reported by Hardy, Beattie, and Woodman (2007) who utilized changes in task difficulty to increase or decrease effort. Results provided some support for the revised model in that hysteresis was observed in a high cognitive anxiety condition as effort was manipulated.

CONCEPT   If cognitive state anxiety is high, an increase in physiological arousal can result in a sudden and large decrement in athletic performance.

APPLICATION   Large and sudden decrements in performance will not occur if cognitive state

anxiety can be minimized or eliminated. Failing this, it will be necessary to closely monitor physiological arousal to avoid triggering a catastrophe in performance. If a catastrophe in performance does occur, it is best to give the athlete a rest to allow physiological arousal to return to a low level.

Technically, the three-dimensional model illustrated in figure 8.3 describes what has been called the **"cusp" catastrophe model.** Higher-order models in which variables such as personal control and self-confidence are included are called **"butterfly" catastrophe models** (Edwards, Kingston, Hardy, & Gould, 2002; Hardy, Woodman, & Carrington, 2004). Utilizing driving off a tee in golf, Hardy, Woodman, et al. (2004) demonstrated that self-confidence moderates the relationship between arousal, cognitive anxiety, and performance. Specifically, with a high level of self-confidence, a catastrophe in performance would not be observed unless both somatic and cognitive anxiety were very high.

Hanin's Individual Zone of Optimal Functioning (IZOF) Theory

I couldn't have played any better. In the beginning, in the middle of the second set, I was on fire. In all aspects of my game, from my serving to my groundstrokes, I was playing in a zone. It was as well as I could play, plain and simple.

(Pete Sampras on winning Wimbledon against Andre Agassi in Alexander, 1999.)

The concept of being in the zone or being within an individual zone of optimal functioning (IZOF) was first introduced by the Russian psychologist Yuri Hanin (1986) as it related to the emotion of state anxiety. Since those early beginnings, the concept of a zone of optimal functioning

has evolved from a focus on anxiety, to a focus on emotions generally, and most recently to a focus on a complex probabilistic model. In order to avoid unnecessary confusion, these three phases will be discussed sequentially.

Original IZOF Model with a Focus on Anxiety

Developed by Yuri Hanin (1989), **individual zone of optimal functioning** (IZOF) theory also questions the two basic assumptions of inverted-U theory, but more specifically the notion that a moderate level of state anxiety results in best performance. IZOF theory postulates that the level of optimal state anxiety best for one athlete may be very different from that optimal for the next athlete. Hanin (1986), for example, reported that a group of 46 elite female rowers had a mean optimal **prestart state anxiety** (precompetitive) of 43.80, with individual levels ranging from 26 to 67. Thus, for some athletes, the optimal level of state anxiety was very low, while for others it was very high. State anxiety was measured using a Russian version of Spielberger's State Anxiety Inventory (SAI). Hanin's concept of a zone of optimal functioning, as it relates to anxiety, has been discussed in detail by Raglin and Hanin (2000).

According to Hanin, if an athlete's optimal prestart state anxiety level can be determined, it should be possible to help an athlete achieve that ideal level through arousal control techniques. An athlete's optimal prestart anxiety level can be determined either directly or *retrospectively*. Direct measurement of optimal prestart anxiety

Playing "in the zone" requires outstanding skill as well as optimal positive and negative affect. Courtesy Ball State University Sports Information.

level is accomplished by actually measuring state anxiety immediately before a number of competitions and determining the level of anxiety that corresponds to the best performance. Since this method of determining optimal prestart anxiety is often time-consuming and impractical, the retrospective or **recall method** offers an attractive alternative. In the recall method, athletes are merely asked to reflect upon past performances and to complete the SAI according to how they remember feeling immediately before their best-ever performance.

The notion that an individual's recalled optimal precompetitive anxiety level is essentially the same as that obtained through actual observation has been the topic of several investigations

(Annesi, 1997; Harger & Raglin, 1994; Imlay, Carda, Stanbrough, Dreiling, & O'Connor, 1995; Russell & Cox, 2000; Tenenbaum & Elran, 2003; Tenenbaum, Lloyd, Pretty, & Hanin, 2002). Correlations between actual and recalled optimal precompetitive anxiety are relatively high (r = .95) when the recalled information is obtained within two days of the target competition. Correlations drop off significantly, however, with an increase in the time interval between actual event and recalled optimal precompetitive anxiety. In summary, the use of recalled optimal affect scores is a viable option if the actual scores cannot be obtained, but their accuracy may be limited in some cases.

Once optimal prestart state anxiety is determined, a zone of confidence (confidence interval) is placed around it. The upper and lower boundaries of the IZOF are established by adding and subtracting four points to or from the optimal prestart state anxiety score. This procedure allows for error in selecting the optimal level of anxiety. Hanin reported that four anxiety points correspond to a .5 standard deviation of observed precontest optimal state anxiety scores. Therefore, an IZOF is defined as an individual's optimal prestart level of state anxiety, plus or minus a population estimate of a .5 standard deviation. Based on Hanin's theory, it would be expected that best performance would be achieved when state anxiety was within this zone, as opposed to some "moderate" level of state anxiety. By monitoring an athlete's prestart state anxiety, it should be possible to utilize some form of intervention to increase or decrease state anxiety to move it into the IZOF. The concept of the IZOF, relative to precompetitive state anxiety, is illustrated in figure 8.4 for two different athletes.

Strong support for the concept of an individual zone of optimal functioning (IZOF) has been reported by Prapavessis and Grove (1991), Raglin and Turner (1993), and Turner and Raglin (1996). In all three of these investigations, predictions based on IZOF theory were compared to predictions based on Morgan's mental health model approach (discussed in chapter 7) or upon

CONCEPT   In the absence of an actual ideal pre-competitive state anxiety score, an estimate may be obtained by asking the athlete to complete a state anxiety inventory relative to how she retrospectively recalls feeling before her best performance.

APPLICATION   Once the ideal precompetitive anxiety score is identified, a zone of optimal functioning can be easily formed by adding and subtracting .5 standard deviations. In the case of Spielberger's SAI, the zone would range from four points below to four points above the ideal score.

inverted-U theory. In each case, the results favored IZOF theory.

Of particular interest to IZOF theory is an applied investigation reported by Annesi (1998). In this study, Annesi patiently identified the actual IZOFs of three elite adolescent tennis players. After establishing the IZOF for each athlete, the athlete was instructed in anxiety adjustment techniques. In the second phase of the investigation, athletes self-measured anxiety level prior to competitive matches and used their anxiety adjustment skills to move precompetitive anxiety into their predetermined IZOF. Results of the study showed that the self-monitored intervention was successful in bringing their tennis performance to a level

above where it had been before the intervention started. This was an important study, because it demonstrated that Hanin's concepts could be applied by athletes prior to competition.

An interesting study reported by Raglin and Morris (1994) provides some perspective. They showed that collegiate volleyball players tended to perform within their predetermined IZOF when they were playing difficult matches against highly skilled opponents. When they were playing easy matches against less skilled opponents, however, their precompetitive anxiety levels tended not to be in their predetermined IZOF. It is not generally necessary that athletes be in their zones of optimal functioning against lesser competition. They will

FIGURE 8.4 | Two athletes (A and B) exhibit different bell-shaped curves relative to state anxiety and performance. Best performance occurs within IZOF for each athlete.

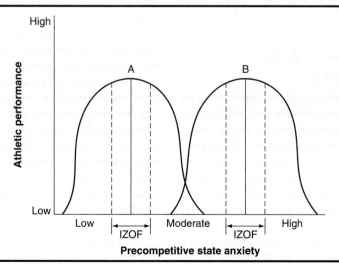

CONCEPT An athlete will perform best if her state anxiety is within a certain zone of optimal functioning.

APPLICATION Once an athlete's zone of optimal functioning has been determined (directly or through retrospection), arousal control techniques can be utilized to assist the athlete in achieving the optimal-level prestart state anxiety. Some athletes monitor prestart pulse rate as a means of determining if they are within their IZOF.

likely prevail anyway. This explains, however, why it is possible for a weaker team to defeat a stronger team on occasion. If a strong team overlooked a supposedly weak team or failed to take it seriously, it is possible that its players could suffer an unexpected loss before they could appropriately adjust their arousal levels. We will discuss more on this important topic in part 4.

Finally, in support of the IZOF model concept is an investigation in which functional magnetic resonance imaging (fMRI) was utilized to demonstrate the presence of an IZOF (Ferrell, Beach, Szeverenyi, Krch, & Fernhall, 2006). In this study, eight highly skilled archers were hypnotized and asked to visualize superior IZOF like performance and normal performance while being scanned using the fMRI technology. Results suggested that the neural records of the visualized superior performances could be distinguished from the normal non-IZOF performance.

The IZOF Model Involving Emotion Generally

In the previous section, we focused on forming an IZOF around an optimal level of competitive state anxiety to predict performance. In recent years, Hanin and others have moved from a focus on a single emotion (anxiety) to a focus on emotions generally, of which anxiety is just one example. It makes sense that positive and negative emotions, as opposed to just the negative emotion of anxiety, should determine the zone of optimal functioning. Technically, it would be possible to form IZOFs around multiple emotions, but this would not be feasible nor would it be practical in terms of application. Two recent studies provide constructive suggestions as to how emotions generally could be utilized in determining an IZOF involving multiple emotions (Hagtvet & Hanin, 2007; Robazza, Bortoli, & Hanin, 2006).

For our discussion here, we will focus on the Hagtvet and Hanin (2007) study in which 12 skilled ice hockey players served as participants. In this the athletes completed a 28-item aggregated sport-specific emotion scale relative to recalled best and worst games. Resultant emotions were plotted and categorized as a function of emotional intensity and aggregated emotional scores. Relative to *best performance,* an inverted-U relationship was observed between emotional intensity and category of emotion as illustrated in figure 8.5. As can be observed in this figure, and moving from left to right, the four categories of emotions are (a) unpleasant (negative) dysfunctional emotions, (b) unpleasant (negative) functional emotions, (c) pleasant (positive) functional emotions, and (d) pleasant (positive) dysfunctional emotions. Generally speaking, best performance is realized when pleasant functional emotions such as confidence and determination are very high and unpleasant dysfunctional emotions such as fatigue, fear, and discouragement are very low. Based on this investigation, **unpleasant dysfunctional emotions** include the emotions of fatigue, sorry, inactive, helplessness, doubtful, afraid, and discouraged. **Unpleasant functional emotions** include the emotions of nervous, concerned, anxious, annoyed, tense, intense, and angry. **Pleasant functional emotions** include the emotions of excited, inspired, brave, determined,

CONCEPT Just as an IZOF can be formed around an optimal level of competitive anxiety, an IZOF also can be formed around the more general notions of positive and negative affect. The athlete who is playing at peak performance is probably in the zone of optimal performance relative to a whole array of distinct emotions, and not just anxiety.

APPLICATION Precompetitive measures of positive and negative affect can be obtained using the Positive and Negative Affect Scale (PANAS; Watson, Clark, & Tellegen, 1988). Through practice, an athlete can learn to recognize when she is in her personal zone of optimal functioning. Once the zone is determined, interventions such as those discussed in part 4 of the text can be applied to increase or decrease various emotions.

---

confident, quick, and active. Finally, **pleasant dysfunctional emotions** include lighthearted, nice, glad, cheerful, calm, relaxed, and delighted.

The Probabilistic Model for Determining the IAPZ

The **probabilistic model** for determining affect and emotions associated with different levels of performance was first proposed and demonstrated by Kamata, Tenenbaum, and Hanin (2002). This was followed by a series of studies designed to

illustrate how the model could be applied with sports such as car racing, archery, and tennis (Edmonds, Mann, Tenenbaum, & Janelle, 2006; Johnson, Edmonds, Moraes, Filho, & Tenenbaum, 2007; Johnson, Edmonds, Tenenbaum, & Kamata, 2007). In all of these investigations, the Affect Grid (Russell et al., 1989) was employed to measure pleasure and felt arousal on a 9-point scale. In addition, heart rate was often included as an independent measure of physiological arousal. In all cases, measures were recorded and associated with actual performance.

FIGURE 8.5 | Intensity of categories of emotion associated with best performance.

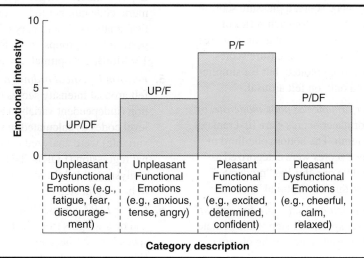

Source: Based on Hagtvet, K. A., & Hanin, Y. L. (2007). Consistency of performance related emotions in elite athletes: Generalizability theory applied to the IZOF model. *Psychology of Sport and Exercise, 8,* 47–72.

Classic IZOF theory, in its simplest form, relied on forming a zone around the optimal level of anxiety associated with best or optimum performance. Poorer performance was above or below the IZOF. This was somewhat theoretical, as best performance often occurred outside of the calculated IZOF. With the introduction of the probabilistic model came new terminology, in which the IZOF was dropped in favor of the term **individual affect-related performance zone** (IAPZ). As defined, the IAPZ was linked with the notion that probabilities could be calculated relative to whether a specific level of affect would fall within the various possible levels of performance. The process of determining the IAPZs for athletes is at once elegant, but also extremely complicated and tedious. Recognizing this, Johnson, Edmonds, Kamata, and Tenenbaum (2009) provided the procedural steps that may be used to derive an athletes' individual affect-related performance zone (IAPZ). In the paragraphs that follow, we will briefly discuss and clarify the steps involved using data from a female international archer shooting from a distance of 30 meters.

1. *Collect data.* For each series (e.g., 10 arrows) of arrows shot, performance was recorded and the Affect Grid completed. This would yield a performance score, a pleasure score, and a felt arousal score for each series of arrows. In this illustration, felt arousal scores were used as the example. Pleasure scores could also have been plotted, but for simplicity, we focused only on felt arousal.

2. *Categorize performance as poor, moderate, or optimal.* Performance scores were first ranked from top to bottom. The bottom one-third of the performance scores were categorized as "poor," the middle one-third as "moderate," and the top one-third as "optimal."

3. *Calculate mean felt arousal score for optimal performance group.* In this step you calculate the mean felt arousal score for the observations that belong to the optimal performance group. In this example, the mean of this group was 6.06 (range was 1–9).

4. *Calculate new performance categories.* Regardless of affect, all observations originally belonging to the optimal performance (OP) category were coded 2. Observations originally grouped as being in the moderate category (step 2) were coded 1 or 3 depending on whether their felt arousal score was above or below the optimal groups' mean felt arousal score (i.e., 6.08). If the felt arousal score was above 6.08, the observation was coded 3 and assigned to the moderate/above (Mo/A) performance group. If the felt arousal score was below 6.08, the observation was coded 1 and assigned to the moderate/below (Mo/B) performance group. Similarly, observations originally grouped as being in the poor category were coded 0 or 4 depending on whether their felt arousal score was above or below the optimal group's mean felt arousal score (i.e., 6.08). If the felt arousal score was above 6.08, the observation was coded 4 and assigned to the poor/above (P/A) performance group. If the felt arousal score was below 6.08, the observation was coded 1 and assigned to the poor/below (P/B). In this way, all felt arousal observations were reassigned to performance categories and given a numeric code number to be entered into a statistical analysis. A summary of the codes and performance groups are as follows: 0 = P/B, 1 = Mo/B, 2 = optimal, 3 = Mo/A, 4 = P/A.

5. *Perform logistical ordinal regression.* Actual felt arousal intensity scores of each observation (independent variable) and performance level codes as calculated in step 4 (dependent variable) were analyzed using logistical ordinal regression (LOR). The output from this analysis yielded the slopes and beta weights to be used in step 6.

6. *Create IAPZ curves.* Utilizing generated slopes and beta weights from the LOR and utilizing a special spreadsheet obtained from Johnson, Edmonds, Kamata, et al. (2009), an IAPZ curve was generated as illustrated in figure 8.6 for felt arousal.

FIGURE 8.6 | Archery performance IAPZ probability curves associated with felt arousal performance categories from left to right are poor below optimal (P/B), moderate below optimal (Mo/B), optimal performance (OP), moderate above optimal (Mo/A), and poor above optimal (P/A).

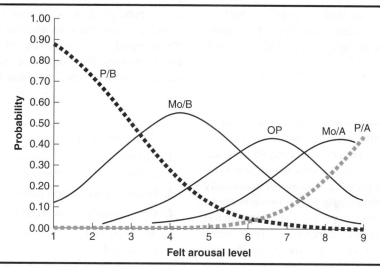

Source: Adapted with permission from Johnson, M. B., Edmonds, W. A., Kamata, A., & Tenenbaum, G. (2009). Determining individual affect-related performance zones (IAPZs): A tutorial. *Journal of Clinical Sport Psychology, 3* (I), 34–57.

With an IZOF curve for anxiety we could hypothesize that optimal performance would be associated with anxiety scores within the zone and less than optimal performance either below or above the IZOF (figure 8.4). With the IAPZ curves illustrated in figure 8.6, we are actually able to look at probabilities associated with performance categories. For example, with a felt arousal level of 7.0 we can see that the probability of that score being associated with the P/B, Mo/B, OP, Mo/A, or P/A performance category is .04, .20, .45, .32, and .10 respectively. Speaking more generally, we can be confident that for this archer, felt arousal scores below 2 are almost certainly going to yield poor performance, while a score of 4 would likely yield moderate performance. Furthermore, optimal performance is most likely to occur when felt arousal is between 6 and 7, and scores approaching 9 are likely to yield moderate or poor performance. For this specific case, the probabilistic model provides excellent information for this particular athlete (archer) to be able to maximize her perfor-mance. At least in the case of felt arousal she knows that maintaining a felt arousal level around 6 to 7 will give her the best chance of performing well. It remains to be seen if the complexity of the IAPZ generation procedure is feasible for coaches and sport psychologists generally.

Flow: The Psychology of Optimal Experience

I know that in some sports they talk about the zone, the place where your mind goes, and when you surf the best, you are in the zone. You are there alone. It is you, the wind, the waves, the salt in your mouth and the vision of the bumps and the chop and the sucking phase. There is nothing else there. There is nothing else in your mind. There is nothing else that matters. For a moment in time, time stands still and you are able to control the most uncontrollable because everything becomes slow motion and that's when you know you are surfing the best.

(Partington, Partington, & Olivier, 2009, p. 176)

CONCEPT When the conditions are just right, the athlete may enjoy a psychological experience that yields both high performance and personal ecstasy. Flow is an end in itself, something that is to be enjoyed and appreciated. It is sometimes, but not necessarily, associated with peak performance.

APPLICATION Conditions necessary for Flow to occur are listed in table 8.1. They include a positive mental attitude, positive affect, attentional focus, perception of being well prepared physically, and a oneness with teammates and/or coach. These are all attributes that an athlete should strive for at all times. If at some time they yield the ecstasy of the flow experience, this is all the better.

Mihaly Csikszentmihalyi (pronounced cheeks-sent-me-high) is credited with being the originator of the flow concept. Flow is not an acronym, but a way of expressing a sense of seemingly effortless and intrinsically joyful movement. As originally conceptualized by Csikszentmihalyi (1990), an individual experiences **flow** when engaged in an interesting activity for its own sake and for no other external purpose. In recent years, however, flow has been associated with Hanin's notion of an individual zone of optimal functioning (IZOF). Thus, the term "peak performance" is often used to describe the concept of flow. In reality, however, it is not necessary to have a peak or optimal performance in order to experience flow.

The individual most responsible for applying the principles of flow to sport and exercise is Susan Jackson. As defined by Jackson (1995), "Flow is a state of optimal experiencing involving total absorption in a task, and creating a state of consciousness where optimal levels of functioning often occur" (p. 138). In his original conceptualization of the flow construct, Csikszentmihalyi (1990) described flow as an end in itself, something that is to be enjoyed and appreciated. The key term in the flow construct is that of the **autotelic experience.** An autotelic experience is "a self-contained activity, one that is done not with the expectation of some future benefit, but simply because the doing itself is the reward" (p. 67). The nine defining characteristics of the flow experience are these (Csikszentmihalyi, 1990):

1. Requirement of a challenge/skill balance.
2. Merging of action and awareness (sense of automaticity and spontaneity).
3. Goals that are clearly defined.
4. Clear, unambiguous feedback.
5. Total concentration on the skill being performed.
6. Sense of being in control without trying to be in control (paradox of control).
7. Loss of self-awareness (becoming one with the activity).
8. Loss of time awareness.
9. Autotelic experience (end result of all of the above).

The nine defining characteristics of the flow experience form the basis of two instruments developed to measure flow (Jackson & Eklund, 2002). The Flow State Scale-2 (FSS-2) is a 36-item instrument designed to measure situation-specific flow, while the Dispositional Flow Scale-2 (DFS-2) is a 36-item instrument designed to measure flow as a personality trait. Psychometric studies have confirmed the factor structure and psychometric properties of both scales (Kawabata, Mallett, & Jackson, 2008; Martin & Jackson, 2008). To be used when time and convenience are important issues, short forms of the FSS-2 and DFS-2 have also been developed (Jackson, Martin, & Eklund, 2008; Martin & Jackson, 2008). In addition, a short scale has been developed to measure core

TABLE 8.1 | Factors Believed to Facilitate or to Prevent the Occurrence of the Flow State

Effect on Flow State	Factor
Facilitate	1. Development of a positive mental attitude. 2. Positive precompetitive affect. 3. Positive competitive affect (during contest). 4. Maintaining appropriate attentional focus. 5. Physical readiness (perception of being prepared). 6. Unity with teammates(s) and/or coach.
Prevent	1. Experiencing physical problems and mistakes. 2. Inability to maintain appropriate attentional focus. 3. Negative mental attitude. 4. Lack of audience response.

flow (Martin & Jackson, 2008). **Core flow** is defined as the degree to which an individual is absorbed in a task.

As mentioned earlier, it has been tempting for some authors to use the terms "peak experience" or "peak performance" as identical to the flow experience. Flow is a combination of emotional ecstasy and personal best performance. An athlete may perform a personal best in track and field event, yet not really consider the total experience as a peak moment. Conversely, one may experience an autotelic experience in sport and not realize a personal best score in terms of performance. In studying the flow experience Jackson identified factors believed to facilitate flow, as well as other factors believed to prevent the occurrence of the flow state. These factors are listed in table 8.1.

One interesting way to view the flow experience is as a positive interaction between skill and challenge. This concept, referred to as the **orthogonal model of flow,** is illustrated in figure 8.7 (Stavrou, Jackson, Zervas, & Karteroliotis, 2007). The flow experience is most likely to occur when the athlete is highly skilled, yet feels personally challenged by the competition that she faces. If the athlete feels personally challenged by the competition, yet feels that her skills are not up to the challenge, anxiety is likely to occur. Apathy is the likely outcome when an individual with a low skill

level is confronted with a nonchallenging situation. Finally, boredom will likely ensue when a highly skilled athlete is confronted with a nonchallenging competitive situation.

In an investigation reported by Jackson, Ford, Kimiecik, and Marsh (1998), dispositional flow was measured in 398 athletes participating in Masters Games in a setting separate from competition. Measures of trait anxiety, goal orientation, intrinsic motivation, and perceived ability were

FIGURE 8.7 | The orthogonal model of flow in sport is associated with a high level of skill and a high level of personal challenge.

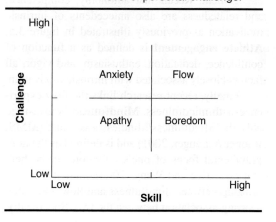

taken on the athletes at the same time dispositional flow was measured. In addition, flow state was measured for all participants immediately after a competitive event associated with the games. Three important findings emerged from this research:

1. Both trait and state measures of flow are correlated with perceived ability. This finding supports the concept illustrated in figure 8.7 that flow is associated with high levels of skill and challenge.

2. Both trait and state measures of flow are negatively correlated with competitive trait anxiety. This confirms the notion, listed in table 8.1, that positive and not negative affect facilitates the flow experience. It also suggests that anxiety (worry) is the antithesis of flow.

3. Both trait and state measures of flow are positively correlated with intrinsic motivation. By definition, the flow experience should be related to intrinsic motivation, because it occurs while one is performing a task that is interesting and enjoyable.

While flow has been discussed in this chapter as linked with the IZOF, it is closely associated with intrinsic motivation (Martin & Cutler, 2002). This point is further confirmed in an investigation reported by Hodge, Lonsdale, and Jackson (2009). Hodge et al. showed that autonomy, competence, and relatedness are antecedents of flow athlete engagement. Recall that autonomy, competence, and relatedness are also antecedents of intrinsic motivation as previously illustrated in figure 3.5. **Athlete engagement** is defined as a function of confidence, dedication, enthusiasm, and vigor, all factors closely associated with intrinsic motivation.

Finally, recent research links the flow experience with mindfulness. **Mindfulness** is measured with the Mindfulness/Mindlessness Scale (MMS; Bodner & Langer, 2001) and is defined as the nonjudgmental focus of one's attention on the here and now. Kee and Wang (2008) studied the relationship between mindfulness and flow and found a strong association between the two. Specifically,

mindfulness is predictive of a challenge-skill balance, merging of action and awareness, clear goals, concentration, and loss of consciousness. These are all defining characteristics of the flow experience.

Jones's Directionality Theory

> People are a little nervous right now, but that can be a good thing. You can turn that anxiety into competitiveness on the court and that helps you out. (Logan Tom, member of year 2000 USA Women's Olympic Volleyball team, cited in Moore (2000))

In the previous two sections on catastrophe theory and IZOF, the intensity of anxiety or of any emotion was the focus of our attention. If an athlete received a precompetitive cognitive state anxiety score of 30 out of a possible 36, we would say that the intensity of state anxiety for that athlete was relatively high. If the score was 15 we would say that the intensity of cognitive anxiety was very low. Jones (1991) identified this measure of anxiety as the **intensity component of anxiety**, or of any emotion. He further argued in this same article that the intensity of anxiety was not as important as the athlete's perception of whether his anxiety intensity was facilitative or debilitative relative to a subsequent competitive event. Jones labeled this facilitative or debilitative perception the **direction component of anxiety**, or of any emotion. Thus, the important question is not whether an athlete has a high or low level of anxiety intensity, but whether he perceives that this specific level will help or hinder his performance. Not long after conceptualizing the direction component of anxiety, Jones and colleagues allowed that a third component of anxiety existed, and that was the frequency component. According Swain and Jones (1993), the **frequency component of anxiety** assesses the degree to which anxiety symptoms were experienced. Consequently, Jones and colleagues (Jones & Swain, 1992; Swain & Jones, 1993) revised the Competitive State Anxiety Inventory-2 (CSAI-2) to measure, in addition to intensity, the direction and frequency components of competitive state

TABLE 8.2 | Correlations Among Intensity, Direction, and Frequency for Somatic Anxiety, Cognitive Anxiety, and Self-Confidence (based on Martinent et al., 2010)

CSAI-2R Scales	Correlation Contrasts (*r*)		
	I/D#	I/F	D/F
Somatic anxiety	−.31	+.47	+.07
Cognitive anxiety	−.44	+.69	−.35
Self-confidence	+.83	+.30	+.14

\# Correlation (*r*) between intensity (I) and direction (D)

anxiety. For every item on the CSAI-2, in addition to evaluating the intensity of the experienced item on a scale from 1 to 4, the athlete was asked to indicate on a scale of −3 to +3 the directional effect of the item and on a scale of 1 to 7 the frequency component of the item. In the case of directionality, a positive score would suggest a facilitative effect whereas a negative score would suggest a debilitative effect. Martinent et al. (2010) did the same thing with the CSAI-2R (Cox et al., 2003).

While we will consider the frequency component of anxiety in this section, our primary focus will be on the directional component. Correlations among the intensity, direction, and frequency components of the three factors measured by the CSAI-2R were reported by Martinent et al. (2010) and displayed in table 8.2.

As we can observe in table 8.2, the correlations between *intensity and direction* are negative for the two anxiety measures, but high and positive for self-confidence. The negative correlations for somatic and cognitive anxiety indicate that as intensity increases, direction decreases. The correlations between *intensity and frequency* for all three CSAI-2R measures are positive, indicating that as intensity increases, so does frequency. The correlations between *direction and frequency* for somatic anxiety and self-confidence are weak but positive, while for cognitive anxiety the correlation is negative suggesting that as direction increases, frequency decreases. Taken together, these correlational results suggest that (a) intensity and direction are inversely related for somatic anxiety

and cognitive anxiety, but positively related for self-confidence; (b) intensity and frequency are positively related for all three measures of the CSAI-2R; and (c) direction and intensity are inversely related for cognitive anxiety.

Research supports the position that the direction component of anxiety is predictive of athletic performance. The Jones group has reported the results of numerous studies that show successful athletes can be distinguished from less successful athletes based on directional but not intensity anxiety scores (Jones & Hanton, 1996; Jones, Hanton, & Swain, 1994; Jones & Swain, 1995). In addition, Perry and Williams (1998) reported an investigation in which novice and skilled tennis players were differentiated based on anxiety direction scores.

Directionality versus IZOF

From an applied perspective, clear differences emerge between Hanin's theory of individual zones of optimal functioning (IZOF) and Jones's theory of directionality. In the case of IZOF, obtained precompetitive state anxiety is compared with an established zone of optimal functioning relative to state anxiety. If this obtained score is either below or above the predetermined IZOF, behavioral and/or cognitive interventions are applied to raise or lower precompetitive anxiety. A markedly different strategy emerges if you subscribe to the directionality theory of precompetitive anxiety. Instead of concluding that high anxiety is a negative thing, the athlete is taught to view anxiety as a natural by-product of competition. The athlete is taught to view high levels of anxiety as being facilitative to best performance. Athletes are taught to restructure their conscious thought relative to experiencing either somatic or cognitive state anxiety prior to a competition (Eubank, Collins, & Smith, 2000).

Changing Perceived Direction of Precompetitive State Anxiety

From table 8.2, we observed that negative correlations exist between the intensity and direction components of anxiety for somatic and cognitive anxiety ($-.31$, $-.44$) respectively. This would suggest that as the intensity of anxiety increases, the direction shifts from being facilitative to more debilitative. Research, however, suggests that the direction of anxiety can be shifted from debilitative to facilitative through psychological interventions designed for that purpose (Hanton & Jones, 1999a; Page, Sime, & Nordell, 1999; Thomas, Maynard, & Hanton, 2007).

In the Page et al. (1999) investigation, five weeks of imagery training was effective in helping athletes to view precompetitive state anxiety as being conducive to good performance as opposed to debilitating. In the Hanton and Jones (1999b) and Thomas, Maynard, et al. (2007) investigations, a **multiple baseline single subject design** (MBSSD) was employed to see if psychological skill training could be effective in training athletes to adopt a more facilitative perception of the influence of anxiety upon performance. In both of these studies, the three female hockey players and four male swimmers who served as participants were initially identified as consistently interpreting precompetitive state anxiety as debilitating. The MBSSD is a research design in which a small number of participants achieve a stable performance baseline prior to receiving a behavioral or cognitive intervention of some kind (e.g., imagery, cognitive restructuring, mental skills training). Following the intervention, performance trials continue to be monitored and compared to preintervention trials. Criteria for determining a significant effect are identified by Hrycaiko and Martin (1996).

In these two studies in which the MBSSD was applied, participants who initially viewed anxiety as debilitating to performance came to view anxiety as being facilitative to performance.

Anxiety Direction and Frequency Relative to Time-to-Event

In chapter 7 we learned how time to event affects the intensity of precompetitive cognitive and somatic anxiety (see figure 7.3). The intensity of cognitive anxiety starts relatively high and increases gradually to start time. It thereafter fluctuates throughout the contest as the probability of success changes. Conversely, the intensity of somatic anxiety starts low and increases rapidly up to the beginning of the event but then drops precipitously once the event began.

As reported by Thomas, Maynard, and Hanton (2004), however, the pattern is different for the direction component of precompetitive state anxiety of national and regional level athletes. Using prestart times of 7 days, 48 hours, 24 hours, and 1 hour their data showed that the directional scale was flat for cognitive anxiety and somatic anxiety up to 24 hours before competition but then dropped significantly 1 hour prior to start time. This would suggest that the participants became less certain about the facilitative benefits of anxiety as the time-to-event got closer. In the case of the frequency component of anxiety, both cognitive and somatic anxiety frequency scores increased in a sharp linear fashion for 7 days to 1 hour before competition. Relative to the frequency of somatic anxiety, this pattern was nearly identical to that observed in figure 7.3 for anxiety intensity. This observation is to be as expected given the positive correlation between somatic anxiety intensity and frequency scores (table 8.2).

In a subsequent investigation by Thomas, Hanton, and Maynard (2007), involving elite female hockey players, two extreme groups were formed in terms of direction of anxiety (facilitators and debilitators). Using a qualitative design, participants were interviewed across three time periods (1 to 2 days prior to match, prestart on day of match, and post match). Results of the investigation showed that (a) 1 to 2 days prior to competition, frequency and intensity of anxiety was increasing for participants in both groups, but the facilitators actively engaged in coping strategies to counter the increased anxiety; (b) on the day of the match, frequency and intensity of anxiety was again increasing, and again only the facilitators were actively engaging in coping strategies to counter the increased anxiety; and (c) post match, the debilitators focused their attention on mistakes that had been made, while facilitators used coping strategies to replace negative post match thoughts with positive thoughts. Thus, it would appear that one difference between directional debilitators and facilitators was their coping skills and mental skill training (to be discussed in part 4).

Other Research Relationships Related to Direction of Anxiety

Hanton and Connaughton (2002) reported an interesting study involving swimmers in which perceived personal control served as a moderator between the intensity and direction components of anxiety. As illustrated in figure 8.8, intensity of somatic and cognitive anxiety has a facilitative effect upon performance and self-confidence if the athlete perceives she has the ability to control the debilitative effects of state anxiety. Conversely, if the athlete does not feel that she has personal control over the debilitating effects of anxiety, then a decline in performance and self-confidence will follow.

In another investigation (Mellalieu, Neil, & Hanton, 2006), elite and nonelite athletes served as participants to determine if self-confidence mediates the relationship between anxiety intensity and anxiety direction.

The results of the investigation showed that the relationship is moderated by level of skill. For *elite athletes*, self-confidence does not mediate the relationship between somatic intensity and somatic direction, but it does mediate the relationship between cognitive intensity and cognitive direction. For *nonelite athletes*, self-confidence is a partial mediator between intensity and direction for both somatic anxiety and cognitive anxiety. This means that anxiety intensity affects anxiety direction both directly and through self-confidence. In general, we might conclude that self-confidence is instrumental in determining the effect that anxiety intensity has upon anxiety direction.

Finally, while the focus of this section has been on the directional effects of anxiety upon athletic performance, it is important to recognize that the effect of every emotion upon performance can

FIGURE 8.8 | Whether anxiety is perceived as facilitating or debilitating depends on perception of personal control.

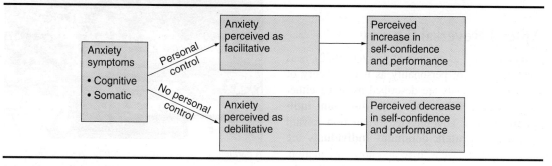

Source: Based on Hanton, S., & Connaughton, D. (2002). Perceived control of anxiety and its relationship to self-confidence. *Research Quarterly for Exercise and Sport, 73,* 87–97.

CONCEPT Intensity of competitive state anxiety is an indicator of the absolute level of state anxiety associated with a competitive situation, whereas direction of competitive state anxiety is the athlete's perception of whether the manifested intensity is debilitative or facilitative relative to performance.

APPLICATION From the perspective of individual differences, it is more important for the coach or teacher to know whether an athlete perceives a certain level of anxiety to be positive or negative than for her to know the absolute level. Two athletes may exhibit high levels of somatic and cognitive anxiety immediately prior to competition, but one of them may view these high levels as having a positive, or facilitative, influence on the competition. This knowledge should provide the coach with valuable information as to how to best prepare the athlete for competition.

---

be considered in terms of the intensity, direction, and frequency components. Martinent and Ferrand (2009) reported on a study involving 11 French National level male table tennis players in which nine specific emotions were identified (anger, anxiety, discouragement, disappointment, disgust, joy, relief, serenity, and hope). In addition, four categories of directional influence emerged for each emotion (positive, negative, neutral, and no perceived influence). Depending on the situation, every identified emotion can have either a positive or a negative directional effect. For example, the negative emotion of anger can facilitate (positive) performance by increasing motivation, or a debilitating effect by decreasing concentration. Conversely, a positive emotion such as joy could facilitate performance by having a positive effect on motivation or a debilitating effect by causing the athlete to be overly confident.

Apter's Reversal Theory

Reversal theory, as proposed by Apter (1982), is as much a theory of personality as it is a theory of arousal. Individuals are described as being either telic or paratelic dominant. **Telic-dominant individuals** have a goal-directed orientation toward life, while **paratelic-dominant individuals** are fun-loving and have a "here-and-now" orientation. At the same time, however, Apter notes that the telic and paratelic orientations are not enduring

traits or personality dispositions. While an individual tends to be dominant in either the telic or the paratelic orientation, each person has the capability

A paratelic orientation may be conductive to a Flow experience. Courtesy University of Missouri–Columbia Sports Information.

FIGURE 8.9 | The hypothesized relationship between arousal and hedonic tone (pleasure seeking) for the anxiety-avoidance (telic) and the excitement-seeking (paratelic) systems.

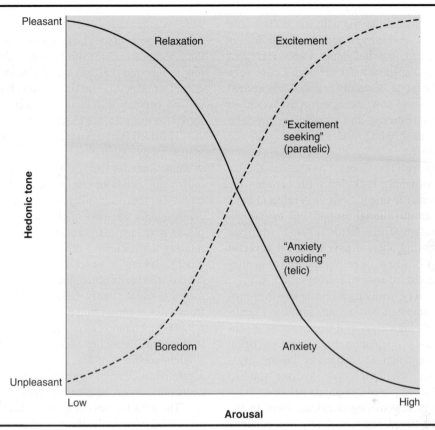

Source: Adapted from Apter, M. J. (1982). *The experience of motivation: The theory of psychological reversals.* London, New York: Academic Press.

to switch back and forth between the two. **Reversal theory** receives its name from this proclivity toward switching back and forth between the two orientations. Apter's concept of reversal theory is described in detail by Apter (1984) and by Kerr (1997).

Reversal theory is described as having characteristics associated with both drive theory and inverted-U theory. In drive theory, the organism seeks to reduce drive (anxiety) by satisfying the craving for such needs as food, water, or sex. Drive reduction has the effect of moving an organism from a state of being aroused to a state of relaxation. In inverted-U theory, the organism seeks to overcome boredom by

increasing arousal. In this case, a moderate increase in arousal brings on the desirable psychological state of excitement. Combining these two conditions into a single theory (reversal theory) produces a hedonic goal (pleasure seeking) to bring about a situation of relaxation or excitement, as opposed to anxiety or boredom. Reversal theory as explained in these terms is illustrated in figure 8.9. As can be observed in this figure, the objective is to increase hedonic tone, not to increase or decrease arousal.

The two curves in figure 8.9 are representative of the two frame-of-mind orientations in reversal theory. The orientation leading from anxiety (an unpleasant condition) to relaxation is labeled the telic mode, while the orientation leading from boredom (also an unpleasant condition) to excitement is labeled the paratelic mode. The telic mode is goal oriented and serious. While in this frame of mind, the individual views increased arousal to be unpleasant and stressful. Conversely, the paratelic mode is activity oriented and excited with the here-and-now. Increased arousal could be viewed as threatening and stressful in the telic mode and as exciting and exhilarating in the paratelic mode.

Because reversal theory hypothesizes the involuntary switching back and forth between the telic and paratelic orientations, it is referred to as being **metamotivational** as opposed to motivational in nature. Three factors interact with one another to bring about a **psychological reversal** (Apter, 1984). These three factors are (a) contingent events, (b) frustration, and (c) satiation.

A true story involving a female skydiver provides an example of how a *contingent event* facilitated a psychological reversal from a paratelic sensation seeking orientation to a telic sensation avoiding orientation. The subject of this investigation was an experienced female skydiver who had successfully completed 298 jumps before an associate died in a skydiving accident. Prior to the death of her friend, she was clearly in a paratelic thrill-seeking mode in which she enjoyed a feeling of safety in the face of extreme danger. This feeling of safety in the face of danger is referred to as a **protective frame** of reference or a "psychological bubble." When her friend died, her bubble burst and she experienced a psychological reversal that thrust her into a telic sensation avoiding psychological orientation. As a result of the psychological reversal, she gave up skydiving and went into a phase of deep depression (Kerr, 2007).

The following describes an infamous Olympic incident that could be an example in which *frustration* caused a reversal. In the 1972 Munich Olympic Games, members of the U.S.A. men's basketball team leaped and hugged one another with joy (paratelic mode) when they believed they had won

the gold medal against the then Soviet Union. This psychological frame of mind quickly changed to the telic mode when they were informed that the game was not over and that three seconds were being put back on the clock. It was during these last three seconds, and the third questionable opportunity to inbound the ball, that the Soviets won the game by one point. The U.S. players boycotted the medals ceremony, refusing to accept the silver medal for second place (Smith, 1992).

The third factor that can bring about a change in metamotivational mode is *satiation,* or an innate dynamic force for change. As the period of time an individual spends in one metamotivational mode increases, the probability of a reversal also increases. This situation might occur with a tennis player who has just spent two hours working on refining his backhand drive down the line (telic mode). Taking a water break, he meets some friends who invite him to join in a friendly game of mixed doubles. Partly from satiation and partly from a desire for a change, the tennis player experiences a metamotivational reversal from the telic to the paratelic mode. Suddenly, the tension and singlemindedness of his practice session shifts to a carefree feeling of enjoyment, enthusiasm, and excitement about the game of tennis.

The attractiveness of reversal theory is closely associated with its flexibility and dynamic nature. The theory underscores the importance of taking a situation-specific and individualistic approach to studying the relationship between arousal and performance. If an athlete is in the telic mode, increased arousal could result in a state anxiety level that could cause a decrement in performance. Conversely, if an athlete is in the paratelic mode, decreasing arousal through some sort of intervention could actually bring about boredom. Neither of these scenarios is likely to have a facilitative effect on athletic performance. A great deal of care must be used to determine the appropriate approach to use with an athlete who is suffering from a decrement in athletic performance. From a reversal theory perspective, figure 8.10 illustrates the various options that are available to the athlete

CONCEPT   In addition to arousal control (to be discussed in part 4), reversal theory offers a second strategy for dealing with boredom and/or anxiety in sport.

APPLICATION   Athletes should be instructed in the thought process necessary to reinterpret the ways in which they respond to high and low arousal. If interpreted differently, the boredom of waiting for the next round of competition could be viewed as relaxing. Additionally, the anxiety associated with worrying about an important competition could be reinterpreted as excitement about a stimulating opportunity.

FIGURE 8.10 | Possible options available to the athlete experiencing high anxiety while in telic mode, or boredom while in paratelic mode.

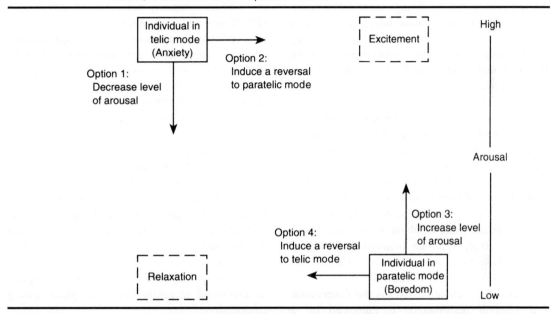

Source: Adapted from Kerr, J. H. (1989). Anxiety, arousal, and sport performance: An application of reversal theory. In D. Hockfort & C. D. Spielberger (Eds.), *Anxiety in sports: An international perspective* (p. 148). New York: Hemisphere Publishing Corporation.

who is experiencing either debilitating state anxiety or boredom.

An athlete suffering from debilitating anxiety while in the *telic mode* has two possible options open to her. The first option is to decrease the level of arousal through a stress management strategy (progressive relaxation). The second option is to induce a reversal to the paratelic mode. If this can be accomplished, the athlete will view the anxiety-provoking situation as exciting and challenging (pleasurable), as opposed to threatening and unpleasant.

Similarly, an athlete who is suffering from boredom while in the *paratelic state* has two options available to her. The first option is to increase the level of arousal to induce a sense of excitement (psyching-up strategy). The second option is to induce a reversal to the telic state. If this can be accomplished, the athlete will view the unpleasant situation as relaxing and tranquil as opposed to boring.

As shown in figures 8.9 and 8.10, reversal theory posits that athletes seek an increase in hedonic tone as they strive for excellence. The bored athlete strives for more excitement and enthusiasm, and the distressed athlete strives for calm and relaxation. Increased hedonic tone should result in improved athletic performance. Individuals with a strong paratelic orientation should seek involvement in sports that involve excitement and some physical risk (e.g., skiing, surfing, diving); those with a strong telic orientation should pursue safe, low-risk sports associated with relaxation and low arousal (e.g., archery, golf, walking). Best performance from an athlete should occur in conditions associated with pleasant moods and in situations in which an athlete's preferred level of arousal is matched by his actual felt level of arousal (Males & Kerr, 1996).

Qualitative research with elite male slalom canoeists leads to the observation that a predominantly telic orientation is displayed most often during situations that require hard work, staying focused, and following rules. A paratelic orientation occurs most often during the actual race. The great spontaneity and exhilaration associated with a paratelic orientation are believed to be linked with the flow experience discussed earlier in this chapter (Males, Kerr, & Gerkovich, 1998).

Related to activation level is the observation that strength performance is enhanced by a paratelic reversal associated with pleasant excitement (Perkins, Wilson, & Kerr, 2001). Other investigations that have shown support for reversal theory applications in sport include Kerr and Vlaswinkel (1995), Males et al. (1998), Purcell (1999), Hudson and Bates (2000), and Cromer and Tenenbaum (2009).

While researchers have tended to focus on the telic-paratelic state pair, three additional bipolar pairs are mentioned by Apter (1982). In addition to the telic-paratelic pair, there is the negativist-conformist pair, the autic-alloic pair, and the mastery-sympathy pair. Hudson and Walker (2002) reported a qualitative investigation that involved five members of a university golf team. During a round-robin golf tournament, 17 psychological reversals were noted, with each golfer experiencing between one and five reversals. Of these 17 reversals, 65 percent were attributed to a contingent event, 29 percent to frustration, and 6 percent to satiation. The most frequently reported metamotivational states were paratellic (29 percent); telic (27 percent); and autic, or focused upon self (27 percent). This only left 17 percent to be distributed among the remaining five states. Most reversals were related to the telic-paratelic and autic-alloic pairs. The researchers concluded that psychological states do not remain constant across an athletic event, underscoring the importance of preparing athletes to manage and respond to unwanted reversals that take place during competition.

Summary

In this chapter we introduced and discussed alternatives to inverted-U theory. Several theories have been posited to explain alternative or more detailed explanation of how and why increased arousal and anxiety influence athletic performance. These include multidimensional theory, catastrophe theory, zone of optimal functioning theory, psychological flow, direction of anxiety theory, and reversal theory.

Martens' multidimensional anxiety theory is based on the notion that anxiety is multidimensional in nature and is composed of a cognitive anxiety component and a somatic anxiety component. The theory hypothesizes a negative linear relationship between cognitive state anxiety and athletic performance, and an inverted-U relationship between somatic anxiety and performance.

Fazey and Hardy's catastrophe model was introduced as a theory of performance and arousal that specifically rejects the inverted-U concept of a smooth quadratic curve relationship between increased arousal and performance. The relationship between physiological arousal and athletic performance is believed to take the form of the inverted-U when cognitive anxiety is low, but to take a very different form when cognitive anxiety increases. At a high level of cognitive anxiety, performance increases gradually as in the inverted-U, but at some point as arousal continues to rise, performance will show a catastrophic drop-off.

Developed by Yuri Hanin, individual zone of optimal functioning (IZOF) theory also questions the basic assumptions of inverted-U theory, but more specifically the notion that a moderate level of state anxiety results in best performance. In IZOF theory an optimal level of precompetitive state anxiety is identified and a narrow band of anxiety functioning created around it. The IZOF, or band of optimal functioning, is generally considered to be the optimal level of anxiety plus or minus one-half of a standard deviation. The athlete attempts to adjust his level of precompetitive anxiety so that it falls within the IZOF.

The concept of an IZOF for anxiety has expanded to include a focus upon emotions generally, as opposed to just anxiety. Other categories of emotion that fit the IZOF mode include unpleasant dysfunctional emotions, unpleasant functional emotions, pleasant functional emotions, and pleasant dysfunctional emotions. Another theoretical advancement related to IZOF is the adoption of a probabilistic model for determining an individual affect-related performance zone (IAPZ). As defined, the IAPZ is linked to the notion that probabilities can be calculated as to whether a specific level of affect would fall within the various levels of performance.

Flow is experienced when a person engages in an interesting activity for its own sake and for no other external reason. Flow is defined by Jackson (1995) as a "state of optimal experiencing involving total absorption in a task, and creating a state of consciousness where optimal levels of functioning often occur."

Flow is measured with the Flow State Scale-2 (FSS-2) and the Dispositional Flow Scale-2 (DFS-2). In addition, short forms of the FSS-2 and DFS-2 have been developed.

A precompetitive administration of the Competitive State Anxiety Inventory-2 (CSAI-2) yields an intensity measure for cognitive and somatic state anxiety. Directionality theory posits that the athlete's perception of how intensity affects performance is more important than the intensity itself. Jones labeled the perception aspect as the direction component of precompetitive state anxiety. Rather than attempting to adjust precompetitive anxiety as in IZOF theory, directionality theory posits that the athlete's perception of how precompetitive anxiety affects performance should be changed.

Apter's reversal theory has characteristics associated with both drive and inverted-U theory. While in a telic frame of mind, the athlete seeks to reduce the level of arousal in order to bring about a state of relaxation. While in a paratelic frame of mind, the athlete seeks to increase arousal in order to increase excitement. The individual's ability to switch back and forth between telic and paratelic modes is referred to as psychological reversal.

Critical Thought Questions

1. In your opinion, are the alternatives to inverted-U theory really clear alternatives, or are they in fact modifications in the theory's predictions? Explain.

2. How would you go about testing Fazey and Hardy's catastrophe theory in an applied setting?

3. What do you like most and least about catastrophe theory? Justify and explain your answers.

4. Describe the evolution of thinking regarding individual zone of optimal functioning theory. Which approach do you favor from an applied perspective and why?

5. Discuss in your own words the process whereby the individual affect-related performance zone (IAPZ) can be formed. What are the strengths and weaknesses of this approach?

6. Can you teach an athlete to experience flow? Would you want to do this? Why would you want to do this? Explain.

7. If an athlete exhibits an alarmingly high level of precompetitive state anxiety, but then indicates that she believes it will facilitate good performance, how would you advise this athlete?

8. Explain how you would propose to utilize reversal theory in enhancing athletic performance in the face of alarmingly high precompetitive state anxiety.

Glossary

athlete engagement As related to flow, the process of being psychologically engaged in an activity while exhibiting confidence, dedication, enthusiasm, and vigor.

autotelic experience An experience that is entered into as an end in itself. The doing is its own reward.

butterly catastrophe model Four-dimensional catastrophe theory model in which self-confidence (or some other variable) is added as a fourth dimension.

catastrophe theory A theory of arousal that predicts that small incremental changes in arousal can result in a catastrophic decline in performance.

core flow Degree to which an individual is absorbed in a task.

cusp catastrophe model Three-dimensional catastrophe model (*see* Catastrophe theory).

direction component of anxiety An athlete's perception of whether a specific intensity level of anxiety is facilitative or debilitative relative to performance.

flow An experience that is an end in and of itself, to be enjoyed and appreciated.

frequency component of anxiety How often anxiety symptoms are experienced.

hysteresis In catastrophe theory, the point at which performance drops off and recovers at different points along the arousal continuum.

individual affect-related performance zone Linked with the Probabilistic model in which individual affect-related performance zones (IAPZs) are calculated.

individual zone of optimal functioning Hanin's notion that best performance occurs within a zone of optimal state anxiety or affect.

intensity component of anxiety The absolute level of anxiety as measured by an anxiety inventory.

intraindividualized scores An athlete's repeated scores, standardized using the athlete's own mean and standard deviation (*see* Ipsative z-score).

ipsative z-score An athlete's repeated scores, standardized using the athlete's own mean and standard deviation (*see* Intraindividualized scores).

metamotivational A term used by Aptner to describe how motivation shifts from a telic mode to a paratelic mode in reversal theory.

mindfulness As related to flow, the nonjudgmental focus of one's attention on the here and now.

multidimensional anxiety theory An anxiety theory based on the notion that anxiety has both cognitive and somatic components.

multiple baseline single subject design Research design in which a small number of participants achieve a stable performance baseline prior to receiving a behavioral or cognitive intervention of some kind. Pre-and post-intervention performance scores are compared.

orthogonal model of flow A positive interaction between skill and challenge. Flow occurs only when both skill and task difficulty are high.

paratelic-dominant individual A person with the personality orientation to be fun-loving and have a here-and-now perspective on life.

pleasant dysfunctional emotions As used in IZOF theory, pleasant emotions such as light-hearted, nice, and glad may have a negative effect on performance.

pleasant functional emotions As used in IZOF theory, pleasant emotions such as excited, inspired, and brave may have a positive effect on performance.

prestart state anxiety Level of state anxiety just before an event starts (i.e., precompetitive anxiety).

probabilistic model A zone of optimal functioning model in which performance categories are predicted based on calculated probabilities.

protective frame Feeling of safety in the face of extreme danger.

psychological reversal The involuntary switching back and forth between a telic and a paratelic orientation.

recall method In IZOF theory, the retrospective determination of optimal level of competitive state anxiety.

reversal theory A theory of personality and arousal proposing that an individual's psychological orientation switches back and forth between the telic and the paratelic modes.

standard deviation On the average, the extent to which a group of scores deviates from the group mean.

telic-dominant individual A person with the personality orientation to be goal oriented and to have a serious perspective on life.

unpleasant dysfunctional emotions As used in IZOF theory, unpleasant emotions such as fatigue, doubtful, and afraid may have a negative effect on performance.

unpleasant functional emotions As used in IZOF theory, unpleasant emotions such as nervous, concerned, and anger may have a positive effect on performance.

z-score A standardized score in which a group mean is subtracted from an athlete's score; the difference is then divided by the group standard deviation.

PART 4

Cognitive and Behavioral Interventions

In an earlier chapter on anxiety, stress, and mood relationships (chapter 7), we introduced the case study of a young high school athlete named Ryan. Recall that Ryan was an extremely gifted multiple-sport athlete who experienced difficulty in dealing with anxiety while competing in track events. Specifically, he would become so anxious prior to sprinting and hurdling events that he literally could not run efficiently. During practices, however, Ryan experienced little or no tension and anxiety. During three years of high school track, he had never lost a race during practice with teammates.

It was clear that Ryan was going to be a track "dropout" if some sort of intervention were not provided. Ryan's father talked to a professor of sport psychology at the local college to find out if something could be done to help Ryan. After three weeks of studying Ryan's anxiety response to competition, the sport psychologist concluded that an individualized intervention program could be developed to help him. The program that was recommended was one very similar to autogenic training, described in chapter 9. In this program, Ryan learned what caused his anxiety and how to cope with it when it occurred. Ryan's success at reversing the damaging effects of anxiety did not happen overnight. However, during his senior year he made up for many of his earlier failures by setting a state record in the 200-meter sprint.

In part 3 of the text, we discussed the concepts of arousal and anxiety in great depth. You are now familiar with both of these terms and aware of several theories that purport to explain the relationship between arousal/anxiety and performance. Too much or too little arousal may result in poor athletic performance. Consequently, the goal for the athlete and the coach is to identify the optimal level of arousal for any particular event.

The purpose of this part of the book is to introduce and explain various coping and intervention strategies designed to control or modify anxiety, arousal, and stress as defined in part 3 of the text. Topics to be addressed in chapters 9 through 12 include (a) coping and intervention strategies in sport, (b) goal setting in sport, (c) imagery and hypnosis in sport, and (d) psychological skills training. ⌘

CHAPTER 9

Coping and Intervention Strategies in Sport

KEY TERMS

Abdominal breathing
Affirmation statements
Anxiety/stress spiral
Autogenic training
Automated coping strategies
Biofeedback
Bulletin board
Chest breathing
Coping
Coping conceptual framework
Coping strategies
Coping strategy dimension
Coping style
Coping style dimension
Deep breathing
Dispositional hypothesis
Dynamic hypothesis
Emotion-focused coping strategy
Fan support
4 Ws of self-talk
Generalizability of coping skills
Immediate mobilization
Individual self-energizing strategies
Integrative mind-body training
Mantra
Matching hypothesis
Meditation
Mental device
Pep talk
Proactive coping strategies

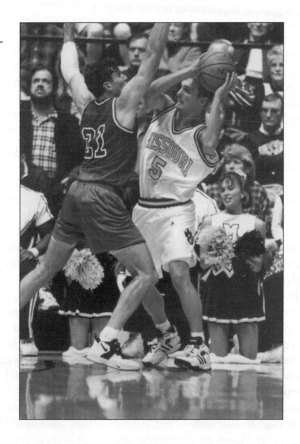

Problem-focused coping strategy
Progressive relaxation
Relaxation response
Self-activation
Self-energizing strategies

Self-talk
Self-thought
Stress management
Team energizing strategies
Transcendental meditation

In this very important chapter on coping and intervention strategies in sport, we are going to introduce and discuss four major topics that relate to coping and intervention. These include (a) coping strategies in sport, (b) self-talk as an intervention, (c) relaxation strategies used in sport, and (d) arousal energizing strategies. Subsequent chapters in this part of the text will build on the behavioral and cognitive interventions introduced in this chapter.

While it may seem obvious to most students of sport psychology, it is important to briefly distinguish between the concepts of behavioral and cognitive interventions. A behavior is something that can be observed, so when we talk about a behavioral intervention we are talking about an intervention that changes the way an athlete behaves. This usually involves changing the environment in some way, or changing the way an athlete prepares for competition. For example, teaching an athlete how to breathe in preparation for a free throw in basketball would be a behavioral intervention. Conversely, a cognitive intervention has to do with the way athletes think and analyze situations. We can observe the effects of a cognitive intervention, but we can't see an athlete think. That is, we can't get inside of the athlete's head and observe how she thinks. Nevertheless, restructuring how an athlete thinks about competition or how she thinks about confidence can have a powerful effect on behavior or performance. For example, the use of imagery as a way to improve technique in a sport skill would be a cognitive intervention. Sometimes cognitive and behavioral interventions are combined and intertwined into a single intervention.

Another important concept to understand before we begin this chapter is the distinction between the terms *psychological intervention* and *coping strategy*. While these two terms are very similar and are often used interchangeably, there are some important differences. Think of a psychological intervention (behavioral or cognitive) as something that the coach or sport psychologist uses to intervene on the athlete's behalf. For example, if the sport psychologist uses a stress management technique to

teach an athlete how to reduce pregame anxiety, this would be an example of an intervention designed by someone else to help the athlete. However, if the athlete is able to personalize and claim ownership of the newly discovered stress management skills and to integrate them into her own repertoire of psychological skills, then they become personal coping skills. So, what was once an intervention provided by the coach or sport psychologist can later become a personal coping strategy or skill.

Coping Strategies in Sport

> My third maxim was to endeavor always to conquer myself rather than the order of the world, and in general accustom myself to the persuasion that except our own thoughts, there is nothing absolutely in our power. (René Descartes, *Discourse on Method,* Part III)

Coping has been defined by Lazarus and Folkman (1984) as "constantly changing cognitive and behavioral efforts to manage specific external and/ or internal demands that are appraised as taking or exceeding resources of the person" (p. 141). Referring back to figure 7.2, we are reminded that the stress response is the end result of a perceived imbalance between the demands of the situation and an appraisal of coping resources. To address the debilitating effects of the stress response, the athlete intervenes with active coping responses.

Consistent with the stress process shown in figure 7.2 is the interaction model shown in figure 9.1. As an extension of Cerin, Szabo, Hunt, and Williams (2000), the interaction model was proposed by Mellalieu (2003) to show how the stress process is influenced by mood state, personal factors, situational factors, and attentional processing; all of these are factors we have discussed in previous chapters. The stress process, including coping, is shown as the central feature in the interactional model. Thus, figure 9.1 shows a much more complex and complete picture as to how coping plays a central role in the stress process, and how emotions influence performance. Research confirms

FIGURE 9.1 | The Interactional Model of the Stress Process, showing how coping with emotions is influenced by mood, attention, personality, and situational factors.

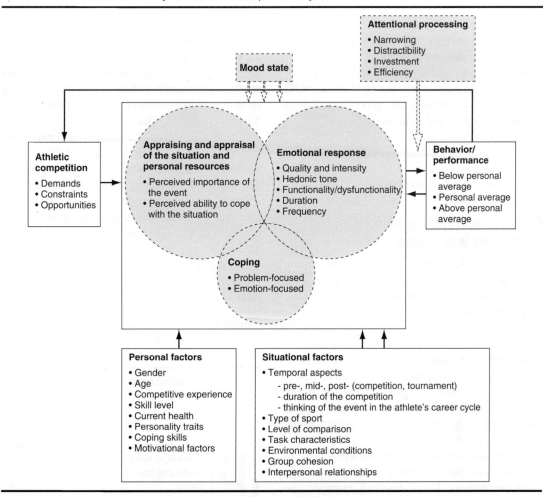

Source: Mellalieu, S. D. (2003). Mood matters: But how much? A comment on Lane and Terry (2000). *Journal of Applied Sport Psychology, 15,* 99–114. Reproduced with permission of Taylor & Francis, Inc. http://www.taylorandfrancis.com

that cognitive appraisals of stressful situations influence the use of coping strategies (Anshel, Jamieson, & Raviv, 2001), and that unexpected stressors present additional challenges to the coping process (Dugdale, Eklund, & Gordon, 2002).

Coping involves a personal response on the part of the athlete to address the stress response. The athlete feels anxious in a competitive situation

and tries to use personal coping resources to reduce the anxiety. The use of various relaxation or arousal management procedures to reduce anxiety is commonly referred to as **stress management.** When an athlete uses a stress management technique or any other cognitive or behavioral intervention, this is a form of coping. Thus, any sort of intervention, if it is self-applied, can appropriately be called a coping skill. Sometimes, however, an athlete's coach may determine that the athlete's own coping attempts are not working and decide to intervene with a planned cognitive or behavioral intervention.

In the balance of this section we will focus our discussion on (a) a conceptual framework for coping strategies and styles, (b) measurement of coping skill, (c) the dynamic nature of coping skill, (d) factors that enhance the generalizability of coping, (e) factors that influence coping effectiveness, and (f) sources of stress and coping strategies used by athletes. In subsequent chapters of part 4 of the text, we will address other ways of preparing athletes for optimal performance.

Conceptual Framework for Coping Strategies and Styles

Lazarus and Folkman (1984) indicated that **coping strategies** are of two types: problem-focused and emotion-focused. **Problem-focused coping strategies** center on alleviating the environmental stimulus that is causing the stress response. If a right-handed baseball player is very anxious when batting against left-handed pitchers, an appropriate problem-focused coping strategy might be to get more experience hitting against left-handed pitchers during practice. Other common names for problem-focused coping include the terms task focused coping, action coping, and cognitive coping.

Emotion-focused coping strategies seek to regulate emotions in order to reduce or manage cognitive distress. In the baseball example, the batter would focus his coping on controlling his emotions through anxiety reduction techniques. Instead of attacking the source of the problem, the athlete seeks to reduce or eliminate the symptoms associated with the stress. Emotion-focused coping is often referred to as behavioral coping.

Several authors have proposed a third coping strategy and called it "avoidance coping" (Anshel & Sutarso, 2007; Endler & Parker, 1990; Grove & Heard, 1997). While this approach is consistent with the literature, it is somewhat illogical, in that problem- and emotion-focused coping strategies

are clearly approach strategies, while an avoidance strategy is not. This problem of incongruence was addressed by Anshel, Williams, and Hodge (1997) when they proposed the two-dimensional **coping conceptual framework** illustrated in figure 9.2. As you can see in this figure, the two dimensions of coping include the situation-specific **coping strategy dimension** and the dispositional **coping style dimension** (Anshel & Si, 2008; Holt, Berg, & Tamminen, 2007). Thus, there are two levels of coping strategy (problem/emotion) and two levels of **coping style** (approach/avoidance). From a dispositional perspective, some athletes will prefer an approach style of coping while others will prefer an avoidance coping style. From a practical perspective, however, it is easy to see how three as opposed to two categories of coping strategy emerge from the sport literature. It is impractical to try to classify avoidance coping as being either problem or emotion focused. Instead, researchers have tended to classify coping strategies such as

FIGURE 9.2 | Conceptual framework for studying coping styles and strategies and examples.

| | **Dispositional coping style dimension** | |
	Approach	Avoidance
Problem Focused	Analyze reasons why errors were made and correct them	Apply a mental distraction
Emotion Focused	Use progressive relaxation to reduce stress	Vent unpleasant emotions, cry

Situation specific coping strategy dimension

Source: Based on Anshel, M. H., Williams, L. R. T., & Hodge, K. (1997). Cross-cultural and gender differences on coping style in sport. *International Journal of Sport Psychology, 28,* 141–156.

employing a mental distraction, distancing, venting emotions, resignation, and disengagement as simply being examples of an avoidance coping strategy (Compas, Connor-Smith, Saltzman, Harding-Thompson, & Wadsworth, 2001; Nicholls, Polman, Morley, & Taylor, 2009; Reeves, Nicholls, & McKenna, 2009). In the literature, the terms *coping style* and *coping strategy* are often used interchangeably.

While figure 9.2 is completely consistent with Lazarus and Folkman's original conceptualization of problem- and emotion-focused coping strategies, some sport psychologists have conceptualized a cognitive versus behavioral classification of approach-style coping strategies (Anshel & Sutarso, 2007; Nicholls, Holt, & Polman, 2005). While emotion-focused coping strategies are by definition behavioral in nature, problem-focused coping strategies can be either cognitive or behavioral in nature. Consequently, when we divide up the approach-coping strategies into cognitive- and behavioral-focused as opposed to problem- and emotion-focused, this changes the classification system, and not just the names we give the coping strategies.

Measurement of Coping Skill

Several different pencil-and-paper inventories have been developed to measure coping resources. Among them are the Ways of Coping Checklist (WOCC; Crocker, 1992; Folkman & Lazarus, 1985); the COPE and MCOPE instruments (Carver, Scheier, & Weintraub, 1989; Crocker & Graham, 1995); Coping Inventory for Stressful Situations (CISS; Endler & Parker, 1990); the Coping Style in Sport Survey (CSSS; Anshel et al., 1997); the Coping Function Questionnaire (CFQ; Kowalski & Crocker, 2001); and the Coping Inventory for Competitive Sport (CICS; Gaudreau & Blondin, 2002).

The Coping Style in Sport Survey (CSSS) was developed by Anshel et al. (1997) to reflect the coping styles and strategies conceptual framework illustrated in figure 9.2. The CSSS is composed of 134 items associated with seven common sports-related stressors. The athlete's task is to indicate how she would usually respond relative to the following acute stressors:

1. After making a physical or mental error
2. After being criticized by the coach
3. After observing my opponent cheat
4. After experiencing intense pain or injury
5. After receiving a "bad" call by the official
6. After successful performance by an opponent
7. After poor environmental conditions such as bad weather, poor ground/court conditions, or negative crowd reactions

The Dynamic Nature of Coping Styles and Strategies

Sport psychologists have been interested in knowing if athletes' coping strategies are dispositional in nature or if they are consistent with a dynamic

CONCEPT Athletes utilize a dynamic as opposed to dispositional approach to coping with stress. Different situations require different coping applications.

APPLICATION The dynamic nature of coping and the principle of specificity highlight the

importance of learning many different kinds of coping styles and strategies. If an athlete has numerous ways in which to cope with adversity, she will be more likely to find one that will be effective in a specific situation.

---

process. The **dispositional hypothesis** posits that athletes have a certain learned or innate way of coping with all stress-related situations. Conversely, the **dynamic hypothesis** posits that athletes' coping responses are dynamic and fluid, changing from situation to situation.

Applied research has generally supported the hypothesis that coping strategies and styles are dynamic and fluid. Research involving U.S. Olympic wrestlers, U.S. National Champion figure skaters, and elite Korean athletes all confirms this hypothesis. Elite athletes do not simply apply the same coping strategy to every situation, but rather select different strategies to fit different situations (Gould, Eklund, & Jackson, 1993; Gould, Finch, & Jackson, 1993; Park, 2000). The dynamic hypothesis was also supported by research reported by Crocker and Isaak (1997), Grove and Heard (1997), and Anshel and Si (2008).

While the majority of research supports the dynamic transitional hypothesis over the dispositional hypothesis, there are a few exceptions (Giacobbi & Weinberg, 2000; Louvet, Gaudreau, Menaut, Gentry, & Deneuve, 2007). The Louvet et al. study is of particular interest, because it provides support for both models. In this study, coping strategies were measured three times across a six-month competitive soccer season. Fifty percent of the participants exhibited stable unchanging coping strategies across the three time periods, while the other 50 percent showed significant dynamic changes across the three time periods.

Factors That Enhance the Generalizability of Coping

The skills athletes acquire to deal with anxiety, low self-confidence, and other stressful sport-related situations may generalize to other more global life situations. This means that if an athlete can learn to cope with failure (or success) in an athletic situation, the coping skill may be transferred to another sport situation or even a stressful nonsport situation (e.g., illness, financial setback, loss of job, loss of friend).

In this regard, Smith (1999) identified five different factors that can facilitate the **generalizability of coping skills** to other situations. These factors are as follows:

1. *Recognition of stimulus generality* Many stressful life situations are very similar to athletic situations. Recognizing the similarity and recalling the specific coping strategy that was effective in the athletic situation will facilitate transfer of coping skill to another situation.

2. *Broad application of coping skill* Some coping skills are very specific to a specific athletic situation, but others are very broad. Progressive relaxation, for example, is a broad coping skill that should generalize to numerous sport and nonsport situations.

3. *Personal significance of coping application* A coping skill that was effective in reducing stress related to an issue of great personal

CONCEPT Factors such as stimulus generality, broad application, personal significance, being in control, and learned resourcefulness are all important in enhancing the generalizability of coping skills.

APPLICATION As coaches teach and athletes learn coping skills, it is important to understand the broad potential application of these skills. In a sense, all coping skills should be taught with the thought in mind that they should transfer to other situations as well. Coping skills learned in sport situations should generalize to the nonsport environment, and vice versa. To accomplish this, the athlete and coach must think in terms of broad application and ways of enhancing generalizability.

significance will be remembered. Coping skills that have proven to be personally important will generalize to other situations.

4. *Internal locus of control of coping skill* When an athlete claims "ownership" of a coping skill, it is more easily transferred to other situations.

5. *Learned resourcefulness* Learning a specific coping skill to address a specific life stress is effective, but it is narrow-minded. The resourceful individual looks for broader application of all coping skills and learning experiences.

Factors That Influence Coping Effectiveness

Research shows that female athletes are more effective at employing coping strategies than are male athletes. Women use emotion-focused coping better than men and they benefit more from social support (Hammereister & Burton, 2004). Both approach and avoidance styles of coping can be effective in the short run, but only approach styles are effective long term (Kim & Duda, 2003). The **matching hypothesis** states that coping resources should be matched with stressors for maximum effectiveness. For example, a cognitive coping strategy might be more effective in addressing the debilitating effects of cognitive anxiety than an emotion-focused coping strategy

Cyclists coping with competition and the environment.
Eyewire/Getty Images.

(Campen & Roberts, 2001). Related to motivation is the observation that the effectiveness of coping in sport is connected to an athlete's perception of self-determination (Amiot, Gaudreau, & Blanchard, 2004). Autonomous motivation is linked to

CONCEPT   Factors such as sex of athlete, match between stressor and coping strategy, coping style (approach/avoidance), and self-determination (intrinsic motivation) all have an influence on the effectiveness of an athlete's attempts to cope with adversity.

APPLICATION   From an applied perspective, nothing can be done about the sex of the athlete, but a great deal can be done about matching the coping strategy with the stressor, developing self-determination, and ultimately influencing the long-term effectiveness of coping. An approach coping style should be encouraged by coaches, as this will lead to greater likelihood of goal attainment. Furthermore, as we learned in chapter 3, coaches must continually focus on the development of intrinsic motivation, as opposed to a reliance on external rewards.

---

an approach style of coping, whereas less self-determined motivation is linked to an avoidance style of coping.

The most effective coping strategies are those that are used most frequently, are proactive in nature, and are well practiced and learned (Holt et al., 2007; Nicholls, Holt, Polman, & Bloomfield, 2006). **Proactive coping strategies** are those in which the athlete anticipates in advance potential stressors and prepares for them. In a similar vein, **automated coping strategies** are those that are well practiced and frequently used. Strategies associated with effective coping include such things as thinking ahead, being relaxed, following planned routine, optimizing emotions, reappraising, and seeking social support. Conversely, Ineffective coping is associated with trying too hard, speeding up, routine changes, negative thinking, and failure to use coping to deal with stress (Nicholls, Holt, & Polman, 2005). Athletes who effectively cope with stress tend to use problem-focused coping strategies as opposed to avoidance strategies (Gaudreau & Blondin, 2004). A case in point is an investigation in which 65 male members of a soccer academy were tracked across 15 years to determine which athletes were successful in reaching their goal to play on professional teams and which were not. The two groups of athletes differed significantly on three factors including goal · commitment and motivation,

problem-focused coping skills, and need for social support (Van Yperen, 2009).

In summary, we can give at least three explanations for coping effectiveness. These include (a) the matching or goodness of fit hypothesis, (b) function of selection of coping response, and (c) automaticity of coping response. Relative to the matching hypothesis it might seem obvious that a cognitive stressor would be best addressed with a cognitive coping response, but there is another issue involved relative to the goodness of fit hypothesis. This is the principle of *perceived controllability*. If a stressor is believed to be controllable, then a problem-focused coping response would be most effective. Conversely, if a stressor is perceived to be uncontrollable, then an emotion-focused coping strategy would be most effective (Nicholls, Holt, & Polman, 2005). This principle is illustrated in figure 9.3

Sources of Stress and Coping Strategies Used by Athletes

Numerous recent studies have been conducted and reported by researchers relative to sources of stress experienced and coping responses selected. While some common themes emerge from these investigations, much of what is reported is situation specific in terms of age, sport, skill level, and gender (Anshel & Sutarso, 2007; Buman, Omli, Giacobbi, &

FIGURE 9.3 | Coping strategy effectiveness as a function of perceived controllability (based on Nicholls, Holt, & Polman, 2005).

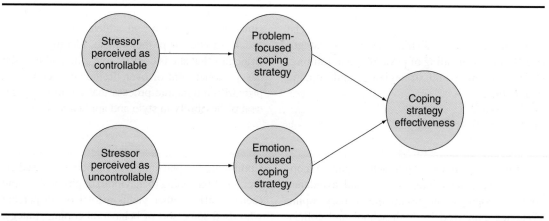

Brewer, 2008; Giacobbi, Foore, & Weinberg, 2004; Nicholls, Holt, & Polman, 2005; Nicholls, Holt, Polman, & Bloomfield, 2006; Nicholls, Holt, Polman, & James, 2005; Park, 2000; Reeves et al., 2009; Sager, Lavallee, & Spray, 2009). While each study is interesting relative to stressors identified and coping responses selected, the specificity of each study makes it impractical to review each separately. Consequently, common sources of stress and coping responses will be briefly summarized in separate sections.

Sources of Stress Anshel and Sutarso (2007) reduced a multitude of perceived stressors down to those related to athletes' performance and those related to the coach. Commonly mentioned sources of stress for professional male rugby players include worry about injuries, mental errors, and physical errors (Nicholls, Holt, Polman, & Bloomfield, 2006). Elite female soccer players identify coach/player communication, competitive stressors (anxiety, mistakes, evaluations, playing time), pace and demand of international soccer, fatigue, and opponent distractions as common sources of stress (Holt & Hogg, 2002). Several studies looked at sources of stress in golfers (Giacobbi et al., 2004; Nicholls, Holt, Polman, &

James, 2005). Common sources of stress associated with golf include concern about mental errors, physical errors, opponents playing well, weather conditions, and competitive stress. Fear of failure was identified as a common source of threat among elite 14–17-year-old British athletes (Sager et al., 2009). Important sources of fear of failure in these young athletes included (a) fear of experiencing shame and embarrassment, (b) fear of devaluing one's self-estimate, (c) fear of important others losing interest, (d) fear of an uncertain future, (e) fear of upsetting significant others, and (f) fear of performing poorly. Finally, Reeve et al. (2009) reported on a developmental study involving male members of a soccer academy. In this investigation, participants were divided into two groups based on age and then contrasted in terms of perceived sources of stress (12–14 and 15–18 years). Both groups were equally concerned about making errors, team performance, coaches, team selection, opposing teams, and individual performance. The early adolescent group experienced greater stress associated with family concerns, whereas the older adolescent group experienced greater stress associated with physical demands, contractual issues, playing at a higher level, and mental stress.

CONCEPT Elite athletes tend to use an approach style of coping, with the majority of the strategies being problem or action focused. The vast majority of coping strategies may be categorized under the heading of psychological training, physical training and strategizing, and somatic relaxation.

APPLICATION While coping strategies tend to be of the approach variety, they vary greatly from situation to situation and athlete to athlete. The coach should help the athlete identify coping strategies that she is comfortable with and that she has personal control over. Remember, coping is primarily a dynamic process that requires a great deal of flexibility in style and application.

Coping Responses Approach cognitive coping, approach behavioral coping, and avoidance cognitive coping strategies are the primary coping strategies employed by high school and college athletes for dealing with performance and coach stressors. Among these three, approach behavioral coping was found to be most effective in dealing with both performance and coaching stress (Anshel & Sutarso, 2007). When approach coping strategies were conceptually categorized as being either problem or emotion focused, it was the problem-focused coping strategies that were used the most across studies (Nicholls, Holt, Polman, & Bloomfield, 2006; Nicholls, Holt, Polman, & James, 2005; Sager et al., 2009). When approach coping strategies were conceptually categorized as being either cognitive or behavioral in nature, there was a nearly equal split between which strategy was used the most (Anshel & Sutarso, 2007; Nichols, Holt, & Polman, 2005). A case in point was a study involving marathon runners in which the identified source of the stressor was dealing with "hitting the wall" near the end of the race (Buman et al., 2008). In this study involving 57 athletes, 51 percent indicated that they used cognitive coping strategies to deal with the stress (e.g., dissociation, self-talk, mental reframing), 44 percent said they tried physical effort coping strategies (e.g., slow pace, hydration, pain killers, supplements), 12 percent indicated trying emotion-focused strategies (e.g., social support from other runners, emotional regulation), and 30 percent admitted to not using any kind of coping strategy.

Combining the percentage of runners who used either emotion coping (behavioral) or physical coping (behavioral) together yields a total of 56 percent who used some sort of behavioral coping strategy. Thus, the percent who tried a behavioral strategy (56 percent) was nearly equal to the number who tried a cognitive strategy (51 percent).

Self-Talk as an Intervention

> When you step into the water you have to tell yourself a thousand times "I can swim the channel. I can swim the channel." I can't tell you how many times over the past year, two years I have said that to myself. (An athlete's self-talk thoughts on preparing to swim the English Channel, a distance of approximately 27 miles; Hollander & Acedvedo, 2000, p. 6)

It is an observed fact that athletes engage in self-talk during practice and competition (Cutton & Landin, 2007; Hardy, 2006; Van Raalte, Brewer, Rivera, & Petitpas, 1994; Van Raalte, Cornelius, Brewer, & Hatten, 2000). Sometimes the self-talk is positive in nature and sometimes it is negative in nature.

While the primary purpose of this section is to discuss the beneficial effects of positive self-talk on athletic performance, we would be remiss to ignore negative self-talk entirely as it has been reported to occur twice as often as positive self-talk in junior tennis players (Van Raalte, Brewer, et al., 1994). In a cross-cultural study, Peters and Williams (2006) reported on a study in which a higher proportion of negative self-talk thoughts to positive thoughts predicted decreased dart-tossing performance in American-born college students, but predicted increased performance in Asian-born college students. This result suggests that the effect of negative thoughts on performance may be culturally biased. Notwithstanding this conflicting result, Hatzigeorgiadis and Biddle (2008) reported on an investigation, associated with a timed 2.5 mile race, in which negative self-talk predicted (a) a decrease in cognitive anxiety direction (more debilitative), (b) an increase in cognitive anxiety intensity, and (c) a decrease in running performance compared to prestart goal. While more research is needed on the effect of negative self-talk on performance, at this point we conclude that negative self-talk should be discouraged. From this point on, our discussion will focus only upon positive self-talk.

Consistent with Hardy, Gammage, and Hall (2001), we will define **self-talk** as overt or covert personal dialogue in which the athlete interprets feelings, perceptions, and convictions and gives himself instructions and reinforcement. Perhaps one of the best explanations of the nature and function of self-talk was provided by Hardy, Gammage, et al. (2001). In this excellent paper, the authors discuss research that focuses upon the where, when, what, and why of self-talk. They referred to these factors as the **4 Ws of self-talk**.

The Where and When of Self-Talk

Athletes use self-talk in both sports-related and non-sports-related venues. Sports-related venues include such places as the practice environment, the competitive environment, the dressing room, and the bench. Non-sports-related venues include the home or any quiet place. Next to sports-related venues, the home is the second most common place for self-talk to take place. Within the sports-related environment, the most common time for self-talk to take place is during competition, with "during practice" being a distant second. Self-talk takes place equally either before or during competition. Relative to the competitive season, self-talk increases

linearly as the season progresses from preseason through early season to late season. Individual sport athletes report using self-talk to a greater degree than team sport athletes, and more highly skilled athletes use it more frequently than less skilled athletes (Hardy, Gammage, et al., 2001; Hardy, Hall, & Hardy, 2004).

The What of Self-Talk

The what of self-talk represents the content of self-talk. By far, the most documented "what's" are structure and task instruction. *Structure* of self-talk describes the use of cue words, phrases, and sentences, of which phrases are the most common. *Task instruction* is usually specific as opposed to general in nature (Hardy, Gammage, et al., 2001).

Self-talk can be in the form of words actually spoken, or in the form of thoughts that come into one's mind. These thoughts can be either positive or negative. As a psychological method for improving self-confidence, self-talk must be positive in nature and lead to positive feelings about an athlete's ability. Evidence exists to support the use of self-talk for the purpose of enhancing self-confidence. Self-talk is a strategy used by both junior and professional tennis players (DeFrancesco & Burke, 1997; Gould, Russell, Damarjian, & Lauer, 1999). In addition to demonstrating the effectiveness of self-talk in a study involving female collegiate tennis players, Landin and Herbert (1999) discuss the different types of self-talk as well as guidelines for its implementation. Three primary categories of self-talk include task-specific statements, encouragement and effort, and mood words. These three categories are further clarified below:

1. *Task-specific statements relating to technique* This category of self-talk refers to words or statements that reinforce technique. For example, in the tennis volley, the word "turn" might be used in association with preparation for stepping into the volley.

2. *Encouragement and effort* This category of self-talk refers to words or statements that provide self-encouragement to persevere

or to try harder. For example, the phrase "You can do it" might be used in preparation for an anticipated play at home plate in softball.

3. *Mood words* This category of self-talk refers to words that precipitate an increase in mood or arousal. For example, the mood words "hard" or "blast" might be used in conjunction with a play in football or soccer.

For self-talk to be effective, it is suggested that self-talk statements be (a) brief and phonetically simple, (b) logically associated with the skill involved, and (c) compatible with the sequential timing of the task being performed. In the Landin and Herbert (1999) investigation, the skill being practiced was the tennis volley. Two important components of executing the volley are the split stop, referring to the position of the feet prior to executing the volley, and the shoulder turn in preparation for the actual stroke. Key words used for self-talk were "split" and "turn," spoken in rhythm with the timing of the actual execution of the skill.

The Why of Self-Talk

The why of self-talk describes its role and function. The two main functions of self-talk are cognition and motivation. The cognitive component of self-talk is used to assist in skill development, skill execution, improvement in performance, and execution and planning of strategy. The motivational component of self-talk is instrumental in developing self-confidence, focusing attention, controlling arousal, and maintaining drive (Hardy, Gammage, et al., 2001).

Williams, Zinsser, and Bunker (2010) identify specific uses or functions of self-talk. From their perspective, one of the most important uses of self-talk is the building and enhancing of self-efficacy and self-confidence. This position is further reinforced by Conroy and Metzler (2004), who studied the association between self-talk and state anxiety. An association between self-talk and reduced anxiety would also provide evidence of an association between self-talk and self-confidence, because of

the strong negative association between state anxiety and self-confidence (Cox, Martens, et al., 2003). A partial summary of the Williams, Zinsser, et al. (2010) list is as follows:

1. *Building and developing self-efficacy* Self-talk is effective in stimulating thoughts and feelings that lead to the belief that a person is competent and able to perform a task efficiently and effectively.

2. *Skill acquisition* Learning a new skill requires persistence, effort, and dedication. Self-talk can be effective in helping the athlete to continue to work hard in order to achieve a worthwhile goal. In becoming proficient in a new skill, the athlete changes bad habits and learns new good habits.

3. *Creating and changing mood* Effective use of mood words can either create a desired mood or change an undesirable one. Words are powerful motivators because of the meaning that they convey. In an effort to increase power needed to get out of a sprinter's block quickly, the athlete might say the words "go" or "explode" as she powers forward.

4. *Controlling effort* Athletes need to be able to sustain effort throughout long practices or competitions. Self-talk can suggest to the athlete the need to increase effort when it is needed or to sustain effort when it is deemed beneficial for performance learning or enhancement. During long practices, boredom can be a challenge that must be overcome. Self-talk words and phrases such as "pick it up," "stay with it," or "pace" can be effective in controlling effort.

5. *Focusing attention or concentration* As with maintaining effort, it is often necessary to remind yourself to stay focused or to concentrate on the task at hand. Athletes often get tired, and when this happens, their concentration can easily wander. If the mind wanders when the coach is teaching an important concept relating to the athlete's role

TABLE 9.1 | Examples of Self-Affirmation Statements to Be Used by the Athlete

Sport Situation	Affirmation Statement
Goalie in Soccer	"Nothing gets by me"
Server in Tennis	"I can hit a strong and accurate first serve"
Shooter in Basketball	"Nothing but net for me"
Receiver in Volleyball	"I am a consistent and accurate passer"
Quarterback in Football	"I have a cannon for a throwing arm"
Wrestler	"I am strong as a bull"
Golf	"I have the perfect swing"

on the team, it is imperative that he heighten and maintain concentration. Such words and phrases as "focus," "stay with it," or "now" can help the athlete stay focused.

Feelings of confidence, efficacy, and personal control will be enhanced if coaches and sport psychologists assist the athlete in preselecting and constructing **affirmation statements** that can be used during competition or during preparation for competition. These are statements that affirm to the athlete that she possesses the skills, abilities, positive attitudes, and beliefs necessary for successful performance. These self-affirmation statements must be both believable and vivid. Do not leave it to the athlete to come up with these important thoughts or statements at the exact moment that they are needed, but prepare them in advance. Some examples are illustrated in table 9.1.

Research suggests that there is a matching relationship between self-talk cues and function of self-talk. For example, a self-talk statement suggesting greater anxiety control (e.g. relax, you can do it) results in an increase in measured functional control of anxiety. Similarly, a self-talk statement suggesting greater attentional focus should result in an increase in measured functional control for attention (Hatzigeorgiadis, Zourbanos, & Theodorakis, 2007). As already mentioned, self-talk is an effective intervention for increasing self-confidence and self-efficacy. This has been recently verified in research involving the forehand drive in tennis (Hatzigeorgiadis, Zourbanos, Goltsios, & Theodorakis, 2008; Hatzigeorgiadis, Zourbanos, Mpoumpaki, & Theodorakis, 2009). In addition, these two investigations also demonstrated that self-confidence and self-efficacy mediate the relationship between self-talk and athletic performance as illustrated here:

Self-Talk → Self-Confidence → Performance

Measuring Self-Talk

Pencil and pencil inventories designed to measure self-talk in sport are of a relatively recent origin, beginning in the year 2000 with the Thought Occurrence Questionnaire for Sport (TOQS; Hatzigeorgiadis & Biddle, 2000). The TOQS is an instrument that asks the athlete to report on negative thoughts (worry), task irrelevant thoughts, and thoughts of escape. Since that time, five additional inventories have been developed. These instruments can generally be classified as a function of the 4 Ws of self-talk (where, when, what, and why), but some variations on those themes have emerged. A summary of the inventories that have been developed and used by practitioners and researchers are illustrated in table 9.2.

Research Support for Self-Talk

Theodorakis, Weinberg, Natsis, Douma, and Kazakas (2000) and Hardy (2006) provide excellent reviews of research that shows general support for the use of self-talk strategies to improve performance in exercise and sport tasks. In addition, Theodorakis et al. (2000) report the results of

CONCEPT   Self-talk is an effective technique to control thoughts and to influence feelings. Thoughts and feelings can influence self-confidence as well as performance.

APPLICATION   Thoughts that come into an athlete's mind during competition can be either positive or negative. These thoughts are a form of self-talk. The athlete must learn to control his thoughts and to structure them to his advantage. This is effectively accomplished through self-talk. The athlete must carefully preselect the actual words and phrases used during self-talk and consider them for maximum effectiveness. The coach or sport psychologist can assist the athlete in this regard.

TABLE 9.2 | Inventories Designed to Measure Self-Talk

Valence	Inventory Name	Reference	Purpose
Negative	Thought Occurrence Questionnaire for Sport (TOQS)	Hatzigeorgiadis and Biddle (2000)	Covert thoughts (worry, irrelevant, escape)
	Negative Self-Talk Questionnaire (NSTQ)	Hardy, Roberts, and Hardy (2009)	Motivation to change, awareness of use, and content
Positive	Self-Talk Use Questionnaire (STUQ)	Hardy, Hall, and Hardy (2005)	Where, When, What, Why, and How
	Self-Talk Questionnaire (S-TQ)	Zervas, Stavrou, and Psychountaki (2007)	Why (function)
	Functions of Self-Talk Questionnaire (FSTQ)	Theodorakis, Hatzigeorgiadis, and Chroni (2008)	Why (function)
	Automatic Self-Talk Questionnaire for Sports (ASTQS)	Zourbanos, Hatzigeorgiadis, Chroni, Theodorakis, and Papaioannou (2009)	What (content and structure)

experiments designed to contrast the efficacy of "motivational" and "instructional" self-talk strategies compared to a control condition.

Research by Hatzigeorgiadis, Theodorakis, and Zourbanos (2004) provides strong experimental support for the efficacy of self-talk as an intervention or coping strategy for improving athletic performance. Utilizing water polo athletes and two different water polo tosses, they investigated the relative effectiveness of two different types of self-talk (instructional/motivational) on tossing performance. Both types of self-talk were more effective than a control group for improving either tossing task. The study also showed a significant decline in attentional distraction during experimental testing compared to the control group, leading the researchers to conclude that reduced attentional distraction was one important explanation for the effectiveness of self-talk. Similarly, experimental support for the efficacy of self-talk in improving basketball performance has been reported (Perkos, Theodorakis, & Chroni, 2002; Theodorakis, Chroni, Laparidis, Bebetos, & Duoma, 2001).

Additional support for the efficacy of using self-talk to improve athletic performance has been reported using a single-subject multiple-baseline design. If athletes improve performance following the intervention compared to their control performance, this is evidence of the effectiveness of self-talk. In a study involving five junior ice

CONCEPT An important part of any relaxation procedure is to focus attention on a mental device.

APPLICATION Two mental devices are highly recommended for the athlete. The first is to take a deep breath and exhale slowly, and the second is the use of a *mantra,* or key word or phrase. Athletes can focus on the key phrase and slow air release as they relax.

---

hockey goaltenders, goal save performance was monitored across a six-month season. Results showed that self-talk was effective in improving goal-tending performance across the season (Rogerson & Hrycaiko, 2002). Similarly, in a study involving four elite female youth soccer players, soccer goal shooting performance was improved compared to a control subject as well as to their own preintervention (self-talk) performance (Johnson, Hrycaiko, Johnson, & Halas, 2004).

Relaxation Strategies Used in Sport

> I think a lot of it has to do with me pressing. It's in my head. I'm trying harder, and the harder I try, the worse it goes. I've just got to try and relax. But the more I miss, the harder it is to relax, so it's just a vicious circle.
>
> (Jeff Jaeger, place kicker, Cleveland Browns, 1987)

While some athletes may suffer from low levels of arousal, the more difficult problems occur with athletes who experience excessively high levels of anxiety and tension. For these athletes, any strategy calculated to heighten arousal can only cause greater anxiety and tension. Typically, what happens is that an initial increase in anxiety leads to a decrease in performance. This decrease in performance itself results in even greater anxiety, resulting in the **anxiety/stress spiral.** There is only one way out of this spiral, and that is to reverse the process by reducing the anxiety and tension. *Relaxation procedures* can effectively reduce tension and anxiety associated with sport. In this section, we will discuss some of them.

Four prevalent relaxation procedures can be adequately categorized under the broad heading of relaxation. These are (1) progressive relaxation, (2) autogenic training, (3) meditation, and (4) biofeedback. Each procedure is unique, but they all yield essentially the same physiological result. That is, they all result in the **relaxation response.** The relaxation response consists of physiological changes that are opposite to the "fight or flight" response of the sympathetic nervous system. Specifically,

Athletes engage in self-talk to help them prepare to execute a skill. Courtesy University of Missouri–Columbia Sports Information.

procedures such as progressive relaxation, autogenic training, and meditation result in decreases in oxygen consumption, heart rate, respiration, and skeletal muscle activity, while they increase skin resistance and alpha brain waves.

Four different factors are necessary for eliciting the relaxation response. Each of these factors is present to some degree in the specific relaxation techniques that we will discuss. These four elements or factors are (1) a **mental device,** (2) a passive attitude, (3) decreased muscle tone, and (4) a quiet environment. The mental device is generally some sort of word, phrase, object, or process used to shift attention inward.

Before discussing specific relaxation procedures, it is essential that the issue of *need* be addressed. Except in a general way, athletes who are *not* overly aroused may not benefit from relaxation intervention. In fact, the danger exists that an athlete who is "misdiagnosed" by his coach as tense and anxious may become drowsy and broadly focused as a result of arousal reduction. This problem is identified because coaches may be inaccurate estimators of athletes' competitive state and trait anxiety (Hanson & Gould, 1988). A coach should make sure that an athlete is actually suffering from anxiety and tension before applying an arousal adjustment intervention.

In this section we will discuss specific relaxation techniques that are designed to bring about the relaxation response. Mastering the technique of **deep breathing** for the purpose of relaxation and relieving tension is an important component of each of the relaxation techniques we will discuss. As explained by Davis, Eshelman, and McKay (1995), two patterns of breathing are typically used: chest or thoracic breathing, and abdominal or diaphragmatic breathing. **Chest breathing** is usually associated with emotional distress and is often shallow, irregular, and rapid. Conversely, **abdominal breathing** is associated with relaxation and is often deep, regular, and slow. In practicing the relaxation procedures introduced in this chapter, the athlete must practice relaxing through deep breathing. The process of deeply inhaling and exhaling in

a slow rhythmic fashion is very relaxing to the body and mind. Deep breathing can be practiced at any time or in any place (e.g., a basketball free-throw line), but it is most effective while sitting or lying down on one's back in a comfortable position. Each time the athlete breathes out, she should imagine that she is expelling tension from her body. When practicing deep breathing, place one hand lightly on your chest and the other on your diaphragm. You should feel small amounts of movement under the hand resting on the chest, and large rhythmic movement under the hand on the diaphragm.

When learning relaxation strategies for the purpose of performance enhancement, it is critical that the athlete have in mind some optimal level of arousal or relaxation that he is seeking. Becoming too relaxed just before an event requiring great physical exertion may be worse than being overly aroused or anxious. In this regard, advice given by Dan O'Brian, the U.S. 1996 Olympic decathlon champion, is instructive (O'Brian & Sloan, 1999). Dan mentioned two principles that he believes are of great importance when preparing for optimal performance in the decathlon:

1. "The athlete has to be able to turn it on and then turn it off in a short period of time."

2. "Give me a 90 percent effort, not 100 or 110, for best performance."

Dan's first principle underscores the importance of mastering relaxation and arousal energizing strategies for the purpose of immediate application. During one phase of preparation for competition, an athlete is trying to relax and conserve energy. Yet in another phase, perhaps separated by minutes, he has to be able to activate the arousal response in anticipation of maximal effort. Dan's second principle underscores the important concept that best performance, regardless of activity, is probably not at a super-aroused level. Baseball pitchers routinely comment that they have their best "stuff" when they are a bit fatigued and not trying to throw 100 mph fastballs. With these preliminary principles and reminders firmly in mind, we now turn to a discussion of specific

CONCEPT It is difficult for a coach to accurately estimate an athlete's level of competitive state anxiety.

APPLICATION If a coach believes that an athlete is suffering a decrement in performance due to elevated competitive state anxiety, she should

consider recommending an arousal control intervention. However, before actually referring the athlete for treatment, the coach should make sure that she has not misdiagnosed the athlete. This can be accomplished through the administration of a state anxiety inventory, discussed in chapter 7.

CONCEPT Deep breathing is associated with relaxation and involves expanding the abdominal area more than the chest.

APPLICATION The athlete should practice deep breathing in order to feel the difference between

breathing with the diaphragm and breathing with the chest. Deep breathing involves rhythmic breathing as opposed to shallow, irregular, fast breathing. In deep breathing, each phase of expiration should be mentally linked with the feeling of expelling pent-up tension and anxiety.

relaxation strategies used by athletes to reduce anxiety and to control physiological arousal.

Progressive Relaxation

Modern progressive relaxation techniques are all variations of those outlined by Edmond Jacobson (1929, 1938). Jacobson began his work with progressive relaxation in the early part of the twentieth century. It was Jacobson's basic thesis that it is impossible to be nervous or tense in any part of the body where the muscles are completely relaxed. In addition, Jacobson believed that nervousness and tenseness of involuntary muscles and organs could be reduced if the associated skeletal muscles were relaxed. According to Jacobson, an anxious mind cannot exist in a relaxed body.

Jacobson's **progressive relaxation** procedure requires that subjects lie on their backs with their arms to the side. Occasionally a sitting posture in a comfortable chair is recommended. In either case, the room should be fairly quiet and arms and

legs should not be crossed, to avoid unnecessary stimulation. While the goal of any progressive relaxation program is to relax the entire body in a matter of minutes, it is essential that in the beginning the subject practice the technique for at least one hour every day. Once the relaxation procedure is well learned, the relaxation response can be achieved in a few minutes.

Jacobson's method calls for the subject to tense a muscle before relaxing it. The tensing helps the subject recognize the difference between tension and relaxation. Once the subject can do this, he should be able to relax a limb completely without tensing it first. Jacobson warns that only the first few minutes of any relaxation session should be devoted to muscle tensing. The remaining time should be devoted to gaining complete relaxation. For a muscle to be considered relaxed, it must be completely absent of any contractions and must be limp and motionless.

Jacobson's full progressive relaxation procedure involves systematically tensing and relaxing

CONCEPT   Learning how to relax the muscles of the body is a foundation skill for all stress management and intervention strategies.

APPLICATION   As a first step in learning how to control anxiety and stress, the athlete must become proficient at relaxing the mind and the body.

specific muscle groups in a predetermined order. Relaxation begins with the muscles of the left arm and proceeds to those of the right arm, left and right legs, abdomen, back, and chest and shoulders, concluding with the neck and face muscles. The full training procedure lasts many months. In the beginning stages, an entire session should be devoted to the total relaxation of a single muscle group. While it is unrealistic to expect an athlete to devote this much time to learning to relax, Jacobson's point is well taken. A well-developed relaxation training program requires a great deal of practice in the beginning. It is unrealistic to expect an athlete to elicit the relaxation response at will after only one or two 15-minute practice sessions. However, after several months of practice and training, it should be possible to evoke the relaxation response in a matter of seconds.

Abbreviated versions of Jacobson's full 40-session procedure have been proposed (Davis, Eshelman, et al., 1995; Greenberg, 2009). A review by Carlson and Hoyle (1993) provided evidence that abbreviated progressive relaxation training procedures are effective in reducing anxiety, tension, and stress. Numerous variations of Jacobson's original progressive relaxation procedure have proved to be effective. For example, it is not necessary that the procedure always start with the left arm. And in some cases a muscle contraction could be best accomplished by applying resistance to an immovable object.

The ultimate goal of any relaxation training program is to evoke the relaxation response to counter stress in a specific situation. For example, a professional golfer does not have 30 minutes to relax prior to a $15,000 putt. The golfer must be able to accomplish this while waiting to putt, a skill that takes many hours of practice to master.

Research has clearly shown that progressive relaxation procedures are effective in eliciting the relaxation response. Additionally, numerous investigations have shown that when used in conjunction with other cognitive or arousal control interventions, it is associated with increased sports performance. Greenspan and Feltz (1989) critically reviewed nine investigations in which forms of relaxation intervention were involved. The majority of the studies showed that increased performance was associated with arousal control in combination with some other cognitive technique. Few studies, however, have shown that progressive relaxation procedures alone effectively enhance performance. For example, Wrisberg and Anshel (1989) showed that relaxation used in conjunction with imagery was effective in enhancing the basketball shooting performance of young boys. Neither imagery nor relaxation training alone was effective in enhancing shooting performance. In conjunction with adequate preparation, muscle relaxation training is effective in enhancing an athlete's tolerance to pain (Broucek, Bartholomew, Landers, & Linder, 1993).

Autogenic Training

Autogenic training and progressive relaxation both elicit the relaxation response. Whereas progressive relaxation relies upon dynamic contracting and relaxing of muscles, **autogenic training** relies upon feelings associated with the limbs and muscles of the body. Autogenic training is very similar to autohypnosis, and is based upon early research with hypnosis. The procedure was first developed by the German psychiatrist Johannes Schultz (Schultz & Luthe, 1959). In working with hypnotized patients, Schultz noted that they invariably reported two bodily sensations associated with the

CONCEPT Meditation, if properly used, can result in the relaxation response and offers an excellent vehicle for practicing and refining selective attention skills.

APPLICATION Meditation offers the individual sport athlete one of the best tools for relaxing and learning to control attention in preparation for athletic competition. Sporting events such as diving, gymnastics, and field events (track and field) could effectively utilize meditation as a means to prepare for the next dive, routine, or toss.

---

relaxation response. These two sensations were heaviness in the limbs and a feeling of general warmth in the body, arms, and legs. In its simplest form, autogenic training consists of a series of mental exercises designed to bring about these two bodily states. Limbs feel heavy because of a total lack of muscle tension, and the body feels warm due to dilation of blood vessels (a parasympathetic nervous system response).

Various authors have suggested different exercises and self-statements to bring about the relaxation response using autogenic training (Davis, Eshelman, et al., 1995; Greenberg, 2009). Essentially, autogenic training is composed of three component parts that are often intermingled. The first and most important part is the six initial steps designed to suggest to the mind a feeling of warmth in the body and heaviness in the limbs. These six self-statement steps are as follows:

1. Heaviness in the arms and legs (beginning with the dominant arm or leg)
2. Warmth in the arms and the legs (again, beginning with the dominant arm or leg)
3. Warmth in the chest and a perception of reduced heart rate
4. Calm and relaxed breathing
5. Warmth in the solar plexus area
6. Sensation of coolness on the forehead

The second component part of autogenic training involves the use of imagery. In this step, the subject is encouraged to visualize images of relaxing scenes while at the same time focusing upon feelings of warmth and heaviness in the arms and legs. The third component of autogenic training involves the use of *specific themes* (Davis, Eshelman, et al., 1995) to assist in bringing about the relaxation response. One particularly effective specific theme is the use of self-statements to suggest to the mind that the body is indeed relaxed.

As with progressive relaxation, research has clearly shown that when used properly, autogenic training is effective in bringing about the relaxation response (Benson, Beary, & Carol, 1974). Autogenic training requires several months and a great deal of practice to master. Once mastered, it can be utilized to bring about the relaxation response in a matter of minutes. Whereas the relaxation benefits of this technique are well documented, very little evidence exists to suggest that autogenic training by itself enhances athletic performance. Spigolon and Annalisa (1985) provide anecdotal evidence to suggest that autogenic training is related to improved athletic performance.

More recently, Groslambert, Candau, Grappe, Dugue, and Rouillon (2003) provided evidence that demonstrated the effectiveness of autogenic training in the French Biathlon. The biathlon is a winter sport that combines cross-country skiing with rifle marksmanship. Compared to a classical training condition, a condition that included six weeks of classical training plus autogenic training demonstrated greater improvement in terms of standing stability control while shooting. No difference, however, was noted for marksmanship.

Various authors have outlined autogenic training and relaxation programs that can be adopted by the athlete (Greenberg, 2009). Table 9.3 includes a

TABLE 9.3 | Suggested Instructions and Statements That May Be Included in an Autogenic Training Presentation

1. Locate a quiet room or environment where you will not be disturbed.
2. Find a comfortable area where you can sit or lie down on your back.
3. Close your eyes and put away thoughts of the outside world.
4. Begin by practicing some deep breathing to help you to relax.
5. Slowly inhale, exhale, inhale, exhale, inhale, exhale.
6. Each time you exhale, *feel* the tension being expelled from your body.
7. Now that you are feeling relaxed and your breathing has stabilized, begin suggesting to yourself that your limbs are beginning to feel heavy.
8. "My right arm feels heavy," "my left arm feels heavy," "both of my arms feel heavy," "my right leg feels heavy," "my left leg feels heavy," "both of my legs feel heavy," "my arms and legs feel heavy."
9. "My right arm feels warm," "my left arm feels warm," "both of my arms feel warm," "my right leg feels warm," "my left leg feels warm," "both of my legs feel warm," "my arms and legs feel warm."
10. "My chest area feels warm and my heartbeat feels slow and regular."
11. Focus for a few minutes upon your heart rate, while at the same time repeating to yourself that your heartbeat feels slow and regular.
12. Focus for a few minutes upon your breathing, while at the same time repeating to yourself that your respiration feels calm and relaxed.
13. Repeat several times: "My stomach area feels warm."
14. Repeat several times: "My forehead feels cool."
15. While experiencing feelings of warmth and heaviness in your limbs, warmth in your solar plexus and coolness in your forehead, imagine to yourself that you are on a warm sandy beach enjoying a cool lemonade while watching the waves flow in and out.
16. While enjoying this relaxing visual image (or some other one), repeat relaxing statements to yourself.
17. "I feel quiet."
18. "I feel warm and relaxed."
19. "My mind is at ease."

series of instructions and statements that can be used for teaching athletes to relax using autogenic training. Using this list and others, the athlete could develop and record her own autogenic training tape.

Meditation

Meditation, as a form of relaxation, is tied directly to the concepts of selective attention discussed in chapter 6. In practicing **meditation,** the individual attempts to uncritically focus his attention on a single thought, sound, or object. Meditation will result in the relaxation response if practiced in a quiet environment that is associated with a passive attitude and decreased muscle tone.

The practice of meditation as a form of relaxation and thought control had its origin in Eastern cultures more than four thousand years ago. The individual most responsible for exporting meditation to the Western cultures was Maharishi Mahesh Yogi of India. Referred to as **transcendental meditation,** Maharishi Mahesh Yogi's brand of meditation has been widely accepted in the United States and throughout the world. Other forms of Eastern culture meditation practices include Chakra yoga, Rinzai Zen, Mudra yoga, Sufism, Zen meditation, and Soto Zen (Greenberg, 2009). The most common *mental device* used in transcendental meditation is the repetition of a **mantra.** The mantra is a simple sound selected by the instructor as a mental concentration device. One such sound, "om" or "ahhom," has been popular. Other mental devices that have been used in meditation include the *mandala* (a geometric figure), *nadam* (imagined sounds), and *pranayama* (breathing).

In practice, the participant sits in a comfortable position with eyes closed. The participant concentrates on deep breathing while at the same time repeating the mantra. The sound of the mantra soon disappears as the mind experiences more subtle thought levels and finally arrives at the source of the thought. While most Oriental approaches teach a sitting meditation position, both Zen and transcendental meditation emphasize that standing or sitting are acceptable. Davis, Eshelman, et al. (1995) and Greenberg (2009) offer excellent ideas for enhancing and facilitating the meditation experience. Similar to transcendental meditation, Tai Chi is a moving form of meditation which originated in China. The stress reduction effects of Tai Chi are comparable to those received from moderate physical exercise.

While it is clear that the various forms of meditation can reduce anxiety and tension by evoking the relaxation response, it is not clear whether its practice has a facilitative effect on athletic performance. Like the effects of other forms of relaxation, the effects of meditation upon athletic performance are likely to be indirect. Meditation has a direct effect on reducing anxiety, tension, and stress, which in turn should have a facilitative effect on the performance of the anxiety-prone athlete. Attempts to link meditation training directly with improved athletic performance have met with mixed success. Meditation seems to be beneficial for performing gross motor skills such as the 50-meter dash, agility tasks, standing broad jump, and coordination tasks (Reddy, Bai, & Rao, 1976). But it seems to be of little facilitative value for performing fine motor tasks such as the rotary pursuit, mirror tracing, or pistol shooting (Hall & Hardy, 1991).

Integrative Mind-Body Training

Spearheaded by Yi-Yuan Tang, **integrative mind-body training** (IMBT) is a modern meditational approach to controlling the autonomic nervous system (Tang, Ma, Fan, et al., 2009; Tang, Ma, Wang, et al., 2007; Tang & Posner, 2009). Integrative mind-body training comes from the Eastern tradition with a focus upon achieving a mental state that lends itself to improved attention and self-regulation of the autonomic nervous system (ANS). Western approaches to relaxation have focused almost exclusively upon attention training that can be mentally fatiguing and therefore counterproductive to achieving and maintaining the relaxation response. The focus of IMBT is upon attention state training (AST) and not upon traditional Western style attention training. The goal of AST is to create a mental state of mind that facilitates enhanced arousal control, improved attention, and improved performance.

Traditional relaxation methods require focused effortful attention to achieve improved attention and relaxation. In contrast, the IMBT method focuses upon achieving a natural state of restful alertness that allows a high degree of body awareness, breathing, and external instruction from either a live instructor or from an instructor on a compact disk. Thought control is achieved gradually through posture, relaxation, body-mind harmony and balance. There is no effortful internal struggle to control thought or to achieve the relaxation response. Mental imagery, to be discussed in chapter 11, is an integral part of the IMBT method. IMBT integrates key components of body relaxation, breathing adjustment, mental imagery, and mindfulness training. IMBT focuses upon body-mind health, balance, and purification. In the final analysis, IMBT utilizes attentional state training to create a mental state that is receptive to reduced stress, focused attention, and mood regulation.

Research reported by Tang, Ma, Fan, et al. (2009) contrasted five days of integrative mind-body training with an equal amount of traditional relaxation training. Results showed that the IMBT group showed superior regulation of the autonomic

CONCEPT Biofeedback is an effective and powerful tool for reducing the debilitating effects of anxiety and stress.

APPLICATION If an athlete cannot control anxiety and stress using progressive relaxation, autogenic training, meditation, or integrative mind body training, then biofeedback training should be attempted. To begin biofeedback training, it may be necessary to identify a professional therapist. Equipment necessary for biofeedback training may not be readily available to the athlete or coach.

---

nervous system as evidenced through brain imaging data, heart rate control, respiration, and skin conductivity. In a related investigation, Marks (2008) reviewed research that provided evidence that meditation generally is supported by identifiable neuroanatomical changes in the brain as shown through functional magnetic imaging (fMRI) and the EEG.

Biofeedback Training

It has been demonstrated that humans can voluntarily control functions of the autonomic nervous system. Biofeedback is a relatively modern technique that is based upon this principle (Davis, Eshelman, et al., 1995; Greenberg, 2009; Tenenbaum, Corbett, & Kitsantas, 2002).

Biofeedback training uses instruments to help people control responses of the autonomic nervous system. For example, a participant monitors an auditory signal of her own heart rate and experiments with different thoughts, feelings, and sensations to slow the heart rate. Once the participant learns to recognize the feelings associated with the reduction of heart rate, the instrument is removed and the participant tries to control the heart rate without it. This is the goal of the biofeedback therapist. People suffering from chronic anxiety or illnesses caused by anxiety can often benefit from biofeedback training, because when they learn to reduce functions of the sympathetic nervous system, they are indirectly learning to reduce anxiety and tension. Biofeedback is essentially the same as progressive relaxation, autogenic training, and meditation. Using the latter three techniques, the participant relaxes; this lowers arousal and decreases the activity of the sympathetic nervous system. With biofeedback, the participant begins by lowering certain physiological measures with the help of an instrument. This decreases arousal and increases relaxation.

Instrumentation Theoretically, biofeedback can be very useful to athletes who suffer from excessive anxiety and arousal. If athletes could be trained to control their physiological responses in the laboratory, they should be able to transfer this ability onto the athletic field. The main drawback to biofeedback in athletics is expense. The cost of purchasing a machine for measuring heart rate, EEG, EMG, or GSR changes is out of reach for the average school's athletic budget. However, not all biofeedback measurement techniques are expensive, and many are still in the experimental stages. Some of the basic measurement techniques used in biofeedback training are as follows.

Skin Temperature The most commonly used and least expensive form of biofeedback is skin temperature. When an athlete becomes highly aroused, additional blood is pumped to the vital organs. Part of this additional blood supply comes from the peripheral blood vessels, leaving the hands feeling cold and clammy. Thus, the effect of stress is to decrease the skin temperature of the extremities. Participants can monitor skin temperature to discover what kinds of responses, thoughts, and autogenic phrases are most effective in increasing it. Typically, participants are trained to use progressive relaxation techniques and autogenic phrases to assist them in the biofeedback process. Although sophisticated instruments are available,

CONCEPT   Biofeedback training is effective in facilitating athletic performance.

APPLICATION   The use of biofeedback equipment for learning how to monitor and manipulate physiological arousal as a means of controlling and eliminating debilitating negative affect has proven to be very effective. If an athlete's performance is negatively influenced by inappropriate high (or low) levels of arousal, then biofeedback training can help. The availability of biofeedback equipment and trained clinicians should be investigated.

FIGURE 9.4 | Skin temperature can be monitored with a cardboard-backed thermometer.

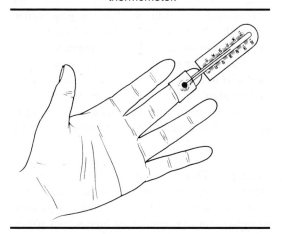

Source: From *Biofeedback: An introduction and guide* by David Danskin and Mark Crow. Reprinted by permission of Mayfield Publishing Company. Copyright © 1981 by Mayfield Publishing Company.

a simple and inexpensive cardboard-backed thermometer can be used to monitor skin temperature. The cardboard is cut off just above the bulb and the thermometer is taped to the finger, as illustrated in figure 9.4. Similarly, small skin sensors can be attached to the fingers to register temperature changes.

Electromyography   Another very popular biofeedback technique employs the use of an electromyographic feedback instrument (EMG). Electrodes are attached to a particular group of muscles in the arm or forehead, and the subject tries to reduce muscular tension by using auditory or visual cues of muscle electrical activity. Auditory cues typically come through earphones in the form of clicks. Visual cues come through an oscilloscope that the participant watches.

Electroencephalogram   A third major instrument used for biofeedback is the electroencephalogram (EEG). Use of the EEG is commonly called brainwave training. Tiny electrical impulses from billions of brain cells can be detected by electrodes placed on the scalp and connected to an EEG. Four basic types of brain waves are associated with EEG recordings. Beta waves predominate during periods of excitement and high arousal. Alpha waves predominate when the participant relaxes and puts his mind "in neutral." It is the alpha waves that the participant tries to produce.

Other Methods   While skin temperature, EMG, and EEG are the most common methods used in biofeedback training, several others are used to a lesser degree, including the galvanic skin response (GSR), heart rate, and blood pressure. In addition to these six biofeedback methods, other potential techniques include monitoring of respiration rate, vapor pressure from the skin, stomach acidity, sphincter constriction, and blood chemistry.

Biofeedback and Performance   In a laboratory setting, the athlete learns to control the autonomic nervous system. The feelings and experiences associated with learning how to reduce sympathetic nervous system responses in the laboratory are then transferred to the athletic environment. In some cases, biofeedback may be practiced in the athletic environment. For example, Costa, Bonaccorsi, and Scrimali (1984) reported the use of biofeedback training with team handball athletes to reduce precompetitive anxiety.

The difference between success and failure of two equally matched athletes often depends on an individual's ability to cope with the perceived stress of competition. Biofeedback provides a way for athletes to determine their levels of physiological arousal and to learn how to make conscious changes calculated to reduce anxiety and improve performance. A number of scientific investigations have been conducted to determine the effect of biofeedback on athletic performance. Zaichkowsky and Fuchs (1988) reviewed 42 studies that examined the effect of biofeedback training on sports and athletic performance. Of these 42 studies, 83 percent found biofeedback training to be successful in facilitating sport and athletic performance, as well as beneficial to the athlete's well-being. More recently, Petruzzello, Landers, Hatfield, Kubitz, and Salazar (1991); Boutcher and Zinsser (1990); and Blumenstein, Bar-Eli, and Tenenbaum (1995) have reported that biofeedback training is highly effective in eliciting the relaxation response and moderately effective in facilitating improved performance in athletes.

Arousal Energizing Strategies

In the previous section we discussed strategies that athletes use to relax and to reduce anxiety and arousal associated with the stress response. In this section we will discuss arousal energizing strategies needed to obtain peak performance. Often athletes need to be "psyched up" or energized to prepare them for competition. As Dan O'Brian said in the previous section, the athlete needs to be able to "turn it on and then turn it off." The skill, however, comes in knowing when to turn it on and when to turn it off or down. In this section we will be talking about "turning it on," but at the same time we need to be aware of the dangers of getting the athlete overly energized and psyched up. Let us

discuss this issue a little more before moving on to a discussion of specific psyching-up strategies.

It was reported several years ago (McCallum, 1994) that the Milwaukee Brewers professional baseball team brought in a California motivational group called Radical Reality to "motivate" its players. During one of the presentations, one of the Radicals ripped a phone book in two with his bare hands. The next day, one of the team's pitchers tried to duplicate the phone book stunt and dislocated his left shoulder. The rookie right-hander was scratched from his next scheduled pitching rotation and reassigned to a minor league team. This example of misdirected "psyching up" underscores the danger of undifferentiated attempts to raise or lower the arousal level of athletes.

Coaches have been looking to the sport psychologist to learn how to maintain optimal levels of arousal in athletes. This is a most promising development, since many coaches have improperly prepared their athletes for competition. The typical approach has been to "psych up" the athlete through various kinds of pep talks and activation techniques. There is, of course, a proper time to get athletes excited and aroused, but often these techniques are applied at the wrong time. It is commonplace, for example, to see high school volleyball coaches leading their players in cheering and psyching-up sessions immediately before a match. Generally, these athletes have only an intermediate level of skill, and the extra arousal serves only to induce unforced errors. This problem is illustrated in figure 9.5. Each athlete in this figure begins with a different initial level of arousal. Increasing arousal affects each athlete differently. In most cases, intervention procedures are best applied on an individual basis; each athlete should be treated differently. Some will need a pep talk, but others may need an entirely different form of intervention.

As can be observed in figure 9.5, using a pep talk to increase the arousal level of four different athletes has interesting ramifications. Only in situations 1 and 2 did the pep talk have the desired effect. In situation 3, the athlete was already at an optimal level of activation, and it was destroyed

CONCEPT   Group activation strategies such as pep talks may help some athletes reach an optimal level of arousal, but may cause others to become overaroused.

APPLICATION   Indiscriminate use of activation procedures to psych up athletic teams should be avoided. Instead, help each athlete to find her own optimal arousal level.

FIGURE 9.5 | The effects of a pep talk on the activation levels of four different athletes.

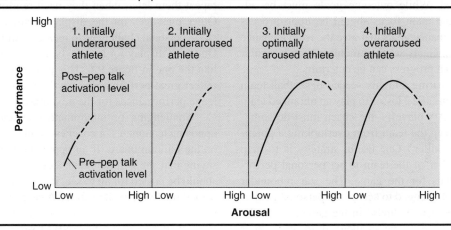

by the coach's pep talk. In situation 4, the athlete was overactivated to begin with; the intervention was totally inappropriate. How many coaches overactivate their athletes by their pregame locker room pep talks? It is also important to recall the important lesson learned from our earlier discussion on catastrophe theory (chapter 8). When an athlete has a high level of cognitive state anxiety, it is possible that even a small increase in physiological arousal could result in a large catastrophic decrement in performance.

This section will be divided into two major parts: (a) team energizing strategies, and (b) individual energizing strategies. **Team energizing strategies** are those strategies that deal with the team as a whole and are generally orchestrated by the coach. They include such things as team goal setting; pep talks; bulletin boards; publicity and news coverage; fan support; and coach, athlete, and parent interactions. **Individual self-energizing strategies** are those strategies that the individual

uses to induce immediate activation and alertness. From the perspective of the individual, these latter techniques are also referred to as individual psyching-up strategies.

Team Energizing Strategies

As a coach prepares for the season, she recognizes the need to set into motion a number of initiatives designed to keep the team focused and energized for the entire season. At the beginning of the season, the athletes are generally energized and excited about the new season and the new challenges. This initial enthusiasm and excitement, however, can diminish across a long season if efforts are not set into motion to maintain it. This is especially true if the team or individual athletes get mired in a losing streak or a period of energy-draining situations.

Team Goal Setting   As proposed by Locke and Latham (1990), goal setting is motivational in nature and is used by athletic teams as a way to energize individual athletes. Chapter 10 of the text is dedicated to the details of the goal-setting process. The coach should provide the leadership in this process, but the athletes must be equal partners in deciding what they want to accomplish as a team and as individuals during the current competitive season. The coach then lays out for the team a plan whereby the goals set by the team can be accomplished. While outcome goals must be addressed, the main focus should be upon process and performance goals that give the team a chance to succeed. Goals are then monitored on a regular basis so that progress can be determined.

In preparing a highly seeded basketball team with 28 wins and 2 losses to play an unranked team in the NCAA playoffs, the coach must do something to keep the team from overlooking a potential "giant killer." One useful strategy is to help each member of the team to set personal performance goals for the game. The star rebounder might be challenged to accept the personal goal of getting thirteen "bounds" in the game. Similarly, the guards might be challenged to keep their turnovers below three between them. With each member of the team working to achieve realistic but moderately difficult goals, it is likely that the team as a whole will perform well.

Pep Talks   A **pep talk** by the coach or a respected member of the team is the most common method now used to increase the activation level of athletes. But like any verbal communication, it can be either effective or ineffective. Perhaps the most important element of the pep talk is an emphasis on the ingredient that is lacking in the team. If the team is obviously taking an opponent lightly, it must be impressed upon them that on a given night, any team can pull off an upset. Some of the elements of an effective pep talk may include personal challenges, stories, poems, silence, reasoning, and voice inflections.

Bulletin Boards   In many ways the messages on a **bulletin board** are identical to those in a pep talk, but they are visually rather than verbally conveyed. Poster-board displays should be placed where team members cannot miss them. Such places as locker room dressing areas and confined training areas are ideal. The bulletin board should always convey positive, motivating thoughts and ideas. Catchy phrases such as "when the going gets tough, the tough get going" can be effective. Athletes remember these simple phrases and will repeat them later, when they need reinforcement. Other messages on the display board might include personal challenges to members of the team. One such display for a volleyball team might look like the one in figure 9.6. This poster could either reflect great performances for the season or challenge performances for the next match.

Challenging or inflammatory statements by opposing teammates or coaches should also appear on the bulletin board. If an opponent is quoted as saying that she will dominate a certain player, this should be posted for all to see. It will give the team something to get excited about. A case in point was game six of the first round of the 2003 National Basketball Championship (NBA) series between the Portland Trail Blazers and the Dallas Mavericks. In response to a blowout victory against Dallas in game six of the series, Portland guard Ruben Patterson was quoted in the news coverage as saying that he could see fear in the eyes of the Dallas players. Dallas coach Don Nelson prominently displayed the quote in the Dallas locker room in preparation for game seven in Dallas. The Dallas Mavericks eliminated Portland with a 107–95 game seven victory (Thamel, 2003).

Publicity and News Coverage   The school newspaper and other advertisements can be very helpful in generating team spirit. If the members of the team sense that the student body is behind them, they will work harder to get prepared. Ads can be placed in the newspaper by the coach to call attention to an important game or contest. These same ads can be used to recruit new players for the team. For many teams, publicity comes easy, but for others it does not. It may be necessary to cultivate a close relationship with the media and school

FIGURE 9.6 | Poster showing performance goals for a volleyball team.

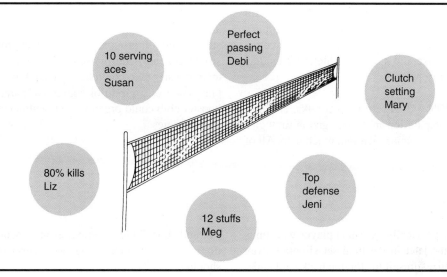

Source: From Voelz, C. (1982). *Motivation in coaching a team sport.* Reprinted by permission of American Alliance for Health, Physical Education, Recreation and Dance, 1900 Association Drive, Reston, Virginia 22091.

sports reporters. Invite them to games and send them positive information about players and upcoming contests.

Fan Support Those who enjoy sport for its recreational value do not need people watching in order to enjoy the game. However, if you practice 10 to 15 hours a week and have a 20-game schedule, it doesn't hurt to have **fan support.** Fans tell the athletes that what they are doing is important to people other than themselves. A full season of daily basketball, football, or tennis can burn out many players. Those responsible for promoting the team must do all they can to get people to support the team by coming to watch and cheer for them.

Coach, Athlete, and Parent Interaction The interactions between an athlete's parents, the athlete, and the coach are an often-overlooked source of motivation for an athlete. Coaches are often wary about the overinvolved and demanding parent. However, often just the opposite situation

occurs, and parents are excluded from active involvement in motivating a young athlete. Parents provide tremendous support for an athlete's involvement that sometimes goes completely unnoticed. Parents provide transportation for games and practices, and sacrifice vacations and leisure time to watch their son or daughter perform. When called on, they are observed serving as scorekeepers, "water boys," bus drivers, and sometimes assistant coaches. What a tremendous source of support and motivation a parent can be when properly nurtured, cultivated, and appreciated!

Immediate Self-Energizing Strategies

In the paragraphs above we talked about team strategies for energizing athletes for the duration of a season. Individual athletes, however, also need to be able to energize themselves for **immediate mobilization.** A basketball player who sits on the bench for three-quarters of the game and is then inserted into the lineup is not ready to play

CONCEPT Goal setting, pep talks, bulletin boards, publicity and news coverage, fan support, and coach and parent interaction, are all effective ways to energize and motivate athletic teams during a long season.

APPLICATION Goal setting, pep talks, and bulletin board preparation are all energizing strategies that a coach can manage without much help. All of the other energizing strategies, however, take time and organization and will require the assistance of student support groups, parent support groups, assistant coaches, and the school administration. A team booster club could be organized by an assistant coach or a group of supportive parents. The booster club could organize and facilitate energizing strategies.

mentally or physically. A tennis player who finds his two-game lead in the final set slipping away has to energize himself to stop the backward slide. An earlier quote by Dan O'Brian is of particular significance here. Recall that he said you have to be able to "turn it on and then turn it off." We learned how to turn it off earlier in this chapter, and now we learn how to turn it on. Most of the strategies we will mention in the following paragraphs have already been introduced in earlier sections and chapters of the book. **Self-energizing strategies** to be discussed include individual goal setting, self-talk, attentional focus, imagery, and self-activation.

Individual Goal Setting Individual athletes set long-term goals to help motivate them for the long haul across a season. However, successful athletes also use goal setting to motivate and energize them for an approaching competition. To be effective, these immediate goals must be phrased silently or verbally just before the event occurs. Goal setting that is contiguous with an event is a form of positive self-talk containing specific goal parameters. For example, when the "hit and run" play is on in baseball, the batter's stated goal might be, "Make contact." In tennis, the serve receiver's goal on the first serve might be, "Block it back." In the waning moments of a basketball game, the power forward's goal might be, "Take it hard to the rim and score." Goal setting, even in acute situations, is highly motivating and energizing, and should be used often.

Self-Talk Self-talk was introduced earlier in this chapter as an intervention strategy. Here we introduce the concept as a means of energizing the athlete to greater activity and effort. Self-talk, or even **self-thought,** should always be used with a positive frame of reference. Actually phrasing and verbally stating cues that remind the athlete of the need to generate greater energy can be effective. As the fullback leads the way into the defensive line in football, he picks his target and thinks or says, "Explode." As the basketball player sets a blind screen in anticipation of hard contact, she says or thinks, "Hold." As the tennis player aims for a backhand passing shot down the line, he says or thinks the word, "Blast." Other key words that are symbolic of greater energy and activation include "now," "go," "deep," "hit," and "power."

Attentional Focus Attentional focus was introduced in chapter 6 of the text. Increased attention is associated with increased physiological arousal. Consequently, strategies designed to narrow attention will also result in activation and greater energy. Narrowed attention occurs when we gate out irrelevant cues that may serve as distractors. It is instructive to think of the linebacker

CONCEPT Personal goal setting, self-talk, attentional focus, imagery, and self-activation are effective in energizing the athlete to greater levels of activation.

APPLICATION Dan O'Brian's wise statement that you have to be able to "turn it on and then turn it off" when you need to is extremely appropriate here. Athletes are not always optimally aroused for competition. Sometimes they are overaroused and sometimes they are underaroused. When the athlete is underaroused and needs to be immediately energized, a pep talk from a coach or another athlete might help, but usually it is a personal thing. The athlete has to be able to "turn it on" when she needs to. The methods reviewed in this section are all effective in energizing athletes. Coaches should help athletes learn how to use these energizing techniques to their advantage.

in American football as he focuses his attention on the running back and says to himself, "You are mine." The goalie in soccer focuses her attention on the ball and says to herself, "Be fearless and smother the ball." There are certain situations in sport in which maximum effort and maximum arousal are necessary for success. When these situations occur, the athlete has to be fully attentive and fully activated.

Imagery As we will learn in chapter 11 of this book, imagery has both a cognitive and a motivational function. It is the motivational function that makes imagery a viable energizer. As the tennis player prepares for an important serve, he visualizes the ball "leaping" off his racket and "exploding" into the backhand corner of the opponent's receiving court. As the spiker in volleyball approaches the net, she visualizes herself "smashing" the ball over the block and into the unprotected deep down-the-line corner of the opponent's court. In golf, the golfer sees himself "drive" the ball in a low trajectory deep into the middle of the fairway. Visualizing successful outcomes in situations requiring activation and strong effort is motivating and energizing.

Listening to Music Music, often employed as a way to relax, can also be a powerful energizer (Bishop, Karageorghis, & Loizou, 2007; Bishop, Karageorghis, & Kinrade, 2009. Utilizing competitive tennis players as participants, Bishop, Karageorghis, and Kinrade (2009) studied the effects of manipulating the tempo (speed) and intensity (loudness) of a music selection upon choice reaction time, felt arousal, pleasantness, and heart rate. This study confirmed that increasing the intensity of a music selection effectively increases felt arousal, while increasing the temple increases both felt arousal and perceived pleasantness. Increasing the intensity of the music has the effect of increasing choice reaction time speed (quicker).

Self-Activation In addition to all of the energizing techniques mentioned above, successful athletes develop their own methods for energizing themselves on a moment's notice. This is called **self-activation.** Jimmy Conners, a former tennis great, would slap himself on the thigh in conjunction with various self-talk statements to get himself activated late in the match. Dennis Rodman, of Chicago Bulls basketball fame, had the curious habit of going back into the tunnel leading to the locker room and riding a stationary bicycle at high speeds to elevate his heart rate. John Rocker, fiery reliever for the Atlanta Braves baseball team, liked to sprint onto the field for his relief appearances. Every successful athlete learns ways to self-activate and energize himself when he needs to.

8. Practice your deep breathing skills and explain why you feel deep breathing is effective in helping a person to relax.

9. Of the five methods of relaxation discussed in this chapter, which one do you like the best? Explain why.

10. Each of the relaxation methods discussed in this chapter takes hours and weeks to master. How, then, can these methods be utilized by an athlete who must be able to bring on the relaxation response in a matter of minutes, or even seconds?

11. What is the practical application of biofeedback for a high school football team?

12. Exactly how do you go about matching a relaxation intervention with an athlete's anxiety and stress symptoms?

13. News coverage given by local newspapers and radio talk shows is not always positive. How do you go about protecting athletes from negative news coverage that is demotivating?

14. Develop a brief training manual teaching athletes how to immediately energize themselves in preparation for competition.

Glossary

abdominal breathing Deep breathing, associated with relaxation, that takes place at the level of the abdomen or diaphragm.

affirmation statements Statements that affirm to the athlete that he possesses the skills, abilities, positive attitudes, and beliefs necessary for successful performace.

anxiety/stress spiral The circular effect of anxiety causing poor performance that results in even more anxiety.

autogenic training A relaxation training program in which the athlete attends to body feedback.

automated coping strategies Coping strategies that are well practiced and frequently used.

biofeedback A program in which the athlete learns to elicit the relaxation response with the aid of physiological measurement equipment.

bulletin board Vehicle used to visually motivate members of a team by displaying and posting material that the coach feels is for the good of the cause.

chest breathing Shallow breathing, associated with anxiety, that takes place at the level of the chest or thorax.

coping Constantly changing cognitive and behavioral efforts to manage specific external and/or internal demands that are appraised as taking or exceeding the resources of the person.

coping conceptual framework A two-dimensional coping framework for considering coping style and strategy.

coping strategies Ways of alleviating the debilitating effects of the stress response.

coping strategy dimension A conceptual dimension of coping that is situation specific and includes the problem and emotional coping strategies, or in some cases cognitive versus behavioral strategies.

coping style An approach to alleviating the debilitating effects of the stress response.

coping style dimension A conceptual dimension of coping that is dispositional (trait) in nature, and includes the approach and avoidance styles of coping.

deep breathing Breathing that takes place at the level of the abdomen and diaphragm, as opposed to the chest and thorax.

dispositional hypothesis The hypothesis that athletes have a certain learned or innate way of coping with all stress-related situations.

dynamic hypothesis The hypothesis that athletes' coping responses are dynamic and fluid, changing from situation to situation.

emotion-focused coping strategy Coping strategy in which the individual attempts to alleviate the stress response by regulating emotions.

fan support Getting people who support a team to come to watch them play regardless of their win/loss record.

4 Ws of self-talk The where, when, what (content), and why (function/use) of self-talk.

generalizability of coping skills The notion that coping skills learned in the sporting environment can transfer to nonsport real-life situations.

immediate mobilization The need for an athlete to "turn it on" just before competition in order to be optimally prepared.

individual self-energizing strategies Strategies that the individual uses to induce immediate activation and alertness.

integrative mind-body training Modern mind-body meditational approach to controlling the autonomic nervous system.

mantra A key phrase or mental device used in transcendental meditation to help the athlete focus attention internally.

matching hypothesis The attempt to develop a closer match between precompetitive affect and psychological adjustment.

meditation A form of relaxation that applies directly to the concepts of selective attention.

mental device A word, phrase, object, or process used to help elicit the relaxation response.

pep talk The practice by the coach or an influential individual of talking to the team just before competition to energize and motivate them.

proactive coping strategies Potential stressors are anticipated in advance and matching coping strategies are preselected.

problem-focused coping strategy Coping strategy in which the individual attempts to alleviate the stress response by eliminating the environmental stimulus that is causing the stress.

progressive relaxation A muscle relaxation procedure in which skeletal muscles are systematically tensed and relaxed.

relaxation response Physiological changes that reverse the effect of the sympathetic nervous system.

self-activation Methods developed by successful athletes for energizing themselves on a moment's notice.

self-energizing strategies Strategies calculated to self-energize or activate an athlete immediately before a specific event or situation.

self-talk An effective overt or covert cognitive technique for reinforcing situation-specific self-confidence and ultimately behavior.

self-thought Self-talk statements that are not actually spoken but are mentally framed as thoughts.

stress management The use of various relaxation or arousal management procedures to reduce anxiety.

team energizing strategies Energizing strategies that focus upon the team as a whole and are generally orchestrated by the coach.

transcendental meditation A relaxation procedure that originated in India and features the repetition of a mantra to elicit the relaxation response.

Goal Setting in Sport

KEY TERMS

Action-oriented goal
Behavioral goal
Goal attributes
Goal difficulty
Goal setting
Goal-setting paradox
Goal striving
Learning strategies
Long-range goal
Measurable goal
Mobilizing effort
Multiple goal strategy
Needs assessment
Observable goal
Outcome goal
Performance goal
Persistence
Process goal
Process goal paradox
Realistic goal
Self-concordance model

Short-range goals
SMART

Specific goal
Timely goal

In 2004 Lance Armstrong and his United States Postal Service cycling team made history. Armstrong was the only person in the history of the Tour de France cycle race to win the race six years in a row. In 2005, sponsored by The Discovery Channel, Armstrong gained his seventh victory in a row. Lance Armstrong and his teams are part of this decade's greatest sport dynasties. Lance Armstrong overcame testicular cancer in 1996 and 1997 to win his first Tour de France in 1999. This is without a doubt one of the greatest sports-related motivational stories in history. Undoubtedly, team and individual goal setting played a major role in this great accomplishment (Murphy, 2004; Price, 2004).

Currently, it can be said that Michael Phelps is the greatest Olympic athlete of all time. In the 2008 Beijing Summer Olympics, he won 8 gold medals (including three relays) for the United

States. In each of these races, except one (100 m butterfly), he set a new world record. Interestingly, it was his gold medal and Olympic record in the 100 m backstroke that was most memorable. In this race, he came from behind to beat Milorad Cavic by .01 sec. By winning 8 gold medals he eclipsed Mark Spitz who had won 7 gold medals in the 1972 Munich Olympic Games. Overall, at age 23, Michael Phelps owned 16 Olympic medals, 14 of which were gold. In winning 8 gold medals in the 2008 Olympic Games, Phelps swam 17 races in eight events, three of which were relays. This meant that he had 38 opportunities for a false start and countless chances for a stroke or turn violation (Casey, 2008; McDonell, 2008). These amazing accomplishments were undoubtedly accomplished through dedicated training, competition, and effective goal setting over a long period of time.

As we shall learn in this chapter, goal setting is about cognition and motivation. By its very nature it is cognitive, because the athlete has to think and plan for the future. It is also motivational in nature, because the very process of setting goals is energizing. Each year of Lance Armstrong's Tour de France victory had to begin with both team and individual goal setting in order to get them on target for another grueling season of training and competition.

It is important to point out the similarities and differences between goal perspective theory, discussed in chapter 4, and goal setting, discussed in this chapter. Goal orientation is about the different ways that athletes think about ability. The task-goal-oriented athlete does not have to defeat an opponent in order to feel successful. She simply has to believe that she tried hard, did her best, and made some improvement—and that's the goal. Conversely, the ego-goal-oriented athlete cannot feel successful unless she has performed better than another person or another team—and that's the goal. Goal setting, however, focuses on the mechanics of how one can set goals and how those goals can be energizing and motivational. There are, of course, some similarities between goal orientation theory and goal setting. Some of these similarities will be further investigated later on in this chapter.

As illustrated in the previous examples involving Lance Armstrong and Michael Phelps, it takes a lot of work and dedication to become a world champion in any sport. An accomplishment of this magnitude is realized only through the judicious setting of daily, weekly, and long-term personal goals. **Goal setting** is a theory of *motivation* that effectively energizes athletes to become more productive and effective (Latham & Locke, 2007; Locke & Latham, 1990). Goals set by athletes represent either internal or external motivation, depending on whether or not the goals are internalized and personalized. Simply stated, Locke and Latham's (1985) basic theory is that (a) a linear relationship exists between degree of goal difficulty and performance, and (b) goals that are specific and difficult lead to a higher level of performance than "do your best" goals. In 1990, Locke and Latham reported that 354 out of 393 industrial, organizational, and academically based studies supported their theory. We turn now to a discussion of goal setting as it is applied in the sport and exercise setting. Important topics to be discussed in this chapter include (a) basic types of goals and their effectiveness; (b) reasons goal setting results in improved performance; (c) principles of effective goal setting; (d) a team approach to goal setting; (e) goal management strategies; (f) common goal busters; (g) goal setting, self-determination and goal perspective relationships, and, (h) what the elite athlete can teach us about goal setting.

Basic Types of Goals and Their Effectiveness

Three basic types of goals have been identified in the sport psychology literature (Kingston & Hardy, 1997). These three different types of goals are outcome goals, performance goals, and process goals.

Outcome Goals

Outcome goals focus on the outcomes of sporting events and usually involve some sort of interpersonal comparison. A typical outcome goal might be to win a basketball game, place first in a volley-ball tournament, defeat an opponent in tennis, or finish the season with a winning record. It is very typical for coaches to speak in terms of the number of wins they hope to have in a particular season.

Performance Goals

Performance goals specify an end product of performance that will be achieved by the athlete relatively independently of other performers and the team. A typical performance goal for an individual athlete might be to strike out seven batters, score twenty-five points in a basketball game, serve five aces in a tennis match, or get fifteen kills in a volleyball game. Intuitively, athletes and coaches should prefer performance goals to outcome goals for two fundamental reasons. First, if performance goals are accomplished, there is a good possibility that outcome goals will also be accomplished. Second, personal satisfaction can be realized from the achievement of performance goals even if outcome goals remain unfulfilled.

A conflict arises, however, if the athlete places the accomplishment of personal performance goals above team outcome goals. Team goals focus on team members working together to achieve a common team objective, while individual goals often focus upon individual statistics. A high school basketball player who glories in scoring 25 points per game may do so at the demise of the synergy of the team as a whole.

Process Goals

Process goals focus on specific behaviors exhibited throughout a performance. A typical process goal for an athlete might be to keep the left elbow straight while executing a golf drive, to keep the elbow down and wrist firm in the tennis backhand, or to focus on the spiker and not the ball in volleyball blocking. Each of these behaviors reflects proper and effective technique for executing a specific athletic task. If the athlete is successful in set-

Professional athletes set specific performance goals for themselves and design their training approach in a way that helps them meet those goals. Courtesy Photolink/ Getty Images.

ting and meeting process goals, improved performance and outcome should be the result.

As we learned in chapter 6, the conscious processing hypothesis posits that conscious processing under pressure may disrupt the smooth execution of a well-learned motor skill (e.g., step-by-step monitoring). Yet, in this section we are suggesting that attending to a process goal, such as keeping the left elbow straight (right-handed golfer) while executing a golf swing, is a beneficial goal type. This apparent contradiction is referred to in the literature as the **process goal paradox.** An investigation reported by Mullen and Hardy

(2010), however, clarifies that if the process goal is holistic in nature, instead of focusing on a body part, it should not interfere with executing a motor skill. A holistic process goal is one in which the athlete focuses upon the process of executing a smooth golf swing or other sport skill.

Which Type of Goal Is Best?

Numerous investigations have been conducted contrasting the three different types of goals. Kingston and Hardy (1997) contrasted the effectiveness of performance goals with that of process goals in club golfers relative to their skill improvement and psychological skill development. After a 54-week training period, they observed that both performance and process goals resulted in improved performance, whereas a control group with no goals did not show improvement. In addition, the researchers observed that process goals were superior to performance goals in terms of realizing improvements in anxiety management and selected psychological skills.

Burton, Weinberg, Yukelson, and Weigand (1998) categorized 570 collegiate athletes as either less or more effective in the use of goal setting. The more effective athletes relative to goal setting reported that process goals were more important to them than a combination of performance and outcome goals (product goals).

Filby, Maynard, and Graydon (1999) assigned college-age soccer players to one of five goal groups. The five groups were characterized by (a) no goals (control group), (b) outcome goals only, (c) process goals only, (d) outcome and process goals, and (e) outcome, performance, and process goals combined. After five weeks of training, results showed that the two **multiple goal strategy** groups outperformed the other three groups. Relatively speaking, the group exhibiting the lowest level of improvement was the "outcome only" group. The efficacy of the multiple goal strategy was also supported by Steinberg, Singer, and Murphy (2000).

As illustrated in figure 10.1, research supports the position that a multiple goal strategy is best. Used in isolation, outcome goals are probably the least effective, but when used in conjunction with performance and process goals, they are helpful. It would seem that a goal-setting strategy that uses all three types of goals is best for the athlete in terms of psychological development as well as performance improvement. The important thing for the athlete and coach is that they understand clearly the distinctions between the three and use them all effectively.

Reasons Goal Setting Results in Improved Performance

According to Locke, Shaw, Saari, and Latham (1981), there are four basic ways in which goal setting can influence performance. Because it is important for the athlete and the coach to understand why goal setting is effective, these four explanations plus one more will be discussed.

Directed Attention

Goal setting causes the athlete to focus her attention upon the task and upon achieving the goal

FIGURE 10.1 | Athlete should focus on a combination of outcome, performance, and process goals.

relative to the task. When she has no specific goal, the athlete's attention wanders from one thought to another without any particular direction. Setting a specific goal causes the athlete to focus her attention on that goal and upon the task that is associated with that goal.

Effort Mobilization

Once an athlete's attention is directed toward a particular goal, it is necessary for the athlete to put forth the effort necessary to achieve that goal. The very act of increasing or **mobilizing effort** will have a positive effect upon improved performance. Consider the bowler who wishes to consistently bowl a score of around 250. To bowl consistently in this score range, the athlete must be able to follow a strike with another strike, or at least a spare. Goal setting will

have the effect of increasing the athlete's effort during practice so that she can accomplish this goal.

Persistence

A third way that goal setting influences performance is through **persistence.** Many athletes can focus their effort and attention on improving a skill for a few minutes or even for a whole practice, but to be successful, an athlete must persist for a long period of time. Persistence is a by-product of effective goal setting. As long as the goal is present and the athlete wants to obtain the goal, he will persist in the effort needed to accomplish it. Thirty days after winning the U.S. Open by 15 strokes, Tiger Woods won the British Open by eight strokes. In so doing, he accomplished a career Grand Slam at age 24, two years younger than Jack Nicklaus was when he accomplished it. Woods now holds the record for most strokes under par in the Masters, the U.S. Open, and the British Open. How did he get to be a "physical genius" at such a young age? Here's a clue. He sometimes required himself to hole one hundred six-foot putts consecutively, using only his right hand during practice (Rushin, 2000). This is persistence, and it requires goal setting to gain that kind of skill and persistence during practice.

Development of New Learning Strategies

Goal setting promotes the development of new **learning strategies.** Without goals for improvement, an athlete is content to get along with the learning strategies and skills that she currently possesses. Setting of new goals not only directs attention, mobilizes effort, and nurtures persistence, but it also forces the athlete to learn new and better ways of accomplishing a skill or task. A post-up player in basketball may be relatively successful in scoring 12 points a game using a drop-step move, but more than one move is necessary if he wants to score 20 points a game. Once a basketball player sets a personal goal to score more points on offense, he must learn new skills and techniques to make this possible.

CONCEPT Goal setting improves performance by directing attention, increasing effort and persistence, motivating the athlete to learn new learning strategies, and by increasing positive affect.

APPLICATION Goal setting is one of the best motivational strategies available to the athlete.

The coach and the athlete must learn effective goal-setting techniques. Ineffective goal setting can actually do more harm than good, because it can raise expectations that the athlete cannot realize. In the pages that follow, principles of effective goal setting will be discussed in detail.

Increase in Positive Affect

Positive affect is linked to increased motivation, performance, and commitment (McCarthy, Jones, Harwood, & Davenport, 2010). Therefore, evidence that goal setting can increase positive affect is indirect evidence that goal setting can improve performance. Using a single-subject multiple-baseline design. McCarthy et al. (2010) were able to demonstrate that a goal-setting intervention increases positive affect in young multi-event athletes. An additional explanation for how goal setting increases performance is through the mechanism of increasing positive affect.

Principles of Effective Goal Setting

We are now aware that there are three different types of goals and that goal setting improves performance by directing attention, increasing effort and persistence, and motivating athletes to learn new strategies. In the pages that follow we will learn about principles of effective goal setting. Goal setting must be well planned and effective if it is to result in desirable performance results. The principles of effective goal setting are also summarized in table 10.1.

Make Goals Specific, Measurable, and Observable

It is difficult to determine if a general nonspecific goal has been achieved. If a tennis player sets a general goal to become a more accurate and effective server, how does she know if she has achieved this goal? One source of information could be her win/loss record, but this could be misleading, as the skill of the opponents could have changed. Wins would go up if she played weaker opponents, but this would not be evidence of her improved serving ability. The terms *specific, measurable,* and *observable* are all related to one another. A **specific goal** is one that focuses exactly on the goal to be achieved. For example, "shooting 80 percent accuracy in free-throw shooting" is specific, but "becoming a better basketball player" is not. A **measurable goal** is one

TABLE 10.1 | Principles of Effective Goal Setting

1. Make goals specific, measurable, and observable.
2. Clearly identify time constraints.
3. Use moderately difficult goals; they are superior to either easy or very difficult goals.
4. Write goals down and regularly monitor progress.
5. Use a mix of process, performance, and outcome goals.
6. Use short-range goals to achieve long-range goals.
7. Set team as well as individual performance goals.
8. Set practice as well as competition goals.
9. Make sure goals are internalized by the athlete.
10. Consider personality and individual differences in goal setting.

that you can quantify, in the sense that you know exactly how close you are to achieving the goal. The general goal "to become a better server in tennis" is not measurable, because you don't know when you have achieved the goal. An **observable goal** is one that you can measure, because you can observe it. For example, the goal "to hit 80 percent of my free throws" is observable as well as measurable, because if I shoot with 75 percent accuracy, I know I have fallen short. Observable performance goals are also referred to as **behavioral** or **action-oriented goals.** Good goals are those that you can measure, and the only way you can measure them is by observing them in behavioral terms. If a goal is specific, measurable, and observable, you will be able to watch the athlete in action and observe whether he is realizing the goal or behavior.

Clearly Identify Time Constraints

In tennis, it does little good for a player to set a goal to serve 60 percent of her first serves into the court if she doesn't specify when she plans on accomplishing this goal. Is this goal to be accomplished by the next major tournament? By the end of the season? By the end of her collegiate career? Stating a long-range goal without specifying the time component of the goal introduces uncertainty into the goal-setting process. Setting time constraint goals that are too short can make a goal seem unreachable and discourage the athlete. Setting time constraint goals that are too distant can also have negative ramifications. If an athlete is given eight weeks to accomplish a goal that can be accomplished in a shorter period of time, she will take the whole eight weeks to accomplish the goal (Tenenbaum, Bar-Eli, & Yaaron, 1999).

A well-stated goal should be **timely** in the sense that it specifies time constraints associated with the goal, but also timely in the sense that it reflects an appropriate amount of time to accomplish the goal. The timeliness of a goal can add to the motivational characteristics of the goal. If the time constraint is too long, the athlete may procrastinate over the achievement of the goal, while if it is too short, the athlete will view it as unrealistic.

Use Moderately Difficult Goals; They Are Superior to Either Easy or Very Difficult Goals

Most of the goal-setting research in sport and exercise has been conducted in this specific area. For maximum performance, Locke and Latham (1990) argued that goals should be so difficult that only 10 percent of individuals can reach them. Research in sport and exercise, however, has failed to support this level of **goal difficulty.** For example, a statistical summary (meta-analysis) of 36 studies conducted in sport and exercise concluded that moderately difficult goals are best (Kyllo & Landers, 1995). Recently, 52 percent of Olympic athletes indicated a preference for moderately difficult goals, whereas only 25 percent preferred very difficult goals (Bueno, Weinberg, Fernández-Castro, & Capdevila, 2008; Weinberg, Burton, Yukelson, & Weigand, 2000). Similarly, coaches have expressed frustration with difficult goals because their athletes get discouraged when goals seem unattainable (Weinberg, Butt, & Knight, 2001).

A study by Bar-Eli, Tenenbaum, Pie, Btesh, and Almong (1997) supported this conclusion in a study involving 346 male ninth- and tenth-grade Israeli students from 15 high schools. The students from each school were randomly assigned to one of 15 sit-up treatment conditions. The first five schools participated in the study for four weeks, the next five schools for six weeks, and the last five for eight weeks. Within each group of five schools, there were five goal training conditions: "do," "do your best," "improve by 10 percent" (easy), "improve by 20 percent" (moderately difficult), and "improve by 40 percent" (very difficult). The results showed that the three groups receiving specific goals outperformed the two groups given nonspecific assignments ("do" or "do your best"). Results further showed that the moderately difficult goal group generally outperformed the easy and very difficult groups, although some variability of results occurred as a function of length of training period.

One of the controversies associated with goal difficulty research in sport and exercise has been the problem of controlling for social comparison between members of different training groups. Specifically, participants in the control group who were told "do your best" routinely reported setting goals. This problem was solved in the Bar-Eli et al. (1997) study by using a large sample size and 15 different schools. In this design, participants in one group could not be influenced by members of another group because they belonged to a different school. Therefore, this was a very important study and the reason that it was presented in some detail here.

Goals should be moderately difficult, so that athletes must work hard and extend themselves in order to meet them. At the same time, however, a goal must be **realistic,** in the sense that the athlete must believe that the goal is achievable. If a goal is perceived by an athlete as not being realistic or achievable, she may become discouraged and not try to achieve the goal. The acronym **SMART** has been used by sport psychologists to help athletes remember five important characteristics of well-stated goals that have been discussed in the paragraphs above. Goals should be Specific, Measurable, Action-oriented, Realistic, and Timely (Weinberg & Gould, 1999). The SMART acronym is useful in helping athletes to remember these five important characteristics. The SMART principle is illustrated in figure 10.2.

Write Goals Down and Regularly Monitor Progress

An effective goal is one that you write down and monitor regularly to determine if you are making progress. You must take care to avoid making this a laborious and tedious task. If you have set a goal that you truly want to achieve, then writing it down and knowing how you are doing relative to achieving the goal is of critical importance. An effective goal is not one that you think about and then forget. An effective goal is also not one that you write down, place in a time capsule, and then open

FIGURE 10.2 | Athletes and coaches must be SMART when setting goals.

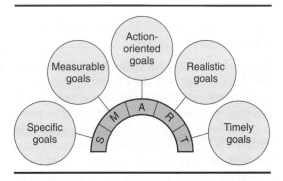

up a year later to see if you have accomplished it (Weinberg, Butt, Knight, & Perritt, 2001).

Monitoring performance and process goals in a dynamic sport such as tennis or basketball will require assistance from coaches or statisticians to keep track of what occurs during a game or match. It is fairly common for coaches to record player performance statistics in sports such as tennis, basketball, and volleyball, but it is less common for them to monitor process goals. Unless matches and games are videotaped for replay, athletes have no way of knowing on a consistent basis if their process goals, such as maintaining certain body alignments, are being realized.

Effective goal setting usually involves more than the athlete. A case in point is an ecologically valid goal-setting study in which goal-setting effectiveness was observed in four youth speed skaters across an actual competitive season (Wanlin, Hrycaiko, Martin, & Mahon, 1997). A multiple baseline design was used in which each athlete received training and monitoring in goal setting across 12 weeks. Each athlete started the goal intervention at different points in time during the 12 weeks. Results showed an increase in positive practice behaviors and a decrease in negative practice behaviors following introduction of the goal-setting intervention. All three experimental skaters made small improvements in racing times following the goal-setting intervention. Similar results were obtained for three elite amature boxers in which a multiple baseline single subject design was also utilized (O'Brien, Mellalieu, & Hanton, 2009).

Use a Mix of Process, Performance, and Outcome Goals

As already mentioned in a previous section, a multiple goal strategy will yield the best performance and psychological results. One should never use an outcome goal strategy by itself. Outcome goals (success/failure) serve a useful purpose when used in conjuction with process and performance goals, but by themselves they can lead to a loss of motivation. An athlete has a great deal of personal control over process and performance goals, but not so much over outcome goals. The individual athlete has only a limited amount of control over the outcome of a team sport game such as baseball or soccer. The individual athlete has more control over the outcome of an individual sport contest, but even there personal control is limited by external causes such as skill difficulty. For example, you could run the race of your life, post a personal best on the 5K, and still lose to a faster runner.

Use Short-Range Goals to Achieve Long-Range Goals

If you have ever climbed a high mountain, you will be able to relate to the importance of this principle. When you set out to climb to the top of a mountain peak, your **long-range goal** is to be on top of the mountain looking down within a certain time frame. As you begin the steep climb, however, you almost immediately start making **short-range goals.** For example, you might see a plateau about one hundred feet up and set a goal to get to that point before stopping for a rest. This process continues until you make your last one-hundred-foot short-range goal to reach the top of the mountain before stopping to rest.

The efficacy of setting both short- and long-range goals is supported in the sport psychology literature (Bar-Eli, Hartman, & Levy-Kolker, 1994; Gould, 2010).

Set Team as Well as Individual Performance Goals

Normally, when we think of team goals, we think in terms of outcome goals. For example, we might set a goal for the team to make the playoffs at the end of the season. Performance goals can be set for a group or a team just as they can be set for an individual. This principle is illustrated in a study reported by Johnson, Ostrow, Perna, and Etzel (1997). The five-week bowling performance of 12 bowlers who set individual goals to knock down a certain number of pins was compared with the bowling performance of 12 bowlers who set a team goal to knock down a specific number of pins as a team. The results showed that the group that set goals as a team performed better than the individual-goal group.

Set Practice as Well as Competition Goals

Weinberg, Burke, and Jackson (1997) sampled the goal-setting beliefs and practices of 240 youth tennis players and discovered that they viewed practice goals as being very effective in improving tennis performance. Successful Olympic athletes also value the importance of goal setting for practice as well as competition (Orlick & Partington, 1988). Coaches recognize the critical importance of effective practices to prepare for competition. How an individual or team performs during practice will be directly correlated with performance in competition. It is also important to recognize that athletes spend much more time practicing their sport than they do actually competing in the sport.

There are a number of ways in which practice goals could help an athlete achieve competitive performance goals. If a basketball player has a competition performance goal to hit 45 percent of her field goal attempts, then she should have the same goal for practice. It makes no sense to practice with no goal in mind relative to individual performance and then expect to achieve competitive performance goals. If I am going to be a good shooter during competition, then I had better be a good shooter in practice as well. Setting practice goals is the way to accomplish competition goals.

Munroe-Chandler, Hall, and Weinberg (2004) reported the results of an investigation in which a comparison was made between the types of goals set by 249 athletes representing 18 different sports. Results generally showed similarities between goals set during practice and those set for competition, but some differences were noted as well. For example, goals set during practice tended to be more subjective (e.g., train effectively, have fun) whereas during competition they were more objective (e.g., win, get a medal or trophy). Mental preparation goals and strategy goals were the most frequently cited goals for both competition and training. Skill improvement and execution goals were used more frequently in training than in competition.

Make Sure Goals Are Internalized by the Athlete

Perhaps one of the most important ingredients of good goal setting is that goals are accepted and internalized by the athlete (Locke, 1991). If an athlete sets her own goals, it is relatively certain that she will internalize them. Conversely, if goals are assigned to the athlete by the coaching staff, it is possible that the athlete will not feel ownership for the goals. Does this mean that the athlete should always set her own goals without involvement from the coaching staff? Not necessarily. It only means that the athlete must accept and internalize the goals she either sets for herself or is assigned by the coach. Expecting athletes to set their own goals is not always the best strategy, because they may not be aware of effective goal-setting principles.

Based on their meta-analysis, Kyllo and Landers (1995) concluded that in sport it is best to let athletes either set their own goals or participate in the goal-setting process. Locke and Latham (1990), however, have argued that participative goals do not necessarily yield better performance results than assigned goals, as long as the leader is supportive and goal instructions are clear. With this background in mind, Fairall and Rodgers (1997) reported an investigation in which 67 collegiate track and field athletes served as participants. The athletes were instructed in principles of effective goal-setting and randomly assigned to one of three goal-setting conditions: athletes set their own goals, goals were set by the coach, and coach and athletes mutually agreed upon goals. Goal-setting effectiveness was evaluated as a function of measured **goal attributes** (clarity, commitment, influence, certainty, satisfaction, acceptance, and participation). Results of the investigation showed that the three goal-setting groups did not differ in terms of measured goal attributes, even though they clearly differed in terms of perceived involvement in the goal-setting process. This led the researchers to conclude that "there is no advantage to participative or self-set goals over assigned goals in terms of goal attributes" (p. 14). Athletes must accept and internalize their goals regardless of who initially wrote the goals down. Athletes must feel as though they are in control (self-determination), but it is not necessary for athletes to set their own goals in order to feel this way.

An interesting twist to this discussion comes from a recent investigation reported by Elston and Ginis (2004). They looked at the difference

Youth sport participants express glee over achieving a team goal. © Digital Vision/PunchStock.

CONCEPT Effective goal-setting practices are a function of being aware of and adhering to the 10 goal-setting principles discussed above and listed in table 10.1.

APPLICATION Most athletes set goals, but very few know how to set effective goals. It is even more challenging to write the goals down in a form that makes them motivational, measurable, and achievable. Coaches should work together and with athletes in learning how to write good goals. Start by reviewing the list of principles outlined in table 10.1. Once the principles are clear and understood by everyone, visually display a short list of poorly written goal statements and ask the athletes to show how each could be improved. From there, get more specific and consider a couple of actual goal statements specific to athletes in the room. See table 10.2 for examples of poor and correctly written goal statements.

TABLE 10.2 | Examples of Improperly and Properly Written Goal Statements for Tennis

Goal Type	Poorly Written Goals	Rewritten and Improved Goals
Process	1. Improve tennis backstroke technique.	1. Execute backstroke with firm wrist and with elbow pointed down.
Performance	2. Improve first-serve effectiveness.	2. During competition, serve no less and no more than 60 percent of first serves into court by end of third tournament.
Outcome	3. Improve win/loss percentage over previous year.	3. Maintain number two ranking on team and win five of seven dual-meet matches prior to playoffs.

between self-set versus assigned goals in terms of developing self-efficacy. Based on previous research, they hypothesized that a self-set goal strategy should be superior for a familiar task, but for an unfamiliar task an assigned goal strategy should be superior. Conceivably, the assigned goal strategy would be better for an unfamiliar task, because it instills confidence in the goal recipient to know that an expert believes he can achieve the assigned goal. The unfamiliar task selected for the study was hand grip strength using a hand grip dynamometer.

Results showed that consistent with the researchers' expectation, an assigned goal is superior to a self-set goal in terms of developing self-efficacy to achieve a goal on an unfamiliar task. This result appears to be due to the confidence generated when an expert (coach) believes that the goal can be accomplished. This does not alter the need for the participant to internalize goals, but it provides additional insight into the cognition involved in goal setting.

Consider Personality and Individual Differences in Goal Setting

When coaches are involved in the goal-setting process, they should take into consideration personality differences. Lambert, Moore, and Dixon (1999) observed that national-level female gymnasts who exhibited an internal locus of causality disposition performed best when they used a "set your own goals" strategy; in contrast, gymnasts who exhibited an external locus of causality performed best when they used a "coach-set goals" strategy. Likewise, Theodorakis (1996) noted that the psychological characteristics of self-efficacy, satisfaction, and commitment have a direct effect upon goal setting, which in turn has a direct effect upon performance. Finally, Pierce and Burton (1998) reported that a season-long goal-setting program for gymnasts was more effective if the athletes exhibited the personality characteristic of being task oriented as opposed to ego oriented.

These few studies do not provide enough evidence to warrant tailoring goal-setting training stategies on the basis of personality profiles, but they do alert the coach to be aware of individual differences when setting team and individual goals. The failure of a particular goal-setting plan to work with a particular athlete may be due to the personality and psychological characteristics of the athlete, and not the goal-setting strategies employed.

A Team Approach to Setting Goals

Botterill (1983) identified a number of elements that are important in developing a goal-setting system to be used by coaches. Gould (2010) reduced these elements down to three critical components. The three components of a team approach to setting goals are (a) the planning phase, (b) the meeting phase, and (c) the evaluation phase.

The Planning Phase

It would be folly for a coach to stage a goal-setting meeting with her athletes without first doing a needs assessment. In a **needs assessment,** the coaching staff carefully reviews the team as a whole, and each individual, relative to areas of needed improvement. Start with the team as a whole and list the strengths and weaknesses of the team. From the list of weaknesses, you can articulate specific team needs and write them down. From the list of team needs, you may conclude that the team needs to improve in team cohesion (togetherness), physical fitness, and ball handling skills (too many turnovers). From these team needs, you should write down specific goals that state in observable terms if and when team goals are achieved—for example, "when training camp begins, each member of the team will be able to run 3 miles (5K) in less than 24 minutes."

In a similar fashion, the coaching staff considers the strengths and weaknesses of each athlete on the team, one athlete at a time. These could be called "areas of needed improvement" instead of weaknesses. Areas of needed improvement are listed for each athlete on the team. Following this exercise, goals should be written that are specific, measurable, and realistic. They should be written and planned in a way consistent with the SMART principle and with each of the principles listed in table 10.1. Before the coaching staff approaches the team and individual athletes, they must have done their "homework" and preplanning.

Before moving into the meeting phase, the coach must carefully consider how best to approach the athletes with the needs assessment and goals for the team and individual athletes. Athletes must accept and internalize the goals that coaches give them. This is best accomplished by involving the athletes in the actual goal-setting process. There is no sense in approaching this step from a dictatorial perspective, because if the athlete does not internalize a goal, then it is not his.

In addition to considering how to involve the athletes in the goal-setting process, the coach must plan how to implement the goal-setting process and to monitor it once it is implemented. Who will monitor the team goals? Who will monitor individual athletes' goals? How much of the actual monitoring will be done by the coaching and support staff and how much by the athlete? These questions must be considered during the planning phase.

The Meeting Phase

If the planning phase was carefully considered and implemented, then the meeting phase should go smoothly. The most straightforward component of the meeting phase is the initial meeting, in which team goals can be reflected upon and discussed. This can be a very useful meeting in terms of discussing the previous year's performance and giving a realistic assessment of what to expect for the future. Coaches should educate athletes on the differences between outcome, performance, and

FIGURE 10.3 | Sample performance goal-setting form for the sport of volleyball.

Goal-Setting Form for Volleyball

Name _Jane_   Position _Strong side_   Date _Sept._

Skill	Evaluation +	Evaluation 0	Evaluation −	Specific Need	Specific Goal
Serving	✓				
Serve Reception			✓	inconsistent passes to setter	75% plus passes with no aces by Oct 15th
Setting	✓				
Spiking			✓	getting blocked	increase angles, 75% in court efficiency by Oct 15th
Blocking		✓			
Digging		✓			

process goals. Process and performance goals tell the athletes exactly what they must do as a team to accomplish outcome goals.

In a subsequent meeting, coaches should instruct athletes on the SMART principle and on how to write and put into words their own personal goals. Once they have accomplished this, athletes should be given time to reflect on their personal goals, and then a time should be scheduled for each athlete to meet with the coach. During the one-on-one meeting with the athlete, the coach compares the athlete's goal statements with those written by the coach during the planning phase. Together, coach and athlete mutually agree on goals to be targeted. If time is a major issue, this whole process can be speeded up by having the coach assign individual goals to the athlete and then meet with him briefly to make sure they are acceptable to the athlete. Recall that Fairall and Rodgers (1997)

demonstrated that assigned goals are as effective as participatory or self-set goals in terms of realizing selected goal behaviors. Illustrated in figure 10.3 is a goal-setting form that a volleyball player could use for setting personal performance goals.

In addition to setting clear, measurable goals, coaches must implement a plan or strategy to achieve the stated goals. Let's say a runner accepts the goal to run a 5K (3-mile) race in less than 21 minutes before the first competitive meet of the season. An exact plan or strategy must be implemented to give the athlete a reasonable chance to accomplish that goal. If the goal is a difficult one and no plan is in place to accomplish it, the athlete probably will not meet it. In addition to setting goals, coaches must assist athletes in developing a plan to accomplish the goal. In the case of the 5K race, it would be wise to determine exactly how much time must be shaved

CONCEPT From a team perspective, a goal-setting system is based upon a planning phase, a meeting phase, and an evaluation phase.

APPLICATION All three phases are important, but from the coach's perspective, the planning phase is most important. Without good planning and an effective needs analysis, the subsequent meeting and evaluation phases will be ineffective. This is where the coach does her homework in preparation for the season. With a good goal-strategy planning session, the coach can enter the meeting with athletes knowing where the team and each of the athletes stand relative to the upcoming season.

---

off the athlete's current running pace, as this will certainly determine strategy. Let's say the runner needs to shave three minutes off his time. This is quite a bit, so a sufficient time frame will be necessary to accomplish it. A series of short-range goals should be set to help break the long-range goal into smaller units. Coach and athlete must decide what daily running schedule would be most beneficial for the athlete. Would it be best to focus on the 5K, or would running some longer training races along with some sprints be helpful? The point is that a detailed strategy must be decided upon if the athlete has any hope at all of achieving a difficult goal. Every goal must have a plan by which to achieve it.

The Evaluation Phase

The evaluation phase of goal setting should take place at the end of the competitive season, but also throughout the season. Goals set by the team and by individuals should be monitored regularly. Monitoring of process and performance goals should take place following each competition, as well as after practice sessions. It is critical to the evaluation component of goal setting that performance statistics be kept on every game and match. Team and individual statistics should be posted after each competition so that athletes can review their own personal goals. If feasible, competition and practices should be videotaped so that process and technique goals can be evaluated. Outcome goals are easier to monitor because they relate to success or failure. Where it is clear that an athlete is falling short of performance goals, the coach should schedule a one-on-one meeting with that athlete, so that they can reevaluate goals in terms of achievability as well as athlete commitment. Without constant monitoring, feedback, and evaluation, the goal-setting process will not be effective.

Common Goal-Setting Pitfalls

Principles listed in table 10.1 identify ways in which goal setting can be made more effective. In a sense, the reverse is also true. Failure to consider the principles of effective goal setting would represent 10 different ways to undermine the goal-setting process. In practice, though, there are several common pitfalls, or reasons goal setting does not result in improved performance. These pitfalls come under the general headings of (a) poorly written goal statements, (b) failure to devise a goal-attainment strategy, (c) failure to follow the goal-attainment strategy, (d) failure to monitor performance progress, and (e) discouragement.

Poorly Written Goal Statements

One common problem for athletes is that their goals are so vague and general that they cannot tell if they are making progress (Weinberg et al., 1997). Violation of the SMART principle in setting goals is the most common reason goals are not met. Among other things, a goal must be specific, measurable, action oriented, realistic, and timely.

CONCEPT Goal setting is an effective motivator of behavior that leads to improved performance, but there are common pitfalls that can interfere with the effectiveness of a goal-setting program.

APPLICATION Two of the most critical pitfalls to effective goal setting relate to the goal-setting plan or strategy designed to achieve a goal. Setting a goal without designing a plan to achieve the goal is a little like making a wish and doing nothing about making the wish come true. Failure to devise a plan to achieve a goal is a major pitfall in goal-setting effectiveness. Related to this is the pitfall of not following the goal strategy or plan once it has been devised. Step one is to set a measurable goal. Step two is to devise a plan to achieve the goal. Step three is to follow the plan.

Failure to Devise a Goal-Attainment Strategy

A goal without a plan to achieve the goal almost always results in ineffective goal setting. An athlete sets a goal to shoot par golf. Now, exactly what goal strategy plan is set in place to help the athlete accomplish that goal? Without a well-conceived plan to improve drive distance and accuracy, approach shot accuracy, and putting accuracy, it is unlikely the athlete will achieve the goal.

Failure to Follow the Goal-Attainment Strategy

Once a goal-attainment strategy or plan has been decided upon, it is necessary to follow the plan. A man sets a goal to reduce his body fat from 45 percent to 30 percent in 18 months using a scientifically sound program of daily exercise and the restriction of processed foods high in fat, sugar, and salt. Not completely committed to the program, the man fails to lose any weight during the first six months, so he gives up and decides goal setting does not work.

Failure to Monitor Performance Progress

If you are a quarterback in college football, and your goal is to increase pass completion percentage, you won't have to worry about monitoring your progress, because the coach will tell you exactly how many passes you attempted, and how many were completed. This may not be the case, however, in a small high school, or even during practice in college. Failure to monitor measurable and observable progress in sport makes it impossible to tell if goal setting is working.

Discouragement

There are many ways that discouragement can sabotage the effectiveness of goal setting in sport. Here are a few of them:

Goal Difficulty Athletes get discouraged with goal setting when the goal appears too difficult or unrealistic. If performance is being monitored, adjustments in goals can be made. If the goals are too hard and seem impossible to obtain, it makes sense to adjust the goal to make it more reasonable.

Use of Outcome Goals When an athlete sets only outcome goals and does not realize the goals, this can be very discouraging. If your goal was to win seven of ten soccer matches, and you have already lost five games with only five to go, what do you have to work for? Nothing, really. Revising the outcome goals down from 70 percent wins to 30 percent wins might help, but it would be better if you started to focus on achieving performance and process goals. It is never too late to start setting personal performance goals. Maybe you can't win the soccer match, but you can make five defensive tackles per game if you work hard at it.

Too Many Goals Sometimes the coach sets too many goals for the athlete to accomplish. Perhaps it is the athlete who is setting too many goals for herself. Whatever the reason, athletes can get discouraged when they try to accomplish too many things at once. If an athlete is just learning to play the game of tennis, there are numerous areas of needed improvement. The athlete should not try to accomplish too much at once. She should slow down and focus upon one goal at a time. This is called information overload, a topic covered in the chapter on attention.

Goal Setting, Self-Determination, and Goal Perspective Relationships

At the beginning of this chapter we discussed briefly the difference between goal-setting theory and goal-perspective theory. We also indicated at that time that we would revisit the discussion and discuss similarities between the two later in the chapter. In addition to discussing important relationships between goal setting and goal orientation, we will also mention some relationships between goal-setting theory and self-determination theory.

Self-Determination Theory and Goal-Setting Theory

Research on this topic is sparse, but what we do have access to is based upon the self-concordance model proposed by Sheldon and Elliot (1999). The **self-concordance model** addresses the process of goal striving and its effect on well-being within the broad conceptual framework of self-determination theory (SDT), in which **goal striving** is defined as the process of striving to set and to achieve goals. Within this framework, there are two kinds of goal striving:

1. Striving for personal goals that are based upon *autonomous motivational regulation,* which leads to sustained effort.

2. Striving for personal goals that are based upon *externally controlled motivational regulation,* which leads to initial effort that is not sustainable.

Based upon the self-concordance model, Smith, Ntoumanis, and Duda (2007) reported on an investigation in which they asked the following question: Does striving for goals reflect an athlete's inner core values and beliefs (autonomy), or does it reflect a response to internal and external pressure (controlling)? As part of the investigation, they measured (a) personal goals, (b) autonomous goal striving, (c) controlled goal striving, (d) coach autonomy support, (f) effort, (g) goal attainment, (h) psychological need satisfaction (autonomy, competence, relatedness), and (i) relative well-being in 210 British athletes. The results of the Smith, Ntoumanis, et al. (2007) investigation showed that autonomous goal striving (AGS) has a direct effect upon effort (E), which has a direct effect upon goal attainment (GA), which has a direct effect upon psychological need satisfaction (PNS), which has a direct effect on relative well-being (WB) as shown in the following string:

$$AGS \rightarrow E \rightarrow GA \rightarrow PNS \rightarrow WB$$

Mediation tests were conducted to confirm that (a) effort mediates the relationship between autonomous goal striving and goal attainment; (b) goal attainment mediates the relationship between effort and psychological needs satisfaction; and (c) psychological needs satisfaction mediates the relationship between goal attainment and relative well-being. Thus, the answer to the first part of the research question is that striving for goals reflects an athlete's inner core values and autonomy beliefs. Results also showed that controlled goal striving has a direct attenuating effect upon relative well-being. Thus, from a self-determination perspective, controlled goal striving (motivation) has little or no effect upon effort, goal attainment, or need satisfaction, but does have a direct negative effect upon perceived well-being.

An observed interaction between coach autonomy support and autonomous goal striving, in predicting need satisfaction, leads to the conclusion that autonomous goal striving moderates the relationship between coach autonomous support and need satisfaction. Athletes' need satisfaction increases as coach's autonomy support increases, but it increases at a faster rate when autonomous goal striving is high as opposed to when it is low. The highest level of need satisfaction occurs when coach's autonomy support is high and athletes' autonomy goal striving is also high.

In a follow-up investigation (Smith, Ntoumanis, & Duda, 2010), it was further observed that autonomous goal motives mediate the relationship between coach autonomous supportive behavior and relative well-being; and that controlled goal motives mediate the relationship between coach controlling behaviors and well-being attenuation.

Goal-Perspective Theory and Goal-Setting Theory

Serious theory testing associated with goal setting had its inception with the published research of Locke and Latham (1985), and achievement goal orientation with the published research of Nicholls (1984, 1989). Since that time the two theories have generated their own independent literature. Early on, Duda (1992) mused that ego-oriented athletes would likely favor outcome goals. Actual merging of these two literatures, in a research investigation, occurred in a business study reported by Seijts, Latham, Tasa, and Latham (2004). The merging of these two lines of inquiry has been challenging, as goal-setting research has typically been straightforward with a focus upon effort and persistence, while goal-orientation research has been complex with a focus on ability and perceived competence.

In the Seijts et al. (2004) investigation, three goals were measured including specific-performance goals, do-your-best goals, and learning goals (like process goals). In addition, three kinds of achievement goal orientations were measured including a learning (task) goal orientation, a performance-approach goal orientation, and a

performance-avoidance goal orientation. The performance task (dependent variable) in this study was a complex decision-making problem with the goal of increasing simulated market shares. Two basic conclusions were drawn from this research. The first was that "do-your-best" and "specific high-difficulty goals" mediate a positive relationship between a learning-goal (task) orientation and performance on the target task as illustrated here:

Task Orientation→Goal Setting→Performance

The second basic conclusion was that "do-your-best goals" mediates a negative relationship between a performance-goal orientation and performance on the target task.

In a second investigation, Wilson, Hardy, and Harwood (2006) had rugby union players complete inventories that measured their perception of the importance of process goals and their achievement-goal orientations. Results of this investigation indicated that task-goal orientation was positively associated with the perceived importance of process goals, while an ego (performance) goal orientation was negatively associated with the perceived importance of process goals. Thus, it would seem that process goals are valued by athletes possessing a task-goal orientation, but not by those possessing an ego-goal orientation.

In a final investigation, Stoeber et al. (2009) measured the goal orientations and performance and outcome goals of 339 triathletes prior to a race. The dependent variable was time to complete the race. One important outcome of this investigation was that personal goal setting (performance goal + outcome goal) mediated a positive relationship between a performance-approach (PA) goal orientation and race performance as indicated below:

PA Orientation→Personal goals→Performance

Each of the studies reviewed above suggest that goal-setting research and goal-orientation research have important relationships that need to be investigated. It is likely that the interaction between these two theories will become the subject of important investigation in the years to come.

What the Elite Athlete Can Teach Us about Goal Setting

While almost everyone has had experience at goal setting, most are only moderately effective in achieving their goals. This is the **goal-setting paradox** that we are confronted with (Burton, Pickering, Weinberg, Yukelson, & Weigand, 2010). An important investigation reported by Burton et al. (2010) provides some interesting insights relative to the goal-setting practices and beliefs of prospective Olympic athletes.

Burton et al. administered a battery of inventories to 338 prospective Olympic athletes, providing the researchers with important information about (a) goal-setting effectiveness (short-term goals, competitive goals, and psychological goals), (b) goal-setting frequency (short, long, and psychological), (c) goal commitment (outcome goals, and process goal involvement), (d) goal barriers, and (e) sport confidence and success. Based upon the goal-setting

effectiveness results, the athletes were grouped into one of four clusters (cluster analysis). The four clusters of athletes differed as a function of short-term goal effectiveness, competitive-goal effectiveness, and psychological-goal effectiveness). The cluster highest in all three of these measures was referred to as the multifaceted or effective goal-setting group, while the cluster lowest in the three measures was referred to as the goal nonbelievers. The two in-between clusters were labeled the disillusioned process and competitive goal setters.

These four emerging goal-setting clusters were then statistically contrasted on all of the remaining variables (i.e., goal-setting frequency, goal commitment, goal barriers, and sport confidence). The results of these analyses revealed that the multifaceted or effective goal-setting cluster scored higher on all of these variables compared to the other three clusters, and in particular the goal nonbelievers. These results make it clear that not all elite athletes are effective goal setters. However, those who are effective goal setters reap the benefits of performance improvement, goal achievement, and psychological goal achievement.

Summary

Goal setting is a theory of motivation that energizes athletes to become more productive and effective. The three basic types of goals are outcome, performance, and process. Research supports a multiple goal strategy in exercise and sport. Goal setting influences behavior through directed attention, effort mobilization, persistence, and the development of new learning strategies.

Ten principles of effective goal setting were identified and discussed:

1. Make goals specific, measurable, and observable. Observable goals are also referred to as being action oriented and behavioral in nature.

2. Clearly identify time constraints.

3. Use moderately difficult goals; they are superior to either easy or very difficult goals.

4. Write goals down and regularly monitor progress.

5. In setting goals, use a mix of process, performance, and outcome goals.

6. Use short-range goals to assist in achieving long-range goals.

7. Set team as well as individual performance goals.

8. Set goals that relate to practice as well as competition.

9. Make sure goals are internalized and accepted by the athlete.

10. In setting goals, consider personality and individual differences.

An effective team goal-setting system requires an effective planning phase, a productive meeting phase, and an evaluation phase. All three phases are important, but without effective planning, goal setting will suffer. In addition to setting clear, measurable goals, a plan or strategy must be implemented to actually achieve the goals.

Common goal-setting pitfalls include (a) poorly written and conceived goal statements, (b) failure to devise a goal-attainment strategy, (c) failure to follow the goal-attainment strategy, (d) failure to monitor performance progress, and (e) discouragement.

Discouragement is often associated with goals being too difficult, too many goals, and the inappropriate use of outcome goals.

Goal-setting research and theory was further discussed as it related to self-determination theory and goal perspective theory. Research shows that striving for personal goals that are based on autonomous motivational regulation results in greater effort and task performance. Conversely, research shows that striving for personal goals that are based on externally controlled motivational regulation does not lead to increased effort and persistence, but leads to a reduction in perceived well-being. Relative to goal perspective theory, research shows that the kind of goals set by athletes moderates the relationship between goal orientation and task performance.

Critical Thought Questions

1. Locke and associates clearly state that a linear relationship exists between goal difficulty and performance, and that difficult goals lead to a higher level of performance. Yet, research in sport and exercise concludes that moderately difficult goals are superior to very difficult goals in facilitating performance. Discuss this apparent conflict and express your opinion on why differences in research conclusions exist.

2. If you were limited to just one type of goal, which type would you select, and why? Which type would you not select, and why? What is the wisdom and support for the multiple goal strategy concept?

3. Why was the Bar-Eli et al. (1997) study important relative to controlling for the effect of social comparison? What does this investigation show relative to goal difficulty and performance?

4. Should athletes set their own goals or should the coach be involved in this process? What does the research say about this? What are goal attributes? What do you think is the best approach in light of the Fairall and Rodgers (1997) research results?

5. Look at figure 10.3 and see if you can improve on this form. Create separate forms for an individual sport and a team sport that you are familiar with.

6. Why do you think that the goal-setting literature and the goal-orientation literature has emerged relatively independent of each other for so many years?

7. What are some of the advantages and disadvantages that you can see for merging the two theories in future research (see question 6)?

8. At this point, what are some conclusions that you can draw about the relationship between goal setting and achievement-goal orientation?

Glossary

action-oriented goal A goal that, when achieved, is observable in behavioral terms.

behavioral goal A goal that, when achieved, is observable and action oriented. You can see the athlete perform the goal behavior.

goal attributes The characteristics of effective goals (e.g., clarity, commitment, influence, certainty, satisfaction, acceptance, and participation). These goal attributes are precursors to good performance.

goal difficulty The difficulty associated with accomplishing a goal. For example, a goal can be considered easy, moderately difficult, or very difficult to achieve.

goal setting A theory of motivation that effectively energizes athletes to become more productive and effective through using goals.

goal-setting paradox while almost everyone has had experience at goal setting, most are only moderately effective in achieving their goals.

goal striving The process of striving to set and to achieve goals.

learning strategies Effective goal setting encourages development of new ways to accomplish things.

long-range goal A goal that is distal, in the sense that it is going to take a longer time to accomplish. A number of shorter or more proximal goals will need to be achieved before the long-range goal can be realized.

measurable goal A goal whose accomplishment can be determined in a quantitative sense.

mobilizing effort By-product of effective goal setting that suggests increased effort.

multiple goal strategy A strategy in which process, performance, and outcome goals are utilized.

needs assessment A review by coaching staff of the team as a whole as well as individuals, relative to areas of needed improvement.

observable goal A goal in which goal attainment can be observed and monitored in behavioral terms.

outcome goal A goal in which the focus is upon the outcome of a sporting event and usually involves some sort of social comparison.

performance goal An end product that will be achieved by the athlete independently of other performers and of outcome.

persistence Sustained effort over a long period of time; a by-product of effective goal setting.

process goal A goal in which the focus is on a specific behavior exhibited throughout a performance.

process goal paradox The notion that process goals are considered desirable, while at the same time acknowledging that conscious processing may disrupt the smooth execution of a well-learned motor skill.

realistic goal A goal that is realistic in the sense that the athlete believes that it can be attained.

self-concordance model The process of goal striving and its effect on well-being within the broad conceptual framework of self-determination theory (SDT).

short-range goals Goals that are achieved along the way toward achieving a long-range goal. Long-range goals are more distal, while short-range goals are more proximal.

SMART Acronym to help athletes remember that goals should be specific, measurable, action oriented, realistic, and timely.

specific goal A goal that focuses exactly on the goal to be achieved.

timely goal A goal that appropriately specifies time constraints associated with its achievement.

11 CHAPTER

Imagery and Hypnosis in Sport

KEY TERMS

Applied model of imagery use
Cognitive-behavioral
  intervention
Cognitive component
Cognitive function of imagery
Cognitive intervention
External imagery
4 Ws of applied sport imagery
Functional equivalence
  hypothesis
Heterohypnosis
Hypnosis
Hypnotic induction
Imagery
Imagery perspective
Internal imagery
Kinesthetic sensitivity
Mental practice
Motivational function
  of imagery
Negative imagery
Neutral hypnosis
Paivio's conceptual model
  of imagery
PETTLEP-based imagery
Positive imagery
Posthypnotic suggestions
Psychoneuromuscular theory
Real-time imagery

Self-hypnosis
Stress inoculation training
Stress management training
Subliminal muscle activity

Symbolic learning theory
Visual motor behavior
  rehearsal
Waking hypnosis

The following quotation provides an example of perfectly realized and imagery-aided athletic accomplishment:

> And then it happened, just as they'd pictured it. Fully stretched out on his one-arm sequences. Flipping high and free above the bar. The crowd noise building, all eyes riveted, and the final tumbling release that ended with him sticking his landing as firmly as a plug into a socket. Another flawless routine. (Swift, 2004, p. 47)

This quotation describes the emotion associated with Paul Hamm's final performance on the high bar that won him the 2004 Olympic gold medal for best all-around male gymnast. Previous to this performance, Hamm had fallen from the vault, requiring a near-perfect performance on both the parallel bars and the high bar.

Successful athletes use imagery and visualization to their advantage. Not all athletes are able to verbally describe exactly how they use imagery, but some can. Jack Nicklaus, one of the greatest golfers of all time, not only used imagery, but was able to describe in detail how he used it. The following quotation provides an eloquent description of how this great athlete used imagery prior to every shot:

> I never hit a shot, not even in practice, without having a very sharp, in-focus picture of it in my head. It's like a color movie. First, I "see" the ball where I want it to finish. . . . Then the scene quickly changes and I "see" the ball going there. . . . Then there is sort of a fade-out, and the next scene shows me making the kind of swing that will turn the images into reality. (Nicklaus, 1974, p. 79)

Other great athletes who have commented on the use of imagery in preparing for competition include Michael Jordan and Phil Jackson (Jackson & Delehanty, 1995) in basketball, Chris Evert in tennis, Greg Louganis in diving, Mike Piazza in baseball, and Nancy Kerrigan in figure skating. Clearly, imagery has been useful for great athletes.

Imagery is a **cognitive intervention** technique that we will discuss in detail in this chapter.

Topics to be discussed include (a) defining imagery, (b) mental practice as a learning application, (c) evidence that imagery works, (d) theories of why imagery works, (e) the 4 Ws of applied sport imagery, (f) measurement of imagery, (g) developing imagery skills, (h) cognitive-behavioral intervention programs, and (i) hypnosis in sport.

Defining Imagery

Imagery may be defined as using one's senses to create or recreate an experience or visual image in the mind that at times may seem to be as real as seeing the image with our physical eyes (Vealey & Greenleaf, 2010). An expansion of this brief definition clarifies that (a) an image can be created in the mind in the absence of any external stimuli, (b) an image may involve one or more physical senses, and (c) an image is created from information stored in the sensory store, working memory, or long-term memory.

In a real sense, the brain cannot tell the difference between an actual physical event and the vivid imagery of the same event (Szameitat, Shen, & Sterr, 2007). Most everyone has experienced either dreams or daydreams that are so vivid and lifelike that for a moment we truly believe they are real. For this reason, imagery can be used by the brain to provide powerful repetition, elaboration, intensification, and preservation of important athletic sequences and skills.

We don't know exactly how vivid visual images are created in our minds, but scientists have speculated that the act of seeing things in our "mind's eye" employs the same brain circuitry that we use when seeing things with our physical eyes (Zimmer, 2010). A case in point is a patient that scientists named MX. Patient MX suffered a literal loss of his ability to see visual images in his brain through a side effect of vascular surgery. While he could no longer visualize images in the brain, he still had full ability to see physical objects and to describe unseen objects and scenes. As explained by Zimmer (2010), the brain lesions did not destroy the patient's ability to recognize faces or

CONCEPT   When used in conjunction with actual practice, mental practice effectively enhances motor performance. Mental practice by itself is more effective than no practice, and in certain circumstances is as effective as actual practice.

APPLICATION   In order to realize maximum performance, athletes should be taught to mentally practice sports skills in conjunction with actual practice. In addition, mental practice should be used by itself in situations where actual practice is not practical (e.g., waiting in the locker room).

CONCEPT   The more skillful and experienced an athlete is, the more he will be able to benefit from the use of mental practice.

APPLICATION   To avoid discouraging young athletes from the use of mental practice, make sure that they are familiar enough with the activity to know the difference between a good and a bad performance. An athlete must know what a skill looks like and how it feels in order to effectively mentally practice it.

other visual information, but it did destroy an essential brain region responsible for creating images. Visual imagery works in conjunction with the same brain circuits that allow us to see things with our physical eyes. The research with MX, however, demonstrated that a specific region in the brain is responsible for seeing things in our mind's eye. When this region was destroyed through a lesion, MX's ability to visualize things not seen with his physical eyes was lost to him.

Other terms that have been used as synonyms to imagery include *cognitive and symbolic rehearsal, mental rehearsal, visualization,* and *mental or covert practice.* Some distinction, however, can be made between imagery and mental practice. In the case of learning, imagery is used by the learner in conjunction with physical practice to strengthen the learning pattern. Used in this way, imagery is referred to as mental practice. In the case of performance preparation, imagery is used to prime or prepare the athlete for correct execution of a physical skill. Used in this way, imagery is referred to as mental rehearsal (Rushall & Lippman, 1998). In the following section we will discuss the specific role and function of mental practice in learning.

Mental Practice as a Learning Application

The **mental practice** literature is very instructive relative to the general application of imagery to sport. Among other things, the mental practice literature provides evidence that imagery is an effective cognitive process for enhancing learning and performance of motor skills. Excellent literature reviews conclude that mental practice is more effective than no practice, but less effective than physical practice. Mental practice used in a complementary fashion with physical practice often

CONCEPT   Mental practice is more effective in enhancing the learning of a motor skill that has a large cognitive component than in enhancing learning of one with a large motor component.

APPLICATION   Mental practice is an important adjunct to the learning of almost all sport skills.

However, it is important to recognize that the beneficial effects of mental practice will be greater for tasks that have a larger cognitive component. This should not discourage the athlete from using mental practice in all sports situations, but it will help to explain why it is more effective in one situation than in another.

---

yields the best results (Caliari, 2008; Feltz & Landers, 1983; Grouios, 1992; Hinshaw, 1991; Smith, Wright, & Cantwell, 2008.) The literature suggests that in addition to physically practicing a sport skill, the athlete should spend a small amount of time rehearsing execution of the skill in her mind. Mental practice can occur prior to actual physical practice (mental rehearsal), or it can occur at a time when physical practice is not possible (e.g., while traveling, in the locker room, while resting). Research with mental practice has also revealed several principles that enhance the effectiveness of mental practice.

Skill Level of the Athlete

An important finding associated with mental practice is that advanced performers benefit from mental practice to a much greater extent than beginners (Feltz & Landers, 1983). Clark (1960) compared the effect of mental practice with that of physical practice in the learning of the Pacific Coast one-hand basketball foul shot. He placed 144 high school boys into physical and mental practice groups on the basis of varsity, junior varsity, or novice experience. All subjects were given a 25-shot pretest before and a 25-shot posttest after 14 days of practice (30 shots per day). Results showed that mental practice was almost as effective as physical practice for the junior varsity and varsity groups, but physical practice was far superior to mental practice for the beginners. Corbin (1967a, 1967b) observed similar results using a

wand-juggling task. From the results of these studies, it seems clear that for mental practice to facilitate performance, a certain amount of skill is necessary. In other words, a coach or teacher should not expect mental practice to be effective with athletes who are unskilled in their sports. The more skillful they are, the more useful mental practice will be for them.

Cognitive Component of the Skill

Mental practice is most effective for activities that require some thinking and planning (Hird, Landers, Thomas, & Horan, 1991; Ryan & Simons, 1981). Different sports skills vary as a function of the amount of cognitive processing that is required. A finger maze would be an example of a task that has a large **cognitive component.** The most challenging aspect of learning to move through a finger maze is remembering when to turn left and right. This is something that can be learned in advance, and then the task becomes quite easy. Mental practice should be very helpful in a task of this nature. Mental practice should be less effective in a motor task that has a small cognitive component. A bench press in weight lifting would be an example of a motor skill that would seem to have a small cognitive component. Later, we will learn that imagery has both a cognitive and a motivational function. It is possible that weight lifting could benefit from the motivational use of imagery, but not from its cognitive use.

CONCEPT In the case of quality physical practice, more seems to be better, but in the case of quantity mental practice, more is not necessarily better.

APPLICATION There may be an optimal amount of time that an athlete can mentally practice a physical task in one sitting. Once that amount of time has been exceeded, continuing to mentally practice may yield diminishing returns. An athlete should be encouraged to mentally practice a task until attention fades, and then to turn to other things.

Time Factors and Mental Practice

When it comes to mental practice, more is not necessarily better. Using a basketball task, Etnier and Landers (1996) demonstrated that when an athlete holds physical practice constant, mentally practicing for one to three minutes is more beneficial than mentally practicing for five to seven minutes. In this same study it was also demonstrated that mental practice preceding physical practice may be more beneficial than mental practice following physical practice. This gives greater credence to the use of mental rehearsal immediately prior to competition.

Evidence that Imagery Works

We have already provided evidence that mental practice is an effective companion to physical practice in enhancing the learning of motor skills. In addition, the literature is full of studies that have demonstrated the efficacy of mental imagery in (a) enhancing the thoughts and emotions of athletes, (b) facilitating cognition and motivation, and (c) demonstrating its use by successful athletes. For example, Weinberg (2008) and Vealey and Greenleaf (2010) have provided summaries of documented evidence of the many beneficial effects of visual imagery as used by athletes. In addition, a recent review of imagery research reveals numerous studies that document the effectiveness of imagery interventions in improving performance, cognition, and motivation (Bell, Skinner, & Fisher, 2009; Cumming, Nordin, Horton, & Reynolds, 2006; Jordet, 2005; Malouff, McGee,

Halford, & Rooke, 2008; Post, Wrisberg, & Mullins, 2010; Rymal & Ste-Marie, 2009; Smith, Wright, Allsopp, & Westhead, 2007; Wakefield & Smith, 2009). A summary of research support for the effectiveness of imagery in sport and exercise is illustrated in figure 11.1. Notwithstanding all of the research support for the effectiveness of imagery in enhancing the athletic experience, it is well to remind the reader that this only applies to effective and well-presented imagery interventions and experiences.

Theories of Why Imagery Works

While a great deal of research has been published relative to the effectiveness of imagery and mental practice in sport, sport psychologists know less about the reasons they are effective, how they work, and what mechanisms are involved. Why should mentally practicing or imaging a physical task result in improved learning and performance? A number of possible explanations to this basic question have been proposed. For the sake of brevity and simplicity, only three theoretical explanations will be discussed.

Psychoneuromuscular Theory

Psychoneuromuscular theory posits that imagery results in subliminal neuromuscular patterns that are identical to the patterns used during actual movement. Even though the imagined event does not result in an overt movement of the musculature, subliminal efferent commands are sent from the brain to the muscles. In a sense, the neuromuscular

FIGURE 11.1 | Summary of research support for the effectiveness of imagery.

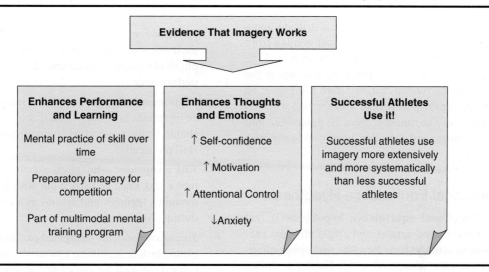

Source: Vealey, R. S., & Greenleaf, C. A. (2010). Seeing is believing: Understanding and using imagery in sport. In J. M. Williams (Ed.), *Applied sport psychology: Personal growth to peak performance* (pp. 267–304). New York: McGraw-Hill publishers. (p. 272, Fig. 14.1).

system is given the opportunity to "practice" a movement pattern without really moving a muscle. A study reported by Jowdy and Harris (1990) confirms that increased electrical activity in the muscles is associated with mental practice and imagery, regardless of the type of imagery used (kinesthetic or visual). Additional research reported by Slade, Landers, and Martin (2002) and Smith and Collins (2004) continued to provide evidence of subliminal electrical activity in the muscles of passive limbs during imagery. However, subliminal activity does not necessarily mirror the electrical activity of the physically involved limb. Nevertheless, it is believed that imagery assists the brain in developing a motor schema for executing a particular motor pattern.

Symbolic Learning Theory

Symbolic learning theory differs from psychoneuromuscular theory in that subliminal electrical activity in the musculature is not required. Mental practice and imagery work because the

individual literally plans her actions in advance (Janssen & Sheikh, 1994). Motor sequences, task goals, and alternative solutions are considered cognitively before a physical response is required. The shortstop in softball provides an excellent example of this theory in action. Prior to each pitch to the hitter, the shortstop cognitively reviews in her mind the various possible events and the appropriate response for each event. If there is one out in the eighth inning, the bases are loaded, and the score is tied, the shortstop's play will depend upon the type of ball that is hit to her. By mentally rehearsing the various stimuli and possible responses before each pitch, the shortstop can improve her chances of making the correct play.

As an illustration, the following true story involving Little League baseball is related. The game was in the last inning with the home team holding a 2 to 1 lead, two out, and a runner on third base. So, think to yourself: if the ball is hit on the ground, where is the play? Yes, the play is at first base. Every infield player should have been mentally rehearsing the play in the event the ball were hit to him. What happened, though, was that the ball was hit on the ground to the pitcher, who fielded the ball cleanly and threw a strike to home plate in time to easily tag the runner coming from third base out. But the catcher, who expected the play to be to first, was not even looking at the pitcher or the runner charging from third base; he was looking towards first base as the ball whistled by his head. The runner scored, the game went into extra innings, and the other team eventually won the game.

Functional Equivalence Hypothesis

The **functional equivalence hypothesis** is that mentally imaged actions and actual physical execution of actions share the same neurophysiological processes (Jeannerod, 1995; Guillot & Collet, 2005; Smith, Wright, et al., 2007; Szameitat et al., 2007). This would seem to imply that in the early stages of learning, there should be less functional equivalence than in the later stages of learning. In the later stages of learning a motor skill, such as serving a tennis ball, imaging a tennis serve should be functionally equivalent to an actual serve. Based on the functional equivalence hypothesis, Holmes and Collins (2001) proposed a seven-point functional equivalence checklist to facilitate equivalence. Base on this principle, it was argued that the mental image of executing a physical skill should be identical to the actual physical execution in terms of the following practical components: physical, environment, task, timing, learning, emotion, and perspective. The acronym for these seven components is PETTLEP. Numerous research investigations have been generated in which **PETTLEP-based imagery** interventions have been based (Guillot & Collet, 2005; Holmes & Collins, 2001; O & Hall, 2009; O & Munroe-Chandler, 2008; Smith, Wright, et al., 2007; Smith, Wright, & Cantwell, 2008; Wakefield & Smith, 2009). Generally speaking, research supports the PETTLEP approach to applying imagery intervention and to the functional equivalency hypothesis. However, additional research is needed.

A clear description of each PETTLEP imagery component is presented below:

- *Physical component*—Imagery should be most effective when it includes all of the physical sensations experienced during actual performance.

- *Environmental component*—The imagined environment in which the skill is executed should be the same as when performing the skill physically.

- *Task component*—Imagined execution of a motor task must be carried out with the same thoughts, feelings, and actions as are present during physical execution.

- *Timing component*—Imagined execution of a timing task (e.g., hitting a baseball) must be carried out with the same emphasis on speed and pace as in the actual task.

- *Learning component*—As the skill level of the performer moves from being cognitive to autonomous, correct emphasis must be placed on the appropriate actions associated with the applicable stage of learning.

- *Emotion component*—To achieve functional equivalence during imagery, the athlete must experience the same emotions as during physical execution of the task.

- *Perspective component*—As either an internal or external visual perspective may be utilized, a situation specific individualized approach to imagery should be considered.

4 Ws of Applied Sport Imagery

Based upon the groundbreaking work of Munroe, Giacobbi, Hall, and Weinberg (2000) with adult athletes, imagery in sport will now be considered as a function of the "where," the "when," the "what," and the "why" of imagery. Collectively, these are referred to as the **4 Ws of applied sport imagery.** Within each of these functional categories, the theory and research associated with sport imagery will be presented. This includes

CONCEPT When considering imagery use for athletes, it is helpful to consider the where, when, what, and why of imagery use.

APPLICATION The where and when of imagery use has to do with the particular situation in which imagery is used. Typically, it is used most often prior to competition. The why of imagery use has to do with whether you are using imagery to motivate or to make cognitive modifications in skill execution or strategy. The what of imagery use has to do with the actual nature and content of the images. When teaching athletes to use imagery, consider the where, when, what, and why of its use.

---

where imagery occurs, *when* imagery occurs, *what* is occurring relative to the content of imagery, and *why* or for what purpose imagery occurs. In a follow-up investigation, the 4 Ws of imagery was also considered from a developmental perspective with young athletes (Munroe-Chandler, Hall, Fishburne, & Strachan, 2007).

Where and When Imagery Occurs with Athletes

From Munroe et al. (2000) we know that most imagery takes place either during training or during competition, with most taking place in situations associated with competition. Within training, most imagery takes place during practice but some also takes place at home or away from the practice field. Relative to competition, imagery takes place before, during, and after competition, with most taking place before competition in the form of mental rehearsal. Adding to this information is the observation that a high correlation exists between off-season and in-season use of imagery with more highly skilled athletes using imagery the most in both situations (Cumming & Hall, 2002; Hall, Munroe-Chandler, Cumming, Law, & Murphy, 2009). Our understanding of the where and what of imagery use is further reinforced and consistent with research involving dancers (Nordin & Cumming, 2005a, 2007). Finally, research has shown that coaches generally endorse the efficacy of imagery use with their own athletes. Coaches encourage imagery use by their athletes to a greater extent than

they are aware, most often prior to or during competition (visual rehearsal). In addition, coaches at higher competitive levels encourage imagery to a greater extent than coaches of lower skill level teams (Jedlic, Hall, Munroe-Chandler, & Hall, 2007).

What Is Being Imaged by the Athlete

Fournier, Deremaux, and Bernier (2008) introduced the TV analogy to distinguish between the where, when, what, and why of imagery use. While the where and when of imagery use is quite direct and easy to understand, it is a little more challenging to distinguish between the *what* and *why* of imagery use. Using the TV or movie analogy, the *what* of the images you see on the screen is the same as describing the *content* of the images that are viewed. Are the images in black and white or are they in color? Are the images from the perspective of the actor or are they from the perspective of a third person? Are the images presented in real time or in slow motion? Are the images grainy or are they sharp and vivid? These are all questions that describe the what or content of the images being viewed. Conversely, the *why*, the purpose, or function of the image that is being viewed describes the effect that the images are having upon the viewer. For example, the movie or TV images may be instructive or cognitive in nature or they might be motivational or emotional in nature. We will consider *what* is being imaged in this section and the *why* in the next section. In addition to the where, when, what, and why of imagery use, Fournier et al. (2008) further argue for a fifth descriptor associated with imagery that they call the "how" or characteristics of images being viewed. It does seem, however, that most of the *characteristics* (quality) of what is being imaged are logically captured with the *what* or content of the images. Therefore, we will not consider the quality of the images being viewed as a separate category.

The content or "what" of imagery use is illustrated in figure 11.2. From this figure we can see the six aspects of imagery content (column 1) as well as subaspects (column 2) associated with sessions, nature of imagery, and type of imagery. While figure 11.2 provides an excellent consideration of the content of imagery, it does not mean that all possible aspects and subaspects have been identified. For example, the figure shows that the four types of imagery include visual, kinesthetic, auditory, and olfactory; but it could be argued that the sense of taste (gustatory) should be included as a potential imagery type and that each type of imagery, not just visual imagery, should be considered relative to vividness and perspective (internal and external). In the following we will consider research associated with the content of the images being visualized.

The content of imagery has been studied primarily in three areas of figure 11.2. These include the imagery aspects of sessions, nature of imagery, and type of imagery. The focal point of research associated with sessions has been on timing issues associated with duration and frequency of images. The focus of research associated with nature of

FIGURE 11.2 | Illustration showing the content (the what) of imagery.

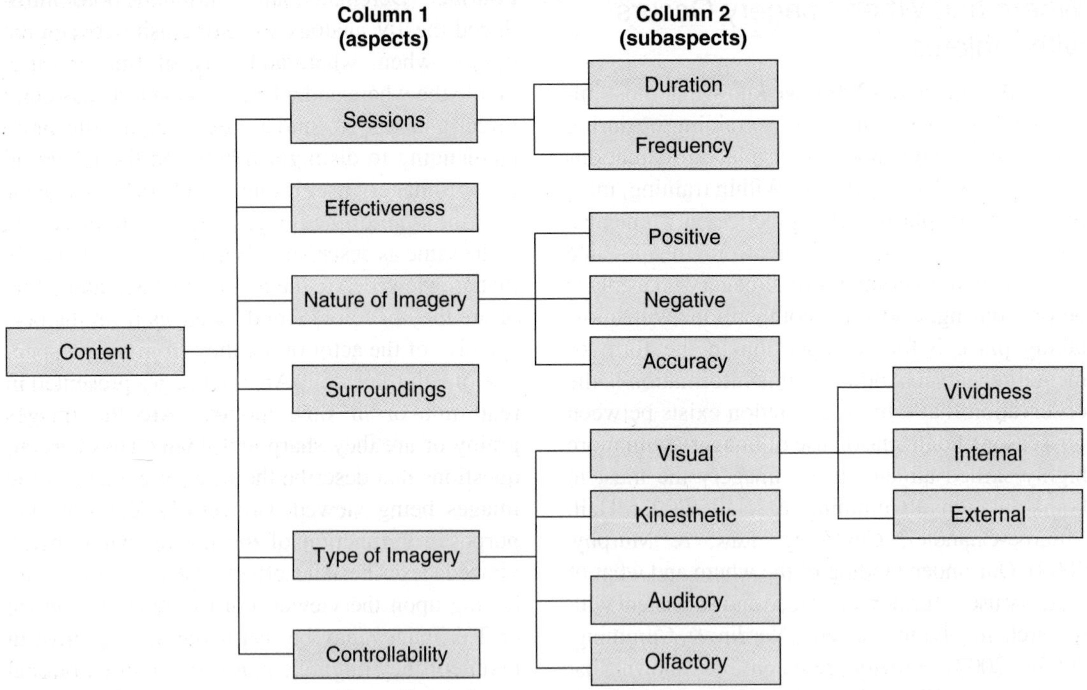

Source: Munroe, K. J., Giacobbi, P. R. Jr., Hall, C., & Weinberg, R. (2000). The four Ws of imagery use: Where, when, why, and what. *The Sport Psychologist, 14:* p. 126, fig. 1. Adapted with permission from Human Kinetics (Champaign, IL).

imagery has been on the facilitative (positive) and debilitative (negative) characteristics of imagery. The focal point of research associated with type of imagery has been upon visual and kinesthetic imagery, while the focus of visual imagery has been upon internal and external perspective.

Timing Issues Associated with Imagery

While the PETTLEP model of imagery suggests that the time to complete an imaged motor task should equal the time to complete the same task physically, a study involving a women's gymnastics floor exercise routine did not bear this out (Calmels & Fournier, 2001). In actuality, the gymnasts reported that imaged movement times were shorter than the same physical floor exercise routine times. However, in a review study involving motor skill imagery, Guillot and Collet (2005) reported that (a) the time durations associated with imaged and actual skilled movements are similar, (b) the speed of a mental image can be manipulated, (c) complex tasks take longer to image than simple ones, and (d) the actual amount of time it takes to complete an imaged motor task is often overestimated. Two additional investigations were reported that studied the use and effectiveness of slow motion, real time, and fast-motion imaged motor tasks. In one investigation it was reported that real-time imagery is used most often by athletes generally, while slow-motion and fast-motion imagery was utilized most by beginners and skilled performers respectively (O & Hall, 2009). **Real-time imagery** is defined as imagery that takes the same amount of time to complete as the execution of the actual physical skill or routine. In a second investigation, soccer dribbling improvement was studied relative to type of imagery intervention that was learned. The results of this study failed to show any performance enhancement advantage associated with completing an imaged task in real time versus slow motion (O & Munroe-Chandler, 2008). In summary, the research seems to suggest that efficacy of using real-time imagery over slow-or fast-motion imagery may vary as a function of skill level of the athlete.

It is also questionable whether the duration of an imaged motor task must be identical to the time it takes to complete the actual task. The duration aspect of imagery may be situation and sport specific, and may vary as a function of individual differences. Based upon the literature, it is recommended that real-time imagery be initially practiced with individual and sport specific adjustments made as needed.

Facilitative and Debilitative Nature of Imagery   Research supports the position that positive imagery is facilitative in nature while negative imagery is debilitative relative to developing self-efficacy and performing a motor skill (Cumming, Nordin, et al., 2006; Nordin & Cumming, 2005b; Short, Bruggeman, et al., 2002). **Positive imagery** is facilitative in nature and involves imaging a successful execution of a sport skill. For example, in mentally rehearsing a successful tennis serve into the opponent's court the server should see the ball land deep in the opponent's receiving court so that a backhand return is necessary. A visualized serve in which the tennis ball hits the net or lands out of bounds would be an example of **negative imagery** to be avoided at all costs. Nevertheless, the student will recall the *ironic effects* phenomenon, introduced in chapter 6, in which the athlete suppresses a negative thought only to have it ironically come to pass. With this in mind, a study reported by MacIntyre and Moran (2007) is relevant. In this investigation, the researchers interviewed seven elite athletes relative to their imagery skills and experiences. The athletes recounted experiencing both positive and negative imagery relative to their personal sport experiences. They further recounted how they were able to restructure negative imagery so that it could be facilitative to a future performance. A few of the athletes reported deliberately imagining errors in their performance so they could use the negative imagery to prepare for "worst case" scenarios in competition. In other words, they used negative imagery as a training device to prepare for challenging situations confronted during competition. This is an intriguing concept that deserves further research and investigation.

Imagery Perspective   There exist two perspectives from which imagery can be applied. The two **imagery perspectives** are internal and external. In **internal imagery,** the athlete imagines herself executing a sport task from within her own body. Shut your eyes and imagine for a moment that you have a basketball in your hand and you are preparing to shoot a free throw. If your perspective at this moment is from within your body looking toward the basket, this is an example of internal imagery. You imagine yourself bouncing the ball a few times, you position yourself for the shot, and you shoot. What do you see? You see your hand releasing the ball and traveling toward the basket. However, you do not see the rest of your body. Internal imagery is very natural for us, because this is the way we actually see the world when we execute a sport skill.

Conversely, external imagery is very unnatural to us. In **external imagery** the athlete imagines herself to be outside of her body watching from a distance. Let's take the basketball free throw example again. Shut your eyes and imagine you are going to shoot a free throw—only this time, imagine that you are outside your body, watching yourself from a distance. You see yourself bounce the ball a few times, position yourself for the shot, and then shoot it. You can see all of these things. You can see, for example, that your right foot is about six inches in front of your left foot, and you notice that your elbow is pointing toward the basket immediately prior to the release of the ball. External imagery provides an excellent perspective from which to observe skill technique and form.

We might assume that internal imagery is superior to external imagery because it is more natural to us. However, it might be the case that because the internal perspective is the natural state of affairs, external imagery might add something new and unique to our perspective. The uniqueness might actually make external imagery more beneficial from a performance enhancement perspective.

Sensory Mode   Earlier we defined imagery as "using one's senses to create or recreate an experience or visual image in the mind." Notice that this definition includes the notion that all of the senses are involved in imagery. This would include vision, hearing, smell, taste, and proprioception (feel). Proprioception is a broad term that refers to tactile and kinesthetic input to the brain. **Kinesthetic sensitivity** informs the brain about movements in the joints and in the muscles.

Both internal and external imagery utilize all five of the body's senses, although different sport skills may benefit more from one perspective than from another (Hardy & Callow, 1999). It has generally been believed, however, that internal imagery utilizes kinesthetic sensitivity to a greater degree than external imagery. This conclusion is based on investigations that have demonstrated greater **subliminal muscle activity** in muscles associated with internal as opposed to external imagery (Barr & Hall, 1992; Harris & Robinson, 1986). These findings have led many sport psychologists to conclude that an internal imagery perspective is superior to an external perspective. This conclusion, however, is premature, because research support has been found for both perspectives.

A study reported by Hardy and Callow (1999) is of particular interest because it shows strong support for the efficacy of an external imagery perspective in combination with kinesthetic imagery. Three separate experiments were reported involving three different closed-loop sport tasks in which form was believed to be important. The three closed-loop tasks (closed to environmental influences) included a karate sequence, a floor gymnastics sequence, and an indoor rock-climbing task. Participants were randomly assigned to one of four experimental conditions. The four conditions were combinations of internal and external imagery with or without a kinesthetic focus. Overall, results of the study concluded that an external imagery perspective with a kinesthetic focus is superior for learning and retention of a motor task that requires good form.

Purpose or Function of Image Being Viewed: The Why

Returning to the TV or movie analogy, when we watch television we do so for a purpose or for a use. It may be for the purpose of being informed, edified, entertained, motivated, and so forth. The same thing applies when we visualize an image in our mind's eye. In discussing the use and function of imagery in sport we will consider (a) Paivio's conceptual model of imagery, (b) Martin's applied model of imagery use in sport, and (c) research related to the conceptual model of imagery function.

Paivio's Conceptual Model of Imagery

Paivio (1985) clarified that imagery has both a cognitive and a motivational function. The **cognitive function of imagery** is the use of mental imagery to experience specific sports skills and to plan strategies in advance of competition. The **motivational function of imagery** is the use of imagery to experience goal attainment, effective coping, and arousal management. One function is primarily cognitive, while the other is primarily motivational. An athlete can use imagery to plan a winning strategy (cognitive function) or to get energized for competition (motivational function).

Paivio further conceptualized the practice of imagery to be either situation specific or general in nature. Thus, **Paivio's conceptual model of imagery** is two-dimensional in nature. The cognitive function could be either situation specific or general in nature; and the motivational function could also be either situation specific or general in nature. Utilizing Paivio's two-dimensional model, Hall, Mack, Paivio, and Hausenblas (1998) developed the Sport Imagery Questionnaire (SIQ) for the purpose of measuring how an athlete uses imagery. In the process of developing the SIQ inventory, they discovered that Paivio's model best fit the data if the motivational-general dimension was divided into arousal and mastery components. As revised by Hall, Mack, et al. (1998) and measured by the SIQ, Paivio's two-dimensional model for imagery use is as illustrated in figure 11.3. As can be observed in this figure, five different independent types or functions of imagery use are hypothesized as follows:

1. *Motivational Specific (MS)* In this type of imagery, the athlete imagines herself in a specific setting that is highly motivating. For example, the athlete might imagine herself making the winning basket in an important basketball game.

2. *Motivational General – Mastery (MGM)* In this type of imagery, the athlete imagines himself in a general sport situation exhibiting the ability to remain focused. For example, the athlete might imagine himself thinking positive thoughts every time he comes to bat during an important game.

3. *Motivational General – Arousal (MG-A)* In this type of imagery, the athlete imagines the ability to control anxiety. For example, the athlete might imagine using deep breathing to stay relaxed during a tennis match.

CONCEPT Using Paivio's two-dimensional framework, five different types of imagery can be conceptualized. Each type of imagery can be utilized by the athlete for a specific purpose.

APPLICATION Paivio's framework for conceptualizing the uses and purposes of imagery makes it much easier for the coach to help an athlete use imagery for a specific purpose. Imagery can be used to enhance skill execution or planning, or it can be used to motivate the athlete in an array of specific and general situations.

4. *Cognitive Specific (CS)* In this type of imagery, the athlete imagines herself correctly executing a specific sport skill during competition. For example, the athlete might imagine chipping a ball onto the green in a golf tournament.

5. *Cognitive General (CG)* In this type of imagery, the athlete imagines himself reviewing team defensive strategies in a team sport. For example, in volleyball, he might imagine the team shifting the defensive formation to defend against a quick attack from the middle.

FIGURE 11.3 | Combination of imagery purpose and application yields five different imagery types.

Purpose

	Motivational	Cognitive
Specific	Motivational Specific (MS)	Cognitive Specific (CS)
General	Motivational General–Mastery (MG-M) / Motivational General–Arousal (MG-A)	Cognitive General (CG)

(Application — Specific / General on vertical axis)

Martin's Applied Model of Imagery Use in Sport Based on Paivio's basic framework of imagery use and the work of Hall, Mack, et al. (1998) to develop the five-factor structure of the SIQ, Martin, Moritz, and Hall (1999) proposed an **applied model of imagery use** in sport. The model as depicted in figure 11.4 shows that depending on the sport situation, the category of imagery use selected determines the outcome. In the model, the effect of imagery use on outcome is moderated or determined by imagery ability. The model predicts that the specifics of outcome are dependent upon the category of imagery use that is selected. In addition, the model hypothesizes that imagery ability moderates or determines the strength of the relationship between imagery function type and specific hypothesized outcomes. For example, it might be shown that the relationship between cognitive specific (CS) imagery and the execution of a chip shot in golf depends on the imagery ability of the golfer. If imagery ability is good, then the predictive relationship between CS imagery and shot execution should be strong, but if imagery ability is poor, then the predictive relationship would be weaker.

Research Related to Martin's Applied Model of Imagery Use Generally speaking, evidence exists to demonstrate that imagery function is predictive of outcomes as illustrated in figure 11.4. For example, several studies show that self-confidence is increased through imagery use (Hall, Munroe-Chandler, et al., 2009; Ross-Stewart & Short, 2009) and that physiological changes occur in response to motivational general–arousal (MG-A) imagery

FIGURE 11.4 | Illustration showing the Martin, Moritz, et al. (1999) applied model of imagery use in sport.

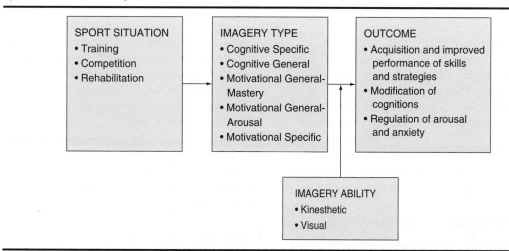

Source: Martin, S. E., Moritz, S. E., & Hall, C. R. (1999). Imagery use in sport: A literature review and applied model. *The Sport Psychologist, 13:* p. 248, fig. 1. Adapted with permission from Human Kinetics (Champaign, IL).

(Cumming, Olphin, & Law, 2007). The most commonly used imagery type is motivational general–mastery (MG-M), but when competitive level and skill type are taken into consideration differences emerge (Arvinen-Barrow, Weigand, Thomas, Hemmings, & Walley, 2007; Gregg & Hall, 2006; Parker & Lovell, 2009; Watt, Spittle, Jaakkola, & Morris, 2008). Athletes in open-skill sports use more motivational general–arousal (MG-A) than closed-skill sport athletes. Elite athletes use more cognitive specific (CS) and cognitive general (CG) imagery than novices. In golf, increased age is associated with decreased imagery use, and practice volume is positively associated with imagery use.

Research shows that a relationship exists between deliberate practice and imagery use (Cumming, Hall, & Starkes, 2005; Nordin, Cumming, Vincent, & McGrory, 2006). Just as deliberate (purposeful) practice is important in physical performance, it is also important in imagery applications. In order for imagery to facilitate learning and performance, the imagery must be relevant, require concentration, and be enjoyable. The principle of individual differences applies to imagery use

(Short, Monsma, & Short, 2004; Short & Short, 2005). Different athletes may use the same image for different functions.

While most of the reported research has utilized athletes as participants, an investigation reported by Short, Smiley, and Ross-Stewart (2005) focused upon imagery use by coaches. Their research showed that imagery types are predictive of coaching efficacy (i.e., motivation, strategy, teaching, and character building). Coaching efficacy was shown to be predicted by motivational general–arousal (MG-A) generally, and by selected imagery types. For example, it was shown that cognitive general (CG) imagery is predictive of game strategy efficacy.

In a specific test of the Martin applied model of imagery, Gregg, Hall, and Nederhof (2005) attempted to demonstrate that imagery ability moderates the relationship between imagery type and track-and-field athlete performance (figure 11.4). This was accomplished by (a) administering the Sport Imagery Questionnaire, (b) administering an inventory designed to measure visual and kinesthetic imagery ability, and (c) obtaining an objective measure of track-and-field performance.

While relationships were observed between imagery and performance and between imagery ability and performance, none of the interactions between imagery use and imagery ability were significant. Consequently, there was no evidence that imagery ability moderates the relationship between imagery use and track-and-field performance. Rather than questioning the efficacy of the model, the authors concluded that the general measure of objective performance was inadequate and difficult to calculate. They recommended further testing of this aspect of the model using either a subjective assessment of performance or objective measures specific to each track-and-field event.

Measurement of Imagery

A plethora of questionnaires have been developed and proposed for the measurement of various aspects of imagery. An incomplete list of questionnaires on imagery is provided in table 11.1. The questionnaires in this list are first categorized

as a function of purpose. Within categories, the questionnaires are listed chronologically by publication date.

Imagery *controllability* refers to the amount of personal control an individual has to change and manipulate images. It is believed that greater personal control is related to imagery effectiveness. Imagery *style* reflects individual differences in the way an individual approaches imagery. Imagery *use* reflects how often an athlete uses imagery and for what purpose. Imagery *vividness* rates the clarity, strength, and distinctiveness of images. In conducting research involving imagery, it is often necessary to take into consideration the athlete's imagery ability in terms of controllability and vividness.

Developing Imagery Skills

Detailed practical suggestions for helping athletes to improve and develop imagery skills are provided by Vealey and Greenleaf (2010). Different aspects and characteristics of imagery ability that an

TABLE 11.1 | An Incomplete List of Imagery Tests Categorized as a Function of Controllability, Style, Use, and Vividness

Imagery Aspect	Questionnaire Name	Source
Controllability	Gordon's Test of Imagery Control (GTIC)	Richardson (1969)
	Group Test of Mental Rotations (GTMR)	Vandenberg and Kuse (1978)
Preferred Style	Individual Differences Questionnaire (IDQ)	Paivio (1971)
	Preferred Imagic Cognitive Style (PICS)	Isaacs (1982)
Imagery Use	Imagery Use Questionnaire (IUQ)	Hall, Rodgers, and Barr (1990)
	Imagery Use Questionnaire for Soccer (IUQ-S)	Salmon, Hall, and Haslam (1994)
	Sport Imagery Questionnaire (SIQ)	Hall, Mack, et al. (1998)
	Athletic Injury Imagery Questionnaire -2 (AIIQ-2)	Sordoni, Hall, and Forwell (2000)
	Revised Exercise Imagery Inventory (EII-R)	Giacobbi, Tuccitto, Buman, and Munroe-Chandler (2010)
Imagery Vividness and Ability	Questionnaire on Mental Imagery (QMI)	Betts (1909)
	Shortened Form of Questionnaire on Mental Imagery (SQMI)	Sheehan (1967)
	Vividness of Visual Imagery Questionnaire (VVIQ)	Marks (1973)
	Movement Imagery Questionnaire (MIQ)	Hall and Pongrac (1983)
	Vividness of Movement Imagery Questionnaire (VMIQ)	Isaac, Marks, and Russell (1986)
	Revised Movement Imagery Questionnaire (MIQ-R)	Hall and Martin (1997)
	Vividness of Movement Imagery Questionnaire – 2 (VMIQ-2)	Roberts, Callow, Hardy, Markland, and Bringer (2008)

Gymnasts use imagery to learn complicated floor exercises. Courtesy University of Missouri–Columbia Sports Information.

athlete might want to develop are found in figure 11.2. Training programs designed to improve and magnify the content of images generally focus upon enhancing controllability and vividness of the images seen. A sample six-step program to enhance imagery ability is provided below:

1. Find a quiet place where you will not be disturbed, assume a comfortable position, and relax completely before beginning. Deep breathing and progressive relaxation are a suggested way to achieve the relaxed state.

2. Practice imagery by visualizing a colored circle that fills the visual field initially and then shrinks to a dot and disappears. Make the circle turn a deep blue. Repeat the process several times, imagining a different color each time. Relax and enjoy the spontaneous imagery that arises.

3. Create the image of a simple three-dimensional glass. Fill the glass with a colorful liquid; add ice cubes and a straw. Write a descriptive caption underneath the image.

4. Select a variety of scenes and images and develop them with rich detail. Include sport-related images such as a swimming pool, a tennis court, and a beautiful golf course next to the ocean. Practice visualizing people, including strangers, in each of the scenes.

5. Imagine yourself in a sport setting of your choice. First, imagine that you are watching other people perform the skill or sport that you are keenly interested in. Project yourself into the image as if you were one of the performers. Imagine yourself successfully performing the task in the scene. Change the sport setting and repeat the process again.

6. End the session by breathing deeply, opening your eyes, and slowly adjusting to the external environment.

Cognitive-Behavioral Intervention Programs Using Imagery and Relaxation

In this section we will discuss three different cognitive-behavioral intervention programs that link imagery and relaxation together into one comprehensive program. A **cognitive-behavioral intervention** is one that combines a cognitive component, such as images, with a behavioral component, such a relaxation. Research has demonstrated that individualized packaged intervention programs are more effective than nonindividualized programs in which participants select their own strategies. Athletes benefit most from intervention strategies that are designed to fit their needs and are presented in a systematic and organized fashion.

CONCEPT Imagery ability can be improved with practice. The more effective an athlete is at controlling the vividness and content of mental images, the more effective imagery will be in terms of cognitive restructuring and motivation.

APPLICATION The effective use of imagery is just like any other skill: it must be practiced and refined. Provide the athlete with specific suggestions as to how imagery ability can be improved and with specific suggestions relative to its application.

CONCEPT VMBR is an effective intervention program that incorporates principles derived from relaxation training and imagery to reduce anxiety, focus attention, and enhance performance.

APPLICATION An athlete who suffers from the debilitating effects of anxiety, as well as a nonaffected athlete, can benefit from Visual Motor Behavior Rehearsal.

Cognitive-behavioral intervention programs designed for performance enhancement and arousal control have one thing in common: they all include a linkage between relaxation training and imagery. The basic notion is that imagery use is enhanced through relaxation training.

Recent information reported by Roberts, Callow, Hardy, Woodman, and Thomas (2010), and Williams, Cumming, and Balanos (2010) should enhance the effectiveness of any intervention program designed to manage anxiety and stress. For example, Williams, Cumming, et al. (2010) demonstrated that an athlete's appraisal of stress-evoking situations can be manipulated through imagery. Furthermore, Roberts, Callow, Hardy, Woodman, et al. (2010) demonstrated that personality characteristics, such as narcissism, can moderate the effectiveness of imagery in controlling anxiety and improving performance.

The three cognitive-behavioral intervention programs to be introduced in this section include Visual Motor Behavior Rehearsal (VMBR), Stress Inoculation Training (SIT), and Stress Management Training (SMT). A summary of the essential components of all three is provided in table 11.2. While our focus

will be upon these three intervention programs, this is not to imply that these are the only programs that are available, or that others are less effective.

Visual Motor Behavior Rehearsal (VMBR)

Visual motor behavior rehearsal (VMBR), originally called visuo-motor behavior rehearsal, was developed by Suinn (1972, 1994) as an adaptation of Wolpe's (1958) desensitization procedures for humans. The process of desensitization was used to help patients to overcome phobias. For example, a patient who feared heights would be desensitized to this phobia through a series of systematic approximations to the fearful stimuli. Although Suinn used VMBR to treat people with depression, he was especially interested in applying the technique to athletes. His particular method of training consisted of (1) relaxing the athlete's body by means of a brief version of Jacobson's progressive relaxation techniques, (2) practicing imagery related to the demands of the athlete's sport, and (3) using imagery to practice a specific skill in a lifelike stressful environment. More recently, Suinn

TABLE 11.2 | Summary of Three Cognitive-Behavioral Intervention Programs That Utilize Imagery and Relaxation

Intervention Program	Characteristic Steps
Visual Motor Behavior Rehearsal (VMBR)	1. Relaxation training for mastery
	2. Practice of imagery in sports-related environment
	3. Sport-specific application of imagery and relaxation
Stress Inoculation Training (SIT)	1. Conceptualization phase
	2. Skills acquisition phase (relaxation, imagery, problem solving, cognitive restructuring)
	3. Inoculation against stress through small manageable steps
Stress Management Training (SMT)	1. Conceptualization of stress phase
	2. Skills acquisition phase (relaxation, imagery, problem solving, cognitive restructuring)
	3. Practice managing strong emotional stress responses

(2000) has referred to VMBR as anxiety management training (AMT).

Basically, VMBR combines relaxation and imagery into one procedure. It also requires the athlete to mentally practice a specific skill under simulated game conditions. Theoretically, this would be better than actual practice, since the practice environment rarely resembles a game situation. Coaches and teachers typically go to great lengths to minimize distractions to their athletes during practice sessions. VMBR teaches the athlete to use relaxation and imagery techniques to create lifelike situations. Going through these stressful experiences mentally should make it easier to deal with the stress of actual competition. Suinn generally recommends the use of internal imagery for VMBR training, but suggests that in addition the athlete should use external imagery to identify performance errors.

Numerous investigations have been reported that demonstrate that VMBR is effective in enhancing athletic performance, as well as in reducing the debilitating effects of overarousal and state anxiety. These include studies involving basketball (Gray & Fernandez, 1990; Kolonay, 1977), karate (Seabourne, Weinberg, & Jackson, 1984), tennis serving (Noel, 1980), pistol shooting (Hall &

Hardy, 1991), and archery (Zervas & Kakkos, 1995). In summary, it appears that VMBR training is effective in reducing an athlete's negative affect relative to the sports tasks mentioned above. Furthermore, the potential for VMBR training to improve athletic performance is very good, but its effectiveness depends on the type of task, the skill level of the performer, and the athlete's ability to relax and use imagery.

Stress Inoculation Training (SIT)

Stress inoculation training (SIT) is a cognitive-behavioral program developed by Meichenbaum (1977, 1985) that incorporates relaxation training, imagery, and other cognitive processes into a single plan. The key element of SIT is the progressive exposure of the athlete to situations of greater and greater stress as a way to inoculate the athlete against the debilitating effects of stress. SIT is composed of three phases. In the *conceptualization phase,* the focus of the sport psychologist is upon establishing a collaborative relationship with the athlete and helping him to better understand the nature of stress and its effect upon emotions and performance. This phase may include interviews, administration of questionnaires, and

CONCEPT Similar to VMBR, SIT effectively reduces stress and has been shown to enhance performance of subjects.

APPLICATION The principle of gradually exposing a fearful athlete to situations of progressively greater threat is one that can be readily applied by the practitioner. As the athlete masters the skills of relaxation and imagery, he will be better prepared to cope with situations of increased difficulty.

CONCEPT Similar to VMBR and SIT, Smith's cognitive-affective SMT program effectively reduces stress and has been shown to enhance performance of athletes.

APPLICATION The principle of helping an athlete to experience competition-like stress through imagery is an effective way to help the athlete overcome real-life competitive stress. The athlete who can visualize herself successfully performing a skill with associated competitive stress is more likely to transfer this ability to a real-life situation.

other strategies to assess the athlete's expectations and goals. During the *skills acquisition phase,* the major objective of the sport psychologist is to help the athlete develop coping skills such as progressive relaxation, cognitive restructuring, imaging, problem solving, and self-instructional training. In the final *application and follow-through phase,* the athlete is encouraged to implement his learned coping skills and responses in day-to-day situations. Small manageable units of stress (whatever distresses the athlete) are introduced to the athlete. The athlete is first asked to imagine himself coping with progressively more threatening scenes while in a relaxed state. In this way, the athlete anticipates stressful interactions and practices ways to behave or cope with them. Next, the athlete is introduced to real-life situations in which the level of stress is gradually increased, allowing the athlete to practice his learned coping strategies. In this graded way, the athlete is inoculated against stress.

Threatening situations are presented through imagery, films, role playing, and real-life situations. For example, if the fear of competition is stressful, the athlete is allowed to experience both imagined and real competitive situations. As soon as the athlete is able to cope with a low level of stress, the situation is changed, and a more stressful situation is presented. In this way, the athlete becomes inoculated against progressively increasing levels of stress. Eventually, the athlete's fear of competition is minimized to such a degree that he can cope with it.

Research with SIT in athletic situations has demonstrated its effectiveness in reducing stress and increasing athletic performance in basketball (Hamilton & Fremouw, 1985), gymnastics (Kerr & Leith, 1993), rappelling (Mace & Carroll, 1985), squash (Mace & Carroll, 1986), and cross-country running (Ziegler, Klinzing, & Williamson, 1982), as well as in increasing athletes' pain tolerance (Whitmarsh & Alderman, 1993).

Stress Management Training (SMT)

Stress Management Training (SMT) is a cognitive-behavioral intervention program developed by Smith (1980) that incorporates relaxation training, imagery, and other cognitive processes. Like Stress Inoculation Training (SIT), SMT is composed of three stages. The significant difference between the two stress management programs is in stage three. SIT emphasizes the ability to manage small incremental changes in stress, while SMT practices managing stress associated with imagined high-stress situations.

In phase one of SMT, the *conceptualization of stress phase,* the athlete is taught to understand the nature of stress generally, and to understand the source of her stress specifically. She learns what causes stress and how to cope with it. During this phase she also learns that she already possesses a number of useful coping strategies for dealing with stress. In phase two, the *skill acquisition phase,* the athlete learns and practices integrated coping responses. The coping responses are based on relaxation, imagery, deep breathing, and other cognitive-behavioral skills. She learns to "trigger" these coping skills through cognitive self-statements. In phase three, the *skill rehearsal phase,* induced affect is used to generate high levels of emotional arousal, which are reduced by the athlete through the application of coping responses learned during skill acquisition. In SMT, the athlete is asked to imagine as vividly as possible a relevant stressful situation. Research supports the use of SMT for reducing stress and for enhancing athletic performance (Crocker, 1989).

Hypnosis in Sport

Like imagery, hypnosis is a cognitive-behavioral process that has both a cognitive function and a motivational function. In a cognitive sense, hypnosis is used to restructure the way athletes think about themselves and about the way they execute and learn new sport skills. In a motivational sense, hypnosis is used to modify emotions, reduce anxiety, increase or decrease arousal, and increase effort. In the initial induction phase, hypnotism is physiologically identical to progressive relaxation, autogenic training, and meditation. All of these intervention strategies are associated with reductions in oxygen consumption, respiration rate, and heart rate (Benson et al., 1974; Coleman, 1976). Yet, following the acceptance of a hypnotic suggestion, the hypnotized individual might display heightened physiological characteristics consistent with motivational suggestions given.

Perhaps because it is poorly understood, hypnosis is not a widely utilized intervention strategy in sport. In a recent qualitative investigation, six applied sport psychologists were interviewed about their use of hypnosis practices (Grindstaff & Fisher, 2006). The research focused upon five guiding questions that resulted in 15 themes. Three of the identified themes refer to stereotypes and misconceptions related to hypnosis.

A dated but well-known application of hypnosis took place before the first heavyweight boxing match between Muhammad Ali and Ken Norton in 1973. Norton reportedly hired a professional hypnotist to help him bolster his self-confidence and reduce prematch anxiety. Norton won the match in a stunning upset, effectively calling attention to hypnosis as a viable intervention strategy.

In the pages that follow, our discussion of hypnosis in sport will focus upon (a) defining hypnosis, (b) facts about hypnosis, (c) achieving the hypnotic trance, (d) self-hypnosis, and (e) hypnosis and athletic performance.

Defining Hypnosis

Providing a simple, widely agreed-upon definition of hypnosis is difficult. It appears that you can obtain as many authoritative definitions of hypnotism as there are authorities to give one. Interestingly, though, most, but not all, will contain the word "suggestion" within the definition. The term *hypnosis* comes from Hypnos, the Greek god of sleep (Kalat, 1999), even though it has long been known that hypnosis is not related to sleep. It may, however, be related to sleepwalking (Weitzenhoffer,

CONCEPT There is general agreement among psychologists that hypnosis is closely associated with the notion of being responsive to suggestions.

APPLICATION If an athlete is already responsive to suggestions, then other forms of intervention such as relaxation, meditation, and imagery may be just as effective as hypnotism.

CONCEPT Some individuals will be more responsive to hypnosis and hypnotic suggestions than others. Through proper preparation, most individuals can benefit from hypnosis, but not all.

APPLICATION Some athletes will be good candidates for hypnosis, but others will not be. If an athlete wants to try hypnosis as an intervention to help him with some problem such as anxiety, refer him to a therapist who is proficient and skilled in its use.

2000). Here are a few definitions that have been offered of **hypnosis:**

> "The uncritical acceptance of a suggestion." (Ulett & Peterson, 1965, p. 13)
>
> "A procedure wherein changes in sensations, perceptions, thoughts, feelings, or behaviors are suggested." (Kirsch & Lynn, 1995, p. 846)
>
> "An induced condition associated with, not just of, hypersuggestibility, and . . . better described as a suggestibility heightening state." (Weitzenhoffer, 2000, p. 229)
>
> "An induced temporary condition of being, a state, that differs mentally and physiologically from a person's normal state of being." (Weitzenhoffer, 2000, p. 221)

The first three definitions all focus upon the word "suggestion" or "suggestibility." Thus, it is generally agreed among psychologists that hypnosis is associated with a situation in which suggestions are more readily accepted and acted upon. The last definition, however, elicits a wide number of dissenters as well as advocates. Clearly, psychologists can agree that hypnosis is closely linked with a heightened suggestibility, but are divided on the efficacy of the last definition. It appears that psychologists cannot agree on the notion that hypnosis is an altered state of consciousness, or even on what an altered state of consciousness is. This is to say, however, not that they fall into two polarized camps on the issue, but that they likely fall along a continuum ranging from total acceptance of the altered state of consciousness concept to total dismissal of the notion (Kirsch & Lynn, 1995).

Facts about Hypnosis and Its Application

Psychologists are divided on what the hypnotic trance is, and on whether there is such a thing as an altered state of consciousness relative to hypnosis, but they are in general agreement about the application of hypnosis (Kirsch & Lynn, 1995). Some agreed upon facts about hypnosis are as follows:

1. The ability to experience a hypnotic phenomenon does not indicate gullibility or personality weakness.

2. Hypnosis is not the same as sleep, nor is it related to sleep.

3. Hypnotic responsiveness depends more on the efforts and abilities of the individual being hypnotized than on the skill of the therapist.

4. While hypnotized, individuals retain the ability to control their behavior, are aware of their surroundings, and can monitor events outside the framework of suggestions given during hypnosis.

5. Spontaneous amnesia or forgetting is relatively rare following hypnosis.

6. An individual does not need to be hypnotized to be responsive to suggestions.

7. The function of a hypnotic induction is to increase suggestibility to a minor degree.

8. Hypnosis is not a dangerous procedure when practiced by qualified researchers and clinicians.

9. Most hypnotized individuals are not faking compliance to suggestions or merely going along with suggestions to be cooperative.

10. Hypnosis cannot increase the accuracy of memory.

11. Hypnosis does not precipitate a literal re-experiencing of childhood events.

Achieving the Hypnotic Trance

Five phases are associated with inducing the hypnotic trance in a participant. They are preparation of the participant, the induction process, the hypnotic phase, waking up, and the posthypnotic phase. Each of these phases will be briefly discussed in the following paragraphs:

Preparation of the Participant   When participants are prepared for hypnotism, they must be relieved of any fears and apprehensions they have about hypnotism. Some myths may need to be exposed. For example, participants may be under the impression that they will lose control, that they will be unaware of their surroundings, or that they will lose consciousness. They must have complete trust in the hypnotist and must want to be hypnotized. They also must be told that they will remain in control at all times and will be able to come out of the hypnotic trance if they want to.

Induction Phase   It is during the **hypnotic induction** phase that the hypnotist actually hypnotizes the participant. There are many induction techniques. The best ones are associated with relaxation, attentional focus, and imagery. In fact, the steps involved in eliciting the relaxation response using these techniques are essentially identical to those in hypnosis. The only difference is that the word *hypnosis* is never used in eliciting the relaxation response whereas it is, and should be used with hypnosis (Grindstaff & Fisher, 2006). It should also be pointed out that in terms of physiological responses, hypnotic induction is identical to the relaxation responses associated with progressive relaxation, transcendental meditation, and autogenic training.

Generally, induction procedures are fairly standard. They are typically composed of a series of suggestions aimed at eliciting the participant's cooperation and directing his attention to thoughts and feelings about being relaxed and peaceful. The selection of an induction technique is generally based on the hypnotist's comfort with it, or her belief that the participant's attentional style or personality is compatible with it. Some of the more common techniques involve fixation on an object, monotonous suggestions ("you feel sleepy"), and imagery. Regardless of which technique is used, the effect is the same. The participant becomes very lethargic, experiences the relaxation response, and becomes very susceptible to suggestions. The hypnotist can use a number of techniques to help the participant become more responsive to hypnotism. Most of these are associated with relaxing the participant and gaining his confidence. Others include using the word *hypnotism* to define the situation and the manner in which suggestions are given. For example, a good time to suggest to the participant that he is becoming tired is when the hypnotist observes that the participant's

Athlete focusing on self-hypnotic suggestions while stretching. © Royalty-Free/Corbis.

eyelids are drooping. The hypnotist must also avoid making suggestions that the participant may fail.

Hypnotic Phase

Once the hypnotic state has been induced, the subject is in **neutral hypnosis.** In this state, physiological responses are identical to those of the relaxation response. The hypnotized participant is generally asked to respond, either in imagination or physically, to suggestions of the hypnotist. Typically, these suggestions are alerting and arousing, and bring about the "alert" trance, or **waking hypnosis.** If participants are asked to carry out suggestions while in a trance, they are doing so in the state of waking hypnosis. Participants may, of course, be given suggestions of deep relaxation while in the hypnotic state. Generally, participants will be given suggestions to carry out after they are awake. These are referred to as **posthypnotic suggestions.** Ken Norton was given posthypnotic suggestions for his fight with Muhammad Ali.

Waking Up

The fourth phase of hypnosis is coming out of the trance. Actually, a hypnotized participant can come out of the trance anytime. The only reason participants do not come out on their own is that they don't want to. The relationship between the hypnotist and the participant can be a very pleasant one. When the hypnotist wishes to bring a participant out of a trance, she does so simply by suggesting that the participant wake up on a given signal. For example, the hypnotist might say, "Okay, when I count to three you will wake up." Occasionally a participant will resist coming out of the trance. If this happens, the participant is taken back into a deep trance and asked why he doesn't want to come out. After a few minutes of discussion and another suggestion to wake up, the participant will generally do so.

Posthypnotic Phase

Suggestions given to participants during hypnosis are often designed to influence them during the posthypnotic phase,

CONCEPT Self-hypnosis, or autohypnosis, can be just as effective as heterohypnosis, and does not place the athlete in a situation of dependence.

APPLICATION If hypnosis skills are taught, self-hypnosis is preferable to heterohypnosis. Self-hypnosis is very similar to autogenic training, meditation, and relaxation.

or after they have come out of the hypnotic trance. Posthypnotic suggestions given to athletes should focus on the way they should feel in certain competitive situations. For example, a baseball player may be told, "when you get into the batter's box, you will find that you feel relaxed and confident." Specific suggestions such as "you'll be able to get a hit almost every time," should be avoided, since failure will tend to undermine the effectiveness of the suggestions.

Self-Hypnosis and Avoiding Negative Suggestions

There are two kinds of hypnosis. The first kind is **heterohypnosis,** and the second is **self-hypnosis,** or autohypnosis. Our discussion up to this point has focused on heterohypnosis, that which is induced by another person, usually a trained therapist or psychologist. Heterohypnosis should be practiced only by skilled professionals. Heterohypnosis is based upon a delicate rapport and trust between the therapist and the client. During periods of hypersuggestibility, the athlete is vulnerable to inadvertent negative suggestions from the hypnotist. A qualified psychologist will be able to avoid making these kinds of mistakes. Having said this, it is also instructive to understand that heterohypnosis is really an extension of self-hypnosis. In heterohypnosis, the participant is hypnotizing herself, with the assistance of the therapist (Kirsch & Lynn, 1998). Therefore, all hypnosis is really self-hypnosis, and all the benefits associated with heterohypnosis are also available in self-hypnosis.

The phases involved in self-hypnosis are identical to those outlined for hypnosis generally. If a coach or teacher wishes to employ self-hypnosis as an intervention strategy for reducing anxiety and improving concentration and imagery, he should go over these steps with the athlete. First, the athlete must be completely comfortable regarding the use of hypnosis. The athlete should begin with the reminder (suggestion) that he is in complete control and can disengage from the hypnotic trance at any time. The induction procedures are the same as those for heterohypnosis. Some common strategies for induction are to sit in an easy chair and stare at a spot on the wall, imagine a blank screen, or look into a mirror.

Posthypnotic suggestions given during self-hypnosis should always be couched in positive terms, stressing what is to be accomplished rather than dwelling on negative things to be eliminated (Wegner, 1997). For example, the athlete may wish to concentrate on being more positive when she prepares to receive a tennis serve from a tough opponent. A suggestion such as "I will feel relaxed and agile" would be better than "I'm going to hit a winner." The second suggestion contains the seeds of defeat, since you can't always hit a winner. Suggestions such as "I won't feel nervous" are negative, because they call attention only to the problem. The athlete should have specific suggestions already in mind before the hypnotic phase begins. In some cases, the athlete could have the suggestions written on a card that she could read during the hypnotic trance.

In our earlier discussion of positive or facilitative imagery, it was emphasized that imaging a success is positive and leads to an increase in performance as well as an increase in self-efficacy (Nordin & Cumming, 2005; Short, Bruggeman, et al., 2002). This same research also showed the *devastating negative effect of imaging a failure* (e.g., imaging the putt missing the hole). This concept is further reinforced by research reported by Beilock, Afremow, et al. (2001), in which an attempt to repress a negative thought was found to be counterproductive. The reason negative thought repression is ineffective is that it calls attention to the negative thought that the individual is trying to avoid. It is better to focus completely on positive thoughts and images and to avoid negative images altogether. A case in point is a true story that was shared with the author by a parent. As you reflect on this story, remember the power of suggestion as it relates to self-hypnosis.

> I was standing at the far end of the track with my daughter's coach prior to a state championship hurdling event my daughter was about to run in. It had rained the night before and despite attempts to dry the track out with new cinders and soil, there were still a few soft spots on the track. As my daughter came around the track on her final warm-up lap, the coach stopped her and said to her, "There is a soft spot in the track at the far end of the track as you begin your final turn. Be careful as you make your jump in that area." That was it and that is all he said, but I had a sickening feeling as the race began and even more as she rounded the fateful turn. Sure enough, as she hit the soft spot she slipped and missed the hurdle. I never really blamed the coach for calling attention to a negative image, but I also knew instinctively that he had inadvertently planted a negative thought in my daughter's mind.
> (N. Kaluhiokalani, personal communication, June, 1990)

As I have thought about this story, I have often reflected on what the coach could have done differently. Rather than calling attention to the negative image of a slip, he could have instructed her to take a few practice jumps around the track, including in the affected area. Thus, without his calling

attention to a negative outcome to avoid, the athlete could have found out for herself how the turf felt and formed positive images of navigating the course.

Hypnosis and Athletic Performance

Is hypnosis effective in facilitating athletic performance? Research on this topic yields a number of basic principles that can be summarized. These important principles are based on extensive reviews and published articles (Baer, 1980; Barker, Jones, & Greenlees, 2010; Ito, 1979; Johnson, 1961; Morgan, 1972; Morgan & Brown, 1983; Ulrich, 1973). A list of basic principles gleaned from the literature is provided below, along with some commentary.

1. The more open and susceptible an athlete is to suggestions, the more likely it is that he will benefit from suggestions given to him under hypnosis. This is also the type of individual who is more likely to be hypnotized.

2. Once an individual is hypnotized, the deeper the trance, the more likely it is that suggestions given under hypnosis will be effective.

3. Positive suggestions are effective in facilitating performance, regardless of whether or not the athlete is hypnotized. This principle underscores the importance of uncritical acceptance of suggestions from the teacher or coach. If an athlete will accept positive suggestions uncritically, it makes little difference whether she is hypnotized at the time or not.

4. General arousal techniques are more useful than hypnotic suggestions in enhancing muscular strength and endurance. Hypnosis tends to relax an athlete. Muscular strength and endurance activities require increased levels of arousal and activation, not relaxation.

5. Negative suggestions almost always cause a decrement in performance. This is perhaps the most important principle of all. Negative

CONCEPT Giving negative suggestions to hypnotized individuals must be guarded against. Positive suggestions may result in a benefit to performance, but negative suggestions almost always are detrimental to performance.

APPLICATION It may seem obvious that one should not give negative suggestions to athletes, whether they are under hypnosis or not. The inexperienced coach or sport psychologist may, however, give negative suggestions without realizing it. For example, telling a hurdler to watch out for soft ground on the first turn of a race may be the equivalent of a negative suggestion, if it is too late for a practice run.

suggestions given to an athlete under hypnosis are particularly powerful. Negative suggestions given to an athlete at any time can be counterproductive. Often, negative suggestions are given inadvertently.

6. Hypnosis may be able to help a successful athlete, but it cannot make a good performer out of a poor one. A lot of practice, goal setting, and physical ability are required to accomplish this.

If properly used, hypnosis may be effective in enhancing the suggestibility of athletes. The heightened suggestibility of athletes may lead to cognitive or behavioral adjustments that may facilitate performance (Barker & Jones, 2006, 2008; Lindsay, Maynard, & Thomas, 2005; Pates, Cummings, & Maynard, 2002; Pates, Cummings, Maynard, & Westbury, 2000; Pates, Maynard, & Westbury, 2001; Pates, Oliver, & Maynard, 2001). Several of the reported studies show an association between hypnosis intervention and increased flow. Recall that the concept of flow was discussed in chapter 8 and that it is associated with attentional focus and with a positive mental attitude.

In conclusion, it is important to not overstate the effectiveness of hypnosis in improving athletic performance. Positive suggestions are beneficial to the athlete, regardless of whether the athlete is hypnotized or not. Hypnosis is not effective in enhancing muscular strength and endurance. Finally, a real danger exists in inadvertently giving an athlete a negative suggestion while he is in a state of hypersuggestibility.

Summary

Imagery is the process of using all the senses to recreate or create an experience in the mind. Other terms that have been used as synonyms to imagery include cognitive and symbolic rehearsal, mental rehearsal, visualization, and mental practice. The mental practice literature provides evidence that imagery is an effective cognitive-behavioral process for enhancing learning and performance of motor skills.

Factors that moderate the relationship between imagery use and performance enhancement include the skill level of the athlete and the cognitive component of the skill. The higher the skill level of the athlete and the larger the cognitive component of the skill, the stronger the relationship between imagery and enhanced performance.

The literature is full of studies that have demonstrated the efficacy of mental imagery in

(a) enhancing the thoughts and emotions of athletes, (b) facilitating cognition and motivation, and (c) demonstrating its use by successful athletes. In addition, a recent review of imagery research reveals numerous studies that document the effectiveness of imagery interventions in improving performance, cognition, and motivation.

Theories of why imagery use enhances learning and performance of sport skills include psychoneuromuscular theory, symbolic learning theory, and the functional equivalence hypothesis. In the final analysis, the best theory might be eclectic in nature and include elements of all three theories.

Based upon the groundbreaking work of Munroe et al. (2000) with adult athletes, imagery in sport was considered as a function of the "where," the "when," the "what," and the "why" of imagery. Within each of these functional categories, the theory and research associated with sport imagery will be presented. This includes *where* imagery occurs, *when* imagery occurs, *what* is occurring relative to the content of imagery, and *why* or for what purpose imagery occurs.

The content or what of imagery was discussed relative to research in the areas of (a) timing associate with imagery, (b) facilitative and debilitative nature of imagery, (c) imagery perspective, and (d) sensory mode. The process of imagery takes place from both an internal perspective and an external perspective. Regardless of which perspective is used, all of the body's senses are utilized.

Paivio's conceptual model of imagery includes a cognitive function and a motivational function. Each of these two functions are categorized as being situation-specific or general. The motivational-general dimension of imagery use was further categorized as being mastery- or arousal-related. Thus the five types of imagery use include motivational-specific (MS), motivational general–mastery (MG-M), motivational general–arousal (MG-A), cognitive specific (CS), and cognitive general (CG). The four Ws of imagery use are where, when, what, and why.

Sixteen different imagery questionnaires were listed and categorized relative to imagery aspect measured. Questionnaires were categorized relative to the imagery aspects of controllability, preferred style, imagery use, and vividness.

Training programs designed to improve and magnify the content of images focus upon enhancing controllability and vividness of the images seen. A sample six-step program designed to enhance imagery ability was presented.

Three cognitive-behavioral intervention programs that include imagery and relaxation were introduced and discussed. These include visual motor behavior rehearsal, stress inoculation training, and stress management training.

Hypnosis is defined as a procedure wherein changes in sensations, perceptions, thoughts, feelings, or behaviors are suggested. Psychologists differ on what is meant by an altered state of consciousness relative to hypnosis.

Eleven specific facts about hypnosis were listed. Included among these facts were the following: (a) responsiveness to hypnotic suggestions is not a sign of personality weakness, (b) hypnotic responsiveness depends more on the individual being hypnotized than on the hypnotist, (c) an individual does not need to be hypnotized to be responsive to suggestions, and (d) the function of a hypnotic induction is to increase suggestibility to a minor degree.

Five phases are associated with inducing the hypnotic trance in a subject. They are preparation of the subject, the induction process, the hypnotic phase, waking up, and the posthypnotic phase. Hypnotic suggestions and posthypnotic suggestions are given during the hypnotic phase.

Heterohypnosis involves a therapist as well as the participant, whereas self-hypnosis involves only the participant. Heterohypnosis is really an extension of self-hypnosis, because the therapist is only helping the participant hypnotize herself.

All the benefits associated with heterohypnosis are also available in self-hypnosis.

Six principles were identified from research on hypnosis and athletic performance. If properly used, hypnosis may be effective in enhancing the suggestibility of athletes. It is important, however, not to overstate the effectiveness of hypnosis in improving athletic performance. Positive suggestions are beneficial to the athlete, regardless of whether the athlete is hypnotized or not.

Critical Thought Questions

1. How might imagery be used to help a fumble-prone running back in football? Devise a plan for accomplishing this goal.

2. Discuss mental practice as an example of applied imagery for enhanced learning and performance. Under what circumstances is mental practice most effective and why?

3. Many sport psychologists have suggested that an internal perspective for imagery use is superior to an external perspective. Why do they claim this, and why might they be wrong? What would be your recommendation to an athlete relative to preferred perspective?

4. Differentiate between the what and why of imagery use. Provide some examples of each and some useful clarifications of how they differ.

5. Discuss Paivio's two-dimensional model of imagery use in sport. Why are there five types of imagery use if the model is two-dimensional in nature? How is imagery use measured?

6. Provide some specific examples of how imagery could be used to learn team strategies and skill development.

7. Provide some specific examples of how imagery could be used to motivate an athlete to greater arousal and effort.

8. Why do you think psychologists disagree on the existence of and meaning of the hypnotic state or trance?

9. In what ways is hypnosis different from and similar to meditation?

10. If you don't believe in the reality of the hypnotic trance, can you still believe in the efficacy of hypnosis as a means to change sensations, perceptions, thoughts, and behaviors? Explain your answer.

11. How do you feel about using hypnosis to assist athletes in anxiety reduction and performance enhancement?

Glossary

applied model of imagery use A conceptual model that shows causal links between sport situation, imagery use, and outcome as moderated by quality of imagery ability.

cognitive-behavioral intervention An intervention for change that includes a cognitive component, a behavioral component, or both.

Psychological Skills Training

KEY TERMS

Athlete-centered sport model

Athletic Coping Skills
  Inventory

Between-play routine

Client

Code of ethics

Mental skills training

Mental toughness

Mindfulness-acceptance-
  commitment

Needs assessment plan

Organizational empowerment
  approach

Ottawa Mental Skills
  Assessment Tool

Performance profiling

Philosophical foundation

Postperformance routine

Preperformance routine

Psychological intervention
  program

Psychological method

Psychological skill

Psychological Skills Inventory
  for Sports

Psychological skills training

Psychological skills training
  program

Resonance

Resonance performance model

Self-regulation

Self-regulation model

Spirituality

Superstitious behavior

Supervisory consulting model

Test of Performance Strategies

Seconds pour away. Agony. Elvis Grbac screams to his teammates. They scream back. The crowd screams louder. Static rushes through Grbac's helmet. It is fourth down. Two yards to go. Seconds pour away. (Elvis Grbac's baptism of fire against the Denver Broncos—Posnanski, 1998)

It is January of 1998 and the Kansas City Chiefs are trailing the Denver Broncos by four points, fourth down, two yards to go for a first down, 34 seconds left in the game, Denver's 20-yard line, Kansas City has no time-outs remaining. Grbac needs a play. The fans in Kansas City are screaming, "Call a play!" The speaker in Grbac's helmet isn't working. He can't hear the play. He looks to the sideline. The coaches are screaming, "Go for the first down!" Grbac can't hear them. He has to do something, so he calls his own play. The wrong play. He goes for the end zone, but the receiver is double teamed, and the pass is batted down. End of game, Denver wins by four.

In retrospect, we might ask, "Given the circumstances, what could Elvis have done differently?" The obvious answer is that he should have gone for the first down—but who is to know if that would have worked? One thing we do know, however, is that Elvis Grbac was not psychologically prepared to deal with that particular situation. What do you do when time is running out and your helmet speaker doesn't work?

The answer is really pretty simple. The situation that confronted Elvis Grbac on that cold January day was just one of many circumstances that he could have been confronted with. Each potential circumstance and scenario should have been visualized and considered in the calm of a practice facility days or even weeks before the situation occurred. A sport psychologist could have helped Elvis prepare for what confronted him that day. What *do* you do when there is no time left and you have to make the play that makes the difference in the outcome of the game? Isn't that what point guards in basketball, quarterbacks in football, and setters in volleyball are supposed to do? This real-life situation provides an excellent example of why athletes need the assistance of a sport psychologist.

This chapter on psychological skills training is the culminating chapter on the general topic (Part 4) of cognitive and behavioral interventions in sport and exercise. In previous chapters in part 4, we discussed coping and intervention strategies in sport, goal setting in sport, and imagery and hypnosis in sport. We bring all of these concepts together now in this chapter on psychological skills training. In this chapter we discuss the following eight topics: (a) psychological skill characteristics of the elite athlete, (b) models of psychological skill development, (c) effectiveness of psychological intervention programs, (d) differentiating between skills and methods, (e) measurement of psychological skills, (f) ethics in sport psychology, (g) delivering sport psychology services, (h) a psychological skills training program, and (i) generalization of sport psychology methods to other application domains.

Psychological Skill Characteristics of the Elite Athlete

Numerous studies and literature reviews have focused on the psychological characteristics of the elite athlete. The thought has been that if these characteristics can be identified they can be studied and used as a template for preparing future Olympians (Krane & Williams, 2010). In a very real sense these characteristics have already been identified through the first 11 chapters of this text. In each chapter, psychological principles have been introduced that relate to successful athletic performance. This included the presentation and citing of research that discussed the relationship between each principle or concept and athletic performance. Based on this, we could theoretically conclude that the elite athlete should possess the following psychological characteristics:

- Personality characteristics that are appropriate for specific sports.

- An internal locus of controllability to both success and failure.

- High self-confidence and belief in ultimate success.

- Intrinsic motivation.

- Strong mastery of goal orientation to athletic achievement.

- Total concentration for the task at hand.

- Ability to regulate emotion and physiological arousal.

- Strong coping skills to confront adversity.

- Ability to set difficult goals and formulate plans to achieve them.

- Ability to use self-talk, imagery, self-regulation, and other psychological methods to build confidence and increase motivation.

- Mental toughness.

Although mental toughness has not yet been discussed in this book, it was added to the list because it represents a culmination of what it takes to be an elite athlete at any level of competition. Below we discuss psychological characteristics of the elite athlete from the perspective of research associated with (a) the Olympic and/or World Championship athlete, (b) the elite youth athlete, and (c) the mentally tough athlete.

Psychological Characteristics of Olympic and/or World-Class Athletes

Studies involving Olympic and/or World Championship athletes provide us with a wealth of information about psychological characteristics of elite athletes (Durand-Bush & Salmela, 2002; Gould, Greenleaf, Chung, & Guinan, 2002; Greenleaf, Gould, & Dieffenbach, 2001). Successful athletes from the 1996 Atlanta Summer Olympics and the 1998 Nagano Winter Olympics had confidence in their ability, were able to make tactical adjustments when necessary, and were prepared for distractions. In addition, elite athletes perceived their coaches to be committed and to have realistic individual and team expectations. Compared to less successful Olympians, the more successful Olympians had a more positive attitude about the Olympics, did not complain as much about housing, and enjoyed good team unity.

Elite Youth Athletes

Young elite athletes, from a broad range of sports, possess a task goal orientation and score high in the psychological methods of imagery use, goal setting, and self-talk (Harwood, Cummings, & Fletcher, 2004). In another investigation, elite youth rugby players took part in a study in which both mental qualities and mental techniques were identified by researchers. *Mental qualities* included such things as enjoyment, responsibility, adaptability, squad spirit, self-awareness, determination, confidence, game sense, concentration, and mental toughness. Identified *mental techniques* included performance strategies, reflection on action, taking advantage of supportive climate, and team-based strategies (Holland, Woodcock, Cumming, & Duda, 2010).

In a two-part set of studies, investigators used one set of elite athletes to discover the psychological characteristics of developing excellence (PCDEs), and another set of elite athletes to confirm the original list of PCDEs and to determine if PCDEs change as a function of stage of development and performance domains (MacNamara, Button, & Collins, 2010a, 2010b). The studies were unique in that current elite *professional* athletes were interviewed *retroactively* in the presence of their parents relative to what they recalled about the developmental stages of becoming an elite professional athlete. In the foundation investigation, seven elite athletes were interviewed, while in the follow-up investigation, 22 elite participants from individual sports, team sports, and music were interviewed. The foundation research identified eight PCDEs that were compared with eight identified from the literature. Due to overlap between the two lists, 13 specific PCDEs were identified as being important for developing mental skills in elite athletes. These 13 PCDEs include the following: motivation, commitment, goal setting, quality practice, imagery, realistic performance evaluations, coping under pressure, social skills, competitiveness, vision of success, work on weaknesses, game awareness, and self-belief. These are the mental skill characteristics believed to be necessary to become an elite professional athlete. Results of the follow-up investigation confirmed the original list of PCDEs and identified a couple of new ones. Most importantly, it was discovered that PCDEs possessed by athletes differed among athletes and between stages of development and kind of activity (team, individual, music). When the athletes were very young, they relied on parents, teachers, and coaches; but as they matured responsibility shifted to autonomous behaviors in later years.

Psychological Characteristics of the Mentally Tough Athlete

In this chapter we define mental toughness and present research that helps us to better understand what it is, how it can be developed, and how it can be measured. For now, however, we define mental toughness by providing two examples of athletes who exhibited it.

The first example is Jim Abbott, the one-handed wonder (Jenkins, 2008). Jim Abbott had one hand, yet he pitched the United States to Olympic Gold in 1988 and went on to pitch 10 seasons in Major League Baseball. He both pitched with his left hand and caught the baseball with his left hand. While pitching he would tuck the baseball glove into his right arm, then after releasing the ball, insert his left hand into the glove and position himself for a defensive play. If he caught the ball, he would reverse the process, tucking the glove into his right arm and pulling the ball out of the glove with his left hand in one motion. His right arm ends in a fleshy nubbin. Jim became and still is an inspiration for all young boys and girls who have similar physical challenges, yet want to excel in a physical game or sport. In his own words: "I know it is hard to do things a little differently from other kids, but believe me, if you stick with it, you can be just as good. Always believe. Anything is possible" (p. 102).

The second example is that of Lindsey Vonn, the favorite to win a gold medal in the women's downhill event in the 2010 Vancouver Winter Olympics (Donaldson, 2010). After crashing so severely in the 2006 Torino Winter Olympics that she was hospitalized, she went on to win a World Cup title and the World Championships in 2009. Then just two weeks before the Vancouver Olympics, during a training run, she fell and severely bruised her shin, making it questionable if she would even be able to race. This was, however, only another setback in a career riddled with setbacks, injuries, and disappointments. Referring to her gold medal run in 2010, she said:

> I felt like I was in a good place mentally. I wasn't too nervous. I was focused. I knew I had to ski an aggressive run if I wanted to medal. This is probably the bumpiest course I've ever run, and I think that's the worst thing you can have for a shin injury. It was definitely a challenge just to make it down, but I was focused and determined, and I just tried not to think about the pain. (p. A8)

While Tutko and Richards (1971) included "mental toughness" in their Athletic Motivation Inventory (AMI), it was not until 2002 that a definitive definition of mental toughness was attempted (Jones, Hanton, & Connaughton, 2002). Jones et al. defined **mental toughness** as follows:

> Mental toughness is having the natural or developed psychological edge that enables you to (a) generally, cope better than your opponents with the many demands (competition, training, lifestyle) that sport places on a performer, and (b) specifically, be more consistent and better than your opponents in remaining determined, focused, confident, and in control under pressure. (p. 209)

The AMI was conceptualized by Tutko and Richards as a personality inventory, and hence, mental toughness was considered to be a personality disposition. Conversely, the Jones et al. definition seems to suggest that mental toughness is composed of both "natural and developed" psychological characteristics. Jones et al. conclude their discussion of mental toughness by identifying and listing 12 attributes of mental toughness. While some aspects of mental toughness may be considered to be innate personality dispositions, the majority of the attributes listed appear to be psychological characteristics that can be developed.

In a follow-up investigation to the Jones, Hanton, and Connaughton (2002) study, Jones, Hanton, and Connaughton (2007) studied 10 elite athletes to categorize attributes of mental toughness under a framework that included (a) attitude and mindset, (b) training, (c) competition, and (d) postcompetition. In a similar vein, Bull, Shambrook, James, and Brooks (2005) used 12 international cricketers to conclude that the athletes' environment influenced the development of mental toughness attributes associated with "tough character," "tough attitudes," and "tough thinking." Also using the Jones, Hanton, and Connaughton (2002) list of attributes and definition of mental toughness as a foundation, Thelwell, Weston, and Greenlees (2005) studied professional soccer players to identify a list of 10 attributes of mental toughness that roughly parallel the 12 identified by Jones et al. In addition, Thelwell et al. tweaked the original Jones et al. definition of mental toughness to replace the words "generally cope better" with the words "always cope better."

Finally, Gucciardi and colleagues reported on four studies that used Australian football athletes as participants (Gucciardi, Gordon, & Dimmock, 2008, 2009a, 2009b, 2009c). These studies yielded two additional definitions of mental toughness, similar lists of attributes or characteristics, and an instrument designed to objectively measure mental toughness in Australian football. While similar to the Jones, Hanton, and Connaughton (2002) definition, the definition provided by Gucciardi et al. (2009a) is instructive:

> Mental toughness is a multifaceted construct made up of multiple key components including values, attitudes, cognitions, emotions, and behaviors that refer to an individual's ability to thrive through both positively and negatively construed challenges, pressures, and adversities. (p. 307)

Based on this definition of mental toughness and 11 characteristics of mental toughness identified by Gucciardi et al. (2008, 2009c) reported on the development and testing of the Australian football Mental Toughness Inventory (AfMTI). The AfMTI is composed of 24 items and four subscales that measure mental toughness as a function of (a) the ability to thrive through challenge, (b) sport awareness, (c) tough attitude, and (d) desire for success. The validity of the AfMTI was established by demonstrating that the four subscales of the AfMTI were correlated with subscales of the Dispositional Resilience Scale (DRS; Bartone et al., 1989), and the Dispositional Flow Scale–2 (DFS-2; Jackson & Eklund, 2002).

It is of particular interest that subscales of the AfMTI are correlated and related to resilience and flow personality disposition measures. This suggests that while the focus of mental toughness is on values, attitudes, cognitions, emotions, and behaviors, the notion that mental toughness also has a personality trait component cannot be easily dismissed. The correlation with resilience is of particular interest, because it is repeatedly mentioned as an attribute possessed by mentally tough athletes (Gucciardi et al., 2008, 2009a). As mentioned in chapter 2, personal resilience drives a person to confront and overcome adversity and has been described as an *innate* righting mechanism (Richardson, 2002).

In addition to the AfMTI, designed using Australian football players, a second inventory was developed using martial arts performers (Creasy, Stratton, Maina, Rearick, & Reincke, 2008; Minnix, 2010). Titled the Mental Toughness Inventory (MTI), this inventory is composed of 20 items that measure the subscales of (a) conviction/determination, (b) commitment, (c) readiness to perform, (d) conditioning, (e) distraction, and (f) shifting focus of attention.

While difficult to define, we do generally recognize mental toughness in athletes when we see and observe it (e.g., Jim Abbott and Lindsey Vonn). There seems to be some innate personality disposition associated with mental toughness, but to a large extent it appears that mental toughness can be

FIGURE 12.1 | Illustration showing an incomplete list of attributes possessed by the mentally tough athlete, a definition of mental toughness, and expected outcomes of mental toughness.

Attributes of Mental Toughness	Definition of Mental Toughness	Consequences of Mental Toughness
• Self-confident and self-assured • Able to focus and concentrate • Intrinsically motivated • Strong work ethic • Committed to excellence • Persistent and determined at all times • Positive attitude, no negativism • Resilient in the face of failure or injury • Thrive on pressure and challenge • Consistent personal values • Emotional intelligence • Physically tough • Gracious in face of success	Mental toughness is a multifaceted construct made up of multiple key components including values, attitudes, cognitions, emotions, and behaviors that refer to an individual's ability to thrive through both positively and negatively construed challenges, pressures, and adversities (Gucciardi et al., 2009a, p. 307).	Mentally tough athletes prepare for and enjoy athletic success. Elite athletes of all sports and all developmental levels possess the attributes associated with mental toughness. Jim Abbott and Lindsey Vonn are examples of elite athletes who possed the attributes associated with mental toughness.

developed in athletes as a function of values, attitudes, cognitions, emotions, and behaviors (Connaughton & Hanton, 2010). Figure 12.1 provides a summary illustration of an incomplete list of attributes of mental toughness, a definition of mental toughness, and expected outcomes associated with mental toughness.

Models of Psychological Skill Development

Some sport psychologists find it useful to look at psychological skill development with the structure of a theoretical model. To this end, four such models are presented and discussed. These include the self-regulation model, the resonance performance model, the athlete-centered sport model, and the mindfulness-acceptance-commitment approach. Each of these models provides useful insight into what is involved in developing psychological skill in sport.

Self-Regulation Model

Within their **self-regulation model,** Cleary and Zimmerman (2001) define **self-regulation** as "self-generated thoughts, feelings, and behaviors that are planned and cyclically adapted based on performance feedback" (p. 187). The model begins with the *forethought phase* (goal setting, strategy choice, self-efficacy), proceeds to the *performance phase* (strategy use, self-monitoring, self-instruction, imagery, attention focusing), and finishes with the *self-reflective phase* (self-evaluation, outcome attribution, self-satisfaction), which in turn feeds back to the forethought phase. Research involving the self-regulation model shows that more successful athletes exhibit superior regulation skills at each phase of the model.

Resonance Performance Model

In a similar vein, Newberg, Kimiecik, Durand-Bush, and Doell (2002) proposed the **resonance performance model** to explain how athletes become elite athletes. The concept of **resonance** is related to the concepts of flow, intrinsic motivation, and emotion. Peak performance in any endeavor begins with a dream that is associated with positive feelings and emotions. To achieve the dream, the performer engages in preparation to help her achieve the dream. Preparation comes in the form of physical and psychological skill development. Along the way to achieving the dream, the athlete will be confronted with obstacles. At this point, the athlete must revisit the dream in order to become more motivated and engaged in her preparation. The key to success is that she not be caught in a loop of going back and forth between the obstacle and the preparation (working harder). She must revisit the dream so that she can again experience the positive feelings and emotions associated with the dream.

Athlete-Centered Sport Model

The **athlete-centered sport model** proposes that sport must contribute to the overall development of the athlete physically, psychologically, and socially (Miller & Kerr, 2002). From a psychological skills development perspective, we are always looking for ways to enhance *performance excellence* (observable, measurable athletic outcomes). That is, we want to foster the development of an athlete who can jump farther, swim faster, and generally perform at an elite level. However, from the perspective of the athlete-centered sport model, this goal is short-sighted and imbalanced. While we are striving for performance excellence, we must also be striving at the same time for *personal excellence*. Personal excellence may include performance excellence, but it also includes all those virtues that make the athlete a better person across a lifetime. As stated by Miller and Kerr (2002), "If high-level sport were delivered in a developmentally appropriate manner, both

performance and personal excellence would be possible at the same time" (p. 141).

Connected to the concept of an athlete-centered sport model is the observation that for many athletes this should include attention to the spiritual well-being of the athlete. A literature review published by Watson and Nesti (2005) pointed to the need to include the concept of **spirituality** within the athlete-centered sport model. Specifically, their investigation suggested the need to (a) integrate spirituality and positive psychology into mental skill training, (b) recognize the connection between spirituality and the flow experience, and (c) include spirituality into consultancy work. Finally, Ridnour and Hammermeister (2008) reported on an investigation that showed a predictive relationship between spirituality, as measured by the Spiritual Well-Being Scale (SWBS; Ellison, 1983), and athlete coping skills.

Mindfulness-Acceptance-Commitment Model

The **mindfulness-acceptance-commitment** (MAC) approach to enhanced athletic performance is closely related to several concepts already introduced in this book (Gardner & Moore, 2007; Moore & Gardner, 2001). They include the notion of positive psychology introduced in chapter one, flow and mindfulness introduced in chapter 8, and integrative mind-body training introduced in chapter 9. These conceptual approaches to psychological self-regulation emphasize a nonjudgmental focus of one's attention on the here and the now. Mindfulness in this model may be measured using the previously introduced Mindfulness/Mindlessness Scale (MMS; Bodner & Langer, 2001) or the Mindfulness Attention Awareness Scale (MAAS; Brown & Ryan, 2003).

As explained by Moore (2009), traditional psychological skill training (PST) programs focus upon teaching athletes to gain control over such internal states as emotions, sensations, and cognitions with the mistaken belief that such personal control will result in a necessary internal state that

Elite athletes possess psychological skills that make it possible for them to experience unprecedented success on the athletic field. The elite athlete is self-confident, highly motivated, and competitive. The athlete-centered sport model also proposes that attention be given to developing the personal excellence as well as the performance excellence of the athlete.

The elite athlete starts with a dream that, through hard work and dedication,

becomes a reality. It is the sport psychologist and coaches' responsibility to provide the motivational climate that makes it possible to achieve the dream. However, even while records are being broken and performance excellence is being achieved, attention must be given to allowing the athlete to grow and develop as a total well-rounded person. The answer is not always more practice and more dedication. Sometimes the answer is simply encouraging the athlete to practice self-reflection and to develop a feeling of autonomy and personal control over his life.

will lead to high-level athletic performance. For example, in the traditional PST approach, an athlete suffering from anxiety and stress would be taught to utilize relaxation strategies designed to reduce and control emotion and anxiety. The MAC approach to high-level athletic performance (peak performance) rejects the notion that "controlling" internal states necessarily leads to peak performance, in favor of a nonjudgmental moment-to-moment acceptance of whatever psychological state the athlete finds himself in. In the MAC approach to developing peak performance, the athlete does not become alarmed with feelings of high emotion, and try to reduce it, but rather accepts it as being what it is (neither good or bad). Once the athlete can learn to do this in an open mindful way, then the emotions that are being experienced can be used in a beneficial way. This should remind the reader of the Jones' directional hypothesis introduced in chapter 8, in which we learned that it is not the absolute intensity of an emotion that is important, but how the athlete interprets the emotion that makes the difference.

In support of the MAC approach to peak performance, Gooding and Gardner (2009) reported on an investigation that showed that mindfulness as measured by the Mindfulness Attention Scale (MAAS) was predictive of game-time free-throw shooting percentage in basketball. In a separate investigation, Kaufman, Glass, and Arnkoff (2009)

subjected selected archers and golfers to a four-week mindfulness sport performance enhancement (MSPE) program based on the MAC approach. As a result of training, the participants increased their scores in state flow, mindfulness, and sport confidence, but not in actual measurable performance.

Effectiveness of Psychological Intervention Programs

A number of literature reviews have been published that verify that planned **psychological intervention programs** are effective in enhancing athletic performance (Greenspan & Feltz, 1989; Vealey, 1994; Weinberg & Comar, 1994). These reviews confirm that of approximately 45 studies reviewed, 38, or 85 percent, have found positive performance effects (Weinberg & Williams, 2010). In addition, as reported below, a number of more recent investigations have supported the effectiveness of psychological interventions.

Three studies were identified that utilized the multiple baseline single subject design (MBSSD) first introduced in chapter 8. The first two studies were very similar in that they both utilized participants who took part in a gymnasium triathlon (rowing, cycling, running). In both studies, a psychological skills training (PST) program based on goal setting, relaxation, imagery, and self-talk was found to successfully improve performance on the endurance tasks (Thelwell & Greenlees, 2001, 2003). In the third study, five male university soccer players who played the midfield position served as participants. Pre- and post-intervention (relaxation, imagery, self-talk) performance data were recorded across nine conference matches in a single season. Skills monitored included number of (a) successful first touches of the ball, (b) successful passes, and (c) successful legal tackles. Results showed that the psychological intervention was effective in enabling small but consistent improvements on the three measured soccer ball handling skills (Thelwell, Greenlees, & Weston, 2006).

Five additional investigations were identified that used experimental designs in which participants were assigned to treatment conditions and studied over time. In a study involving scuba divers, participants assigned to a psychological skill-training program effectively reduced anxiety, increased confidence, and improved performance compared to a control group (Terry, Mayer, & Howe, 1998). In a study involving male youth baseball players, participants were assigned to a psychological skills training (PST) group or to a weight-training control group. The PST group made significant progress toward maintaining skills they learned for up to three months (Grove, Norton, Van Raalte, & Brewer, 1999). In a third investigation, five elite junior tennis players who received PST were contrasted with four who did not across 25 weeks of tennis competition. Results showed that the players who received PST improved their performance and increased their self-confidence (Mamassis & Doganis, 2004). In another study, college-age students learned free-throw basketball- shooting skills under one of five conditions. Condition one received shooting technique instruction only; condition two received instruction plus 12 minutes of practice; while the remaining three groups received instruction, increasing amounts of psychological skill training, and 12 minutes of practice. Following practice, all groups received a posttest on free-throw shooting accuracy. Results showed that the PST groups outperformed

the control groups in free-throw shooting accuracy (Cleary, Zimmerman, & Keating, 2006). In the fifth study, two female varsity golfers completed an inventory designed to measure psychological skills before and after receiving a PST program based on individual zone of optimal functioning principles. Results showed that the two golfers improved their performance as well as measured psychological skills following the intervention (Cohen, Tenenbaum, & English, 2006).

While the five aforementioned studies used relatively long periods of pre-intervention, intervention, and post-intervention, two additional investigations utilized very brief interventions. In the first study, 90 high school long-distance runners completed two "do your best" 1.6-km runs that were separated by a 15-minute time period. During the intervening 15 minutes, participants used earphones to listen to (a) motivational and running technique statements, (b) motivational statements, or (c) silence. Results showed that both intervention groups outperformed the silence group in terms of post-intervention running time (Miller & Donohue, 2003). In the second study, 68 members of an adult female hockey team completed a positive affect scale 15 minutes before and 15 minutes after a game they lost. Before they completed the positive affect scale following the game, they were divided into either an experimental group or a control group. The experimental group received a brief intervention in which they focused on a positive thought and a game-related coping thought for one minute each. Results showed that the athletes who did not receive the brief PST intervention suffered a decrease in positive affect following the game whereas the intervention group did not (Arathoon & Malouff, 2004).

Finally, three studies were identified that provide support for the efficacy of psychological skill training, but were decidedly descriptive and qualitative in nature. In the first study, 115 professional tennis players indicated that they all used some form of psychological skill strategy to enhance performance. In addition, higher ranked players indicated that they used psychological strategies to a greater extent than the lower ranked players (DeFrancesco & Burke, 1997). In the second investigation, eight elite national-level British athletes were identified as having exceptionally high scores on goal setting, imagery, relaxation, and self-talk. These eight elite athletes were then interviewed relative to precompetitive anxiety feelings experienced prior to competition as well as the use of four different advanced psychological strategies used to cope with the experienced anxiety. Results showed that applied psychological strategies (simulation training, cognitive restructuring, preperformance routines, overlearning of skills) enabled participants to interpret anxiety as facilitative, improve performance, and increase self-confidence (Hanton, Wadey, & Mellalieu, 2008). In the third study, participants were 15 elite athletes from various sports who exhibited high scores on imagery, relaxation, self-talk, and goal setting. An interview guide was used to ask each athlete retrospectively to identify cognitive and somatic anxiety symptoms experienced prior to competition and to indicate how they used imagery, relaxation, self-talk, and goal setting to address these symptoms. Results showed that 100 percent of anxiety symptoms were perceived as facilitative following PST application and that all participants experienced an increase in self-confidence as a result of applying the four PST strategies (Wadey & Hanton, 2008).

While not included in the above review of research support for the efficacy of psychological skill training, several recent studies provide additional support. These include investigations involving collegiate athletes generally (Cox, Shannon, McGuire, & McBride, 2010), golfers (Hayslip, Petrie, MacIntire, & Jones, 2010), soccer players (Thelwell, Greenlees, & Weston, 2010), and cross country skiers (von Guenthner, Hammermeister, Burton, & Keller, 2010).

Differentiating between Psychological Skills and Methods

Coaches and athletes often use the terms *psychological skill* and *psychological method* as synonyms, when they actually have different meanings. Vealy (1988) clarified that a **psychological method** is a technique or practice that leads to psychological skill. Examples of psychological methods include goal setting, imagery, progressive relaxation, meditation, self-talk, and hypnosis. Each of these psychological methods, when properly learned and applied, lead to enhanced psychological skill. Conversely, **psychological skill** refers to learned or innate characteristics of the athlete that make it possible or even likely that she will succeed in sport. Examples of psychological skill include intrinsic motivation, self-confidence, attentional control, arousal control, anxiety control, and general self-awareness. A case in point is imagery. Imagery is a psychological method or strategy that may be used to develop psychological skill in visualizing correct performance. It is also used in achieving optimal arousal and optimal attentional control. Similarly,

FIGURE 12.2 | Illustration showing the relationship between psychological method, psychological skill, and performance outcome.

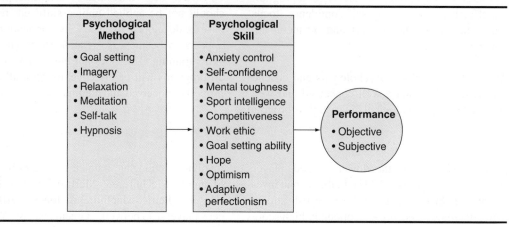

goal setting, relaxation training, and thought control are methods used to develop psychological skills that lead to enhanced performance and self-confidence. Approaching a competitive situation with confidence and with the knowledge that the body and mind are prepared for optimal performance is a psychological skill.

Figure 12.2 shows how psychological methods, psychological skills, and performance outcomes relate to each other. The 12 selected psychological skills were identified by Gould, Dieffenbach, and Moffett (2002) as being possessed by 10 U.S. Olympic champions. It is also of interest to note that coaches are not particularly adept at assessing the psychological strengths and weaknesses of their athletes. Overall, Leslie-Toogood and Martin (2003) reported little agreement between volleyball coaches and their athletes, and between track coaches and their athletes, when it comes to assessing the athletes' mental skills.

Measurement of Psychological Skills

Several inventories have been developed that are designed to measure psychological skills used by athletes. Each of the inventories we will mention

has demonstrated the ability to distinguish among groups of athletes performing at different levels of skill. Before adopting a specific inventory, the practitioner should become familiar with the reliability, validity, and psychometric properties of the selected inventory.

Psychological Skills Inventory for Sports

The **Psychological Skills Inventory for Sports** (PSIS-5) was developed by Mahoney, Gabriel, and Perkins (1987). The PSIS-5 is a 45-item inventory that measures the psychological skills of anxiety control, concentration, confidence, mental preparation, motivation, and team orientation. While the PSIS-5 has exhibited the ability to discriminate among levels of skilled performers, research has questioned the underlying structure of the six factors it measures (Chartrand, Jowdy, & Danish, 1992).

Athletic Coping Skills Inventory

The **Athletic Coping Skills Inventory** (ACSI-28) was developed by Smith, Schutz, Smoll, and Ptacek (1995). The ACSI-28 is a 28-item inventory that measures the psychological skills of coping with adversity, peaking under pressure, goal setting/mental preparation, concentration, freedom from worry, confidence and achievement motivation, and coachability. The ACSI-28 is a modest predictor of hitting and pitching performance among professional baseball players (Smith & Christensen, 1995).

Test of Performance Strategies

The Test of Performance Strategies (TOPS) was developed by Thomas, Murphy, and Hardy (1999). The TOPS is a 64-item inventory that measures a combination of methods and skills of athletes in strategic situations. Factors measured by the TOPS in the *competitive situation* include self-talk, emotional control, automaticity, goal setting, imagery, activation, negative thinking, and relaxation. Factors measured by the TOPS in the *practice situation* include the same factors used in the competitive situation, with the exception that negative thinking is replaced by attentional control.

Notwithstanding the frequent use of the TOPS in research associated with psychological skill training, a confirmatory factor analysis of the structure of the inventory yielded only mixed support (Lane, Harwood, Terry, & Karageorghis, 2004). In response to this criticism of the inventory, Hardy, Roberts, Thomas, and Murphy (2010) developed and tested a revised version of the Test of Performance Strategies (TOPS-2). The revised version is again composed of 64 items, with eight competition (32 items) and eight practice (32 items) subscales.

Ottawa Mental Skills Assessment Tool

The **Ottawa Mental Skills Assessment Tool** (OMSAT-3) was developed by Durand-Bush, Salmela, and Green-Demers (2001). The OMSAT-3 is a 48-item inventory that measures 12 mental skill subscales (four items each). These 12 subscales are then further organized into three conceptual components as follows: *foundation skills* (goal-setting ability, self-confidence, commitment), *psychomotor skills* (stress reactions, fear control, relaxation, activation control), and *cognitive skills* (focusing attention, refocusing attention, imagery ability, mental practice ability, competition planning). Validity testing showed that self-confidence, commitment, stress reaction, focusing, and refocusing were most important in discriminating between elite and less elite athletes.

Ethics in Sport Psychology

As we learned in chapter 1, the Association for Applied Sport Psychology (AASP) is the primary organization within the United States and Canada for professionals interested in applied sport psychology. Members of AASP are bound by a **code of ethics** that governs their interactions with the public and with other professionals. The AASP Ethics Code is based in large part on the Ethical Principles of the American Psychological Association, and is composed of a preamble, six general principles, and 25 standards. Readers are referred to the AASP Web site for details of the ethics code. Here we will only paraphrase the six general principles that govern the conduct of members of AASP.

Principle 1: Competence

AASP members maintain a high standard of competence in their work. In this regard, they recognize the boundaries and limitations of their competence.

Principle 2: Integrity

AASP members practice and promote integrity in the teaching, science, and practice of applied sport psychology. In this regard, they always present themselves and their credentials accurately and forthrightly.

Principle 3: Professional and Scientific Responsibility

AASP members take their professional and scientific responsibilities seriously. It is a member's responsibility to protect the reputation of AASP and the public from members who are deficient in ethical conduct.

CONCEPT Members of the Association for Applied Sport Psychology (AASP) are bound by a set of ethical principles and standards that guide their conduct.

APPLICATION Members of AASP should read and become familiar with the ethical standards that their association subscribes to. They should also take proactive steps to conduct all of their professional interactions in accordance with these guidelines. In addition, the standards should be made available to individuals who receive professional services from AASP members.

Principle 4: Respect for People's Rights and Dignity

AASP members respect the fundamental rights, worth, and dignity of all individuals. An individual's right to confidentiality, privacy, and personal control are respected at all times.

Principle 5: Concern for Others' Welfare

AASP members are personally concerned with and take steps to ensure the personal welfare of individuals they interact with. Conflicts between members or between members and clients are resolved in a manner which minimizes harm and maximizes the concern for the welfare of others.

Principle 6: Social Responsibility

AASP members have a responsibility to share their knowledge and research with members of society. In this regard, their responsibility is to contribute to the common good of society and to protect the rights of individuals as they do so.

Recently, Etzel, Watson, and Zizzi (2004) conducted a Web-based survey of AASP members examining their ethical beliefs and behaviors relative to applied sport psychology. The results of this investigation provided relevant information about the beliefs and practices of AASP members. The survey revealed that females tend to have ethical beliefs and practice ethical behaviors to a greater extent than male members. Relative to background training, the research revealed that members and consultants trained in counseling or clinical psychology express ethical beliefs and exhibit ethical behavior to a greater extent than those trained in physical education and exercise science. Last, but not least, certified AASP consultants tend to have ethical beliefs and exhibit ethical behaviors to a lesser extent than noncertified consultants.

Delivering Sport Psychology Services

Sport psychologists deliver services to athletes in many different ways. The different approaches seem to vary greatly as a function of training, interest, and accessibility. In this section we will consider these different approaches under four major headings that include (a) three types of sport psychologists, (b) philosophical foundations, (c) receptivity of athletes and athletic departments, and (d) building a private practice.

Three Types of Sport Psychologist

In chapter 1 we learned there are three kinds of sport psychologists: research, educational, and counseling/clinical. These three kinds of sport psychologists, however, are not independent of one another. For example, a person could be a university professor and be involved in research, teaching, and the delivery of counseling psychology services to athletes. Another person could be in private practice, consulting with professional athletes, and teaching a course at a university on sport psychology. The point is that there are many different kinds of sport psychologists and many different ways to consult with athletes. The important thing, is that there must be a match between professional training and the services delivered by the consultant.

Individuals who receive training in sport psychology typically find opportunities to deliver services while employed in one of the following five areas:

1. University/college professor (educational, research)

2. University/college counseling center (clinical/counseling)

3. University/college athletic department (educational, clinical/counseling)

4. High school or university/college coaching (educational)

5. Private practice (educational, clinical/counseling)

Although this is an incomplete list of employment opportunities for sport psychologists, it does serve to show how the different types of sport psychologists (clinical/counseling, educational, research) are able to deliver psychological or mental skill services to athletes. When providing psychological skills services to athletes we often think in terms of training possessed by the sport psychologist, but another way to view the qualifications of the sport psychologist is in terms of competencies. Such an approach was taken by Ward, Sandstedt, Cox, and Beck (2005) when they identified 17 athlete-counseling competencies believed to be essential for ethical psychotherapeutic practice with athlete clients. These 17 essential competencies were classified under the headings of (a) attitudes/beliefs, (b) knowledge, and (c) skills. It was proposed that a prospective applied sport psychologist should demonstrate competence in each of the identified competency areas.

Sport psychologists who work as licensed clinical or counseling psychologists must possess specialized training in identifying psychiatric disorders. In this regard, Kamm (2008) identified and classified clinical disorders that may be found in the athlete population. These classifications include (a) mood disorders, (b) anxiety disorders, (c) eating

Wheelchair athletes can benefit from a psychological skills training program. © Royalty-Free/Corbis.

disorders, and (d) attention-deficit/hyperactivity disorders (ADHD). It was Kamm's recommendation that, as a member of a sports medicine team, the sport psychologist should be able to diagnose/recognize and refer for treatment athletes possessing these clinical maladies. Consistent with Kamm, Morse (2008) noted that the five most common areas of mental disturbance experienced by athletes were ADHD, depression, anxiety, addiction, and eating disorders.

Philosophical Foundations

According to Poczwardowski, Sherman, and Ravizza (2004), sport psychology service delivery should be based on a solid **philosophical foundation.** The consultant's philosophy can serve to provide direction when confronted with unique situations for which there exist no textbook solutions. As illustrated in figure 12.3, the model flows from

CONCEPT   The sport psychology consultant must be grounded in terms of a professional philosophy. What are the core values of the sport psychology consultant? How do these core values influence the way that the consultant works with athletes, coaches, and other individuals associated with sport?

APPLICATION   Apply this principle by reviewing the levels shown in figure 12.3 and ask yourself about your own professional philosophy. as it relates to sport psychology consulting. This will be a good exercise regardless of whether you are a student, a student/athlete, a coach, or a sport psychology consultant.

the stable to the dynamic and from the internal to the external. The foundation of the model is the *personal core beliefs* and values of the consultant. If the foundation is flawed, nothing that comes after it can be trusted. Built upon the core beliefs are the *theoretical paradigms* that the consultant operates under. Some consultants will base their approach to behavioral change on psychoanalytic theory, while others embrace a social learning approach or a humanistic approach. Built upon the theoretical paradigm embraced by the consultant is the specific *model of practice* (consultant role) favored by the sport psychology consultant. Potential models of practice include (a) the psychological skills training model, (b) the counseling model, (c) the medical model, (d) the interdisciplinary sport science model, and (e) the supervisory consulting model with an integrative approach. In the **supervisory consulting model,** the consultants work directly with coaches and other professionals within an organization, but do not work directly with athletes. Built upon the selected model of practice are the specific *intervention goals* that are grounded in the philosophical model as a whole. There are as many intervention goals as there are different behavioral issues and problems to deal with. Finally, built upon the intervention goals are the *intervention techniques and methods* selected by the

FIGURE 12.3 | Illustration showing the hierarchical structure of professional philosophy.

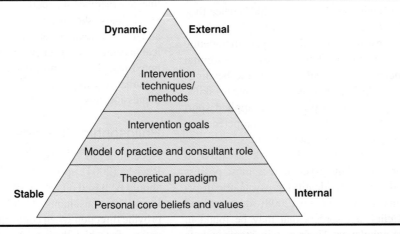

Source: Reproduced with permission of the publisher (Human Kinetics) from Poczwardowski, A., Sherman, C. P., & Ravizza, K. (2004). Professional philosophy in the sport psychology service delivery: Building on theory and practice. *The Sport Psychologist, 18,* 445–463.

consultants to meet the intervention goals. Every practicing sport psychology consultant should be able to describe and verbalize his professional philosophy as it relates to the services that he provides.

Receptivity of Athletes and Athletic Departments

It is believed that scientifically planned and organized PST programs are well received by athletes. A case in point is a qualitative study reported by Dunn and Holt (2003) in which 27 members of a Canadian collegiate ice hockey team reported on their perception of the delivery of a season-long program designed to improve and build upon existing psychological skills. Not only was the feedback positive, but the athletes made useful suggestions regarding logistical issues, multiple roles played by the consultant, and the importance of respect and communication.

Notwithstanding the Dunn and Holt investigation, research continues to suggest that athletes are often wary about working with a sport psychologist. In a study by Maniar, Curry, Sommers-Flanagan, and Walsh (2001) involving 60 collegiate Division I athletes, it was reported that (a) athletes preferred "sport psychology" over "psychology" titled individuals, (b) athletes preferred to consult with a coach, family member, or friend over a psychologist, (c) athletes were generally skeptical about working with a psychologist of any kind because of the stigma attached to the title, and (d) women were generally more receptive than men. In a separate Web-based investigation involving 2,440 collegiate Division I athletes (Wrisberg, Simpson, Loberg, Withycombe, & Reed, 2009), results showed (a) women were again more receptive to the idea of consulting with a sport psychologist than men, (b) team sport athletes were more receptive than individual sport athletes, and (c) athletes who had previous experience with a sport psychologist were more receptive than those with no previous experience.

Two additional studies focused upon the perception and attitude of NCAA Division I athletic directors (AD) toward sport psychology consul-tants (Voight & Callaghan, 2001; Wilson, Gilbert, Gilbert, & Sailor, 2009). Of these two studies, the investigation by Wilson et al. is of particular interest. While only 72 usable Web-based returns were available from a beginning sample of 376 athletic directors (ADs), the results are instructive. The ADs were generally uncertain about the perceived need to have a sport psychologist on their staff, but allowed that a sport psychologist could help athletes deal better with pressure, fine-tune performance, and improve mental toughness. Actual hiring of a full-time sport psychologist did not take place because the psychological needs of the athletes were generally addressed by coaches, counselors, and faculty. Although they thought the services of a sport psychologist was important, they did not think it to be as important as an athletic trainer or a strength coach. Of the 72 responses, three had a full-time sport psychologist on their staff, while 14 had part-time sport psychologists providing services. Fifty-seven percent of the sample had never heard of the Association for AASP and 67 percent were unaware of AASP certification.

Recognizing that psychological skill training is of little value if the athlete is not in the proper frame of mind, researchers developed three companion inventories designed to help the sport psychologist determine if the athlete or an athletic team is in the proper frame of mind to be helped by a sport psychology consultant (Leffingwell, Rider, & Williams, 2001). These three inventories measure (a) the athletes' stage of readiness, (b) pros and cons of using a sport psychologist, and (c) the athletes' belief that a sport psychologist consultant could help him or her.

Building a Successful Practice

As we learned in chapter 1, sport psychology professionals emerge from two distinct but sometimes overlapping disciplines. The first is physical education, often renamed kinesiology, exercise and sport sciences, human movement studies, and the like. The second is psychology (clinical, counseling, or educational). Those who emerge from physical

CONCEPT The initial meeting with the athletes sets the stage for the entire psychological skills training program.

APPLICATION The initial meeting with the athletes must be well planned and organized. The psychological skills training program will be ineffective if this initial meeting does not convince the athletes of the efficacy of psychological skills training. The sport psychologist should be prepared to give concrete examples of how sport psychology can help each athlete achieve peak performance.

education tend to be former athletes with a wealth of experience working with coaches and athletes. Often these individuals will start their professional careers as academicians in a university setting and then gravitate partially or completely to working with professional athletes (e.g., golf and tennis pros). Conversely, those who receive their training through psychology often aspire to become licensed as a counseling or clinical psychologist. Once licensed as a psychologist, they may begin to develop a professional clientele composed of a broad range of clients from the various communities. As these individuals succeed in building their practice generally, they begin to focus more specifically upon clients from the sports environment. These two avenues are not the only ones possible, but they are typical of how sport psychologists get started in their ultimate goal to develop a sport psychology consulting practice.

As a service to the profession of applied sport psychology, Taylor (2008) provided practical advice to emerging professionals to develop their own private consulting business in sport psychology. Taylor's four-part approach to consulting begins with a focus upon **psychological skill training** (PST), or what is increasingly being referred to as **mental skill training** (MST). A strong MST program is based on the principles we have discussed in this text from start to finish. Taylor, however, is quick to point out that equal time and effort must also be dedicated to dealing with personal issues that confront the athlete (personal consulting), consulting with the parents of athletes (parental consulting), and consulting with an athlete's coach (coach consulting). This is a recognition that an athlete's success depends on more than just the athlete–consultant relationship.

Taylor next discusses the personal qualities of the consultant that are necessary for success. First, the sport psychology (SP) consultant must be intrinsically motivated for success and not be controlled by visions of fame and fortune. Second, the SP consultant must be very patient, as it generally takes three to five years to build a small business. Third, the SP consultant must develop multiple skills that go beyond the ability to convey mental skills to athletes. These include counseling skills, public speaking skills, writing skills, and business skills. Fourth, the SP consultant must be very creative, able to think "outside of the box," and transcend traditional patterns and approaches to delivering SP services.

In conclusion, Taylor outlines a five-stage model of professional development. The first stage is to develop the knowledge and competencies associated with being an effective consultant. This will begin in graduate school but continue throughout a lifetime of professional development. Stage two involves developing an identity that differentiates one from all the other sport psychology consultants. Stage three involves developing the credibility and trust necessary to attract and keep clients. In stage four, Taylor suggests that the SP consultant find a niche or specialty within the practice of sport psychology. For example, some sport psychologists have found great success working with professional golfers, while others have found success working with team sport athletes, such as baseball. In stage five Taylor indicates that the consultant must continually find ways to grow his or her business and clientele.

CONCEPT An effective psychological skills training program is based on an assessment plan that allows the sport psychologist to identify an athlete's strengths and weaknesses in terms of psychological skill.

APPLICATION There are many potential approaches to ascertaining the psychological skill profile of an athlete. The method that provides the best and most accurate information is the one that should be employed. The particular assessment technique may vary from athlete to athlete. If the athlete has an accurate perception of his psychological strengths and weaknesses, then the performance profiling method should prove effective. It is really the most direct approach, but it requires self-awareness and trust.

While not specifically addressed by Taylor (2008), Lubker, Watson, Visek, and Geer (2005) also noted the importance of making a good first impression on prospective clients in terms of physical appearance and dress. Finally, Fifer, Henschen, Gould, and Ravizza (2008) offer helpful suggestions as to how the sport psychologist can (a) gain entry to consulting opportunities, (b) identify techniques of assessment, (c) deliver information, and (d) prepare athletes for major competition.

Psychological Skills Training Program

A number of psychological skills training programs have been proposed (Boutcher & Rotella, 1987; Gordon, 1990; Holliday et al., 2008; Lidor, Blumenstein, & Tenenbaum, 2007; Orlick, 1986). In addition to these proposed programs, Weinberg and Williams (2010) provide the basic components that they believe should be considered in developing a psychological skills training program. Illustrated in table 12.1 is a proposed **psychological skills training program** (PSTP) that is based upon the literature. The model is composed of seven discrete but related phases that will be discussed in some detail.

Who Is the Client?

The first and most critical thing that must be determined by the sport psychologist is who the client is. If the **client** is the athletic department of a university, then the athletic department defines the nature of the relationship between the sport psychologist and the athlete or coach. If management wishes to be informed of all ongoing aspects of the PSTP, then this is their right. They may, however, wish to waive that right and give the sport psychologist a free hand in working with the athletes. Regardless of what the relationship is, each party involved must be informed of its nature. If the client is the coach, then the coach defines the nature of the relationship between the sport psychologist and the athlete and coach. Finally, if the athlete is the client, then the athlete defines the nature of the relationship between the sport psychologist and the athlete. Furthermore, regardless of the wishes of the coach or management, consultation between athlete and sport psychologist is confidential and privileged when the client is the athlete.

Related to the question of who is the client is the utilization of the **organizational empowerment approach** to working with athletes. Introduced by Smith and Johnson (1990), the sport psychologist is hired by the organization (e.g., Houston Astros' minor league development league) to train a member of their full-time staff to deliver psychological services to their athletes. This approach empowers the organization to provide psychological services to its own athletes without requiring a full-time sport psychologist on the staff.

TABLE 12.1 | Sample Psychological Skills Training Program (PSTP)

Phase 1: Who Is the Client?

Determine who the client is and develop a working model as to how the PSTP will be delivered.

Phase 2: Initial Meeting with Athletes

The initial meeting is critical in terms of placing an emphasis upon psychological skills training, and getting athletes' and coaches' commitment to the training program.

Phase 3: Education of the Sport Psychologist Relative to Activity

Ideally, the sport psychologist will be an expert on the client's sport from a psychological, biomechanical, physiological, and pedagogical perspective. If not, a period of self-education will be required to help the sport psychologist bridge the gap from being a novice to being fully knowledgeable and conversant about the sport.

Phase 4: Development of a Needs Assessment Plan

In order to develop a needs assessment plan, the sport psychologist must have a working knowledge of athletes' current psychological skills. This can be accomplished only through formal and informal assessment.

1. Interview
2. Performance profiling
3. Observation of athletes during practice and competition
4. Use of objective pencil-and-paper inventories
   a. CSAI-2R   e. TOPS-2
   b. SAS-2   f. ACSI-28
   c. POMS   g. 16-PF
   d. PANAS   h. TAIS

Phase 5: Psychological Methods and Strategies to Be Taught

Based on needs assessment, it will become apparent where the athletes are lacking relative to psychological skills. In this phase, a master plan is developed in terms of what, when, and in what sequence psychological methods are to be taught to address psychological skill weaknesses.

Phase 6: Actual Teaching and Learning of Selected Psychological Methods

1. Psychological methods to be taught, practiced, and applied in competition to enhance psychological skills
   a. Goal setting   d. Imagery
   b. Relaxation   e. Attention skills
   c. Self-talk   f. Self-hypnosis
2. Performance routines to be taught, practiced, and applied in competition to enhance psychological skills
   a. Preperformance routines
   b. Between play routines
   c. Post performance routines

Phase 7: Ongoing and End-of-Season Evaluation of PSTP

For best results, the PSTP must be continually reviewed and evaluated.

Initial Meeting with Athletes

The initial meeting between the sport psychologist and the athletes is pivotal for emphasizing the need for commitment to the PSTP. Coaches and athletes recognize the importance of physical practice and training to prepare for peak performance. Athletes must be equally committed to psychological skills training. A coach who says she is willing to commit 15 minutes at the end of practice to imagery practice and utilization is not committed to psychological skills training. Psychological skills training must be viewed as an equal partner to the practicing of physical skills (Holliday et al. 2008).

Education of the Sport Psychologist Relative to Activity

Athletes find it easier to relate to a sport psychologist who understands the nuances of the sport that the athletes are trying to excel in. If a sport psychologist cannot relate to an athlete's feelings in a critical game situation, she will have difficulty gaining the confidence of the athlete. What does it really feel like to be on the foul line shooting free throws in the final moments of the game? What muscles are involved in executing a complex gymnastics exercise on the high bar? What are the physiological factors associated with fatigue at the end of a marathon? What is the best way to quickly learn how to execute a backhand drive in tennis? A sport psychologist must be more than a psychologist; she must also be an exercise and sport scientist. It is unrealistic to expect the sport psychologist to be an expert performer in every sport that she serves as a consultant in, but it is realistic to expect the psychologist to be an avid student of the game.

Development of a Needs Assessment Plan

In order to develop a **needs assessment plan,** the sport psychologist must determine the psychological skill strengths and weaknesses of each athlete and of a team as a whole. This is accomplished through a series of interviews and test administrations as indicated below.

Interview   An open-ended interview is an important way for the sport psychologist to establish a trusting relationship with the athlete. In this interview, the sport psychologist learns the athlete's attitudes about sport psychology, and his perceptions about psychological strengths and weaknesses.

Performance Profiling   Either as an extension of the personal interview or at another time, the athlete is asked to indicate, using her own labels and definitions, what she feels are important psychological skills for success. The athlete then indicates on a scale of 1 to 10 where she feels she falls on that rating scale. The sport psychologist then produces a bar graph that illustrates the skills the athlete selected and the progress being made from week to week. This process has been labeled **performance profiling** (Gucciardi & Gordon, 2009; Hays, Thomas, Butt, & Maynard, 2010; Weinberg & Williams, 2010). Areas of potential psychological skill improvement may include intrinsic motivation, self-awareness, self-esteem, self-confidence, attentional focus, and arousal control.

Observation of Athletes during Practice and Competition   Regardless of an athlete's perception of personal psychological skill, it is informative to observe the athlete during game-like situations to see how he deals with pressure. This will make it possible to affirm the athlete's belief system about psychological skill. If differences exist between observed and perceived psychological skills, then additional interviews might prove beneficial.

Use of Objective Pencil-and-Paper Inventories   Throughout this text we have introduced psychological inventories for assessing anxiety and mood (CSAI-2R, SAS-2, POMS, PANAS), psychological skill and technique (TOPS-2, ACSI-28), and personality (16-PF, TAIS). Where appropriate, these inventories should be administered and carefully evaluated relative to other subjectively determined information.

All of the inventories listed above and also listed in table 12.1 are used extensively by practicing sport psychologist consultants and by sport psychology researchers. As are all pencil-and-paper tests, all of the inventories listed in table 12.1 are subject to athlete distortion, i.e., "faking good" or "faking bad." In order to minimize the damage caused by an athlete's "faking good" on an inventory, it is often recommended that the short form of the Marlowe-Crowne Social Desirability Scale (MC-SDS) also be administered (Reynolds, 1982). Each of the 13 items on the MC-SDS describe a socially desirable or undesirable behavior that is relatively unlikely. A high score on the MC-SDS is thought to indicate socially desirable responding. If

CONCEPT   Preperformance routines are effective strategies for channeling an athlete's attention to the execution of a motor skill.

APPLICATION   A young athlete needs assistance in crafting a preperformance routine that fits his personality. All preperformance routines need not be identical. However, they should cause the athlete to focus attention upon appropriate stimuli and should be of uniform length. The sequencing of activities within the routine should also remain unchanged from one preperformance to the next.

---

an athlete gets a high score on the MC-SDS, there is a good possibility that she has "faked good" on other companion inventories.

While not mentioned anywhere else in this text and not listed in table 12.1, a Multilevel Classification System for Sport Psychology (MCS-SP) has been proposed (Gardner & Moore, 2004). Much like the Diagnostic and Statistical Manual of Mental Disorders (DSM-IV; American Psychiatric Association, 2000), the MCS-SP proposes to categorize athletes relative to their readiness for psychological skills training. To determine where an athlete fits in the MCS-SP, it is necessary that the athlete go through a three-stage assessment protocol: (a) clinical assessment phase, (b) personal assessment phase, and (c) performance assessment phase. Finally, the much anticipated DSM-5 is due for publication in 2013.

Psychological Methods and Strategies to Be Taught

Based on needs assessment in phase 4, it should be clear to the sport psychologist which areas of psychological skill the athletes are strong in and which areas they are weak in. It is likely that different athletes will exhibit different profiles relative to their psychological skills. Based on this information, the sport psychologist develops a master plan detailing how to enhance psychological skill through the application of various psychological methods, strategies, and techniques. Timing and sequencing of the delivery of psychological methods are also determined at this time.

Actual Teaching and Learning of Selected Psychological Methods

During this phase, the actual teaching of psychological methods is carried out. Each psychological method is taught with a specific purpose in mind in terms of enhancing psychological skill. For example, if the athlete is lacking in the psychological skill of displaying self-confidence prior to competition, self-talk, self-hypnosis, and imagery might prove to be particularly effective.

Psychological Methods to Be Taught and Practiced   Throughout this text and especially in this part, of the text, psychological methods effective in enhancing psychological skill and, hence, skilled performance, have been introduced. An incomplete list of potential psychological methods to be taught include goal setting, relaxation, self-talk, imagery, attention skills, and self-hypnosis.

Performance Routines   Performance routines can be categorized as preperformance, between-play, or postperformance in nature. **Preperformance routines** take place immediately preceding the initiation of a shot or play. Preperformance routines are most effective in self-paced sports and events that allow time for the athlete to prepare in a stable and predictable manner. Serving in tennis would be a self-paced event.

As defined by Foster and Weigand (2006), a preperformance routine is defined as involving "cognitive and behavioral elements that *intentionally*

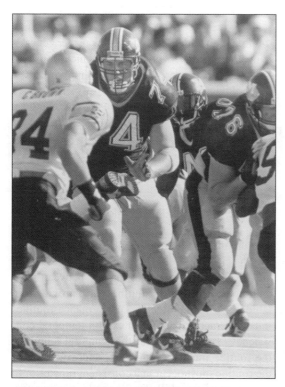

Football offensive linemen benefit from mental skill preparation. Courtesy University of Missouri–Columbia Sports Information.

help regulate arousal and enhance concentration" (p. 167). Conversely, Foster and Weigand define **superstitious behavior** as "behavior which does not have a clear technical function in the execution of a skill, yet which is believed to control luck and/or other external factors" (p. 167). On the surface, it may be difficult to tell if baseball batters are engaging in a preperformance routine or in superstitious behavior when they go through a series of repetitive bat, shoe, and glove adjustments/movements prior to stepping into the batting box. Interestingly, the Foster and Weigand research shows that asking free-throw shooters in basketball to remove well-learned superstitious behavior from their preperformance preparation results in a decrement in performance. This, however, is probably due

to disruption of their normal preperformance preparation.

Numerous studies have demonstrated the effectiveness of teaching athletes to learn and utilize well-learned preperformance routines (Czech, Ploszay, & Burke, 2004; Hill & Borden, 1995; Lidor & Mayan, 2005; Lidor & Singer, 2000; Mesagno, Marchant, & Morris, 2008). Different hypotheses have been posited to explain the beneficial effects of a preperformance routine, including the distraction and self-focus theories discussed in chapter 8 on attention. A preperformance routine could cause the athlete to focus upon relevant stimuli (distraction hypothesis) or to focus externally away from the automatic execution of the skill (self-focus theory). Research also shows that the preperformance routine can be enhanced by including a tactile component to the routine. For example, the athlete can benefit from bouncing and spinning the basketball prior to executing a free-throw shot (Lidor & Mayan, 2005). Finally, research indicates that preperformance routines are highly individualistic; their development is dependent upon the coping resources, personality, and situational appraisals of each athlete (Cotterill, Sanders, & Collins, 2010).

As explained by Singer (2002), the preperformance routine is a five-step process. These five steps are as follows:

1. *Readying*   In this step, the athlete uses coping skills to create an atmosphere of self-confidence, internal attentional focus, arousal adjustment, and emotional control (may involve repetitive physical actions).

2. *Imaging*   The athlete images a successful outcome.

3. *Focusing attention externally*   Attention is focused on a relevant external cue or thought.

4. *Executing with a quiet mind*   The athlete stays calm and thinks positive thoughts as the skill is executed.

5. *Evaluating*   If time allows, the execution and outcome of the skill, as well as the preperformance routine, are evaluated.

CONCEPT Psychological methods found to be effective in the sport domain for enhancing performance excellence as well as personal excellence can be equally effective in business, the arts, music, and the military.

APPLICATION Sport psychologists who are expert in the application of psychological skill

training with athletes should also consider generalizing their skills to other performance domains. Just as athletes are interested in improving their psychological skills for purposes of performance enhancement, so are dancers, business executives, performing artists, and military/police officers.

Between-play routines take place during breaks in the action of games such as tennis, basketball, volleyball, and baseball. For example, what should baseball outfielders be thinking about or doing during the period of time the catcher is warming up a relief pitcher? One possibility would be to engage in relaxing conversation with teammates or fellow competitors. Another would be to imagine restful scenes on a secluded beach or a walk along a mountain stream.

Postperformance routines take place during the period of time immediately following the execution of a skill, or even following a game or match. There is a natural tendency in sport to dwell on the negative aspects of an unsuccessful performance. A planned postperformance routine would include a strategy to clear the mind for the next performance or the next match and to save critical analysis for the practice field. A dramatic case in point is the *closer* in baseball. Lots of pitchers can save 30 games in a single season, but few can do it across multiple seasons. Trevor Hoffman of the San Diego Padres was an exception. In 2001 he was the only active pitcher to have saved 30 or more games in each of the past six years. For closers, the cruelest, most negative statistic is the *blown save*. This occurs when the closer enters the game in late innings with a lead and loses the game. When Hoffman suffered a blown save, he had a *postgame emergency routine* to deal with it. "First, while sitting alone in the dugout, he reflects on what just happened; then, even after his worst outings, he goes to the clubhouse and fields questions

from the media. . . . Finally, alone, he finds something positive amid the despair. He won't leave the stadium until he is sure the virus is under control" (Verducci, 2001, p. 84).

Examples of preperformance, between-play, and postperformance routines are provided in table 12.2. To be effective, performance routines must be practiced and must exhibit temporal consistency. This means that the temporal length of the routine must be consistent, and execution of the routine must occur at a consistent time prior to execution of the skill. For example, a preperformance routine for shooting a basketball free throw should always take about the same amount of time to execute, and be initiated at approximately the same point in time relative to releasing the basketball (Wrisberg & Pein, 1992).

Ongoing and End-of-Season Evaluation of a PSTP

If a psychological skills training program extends across an entire sport season, it is imperative that it be evaluated at the end of the season. If psychological inventories were administered during the needs assessment phase of the program, these same inventories can be administered at the end of the season, noting changes and improvements in variables of importance. Taking into consideration task difficulty, a careful review of performance measures recorded throughout the season will provide helpful information about effectiveness of the PSTP. Finally, open-ended

TABLE 12.2 | Examples of Performance Routines Used in Sport

Routine	Sport	Situation	Steps
Preperformance	Golf	Putting	1. Stand behind the ball and "read" the line of the putt.
			2. Approach the ball and take two practice swings.
			3. Align the putter to the target, set the feet, and take two glances at the hole.
Between-Play	Tennis	Changing Courts	1. Take care of your body and your equipment (water and towel off).
			2. Give your mind some relief (focus on positive thoughts).
			3. Focus on strategy for next game.
Postperformance	Volleyball	Passing	1. Clear mind of results of previous pass by yourself or teammate.
			2. Focus on making a perfect pass to the setter.
			3. Use self-talk to remind yourself that you are an excellent passer.

discussions with athletes about the program will provide invaluable information about its effectiveness. In addition to end-of-season evaluations, ongoing evaluation of the program's effectiveness should be obtained at each phase. If an athlete feels uncomfortable about a specific psychological method that she is learning, there is no need to continue it to the end of the program.

Generalization of Sport Psychology Methods to Other Application Domains

Researchers and practitioners in sport psychology have generated a large literature base that informs good practice. Based on the literature, sport psychologists have learned a great deal about facilitating learning and performance in the sport and exercise domains. Cognitive and behavioral intervention methods introduced in this text for enhancing peak performance in sport can be used in other domains, such as music, the arts, the military, police work, and business, for the same purpose (Gould, 2002a, 2002b). As stated by Gould (2002a), "many AASP members are transferring what they have learned about facilitating human performance in

sport to other domains such as music, the arts, business, and the military" (p. 137).

One of the most fruitful areas for applying principles of positive psychology (Seligman & Csikszentmihalyi, 2000) is the business domain. A case in point is Graham Jones (2002), a sport psychologist, who left academia as a full-time endeavor and formed a business consulting company called Lane 4. Although he still has a part-time appointment as Co-Director of the Institute for the Psychology of Elite Performance at the University of Wales, Bangor, his full-time work is as a consultant to business executives. Jones shows links between sport and business in five major areas: (a) organizational issues and similarities, (b) stress and stress management, (c) developing leadership skills, (d) working with high-performance teams, and (e) the need for one-on-one coaching/consultation. He further notes that high-performing business teams learn to create, to unite, and to perform (CUP). The CUP principle in business is equivalent to the sport psychology terms of team building, team work (cohesion), and team effectiveness. In this text, the concepts of team building and team cohesion will be discussed in chapter 15.

Further evidence of the common link between sport and business was provided by Weinberg and

McDermott (2002). In this investigation 10 business executives and 10 sport-related leaders were interviewed to discover commonalities. Results of the investigation revealed more similarities than differences between the two groups of leaders relative to principles of organizational stress. Similarly, LeScanff and Taugis (2002) involved 150 French police officers in a psychological training program for purposes of reducing stress. Results showed that, as with athletes, psychological training skills effectively reduce stress in the French police. Finally, Hays (2002) studied similarities and differences between athletes and performing artists (actors, artists, broadcasters, dancers, musicians) relative to four performance issues. The four issues studied were performance enhancement, developmental issues, injury and retirement issues, and eating disorders. While some differences do exist between athletes and performing artists, it was concluded that both groups can benefit from psychological skills training specific to their area of expertise.

Summary

This chapter began with a discussion of the psychological skill characteristics of the mentally tough elite athlete. The elite athlete possesses psychological skill characteristics that facilitate performance excellence. Some sport psychologists find it useful to look at psychological skill development with the structure of a theoretical model. Four such models were presented and discussed. These include the self-regulation model, the resonance performance model, the athlete-centered model, and the mindfulness-acceptance-commitment model.

Research was summarized that assures us that psychological intervention programs are effective in enhancing performance and changing behavior. A distinction was made between psychological skills and methods used to achieve psychological skill. *Psychological skill* refers to learned or innate characteristics of the athlete that make it possible for him to succeed in sport. *Psychological methods* refer to practices that lead to psychological skill. Four inventories were identified and explained that measure psychological skill. These were the Psychological Skills Inventory for Sports, the Athletic Coping Skills Inventory, the Test of Performance Strategies, and the Ottawa Mental Skills Assessment Tool.

Members of AASP are bound by a code of ethics that governs their interactions with the public and with other professionals. The AASP Ethics Code is based in large part on the Ethical Principles of the American Psychological Association, and is composed of a preamble, six general principles, and 25 standards. Sport psychology delivery should be based on a solid philosophical foundation. The sport psychology consultant's philosophy can serve to provide direction when she is confronted with unique situations for which there exists no textbook solution. A consultant's philosophy should be based on personal core beliefs that provide direction to theoretical paradigms embraced by the consultant.

A sample psychological skills training program (PSTP) composed of seven discrete but related phases was introduced and discussed in detail. The phases included (a) identifying the client, (b) initial meeting with athletes, (c) education of the sport psychologist, (d) needs assessment plan, (e) psychological methods and strategies to be taught, (f) learning of psychological methods, and (g) evaluation. During the learning phase of the PSTP, psychological methods such as goal setting, relaxation, self-talk, imagery, attention skills, and self-hypnosis are taught to athletes. In addition, athletes learn how to develop and use performance routines. Preperformance, between-play, and post performance routines are effective in focusing an athlete's attention on appropriate internal and external cues.

The chapter ends with the topic of generalization of sport psychology methods to areas other than sport. Cognitive and behavioral intervention methods introduced in this text for enhancing peak performance in sport can be used in other domains, such as music, the arts, the military, police work, and business, for the same purpose.

Critical Thought Questions

1. Describe the psychological skill characteristics of the elite athlete. How are they different from those of the nonelite athlete?

2. Describe the characteristics of the mentally tough athlete. How does an athlete get to be mentally tough?

3. Identify and differentiate among the four models of psychological skill development.

4. Provide some evidence to support the proposition that psychological intervention programs are effective in facilitating performance excellence.

5. Why do you think it is important to distinguish between psychological methods and psychological skills?

6. How does a sport psychologist develop a viable and ethically sound philosophy of consulting with athletes?

7. Outline and propose your own psychological skills training program. At each step, explain your reasons and rationale.

8. Develop and present in writing proposed preperformance routines for batting in baseball/softball, free-throw shooting in basketball, putting in golf, and high jumping in track and field (or, select four sport situations of your choice).

9. What is superstitious behavior and how does it relate to preperformance routines?

Glossary

athlete-centered sport model A model that proposes that sport must contribute to the overall development of the athlete physically, psychologically, and socially.

Athletic Coping Skills Inventory An inventory, developed by Smith, Schutz, et al. (1995), which assesses psychological skills of athletes.

between-play routine A sequential performance routine that takes place during breaks in the action of an athletic contest.

client The individual or individuals that the sport psychologist contracts with to deliver psychological services.

code of ethics Code that governs how a sport psychologist interacts with the public and with other professionals.

mental skills training Just as deliberate physical practice trains the body and muscles for activity, mental skill training trains the mind for peak performance (*see* psychological skill training).

mental toughness A multifaceted construct made up of multiple key components including values, attitudes, cognitions, emotions, and behaviors that refer to an individual's ability to thrive through both positively and negatively construed challenges, pressures, and adversities.

mindfulness-acceptance-commitment An approach to psychological self-regulation that recognizes a nonjudgmental focus of one's attention on the here and the now.

needs assessment plan A plan, based on an assessment of an athlete's psychological skills, that is designed to address the athlete's needs through a psychological skills training program.

organizational empowerment approach Situation in which a member of an organization is trained by a sport psychologist to deliver psychological services to the member's own organization.

Ottawa Mental Skills Assessment Tool A 48-item inventory that measures 12 mental skill subscales.

performance profiling The cooperative creation by the sport psychologist and the athlete of a profile showing how the athlete ranks on psychological skills deemed important to the athlete.

philosophical foundation The foundation of a philosophical approach to sport psychology consultation is the consultant's personal core beliefs and values.

postperformance routine A performance routine that takes place immediately following the execution of a skill, or following a match or event.

preperformance routine A performance routine that takes place immediately before the execution of a skill.

psychological intervention program An intervention formalized into a program for improving the psychological skills of athletes.

psychological method A technique or strategy used to enhance psychological skill in an athlete.

psychological skill Learned or innate characteristics of the athlete that make it possible or even likely that she will succeed in sport.

psychological skills training Just as deliberate physical practice trains the body and muscles for activity, psychological skills training trains the mind for peak performance (*see* mental skill training).

Psychological Skills Inventory for Sports An inventory, developed by Mahoney et al. (1987), which assesses psychological skills of athletes.

psychological skills training program An organized and systemized program that assesses psychological skill and teaches psychological methods designed to enhance psychological skill.

resonance A key element of the resonance performance model that is related to the concepts of flow, intrinsic motivation, and emotion.

Resonance performance model A model that explains the process by which ordinary athletes become elite athletes.

Self-regulation Self-generated thoughts, feelings, and behaviors that are planned and cyclically adapted based on performance feedback.

Self-regulation model A model that utilizes the concept of self-regulation to explain how psychological skill development takes place.

spirituality A form of positive psychology that recognizes the influence of a higher power.

superstitious behavior Behavior which does not have a clear technical function in the execution of a skill, yet which is believed to control luck and/or other external factors.

supervisory consulting model The sport psychologist works directly with coaches and other professionals but does not work directly with athletes.

Test of Performance Strategies An inventory, developed by Thomas, Murphy, et al. (1999), which assesses a combination of psychological skills and strategies.

PART 5

Social Psychology of Sport

The first four parts of this book have focused upon the individual. Sport psychology, however, involves more than the individual. It also involves sociological factors that affect the individual. Sport sociology is a discipline that focuses upon social relations, group interactions, and sport-related social phenomena. Because groups are composed of individuals, it is often difficult to determine where psychology ends and sociology begins; hence the need for an area of study called social psychology of sport. While it is beyond the scope of a textbook on sport psychology to provide a comprehensive treatment on the topic of social psychology of sport, it is appropriate that selected topics be addressed. Chapters to be discussed in this part of the text include aggression and violence in sport, audience and self-presentation effects in sport, team cohesion in sport, and leadership and communication in sport. Each of these topics impacts the individual in important and different ways.

Athlete aggression and fan violence affect the way that society views and values sport. The behavior of an audience has a powerful influence upon the outcome of an athletic contest and upon the behavior of athletes. Team cohesion affects how well athletes work together and the satisfaction that athletes derive from sport. Finally, the quality of leadership provided by coaches and team leaders has a tremendous impact upon team success and team satisfaction. ⌘

Aggression and Violence in Sport

KEY TERMS

Aggression
Assertiveness
Bracketed morality
Catharsis effect
Circular effect of aggression
False consensus effect
Fan identification
Frustration-aggression theory
Hostile aggression
Instinct theory
Instrumental aggression
Legitimacy of aggressive
  behavior
Mechanisms of moral
  disengagement
Moral reasoning
Peacemakers
Readiness for aggression
Reformulation of frustration-
  aggression theory
Relational aggression

Social learning theory
Transgressive behavior
Troublemakers

I n December of 1999, Latrell Sprewell, of the Golden State Warriors professional basketball team, grabbed his coach, P. J. Carlesimo, by the throat and choked him for 15 seconds, before players could pull them apart (Taylor, 1997). In May of 1999, Wichita State baseball pitcher

Ben Christensen was tossing his warm-up throws while the lead-off hitter for Evansville, Anthony Molina, was standing 30 feet from home plate taking practice swings. Believing that Molina was attempting to "time" his pitches, Christensen threw a fastball at him, hitting him in the left eye, fracturing the eye socket in three places, and leaving his baseball future in doubt. Christensen had been taught by his pitching coach, Brent Kemnitz, that if a batter is standing too close to the plate and timing pitches, you should brush him back. Apparently, 30 feet was too close (Cook & Mravic, 1999).

One of the most repugnant examples of fan violence occurred in 1985 in Europe, where a soccer riot in Brussels left 38 dead and 437 injured after English hooligans attacked panic-stricken Italian fans. The riot occurred prior to the European Cup soccer final in Heysel Stadium in Brussels between Liverpool and Juventus, the soccer team of Turin, Italy. Well-liquored Liverpool hooligans attacked Juventus fans with broken bottles, tin cans, flag sticks, and metal bars. Within minutes, hundreds of Italian fans found themselves pressed against a chain-link fence and a restraining wall. As more bodies pressed against the barriers, they collapsed, pitching hundreds of terrified fans into a hideous pileup in which 31 Italians, 4 Belgians, 2 French, and 1 Briton were killed, most by suffocation. The event has since been referred to as Black Wednesday by shamed residents of Liverpool.

Similarly, more than 40 people were killed and 50 injured at an exhibition soccer match in Johannesburg, South Africa, in 1991. Most of the deaths occurred when panicked spectators were crushed against a fence around the field and trampled by fleeing people. Two children were among the dead. More recently, following a 1996 heavyweight boxing match in New York between Riddick Bowe and Andrew Golota, a confirmed riot ensued. The fight ended after the seventh round as Golota was disqualified for throwing his fourth low blow to Bowe's groin. Thirty-five minutes after the bout, the crowd was ordered to evacuate Madison Square Gardens as riot police rushed in.

Most of the incidences of aggression and violence described in the above paragraphs involved aggression among athletes or violence among fans. In recent years, a number of incidences of aggression and violence have occurred that involve both

fans and athletes. One of the most bizarre incidents took place in Detroit, Michigan, in a nationally televised professional basketball game between the Detroit Pistons and the Indianapolis Pacers (Wilstein, 2004). It all began in the final minutes of the Pistons' 97–82 victory over the Pacers. It started with Ron Artest's hard foul on Ben Wallace and Wallace's retaliatory shove in the face. It should have ended there, but it didn't. Artest retreated to neutral territory and sprawled out on the scorer's table, only to be showered with a cup of water or beer from a fan in the stands. In a rage, Artest went into the stands to pummel the fan, but got the wrong guy. Before it was over there were numerous Pacer players in the stands fighting with fans. This was all displayed and replayed over and over on national television. In defense of the players, Carr (2004) noted that athletes are not prepared to deal with the psychological stresses associated with fan abuse and misbehavior. He noted that they are paid very well for their athletic skills, not for their fan coping skills.

Other examples of violence among fans and athletes have been documented (Price, 2003). On April 30, 1993, during a changeover in a professional tennis match between Monica Seles and Magdalena Maleeva, a man reached over a fence and drove a boning knife into Seles's back. Then in September of 2002, in the ninth inning of a baseball game between the Chicago White Sox and the visiting Kansas City Royals, first base coach Tom Gamboa was leaning forward, knees bent, watching intently as Kansas City Royals' centerfielder Michael Tucker popped a bunt into the air. Suddenly, he was attacked from behind and pummeled by two men who knocked him to the ground, landing him on his head and bent neck.

Even more troubling are acts of premeditated violence carried out by athletes and, in some cases, encouraged by coaches. In an unimportant professional ice hockey game, Todd Bertuzzi of the Vancouver Canucks punched the Colorado Avalanche's Steve Moore from behind, leaving him hospitalized with a broken neck, a concussion, and deep facial cuts. The attack was premeditated and in response to an earlier confrontation between Moore and fellow Canuck teammate Markus Nashlund. From that confrontation, Nashlund had been out with a concussion for three games. The interesting thing about professional ice hockey is that the players know when to hold back. During the Stanley Cup playoffs every year, acts of aggression suddenly diminish, because nobody wants to take a penalty that could ruin a season (Vecsey, 2004). Finally, in a college men's basketball game between St. Joseph and Temple, coach John Chaney ordered a "goon" into the game to wreak havoc on opposing players. The inserted player fouled out in only four minutes, leaving one St. Joseph player with a broken arm. Chaney was suspended for the rest of the regular season (Widman, 2005).

Two of the most widely viewed and publicized examples of athlete aggression and violence occurred relatively recently in the sports of international men's soccer and USA collegiate women's soccer. The first occurred near the end of the men's championship World Cup soccer match between France and Italy in July 2006. With only seconds remaining in regulation time, Italy's Marco Materazzie scored the tying goal. Italy went on to win the match in overtime, but before the goal shootout unfolded, the following horrific even was described by Wahl (2006):

> The greatest soccer player of his generation, perhaps minutes from enjoying his finest hour in his final game, tarnishing his legacy with an outburst so shocking in its violence, so naked in its rage, that it instantly joined Mike Tyson's tear-chomp of Evander Holyfield in the pantheon of Inexplicable Sports Insanity. Fans could only speculate why French midfielder Zinedine Zidane used his head as a battering ram against [Marco] Materazzi with the score tied 1–1 in overtime. (p. 49)

The second incident occurred during a Mountain West Conference semifinal women's soccer match between Brigham Young University (BYU) and the University of New Mexico, that BYU won 1–0. New Mexico women's soccer defender Elizabeth Lambert was caught on camera committing multiple acts of aggression and violent play against BYU forward Kassidy Shumway. In the most violent clip, the video shows Lambert grabbing Kassidy by her pony tail and hauling her forcibly to the turf. The video was seen by millions across America on the Internet, and on news channels, sports channels, and talk shows (Pierce, 2009).

A number of critical questions come to mind as one contemplates the issue of sport aggression. Does participating in or observing violent sporting events serve as a *catharsis,* or release from aggressive tendencies? Conversely, do these events merely teach and encourage further aggression on and off the playing field? If these two questions can be answered, then is it possible to eliminate aggression and violence from sports? If so, how?

In this chapter, these questions and other critically important issues will be discussed. Topics to be addressed include (a) defining aggression, (b) theories of aggression, (c) the catharsis effect, (d) measurement of aggression, (e) fan violence, (f) effects of aggression on performance, (g) situational factors in a sport setting, and (h) reducing aggression in sport.

Defining Aggression

Two factors must be present in order for a behavior to be labeled **aggression** (Berkowitz, 1993). *First,* the behavior must be aimed at another human being with the goal of inflicting physical harm. *Second,* there must be a reasonable expectation that the attempt to inflict bodily harm will be successful. Consequently, the following behaviors, often mislabeled aggression, are not really examples of aggression:

1. Doing destructive violence to an inanimate object such as a door or a water cooler

2. Unintentionally injuring another person during athletic competition

3. Aggressive behavior in which there is no chance for the intended victim to be injured (e.g., aggressor and victim are separated by bars or by teammates)

CONCEPT The difference between hostile and instrumental aggression lies in the perceived goal of the aggressor and not in intent.

APPLICATION Because the intent to harm is present in both forms of aggression, both must be discouraged from an ethical and moral reasoning standpoint.

Over the years, two basic kinds of aggression have been identified. The first is **hostile aggression.** For individuals engaged in hostile aggression, the primary goal is the injury of another human being. The intent is to make the victim suffer, and the reinforcement is the pain and suffering that is caused. This sort of aggression is always accompanied by anger on the part of the aggressor. A good example of hostile aggression occurs when a baseball pitcher throws a high inside fastball at a batter who has angered him. The clear attempt to injure is present, and the goal is to cause suffering. The outcome of the contest is not a factor to be considered. The goal is to harm, not to win. This kind of aggression is often referred to as *violence.*

The second major kind of aggression is **instrumental aggression.** For individuals engaged in instrumental aggression, the intent to harm another individual is present, but the goal is to realize some external goal such as money, victory, or prestige. The aggressor views the aggressive act as *instrumental* in obtaining the primary goal. A parallel baseball example for instrumental aggression would be one in which the pitcher has been "ordered" by his manager to hit a batter in retaliation for some earlier infraction. The pitcher is not necessarily angry at the batter, but sees hitting the batter as instrumental in achieving the team goal of winning the game. In research involving basketball and ice hockey, aggressive acts were categorized as being instrumental in nature two-thirds of the time. (Kirker, Tenenbaum, & Mattson, 2000).

Research also shows that hostile and instrumental aggressive acts may differ as a function of the kinds of explanations that are given by athletes as to why they would carry out an aggressive act (Traclet et al., 2009). Specifically, apologies are offered more often for instrumental athletic aggression than for hostile aggression, and self-justification is offered more often for hostile aggression than for an act of instrumental aggression.

It must be emphasized that neither type of aggression is acceptable. The aggressor is guilty of purposely inflicting harm with the intent to injure another person. This must be discouraged at all levels of competition, especially the professional level, because young athletes everywhere emulate the pros.

A third category of behavior that is often confused with aggression is **assertiveness,** or assertive behavior. Generally, when coaches encourage their athletes to be more aggressive, what they really want is that they be more assertive. Coaches want their athletes to assert themselves and make their presence felt. Assertiveness involves the use of *legitimate* physical or verbal force to achieve one's purpose. However, there is no intent to harm the opponent. Even if an opponent is harmed as a result of a tackle in soccer, it is not necessarily aggression. It is merely assertive play, as long as it is within the spirit of the agreed-on rules and the intent to harm is not present. Assertiveness requires the expenditure of unusual effort and energy, but if there is no *intent* to harm, then any resultant harm is incidental to the game.

As can be observed in figure 13.1, an area of ambiguity lies between instrumental aggression, hostile aggression, and assertive behavior. This is to be expected, since at times only the athlete knows whether an "aggressive" act was intended. From a practical standpoint, it is the job of the official to penalize any behavior that is in violation of the rules, regardless of the intent of the violator.

FIGURE 13.1 | Schematic showing the possible difficulties in discriminating among hostile aggression, instrumental aggression, and assertive behavior.

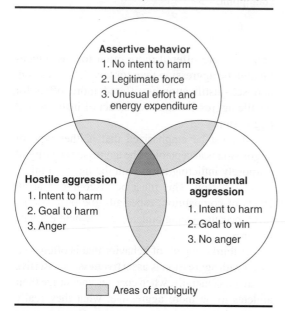

Areas of ambiguity

Source: From Silva, J. M., III. (1979). Assertive and aggressive behavior in sport: A definitional clarification. In C. H. Nadeau (Ed.), *Psychology of Motor Behavior and Sport*. Copyright © 1980 Human Kinetics Publishers, Inc., Champaign, IL. Adapted by permission.

However, most sports make provisions for extraordinary penalties if the behavior is deemed to be intentional and/or dangerous. For clarity, let's return to the baseball pitching example. If in the judgment of the umpire a pitcher purposely throws a pitch at a batter with intent to harm, he must be penalized, regardless of why he did it. However, if a batter has his body over the strike zone, he is inviting an assertive pitcher to throw a fastball over the inside part of the plate. If the batter is hit, it is not the fault of the pitcher and it is not an example of sport aggression.

Researchers have attempted to measure perceived **legitimacy of aggressive behavior** (Rascle, Traclet, Souchon, Coulomb-Cabagno, & Petrucci,

2010). Based on our definition of aggression this would seem to be an oxymoron as the purposeful intent to harm another human should not be considered legitimate. Nevertheless we have the example of boxing and the new ultimate fighting sport in which the clear intent of landing a punch is to harm one's opponent. In this regard, Viseck and Watson (2008) reported on an investigation involving differing levels of competitive ice hockey (youth, high school, collegiate, professional) in which the participants were asked to rate the perceived legitimacy of video clips depicting athletes engaging in five different examples of rule breaking (i.e., slashing, roughing, fighting, elbowing, high sticking). While these examples are clearly against the rules and potentially dangerous, it is difficult to know whether or not they were inflicted with the purpose of harming the opponent. Consequently, the researchers were measuring the perceived legitimacy of various acts of rule breaking that may or may not have been examples of aggression. Nevertheless, the results were instructive, as they showed that the perceived legitimacy of "aggressive behavior" increases as a function of increased age and competitive level. As the level of competitiveness increases, the more inclined the athletes are to consider aggressive behavior to be legitimate in certain circumstances.

While most aggression research focuses upon intended physical harm and sometimes intended verbal harm, relational aggression has also been studied. **Relational aggression** is harming others through such things as social ostracism and malicious rumors. Results of an investigation reported by Storch, Werner, and Storch (2003) show that there is a positive correlation between relational aggression and peer rejection for men and women and between relational aggression and alcohol use for women.

Theories of Aggression

A number of theories have been proposed to explain the phenomenon of aggression. These theories fall into four main categories: instinct theory, social

If looks could kill! Is this an example of aggression or assertive behavior?
Courtesy Kansas State University Sports Information.

learning theory, Berkowitz's reformulation of the frustration-aggression hypothesis, and Bredemeier's theory of moral reasoning and aggression.

Instinct Theory

Instinct theory is based upon the writings of Sigmund Freud and ethologists such as Konrad Lorenz. Freud (1950) viewed aggression as an inborn drive similar to hunger, thirst, and sexual desire. According to Freud, aggression is unavoidable since it is innate, but as with any drive it can be regulated through discharge, or fulfillment. Since humankind is innately aggressive, it benefits society to promote athletic sports and games that provide a socially acceptable outlet for aggression. An important corollary of the biological instinct theory is the notion that aggression results in a

purging, or releasing, of the aggression drive. This purging of pent-up aggression is known as catharsis. According to instinct theory, striking an opposing player serves as a catharsis, or release of pent-up aggression. (Choquet & Arvers, 2003).

Social Learning Theory

Social learning theory posits that aggression is a function of learning, and that biological drive and frustration are inadequate explanations of the phenomenon. While the notion of a catharsis is an important component of biological instinct theory, it has no place in social learning theory. Acts of aggression serve only to lay the foundation for more aggression, and do not result in a reduction or purging of the drive to be aggressive. Perhaps the leading advocate of social learning theory, relative

CONCEPT   According to Berkowitz's reformulation of frustration-aggression theory, a frustrating event creates a readiness for aggression.

APPLICATION   Coaches must look for game situations that could result in aggression. When an athlete becomes frustrated and angry, the coach should take that athlete out of the game to give him time to calm down.

to aggression, is Bandura (1973). Bandura has argued that aggression has a **circular effect.** That is, one act of aggression leads to further aggression. This pattern will continue until the circle is broken by some type of positive or negative reinforcement. Smith (1980), for instance, argues that violence in ice hockey is due to modeling. Youngsters learn aggression by watching their role models, the professionals, on television or in person. As long as aggression in professional sports is tolerated, children will continue to have adult models of aggressive behavior.

Support was found for social learning theory in an ice hockey study reported by Sheldon and Aimar (2001). In this investigation, aggressive behaviors were noted 15 seconds before and after successful and unsuccessful behaviors (e.g., score, steal). Results showed that a disproportionate number of successes were preceded by aggression as opposed to no aggression. This outcome suggests that aggression is rewarded by success. Other research supports the proposition that an individual team member's behavior eventually conforms to the normative behavior of the team (Stephens, 2001; Tucker & Parks, 2001). The study by Stephens (2001) specifically showed that likelihood to aggress was predicted by the players' perception of their teams' pro-aggressive norms.

Reformulated Frustration-Aggression Theory

As originally presented by Dollard, Miller, Doob, Mourer, and Sears (1939), **frustration-aggression theory** proposes that aggression is a natural response to frustration, and that the aggressive act

provides a catharsis, or purging, of the anger associated with the frustration. Frustration caused by events that are believed to be arbitrary or illegitimate are particularly galling to athletes.

Berkowitz's (1958, 1993) **reformulation of frustration-aggression theory** takes into consideration the observation that frustration does not necessarily result in aggression and proposed that frustration creates a **readiness for aggression.** For aggression to actually occur, certain stimuli associated with aggression must be present. These stimuli are cues that the frustrated person associates with aggression. An example of this phenomenon in animals would be the "red flag" for the enraged and frustrated bull. In the presence of frustration, certain stimuli can serve as "triggers" to release a disposition toward aggression in a frustrated individual (Anderson, Deuser, & DeNeve, 1995). Negative affect, associated with frustration, is the fundamental spur to the inclination for aggression. Anger is the root of hostile aggression, but depression is another example of negative affect that can trigger an aggressive act. Illustrated in figure 13.2 are factors that can influence the strength of the impulse to be an aggressor.

Bredemeier's Theory of Moral Reasoning and Aggression

Based upon Jean Piaget's theory of cognitive development, Bredemeier's theory of **moral reasoning** as it relates to aggression proposes that an individuals' willingness to engage in aggression is related to her stage of moral reasoning (Bredemeier, 1994; Shields & Bredemeier, 2007). Because human

CONCEPT A relationship exists between an athlete's level of moral and ethical reasoning and her willingness to engage in acts of aggression.

APPLICATION Coaches and teachers can best control athletes' aggression by appealing to their sense of right and wrong. Athletes must be taught that aggression is just as wrong during an athletic contest as it is in normal everyday life.

aggression is viewed as unethical, Bredemeier reasoned that a relationship should exist between the level of moral reasoning and acts of overt athletic aggression. Contact sport, because it seems to legitimize acts of aggression, may actually slow a person's moral development. The three stages of moral development include the preconventional, the conventional, and the postconventional stages (Chow, Murray, & Feltz, 2009; Shields & Bredemeier, 2007). In the *preconventional stage*, the individual is concerned with rewards, punishment, and one's own welfare. In the *conventional stage*, the individual is concerned with group or team norms. In the *postconventional stage*, the individual is guided by moral principles. The higher the stage of moral development, the less likely it is that an athlete will engage in unethical aggressive behavior.

FIGURE 13.2 | Illustration showing factors that can influence the strength of an impulse to commit an act of aggression.

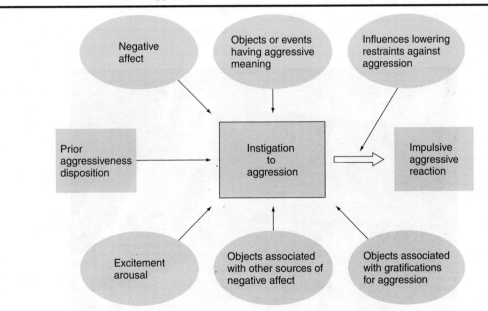

Source: Reproduced with permission from Berkowitz, L. (1993). *Aggression: Its causes, consequences, and control.* Philadelphia, PA: Temple University Press (figure 3.6, p. 71).

CONCEPT   Sport-related aggression is not cathartic in the sense that it reduces the desire for more aggression. Aggression begets more aggression as the behavior becomes reinforced and learned.

APPLICATION   Aggression on and off the athletic field must be discouraged and penalized as unacceptable behavior. Coaches must take the lead in making sure that an athlete is not rewarded in any way for perpetuating an act of aggression. Aggression is unacceptable in any environmental situation, including the athletic field.

The level of morality necessary for everyday life is often suspended during athletic competition. Bredemeier refers to this suspension of ethical morality as **bracketed morality.** Athletic teams create a "moral atmosphere" that may be conducive to the willingness to be aggressive (Chow et al., 2009; Stephen & Bredemeier, 1996; Tucker & Parks, 2001). In this regard, it should be emphasized that coaches, parents, and society as a whole contribute to the moral atmosphere and the development of moral reasoning in an athlete.

Consistent with other researchers (Bandura, Barbaranelli, Caprara, & Pastorelli, 1996; Long, Pantaleon, Bruant, & d'Arripe-Longueville, 2006), Corrion, Long, Smith, and d'Arripe-Longueville (2009) identified eight **mechanisms of moral disengagement** that allow an athlete to disengage from usual moral standards and engage in transgressive behavior. Different categories of **transgressive behavior** include (a) using rules to one's advantage, (b) unintentional fouls or violations, and (c) aggressive behavior in which there is a perceived attempt to harm. Listed in descending order of frequency of use are the eight identified mechanisms of moral disengagement identified in this investigation:

1. Displacement of responsibility (it's not my fault).
2. Attribution of blame (it's not my fault).

In boxing, the goal is to inflict harm. Eyewire/Getty Images.

CONCEPT   In ice hockey, individuals most likely to take part in fan violence are young males who travel in packs, have a recent history of fighting, like to watch fights, attend hockey games in the hope of seeing fights, react impulsively, and score high on the trait of aggressiveness.

APPLICATION   Knowing the physical and mental psychological profile of potential troublemakers should make it possible for sporting event organizers to take precautions that could prevent fan violence. The number one precaution would be for records to be kept, so that those who have a history of fighting can be either closely watched or barred from admission. Fan violence seems to be precipitated primarily by individuals who come to athletic events hoping to see or take part in violence, and who have a recent history of fighting. In ice hockey, troublemakers tend to be young males who travel in packs. However, it would be unfair to assume that all young males in groups are troublemakers.

3. Minimizing or ignoring the consequences (it's not serious).

4. Euphemistic labeling (common rule breaking).

5. Diffusion of responsibility (everybody does it).

6. Moral justification (the action was justified).

7. Advantageous comparison (comparison with daily life or other sport context).

8. Dehumanization (dehumanize opponent or recipient of aggressive act).

In this investigation, justifications 1 through 5 were identified the most by the athletes, while dehumanization was rarely identified. These identified mechanisms are important because humans often possess an innate need to find some justification for their unethical behaviors.

The Catharsis Effect

Introduced earlier, the **catharsis effect** represents a release of pent-up frustration that makes one feel better. It is a purging of the anger and frustration associated with not being able to accomplish a goal. Venting frustration upon a punching bag or some other inanimate object may serve as a useful catharsis. Venting frustration upon another human being, however, is an unacceptable behavior that is likely to lead to more aggression. Research supports the position that aggression begets more aggression, and that it can become learned behavior. If an act of aggression is precipitated by frustration, it may seem to give an immediate cathartic effect, but this feeling of catharsis is quickly followed by feelings of remorse, penalties, and likely escalation of tension and more aggression. *Aggression is not cathartic in the sense that it leads to a reduction in the desire to aggress.* Aggression leads to an increase in aggression as tempers flare and as the behavior becomes learned. This is especially true if aggression is rewarded by fans, by coaches, or by morbid gratification from having inflicted harm on another human being (Russell, 1999).

Measurement of Aggression

A number of inventories have been developed to measure aggressiveness as a personality disposition or trait. Two of these inventories are the Aggression Questionnaire (Buss & Perry, 1992) and the Aggression Inventory (Gladue, 1991). Sport-specific inventories include the Athletic Aggression Inventory (Bredemeier, 1978), the Continuum of Injurious Acts (Bredemeier, 1985), and the Competitive Aggressiveness and Anger Scale (Maxwell & Moores 2007, 2008; Visek, Maxwell, Watson, & Hurst, 2010).

CONCEPT Aggressive play may facilitate performance in some situations and in some sports, but hinder performance in other situations. From an ethical and moral perspective, aggressive (not assertive) play must be severely penalized by referees and umpires, as well as by coaches and team managers. It also must not be subtly promoted by management to boost ticket sales.

APPLICATION Coaches who want to be successful will not encourage aggression. An unpenalized act of aggression may help a team or individual win an athletic contest now and again, but over the long haul it will be a serious handicap and distraction. A coach's position on acts of aggression must be made perfectly clear. A player who gains an unfair advantage over an opponent through aggressive play must be taken out of the game, even if he is the star player.

The actual measurement of aggression, however, is much more difficult. Because aggression is defined as the intent to harm another human being, the measurement device must be able to capture this intent. This approach generally requires the use of trained observers using a standardized checklist of some kind, as well as videotaping (Sheldon & Aimar, 2001).

While not a state measure of aggression, the Judgements about Moral Behavior in Youth Sport Questionnaire (JAMBYSQ; Stephens, Bredemeier, & Shields, 1997) provide a way to measure aggressive tendencies consistent with Bredemeier's theory of moral reasoning and aggression. The JAMBYSQ measures an athlete's self-described behavior as a function of (a) lying to an official, (b) cheating by breaking a rule, and (c) hurting an opponent in a game situation. Questions related to "hurting an opponent in a game situation" measure three aspects of aggression:

1. Team norm for aggression (would teammates engage in aggressive acts?).

2. Stage of moral development (preconventional, conventional, postconventional).

3. Self-described likelihood to engage in acts of aggression.

Evidence suggests that team norms for aggression, stage of moral development, and likelihood to engage in aggression are all predictive of actual state aggression in sport (Shields & Bredemeier, 2007; Traclet et al., 2009).

Fan Violence

Most of our discussion in this section has focused upon acts of aggression on the part of sport participants. Unfortunately, however, some of the worst examples of sports aggression and violence occur among the fans watching an athletic contest. This chapter was prefaced with examples of both athlete aggression and fan violence. Intense rivalries, nationalism, and alcohol abuse are major factors contributing to fan violence. Every sports event is attended by individuals who may instigate fan violence. These are individuals who score high in the personality dispositions of anger and physical aggression. These individuals are attracted to violence and fighting among fans, and exhibit a false belief about the willingness of other fans to join in acts of violence. The **false consensus effect** emboldens individuals with a disposition for violence to believe that other fans share their infatuation for fighting and would willingly join them in precipitating an altercation (Russell, 1995; Russell & Arms, 1995).

Research involving ice hockey fans has provided important information about the type of individual who is most likely to take part in fighting and violence (Arms & Russell, 1997; Russell, 1999; Russell & Arms, 1998; Russell & Mustonen, 1998). In carrying out this line of research, trained assistants conducted brief interviews and administered inventories to randomly selected hockey fans during breaks in the action. Results show that the individuals most likely to take part in fan violence are young

CONCEPT Acts of aggression occur more frequently among losing teams, during games with high point differentials, and after the first quarter of play.

APPLICATION Athletes who have a history of aggression should be closely monitored during these situations.

males who travel in packs, have a recent history of fighting, like to watch fights, attend hockey games in hopes of seeing fights, react impulsively, and score high on the trait of aggressiveness. If a fight were to break out nearby in the stands, 61 percent of the fans interviewed said they would watch, 26 percent said they would try to stop the fight (peacemakers), 7 percent said they would applaud or join in (troublemakers), and the remainder said they would leave the area. **Peacemakers** are not older or of larger stature than other fans; yet, they are willing to risk harm by intervening. **Troublemakers** tend to be young, small in stature, and have a history of violence and fighting.

Another factor that has been shown to be associated with fan violence is the degree to which fans identify with a sports team. **Fan identification** refers to the psychological connection that individuals have with their team. A study reported by Dimmock and Grove (2005) showed that highly identified professional sport fans feel less control over their behavior at games than moderately identified fans and slightly identified fans.

Effects of Aggression on Performance

Conventional wisdom argues that acts of aggression on the part of an athlete will constitute a distraction and result in a decrement in performance. Not only are aggressive acts on the part of an individual distracting to the individual, but also they are likely to be distracting to the team as a whole. Research shows, for example, that the lower a team is in the standings, the more likely it will be to engage in aggression. An exception to this general observation may be in the sport of ice hockey, where it is often

difficult to separate legitimate force (assertiveness) from illegitimate force (aggression). Because hostile aggression is associated with anger and hence with an increase in physiological arousal, it is possible that for some individuals an increase in anger may produce a level of physiological arousal conducive to best performance. Conversely, it may produce a level of arousal that is above an athlete's zone of optimal functioning and cause a decrement in performance.

Hard-fought assertive play on the part of athletes in team sports such as American football, rugby, and ice hockey is important for team success. Forceful physical contact in ice hockey is both necessary and well within the rules of the game, but aggressive play with an intent to harm is not within the rules and is penalized. An offending player is sent to the penalty box for two-minutes, leaving his team short-handed for that period of time. This is referred to as a "power play," and it is a time when goals are often scored against the short-handed team.

Situational Factors in a Sport Setting

Much of the research in sport-related aggression has dealt with situation-specific factors. Factors associated with the occurrence of aggression in sport-specific situations among athletes are as follows:

1. *Environmental temperature* Using archival data from major league baseball games played during the 1986, 1987, and 1988 seasons, Reifman, Larrick, and Fein (1991) observed a linear relationship between hit batters and environmental temperature. The

data suggest that higher temperatures lead major league pitchers to become more aggressive in pitching to batters.

2. *Perception of victim's intent*   If athletes perceive that an opponent's intent is to inflict harm, they are more likely to respond with aggression against the opponent. This means that perception of an opponent's aggressive intentions may be more salient than such things as defeat and competition. When athletes perceive that their opponents' rough play is intentional and designed to inflict harm, they are more likely to respond with aggression than if they perceive that the roughness is incidental (Harrell, 1980; Stephens, 2000).

3. *Fear of retaliation*   To some degree, the fear of retaliation on the part of the individual who is the target of aggression can inhibit another player from initiating that aggression. A basketball player is a little less likely to elbow her opponent in the ribs if she fears similar treatment from the opponent. This sort of respect for an opponent's ability to "give as good as she gets," however, can quickly escalate into open aggression and counteraggression (Knott & Drost, 1972).

4. *Structure of the game*   Two of the earliest studies of game variables and aggression were conducted by Volkamer (1972) with soccer and Wankel (1972) with ice hockey. These studies were quickly followed by investigations by Lefebvre and Passer (1974) with soccer, Cullen and Cullen (1975) with ice hockey, Martin (1976) with basketball and wrestling, Russell and Drewery (1976) with soccer, and Engelhardt (1995) with ice hockey. Following is a summary of the findings with respect to game variables:

   a. *Point differential*   More aggressive penalties occur as the game score differential increases. When teams are tied or the scores are close, aggression is at a minimum.

   b. *Playing at home or away*   Whether home or visiting teams display more aggressive behavior may depend on the nature of the aggression and the type of game involved. Soccer teams tend to be more aggressive when playing away from home, whereas aggression is almost equal for home and visiting ice hockey teams.

   c. *Outcome of participation*   Consistent with the frustration-aggression hypothesis, members of losing teams are observed to be more aggressive than members of winning teams.

   d. *League standings*   The lower a team is in the standings, the more its members engage in aggression. The lowest incidence of aggression occurs with teams in first place.

   e. *Periods of play*   As a general rule, acts of aggression increase as the game proceeds. Clearly, the lowest number of acts of aggression occurs during the first period of play. This finding may be related to point differential.

5. *Rivalry, familiarity, and frequency of play* Intradivisional play in professional ice hockey is associated with significantly more incidents of aggression among players than interdivisional play (Widmeyer & McGuire, 1997). Intradivisional play features frequent competition among teams that are geographically close to each other (cities) and that have intense rivalries. As players become more familiar with one another due to frequency of play, and as the rivalries become more intense due to geographical location, aggression becomes more frequent.

6. *Personal characteristics of athlete*   Research has demonstrated that there are a number of personality-related factors that are predictive of potential aggressive behavior or actual aggression. Athletes who exhibit high levels of ego (performance) goal orientation are more

likely to exhibit aggressive behavior than those low on this personality disposition (Dunn & Dunn, 1999; Rascle, Coulomb-Cabagno, & Delsarte, 2005; Stephens, 2001). In addition, individuals high in ego goal orientation are more likely to engage in dating violence (Merten, 2008). Athletes who possess the trait of reactive anger are more likely to exhibit angry outbursts, while those who possess the trait of anger control are more likely to exhibit the ability to control their anger and to engage in problem and emotion focused coping associated with aggressive tendencies (Bolgar, Janelle, & Giacobbi, 2008). Athletes who exhibit antisocial behavior generally and toward opponents specifically are predisposed to commit acts of aggression (Kavussanu & Boardley, 2009; Kavussanu, Stamp, Slade, & Ring, 2009). Finally, athletes who score high in obsessive passion are more likely to display aggressive behavior than those who are low in this characteristic or high in harmonious passion (Donahue, Rip, & Vallerand, 2009).

7. *Athlete and sport differences*   Aggressive behavior may differ as a function of type of sport. One study demonstrated numerous differences between the sports of men's basketball and ice hockey relative to aggressive behavior and aggressive play: ice hockey athletes commit greater numbers of acts of aggression; aggression is more acceptable in ice hockey than basketball; and verbal abuse of referees is more common in basketball than ice hockey (Kirker et al., 2000). Despite suggestions to the contrary, athletes do not engage in dating violence, sexual assault, or off-field aggression more often than nonathletes (Merten, 2008; Smith & Stewart, 2003). Finally, research shows that perceived legitimacy of aggressive behavior in ice hockey increases as the athlete increases in age and experience (Viseck & Watson, 2005).

8. *Coach characteristics*   Coaches can, of course, have a direct effect upon an athlete's aggressive behavior simply by instructing an athlete to inflict pain or injury upon an opposing player or players. A case in point would be a baseball manager ordering his pitcher to throw at an opposing batter in retaliation for an earlier incident, or in the case of men's collegiate baseball where the coach inserts a "goon" into the game to wreak havoc on opposing players (Widman, 2005). Setting these direct effect examples aside, consider the subtle relationship between the coach characteristics and player-aggressive behavior. In a study reported by Chow et al. (2009) involving youth soccer teams we learn that a player's self-assessed likelihood to display aggressive behavior is related to (a) the coach's sex, (b) the coach's playing experience, and (c) the coach's perception of the team's ability. Athletes are more likely to assess themselves as being aggressive if their coach is a male, their coach has lots of personal playing experience, and the coach perceives his team as lacking in ability.

Reducing Aggression in Sport

Aggression in sport can be curtailed, or at least minimized, if all concerned are interested in doing so. The sad part is that some of the most influential people actually promote rather than discourage violence because they believe it increases revenue. As long as this attitude is allowed to continue, there is little hope of solving the problem. If it is allowed to continue on the professional level, it will continue to be promoted at the lower skill levels. Athletes in the youth leagues emulate their heroes on the collegiate and professional levels. They watch their sport heroes receive awards, applause, money, and adulation for behavior that borders on open aggression, and they want to become like them.

Research shows that angry feelings and angry behavior, the precursor to hostile aggression, can be modified through anger awareness training and role playing (Brunelle, Janelle, & Tennant, 1999). Athletes can learn to control their feelings of hostility and anger. Role playing is particularly effective in reducing an athlete's angry feelings and behavior. The effects of anger management training and role playing persist after training ceases. In the two sections that follow, specific suggestions are given as to how aggression by athletes and violence by fans can be reduced or eliminated. These suggestions are based upon the literature generally, but also upon an important position paper endorsed by the International Society of Sport Psychology (Tenenbaum, Stewart, Singer, & Duda, 1997).

Curtailing Aggression and Violence by Athletes

1. Young athletes must be provided with models of nonaggressive but effective assertive behavior.

2. Athletes who engage in aggressive acts must be severely penalized. A case in point was the two-game suspension of University of Utah's starting basketball guard, Luka Drca, by his coach, Jim Boylen, for an intentional foul inflicted on an opposing University of Oklahoma player. The suspension was not mandated by the league, but Boylen suspended the player anyway, stating, "His behavior was unacceptable and does not represent what our program is about" (Utah's Drca Suspended, 2008, p. D2).

3. The penalty or punishment that an athlete receives for an act of aggression must be of greater punitive value than the potential reinforcement received for committing the act. On balance, it must be demonstrated that aggression does not pay.

4. Coaches who encourage or even allow their athletes to engage in aggressive behavior should be fined, censored, and/or suspended from their coaching duties.

5. External stimuli or cues capable of evoking hostile aggression on the field of play should be removed. An example of an aggressive cue might be the antics of an overly zealous fan displaying an inflammatory sign.

6. Coaches and referees should be encouraged to attend in-service training workshops on dealing with aggression on the part of players.

7. In addition to receiving punishment for acts of aggression, athletes should receive rewards and praise for showing restraint and patience in emotionally charged situations.

8. Strategies and coping skills designed to curtail acts of aggression should be practiced.

9. Social interaction between members of opposing teams should be encouraged by coaches and managers during the days leading up to a contest.

Curtailing Aggression and Violence by Fans

1. Potential troublemakers should be closely supervised. Fans with a history of violence and fighting should be identified and denied admission.

2. The sale, distribution, and use of alcoholic beverages at sporting events should be limited and controlled.

3. Athletic events should be promoted and encouraged as family affairs. The best way to do this is to promise a family-like environment and to provide financial incentives for family attendance.

4. The media should promote responsible behavior on the part of the fans by not glamorizing acts of aggression on the field of play and by not promoting a sense of friction or dislike between the players and fans of the two competing teams.

5. As with athletes and coaches, fan aggression must be swiftly and severely punished.

Summary

Two factors must be present in order for a behavior to be labeled aggression. First, the behavior must be aimed at another human being with the goal of inflicting physical harm. Second, there must be a reasonable expectation that the attempt to inflict harm will be successful. There are two kinds of aggression, hostile and instrumental. In hostile aggression the goal is to harm, while in instrumental aggression the goal is to obtain some external goal, such as victory. Assertiveness is not aggression, but because legitimate physical force is often used, it is often confused with aggression. Perceived legitimacy of aggressive behavior increases as a function of increased age and level of competition.

Theories of aggression discussed include instinct theory, social learning theory, Berkowitz's reformulation of the frustration-aggression hypothesis, and Bredemeier's theory of moral reasoning and aggression. Instinct theory posits that aggression is a catharsis that results in a reduced drive to aggress. Social learning theory posits that aggression is a learned behavior that does not result in a catharsis. Berkowitz's reformulation of frustration-aggression theory focuses upon the notion that frustration results in a readiness to aggress, but not necessarily in aggression. Bredemeier's theory of moral reasoning and aggression links an individual's stage of moral reasoning with the willingness to show aggression. Stages of moral reasoning include the preconventional, conventional, and post-conventional stages. Important concepts discussed as they relate to morality and aggression include bracketed morality, mechanisms of moral disengagement, and transgressive behavior.

Individuals likely to precipitate fan violence tend to be young males who travel in packs, have a recent history of fighting, like to watch fights, are impulsive, and score high on the trait of aggressiveness. In every incident of fan violence there will be onlookers, peacemakers, and troublemakers. The onlookers are likely to constitute the clear majority of the fans, while approximately 26 percent say they would try to stop the fight (peacemakers), and 7 percent would join in or encourage others to join in the violence (troublemakers).

Research has demonstrated that there are certain situational factors that are associated with aggression on the part of athletes. A knowledge of these situational factors is likely to help reduce aggression in sport. Recommendations are given for reducing aggression among athletes and reducing fan violence.

Critical Thought Questions

1. The discussion in this chapter has focused upon aggression and physical harm. How could the operational definition of aggression be revised to include psychological harm?

2. Which theory of aggression do you think provides the best explanation of aggressive behavior in sport? Explain.

3. Discuss the concept of catharsis relative to instinct theory, frustration-aggression theory, and social learning theory.

4. Can a researcher differentiate between aggressive behavior and assertive behavior when using archival data? Explain.

5. Discuss situational factors associated with athlete aggression. Can you add to test list? How can this information assist in reducing athlete aggression?

6. Add to the list of strategies for curtailing aggression among athletes and violence among fans.

7. Why do you think that there is a general belief that athletes are more likely to commit acts of aggression than non-athletes? What can be done to dispel this myth?

Glossary

aggression A sequence of behaviors in which the goal is to injure another person.

assertiveness The expenditure of unusual effort and energy to achieve an external goal.

bracketed morality The suspension of ethics, or morality, during athletic competition.

catharsis effect The purging of anger and frustration associated with not being able to accomplish a goal.

circular effect of aggression The pattern in which one act of aggression leads to further aggression.

false consensus effect The belief on the part of some violence-prone fans that others share their infatuation for fighting and would willingly join them in precipitating an altercation.

fan identification The psychological connection or identification that individuals have with their teams.

frustration-aggression theory As originally conceived by Dollard et al. (1939), the theory that frustration always results in aggression.

hostile aggression Aggression against another human being with the intent to harm; the reinforcement or goal is to inflict pain and suffering on the victim. It is always accompanied by anger.

instinct theory The theory that human aggression is an innate biological drive that cannot be eliminated, but must be controlled through catharsis for the good of humankind.

instrumental aggression Aggression against another human being with the intent to harm; the reinforcement is to obtain some external goal, such as victory or prestige.

legitimacy of aggressive behavior The perception on the part of athletes that aggressive behavior may be justified in varying degrees depending on the situation.

mechanisms of moral disengagement Perceptions that allow individuals to justify in their own mind acts of athletic aggression.

moral reasoning An individual's capacity to understand and embrace standards of moral behavior. Bredemeier asserts that an individual's willingness to engage in aggression is related to her stage of moral reasoning.

peacemakers Those who try to make peace when a riot occurs. Peacemakers are contrasted with those who watch and those who incite.

readiness for aggression According to Berkowitz, the condition of being primed for aggression because of frustration. Aggression does not occur unless an aggressive cue is presented to the frustrated person.

reformulation of frustration-aggression theory Berkowitz's theory that frustration does not necessarily result in an aggressive response, but does result in a readiness for aggression.

relational aggression Harming others through such things as social ostracism and malicious rumors.

social learning theory Relative to aggression, a theory that posits that aggression is a function of learning, and that biological drive and frustration are inadequate explanations for aggression.

transgressive behavior Categories of behavior that are violations of good conduct in sport (e.g., using rules to one's advantage, unintentional violations of rules, aggressive behavior in which there is a perceived attempt to harm another person).

troublemakers Those who incite and take part in a riot. Troublemakers are contrasted with those who watch and those who try to make peace.

CHAPTER 14

Audience and Self-Presentation Effects in Sport

KEY TERMS

Archival data
Audience density
Away court disadvantage
Dysfunctional assertive
  behavior
Functional assertive
  behavior
Home advantage
Home disadvantage
Hostile crowd
Impression construction
Impression management
Impression motivation
Interactive audience
Self-attention
Self-handicapping
Self-presentation
Social facilitation
Zajonc's model

When the crowd gives to the athlete, the athlete gives back to the crowd. (Dan O'Brian, U.S.A., 1996 Olympic Decathlon Champion; O'Brian & Sloan, 1999).

Perhaps no social-psychological effect is more important to athletic performance and outcome than the audience, or spectator, effect. The evidence is clear, for example, that there is significant advantage to playing at home in baseball, football, basketball, ice hockey, and soccer. The perception of a home court advantage is especially evident in men's collegiate basketball and professional soccer.

In professional sports, two well-publicized examples of the home court advantage may be cited. Sports writers, during the Larry Bird era, coined the phrase "Celtic Mystique," when referring to the win-loss record of the Boston Celtics basketball franchise when playing at Boston Gardens. Prior to losing game number four to the Los Angeles Lakers in the 1987 NBA championship series, the Celtics had won 94 of their previous 97 games in "friendly" Boston Gardens. The 1987 World champion Minnesota Twins baseball team won 70 percent of its regular-season home games. In addition, the Twins won all their post-season home games when they defeated the heavily favored Detroit Tigers for the American League Pennant, as well as all their home games against the St. Louis Cardinals in the World Series.

While many variables may help create the home court or home field advantage, none seem to be as important as the presence of a supportive audience. Determining how and why an audience presence affects athletic performance is the focus of this chapter. Major topics to be discussed in this chapter include (a) social facilitation, (b) effects of an interactive audience on performance, and (c) self-presentation effects in sport.

Social Facilitation

Social facilitation research is based on the notion that the presence of an audience of one or more spectators can facilitate performance. This is an appealing concept, since almost everyone has experienced the desire to perform better when friends, family, or members of the opposite gender are watching.

Research in the area of social facilitation was significantly influenced by the work of Robert Zajonc (pronounced "science"). Zajonc's classic paper on the topic remains the single most critical factor in the development of social facilitation as a field of inquiry (Zajonc, 1965). Based upon drive theory (see chapter 7), **Zajonc's model** proposed that the presence of an audience has the effect of increasing arousal (drive) in performing participants. Since increased arousal facilitates the elicitation of the dominant response, the presence of an audience will enhance the performance of a skilled individual while causing a decrement in the performance of an unskilled individual. This concept is illustrated in figure 14.1 for athletic competition.

FIGURE 14.1 | Drive theory prediction of the influence of a crowd on the performance of athletes of differing skill levels.

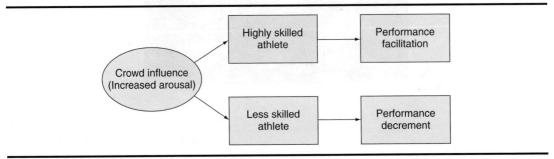

CONCEPT The presence of a supportive and emotionally arousing crowd translates into a home court advantage in many situations.

APPLICATION Since the home court advantage is a function of fan support, it is important to capitalize on this advantage by filling the stadium or fieldhouse. Additionally, the band, the cheering squad, and publicity should be used to generate excitement and enthusiasm.

While Zajonc's model generated hundreds of research investigations, it suffered a fatal flaw from the perspective of sport psychology research. Social facilitation was defined as "consequences upon behavior which derive from the sheer presence of other individuals" (Zajonc, 1965, p. 269). To test the model, researchers were obligated to focus on the "sheer presence" of an audience with no interaction between the performer and the audience. Since this situation *rarely* occurs in competitive athletics, the research generated from testing the model is not easily applied to sport. Therefore, the balance of this chapter will be devoted to research in which an interactive relationship between participants and spectators is assumed. For a review of social facilitation research, the reader is referred to Cox (1990).

Effects of an Interactive Audience on Performance

Perhaps the most interesting topic associated with the **interactive audience** is that of the **home advantage.** The fact that the home advantage exists in such team sports as basketball, baseball, football, ice hockey, and soccer is well documented (Bray, 1999; Bray, Law, & Foyle, 2003; Brown et al., 2002). In addition to the concept of a home court advantage in traditional team sports, we also have evidence of a home country advantage relative to the Olympics (Leonard, 1989) and to individual sports (Bray & Carron, 1993).

While the presence of a supportive audience is the most critical factor in the home court advantage

in sport, this does not rule out the observation that other factors contribute to this advantage. Following a review of the literature, Pollard (2006) provided a very useful model that shows how seven different factors can contribute to the home court or field advantage. As illustrated in figure 14.2, these seven different factors may have either direct or indirect effects on the home advantage. According to the model, crowd support, familiarity, travel, and territoriality have both a direct effect as well as two indirect effects upon the home advantage. For example, a supportive audience (crowd support) has a direct effect upon the home advantage, an indirect effect through the referees, and an indirect effect through psychological factors (the thoughts and actions of players, coaches, and referees). Notwithstanding the potential influences these other factors have on the home court advantage, researchers have shown that the influence of such things as travel (Courneya & Carron, 1991) and lack of facility familiarity (Moore & Brylinski, 1995) are trivial compared to the crowd's influence. A corollary to the facility familiarity issue, however, was studied by Wilkinson and Pollard (2006). In this investigation the researchers wondered whether moving into a new home stadium would change the home court/field advantage. Data for their study came from 40 professional baseball, basketball, and hockey teams that moved into new facilities between 1987 and 2002. Results showed that compared to the previous year (old stadium), home-winning percentages dipped from 59.63 percent to 57.36 percent for the first year, and recovered to 59.02 percent for the second year in the new facility. Changing to a new facility is associated with a slight drop in home-winning percentage, but recovers quickly after one year.

FIGURE 14.2 | Interrelationship of factors associated with home court/field advantage in sport.

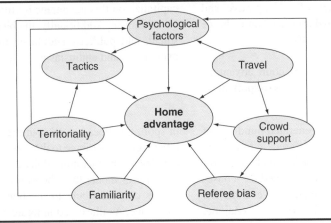

Source: Reproduced with permission from Pollard, R. (2006). Home advantage in soccer: Variations in its magnitude and a literature review of the interrelated factors associated with its existence. *Journal of Sport Behavior, 29,* 169–189.

In this chapter, we focus on the most viable explanation for the home court advantage: the presence of a supportive and interactive audience.

Why Is There a Home Court Advantage?

The most plausible explanation for the home advantage in sport is the presence of a supportive and interactive audience. But how does this work? Does the audience energize the home team, or does it inhibit the performance of the visiting team? The best available answers for these questions come from two separate investigations.

The first investigation of interest, reported by Varca (1980), involved collegiate men's basketball games played during the 1977–78 season in the Southeastern Conference. Varca tested the hypothesis that the home court advantage was attributable to more functional assertive play on the part of the home team and more dysfunctional assertive play on the part of the visiting team. Increased arousal caused by the supportive crowd was believed to facilitate assertive play. In Varca's terminology, **functional assertive behavior** in basketball included superior performance in the skills of rebounding, steals, and blocked shots, while **dysfunctional assertive**

behavior was limited to personal fouls, a behavior believed to inhibit performance. As predicted by Varca's hypothesis, significant differences were noted between home and away teams on the functionally assertive skills of stealing, blocking shots, and rebounding. The home teams enjoyed a superiority in these three important skills. Additionally, the visiting teams had significantly more fouls than the home teams. Varca's research is very helpful in explaining why the presence of a roaring crowd could facilitate the home team's performance, but inhibit that of the visiting team. The skills involved in rebounding, stealing, and blocking shots are closely associated with strength and speed. These are the kinds of skills that are facilitated by very high arousal. While trying to negate the functional assertive behavior of the home team, the visiting team gets whistled for personal fouls. This causes increased frustration, and more dysfunctional behavior results.

The second study of interest was reported by Silva and Andrew (1987). Based on previous research, the investigators knew that the home team won more games than did the visiting team in collegiate basketball. They hypothesized, however, that the advantage favoring the home team was due not to increased performance caused by a supportive audience, but to inferior performance on the

CONCEPT Winning on the road can be enhanced by understanding the nature of the home court advantage.

APPLICATION When playing away from home, it is important that the coach develop a careful game plan and stay with it. The game plan should emphasize patience on offense, tactics to keep the crowd calm, and careful avoidance of penalties and fouls.

---

part of the visiting team—sort of an **away court disadvantage,** as opposed to a home court advantage. **Archival data** from 418 men's collegiate basketball games played in the Atlantic Coast Conference from 1971 to 1981 were utilized in the investigation. The unique aspect of this investigation was that performance of players during actual competition was compared with a pregame standard of good performance provided by coaches. While home teams did exhibit superior game statistics when compared to visiting teams, this occurred not because the home teams exhibited game statistics better than expected, but because the visiting teams exhibited game statistics worse than expected. In other words, the home crowd facilitates expected performance in the home team but less than expected performance in the visiting team.

When Is the Home Court/Field a Disadvantage?

Is playing at home always an advantage, or can it sometimes be a disadvantage? For a number of reasons, playing at home can create a **home disadvantage.** One reason might be that the fans expect you to win at home; this can result in additional pressure to play well. A second reason might be that playing before a very vocal and supportive audience can raise arousal to a level that results in a decrement of performance.

> Sometimes, playing at home in the postseason isn't an advantage. You get so charged up that you lose focus of what you have to do.
>
> (Joe Torre, New York Yankees manager; Walker, 1996.)

A case in point is the above observation by Joe Torre, manager of the New York Yankees baseball team, following the loss of the first two games of the 1996 World Series while playing at home. The Yankees went on to win the series in six games. In this series the Atlanta Braves lost three straight games at home as well. According to Baumeister and Steinhilber (1984), this is the heightened **self-attention,** or self-awareness, effect that can plague home teams during important home games. The presence of a supportive audience may have the effect of increasing the cost of not winning when you are expected to. The athlete or athletes begin to "press," which interferes with the execution of skillful play (Jordet, 2009; Wallace, Baumeister, & Vohs, 2005).

Butler and Baumeister (1998) asserted that for self-attention reasons, participants may adopt a cautious performance style that, in the presence of a supportive audience, may lead to suboptimal performance (e.g., trying too hard to please the hometown fans in a critical game situation). Law, Masters, Bray, Eves, and Bardswell (2003), however, demonstrated that this effect would occur only if the athletes possessed explicit knowledge as opposed to conceptual or implicit knowledge of how to perform a skill. For example, a tennis player who possessed only a conceptual understanding of how to hit a topspin tennis drive should not suffer a performance decrement in the presence of a supportive audience. Conversely, a tennis player who possessed detailed technical knowledge (explicit knowledge) of how to hit a topspin tennis drive may suffer a performance decrement in the presence of a supportive audience. This takes us back to

CONCEPT Playing before a supportive but expectant audience can increase the cost of not winning, thereby leading to self-attention and "pressing" on the part of an athlete or a team.

APPLICATION There are lots of examples of the self-attention effect in sport. It often happens when a new player replaces a popular home-town favorite on the team roster. Expectations are high and the player tries too hard to please the crowd. A sport psychologist or informed coach can help an athlete in this situation by teaching him patience and by building the athlete's self-confidence.

our study of attention in chapter 6, where we learned about the debilitative performance effects of disrupting the automatic nature of a motor task. Due to self-attention, the supportive crowd causes the athlete to revert back to attending to the explicit-knowledge details of executing a motor skill.

While the self-attention hypothesis provides a viable explanation for why the home team and some home-team players may play poorly in important games, this is not a universally accepted and observed phenomenon. A case in point is a study reported by Tauer, Guenther, and Rozek (2009), in which they studied over 50 years of National Basketball Association (NBA) data from 1947–2005. During that period of time they did not observe evidence of a home court "choke," but did observe lots of evidence of a home court advantage. They, however, did not rule out the potential negative effect that playing at home might have on certain players. That is, some players may suffer a decrement in performance due to self-attention and a disruption of their normal automatic execution of a motor skill. Failure to hit clutch basketball free throws during the last few minutes of a close game is an example of "choking" under pressure and may well be due to self-attention.

Audience Characteristics

Having determined that a home advantage usually exists in sport and that this advantage is related to the presence of a supportive and interactive audience, we should now examine characteristics of the audience. Do certain audience characteristics lead to a greater home advantage? This question will be discussed in the following paragraphs.

Crowd Size, Intimacy, and Density There is evidence in professional baseball that crowd size makes a difference. Schwartz and Barsky (1977), for example, demonstrated that audience size is related to performance in baseball. The winning percentage of home teams increased as the size of the crowd increased. This effect is most pronounced when first-division home teams play visiting teams from the second division (those with fewer wins). Also based upon the Schwartz and Barsky data is the observation that sports such as basketball and ice hockey enjoy a greater home advantage than baseball and football. Since baseball and football normally accommodate a far greater number of fans than basketball and/or ice hockey, factors such as audience density and audience intimacy may be more important than size for creating the home court advantage (Agnew & Carron, 1994). **Audience density** and audience intimacy are related to how tightly packed together the fans are and how close they are to the field of play. Successful teams that opt to move out of smaller, more intimate facilities into larger ones often do so at the expense of crowd density and intimacy.

Crowd Hostility It is generally understood that a supportive and friendly crowd will help the home team. What is the effect, however, of a seemingly **hostile crowd** on player performance? Research by Greer (1983) demonstrated that sustained hostile spectator protests have a clearly negative impact on

CONCEPT A supportive audience is important for the home team. However, the home team should make sure that the mood of an audience does not turn ugly and hostile.

APPLICATION It is unethical and unsportsmanlike to promote fan hostility in support of the home team. Coaches, managers, and team officials are morally obligated to avoid such a situation.

the visiting team. Home basketball games of two Division I basketball teams were monitored and studied. Observations of sustained spectator protest were identified and studied relative to subsequent skill performance. Following episodes of sustained fan protest (usually directed at officials), the performance of athletes was monitored for five minutes of running game time. The results of the research showed a slight improvement in the performance of the home team, paralleled by a more significant and pronounced decline in performance of the visiting team following spectator protest. The negative effects of hostile crowd noise upon visiting teams and upon officials is further documented by Unkelbach and Memmert (2010).

Arie Selinger, former head coach of the U.S. women's national volleyball team, can attest to the devastating effect of a hostile audience (Steers, 1982). Arie took his heavily favored women's team to Peru in 1982 to compete in the World Championships. Everything went according to plan until the U.S. team played Peru. That was when the crowd took over. For two hours, it was impossible for players, coach, or officials to communicate verbally. The highly unsportsmanlike fans were armed with whistles and noisemakers. Each time a U.S. player went back to serve, the noise was deafening. "The sound came down like thunder. You could feel the vibrations. You're totally disoriented. It's a terrible experience," said Coach Selinger. A father of one of the athletes summed it up this way: "The team prepared for nine months to win the World Championships and they were beaten by a wireless microphone and fifteen thousand plastic whistles."

Sometimes it is not necessarily the entire crowd that is hostile, but a small and highly vocal section of the crowd. A case in point is the "Antlers," a rowdy, raucous, almost-anything-goes men's basketball student jeering section composed of University of Missouri–Columbia undergraduates wearing black T-shirts, goofy hats, and painted faces. The antics of the "Antlers" are at times so offensive that they have to be censured by university administrators (Fallstrom, 1993).

Home Court Advantage and Team Quality

From the previous discussions we understand that the home team usually enjoys a home court or field advantage. At least, we know that the home team wins more often than the visiting team. This advantage is more noticeable in basketball and ice hockey (63 percent) compared to football (60 percent) and baseball (53 percent), but it is a consistent observation on most levels of play. What these statistics do not reveal, however, is the effect of team quality on home court advantage. Bray (1999) studied archival data from the National Hockey League (NHL) across nearly 20 years, and over thirty thousand games. For most of the designated period of time, 26 teams were involved in an 80-game schedule (40 at home, 40 away). By grouping teams as a function of winning percentages, Bray was able to report that the home winning percentages of low-, average-, and high-quality teams were 32 percent, 52 percent, and 70 percent, respectively. Conversely, away winning percentages of low-, average-, and high-quality teams were 17 percent, 35 percent, and 52 percent, respectively. It is an advantage to play at home in the NHL, but the chances of winning at home are far greater for high-quality teams as opposed to lower-quality teams.

The *"Antlers" provide raucous and sometimes rowdy support for the home team.* Courtesy University of Missouri–Columbia Sports Information.

Madrigal and James (1999) conducted a similar investigation involving archival data from 10 years of women's Big Ten basketball (1,800 games). Their analysis showed that over the ten-year period, the home teams won 61 percent of the contests. When the percentage of games won by home teams was considered as a function of team quality, strong teams defeated other strong teams, moderately strong teams, and weak teams at home 70 percent, 86 percent, and 95 percent of the time, respectively. High-quality teams performed better at home than away in terms of field goal percentages, steals, and fouls, when they played the same opponent in the same season.

Conversely, for low-quality teams, the opposite was observed; they performed better away than at home on these same skills. Factors that contributed most to the home team advantage, after controlling for team quality, were crowd density, rebounds, steals, and field goal shooting percentage.

From these two investigations, involving two different team sports, it seems clear that team quality is a *moderating variable* that determines the strength of the relationship between playing at home and winning percentage. Winning at home occurs more often for high-quality teams than for low-quality teams.

CONCEPT Team quality is a more powerful predictor of whether or not a team will win a contest than where the game is being played. When two teams of equal quality play each other, the home team should have the advantage.

APPLICATION Teams and coaches should worry less about whether they are playing at home or away and focus more on team quality. The stronger and better team should have the advantage regardless of whether the game is at home or away. In those cases where teams are of equal quality, the home court or field advantage can have a powerful effect upon the outcome of the game. Regardless of where a game is being played, a quality team should always enter a contest believing they are the best team and that they will win if they play as well as they should. The focus should be upon execution and quality of play and not upon the crowd or the facility.

Players' Perceptions of Home Court Advantage

The majority of research on home court advantage has been generated using archival data. Seldom have athletes been asked in a systematic way about their perception of the phenomenon. Bray and Widmeyer (2000) asked 40 collegiate female basketball players about their perceptions of the home court advantage. The athletes indicated that they believed there was a home court advantage in their league, and that about 61 percent of the games were won by the home team. They further indicated that they felt that home court familiarity and crowd support were the primary factors determining the home court advantage. Athletes indicated that they believed that travel considerations were of borderline importance, and that special "house rules" associated with the building they played in were of no consequence. Finally, athletes believed that they were more self-confident when they played at home than when they played away.

Self-Presentation Effects in Sport

Earlier in this chapter we introduced Zajonc's model of social facilitation, which proposes that the arousal associated with the presence of an audience could either facilitate or inhibit the performance of an athlete. We further learned that the tenets of Zajonc's model are grounded in drive theory. However, these same relationships can be explained through a principle of social psychology called **self-presentation.** "Self-presentation, also called impression management, refers to the processes by which people monitor and control how they are perceived by other people" (Leary, 1992, p. 339). As explained by Leary and Kowalski (1990), **impression management** or self-presentation has two components. The first component of impression management is impression motivation, while the second is impression construction. **Impression motivation** involves the process that causes a person to be concerned about how she is perceived by others and her attempts to regulate other people's impression of her. **Impression construction** deals with the types of images a person wants to construct for people to see. The 33-item Self-presentation in Sport Questionnaire (SPSQ; Wilson & Eklund, 1998) was developed to measure four aspects of self-presentation: (a) appearing athletically untalented, (b) physical appearance, (c) fatigue or lacking energy, and (d) performance and composure inadequacies. A revised version of the SPSQ (SPSQ-R) is composed of 21 items (McGowan, Prapavessis, & Wesch, 2008).

As illustrated in figure 14.3, an athlete's efforts to regulate other people's (the audience's) impression of him can result in either a positive performance effect or a negative performance effect. In

FIGURE 14.3 | Self-presentation in sport may be manifested as a function of social facilitation, self-attention, or self-handicapping.

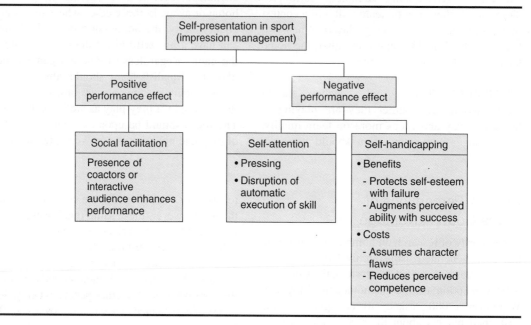

the case of a positive performance effect, it is impression motivation and not physiological arousal that causes an increase in performance (Carron, Burke, & Prapavessis, 2004). Conversely, if efforts to regulate people's image do not go well, a decrement in performance could result. We introduced this earlier in this chapter when we were talking about the home field/court disadvantage. While playing at home, the athlete may try too hard to impress the home team crowd. Pressing results in *self-attention,* which tends to disrupt the automatic execution of a motor task. This causes the athlete to fall back into attending to the details of the execution of a motor task.

As can be seen in figure 14.3, there is another way that impression management associated with self-presentation can lead to a decrement in performance. This is through **self-handicapping.** Self-handicapping is a form of self-presentation because the athlete is attempting to regulate the impression that other people have of her. As

stated by Leary (1992), "[R]esearch has demonstrated that self-handicapping has a strong self-presentational component. People are more likely to self-handicap when others will be aware of their handicaps, suggesting that people erect such handicaps, in part, to protect their social images in the face of failure" (p. 346). In self-handicapping individuals make preplanned proactive use of effort reduction and performance excuses in order to protect their self-esteem from potential negative feedback within a social evaluative setting. For example, a tennis player fearing that she is going to be defeated by a superior player in a weekend tournament misses three days of practice during the week leading up to the match. This makes it possible for the athlete to make the argument to herself and to those she hopes to influence that her poor performance was due to lack of practice, and not to lack of ability or skill. If an athlete is effective in self-handicapping, he can look good if he performs poorly because of the

CONCEPT Efforts to regulate impressions that other people have of you may result in self-handicapping. Self-handicapping involves the attempt on the part of the athlete to protect the athlete against a loss of self-esteem by establishing an a priori excuse for performing poorly. Self-handicapping is related to low task and high ego orientation, and to the perception of a competitive environment.

APPLICATION The use of self-handicapping to attempt to regulate the impressions that others have of us is a common practice. It is a practice, however, that should be discouraged, because it is misleading and because it could result in other people not believing us or discounting our precompetitive attributions for failure. While self-handicapping does not necessarily result in a decrement in performance, it is manipulative and it creates an expectation of failure. Take a positive approach with the athlete: teach her to "think positive" and to try her best at all times.

pre-established cause, but also look great if he succeeds in the face of so many obstacles. Thus, the benefit of effective self-handicapping is to protect self-esteem after failure and to augment perceptions of ability after success. However, there are potential costs associated with ineffective self-handicapping. If the athlete is not convincing, or the audience does not believe the athlete's predetermined explanations for failure, others may come to perceive that the athlete suffers from a character flaw (Prapavessis, Grove, & Eklund, 2004).

A number of investigations have linked *self-handicapping* with *goal perspective theory* (Elliot, Cury, Fryer, & Huguet, 2006; Ommundsen, 2001, 2004; Ryska, Zenong, & Boyd, 1999). In all of these investigations, athletes who score high in the disposition to self-handicap also score low in

Female gymnast performing her floor exercise doing the splits in front of a large crowd. © 2009 Jupiterimages Corporation.

dispositional task goal orientation. Athletes who practice self-handicapping are less likely to value hard work, effort, and long-term dedication to learning a task. Research also shows that self-handicapping mediates the relationship between goal perspective and performance (Elliot et al., 2006). The disposition to self-handicap may be measured using the Self-Handicapping Scale (Jones & Rhodewalt, 1982).

Other recent research suggests that *self-handicapping* may be associated with directional cognitive anxiety. Specifically, Coudevylle, Ginis, Famose, and Gernigon (2008) reported an increase in the perception that cognitive anxiety facilitates basketball shooting performance following self-handicapping. In another study, adolescent elite rock climbers identified six impediments to their competitive performance, four of which were considered potential self-handicapping examples (Ferrand, Tetard, & Fontayne, 2006).

Relative to *self-presentation,* research has linked self-presentation behaviors to reduced athletic identity and to positive and negative health behaviors. Following the traumatic experience of not being selected to an all-star team, young women described themselves as being less identified with athletics in order to protect their self-image (Grove, Fish, & Eklund, 2004). A young man who practices risky driving practices to impress a young woman is engaging in negative health behavior. Conversely, a young woman who takes up a regular exercise program to impress a boyfriend is engaging in positive health behavior (Ginnis & Leary, 2004).

Summary

Zajonc's model and social facilitation research were based on the notion that the presence of an audience of one or more spectators can facilitate performance. Because Zajonc's model was based on the effect that the "sheer presence" of an audience had on performance, interactive audiences were ruled out. Because athletic competition almost always involves an interaction between athletes and spectators, Zajonc's model cannot be easily applied to sport. Therefore, the focus of this chapter was upon the effects of interactive audiences on performance.

It is well documented that the home team wins most athletic contests, but less is known about the reasons for this advantage. Research was reviewed that suggests that an audience generates functional assertive behavior in home team athletes and dysfunctional assertive behavior in visiting team athletes. Research also suggests that the home court advantage may be more of an away court disadvantage, because visiting team athletes often play below their normal level of play.

Some athletes perform better away than they do at home. This is known as the home court disadvantage. It is believed that this occurs when athletes try too hard to please the hometown fans and begin to "press." This is the self-attention effect, which interferes with skillful play.

While the size of the crowd may be an important predictor of team performance, the density of the crowd and crowd intimacy are even more important. Related to the density of the crowd is the mood of the audience. A hostile and protesting crowd can have a particularly negative effect on the visiting team as well as the officials. Team quality seems to moderate the relationship between playing site and team performance. The home court advantage is much stronger for high-quality teams than for lower-quality teams.

Self-presentation refers to the processes by which athletes monitor and control how they are perceived by other people. Self-presentation is also called impression management, and is composed of impression motivation and impression construction.

When an athlete is successful in regulating how others perceive him, social facilitation is the end result. When he is unsuccessful, the end result is self-attention. Self-handicapping is a form of self-presentation, because the athlete is attempting to regulate the impression that other people have of him.

Critical Thought Questions

1. How can the home team best take advantage of the home court advantage when playing a team of equal quality and ability? Devise a game plan in your favorite team sport.

2. How can the visiting team best prepare for an away contest when playing a team of equal quality and ability? Devise a game plan in your favorite team sport.

3. As a sport psychologist, how would you suggest working with an athlete who suffers from self-attention in front of the home crowd?

4. Imagine coaching a basketball team (or sport team of your choice) in front of an abusive and hostile crowd. Consider the fact that you will not be able to communicate with your athletes without shouting. Devise a game strategy for this situation.

5. Discuss self-handicapping as a strategy for regulating the impression that other people have for an athlete. Give specific examples in yourself and in athletes you have observed who have used self-handicapping to regulate other people's impression. Discuss the pros and cons of self-handicapping.

Glossary

archival data Data that have been saved from earlier games. Generally, official records from collegiate and professional team games are kept for many years.

audience density How crowded an audience is; how close to and intimate with the players the audience is.

away court disadvantage The notion that teams win more often at home not because of a home court advantage, but because of an away court disadvantage for the visiting team.

dysfunctional assertive behavior Aggressive or assertive behavior, such as fouling, that interferes with successful performance.

functional assertive behavior Aggressive or assertive behavior, such as rebounding, stealing, and shot blocking in basketball, that facilitates successful performance.

home advantage The notion that playing an athletic contest at home is an advantage.

home disadvantage The idea that if athletes try too hard to please an expectant audience, playing at home may actually be a disadvantage.

hostile crowd An audience that is hostile and threatening to the visiting team in a sustained and noisy way.

impression construction The process of constructing images of oneself for other people to see.

impression management The process by which people monitor and control how they are perceived by other people.

impression motivation A personal concern about how she is perceived by others and her attempts to regulate other people's impression of her.

interactive audience   An audience or crowd that interacts in various ways with the athletes. Usually the interaction is visual and auditory.

self-attention   The tendency of an athlete to "press," or try too hard to please the crowd, when playing in front of an expectant home crowd.

self-handicapping   A form of self-presentation in which people make preplanned proactive use of effort reduction and performance excuses in order to protect self-esteem.

self-presentation   The process by which people monitor and control how they are perceived by other people.

social facilitation   The benefits or detriments associated with the presence of an interactive audience.

Zajonc's model   A model of social facilitation based upon drive theory.

CHAPTER 15

Team Cohesion in Sport

KEY TERMS

Coactive sports
Conceptual model of team
  cohesion
Consequences of team cohesion
Determinants of team cohesion
Direct intervention approach
Direct measurement approach
Direction of causality
Dyadic self-determination
Dyadic sport
Group Environment
  Questionnaire
Indirect intervention approach
Indirect measurement approach
Interactive sports
Personal satisfaction
Social cohesion
Task cohesion
Team building
Team cohesion
Team efficacy
Youth Sport Environment
  Questionnaire

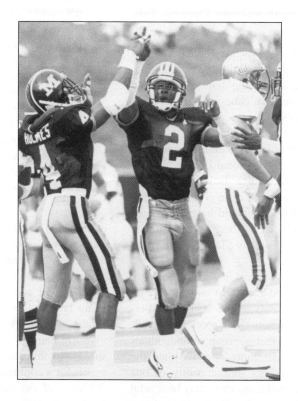

Intuitively, athletes, coaches, and sport enthusiasts understand that there is more to athletic success than the collective individual skills of the members of a team. Sport psychologists refer to this extra team ingredient as *group* or *team cohesion*. Athletes have described the presence or absence of team cohesion in interesting ways:

Naturally there are going to be some ups and downs, particularly if you have individuals trying to achieve at a high level. But when we stepped in between the lines, we knew what we were capable of doing. When a pressure situation presented itself, we were plugged into one another as a cohesive unit. That's why we were able to come back

so often and win so many close games. And that's
why we were able to beat more talented teams.
(Michael Jordan, Chicago Bulls;
Jordan, 1994, p. 23.)

We've got a funny chemistry here. It's a strange
mixture of guys. They're all good guys; I don't have
any personal problems with any of them. They are
guys who have great talent and good dispositions,
but the mix—something's not there. I can't really
explain it other than it's a strange chemistry.
(Rob Murphy, Cincinnati Reds;
Kay, 1988, p. 15.)

The first quotation was by Michael Jordan, arguably
the best professional basketball player in the history of the game, describing how the Chicago
Bulls played together as a cohesive unit to defeat
more talented teams. The second quotation was
by Rob Murphy, a relief pitcher on the 1988
Cincinnati Reds major league baseball team. After
being picked to win the National League West in
1988, the Reds suffered a lackluster season.
Murphy made his comment in an effort to explain
how the talent-laden Reds could have performed
so poorly on the field. He attributed it to a "strange
chemistry," or what was likely a lack of team cohesion among the players.

The sports pages of local newspapers are full
of examples of talented teams that failed to live up
to expectations, or less talented teams that performed far above expectations. In sport, it is a well-
established principle that a group of individuals
working together is far more effective than the
same individuals working independently of one
another. On a basketball team, there may be several
individuals capable of scoring 20 or more points a
game. However, in the interest of team success, the
coach may require that one or more of these athletes assume nonscoring roles. For example, a point
guard has the primary responsibility of setting up
plays and getting the offense started, while the
power forward must "crash" the boards and get
offensive and defensive rebounds. Athletes who
play these specialized roles rarely score as many

points as shooting guards or forwards. Yet, out
of the desire to be "team players," these athletes
accept less glamorous roles for the common good
of the team. Thus, as a group or team evolves, a
certain structure develops. This structure varies
from group to group and situation to situation, but
it is critical for team success.

When the Pistons won, I thought there might be
hope yet for the National Basketball Association.
A group of virtual unknowns who played together
as a team beat a more talented team built around
four superstars. How old-school can you get?
There's an art to putting together a team that can
compete with any other team. It isn't just a matter
of having talent at each position, or matching up
with other teams position by position. The players
have to be able to play the game, to want to play
together, to be willing to pick one another up and
to be capable of making intelligent decisions.
(Oscar Robertson (2004) commenting on the
Detroit Pistons' defeat of the Los Angeles Lakers
in the 2004 NBA Championship series.)

Not only do members of successful teams
have the ability to work together (teamwork), they
also enjoy a certain attraction to one another. In
this respect, it seems logical that teams composed
of members who like each other and enjoy playing
together will somehow be more successful than
teams lacking this quality. In 1979, the Pittsburgh
Pirates won the World Series. Their theme was
"We Are Family," suggesting that they owed their
success to this ability to get along and work together for a common goal. Ironically, the Oakland
Athletics of the early 1970s and the New York
Yankees in 1978 also enjoyed World Series success, but with well-publicized disharmony within
their ranks.

As a social psychological topic, team cohesion
ranks as a very important factor for enhancing
team performance and feelings of satisfaction
among members. It has evolved as a complex concept that requires study and additional research
before it can be fully understood and appreciated.

CONCEPT Team cohesion is a multidimensional construct that includes both task and social cohesion.

APPLICATION When considering the development of team cohesion among members of a team, it is important that the coach differentiate between task and social cohesion. These two types of cohesion can be developed simultaneously in a team, or they can be developed independently of each other. It is possible to see an athletic team develop a high degree of social cohesion, yet not enjoy athletic success due to poor task cohesion.

In the following sections, team cohesion will be discussed in terms of (a) defining characteristics of team cohesion, (b) a conceptual model of team cohesion, (c) measurement of team cohesion, (d) determinants of team cohesion, (e) consequences of team cohesion, and (f) developing team cohesion.

Defining Characteristics of Team Cohesion

Albert Carron, a prominent sport social psychologist, defined group cohesion as "a dynamic process which is reflected in the tendency for a group to stick together and remain united in the pursuit of goals and objectives" (Carron, 1982, p. 124). Because an athletic team is a group, Carron's definition of group cohesion applies equally well as a definition for **team cohesion.** Intuitively, we know that team cohesion is the elusive ingredient that changes a disorganized collection of individuals into a team.

Fundamental to the study of team cohesion is the understanding of group dynamics. Members of a team or group begin to interact with each other the moment the group is first formed. Once a group is formed, it ceases to interact with outside forces in the same manner that a collection of individuals would. The team becomes an entity in and of itself. From a Gestalt perspective, the whole (group or team) is greater than the sum of its parts.

Over the past 20 years, research on team cohesion has made it clear that one must understand two basic concepts in order to understand the relationship between cohesion and team behavior. The first is the distinction between task and social cohesion, and the second is the distinction between direct and indirect measurement of cohesion.

Task and Social Cohesion

Task and social cohesion are two independent components of team cohesion. Failure to discriminate between the two can result and has resulted in hopelessly confusing results relative to the relationship between athletic performance and team cohesion. **Task cohesion** is the degree to which members of a team work together to achieve a specific and identifiable goal. We see task cohesion on display when a baseball team turns a double play, executes a hit-and-run, or completes a double steal. We see task cohesion on display when a basketball team runs a motion offense or sets up a full-court zone defense. We see task cohesion on display when a volleyball team executes the multiple-attack offense, or defends against the same.

Social cohesion is the degree to which the members of a team like each other and enjoy personal satisfaction from being members of the team. The independence of task cohesion and social cohesion was easily observed in the example of the world champion New York Yankees baseball team of 1978. This was a team that could turn the double play, hit the cut-off man, advance runners, and work together on the field of play better than any other team in baseball. Yet, this was also a team whose members did not like one another.

Team members fought with each other, cliques were formed, and angry words were exchanged both privately and through the media.

If a study had been conducted on the 1978 Yankees to relate task cohesion and team performance, a very high and positive relationship would have been observed. Yet, if a study had been conducted to relate social cohesion and team performance, a very strong negative relationship would have been observed. If care were not taken to distinguish between the two different kinds of team cohesion in this example, confusing results would have been obtained. Such has been the case with numerous early studies on the topic of team cohesion and athlete behavior.

Direct and Indirect Measurement of Cohesion

Just as many early studies failed to differentiate between task and social cohesion, many also failed to differentiate between the two basic approaches to measuring team cohesion (Carron, 1980; Cox, 1985). The **indirect measurement approach** to assessing team cohesion tries to get at team cohesion by asking each team member how she feels about every other member of the team on some basic question (e.g., How much do you like the different members on your team?). Summed scores from team members would represent a measurement of team cohesion. The **direct measurement approach** to assessing team cohesion is direct in the sense that players are asked to indicate how much they like playing for the team (individual attraction) and how well they feel the team functions as a unit (group integration). Research using the indirect approach has generally failed to find a meaningful relationship between team cohesion and team or individual behavior. As with task and social cohesion, it is of critical importance that the approach to measuring team cohesion be reported, as results could vary greatly as a function of the approach. The indirect approach to measuring team cohesion is very rare in sport psychology research today.

A Conceptual Model of Team Cohesion

Building upon the distinction between task and social cohesion and focusing upon the direct measurement approach, Widmeyer, Brawley, and Carron (1985) developed the **conceptual model of team cohesion.** As illustrated in figure 15.1, the conceptual model is based on an interaction between the athlete's group orientation (social versus task) and the athlete's perception of the team. Task and social cohesion are relatively easy concepts to understand, given our discussion on their distinction. Conversely, perception of team is not quite so easy to understand. When an athlete conceptualizes team cohesion, is he thinking about the team as a collective whole (including himself), or is he thinking about his individual attraction to the team (he likes the style of play) and his individual

FIGURE 15.1 | Widmeyer, Brawley, and Carron's conceptual model of team cohesion.

Source: From Widmeyer, W. N., Brawley, L. R., and Carron, A. V. (1985). *The measurement of cohesion in sport teams: The group environment questionnaire.* London, Ontario: Sports Dynamics. Copyright © 1985, Spodym Publishers. Used with permission of the publisher.

CONCEPT   The conceptual approach to looking at team cohesion takes into consideration task and social cohesion as well as the athletes' perceptions of the team.

APPLICATION   The conceptual model takes into consideration the multidimensional nature of team cohesion. If the coach looks at team cohesion from a multidimensional perspective, it will be easier to understand the positive influence of team cohesion on athletic behavior. Social cohesion is different from task cohesion, and individual attraction to the group is different from group integration.

attraction to team members (they are good friends)? If he is thinking of the team as a unit, this is called group integration (GI). If he is thinking about his attraction to the team or to individual members, this is called individual attraction, or attraction to group (ATG). The combination of the two kinds of group orientation and two kinds of perception yields four different dimensions of team cohesion:

1. Group integration–social (GI-S)
2. Group integration–task (GI-T)
3. Individual attraction to the group–social (ATG-S)
4. Individual attraction to the group–task (ATG-T)

Measurement of Team Cohesion

A number of inventories have been developed for measuring team cohesion in sport. An incomplete list of inventories includes the Sports Cohesiveness Questionnaire (SCQ; Martens & Peterson, 1971); the Team Cohesion Questionnaire (TCQ; Gruber & Gray, 1981); the Sport Cohesion Instrument (SCI; Yukelson, Weinberg, & Jackson, 1984); the Group Environment Questionnaire (GEQ; Widmeyer, Brawley, et al., 1985); and the Team Psychology Questionnaire (TPQ: Partington & Shangi, 1992).

Of these five inventories, the **Group Environment Questionnaire** (GEQ) has been sport psychologists' primary inventory of choice over the last 20 years. The GEQ is composed of 18 items that measure the four team cohesion dimensions as illustrated in figure 15.1. Based upon the conceptual model of team cohesion, the GEQ devotes four items to measuring the GI-S dimension, five to the GI-T dimension, five to the ATG-S dimension, and four to the ATG-T dimension. Each item is anchored to an eight-point Likert Scale (1 = strongly disagree, 8 = strongly agree).

Despite the broad use and acceptance of the GEQ since 1985, the factorial integrity of the inventory has been challenged. In particular, an investigation reported by Schutz, Eom, Smoll, and Smith (1994) failed to confirm the hypothesized four-factor structure of the GEQ using a large sample (N = 740) of high school athletes. In addition, it was shown that a different factor structure emerged for the male and female athletes. In response to Schutz et al. (1994), Eys, Carron, Bray, and Brawley (2007) hypothesized that the internal reliability of the GEQ might be improved by converting negatively worded items into positively worded items to avoid response distortion or *response acquiescence*. The results of their investigation confirmed that the internal reliability of three of the four subscales of the GEQ was improved through this change. The researchers did not recommend that the GEQ be revised, but that the psychometric properties of the GEQ continue to be investigated. Also in response to the Schutz et al. (1994) criticism of the GEQ, Eys, Loughead, Bray, and Carron (2009a) investigated the conceptual structure of team cohesion using a qualitative research design in which 56 sport participants between the ages of 13 and 19 years were interviewed. The results of this in-depth investigation revealed that youth sport athletes conceptualized perceptions of task and social cohesion, but not of group integration (GI) and attraction to team (ATG) (see figure 15.1). Perhaps, also, in response to Schutz et al. (1994), Eys, Loughead, Bray, and Carron (2009b), developed the **Youth Sport Environment Questionnaire** (YSEQ). The YSEQ is composed of 18 items that measures task and social cohesion. It was suggested that the YSEQ be used instead of the GEQ when testing youth sport athletes between the ages of 13 to 17.

Determinants of Team Cohesion

Carron (1982) proposed a sport-specific framework for studying team cohesion determinants and consequences. As illustrated in figure 15.2, the basic conceptual framework is composed of four classes of determinants and two classes of consequences.

The basic notion is that there are certain factors that lead to or determine team cohesion, and certain consequences associated with having or not having team cohesion. In this section we will focus attention upon the **determinants of team cohesion;** in the following section, upon the consequences of team cohesion.

In an important study reported by Widmeyer and Williams (1991), factors that determine team cohesion among female collegiate NCAA Division I golfers were investigated and reported. In this investigation, team cohesion was measured using the multidimensional GEQ. The results of this investigation revealed that each specific determinant shown in figure 15.2 was predictive of some aspect of team cohesion. The strongest predictor of team cohesion, however, was **personal satisfaction.** A demonstrated way to develop team cohesion is by cultivating a personal feeling of

FIGURE 15.2 | Illustration showing determinants and consequences of team cohesion.

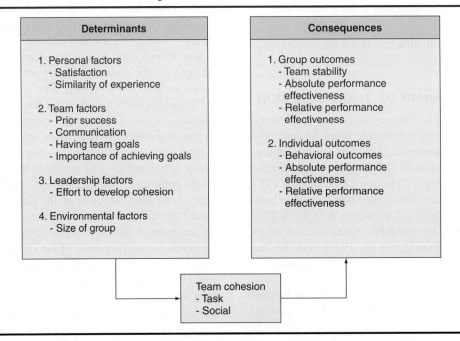

Source: From Carron, A. V. (1982). Cohesiveness in sport groups: Interpretations and considerations. *Journal of Sport Psychology, 4*(2), 131. Copyright 1982 by Human Kinetics Publishers. Adapted by permission.

A tremendous amount of task cohesion and coordinated play is required to execute the "multiple attack" in volleyball. Courtesy Ball State University Sports Information.

satisfaction toward the team and team members. (Aoyagi, Cox, & McGuire, 2008).

Satisfaction may be measured using the Athlete Satisfaction Questionnaire (ASQ; Riemer & Chelladuria, 1998). In addition to being associated with team cohesion, personal satisfaction is predicted by ambiguity and need for clarity (Bray, Beauchamp, Eys, & Carron, 2005). Specifically, as ambiguity increases, satisfaction decreases; however, this negative relationship is more pronounced if the athlete possesses a strong need for team role clarity.

Although the Widmeyer and Williams study was the most comprehensive investigation to date dealing with determinants of team cohesion, other studies have focused upon specific antecedents.

For example, team stability as an antecedent of team cohesion has been studied by Donnelly, Carron, and Chelladurai (1978), with the general finding that team stability fosters cohesion. Similarly, research by Widmeyer, Brawley, and Carron (1990) suggests that team cohesion decreases as team or group size increases.

Communication among team members is another important determinant of team cohesion that has been verified through research (Eccles & Tenenbaum, 2004; Wickwire, Bloom, & Loughead, 2004). Beach volleyball is a **dyadic sport** in which coordinated efforts and communication between two players are required for success. In a qualitative investigation, Wickwire et al. (2004) identified the ability to communicate verbally and nonverbally to be critical components for success and for developing team cohesion in men's international beach volleyball. The same would logically be true of women's beach volleyball and in other dyadic sports such as figure skating, synchronized swimming, badminton, and tennis.

Also demonstrated with athletes involved in dyadic sports (figure skating, synchronized swimming, and badminton) is the observation that individual self-determined motivation is an important predictor of team cohesion (Gaudreau & Fecteau, 2010). As individual self-determination increases, team cohesion increases. The positive association between individual self-determination and team cohesion, however, increases at a faster rate when dyadic self-determination is high. **Dyadic self-determination** moderates the relationship between individual self-determination and team cohesion and is the aggregate of the summed individual self-determination between the two members of a dyadic team.

Another important determinant of team cohesion is team efficacy or collective efficacy as first introduced in chapter 3. **Team efficacy** describes the shared feeling of confidence enjoyed by a team as a whole. It is more than a sum of the individual efficacy beliefs of the members of a team (Ronglan, 2007). Individual team members can possess great self-confidence, but until the team as

CONCEPT The feeling of personal satisfaction with the team as a whole and members generally is the strongest predictor of team cohesion in intercollegiate golf.

APPLICATION Other determinants of team cohesion, such as group size, and interpersonal communication, are of small consequence in developing team cohesion compared to personal satisfaction. Golf coaches who value team cohesion should focus on developing a feeling of satisfaction among team members.

CONCEPT Team cohesion is related to size and stability of a team or group.

APPLICATION It is difficult to maintain team cohesion in teams or groups that are constantly changing and increasing in size. Coaches and leaders who wish to increase cohesion among members must avoid constant turnover and keep groups or subgroups relatively small.

a whole enjoys a feeling of shared collective efficacy, they will not perform consistently well as a cohesive unit (Heuze & Thomas, 2007). In addition, both team cohesion and team efficacy are influenced by the team motivational climate. Specifically, both are increased in the presence of a mastery climate, but reduced in the presence of a competitive or ego motivational climate (Heuze, Sarrazin, Masiero, Raimbault, & Thomas, 2006). Collective efficacy can be measured using the Collective Efficacy Questionnaire for Sports (CEQS; Short, Sullivan, & Feltz, 2005).

Finally, the myth has been perpetuated by some groups and individuals that some form of initiatory *hazing* builds group cohesion among members of fraternities, service clubs, schools, and sport teams. This hypothesis was studied in an investigation reported by Van Raalte, Cornelius, Linder, & Brewer (2007). The results of this study, involving collegiate athletes, revealed that as reports of hazing increase, team cohesion decreases.

This result reveals that hazing is associated with a reduction in team cohesion and not an increase in team cohesion.

Consequences of Team Cohesion

Based on the research, the consequences of high levels of team cohesion are many, and include (a) improved athletic performance, (b) direction of causality for the cohesion–performance relationship, (c) improving team efficacy, (d) future participation and team stability, (e), homogeneity of team cohesion, (f) moderator of disruptive effect of self-handicapping, (g) perceived psychological momentum, and (h) enhanced mood, emotion, and satisfaction.

Improved Athletic Performance

Most research on **consequences of team cohesion** has focused upon performance. The primary question that has been asked is to what degree team cohesion leads to improved team or individual performance. This basic question is also reflected in figure 15.2, where performance is described in terms of individual and group outcomes. Absolute and relative performance effectiveness refer to the difference between winning or losing a contest, as opposed to performing better or worse than the last time. Having a team's performance reduced to a slash in the win or loss column is an absolute measure of performance effectiveness, whereas comparing a team's performance to how well it performed in the last outing is a relative measure of performance effectiveness. A similar dichotomy can be developed for the performance of individual sport athletes. From an absolute performance perspective, a golfer may not have won a golf tournament, but from a relative perspective, she may have improved her score significantly.

Research has consistently shown that a significant relationship exists between team cohesion and athletic performance (Bray & Whaley, 2001; Carron, Brawley, et al., 2004; Carron, Coleman, Wheeler, & Stevens, 2002; Carron & Dennis, 1998; Grieve, Whelan, & Meyers, 2000; Lowther & Lane, 2002; Mullen & Cooper, 1994; Widmeyer, Carron, & Brawley, 1993). This observed relationship is much stronger when task cohesion as opposed to social cohesion is involved, and when interactive as opposed to coactive sports are involved. **Interactive sports** are those team sports, such as volleyball, basketball, and football, that require members of the team to interact with one another. **Coactive sports** are those activities, such as bowling, archery, and riflery, that do not require members of the team to interact with each other for team success.

A meta-analysis published by Carron, Coleman, et al. (2002) is very supportive of the cohesion-performance relationship. This is a very important study, as it shows the strength of the relationship between team cohesion and athletic performance in numerous situations and conditions from 1967 to 2000. For example, it shows relationships using all reported studies, as well as those that used only the Group Environment Questionnaire (GEQ).

When the GEQ was used, the results show (a) a much stronger relationship between cohesion and performance for men compared to women, (b) a slightly stronger relationship for task cohesion compared to social cohesion, and (c) a much stronger relationship for subjective as opposed to objective measures of performance. It is generally believed that a stronger relationship exists between team cohesion and performance for interactive sports compared to coactive sports, but this is not entirely clear in the meta-analysis. The average effect size (measure of strength of relationship) is actually larger for coactive teams compared to interactive teams. It is likely, however, that this is due to the small number of studies that looked at coactive teams.

Direction of Causality for the Cohesion-Performance Relationship

As was briefly mentioned above, numerous investigations have verified that a significant and positive relationship exists between direct measures of team cohesion and performance in both individual and team sports. The issue of **direction of causality,** however, has been a difficult issue to resolve. Does team cohesion lead to or cause successful performance, or does successful performance lead to or cause high team cohesion? As you might guess, this is not a good "either/or" question. It is likely that high team cohesion leads to high performance, but it is also likely that successful performance leads to perceptions of team cohesion. The critical issue is which direction is the most dominant. We would like to think that the direction from team cohesion to successful performance is most dominant. Almost all athletes, however, have experienced the "halo effect" of success. When your team is winning, it is a lot easier to feel at one with your team and with your teammates.

> It was an easy season for me. . . . I'm a lot more comfortable right now . . . when you're winning everybody loves you. (Wesley Stokes, former University of Missouri–Columbia basketball player; Thompson, 2002)

CONCEPT Interactive sport teams, such as soccer, volleyball, and basketball, that enjoy high levels of task cohesion are more likely to experience performance success than equally skilled teams that are low in task cohesion.

APPLICATION It is especially important for interactive teams to work hard to develop task cohesion among members of the team. Coaches should also encourage the development of social cohesion on interactive teams and both task and social cohesion on coactive teams, but these things are less critical to team success than task cohesion is for interactive teams. Coaches should use the GEQ or some other team cohesion measurement instrument of choice to monitor task and social cohesion of interactive team members.

The direction of the relationship between team cohesion and athletic performance has been a subject of discussion and academic debate for over 25 years. Initially, it was assumed that team cohesion leads to improved performance, but then a number of well-controlled studies started to suggest just the opposite, that performance leads to cohesion. Based upon the Carron, Coleman, et al. (2002) meta-analysis, it seems safe to say that a moderately strong relationship exists between team cohesion and athletic performance regardless of direction of relationship, with the strongest relationships being observed when the two are measured concurrently. This relationship is illustrated in figure 15.3. It should be no surprise to anyone, however, that winning an athletic contest would lead to perceptions of increased cohesion among members and that losing a contest would lead to perceptions of reduced team cohesion (Boone,

Beitel, & Kuhlman, 1997; Kozub & Button, 2000; Matheson, Mathes, & Murray, 1997).

Improving Team-Efficacy

The importance of individual self-efficacy in developing self-confidence and in skilled performance was introduced in chapter 3. Research by Kim and Sugiyama (1992) likewise points to the importance of group or team-efficacy in helping teams believe that they will be successful. Teams that have developed high levels of team cohesion tend to exhibit high levels of group efficacy as well. This effect is stronger for task cohesion than for social cohesion (Kozub & McDonnell, 2000). As you will recall, team efficacy was also discussed in a previous section as a determinant of team cohesion.

Future Participation and Team Stability

For young athletes especially, it is important that the sport experience lead to the expectation of continued participation. Sport participants who exhibit high levels of social cohesion also exhibit high scores in the expectation that they will participate in sport during the following season. Thus, social cohesion is a predictor of the intention to continue sport involvement (Spink, 1995). In addition to future participation, team cohesion is also a predictor of team stability. Teams high in team cohesion are more likely to remain together for a longer period

FIGURE 15.3 | Team cohesion leads to increased team performance, but increased team performance also leads to an increase in team cohesion.

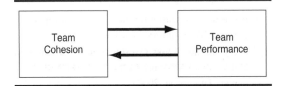

CONCEPT The winning, and even more, the losing, of an athletic contest have a strong effect upon an athlete's perceived team cohesion. This effect may even be stronger than the effect that pre-competitive team cohesion has upon team performance, but it in no way minimizes the importance of developing team cohesion in sport teams. Team cohesion, especially task cohesion, leads to improved performance of interactive team sports.

APPLICATION It is useful to understand that winning or losing can influence perceived team cohesion, but the coach must not allow this information to reduce his efforts to develop team cohesion among members of an athletic team. Team cohesion does lead to improved performance of teams that are required to work together to achieve a common goal.

of time. In an investigation reported by Spink, Wilson, and Odnokon (2010), elite male hockey players from eight teams completed the GEQ at the end of one season, and their team rosters were examined the following season to see who returned to their previous teams. Results confirmed that individuals high in task cohesion returned to their previous teams more often than those low in team cohesion.

Homogeneity of Team Cohesion

It is not enough that starters alone exhibit high levels of team cohesion. Research indicates that homogeneity of team cohesion among both starters and nonstarters is an important predictor of successful team performance. Spink (1992) showed that successful volleyball teams are characterized by high levels of team cohesion on the part of both starters and nonstarters. Conversely, less successful teams are characterized by a lack of homogeneity (agreement) in team cohesion between starters and nonstarters. This observation suggests that the coach must develop high team cohesion among all the members of a team, and not just the starters.

Moderator of the Disruptive Effects of Self-Handicapping

Introduced in chapter 14, self-handicapping represents the strategies athletes use to proactively protect their self-esteem by creating excuses for their

performance in forthcoming events through adopting or advocating impediments for success. Typical excuses might include missing practice due to injury or illness, partying and loss of sleep, school commitments or distractions, and family commitments or distractions. If success follows, the athlete or athletes can always internalize (take credit for) the victory, but if failure follows, they will have numerous external explanations as to why they have failed. This behavior causes disruption in the athlete's preparation for competition, and is therefore referred to as *self-handicapping*. Research (Carron, Prapavessis, & Grove, 1994; Hausenblas & Carron, 1996) indicates that team cohesion has a moderating effect on the trait of self-handicapping. Athletes high on the trait of self-handicapping rated the severity of disruption associated with it as low when team cohesion was low, but high when team cohesion was high. There is something about being a member of a cohesive group that makes athletes sensitive to disruptions associated with self-handicapping.

Perceived Psychological Momentum

Research by Eisler and Spink (1998) demonstrated, using high school volleyball players, that a high level of task cohesion is associated with perceived psychological momentum. As a psychological construct, perceived momentum was introduced in chapter 3. Here we learn that teams that enjoy a high level of task cohesion are more likely to enjoy the benefits of psychological momentum. There are

CONCEPT In addition to increased athletic performance, there are numerous other positive consequences associated with increased team cohesion. These include team-efficacy, sports retention, sensitivity to disruptive effects of self-handicapping, psychological momentum, and mood.

APPLICATION Even if increased team performance is not a direct result of a coach's efforts to increase team cohesion, there are many other positive consequences associated with enhanced team cohesion. Coaches should work to increase the task and social cohesion among members of athletic teams.

Development of social cohesion is an important goal for an athletic team. Courtesy University of Missouri–Columbia Sports Information.

Vallerand, & Provencher, 2009; Lowther & Lane, 2002). Research also shows an association between directional preperformance state anxiety and team cohesion. Athletes who enjoy high levels of team cohesion tend to view preperformance state anxiety as being facilitative of good performance, while those low in team cohesion tend to view preperformance state anxiety as being debilitative in terms of performance (Eys, Hardy, Carron, & Beauchamp, 2003). In an application of self-determination theory (SDT), research reported by Blanchard, Amiot, et al. (2009) shows that team cohesion increases positive emotions as well as individual satisfaction through self-determination constructs. In fact, this study provides additional support for the self-determination model as illustrated in figure 3.5 (chapter 3). Team cohesion (a social factor) predicts psychological need satisfaction (autonomy, competence, relatedness), which in turn predicts self-determined motivation, which in turn predicts both positive emotions and satisfaction.

times in an athletic contest at which the momentum seems to be in one's favor. For teams that are high in task cohesion, this perception of psychological momentum is likely to be more pronounced. Thus, we have another positive consequence of team cohesion.

Enhanced Mood, Emotion, and Satisfaction

Athletes who belong to a cohesive team enjoy increased levels of positive mood compared to teams low in team cohesion (Blanchard, Amiot, Perreault,

Developing Team Cohesion

Given that team cohesion is an important characteristic of successful teams, how can it best be developed? In this section we will address that important question in three different ways. First, we will discuss the development of team cohesion as a process. Second, we will discuss team building as a way to develop team cohesiveness among team members. Finally, we will identify specific interventions calculated to enhance team cohesion.

Team Cohesion as a Process

Very early, Tuckman (1965) described four basic stages that a team must pass through in order to emerge as a cohesive unit. These four stages include forming, storming, norming, and performing. In the *forming* stage, the athletes experience the excitement of new relationships and getting together with teammates for a common goal or cause. In the *storming* stage, the athletes struggle with the frustrations of trying to learn a new team system and of getting acquainted with teammates with whom they may have little in common. During the *norming* stage, members of the team start agreeing upon common goals and establishing what the norms of acceptable and good performance are. Finally, during the *performing* stage, the team is ready to perform as a cohesive unit.

As we look at these four stages of development, it should be clear that team cohesion should be at its lowest during the forming and storming stages. For this reason, if team cohesion is measured during one of these two early stages, one should expect it to be very low. This would be consistent with measuring team cohesion during spring training or some other preseason period of time. If you want to study the relationship between team cohesion and team performance, you should not assess team cohesion during the forming or the storming stage. The best time to measure team cohesion would be during the norming or the performing stage. If team cohesion were low during the performing stage, this could indicate that the team had not progressed as it should, and in reality might not be in the performing stage. Team building is a process that should be helpful for a team to emerge from Tuckman's four stages as a cohesive unit (Bloom, Stevens, & Wickwire, 2003).

Team Building

As described by Newman (1984, p. 27) **team building** is a process to "promote an increased sense of unity and cohesiveness and enable the team to function together more smoothly and effectively." Thus, team building is a process that should lead to cohesiveness among members of a team. In the paragraphs that follow, two *team building models* or approaches will be discussed and presented. These include the direct and indirect intervention approaches.

In the **direct intervention approach** (Eys, Loughead, et al., 2009a; Yukelson, 1997), the sport psychologist works directly with athletes and employees to empower them, through a series of educational seminars and experiences, to develop a shared vision, unity of purpose, collaborative teamwork, individual and mutual accountability, team identity, team cohesiveness, open and honest communication, and trust at all levels. Team building programs based on (a) physical challenges, (b) mutual sharing, (c) and goal setting have been suggested and tested. Using a *physical challenges* approach, Ebbeck and Gibbons (1998) demonstrated that challenging young athletes to work hard to learn physical skills can result in increased perceptions of self-worth, perceived competence, physical appearance, social acceptance, and scholastic competence. Using a *personal-disclosure and mutual sharing* approach, Dunn and Holt (2004), Holt and Dunn (2006), and Pain and Harwood (2009) showed that soccer players and ice hockey players experience increased self-understanding, team cohesion, self-confidence, player ownership, and performance through disclosure of personal stories and engaging in communication exercises. Finally, using *goal setting* as the primary team building intervention, Senecal, Loughead, and Bloom (2008) demonstrated that female high school basketball players gain an increased appreciation for cohesiveness in team sports.

In the **indirect intervention approach,** the sport psychologist teaches coaches and managers how to conduct team building with their athletes or employees. Carron, Spink, and Prapavessis (1997) proposed a four-stage indirect approach for team building. During the initial *introductory phase* the coaches learn about the general benefits of team cohesion. During the *conceptual phase,* the coaches learn to conceptualize team cohesion as a direct result of the team environment, role clarity, conformity to team norms, cooperation, goal setting, and team sacrifices. During the *practical phase*, specific team building strategies are discussed and generated. Finally, during the *intervention phase* actual interventions and strategies identified in the practical phase are applied in a real situation.

Based upon Carron, Spink, et al.'s (1997) four-stage indirect model of team building, Newin, Bloom, and Loughead (2008) conducted an investigation in which they asked peewee-level hockey coaches (a) to implement the team building intervention (stage four) with their respective hockey teams, and (b) to report back to the researchers the results of the intervention. The coaches reported back that the team building activities they implemented were instrumental in improving coach communication, team bonding, and perceived athlete player affective and cognitive gains.

A second indirect approach to team building is the Coach Effectiveness Training Program (CET) as developed by Smith & Smoll (1997a, 1997b). The purpose of the CET program is to teach coaches how to develop athletes who experience true satisfaction and feel interpersonal attraction to the team and team members. Thus, the CET program is an indirect team building program, in that the coach learns how to deliver the program to her own athletes.

Regardless of the team building approach that is implemented, recent research highlights the importance of building social support (Freeman, Rees, & Hardy, 2009) and minimizing jealousy among athletes (Kamphoff, Gill, & Huddleston, 2005). Social support from coaches, parents, and other athletes leads to improved performance, enhanced group cohesion, and increased personal satisfaction. Conversely, jealousy among athletes is an emotion that can minimize team performance, cohesion, and personal satisfaction. Jealousy in sport may be measured using the Sport Jealousy Questionnaire (SJQ-II; Kamphoff et al., 2005).

Specific Interventions Designed to Enhance Team Cohesion

In the process of team building, specific interventions are learned that, if applied, will lead to increased team cohesion among team members. Thirteen specific interventions and strategies for developing team cohesion are listed below:

1. *Acquaint each player with the responsibilities of other players.*   This can be accomplished by allowing players to play other positions during practices. This will give them an appreciation for the importance of other team players. For example, a spiker in volleyball who complains of poor setting should be given the chance to set once in a while.

2. *As a coach or teacher, take the time to learn something personal about each athlete on the team.*   People will come to appreciate and cooperate with those who know little things about them, such as a girlfriend's name, a birthday, or a special hobby.

3. *Develop pride within the subunits of large teams.*   For example, in football, the various special teams need to feel important to the team and take pride in their accomplishments. For smaller units such as basketball teams, this may not be so critical. However, the team as a whole should develop pride in its accomplishments.

4. *Develop a feeling of "ownership" among the players.*   Individual players need to feel that the team is *their* team and not the coach's team. This is accomplished by helping players become involved in decisions that affect the team and them personally. Individual players need to feel that their voice will be heard.

5. *Set team goals and take pride in accomplishments.*   Individuals and teams as a whole must have a sense of direction. Challenging but obtainable goals should be

set throughout the season. When these goals are reached, players should collectively be encouraged to take pride in their accomplishments and then set more goals.

6. *Make sure that each player on the team learns his role and comes to believe it is important.*   In basketball, only five players can be on the floor at one time. The process of keeping the other seven players happy and believing that they too are important is one of the great challenges of teaching and coaching. Each player on the team has a unique role. If players do not feel this, they will not feel they are part of the team, which will detract from team unity.

7. *Do not demand or even expect complete social tranquility.*   While it is not conducive to team cohesion to allow interpersonal conflicts to disrupt team unity, it is equally unrealistic to expect interpersonal conflicts to be completely absent. Anytime individuals are brought together in a group, there is potential for conflict. The complete elimination of any friction may actually suggest a complete lack of interest in group goals.

8. *Since cliques characteristically work in opposition to the task goals of a team, avoid their formation.*   Cliques often form as a result of (1) constant losing, (2) players' needs not being met, (3) players not getting adequate opportunities to play, and (4) coaches who promote the development of cliques through the use of "scapegoats" or personal prejudice.

9. *Develop team drills and lead-up games that encourage member cooperation.*   Many drills are designed solely for the purpose of skill development. Many other drills must be developed that teach athletes the importance of reliance upon teammates. For example, in basketball, drills that emphasize the importance of teammate assists could be emphasized.

10. *Highlight areas of team success, even when the team loses a game or match.*   Since we know from the literature that performance affects feelings of satisfaction and cohesion, the coach must capitalize on this. If a volleyball team played good team defense in a losing effort, point this out to them.

11. *Work to develop collective self-efficacy (team efficacy) in the team.*   Team efficacy is closely associated with team cohesion, so a team that believes it can succeed as a team will have a good chance of performing well. Bring the team along slowly and do not overmatch them early in the season.

12. *Develop a mastery motivational climate for the team.*   A task or mastery climate, with its emphasis upon learning and cooperation, is closely associated with team cohesion. Too much competition among teammates can be counterproductive and lead to a breakdown in team cohesion.

13. *Educate the team as to the destructive effects of jealousy and how to avoid it.*   Jealousy among teammates is negatively correlated with team cohesion and team efficacy and must be avoided.

Summary

Group or team cohesion is defined by Carron as "a dynamic process which is reflected in the tendency for a group to stick together and remain united in the pursuit of goals and objectives." Task and social cohesion are two independent components of team cohesion. Task cohesion reflects the degree to which members work together to achieve a specific goal. Social cohesion reflects the degree to which members of a team like each other and enjoy being members of the team. Both a direct and an indirect approach have been used to measure team cohesion.

The conceptual model of team cohesion is based upon an interaction between the athlete's group orientation (social versus task) and the athlete's perception of the team in terms of individual attraction and group integration. The Group Environment Questionnaire measures four team cohesion dimensions and is based upon the conceptual model of team cohesion.

Determinants of team cohesion include personal satisfaction, team factors, leadership factors, and size of group. Consequences of team cohesion include team stability, behavioral outcomes, and absolute and relative performance effectiveness.

Relative to team and individual performance, research has consistently shown that task cohesion leads to enhanced performance in interactive teams. Based upon the Carron, Coleman, et al. (2002) meta-analysis, it seems safe to say that a moderately strong relationship exists between team cohesion and athletic performance regardless of direction of relationship, with the strongest relationships being observed when the two are measured concurrently.

In addition to increased athletic performance, there are numerous other positive consequences associated with increased team cohesion. These include collective self-efficacy, sports retention, sensitivity to the disruptive effects of self-handicapping, psychological momentum, and positive mood.

The development of team cohesion may be characterized as a process that passes through the four stages of forming, storming, norming, and performing. Team building is described by Newman as a process to "promote an increased sense of unity and cohesiveness and enable the team to function together more smoothly and effectively." Direct and indirect team-building intervention approaches were discussed. Finally, 13 specific interventions were identified that are instrumental in developing team cohesion in athletic teams.

Critical Thought Questions

1. When discussing team cohesion, why is it so critical to differentiate between task and social cohesion?

2. Why is the conceptual model of team cohesion so important to our understanding of this psychological construct?

3. Discuss the determinants of team cohesion illustrated in figure 15.2 relative to the 13 interventions for developing team cohesion. Are there similarities? Should there be?

4. Discuss the issue of direction of causality between team cohesion and athletic performance. Why is this an important concept to understand?

Glossary

coactive sports Activities, such as bowling, archery, and riflery, that do not require members of a team to interact with one another for team success.

conceptual model of team cohesion A model of team cohesion that is based on an interaction between an athlete's group orientation and the athlete's perception of the team.

consequences of team cohesion Outcomes derived from team cohesion.

determinants of team cohesion Factors that cause or determine team cohesion.

direct intervention approach The accomplishment of team building by working directly with the members of a team or group.

direct measurement approach A team cohesion measurement approach that assesses team cohesion by directly asking team members how much they like playing for the team and how well they feel the team functions as a unit.

direction of causality The issue of whether team cohesion causes an improvement in performance or a good performance causes an increase in team cohesion.

dyadic self-determination The aggregate of the summed individual self-determined motivation between the two members of a dyadic team.

dyadic sport A sport, such as beach volleyball, in which coordinated efforts and communication between two players are required for success.

Group Environment Questionnaire A team cohesion measurement instrument designed to measure four dimensions of team cohesion.

indirect intervention approach The accomplishment of team building by teaching coaches and managers how to conduct team building with their athletes and employees.

indirect measurement approach A team cohesion measurement approach that assesses team cohesion by asking each team member how she feels about every other member of the team on some basic question.

interactive sports Team sports, such as volleyball, basketball, and football, that require members of a team to interact with one another.

personal satisfaction The contentment or enjoyment an individual derives from being a member of a sports team.

social cohesion The degree to which the members of a team like each other and enjoy personal satisfaction from being members of the team.

task cohesion The degree to which members of a team work together to achieve a specific and identifiable goal.

team building A process used to promote an increased sense of unity and cohesiveness and to enable a team to function together more smoothly and effectively.

team cohesion A dynamic process that is reflected in the tendency for a group or team to stick together and remain united in the pursuit of goals and objectives.

team efficacy Shared feeling of confidence enjoyed by the team as a whole and not the sum of individual efficacy beliefs.

Youth Sport Environment Questionnaire A youth sport alternative to the Group Environmental Questionnaire that measures social and task cohesion.

Leadership and Communication in Sport

KEY TERMS

Assertiveness training module
Behavioral signature
Centrality
Chelladurai's multidimensional
  model
Coach-athlete dyad
Coach Effectiveness
  Training (CET)
Coaching Behavior Assessment
  System (CBAS)
Coaching competence
Coaching efficacy
Conceptual model of coaching
  efficacy
Consideration
Fiedler's contingency theory
Functional model of leadership
"Great man" theory of leadership
Initiating structure
Jowett model of coach-athlete
  dyad relationship
Leadership behavior model
Life cycle theory
Path-goal theory
Personality paradox
Positive sandwich approach
Propinquity
Reactive behaviors

Relationship motivation
Situation-specific behavior
  theories
Situational behaviors
Situational traits
Spontaneous behaviors
Stacking
Task dependence

Task motivation
3 + 1 Cs model of coach-
  athlete relationship
Transactional leadership
Transformational leadership
Universal behavior theory
Universal behaviors
Universal traits

It is much easier to point to examples of great leadership than it is to explain what great leadership is. For example, in sport, it would be hard to find greater examples of successful leadership than Vince Lombardi, Pat Head Summitt, and John Wooden. The critical questions, however, are these: Why were they great leaders, and can we learn from them?

Vince Lombardi will forever be linked with the unprecedented success of Green Bay Packers professional football. Lombardi had an unquenchable desire to succeed, to excel, and to win. He was famous for slogans placed in locker rooms and upon walls where the players could see them. One of his favorite slogans was, "Winning is not everything. It is the only thing." (Kramer, 1970; Wiebush, 1971). Not to be outdone by Vince Lombardi, George Steinbrenner, former principal owner of the New York Yankees baseball team, was quoted as saying, "For us, winning isn't the only thing, it's second to breathing" (Kepner, 2003).

Pat Head Summitt, women's basketball coach at the University of Tennessee, has enjoyed unprecedented success as a leader and coach. Coach Summitt is one of the most successful coaches in America and ranks with any male coach in terms of success (Wrisberg, 1990).

John Wooden, the most successful basketball coach in college history, won ten NCAA national championships at UCLA. Seven of those wins were in a row, beginning in 1967 and ending in 1973. On Wooden's coaching style, Bill Walton (2000) said this of his former college coach:

> Wooden was a teacher. He taught on a constant basis, from showing us how to put our shoes and socks on, to building a foundation based on the human values and personal characteristics embodied in what he called his Pyramid of Success. All of this was done in the subtlest of ways. While our practices were the most demanding endeavors, both physically and emotionally, that I've ever been a part of, there was always the sense of people having fun playing a simple game.

Sometimes, though, leaders lead simply by example. Pat Tillman's story is both tragic and inspirational (Smith, 2004). While on patrol in the mountains of Afghanistan with other United States Army Rangers, he was killed by friendly fire. This was tragic, but the rest of the story was truly inspirational. Prior to interrupting his National Football League (NFL) career with the Arizona Cardinals, he had signed a three-year, 3.6-million-dollar contract. He gave this up to volunteer for the Army Rangers to fight the Taliban and Al-Qaeda in Afghanistan.

In a sense, the first 15 chapters of this textbook have been dedicated to understanding the psychology of the athlete, while this chapter on leadership is dedicated to understanding the psychology of leadership, or of the athletic coach. To this end, some sport psychologists have pointed out that the sport psychology literature has been primarily devoted to athletes, while the needs and psychological skills of coaches have been largely ignored (Allen & Shaw, 2009; Giges, Petitpas, & Vernacchia, 2004). Consistent with this sentiment, Thelwell, Weston, Greenlees, and Hutchings (2008) reported on a qualitative investigation, in which they interviewed 13 elite-level coaches relative to where, when, and for what purpose coaches use psychological methods to develop psychological skills. Results showed that these coaches use self-talk and imagery more frequently than relaxation training and goal setting.

In some ways, the complexity of the concept of leadership is overwhelming. It is like a puzzle that makes little sense until each piece is put in its place. In an attempt to master this puzzle, this chapter is organized into the following five sections: (a) leadership theory classification system, (b) situations-specific sport models of leadership, (c) predicting coaching outcomes from coaching efficacy and competence, (d) coach-athlete communication and compatibility, and (e) player position, leadership opportunity, and stacking.

FIGURE 16.1 · | A classification scheme for four types of leadership theories.

		Characteristics of leaders	
		Traits	**Behaviors**
Generality of situation	**More universal**	Trait or "great man" theory • Great leaders are born with personality traits that lead to success in all situations.	Michigan and Ohio State studies • Great leaders possess general behavioral characteristics that can be learned.
	More specific	Fiedler's contingency theory • Personality traits that lead to leader effectiveness in one situation may lead to failure in another.	Situation-specific theories • Effective leadership is a function of learned behaviors that are situation specific.

Source: From Behling, O., & Schriesheim, C. (1976). *Organizational behavior: Theory, research, and application.* Boston, MA: Allyn and Bacon. Copyright © 1976 Allyn and Bacon, Inc. Used with permission.

Leadership Theory Classification System

Early interest in leadership centered on the traits or abilities of great leaders. It was believed that great leaders were born and not made. Since these early beginnings, leadership research has evolved from an interest in the behavior of leaders to the notion of situation-specific leadership. The notion of an evolution in leadership thought is useful, but it suggests that the early researchers were somehow naive and behind the times. But a careful analysis of the writings of some of the early researchers reveals that they were as aware of our "modern" concerns for situation-specific leadership as we are today. For example, Metcalf and Urwick (1963, p. 277) quoted management theorist Mary Parker Follett as saying, "Different situations require different kinds of knowledge, and the man possessing the knowledge demanded by a certain situation tends in the best managed business . . . to become the leader of the moment."

Perhaps the most significant contribution to understanding the various approaches to categorizing leadership theory has come from Behling

and Schriesheim (1976). They developed a typology of leadership theory that is illustrated in figure 16.1. Their typology categorizes the four major approaches to studying leadership, according to whether the theory deals with leadership traits or leadership behaviors, and whether the traits or behaviors are universal or situation specific in nature.

Leadership traits are relatively stable personality dispositions such as intelligence, aggressiveness, and independence. *Leadership behaviors* have to do with the observed behavior of leaders and have little to do with their personalities. Traits found in *all* successful leaders are referred to as **universal traits,** as opposed to **situational traits.** Situational traits and **situational behaviors** are those traits and behaviors that may help make a leader successful in one situation, but are of little value in another. Research reported by Cratty and Sage (1964) underscores the time-honored importance of this concept. They conducted a study in which a fraternity pledge class (led by the pledge class president) competed against a loosely organized group of students who did not know one another. The task consisted of going through a maze while blindfolded. The a priori hypothesis

CONCEPT There are four possible explanations for effective leadership. These explanations are that (a) the leader possesses universal personality traits that will make her successful in any situation, (b) the leader possesses universal behaviors that will make her successful in any situation, (c) the leader possesses specific personality traits that will make her successful in some situations but not others, and (d) the leader possesses specific behaviors that will make her successful in some situations but not others.

APPLICATION There are many different theories of leadership. The important principle to understand is that they all can be categorized using the Behling and Schriesheim classification system. Once this has been accomplished, then it is possible to study and test a theory consistent with predictions. In considering a successful leader, it is instructive to see how they fit into the typology illustrated in figure 16.1.

---

was that the pledge class would do better because of their well-established lines of communication and leadership. In fact, the group having no previous association with each other outperformed the pledge class. The reason for this finding was the quality of the leadership. The pledge group tended to rely on the pledge president, who had no specific experience with such things as navigating a maze blindfolded. However, from the independent group, a leader quickly emerged who had obvious skills at navigating the maze. The members of this group turned to him for instructions and tips that allowed them to outperform their competitors. They were not hampered by a leader who had no useful skills for this task.

Universal Trait Theories of Leadership

> I think there are people God put on this earth to be natural-born leaders, and Gary is one of them (Matt Simon's assessment of Gary Pinkel, football coach, University of Missouri–Columbia; Matter, 2000, p. B1).

Trait theory has its origin in the **"great man" theory of leadership,** which suggests that certain great leaders have personality traits and personality characteristics that make them ideally suited for leadership. The heyday of trait leadership theory began with the development of objective personality tests in the 1920s and lasted until the end of World War II. Proponents of trait theory believe

that successful leaders have certain personality characteristics or leadership traits that make it possible for them to be successful leaders in *any* situation. Since these personality traits are relatively stable, it should be possible to identify potential leaders simply by administering a personality inventory. This approach had a great deal of support from social scientists prior to and during World War II, but after the war, support waned rapidly.

The beginning of the decline in trait leadership theory occurred shortly after Stogdill (1948) published his review of 124 trait-related studies. His review and general conclusions led social scientists to discredit the universal trait theory of leadership. It was simply not possible to demonstrate that successful leaders possessed a universal set of leadership traits. A comparable review of sport-related literature led Sage (1975) to make the same conclusion relative to leadership in sport.

Universal Behavior Theories of Leadership

Shortly after World War II, the focus in leadership research turned from universal traits to **universal behaviors** of successful leaders. It was believed that successful leaders had certain universal behaviors. Once these universal behaviors were identified, they could be taught to potential leaders everywhere. This approach to leadership was very optimistic, since anyone could learn to be a successful leader

CONCEPT   There is no such thing as a universal set of personality traits common to all successful leaders.

APPLICATION   Prospective coaches should not be discouraged if they do not share common personality traits with the famous leaders and coaches in sport.

CONCEPT   Leadership behaviors can be learned, while personality traits cannot.

APPLICATION   The distinct advantage of the behavioral approach to effective leadership as opposed to the personality trait approach is that leader behaviors can be learned. Coaches who lack the necessary skills to be effective leaders can learn these skills by studying the universal behaviors possessed by successful leaders.

simply by learning certain predetermined behavioral characteristics. If these universal behaviors could be mastered, then anyone could be a successful leader. Unlike trait theory, the belief was that *leaders are made, not born.* The driving force behind this approach to leadership came from two different sources at approximately the same time: Ohio State University and the University of Michigan.

Two important products or concepts emerged from the universal behavior research conducted at Ohio State University and the University of Michigan during the 1950s and early 1960s. First was the development and refinement of the Leader Behavior Description Questionnaire (LBDQ), from which most of the universal behavior research was derived (Halpin, 1966). Second was the identification of consideration and initiating structure as the two most important factors characterizing the behaviors of leaders. **Consideration** refers to leader behavior that is indicative of friendship, mutual trust, respect, and warmth between the leader and subordinates. Conversely, **initiating structure** refers to the leader's behavior in clearly defining the relationship between the leader and subordinates, and in endeavoring to establish well-defined patterns of organization, channels of communication, and methods of procedure.

These two kinds of behavior are considered to be relatively independent but not necessarily incompatible. That is, a leader could be high in both consideration and initiating structure. It is not necessary, according to the construct, to be high in one and low in the other. Interestingly, the Michigan studies resulted in two nearly identical universal behaviors associated with leadership (Kahn & Katz, 1960).

The two general dimensions of leadership behavior identified in the Ohio State and Michigan studies have provided a basic framework for many leadership theories. Often the terms *initiating structure* and *consideration* have not been used, but compatible terms have been. Yet the general nature of these two categories has resulted in confusion about the terms used to describe them. Table 16.1 presents some of these terms in relation to the labels that have been used. Such leadership styles as authoritarianism, production orientation,

CONCEPT Consideration and initiating structure are the two most important factors characterizing the behavior of leaders.

APPLICATION Coaches and leaders of sport teams should strive to establish well-defined patterns of organization and communication, while at the same time displaying the behaviors of friendship, trust, respect, and warmth.

TABLE 16.1 | Leadership Styles Equivalent to Consideration and Initiating Structure

Consideration	Initiating Structure
Relationship motivated	Task motivated
Democratic	Autocratic
Egalitarian	Authoritarian
Employee oriented	Production oriented
Transformational	Transactional

FIGURE 16.2 | Predicting leadership effectiveness as a function of the universal behaviors of consideration and initiating structure.

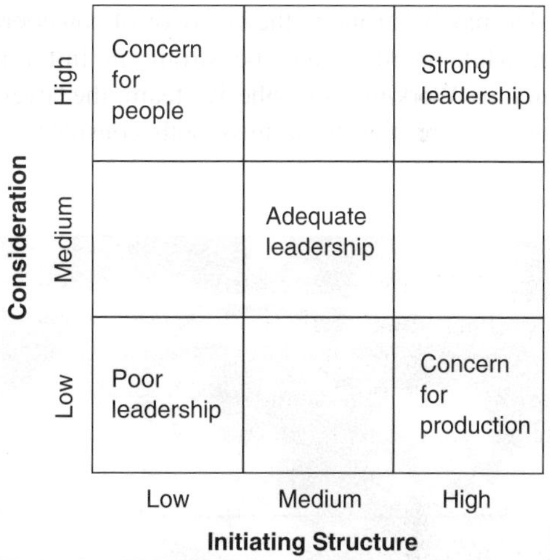

and autocratic leadership are roughly equivalent to the notion of initiating structure. Leadership styles with such labels as democratic, egalitarian, and employee oriented reflect the notion of consideration. Leadership styles that are basically autocratic in nature tend toward behavior that can best be explained in terms of initiating structure or production emphasis. Leadership styles that are basically democratic in nature tend toward behavior that can best be explained in terms of consideration and employee orientation.

Most recently, two additional leadership styles have been identified that are basically equivalent to consideration and initiating structure (Bass & Avolio, 2000; Rowold, 2006). These two styles are the transformational and the transactional leadership styles. **Transformational leadership,** like *consideration,* is based on inspirational motivation, idealized influence, intellectual stimulation, and individualized consideration. Conversely, **transactional leadership,** like *initiating structure,* is based on rewards for productivity, performance monitoring, and error intervention.

The Multifactor Leadership Questionnaire-5X (MLQ-5X; Bass & Avolio, 2000) was developed to measure these two leadership constructs.

If you believe in the **universal behavior theory** of leadership, then you believe that individuals can be taught to be effective leaders by learning how to exhibit the behaviors of consideration and initiating structure in the proper proportions. Organizations that believe in the universal behavior theory conduct management and leadership seminars to teach their managers how to be effective leaders. Theoretically, the most effective leader would exhibit high levels of both consideration and initiating structure. As reflected in figure 16.2,

CONCEPT Leaders tend to be endowed with a disposition toward task motivation or relationship motivation.

APPLICATION Coaches should learn to recognize their own personality dispositions and work to compensate for their weaknesses through personal adjustments or through the help of assistant coaches. If the head coach is a task-motivated person, a relationship-motivated assistant coach might be hired to provide the personal touch. Coaches should also work to improve the favorableness of the situation.

Fiedler's contingency theory has intuitive appeal and some research support (Fiedler, Chemers, & Mahar, 1977). Perhaps the most controversial aspect of the theory is the basic proposition that *leadership training programs are of little value.* Leadership training programs only help the leader learn how to enhance power and influence. However, increased power and influence would not benefit the relationship-oriented person, who does best in a moderately favorable situation. Therefore, Fiedler proposes that there are only two ways to improve leadership effectiveness. The first involves changing a leader's personality. This is unlikely to happen, since core personality dispositions cannot be easily changed. The second approach involves modifying the degree to which the situation is favorable to a certain type of leader. Fiedler suggests that this could be done by adjusting some aspect of organizational structure, or looking for leaders who possess personality characteristics consistent with existing structure and situational favorableness.

Intuitively, one can think of many examples in which Fiedler's theory could apply in sport. Doug Collins, a former coach of the Chicago Bulls professional basketball team, provides a good example. Because of the nature of his emotional volatility, Collins was able to take a young team to near stardom during his early years with the Bulls. His volatile personality was useful in motivating a young and unpredictable team. However, this same personality characteristic became a liability as the Bulls matured as a team and began to tune him out (McCallum, 1991). History records that Collins was fired after the 1988–89 season and replaced by Phil Jackson. It was Jackson who eventually led the Bulls to six World Championships.

A second example would be Johnny Keane. Following the failure of the New York Yankees to win the World Series in 1964, the Yankees fired Yogi Berra, a manager with a light touch, and hired the rules-conscious Johnny Keane.

> It would be the wrong team for him. He was a manager who was better with younger players than older ones, and this was a team of aging stars whose best years were behind them (Halberstam, 1994, p. 352).

The Yankees finished the 1965 season with a losing record of 77–85, and Johnny Keane was fired the following year.

Situation-Specific Behavior Theories of Leadership

Many contingency theories of leadership, or theories that hypothesize an interaction between the leader and the situation, have been studied. The basic difference between Fiedler's contingency theory and those that are to be discussed in this section is that Fiedler insists on looking at relatively stable personality traits, as opposed to behaviors. The theories in this section view leadership as a function of the interaction between *leader behavior* in a specific situation and the situation itself.

Some of the **situation-specific behavior theories** are these: path-goal theory (House & Mitchell, 1974); life cycle theory (Hersey & Blanchard, 1977); adaptive-reactive theory (Osborn & Hunt, 1975); leader-member exchange theory

CONCEPT The basic proposition of path-goal theory is that the function of the leader is to assist the follower in achieving his goals.

APPLICATION To be an effective leader, the coach must assist the athlete in selecting worthwhile goals and by pointing out the "path" to follow to successfully reach goals.

CONCEPT The type of leadership behavior appropriate for any given situation may be mediated by the maturity level of the athlete.

APPLICATION While it is difficult to predict which leadership behavior is best for specific maturity levels, coaches and leaders must be sensitive to the maturity level of the athlete.

(Case, 1998); and the normative model of decision making (Vroom & Yetton, 1973). Unfortunately, space does not allow a thorough review of each of these theories; the first two will be considered because of their potential application to athletics. Situation-specific sport models of leadership will be discussed in the next major section of the chapter.

Path-Goal Theory In Fiedler's theory, the emphasis is on the personality of the leader and the favorableness of the situation. In **path-goal theory,** the emphasis is on the needs and goals of the subordinate or the athlete. In other words, the leader is viewed as a *facilitator.* The coach or leader helps athletes realize their goals. The leader's success is viewed in terms of whether or not the subordinates achieve their goals. Thus, the basic proposition of path-goal theory is that the function of the leader is to provide a "well-lighted path" to assist the follower in achieving goals. This is done by rewarding subordinates for goal attainment, pointing out roadblocks and pitfalls on the path to success, and increasing the opportunities for personal satisfaction. For example, if an athlete's goal

is to break a school record in the mile run, it is the coach's job to provide a training program that is rewarding and enables the athlete to accomplish this goal.

Life Cycle Theory Like path-goal theory, **life cycle theory** places the emphasis in leadership behavior on the subordinates and not on the leader. The appropriate leadership style for any specific situation depends on the maturity of the subordinate. Two types of leadership behavior, conceptualized in terms of relationship behavior (consideration) and task behavior (initiating structure), are possible. The appropriate combination of task and relationship behavior depends on the maturity of the follower. Maturity is defined in terms of the capacity to set and obtain goals, willingness and ability to assume responsibility, and education and/or experience. According to this model, the need for task structure behavior decreases with increased maturity. However, the need for relationship behavior forms an inverted U relative to maturity. At low and high levels of maturity, relationship behavior should be low, but at the moderate levels of maturity it should be high.

Situation-Specific Sport Models of Leadership

In the previous section, we discussed the Behling and Schriesheim (1976) general leadership classification system as illustrated in figure 16.1. In this section we focus upon situation-specific sport models of leadership theory. These are theories that have been proposed by sport psychologists to explain how leader personality traits and leader behaviors lead to desired outcomes in athletes.

Smith's Sport Personality Contingency Model

Smith's Sport Personality contingency model is an example of a sport-specific model that would fit into the lower left-hand quadrant of figure 16.1. Based upon Mischel and Shoda's (1995) cognitive-affective processing (personality) system (CAPS) Smith's (2006) model describes how a leader's personality interacts with the environmental situation to elicit a coaching behavior response. However, before this can happen, the personality and the situation are filtered through a five-element CAPS filtering system as shown in figure 16.4. The five components of the filtering system are as follows:

1. Encodings and personal constructs
2. Beliefs and expectancies
3. Affects and emotional responses
4. Goals and values
5. Skills and self-regulatory competencies

According to the model, the five CAPS elements interact with each other and with the presented situation and personality of the leader to produce the resultant behavioral response. It is this behavioral response that influences athlete behavior. According to Smith, coaches have a coaching **behavioral signature** that is a function of the situation, the leader's personality, and the CAPS filtering elements. Even though the leader's personality remains unchanged, the dynamic CAPS process does not always yield the same behavioral response. This is referred to as the **personality paradox.** The Smith model is classified here as a contingency model, because leader behavior is contingent upon a specific situation and the unchanging personality of the leader. Even though leaders have different coaching behavior signatures, research does suggest that coaches generally exhibit more supportive behaviors compared to instructional behaviors, and more instructional behaviors compared to punitive behaviors.

Situation-Specific Sport Behavioral Models

In this section, we discuss two sport leadership models that are based upon specific leader behaviors. These include Chelladurai's multidimensional model of leadership and Smith's leadership

FIGURE 16.4 | The cognitive-affective personality system (CAPS) leadership model.

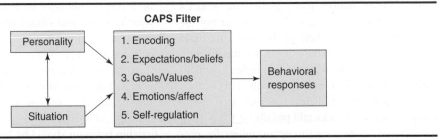

Source: Based on Smith (2006)

behavior model. These two leadership models are examples of leadership theories that fit into the lower right-hand quadrant of figure 16.1.

Chelladurai's Multidimensional Model of Leadership

Chelladurai's (1978, 1993) **multi-dimensional model** of leadership, illustrated in figure 16.5, provides an interactional approach to conceptualizing the leadership process. In this model, athlete satisfaction and performance are viewed as the products of the interaction of three components of leadership: prescribed leader behavior, preferred leader behavior, and actual leader behavior. *Prescribed leader behaviors* are those that conform to the established norms of the organization. In the military, for example, officers are expected to behave in a certain manner in the presence of their subordinates. *Preferred leader behaviors* are those behaviors that are preferred by the athletes. For example, members of a rugby team might prefer that the coach socialize with the team after a game. Finally, *actual leader behaviors* are those behaviors that the leader exhibits, irrespective of the norms or preferences of the team (as perceived by athlete).

Based on the model illustrated in figure 16.5, Chelladurai hypothesized certain consequences of the *congruence* among the three types of leader behavior. As can be observed in figure 16.6, congruence between all three types of leader behavior should promote ideal performance and satisfaction. A laissez-faire outcome is predicted when all three leader behaviors are incongruent with one another. If actual behavior is incongruent with both prescribed and preferred leader behavior, it is expected that the leader will be removed. If the prescribed and actual behaviors are congruent, but both are incongruent with preferred behavior, performance may be high, but athletes may be dissatisfied. Finally, if actual and preferred behavior are congruent, but prescribed behavior is incongruent, athletes may be satisfied, but performance may suffer.

The Leadership Scale for Sport (LSS) was developed by Chelladurai and Saleh (1980) for measuring coaching behavior in sport. Composed of 40 items, the LSS measures the following five coaching behaviors: training and instruction, autocratic behavior, democratic behavior, social support, and positive feedback. Preferred and

FIGURE 16.5 | Chelladurai's mediated multidimensional model of leadership.

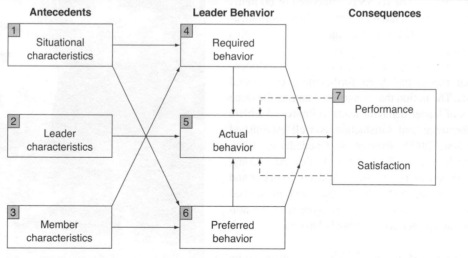

Source: Chelladurai, P. (1993). Leadership. In R. N., Singer, M., Murphey, & L. K. Tennant (Eds.), *Handbook of research on sport psychology* (pp. 647–671). New York, NY: Macmillan. Figure (p. 648) reproduced with permission of Cengage Learning, Inc. (cengage.com/permissions).

FIGURE 16.6 | Leader behavior congruence and outcomes.

Leader Behavior			Outcome
Prescribed	*Actual*	*Preferred*	
+	+	+	Ideal
−	−	−	Laissez-faire
+	−	+	Removal of leader
+	+	−	Performance
−	+	+	Satisfaction

+ Congruence with other types of behavior

− Lack of congruence with other types of behavior

Source: From P. Chelladurai and A. V. Carron, *Leadership.* Copyright © 1978 by the Canadian Association for Health, Physical Education and Recreation. Used with permission of the publisher.

actual (perceived) coaching behaviors are determined by administering the LSS to athletes and asking them to complete the inventory according to the coaching behaviors they prefer or according to the coaching behaviors they observe in their coach. Prescribed coaching behaviors are determined by administering the LSS to coaches and asking them to complete the inventory relative to how they believe they coach. More recently, the LSS was revised (RLSS) by Zhang, Jensen, and Mann (1997). The RLSS is composed of 60 items measuring six behaviors. The six behaviors measured by the RLSS include the original five, plus situational consideration behavior.

General support for Chelladurai's multidimensional model has been forthcoming on several fronts. The notion that congruence among the three types of leader behavior leads to improved athlete performance and satisfaction is well established (Andrew, 2009; Riemer & Chelladurai, 1995, 1998; Riemer & Toon, 2001; Vealey, Armstrong, Comar, & Greenleaf, 1998). Athletes do better and are more satisfied when actual and prescribed coaching behavior of coaches agree with the athletes' own preferred coaching behaviors.

Leadership Behavior Model   As proposed by Smoll and Smith (1989), the **leadership behavior model** is based upon situation-specific behaviors

Communication between coach and athlete is important.
Courtesy University of Missouri–Columbia Sports Information.

CONCEPT Discrepancies between an athlete's preferred coaching behavior and actual (perceived) or prescribed coaching behavior have a measurable effect on the athlete's performance and/or satisfaction.

APPLICATION Athletes enter into the athletic environment with certain predetermined expectations about coaching behavior. Coaches should take this into account as they attempt to motivate athletes to superior performance.

FIGURE 16.7 | Leadership behavior model.

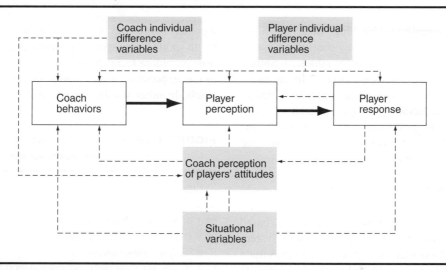

of the leader. As illustrated in figure 16.7, the model's central process is defined with solid lines leading from *coach behaviors* to *player perception* of coach behaviors to *player responses*. In the model, player perception *mediates* the relationship between coach behaviors and player response. The dotted lines in the model represent the effect of various other variables upon the central process. In the model, coach individual difference variables include such factors as goals, intentions, perceptions of self/athletes, and gender. Player individual difference variables include such things as age, gender, perceptions about coach, motivation, anxiety, and self-confidence. Situational factors

include things like nature of the sport, competitive level, success/failure, and team cohesion. The dotted line leading from player individual difference variables to coach behaviors was added to the model to reflect research by Kenow and Williams (1992). Coach behavior is influenced by the coach's perception of the individual athlete. A coach may treat an athlete who exhibits high anxiety or low self-confidence differently from other athletes. To some degree, behaviors exhibited by coaches are grounded in self-determination theory. To measure the controlling aspect of a coach's behavior, Bartholomew, Ntoumanis, and Thogersen-Ntoumanis (2010) developed the

CONCEPT A low correlation exists between a coach's observed behavior and his perception of coaching behaviors.

APPLICATION In order to be effective, a coach needs to be more aware of observed coaching behaviors and less influenced by inaccurate self-perceptions of his behavior. Coaches of youth sports teams could take turns observing each other's reactive and spontaneous behaviors and recording them. The CBAS is very easy to learn. All verbal and body-language responses are categorized into one of 12 categories.

15-item Controlling Coaching Behavior Scale (CCBS). The CCBS measures controlling use of rewards, conditional regard for athlete, intimidation, and excessive personal control. In summary, the leadership behavior model provides a framework for leadership behavior research in sport. Related to the leadership behavior model is the coaching behavioral assessment system and the coach effectiveness training program.

Coaching Behavior Assessment System Coaching behaviors have been studied extensively by Smith and Smoll (1997a). Their research, based upon the **Coaching Behavior Assessment System (CBAS)** as illustrated in figure 16.8, focuses upon reactive and spontaneous behavior of coaches. In the CBAS, a trained observer keeps track of eight different types of reactive behaviors and four different types of spontaneous behaviors.

Reactive behaviors are coach reactions to player or team behaviors. For example, a player makes a mistake and the coach responds by verbally chastising the player. **Spontaneous behaviors** are initiated by the coach and do not occur in response to player behavior.

Research with the CBAS has revealed a number of interesting relationships. When they are working with youth sports athletes, the dominant behaviors of coaches are positive reinforcement, general technical instructions, and general encouragement. The behaviors of keeping control (maintaining order) and administering punishment (punitive behavior) are perceived by players to occur much more often than they actually do.

Another interesting finding is that coaches of youth sports teams spend a greater amount of their time providing technical instruction and feedback to low-expectation youth than to high-expectation youth. In other words, the coach does not favor

FIGURE 16.8 | Coaching behavior assessment system.

Class I. Reactive behaviors
A. Player performs well
   1. Positive reinforcement (R)
   2. Nonreinforcement (NR)
B. Player makes mistake
   3. Mistake-contingent encouragement (EM)
   4. Mistake-contingent technical instruction (TIM)
   5. Punishment (P)
   6. Punitive TIM (TIM + P)
   7. Ignoring mistakes (IM)
C. Player misbehaves
   8. Keeping control (KC)

Class II. Spontaneous behaviors
A. Game-related
   9. General technical instruction (TIG)
   10. General encouragement (EG)
   11. Organization (O)
B. Game-irrelevant
   12. General communication (GC)

Source: From Smith, R. E., Smoll, F. L., & Hunt, E. (1977). A system for the behavioral assessment of athletic coaches. *Research Quarterly, 48,* 401–407. Reprinted by permission of the publisher, the American Alliance for Health, Physical Education, Recreation and Dance.

CONCEPT   Well-planned leadership training programs are effective in teaching coaches how to be good leaders.

APPLICATION   Effective coaching behaviors can be learned. Therefore, coaches should be encouraged to attend training sessions designed to teach effective leadership skills.

the athletes she expects to be the better performers (Horn, 1984; Smoll, Smith, Curtis, & Hunt, 1978).

The CBAS has also been utilized as a measurement tool to determine if behavioral training programs are effective in teaching youth sports coaches to be better and more effective leaders of youth. Research has demonstrated that well-conceived, well-planned efforts to train coaches are effective. Desirable coaching behaviors can be identified and conveyed to new coaches. Furthermore, improved coaching behaviors result in benefit to the young athletes in the form of greater satisfaction and reduced anxiety (Barnett, Smoll, & Smith, 1992; Meeus, Serpa, & DeCuyper, 2010; Smith, Smoll, & Barnett, 1995; Smith, Smoll, & Curtis, 1979).

More recently, research with the CBAS shows that coaches who engage in high frequencies of supportive behaviors, such as positive reinforcement and mistake-contingent encouragement, facilitate the development of teams whose members like the coach and like playing with each other. Conversely, negative interpersonal coaching behaviors, such as punishment and negative criticism, promote the development of teams whose members don't like the coach and don't like playing with each other (Smith & Smoll, 1997a; Smith, Shoda, Cumming, & Smoll, 2009).

Perhaps the most consistent finding involving the use of the CBAS with youth coaches is that there is very little relationship between behaviors actually exhibited by coaches and the coaches' perceptions of their own behaviors. Conversely, children's perception of coaches' behaviors are more highly correlated with actual coaching behaviors. This finding underscores the critical need for objectively recording behaviors of coaches, as their own perception of their behavior is not always accurate. Coaches are simply unaware of how often they really use different kinds of reactive and spontaneous behaviors (Smoll & Smith, 1999).

While the CBAS has been the most widely studied system for observing and documenting coaching behaviors in youth sports, it is not the only one. A case in point is the Arizona State University Observation Instrument (ASUOI) developed by Lacy and Darst (1984). The ASUOI is composed of 17 behavioral categories, seven of which are directly related to instruction. It has been utilized in studying coaching behaviors in American football, tennis, gymnastics, basketball, and soccer. Research with the ASUOI has tended to focus upon behaviors of coaches of adult athletes as opposed to those of youth sport athletes. A case in point is an investigation reported by Becker and Wrisberg (2008), in which coach Pat Summitt's verbal and nonverbal behaviors were videorecorded and coded across six practices during the 2004–05 NCAA Division I women's basketball season using the ASUOI instead of the CBAS. A total of 3,296 behaviors were observed and summarized as follows:

1. Fifty-five percent of all behaviors were directed toward the team while 45 percent were directed toward individuals.

2. Fifty-five percent of all behaviors were instructional in nature while 45 percent were noninstructional in nature (e.g., hustle, praise, scold, management, other).

3. Of the 1,468 noninstructional behaviors, 15 percent involved scolding, 33 percent involved praise, and 24 percent involved hustle encouragement.

CONCEPT Coach effectiveness training is based upon five basic principles derived from research using the Coaching Behavioral Assessment System (CBAS). Two of the principles deal with the importance of deemphasizing winning, and the importance of focusing upon only positive coaching behaviors (positive reinforcement, encouragement, sound technical instruction).

APPLICATION The use of the "positive sandwich approach" provides a means whereby the coach can give reinforcement, encouragement, and technical instructions to an athlete in a completely positive and complimentary way. Young athletes frequently interpret technical instructions to be a form of criticism, so it is important for the youth coach to master and refine her ability to deliver a technical instruction sandwiched between two complimentary statements.

4. No differences in quality or quantity of coaching feedback observed between high- and low-expectancy athletes.

As an extension of the CBAS, Coach Effectiveness Training (CET) was developed to assist coaches in learning leadership skills appropriate for youth sports. A summary of their research findings and the foundation of CET is captured in the following quotation from Smith and Smoll (1997a, p. 17):

> Not surprisingly, we found that the most positive outcomes occurred when children played for coaches who engaged in high levels of positive reinforcement for both desirable performance and effort, who responded to mistakes with encouragement and technical instruction, and who emphasized the importance of fun and personal improvement over winning. Not only did the children who had such coaches like their coaches more and have more fun, but they also liked their teammates more.

Looking once more at the leadership behavioral model as illustrated in figure 16.7, we note that the CBAS was developed by Smith, Smoll, and Hunt (1977) to measure actual observed leadership behaviors. In order to measure player perception of leader behaviors, Smith, Smoll, and Curtis (1978) developed the companion Coaching Feedback Questionnaire (CFQ). Together, the CBAS and the CFQ are referred to as the CBAS-

CFQ. As such, the CBAS-CFQ is a pencil-and-paper inventory, based upon the 12 coaching behaviors identified in figure 16.8, and designed to measure an athlete's perception of coaching behavior.

Chelladurai's multidimensional model of leadership (figure 16.5) and Smoll and Smith's leadership behavior model (figure 16.7) were independently conceptualized and derived. As such, Cumming, Smith, and Smoll (2006) conducted a study to determine if the perceived coaching behaviors measured by the Leadership Scale for Sports (LSS) are related to the perceived coaching behaviors measured by the CBAS-CFQ. Both the LSS and the CBAS-CFQ were administered to 645 high school athletes. Results of the investigation showed that coaching behaviors, derived from the two different theoretical and methodological traditions, were related, and both were similarly related to athlete evaluative responses to their coach's behaviors (i.e., liked playing for coach, coach knowledge, teaching ability).

Coach Effectiveness Training The **Coach Effectiveness Training** (CET) program is based upon over twenty years of research with the CBAS. The stated purpose of the CET is to teach youth coaches how to engage in team building. Effective team building results in teams that have a positive climate, whose members enjoy a sense of satisfaction, and feel attraction to the team as well as to other team members. The purpose of team building is not necessarily a better win/loss record, but the promotion of a more enjoyable and valuable developmental experience for coaches and athletes (Smith & Smoll, 1997a; Smoll & Smith, 1998, 1999). Research supports the effectiveness of the CET-program-in-training coaches to provide a mastery motivational climate for young athletes (Smith, Smoll, & Cumming, 2007; Sousa, Smith, & Cruz, 2008).

A CET workshop lasts approximately two and a half hours. Behavioral guidelines for effective coaching are presented and discussed. The behavioral guidelines are based on a set of five coaching principles, as outlined below (Smith & Smoll, 1997a):

1. *"Winning" is defined not in terms of win-loss records, but in terms of giving maximum effort and making improvements.* The emphasis in the first principle is in creating a mastery climate as opposed to a competitive climate. Coaches learn to make having fun, deriving satisfaction, learning new skills, and developing greater self-confidence and self-esteem the primary goals of the youth sports experience.

2. *Coach-athlete interactions are based on a positive approach that emphasizes positive reinforcement, encouragement, and sound technical instruction.* The three supportive behaviors of positive reinforcement, encouragement, and sound technical instruction represent the three primary ways that coaches should interact with athletes. When they provide corrective instruction, it is recommended that they use the **positive sandwich approach.** In this approach, the coach starts with a compliment, gives a future-oriented instruction, and ends with another compliment. In this way, the instruction is "sandwiched" between two positives. For example, in a tennis-related setting the coach might say this:

   (a) "Way to hustle! You really look strong when you approach the net."

   (b) "Now, if you will stop and square yourself to the net you will look just like a pro when you make your volley shot."

   (c) "Keep up the hard work; you are really improving fast."

3. *Norms are established that emphasize athletes' mutual obligations to help and support one another.* Developing social support, attraction among teammates, and commitment to the team is as much an athlete's responsibility as a coach's responsibility. The coach learns this principle and establishes expected norms for athletes in sharing the responsibility for team building.

4. *Compliance with team roles and responsibilities is promoted by involving athletes in decisions regarding team rules and compliance.* If the athletes are involved in decisions about team rules and expected compliance, they will be able to share in this responsibility. The coach does not want to be placed in a position of using punitive measures to punish noncompliance to team rules.

5. *Coaches obtain behavioral feedback and engage in self-monitoring to increase awareness of their own behaviors.* Coaches are taught how to use the CBAS system, or some simple variation of it, to monitor their positive and negative coaching behaviors. Coaching feedback is critical to the success of the CET program.

Predicting Coaching Outcomes from Coaching Efficacy and Competence

Coaching behavior has been discussed in the previous section as being important for facilitating athlete performance and athlete satisfaction. In this section, we back up a step and ask the question of what leads to the formation of coaching behavior, player satisfaction, and current success. Research by Feltz, Chase, Moritz, and Sullivan (1999) and Sullivan and Kent (2003) suggests that coaching efficacy is a strong predictor of athlete behavior as well as athlete/team satisfaction, performance, and efficacy. As initially proposed by Feltz, Chase, et al. (1999), the **conceptual model of coaching efficacy** is illustrated in figure 16.9. In this model, coaching efficacy predicts outcomes, but it is in turn predicted by efficacy sources such as coaching experience, prior success, perceived skill of athletes, and school/community support. As defined by Feltz, Chase, et al. (1999, p. 765), **coaching efficacy** is "the extent to which coaches believe they have the capacity to affect the learning and performance of their athletes."

In order to measure coaching efficacy, Feltz, Chase, et al. (1999) developed the 24-item Coaching Efficacy Scale (CES). The CES measures the coaching efficacy factors of (a) game strategy, (b) motivation, (c) technique, and (d) character building. Because the original CES was developed using high school and college coaches, a follow-up investigation was conducted using volunteer youth sport coaches (Feltz, Hepler, & Roman, 2009). The results of this investigation confirmed the four-factor structure of the CES.

In another development, Feltz and colleagues (Myers, Feltz, Maier, Wolfe, & Reckase, 2006; Myers, Wolfe, Maier, Feltz, & Reckase, 2006) observed that while the 24-item CES measured coaching efficacy, as completed by coaches, an inventory was not available that measured **coaching competence** (effectiveness) from the perceived perspective of the athlete. Consequently, Meyers et al. developed the 24-item Coaching Competency Scale (CCS). The only difference between the CES and the CCS is the stem that precedes the items. For the CES (completed by coach), the stem reads "How confident are you in your ability to . . .?" While for the CCS (completed by the athlete), the stem reads "How competent is your head coach in his ability to . . .?" In summary, the CES measures coaching efficacy as perceived by the coach, whereas the CCS measures coaching competence as perceived by the coach's athletes.

To accommodate the prediction of coach and player outcomes from both coach efficacy and perceived coach competence, figure 16.9 is presented so that sources, dimensions, and outcomes apply to both coaching efficacy as well as coaching competence. Regardless of whether you are conceptualizing coaching efficacy or coaching competence, both serve as mediators between sources and

FIGURE 16.9 | The conceptual model of coaching efficacy and competence.

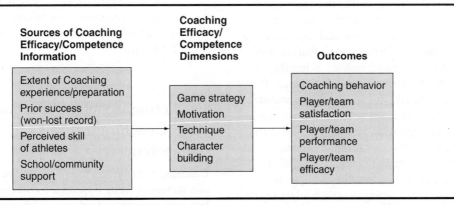

Source: Adapted with permission of the publisher from Feltz, D. L., Chase, M. A., Moritz, S., & Sullivan, P. (1999). Development of the multidimensional coaching efficacy scale. *Journal of Educational Psychology, 91,* 765–76. Published by the American Psychological Association (APA).

outcomes. Research that supports the relationships illustrated in figure 16.9 follows.

Coaching Efficacy as a Mediator between Sources and Outcomes

Utilizing youth sport coaches, Feltz, Chase, et al. (2009) tested and confirmed the hypothesis that *sources of coaching efficacy* (years of coaching experience, years of playing experience, perceived athlete ability, perceived athlete improvement, internal social support, and external social support) predicts *coaching efficacy* (game strategy, motivation, technique, character building) as measured by the CES. While sources of coaching efficacy were generally observed to predict coaching efficacy, some predictors were stronger than others. Internal support (parents) was found to be the strongest source predictor of the efficacy dimensions of motivation and character, while years coaching and playing experience were the strongest source predictors of the efficacy dimensions of strategy and technique. In a second investigation involving coach efficacy and sources of efficacy, Kavussanu, Boardley, Jutkiewicz, Vincent, and Ring (2008) utilized adult coaches to demonstrate that coach gender and years of coaching experience predict coach efficacy. Specifically, being a male coach leads to higher levels of game strategy efficacy compared to being a female coach. In addition, greater coaching experience leads to technique efficacy.

In another investigation involving college coaches, Sullivan and Kent (2003) utilized the CES to test and confirm the hypothesis that coaching efficacy dimensions predict coaching behavior as measured by the Leadership Scale for Sports. Recall that the LSS measures the coaching behavior dimensions of training and instruction, autocratic behavior, democratic behavior, social support, and positive feedback. Study results provided evidence for the conceptual model of coaching efficacy, in that coaching efficacy for motivation and technique were significant predictors of the coaching behaviors of training instruction and positive feedback.

In summary, as illustrated in figure 16.9, sources of coaching efficacy information predicts coaching efficacy (C.E.), which in turn predicts coach behavior and player/team outcomes.

Sources of C.E. → Coaching efficacy → Outcomes

While not a test of the conceptual model illustrated in figure 16.9, an investigation reported by Gould, Collins, Lauer, and Chung (2007) is important because it shows how outstanding and efficacious high school football coaches teach life skills to their athletes (outcome). Through the interview method, these award-winning coaches revealed that to effectively teach life skills to athletes (transfer to life after sport) the teaching must be built into the fabric of their coaching philosophy and not treated as an "add on."

Coaching Competence as a Mediator between Sources and Outcomes

In the previous section, we focused on coaching efficacy, while in this section we turn our attention to coaching competence as the mediator between sources and outcomes. In an investigation reported by Kavussanu, Boardley, et al. (2008), sources of coaching competence information were studied as predictors of coaching competence, as measured by the CCS. Sources of coaching competency information included athletes' gender, athletes' years of sport experience, and the coach-athlete gender match/mismatch (i.e., same or different sex). Results show that athletes' sport experience is a negative predictor of all four measures of coach competence (perceived coaching competence declines as athlete gains experience). In addition, results show that athletes view the coach as being less competent (motivation and character building) if the athlete and coach gender is different.

Finally, Boardley, Kavussanu, and Ring (2008) tested the hypothesis that perceived coaching competence (effectiveness) predicts athlete outcomes in the form of task self-efficacy, enjoyment, commitment, effort, prosocial behavior, and

CONCEPT Each and every coach-athlete interaction is important in developing trust, respect, and cooperation. Of particular concern is the way in which coaches choose to correct athletes' mistakes.

APPLICATION Miller's three-step assertiveness training approach should be used when interacting with athletes. Coaches should learn how to assertively correct athletes' errors and mistakes without coming across as demeaning or threatening.

---

antisocial behavior. In this investigation, using adult rugby players as participants, perceived coaching competence (game strategy, motivation, technique, and character building) was measured using the CCS. Specific results showed that (a) coach motivation competence predicts athlete outcomes of effort, commitment, and enjoyment; (b) coach technique competence predicts task self-efficacy; and (c) character-building competence predicts prosocial behavior. In summary, as illustrated in figure 16.9, sources of coaching competence information predict coaching competence (C.C.), which in turn predicts coach behavior and player/ team outcomes.

Sources of C.C.→Coaching competence→Outcomes

Coach-Athlete Communication and Compatibility

Successful coaches communicate effectively with other coaches, with referees, with parents, with the media, with superiors, and most of all with their athletes. In short, effective coaches are effective and skilled communicators (Yukelson, 2010). Communication is more than dispensing information in an organized and eloquent manner. Information given is not necessarily information received and acted upon. In a 2005 National Football League playoff game between the Minnesota Vikings and the Philadelphia Eagles, the Vikings tried a fake field goal attempt with the holder passing the ball to the wide receiver. However, when the holder turned to pass the ball to the wide receiver, there was no one there. Due to a series of miscommunications, there was an extra player on the field, so the wide receiver walked off the field just before the ball was centered to the holder.

Communication and the Coach-Athlete Dyad

In sport, critical communication takes place constantly among coaches, among athletes, and between the coach and athletes. These communications take place in verbal and nonverbal ways. Nonverbal communication can take place through body language, facial expression, and other symbolic planned and unplanned gestures. Even verbal communications take multiple forms as illustrated in a study involving female collegiate tennis players (Lausic, Tenebaum, Eccles, Jeong, & Johnson, 2009). In this study, categories of coded verbal communications included uncertainty, action statements, acknowledgments, factual statements, and emotional statements.

While all forms of communication are important in developing teamwork, creating team cohesion, and realizing outcome success, our main focus for the balance of this section will be on the communication and observed compatibility that must exist between the coach and the athlete. Figure 16.10 provides a simplified illustration of a compatible and an incompatible **coach-athlete dyad.** While the compatible coach-athlete dyad is based on many dynamic aspects of effective leadership, the two most critical are good communication and the presence of rewarding behavior (Baker, Coté, & Hawes, 2000; Horne & Carron, 1985; Jackson, Knapp, & Beauchamp, 2009; Jowett, 2003; Kenow & Williams, 1999; Martin, Rocca, Caynaus, & Weber, 2009; Schutz, 1966).

CONCEPT   The quality of coach-athlete interaction is a critical factor in team success and satisfaction.

APPLICATION   Perhaps the most important factor in improving coach-athlete interaction is communication. Coaches must encourage two-way communication between themselves and their athletes. If the athletes feel that the coach values their input, they will feel comfortable in a two-way interaction.

FIGURE 16.10 | Some characteristics of compatible and incompatible dyads.

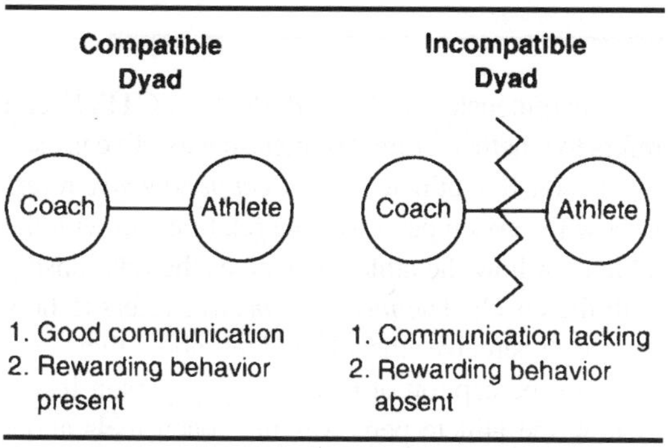

Compatible Dyad

Coach — Athlete

1. Good communication
2. Rewarding behavior present

Incompatible Dyad

Coach ⟩⟨ Athlete

1. Communication lacking
2. Rewarding behavior absent

Communication and Assertiveness Training

Regarding feedback to athletes from coaches, research clearly suggests that a good performance should be followed by praise and helpful information about the performance. In response to a poor performance, the coach should provide encouragement and information that will help the athlete succeed. In correcting a mistake, a coach needs to be assertive (never aggressive), yet avoid damaging the athlete's self-esteem. Miller (1982) suggested assertiveness training for coaches to help them relate better to athletes. In Miller's **assertiveness training module,** the athlete is instructed in three specific steps. Using a volleyball example, actual execution of the module might involve the following three steps:

1. *Describe the situation to the athlete.* "Your defensive assignment was to cover the power angle of that spike."

2. *Tell how it affects the team.* "When you follow through with your assignment, it provides the coverage necessary for an effective team defense."

3. *Tell what you think should be done.* "Focus your attention on your specific assignment and trust your teammates to take care of their assignments."

Coaches have the responsibility to create an environment that encourages athletes to initiate communication freely. Communication between the coach and the athlete must be a two-way street. The athlete must truly believe that he can voice his feelings and concerns openly without reprisal. Table 16.2 contains a number of suggestions from the perspective of the coach for interventions that can facilitate coach-athlete communication (Yukelson, 2010).

Jowett Model of Coach-Athlete Relationship

The balance of this section will be devoted to recent advances in the study of the coach-athlete dyad relationship. Specifically, we will introduce and briefly discuss the **Jowett model of coach-athlete dyad relationship.** The Jowett coach-athlete model is based on the Sprecher, Felmlee, Orbuch, and Willets (2002) social network relationship model. According to the Jowett model, the compatibility of the coach-athlete dyad is based on positive and negative manifestations of closeness (affective aspect), commitment (cognitive aspect), and complementarity (behavioral aspect). *Closeness* refers to mutual respect, common beliefs,

TABLE 16.2 | Selected Practical Suggestions for Facilitating Coach-Athlete
Communication (coaches' perspective)

1. Recognize individual differences among athletes.
2. Use a style of communication that is comfortable.
3. Be honest, sincere, and genuine, but never sarcastic.
4. Be generous with praise and encouragement.
5. Make sure nonverbal communication is consistent with verbal communication (avoid mixed signals).
6. Exercise personal self-control at all times.
7. Be supportive and empathetic to athlete needs.
8. Openly discuss communication needs and shortcomings with individual athletes, as well as with team as a whole.

trust, and love expressed between members of the dyad. *Commitment* refers to dedication, sacrifice, and satisfaction expressed between members of the dyad. *Complementarity* refers to how the coach and athlete complement each other's strengths in terms of roles, tasks, and ability to adapt. Finally, Jowett (2006) introduced the notion of *coorientation* to reflect the degree of agreement that exists between coach and athlete on the three manifestations of closeness, commitment, and complementarity. Together, closeness, commitment, and complementarity are referred to as the 3 Cs model of the coach-athlete relationship. With the addition of the notion of coorientation, the model's name was changed to the extended conceptual **3 + 1 Cs model of coach-athlete relationship.**

Measurement of the Jowett Coach-Athlete Relationship   To measure the 3 + 1 Cs model of coach-athlete relationship, Jowett developed the Coach-Athlete Relationship Questionnaire (CART-Q; Jowett, 2006; Jowett & Ntoumanis, 2003, 2004). The CART-Q is composed of 11 or 13 items that measure the three relationship manifestations of closeness, commitment, and complementarity on a seven-point Likert scale. To measure the fourth construct of coorientation, four versions of the CART-Q are conceptualized. These four versions of the CART-Q are visually illustrated in a two-dimension, 2 × 2 matrix as shown in figure 16.11. The first dimension is labeled DYAD and refers to which member of the dyad is completing the CART-Q. The

second dimension is labeled PERSPECTIVE and refers to whether a direct or meta-perspective is used by the coach or athlete. The *direct perspective* refers to how the coach perceives the relationship with the athlete, or how the athlete perceives the relationship with the coach. The *meta-perspective* refers to how the coach perceives the athlete feels about their relationship (perception of how the other person feels), or how the athlete perceives the coach feels about their relationship. Figure 16.11 illustrates these two dimensions and four quadrants relative to perceived

FIGURE 16.11 | Conceptual model of the 2 × 2 coach-athlete dyad relationship for respect (as an example).

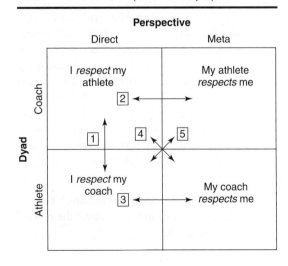

respect (closeness) between the two members of the dyad. The prefix "meta" is typically used to refer to going beyond, higher, or transcending as in *metaphysics*, so in the current case meta-perspective refers to going beyond the obvious (Jackson & Beauchamp, 2010).

The degree of agreement or coorientation between the four different measures of coach-athlete respect is determined by comparing the four 2×2 quadrants in figure 16.11 in five specific ways as follows:

1. Compare "I respect my athlete" direct perspective score with "I respect my coach" direct perspective score.

2. Compare "I respect my athlete" direct perspective score with "my athlete respects me" meta-perspective score.

3. Compare "I respect my coach" direct perspective score with "my coach respects me" meta-perspective score.

4. Compare "I respect my athlete" direct perspective score with "my coach respects me" meta-perspective score.

5. Compare "I respect my coach" direct perspective score with "my athlete respects me" meta-perspective score.

Large differences in the combined comparisons would suggest that the coach-athlete dyad is incompatible and suffers from a lack of closeness, commitment, and complementarity. Conversely, small differences would suggest that the coach-athlete dyad is compatible in terms of closeness, commitment, and complementarity. Summary scores for closeness, commitment, and complementarity are found by summing the item scores that make up each relationship variable.

Research Findings Using the Jowett Model

Application of the Jowett model to the coach-athlete relationship has provided additional insight into this critically important interaction. Jowett and Timson-Katches (2005) utilized a qualitative research design to study the effect that parents have upon the coach-athlete dyad. Their research showed that the quality of the coach-athlete relationship (closeness, commitment, complementarity) is enhanced by parents in three ways: (a) parents facilitate athlete opportunities in sport, (b) parents provide critical information to the coach about the athlete, and (c) parents provide the athletes with emotional support.

Olympiou, Jowett, and Duda (2008) administered the CART-Q (direct and meta-perspective) and a motivational climate inventory to British athletes. Results showed a strong consistent relationship between both direct and meta-perspective measures of closeness, commitment, and complementarity with a mastery motivational climate (role importance, cooperative learning, effort, improvement).

Lafreniere, Jowett, Vallerand, Donahue, and Lorimer (2008) found a consistent relationship between harmonious passion (intrinsic motivation) and both direct and meta-perspective measures of the 3 Cs. Lorimer and Jowett (2009a, 2009b) studied direct and meta-perspective coach-athlete interactions by asking each member of the dyad to independently view and evaluate video clips of the coach-athlete dyad interacting in a training environment. Results show that (a) meta-perceptions of coach and athlete are correlated, (b) both coach and athlete meta-perceptions predict coach-athlete congruence and satisfaction, (c) coach-athlete congruence is higher for individual sports compared to team sports, and (d) coach-athlete congruence increases as the length of the training session increases.

Finally, Rhind and Jowett (2010) reported on an investigation designed to identify strategies calculated to maintain the continuity of the coach-athlete dyad relationship. Based on factors within the Jowett's 3 + 1 Cs coach-athlete dyad model, the researchers identified seven factors that are considered essential for a positive coach-athlete long-term relationship. The first letters of the seven factors form the acronym for the *COMPASS model*. These seven factors are conflict management, openness, motivation, positivity, advice, support, and social networks. If all of these factors are present in a coach-athletic relationship, the dyad will be

CONCEPT The coach can develop leadership skills in young athletes by placing them in team positions requiring observability, visibility, and task dependence.

APPLICATION It is usually the athlete who already possesses leadership ability that becomes

the quarterback in football or the catcher in baseball. Coaches should use this knowledge to help their players develop leadership skills. Young athletes who lack leadership ability could benefit from playing point guard on the basketball team or quarterback on the football team.

---

compatible and will be maintained. The absence of any combination of these factors will result in a negative effect on the compatibility of the dyad. The authors argued that the COMPASS model complements but does not replace the 3 + 1 Cs dyad model.

Player Position, Leadership Opportunity, and Stacking

Beginning with Grusky (1963), a body of literature has evolved that relates an athlete's playing position to future leadership opportunity and to racial bias (stacking). We will first consider the leadership opportunity aspect of this research area, and then consider stacking.

Playing Position and Leadership Opportunity

Most of the research dealing with playing position and leadership opportunity has focused on the sport of professional baseball (Chelladurai & Carron, 1977; Grusky, 1963; Loy & Sage, 1970), but more recently studies have been reported dealing with football (Bivens & Leonard, 1994) and soccer (Norris & Jones, 1998). Basically, what these investigations show is that athletes who play in certain central positions on the playing field benefit from greater leadership opportunity. In the case of professional baseball, it has been clearly demonstrated that former catchers and infielders are selected to be major league managers more often than athletes who played other positions.

Of the six major league managers hired following the strike-shortened 1994 season, four had

been catchers in their playing days. Bob Boone, a manager of the Kansas City Royals, said of his playing days as a catcher, "I managed every game I played in. I just didn't have the control." Dan Duquette, Boston Red Sox general manager, was quoted as saying, "The catcher is involved with every pitch, every pitcher, and he's the only player on the field who has the whole field in front of him" (Chass, 1994, pp. 1, 4).

As illustrated in figure 16.12, and explained by Chelladurai and Carron (1977), the critical factors associated with these findings are task dependence and propinquity. **Task dependence** refers to interaction between players of the same team. Higher task dependence is associated with greater interaction and greater dependence between players. The catcher in baseball interacts with players on her team to a greater extent than any other player. Thus, catching is a position with high task dependence, whereas playing in the outfield is a position with low task dependence. **Propinquity** refers to observability and visibility on the playing field. In baseball and softball, the catcher is the most visible and observable player on the team from the perspective of her teammates. The same could be said for the quarterback in football, the point guard in basketball, the setter in volleyball, and the center halfback in soccer. Athletes enjoying the greatest amounts of task dependence and propinquity have greater leadership responsibility as well as greater leadership opportunity.

Playing Position and Stacking

Related to the concept of playing position and leadership opportunity is the notion of playing position

CONCEPT   Position on an athletic team should be determined on the basis of skill, physical attributes, and athlete preference, and never upon the basis of race, ethnicity, or color of skin.

APPLICATION   There are a lot of myths associated with playing positions on athletic teams. Neither coaches nor athletes should give credence

to these myths. An athlete should be given an opportunity to compete for any position on an athletic team. It is generally the coach that makes the final determination as to where an athlete plays. For this reason, it is also the coach that is ultimately responsible for making sure that stacking does not occur.

FIGURE 16.12 | Categorization of baseball positions on the basis of propinquity and task dependence.

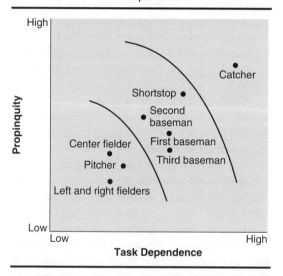

Source: From Chelladurai, P., & Carron, A. V. (1977). A reanalysis of formal structure in sport. *Canadian Journal of Applied Sport Sciences, 2,* 9–14. Reproduced by permission of the publisher.

and stacking. **Stacking** refers to the disproportionate placement of blacks or minorities into positions of low **centrality** relative to task dependence and propinquity. If stacking does occur in sport, African Americans should be underrepresented in positions of high centrality. A position of high centrality would be a position exhibiting high propinquity and high task dependence, such as catcher in

baseball. Studies of centrality and racial segregation have shown that minority players are underrepresented in central positions, where opportunities for leadership are greatest (Hallinan, 1998; Norris & Jones, 1998).

Perhaps of even greater concern than stacking in Major League Baseball (MLB) is the fact that fewer and fewer African American athletes are choosing to play baseball. At the midpoint of the 2003 MLB season, there were only 90 blacks playing in the major leagues, or 10 percent of players on 25-man rosters. This is down from 19 percent in 1995 and down from 27 percent in 1975 (Verducci, 2003). Additionally, the 2005 Houston Astros were the first team since the 1953 New York Yankees, to play in a MLB World Series without a black player on its roster (Antonen, 2005). History records that the Chicago White Sox defeated the Astros in four games.

Possible reasons suggested by Verducci for this disturbing trend include the following: (a) for financial reasons, many blacks are being denied access to expert instruction and groomed playing fields associated with the "pay-for-play" mentality of modern suburbia; (b) there are so few blacks in MLB that there are few role models for young black athletes to emulate; (c) baseball can't match the "buzz"-producing marketing and excitement of football and basketball; and (d) baseball does not provide the opportunity for instant fame and fortune that the National Basketball Association afforded LeBron James when he joined the Cleveland Cavaliers. It would seem, however, that the latter two reasons might discourage white as well as black athletes from focusing on baseball.

Summary

Consistent with Behling and Schriesheim's leadership theory classification system, four different categories of leadership were discussed. These included universal trait theories, universal behavior theories, Fiedler's contingency theory, and situation-specific behavior theories.

Universal trait theory is based upon the notion that great leaders are great men or women who possess universal personality traits that would make them great leaders in any situation. Universal behavior theories are based upon the notion that certain universal behaviors exist that define effective leaders. Research has shown that the universal behaviors are consideration and initiating structure. Individuals can learn to be effective leaders by learning to exhibit these two behaviors, regardless of the situation. Fiedler's contingency theory is based on the notion that leaders possess personality dispositions that will help them be effective leaders in one situation, but not in another. Thus, leadership is contingent upon possessing a certain personality trait suitable for a specific situation. Situation-specific behavioral theories are based on the notion that specific behaviors will help an individual be an effective leader in one situation but not another.

Three situation-specific sport models of leadership were discussed, including (a) Smith's sport personality contingency model, (b) Chelladurai's multidimensional model of leadership, and (c) Smoll and Smith's leadership behavior model. Smith's sport personality contingency model is partially based on the leader's personality, while the other two are based entirely upon leader behaviors. Chelladurai's multidimensional theory posits that effective leadership is a function of congruence between prescribed, actual (perceived), and preferred leader behavior. In the Smoll and Smith model, player perception mediates the relationship between coach behaviors and player response. The coaching behavior assessment system (CBAS) was introduced as a means of measuring coaching behavior and the coach effectiveness training (CET) program was introduced as a means for coaches to engage in team building.

Coaching efficacy and coaching competence were introduced as predictors of coach behaviors and athlete satisfaction, performance, and efficacy. Coaching efficacy is measured using the Coaching Efficacy Scale (CES), and coaching competence is measured using the Coaching Competence Scale (CCS).

Coach-athlete communication and compatibility were discussed as a function of (a) communication and the coach-athlete dyad, (b) communication and assertiveness training, and (c) the Jowett model of coach-athlete relationships. The Jowett $3 + 1$ Cs model of coach-athlete relationships focuses upon positive and negative manifestations of closeness, commitment, and complementarity (3 Cs) plus coach-athlete dyad congruence (coorientation).

Finally, player position, leadership opportunity, and stacking were discussed. Athletes who play in central positions relative to propinquity and task dependence are given greater opportunities for growth as leaders. Minorities are underrepresented in central positions on athletic teams.

Critical Thought Questions

1. Which of the four basic categories of leadership theories do you relate to best? What role would leadership training play in your leadership theory of choice?

2. Identify the three situation-specific sport models of leadership discussed in this chapter. Which of these do you relate to the most? Discuss how your chosen model can

assist you in becoming an effective coach or leader.

3. What are the coach efficacy dimensions that lead to coach and athlete outcomes? Differentiate between coach efficacy and coach competence dimensions in terms of their meaning and how they are measured. Discuss sources or antecedents that lead to coach efficacy and competence.

4. Discuss the importance of communication and compatibility in the coach-athlete dyad. Describe and explain how Miller's assertive training module can assist in establishing good communication between the coach and her athletes. Identify specific examples of how the module can be applied.

5. Discuss the Jowett model of coach-athlete dyad relationship. What is meant by the 3 + 1 Cs model? According to this model how can a good working relationship between coach and athlete be established and maintained?

6. What is the difference between Jowett's 3 + 1 Cs model and the COMPASS model? Which one do you find to be most useful as a coach or leader?

7. Do you think stacking is a problem in youth sports? How about professional sports? Why do you feel this way? Can anything be done about it?

Glossary

assertiveness training module A module proposed by Miller to assist coaches in maintaining positive communication with athletes while at the same time correcting errors.

behavioral signature The proclivity that coaches have to behave in certain consistent ways based on the situation and the leader's personality.

centrality The condition of playing in a position that is highly visible, interactive, and associated with high task interdependence.

Chelladurai's multidimensional model A leadership model in which athlete performance and satisfaction are viewed as products of the congruence of prescribed leadership behavior, actual leadership behavior, and preferred leadership behavior.

coach-athlete dyad The close association between one coach and one athlete.

Coach Effectiveness Training (CET) A coach training system that is based upon 20 years of research with the CBAS.

Coaching Behavior Assessment System (CBAS) A recording system designed to categorize the behavior of coaches during practices and games.

coaching competence Coach effectiveness as perceived by athletes and measured through achieved outcomes.

coaching efficacy The extent to which coaches believe they have the capacity to affect the learning and performance of their athletes.

conceptual model of coaching efficacy A conceptual model that predicts that coaching efficacy leads to effective coaching behaviors.

consideration Leader behavior that is indicative of friendship, mutual trust, respect, and warmth between the leader and subordinates.

Fiedler's contingency theory A leadership theory that is situation specific, but retains the notion of personality traits.

functional model of leadership A team approach to leadership in which one individual is strong in consideration while another is strong in initiating structure.

"great man" theory of leadership A theory of leadership based on the notion that great leaders are born, not made.

initiating structure A leader's behavior in clearly defining the relationship between the leader and subordinates, and in endeavoring to establish well-defined patterns of organization, channels of communication, and methods of procedure.

Jowett model of coach-athlete dyad relationship A social network relationship model that is based upon positive manifestations of closeness, commitment, and complementarity between coach and athlete.

leadership behavior model The Smoll and Smith model of leadership based upon situation-specific behaviors of the leader.

life cycle theory A theory of leadership proposing that the appropriate leadership style for any specific situation depends on the maturity of the athlete.

path-goal theory A theory of leadership in which the emphasis is upon the needs and goals of the athlete. The leader is a facilitator.

Personality paradox The theory that a person's personality remains relatively consistent, yet behavioral outcomes vary greatly from situation to situation.

positive sandwich approach Form of instruction in which the coach starts with a compliment, gives a future-oriented instruction, and ends with another compliment.

propinquity Observability and visibility on the playing field.

reactive behaviors Coach reactions to player or team behavior.

relationship motivation Concern with interpersonal relationships between leader and followers (see consideration).

situation-specific behavior theories Theories that view leadership as a function of specific behaviors effective in one situation but not another.

situational behaviors Behaviors that may help leaders be effective in some situations but not others.

situational traits Personality traits or dispositions that may help leaders be effective in some situations but not others.

spontaneous behaviors Behaviors initiated by the coach that do not occur in response to a players behavior.

stacking The disproportionate placement of blacks or other minorities into positions of low centrality relative to propinquity and task dependence.

task dependence The degree of interaction between members of the same team while executing a task.

task motivation A leader's concern with accomplishing the task at hand (see initiating structure).

3 + 1 Cs model of coach-athlete relationship A coach-athlete dyad model in which compatibility and communication is based upon the 3 Cs (closeness, commitment, and complementarity) plus congruence on the 3 Cs between the coach and the athlete (coorientation).

Transactional leadership Like initiating structure, this type of leadership is based on rewards for productivity, performance monitoring, and error intervention.

Transformational leadership Like consideration, this type of leadership is based on inspirational motivation, idealized influence, intellectual stimulation, and individualized consideration.

universal behavior theory Theory of leadership that proposes the existence of a set of universal leadership behaviors.

universal behaviors Leadership behaviors found in all successful leaders.

universal traits Personality traits found in all successful leaders.

PART 6

Psychobiology of Sport and Exercise

Chapters 13 through 16 (part 5) of this text dealt with several social psychology topics. In a similar fashion, the present part of the text deals with issues that combine psychology with biology. Just as social psychology of sport is viewed as a subset of sport psychology, so also is psychobiology of sport and exercise viewed as a subset of sport psychology. Each of these subset areas could easily be expanded into a separate content area of its own. However, for the purposes of this book, these areas are treated as subsets within the larger discipline of sport psychology. If a university or college curriculum offers a separate course in psychobiology of sport and exercise, this section could serve as an introduction to that course. However, if a separate course is not available, this part of the book will be invaluable to the sport psychology student. The psychobiological issues to be discussed in this part of the text are included in the following three chapters: exercise psychology (chapter 17), the psychology of athletic injuries and career termination (chapter 18), and negative aspects of sport and exercise (chapter 19).

17 CHAPTER

Exercise Psychology

KEY TERMS

Acquired immune deficiency
  syndrome (AIDS)
Acute exercise
Aerobic exercise
Amine hypothesis
Anaerobic exercise
Anxiolytic
Appearance impression
  motivation
Body image
Body mass index
Cardiovascular fitness
  hypothesis
Chronic exercise
Circumplex model
Cognitive behavioral
  hypothesis
Delayed anxiolytic effect
Disconnected values model
Distraction hypothesis
Drive for muscularity
Dual-mode hypothesis
Endorphin hypothesis
Executive function
Exercise adherence
Exercise determinants
Exercise self-efficacy
Exercise self-presentation
  efficacy

Exercise self-schemata
Human immunodeficiency
  virus (HIV)
Immune system functioning
Lactate threshold
Life stress
Mode of aerobic exercise
Natural history of exercise
Physical self-concept

Processes of change
Resistance exercise
Self-schemata
Social interaction hypothesis
Social physique anxiety
Stress inoculation
Theory of planned behavior
Theory of reasoned action
Transtheoretical model

Documentation of the physiological benefits of regular exercise has led to the inclusion of "lack of exercise" by the American Heart Association (1999) as a fourth risk factor for heart disease that can be modified or controlled by the individual. The other three risk factors are smoking, high blood pressure, and elevated cholesterol. Among other things, regular physical exercise helps lower cholesterol, decreases the percentage of body fat, mediates the effects of diabetes, reduces weight, and lowers blood pressure (Paffenbarger, 1994; Pate et al., 1995).

As stated by the President's Council on Physical fitness and Sports (Staff, 1992), "If exercise could be packed into a pill, it would be the single most widely prescribed and beneficial medicine in the nation" (p. 5). Ironically, undocumented reports have emerged that scientists have identified a chemical substance that when injected into rats increases cardiovascular endurance without exercise. In response to these reports, Church and Blair (2009) wrote that these reports are probably too good to be true, as to be effective, such a chemical would need to simultaneously improve a whole array of physiological and psychological outcomes in addition to endurance. They conclude that the benefits of exercise are readily available and encourage health care professionals to actively prescribe physical activity for all individuals and to not wait for the "magic pill."

Notwithstanding the documented physiological benefits of regular physical exercise, Dishman (2001) reports that (a) only 8 to 20 percent of the U.S. population regularly participate in vigorous physical activity; (b) 30 to 59 percent of the U.S. population have relatively sedentary lifestyles; and (c) 50 percent of the individuals who start regular physical activity programs drop out within six months.

In addition to physiological benefits, a large body of literature has been amassed that supports the position that *regular exercise leads to improved psychological affect.* Improved psychological affect is manifested in the form of a reduction in negative affect (e.g., anxiety and depression) and an increase in positive affect (e.g., self-efficacy, vigor, well-being). These consistent findings have led many mental health care professionals to prescribe exercise as a treatment for selected mental health symptoms. Exercise in many cases is as effective as psychotherapy and antidepressant drugs in treating emotional disorders (Babyak et al., 1999, 2000; Faulkner & Biddle, 2004; Nicoloff & Schwenk, 1995).

These conclusions are supported by numerous narrative reviews and meta-analyses (Biddle, 1995; Craft & Landers, 1998; Gillison, Skevington, Sato, Standage, & Evangelidou, 2009; Hamer, Taylor, & Steptoe, 2006; LaFontaine et al., 1992; Leith & Taylor, 1990; Long & Van Stavel, 1995; Mutrie, 2000; North, McCullagh, & Tran, 1990; Petruzzello et al., 1991; Reed & Buck, 2009; Spence, McGannon, & Poon, 2005; Wipfli, Rethorst, & Landers, 2008), as well as recently reported research (e.g., Bixby, Spalding, & Hatfield, 2000; Cox, Thomas, Hinton, & Donahue, 2004, 2006; Focht & Koltyn, 1999; Hale, Koch, & Raglin, 2000; Lochbaum, Karoly, & Landers, 2004; Martin, Waldron, McCabe, & Choi, 2009; Van Landuyt, Ekkekakis, Hall, & Petruzzello, 2000).

Special topics to be treated in this chapter include (a) factors that influence the psychological benefits of exercise; (b) positive effects of exercise on cognitive function; (c) theoretical explanations for the relationship between exercise and improved mental health; (d) exercise adherence and determinants; (e) theories of exercise behavior; (f) fitness as a moderator of life stress; (g) the immune system, cancer, HIV, and exercise; and (h) social physique anxiety, physical self-concept, and body image.

Factors That Influence the Psychological Benefits of Exercise

In the first section of this chapter, we introduce and discuss some, but not all, of the factors that influence the psychological benefits of exercise and physical activity. In particular, we discuss how exercise intensity, exercise mode, special

CONCEPT A relatively large body of literature supports the position that regular exercise (generally, aerobic exercise) is associated with improved psychological affect.

APPLICATION The importance of this scientific finding should not be underestimated. Not only can regular exercise improve cardiovascular fitness, but it is also believed to have a beneficial effect upon the psychological affect of mentally healthy individuals.

---

populations, and other factors such as time of day, music, and social environment can moderate or modify the effects of exercise on mental health.

Exercise Intensity

A large body of literature has emerged that addresses the question of what intensity of exercise is most beneficial in terms of realized psychological benefits. Most of this literature has focused on the **anxiolytic** or anxiety-reducing effects of exercise. Exercise is routinely referred to as being acute or chronic in nature. **Acute exercise** refers to exercise that is of short duration (e.g., 30 minutes), whereas **chronic exercise** refers to long-term exercise (e.g., 12 months). Exercise intensity has mostly been studied relative to acute as opposed to chronic exercise. For example, a group of study participants might be asked to exercise for 30 minutes at a predetermined exercise intensity. In exercise intensity research, most bouts of exercise are aerobic as opposed to anaerobic. **Aerobic exercise** refers to exercise that is accomplished at an exercise intensity that allows for the intake of sufficient oxygen to maintain continuous exercise. This is opposed to **anaerobic exercise,** in which the exerciser does not get enough oxygen to maintain continuous exercise. Anaerobic exercise requires the athlete to breathe hard following exercise in order to replenish stored energy. After a bout of anaerobic exercise, the athlete will need a period of time to "catch her breath." This is not generally necessary with aerobic exercise. Most exercise intensity studies involve participants who complete acute bouts

of aerobic exercise. Most research involving exercise intensity involves aerobic exercise on stationary bicycles or on treadmills. Some researchers, however, are interested in studying the effects of exercise intensity on resistance exercise as opposed to aerobic exercise. **Resistance exercise** usually involves the use of weights or weight training to provide resistance to the muscles. Both aerobic and resistance exercise is linked to beneficial psychological effects. Within this section on exercise intensity, we will briefly (a) summarize aerobic exercise intensity research findings, (b) summarize resistance exercise intensity findings, (c) introduce the Ekkekakis dual-mode hypothesis, and (d) introduce the circumplex model.

Aerobic Exercise Intensity Research The typical research design for this type of research is to first ascertain participants' maximal aerobic capacity (MAC) using either a direct or estimated procedure. Based on laboratory calculated MAC, the participant is assigned to a level of exercise intensity that is a percentage of the MAC. Participants are then asked to exercise on a treadmill (or stationary cycle) at their assigned exercise intensity. Typical levels of exercise intensity are 60 percent (moderate) and 80 percent (high). Depending on the investigation, participants' positive or negative affect (usually anxiety) is measured prior to, during, and after a 20- or 30-minute bout of acute aerobic exercise (or resistance training).

Although the above protocol has yielded variable results, the most common reported finding has been that a moderate bout of acute aerobic exercise

CONCEPT While an acute bout of exercise can result in a measurable reduction in negative mood state, chronic exercise habits are required to maintain these psychological benefits.

APPLICATION In a sense, a single bout of exercise is like a single dose of medication. If the medication, or in this case exercise, is to be of long-term benefit, it must be maintained over a sufficiently long period of time.

is considered to be most effective in reducing negative affect and increasing positive affect compared to a control group (Berger & Motl, 2000; Farrell, Gustafson, Morgan, & Pert, 1987; Steptoe & Cox, 1988). Research reported by Cox, Thomas, Hinton, et al. (2004), however, provides convincing evidence that a bout of relatively intense exercise is superior to a moderate bout of aerobic exercise in terms of reducing state anxiety. This finding is also supported, to some degree, in a meta-analysis reported by Wipfli et al. (2008). Finally, it is important to note that in many cases, an acute bout of aerobic exercise will not result in an immediate decrease in negative affect, but it will result in a decrease following a delay of 30 to 90 minutes. In the case of anxiety, this is known as the **delayed anxiolytic effect** of acute aerobic exercise (Cox, Thomas, & Davis, 2000; Cox, Thomas, Hinton, et al., 2004).

Notwithstanding the efforts of researchers to standardize exercise intensity levels based on percent of maximum aerobic capacity, it is difficult to know if 60 percent or 80 percent of MAC in one study is the same as in another study. This uncertainty has led some researchers to avoid the practice of assigning participants to levels of exercise intensity in favor of asking the participants to exercise at their *preferred* level of exercise intensity. After measuring their MAC and their ventilator threshold (VT), Lind, Joens-Matre, and Ekkekakis (2005) asked the study participants (previously sedentary women) to exercise for 20 minutes at their preferred exercise intensity. As it turned out, their preferred level of exercise intensity was at the beginning of their lactate threshold. The **lactate threshold** or ventilator threshold occurs at the *transition point* between aerobic and anaerobic

exercise, and can therefore be considered to be of high intensity. Furthermore, the participants reported that they enjoyed positive and stable affective responses during and after exercise.

Consistent with a focus on a preferred level of exercise intensity, Ekkekakis, Hall, and Petruzzello (2005) developed the Preference for and Tolerance of the Intensity of Exercise Questionnaire (PRETIE-Q). The PRETIE-Q is a 16-item inventory that measures tolerance and preference for exercise. In a follow-up investigation, Ekkekakis, Lind, and Joens-Matre (2006) established the validity of the PRETIE-Q by showing that the preference scale predicts preferred exercise intensity. Exercising at a preferred level of intensity is important because exercising at an intensity below this level may result in boredom and dropout. Conversely, exercising at an intensity above the preferred level may result in dropout due to overexertion and discomfort. In another related investigation, Lind, Ekkekakis, and Vazou (2008), asked middle-aged sedentary women to exercise on a treadmill for 20 minutes at two levels of exercise intensity (rest in between). In the first case they were asked to exercise at their self-selected preferred level of exercise intensity, while in the second case they exercised at an intensity level that was 10 percent greater than their self-selected preferred level. As predicted, positive affect was higher in the preferred intensity condition compared to the more intense preferred plus 10 percent.

Schneider and Graham (2009) reported on an investigation that suggests that the *personality* of the participant may moderate the effect that exercise has upon affect. Utilizing healthy adolescents as participants, the researchers asked participants to complete two 30-minute bouts of exercise at two different levels of intensity, one at the lactate threshold (high intensity), and the other at 80 percent of the lactate threshold (moderate intensity). Prior to completing the two exercise protocols, all participants completed a personality inventory that measured (a) drive to avoid punishing stimuli (negative characteristic), and (b) drive to approach rewarding behavior (positive characteristic). Results of the investigation showed that participants high in drive to avoid punishing stimuli reported lower levels of positive affect, while those high in drive to approach rewarding behavior reported higher levels of positive affect throughout the two exercise bouts, regardless of exercise intensity. This research suggests that the influence of aerobic exercise on positive mood may have as much to do with the personality of the participant as does exercise intensity. This is a line of investigation that needs further research.

Resistance Exercise Intensity Research

While most intensity research has focused on acute aerobic exercise, many studies have focused on resistance exercise. Resistance exercise usually involves the use of weights or weight training to provide resistance to the muscles. Like acute aerobic exercise, resistance exercise is also associated with beneficial psychological effects (Arent, Alderman, Short, & Landers, 2007; Arent, Landers, Matt, & Etnier, 2005; Bartholomew, 1999; Bartholomew, Moore, Todd, Todd, & Elrod, 2001; Dionigi & Cannon, 2009; Focht & Koltyn, 1999). Relative to resistance exercise intensity, Arent, Landers, et al. (2005) demonstrated that moderately intense resistance exercise (70 percent of 10-RM) was superior to either low- or high-intensity exercise in terms of increasing positive affect and reducing negative affect.

Ekkekakis Dual-mode Hypothesis The

Ekkekakis (2003) dual-mode hypothesis is based upon the observation that exercise above the lactate threshold (LT) may be perceived as unpleasant, while exercise below the LT may be perceived as being pleasant. Therefore, any assigned exercise intensity that is at or above the LT should not be perceived as pleasant to the participant and may have a negative effect on positive affect. Recall, that for any participant, the LT is positioned at the transition point between aerobic exercise (with oxygen) and anaerobic exercise (without oxygen). The **dual-mode hypothesis** hypothesizes two different mechanisms through which affective responses are generated. Proprioceptors from muscles and organs are believed to be primary during bouts of exercise above the lactate threshold, while cognitive appraisal is primary and takes precedence at intensities below the lactate threshold. This should theoretically translate into increased positive affect and reduced negative affect associated with exercise intensity below the lactate threshold and just the opposite above the threshold. Initial support for the new model has been forthcoming (Hall, Ekkekakis, & Petruzzello, 2007; Rose & Parfitt, 2007; Welch, Hulley, Ferguson, & Beauchamp, 2007).

Circumplex Model The circumplex model was

first introduced by Russell (1980) as a way to simultaneously project hedonic tone and felt arousal on the same two-dimensional plane. The concept was applied by Ekkekakis and Petruzzello (2002) as a means of measuring and displaying the effects of exercise on hedonic tone and felt arousal. In applying the circumplex model to exercise, Ekkekakis and Petruzzello utilized the Feeling Scale (FS; Backhouse, Bishop, Biddle, & Williams, 2005; Hardy & Rejeski, 1989) as a way of measuring hedonic tone (pleasure-displeasure), and the Felt Arousal Scale (FAS; Svebak & Murgatroyd, 1985) as a way of measuring felt arousal. The **circumplex model,** as applied to exercise intensity, is illustrated in figure 17.1. As can be observed in this figure, FS is found on the horizontal axis and runs from a -5 (very unpleasant) on the left up to $+5$ (very pleasant) on the right. As also can be observed in the figure, FAS is found on the vertical axis and runs from 6 (highly aroused) on the top down to 1 (under aroused) on the bottom. In application, scores on the FS and FAS

FIGURE 17.1 | The circumplex mode as applied to exercise intensity.

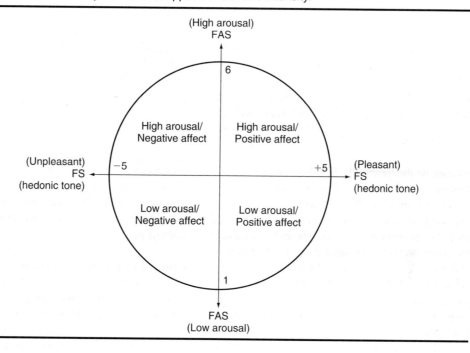

dimensions are plotted on circumplex space to show an exerciser's affective response to exercise as a function of hedonic tone and arousal. Research reported by Backhouse, Ekkekakis, Biddle, Foskett, and Williams (2007) and Bixby and Lochbaum (2008) provide excellent examples of how exercise intensity research can be interpreted using the circumplex model. In the Backhouse, Ekkekakis, et al. (2007) study it was shown that hedonic tone and felt arousal changes as a function of the intensity of the bout of exercise. Hedonic tone (FS) tends to be pleasant prior to and after a demanding 90-minute exercise regime but becomes less pleasant during the actual exercise. Conversely, felt arousal is low prior to and after exercise but is quite high during the strenuous bout of exercise. The Bixby and Lochbaum (2008) investigation observed that multiple modes of preferred and less preferred bouts of exercise were all interpreted as being pleasant and of a low to moderate level of arousal (lower/right quadrant of figure 17.1). Finally, research shows that all

intensities of acute aerobic treadmill running results in increased brain activity and positive affect compared to a resting condition (Woo, Kim, Kim, Petruzzello, & Hatfield, 2010).

Exercise Mode

In terms of grouped data, one particular **mode of aerobic exercise** does not seem to provide greater psychological benefits than another. For example, Cox, Thomas, and Davis (2000) observed no differences in anxiety between treadmill and stepper exercisers following a 30-minute bout of exercise. However, research does show that mode of aerobic exercise does make a difference in terms of energy expenditure. Moyna et al. (2001) exercised participants at three different levels of perceived exertion (light, somewhat hard, and hard) on six different exercise machines. Results showed that energy expenditure at each level of exertion was higher for men on the treadmill and ski simulator, and for

CONCEPT The psychological benefits of regular physical activity are more pronounced for mentally ill individuals than for normal, mentally healthy individuals.

APPLICATION Regular, supervised physical activity is an important adjunct treatment for individuals suffering from anxiety, depression, schizophrenia, and other emotional disorders. Hospitalized individuals would benefit significantly from organized daily physical activity appropriate to their environments.

women on the treadmill, ski simulator, and rowing ergometer, compared to the other modes.

From an individual differences perspective, the greatest positive affect seems to be derived from the mode of exercise that the exerciser labels as most preferred compared to least preferred (Bixby & Lochbaum, 2008; Miller, Bartholomew, & Springer, 2005). In other words, it is not the exercise mode itself that makes the difference (e.g., stepper, rower, cycle, treadmill) but the individual's personal preference.

Because walking is considered to be a different mode of exercise than jogging or running, it is instructive to briefly mention the psychological benefits of walking. In a study reported by Ekkekakis, Backhouse, Gray, and Lind (2008) it was observed that short, self-paced walks increase self-reported energy compared to a control group. In a separate study reported by Focht (2009) it was observed that both outdoor walking and indoor walking improve affective responses. The study, however, also observed that the outdoor walking realized more pleasant affective states and enjoyment compared to walking indoors. This perception is reinforced by research that shows that exercise perceived to be more "green" or natural leads to greater reduction in state anxiety (Mackay & Neill, 2010).

Special Populations

Discussion to this point has focused primarily on the benefits of regular aerobic exercise for normal, healthy individuals. As we have seen, the evidence supporting the beneficial psychological effects of regular aerobic exercise is substantial. We turn our attention now to the beneficial psychological effects of regular physical activity on special populations of people.

Clinical Populations The measurable benefits of regular physical activity are greater for individuals suffering from psychological disorders than for normal individuals (North et al., 1990; Petruzzello et al., 1991). The psychological benefits of aerobic exercise on individuals suffering from clinical depression have been well documented in literature reviews (Craft & Landers, 1998; Mutrie, 2000). Using a meta-analysis procedure, Craft and Landers observed that (a) both aerobic and anaerobic exercise were effective in reducing clinical depression, (b) more depressed individuals benefited the most from exercise, (c) exercise was as beneficial as psychotherapy and drug therapy for reducing depression, and (d) long-term exercise programs were more effective than short-term programs for reducing depression in the clinically ill. The beneficial effects of exercise on depression has also been documented in more recent research (Bodin & Martinsen, 2004; Desha, Ziviani, Nicholson, Martin, & Darnell, 2007; Faulkner & Biddle, 2004; Legrand & Heuze, 2008).

While most research with clinical populations has focused on depression, the beneficial effect of regular exercise has also been observed with individuals suffering from anxiety (Petruzzello et al., 1991), panic disorder (Martinsen, Raglin, Hoffart,

CONCEPT The psychological benefits of exercise extend to all individuals, regardless of age or degree of physical challenge.

APPLICATION We must not lose sight of the need to extend opportunities to be physically active to all populations of people. Children are in particular need, because it is at a young age that exercise behaviors for a lifetime are established. Older adults are also in particular need because of the challenges of growing older. Physical activity can lessen or buffer the debilitating effects of aging, both physiological and psychological. Physically challenged individuals are in need as well, because it is often incorrectly assumed that they are incapable of meaningful physical activity.

& Friis, 1998), and schizophrenia (Faulkner & Sparkes, 1999). Given the difficulty associated with treating schizophrenia, the Faulkner and Sparkes (1999) research is particularly promising. In this study, involving three patients suffering from chronic schizophrenia, improvements associated with exercise were observed in reduced auditory hallucinations and better sleep patterns.

Elderly Adults The elderly are entering a new stage in their lives. They are transitioning from being a father, mother, and provider for others to being responsible for their own happiness and health. In so doing, getting involved in an exercise program helps them to be happier, develop social bonds with other exercisers, and develop a sense of pride and ownership in their exercise program (Bidonde, Goodwin, & Drinkwater, 2009). As with younger adults, exercise and physical activity in the elderly leads to psychological and physiological benefits (Arent, Landers, & Etnier, 2000; Dionigi, 2007; Lampinen, Heikkinen, & Ruoppila, 2000; McAuley, Blissmer, Marquez, et al., 2000; Wilson & Spink, 2009). In addition to improved positive affect, physical activity also has the potential benefit of preserving cognitive functioning that normally declines with age (McLafferty, Hunter, Wetzstein, & Bamman, 2000; Shay & Roth, 1992).

Other Factors

In this section we briefly discuss the potential modifying effects that music and social environment have on facilitating the effectiveness of exercise on mental health.

Music Research suggests that listening to music during exercise can increase positive affect in the exerciser. Not only does listening to music during exercise enhance the beneficial effects of exercise, but it also reduces perceived exertion (Boutcher & Trenske, 1990). Research also suggests that music might improve exercise performance by (a) reducing the perception of fatigue, (b) increasing arousal, (c) encouraging motor coordination, and (d) increasing relaxation (Rendi, Szabo, & Szabo, 2008). Research indicates that motivational music can elicit an ergogenic effect and enhance positive psychological affect during endurance activities (Karageorghis et al., 2009).

Social Environment The social environment associated with exercise has an effect upon the psychological benefits of exercise. In a study reported by Turner, Rejeski, and Brawley (1997), it was observed that exercising in a socially enriched environment results in greater self-revitalization and self-efficacy compared to a socially bland environment. Similarly, McAuley, Blissmer, Katula, Duncan, and Mihalko (2000) observed increases in self-esteem and self-efficacy in older adults who participated in walking or stretching/toning classes. Finally, in a study reported by Wilson and Spink (2009), it was observed that the predictive relationship between social influences and physical activity was stronger for older women who preferred to be active with a friend.

Positive Effects of Exercise on Cognitive Function

Sport psychologists, physical educators, and educators in general have long believed that a positive relationship exists between physical activity and cognitive function. While pioneering research in this area began with Spirduso (1975), it is only recently that consistent evidence has accumulated in support of the relationship. Since 1997, at least three meta-analyses (statistical summaries of research) involving children, adolescents, and adults have been conducted and published that show a significant relationship between exercise and improved cognitive function (Crabbe & Dishman, 2004; Etnier et al., 1997; Sibley & Etnier, 2003). In addition, a review study reported by Tomporowski (2003) showed that for submaximal aerobic exercise, improvements in cognitive function can be observed.

While the Etnier et al. (1997) meta-analysis showed that a relationship exists between exercise and cognitive function, the same analysis also showed that the strength of the relationship declined if only studies that show a cause and effect relationship were considered. In order for a cause and effect relationship to be shown, experimental conditions must be manipulated and a control group included. Many studies have been reported that show an interesting and compelling association between exercise and cognitive function without showing cause and effect (Castelli, Hillman, Buck, & Erwin, 2007; Hillman, Castelli, & Buck, 2005; Stevens, To, Stevenson, & Lochbaum, 2008). Even though the Castelli et al. (2007) study was not experimental in nature, it was very interesting. They regressed three measures of elementary school student academic achievement on age, sex, academic level of school, and physical fitness. After controlling for age, sex, and school, they concluded that aerobic capacity and body mass (measure of obesity) predicted academic achievement. Thus, academic achievement in math

and reading increased as fitness increased and obesity decreased.

In recent years researchers have been interested in more than just establishing an association between physical activity and cognitive function. They have probed deeper to try to understand the brain mechanisms that allow for an improvement in cognitive function associated with exercise. One creative way to study cognitive function is to focus either on (a) information processing speed, or (b) the executive function component of cognitive function. Of the two, executive function is believed to be the truest indicator of improved cognitive function, as it controls planning and selective attention. According to Etnier and Chang (2009), **executive function** of the brain is broadly defined as "a higher order cognitive ability that controls basic, underlying cognitive functions for purposeful, goal directed behavior and that has been associated with frontal [cortical] lobe activity" (p. 470). When planning cognitive function studies it is important that researchers measure executive function in some form or fashion. Etnier and Chang (2009) point out the need for researchers to clearly define executive function and to select multiple tests of the construct. To assist researchers in these goals, Etnier and Chang provided a list of 11 different executive planning tests to select from. As defined by Beilock and Sibley (2007) executive function is an attentional capability that allows for the smooth functioning of working memory (short-term memory) in the face of interference.

A number of creative response time tests have been developed to measure both speed of information processing and executive function. These include the Ericksen flanker task (Ericksen & Ericksen, 1974), the Stroop test (Stroop, 1935), and general reaction time. The Ericksen flanker task was employed in a study reported by Davranche, Hall, and McMorris (2009). In the Ericksen task participants were asked to respond to a central target light that was flanked by distracter lights. In the Davranche et al. study participants who responded to light arrays while exercising did so at a faster rate than a control group.

Two recent investigations utilized the Stroop Test to demonstrate that exercise improves executive brain function (Chang & Etnier, 2009; Sibley, Etnier, & Le Masurier, 2006). In the Chang and Etnier (2009) study, the investigators manipulated the intensity of bouts of resistance exercise. The Stroop test was administered before and after each bout of exercise. In this study, the Stroop word test and the Stroop color test provided measures of information processing speed, while the Stroop color-word test provided a measure of executive function (where the participant can identify the color of a word that spelled a different color). Results of the study showed that as the intensity of the resistance exercise increased so did information processing speed increase. However, in the case of the test of executive function, the relationship between exercise intensity and response time was quadratic in nature. Decision time became faster as exercise intensity increased up to a certain moderate level of intensity, but then became slower as the exercise became very intense. These studies suggest that exercise is associated with improved executive function, but that if the intensity of the exercise is too high, a decline in executive function can occur.

In addition to the Erickson and Stroop tests, other creative studies have employed reaction time as a measure of executive brain function (Chang, Etnier, & Barella, 2009; Ellemberg & St-Louis-Deschenes, 2010; Pontifex, Hillman, Fernhall, Thompson, & Valentini, 2009). While each of these investigations provides experimental support for the hypothesis that exercise improves information processing speed and executive function, the study by Chang et al. (2009) is of particular interest. In this study, the task was to respond physically to a light stimulus while physiological arousal was being manipulated via a stationary cycle. Target heart rates were manipulated from 20 to 90 percent of heart rate reserve. This study was unique, in that simple and complex reaction time (two choice) were fractionated into two parts: (a) premotor cognitive function, and (b) motor peripheral function. The results of the investigation showed that a linear relationship exists between increased aerobic exercise intensity and quicker motor peripheral function reaction time, but not for premotor cognitive function.

Several other recent investigations may be cited that show a cause and effect relationship between exercise and improved cognitive function, but that do not use reaction time as a measure of cognitive function (Beilock & Sibley, 2007; Davis, Tomporowski, et al., 2007; Fontana, Mazzardo, Mokgothu, Furtado, & Gallagher, 2009). Of particular interest, is the Beilock and Sibley investigation: their results suggest that cognitive benefits associated with exercise only benefit individuals initially low in working memory capacity (executive function). In this study, measures of working memory capacity were taken before and after 30 minutes of aerobic exercise at 60 to 80 percent of predicted maximal heart rate. For purposes of analysis, participants were classified into one of four categories of working memory capacity (low, low-moderate, high-moderate, high). Comparisons were made between pre and post measures of working memory for each level of initial memory capacity. Results showed that improvements in working memory capacity occurred only for the participants initially categorized as being low in executive function.

While interesting questions have been raised in the previous reviews, taken together, the investigations reviewed in this section all support the hypothesis that exercise can result in improved cognitive function. This is particularly the case in terms of information processing speed, and conditionally the case in terms of improved executive function. A number of variables have been shown to moderate the relationship between exercise and improved cognitive function, and they need to continue to be investigated (e.g., mode of exercise, intensity of exercise, initial level of working memory).

Finally, an investigation reported by Ekkekakis (2009) is of great importance in identifying the mechanisms involved in facilitating an improvement in cognitive functioning associated with physical activity. As pointed out by Ekkekakis, the prefrontal cortex of the brain has been identified as

CONCEPT Physical activity of the aerobic and resistance exercise variety can result in increased cognitive functioning and academic achievement.

APPLICATION The implications of this research observation are both immense and far-reaching. While numerous moderator variables are likely to be associated with this relationship (variables that modify the relationship), it is clear that regular physical activity should be encouraged in schoolchildren as well as adults at every developmental level. For school children, this can be in the form of frequent breaks from sitting and studying as well as organized physical education and recreational sports.

---

an important cortex structure associated with physical activity and its effects on cognitive functioning. A number of neuroimaging methods have been developed that might be used to study the prefrontal cortex during exercise. These include electroencephalography (EEG), single-photon-emmission computed topography (SPECT), positron-emission tomography (PET), and functional magnetic resonance imaging (fMRI). Each of these neuroimaging methods have advantages and disadvantages associated with movement artifacts, high cost, and/or invasive nature of the test. A fifth method suggested by Ekkekakis is near-infrared spectroscopy (NIRS). After discussing the advantages and disadvantages of this technique, Ekkekakis lists and discusses 28 reported studies that involve exercise and the prefrontal cortex. From the results of this analysis, it appears that mild to moderate exercise results in increased oxygenation (blood flow) of the frontal cortex, while strenuous exercise results in a decrease in oxygenation of this brain site. Ekkekakis concludes the article by discussing three theories that might explain the observed effect, with particular attention to the dual-mode hypothesis discussed in a previous section of this chapter.

Theoretical Explanations for the Relationship between Exercise and Improved Mental Health

Many hypotheses have been proposed to explain why exercise is associated with improved mental health. A number of these hypotheses will be reviewed and discussed in the following paragraphs. The first three explanations are considered to be psychological in nature, while the remaining three are physiological in nature. While it is tempting to subscribe to one hypothesis at the expense of the others, it is likely that the ultimate explanation is eclectic and multidimensional in nature.

Cognitive Behavioral Hypothesis

The basic premise of the **cognitive behavioral hypothesis** is that exercise encourages and generates positive thoughts and feelings that serve to counteract negative mood states such as depression, anxiety, and confusion (North et al., 1990). This theoretical explanation parallels Bandura's theory of self-efficacy, discussed in chapter 3. According to Bandura (1997), when individuals master tasks they perceive to be difficult, they experience an increase in self-efficacy. Exercise is perceived by nonexercisers as a difficult task. When the nonexerciser succeeds in becoming a regular exerciser, she experiences a feeling of accomplishment and self-efficacy. An increase in self-efficacy is helpful in breaking the downward spiral of negative affect associated with depression, anxiety, and other negative mood states.

Social Interaction Hypothesis

The basic premise of the **social interaction hypothesis** is that the social interaction associated with exercising with friends and colleagues is pleasurable and has the net effect of improving mental health (North et al., 1990). While the social interaction hypothesis provides a partial explanation for the psychological benefits of exercise, it does not provide an acceptable complete explanation. Evidence of the psychological benefits of regular exercise abounds, whether the exercising is done in groups or alone. The North et al. (1990) meta-analysis, for example, confirmed that exercising alone and at home results in greater reductions in depression than exercising at other locations (usually with others).

Distraction Hypothesis

The basic premise of the **distraction hypothesis** is that exercise affords an opportunity for individuals to be distracted from their worries and frustrations. Support for this hypothesis comes from Alfermann and Stoll (2000) and from Bahrke and Morgan (1978). Bahrke and Morgan (1978) observed that acute doses of meditation and quiet rest were as effective as exercise in reducing anxiety. The North et al. (1990) meta-analysis, however, concluded that chronic exercise is a more powerful and effective treatment for reducing negative mood than relaxation or other distracting but enjoyable activities. It may be that distraction provides a viable explanation for short-term reduction in depression and anxiety, but not for long-term reduction.

Cardiovascular Fitness Hypothesis

The basic premise of the **cardiovascular fitness hypothesis** is that improved mood state is associated with improved cardiovascular fitness. The cardiovascular fitness hypothesis, however, is not generally supported by the literature (Emery & Blumenthal, 1988; North et al., 1990). The results of the North et al. (1990) meta-analysis suggest that the initial psychological benefits of chronic exercise occur during the first few weeks, before participants experience substantial changes in cardiovascular fitness.

Amine Hypothesis

The basic premise of the **amine hypothesis** is that increased secretion of chemicals that serve as neurotransmitters is related to improved mental health. Neurotransmitters serve to transmit signals from nerve to nerve and from nerve to muscle. Studies have shown that depressed individuals often suffer a decrement in the secretion of various amines, such as norepinephrine, serotonin, and dopamine (North et al., 1990), and that exercised rats experience an increase in brain norepinephrine. Theoretically, exercise stimulates the production of neurotransmitters that in turn have a positive effect on psychological mood (Chaouloff, 1997; Greenwood, Foley, Burhans, Maier, & Fleshner, 2005; Ransford,1982; Schwartz & Kindermann, 1990).

Endorphin Hypothesis

The **endorphin hypothesis** postulates that exercise is associated with brain production of chemicals that have a "morphine-like" effect on the exerciser (pain reduction and general euphoria).

Athlete enjoying the benefits of exercise and competiton.
© Royalty-Free/Corbis.

According to this hypothesis, the morphinelike substance provides a positive modulating effect on mood and emotion. This effect has been referred to, in the popular literature, as the "runner's high." As with the release of neurotransmitters (amine hypothesis), research verifies that intense endurance exercise is associated with the release of three types of endogenous opioids into the bloodstream, of which endorphins are one type (Grossman & Sutton, 1985; Harber & Sutton, 1984; Heitkamp, Schulz, Rocker, & Dickhuth, 1998; Schwarz & Kindermann, 1989, 1992; Thorn, Floras, Hoffman, & Seals, 1990).

While it has been clearly established that intense endurance exercise is associated with the increased release of neurotransmitters and endorphins into the bloodstream, the hypothesis that these blood chemicals are responsible for changes in mood and affect is based largely on logic and not cause and effect research. We do know that

exercise is associated with improved mood and affect, and we also know that intense exercise results in the release of neurotransmitters and endorphins into the bloodstream. Based on these facts, it seems logical to conclude that it is the presence of blood chemicals in the blood that causes improved mood. In partial support of the endorphin hypothesis is a recent animal study reported by Ferreira, Cornilleau, Perez-Diaz, and Cohen-Salmon (2008). In this study, exercised and nonexercised mice were injected with either morphine or a saline solution. On the last day, the mice were injected with naloxone, a drug that induces morphine withdrawal symptoms (jumping and burrowing). The observation that all exercised animals displayed morphine withdrawal symptoms was taken as evidence that exercised animals not injected with morphine were producing endorphins endogenously, and that the endorphins mimic injected morphine.

Exercise Adherence and Determinants

The basic premise of this chapter is that exercise is associated with positive psychological and physiological benefits. The previous sections have reinforced the reality of this strong relationship. In contrast with these positive research findings is the grim reminder that approximately 58 percent of the American population is sedentary, 10 to 25 percent of Americans suffer from mild to moderate depression and anxiety, and 50 percent of the people who start a structured exercise program drop out within the first six months (LaFontaine et al., 1992). With these facts in mind, it becomes clear that another important aspect of exercise psychology is to determine what motivates individuals to start exercising, what motivates them to adhere to an exercise program, and what motivates them to try again after failing the first (or second) time.

A structural model proposed by Sallis and Hovell (1990) provides a framework for studying what these authors call the **natural history of**

FIGURE 17.2 | Four major phases of the natural history of exercise. Transitions denoted by T_1, T_2, and T_3.

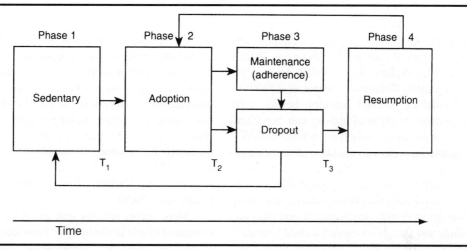

Source: Adapted with permission from Sallis, J. F., & Hovell, M. F. (1990). Determinants of exercise behavior. In K. B. Pandolfi, & J. O. Holloszy (Eds.), *Exercise and Sport Sciences Reviews, 18,* 307–330. Copyright 1990 by Lippincott, Williams & Wilkins, Baltimore.

exercise. The natural history of exercise model, as illustrated in figure 17.2, proposes a framework for studying the *determinants* of exercise behavior.

As depicted in figure 17.2, the determinants of exercise behavior focus on the three *transitions* between the sedentary phase, the adoption phase, the maintenance or dropout phase, and the resumption phase. Research that has been or should be conducted on exercise determinants examines the *three transitions* between the *four phases* of the natural history of exercise.

Transition from Sedentary State to Exercise Adoption (T_1)

Exercise determinants that motivate individuals to make the transition from a sedentary lifestyle to regular exercise are under studied. An exception to this general observation is a study reported by Sallis et al. (1986). In this investigation, 1,400 adults were initially assessed with a battery of potential determinants. One year later these potential determinants were compared with

exercise behaviors. As a result of these comparisons, several predictors of vigorous physical exercise were identified. Based on this investigation, individuals likely to adopt a vigorous exercise lifestyle exhibit the following characteristics:

1. Confidence they can succeed at a vigorous exercise program (exercise self-efficacy).

2. Knowledge about what constitutes a healthy lifestyle, and about the importance and value of regular exercise.

3. The perception that they enjoy a high level of self-control.

4. Good attitudes about the value and importance of regular exercise.

5. Initial condition of not being overweight or obese.

Consistent with Sallis et al. (1986), several studies have documented the importance of *exercise self-efficacy* in starting an exercise program. Highly efficacious individuals experience lower perceptions of effort expenditure during exercise, and report positive affect associated with vigorous exercise. Exercise self-efficacy is negatively impacted by perceptions of obesity. Consequently, initial perceptions of being obese can be a barrier for adopting an exercise program (Lown & Braunschweig, 2008; Martin & McCaughtry, 2008; Welch, Hulley, & Beauchamp, 2010; Williams, Dunsiger, et al., 2008).

For children, parental attitudes, beliefs, and support relative to physical activity can be either strong determinants or strong barriers toward adopting an active lifestyle. Parents (as well as siblings and friends) can make a big difference as to whether or not a young person seeks out opportunities to be active or not. Television, video games, and other sedentary activities provided by parents and enjoyed by siblings and friends counteract a child's natural desire to be physically active (Anderson, Hughes, & Fuemmeler, 2009; Jago et al., 2009; Kimiecik & Horn, 1998; Martin & McCaughtry, 2008).

For older adults, loneliness can be a barrier to adopting an exercise program. This may seem particularly counterintuitive, as getting involved with other adults in physical activity should make one less lonely. However, it is a little bit like the problem of obesity in children. The perception of being obese may result in reduced confidence and hence a reluctance to try exercise. With older adults, getting involved in physical activity will give rise to a good or bad mood. Being able to interpret the mood in a positive way will determine if the person seeks out other opportunities to be physically active (Hawkley, Thisted, & Cacioppo, 2009). For adults, adopting a physically active lifestyle may also have a lot to do with the community in which they live. Progressive communities are proactive in establishing a community coalition for developing exercise opportunities within the community (Whaley & Haley, 2008).

Transition from Adoption to Maintenance or Dropout Status (T$_2$)

The statistics that only 20 percent of all adult North Americans exercise regularly, and that 50 percent of all adults who begin an exercise program drop out within six months, are alarming (Dishman, 2001). The positive psychological and physiological benefits associated with regular physical activity cannot be realized in the absence of exercise. Most of the research that has been conducted on exercise determinants has focused on the transition from adoption to maintenance (T$_2$ in figure 17.2). This area of research is referred to as **exercise adherence,** or the degree to which exercisers adhere to their exercise programs. Excellent reviews of exercise adherence research have been provided by Carron, Hausenblas, and Mack (1996); Dishman (1987); Sallis and Hovell (1990); and Burke, Carron, Eys, Ntoumanis, and Estabrooks (2006).

More recent reviews and investigations have continued to add to the body of knowledge relative to exercise adherence. These studies have sharpened our understanding of how such factors as group cohesion, equipment accessibility, self-efficacy, intrinsic motivation, and social physique anxiety determine or are predictive of exercise adherence. In group exercise programs, *group cohesion* developed among the members of the exercise group increases exercise adherence (Burke, Carron, et al., 2006; Estabrooks, 2000). Placing a treadmill in the home (*accessibility*) of obese female exercisers increases the likelihood that they will adhere to their exercise program (Jakicic, Winters, Lang, & Wing, 1999; Kerr, Norman, Sallis, & Patrick, 2008; Oman & King, 2000). A recent narrative review shows the importance of *exercise self-efficacy* in predicting exercise adherence. Exercisers who believe they can succeed at a regular exercise program do succeed (McAuley and Blissmer, 2000). Self-efficacy is also important in facilitating adherence to exercise resistance programs involving older adults (Neupert, Lachman, & Whitbourne, 2009). Furthermore, self-efficacy for coping with exercise barriers enhances the probability of former high school students of remaining physically active during their freshman year of college (Bray, 2007). Age is a moderator of the relationship between *social physique anxiety* and exercise adherence. Younger obese women

CONCEPT   An incomplete list of determinants of both exercise adherence and nonadherence has been identified through research.

APPLICATION   Once an individual has committed to a vigorous long-term program, it is the responsibility of the exercise psychologist and fitness leader to help him maintain a lifelong commitment to regular exercise. Knowledge of the determinants of exercise adherence and nonadherence should be used to anticipate potential dropouts. Planned intervention strategies should be applied, when needed, to maintain motivation and commitment.

who are high in social physique anxiety tend to be exercise program dropouts, whereas older women high in the construct are less likely to drop out (Treasure, Lox, & Lawton, 1998). A summary of determinants of exercise adherence and nonadherence is provided in table 17.1.

Research continues to reinforce the importance of good weather, personal convenience, and a paucity of debilitating stressful life events on

TABLE 17.1 | Primary Determinants of Adherence and Nonadherence to Vigorous Exercise Programs

A. Determinants of Exercise Adherence

1. Available time
2. Behavioral coping skills
3. Equipment and facility accessibility
4. Exercise self-efficacy
5. Group cohesion
6. High risk of heart disease
7. Intrinsic motivation
8. Personal perception of good health
9. Social support

B. Determinants of Exercise Nonadherence

1. Being a blue-collar worker
2. Being overweight or obese
3. Mood state disturbances relative to exercise
4. Physical discomfort during exercise
5. Being a smoker
6. Social physique anxiety

exercise adherence (Oman & King, 2000; Salmon, Owen, Crawford, Bauman, & Sallis, 2003). Some factors that might make it more conducive to continue exercising include variability, frequency, and intensity of exercise (Glaros & Janelle, 2001; Perri et al., 2002). Adherence levels of previously sedentary individuals can be increased by varying exercise mode so that it does not get boring; by increasing the frequency of exercise bouts during a week, and by maintaining moderate- as opposed to high-intensity exercise bouts.

While it is important to avoid prolonged bouts of overly intense exercise, research reported by Anton et al. (2005) is instructive. Their research shows that exercise intensity moderates the relationship between past exercise history and future adherence to an exercise program. Exercisers who have a past history of exercising at a high level of intensity are better adherers to an exercise program than are moderate-intensity exercisers. Ekkekakis's dual-mode model (2003) provides theoretical background for what constitutes excessively intense exercise (Williams, 2008).

Research shows that exercise imagery is positively associated with exercise motivation, self-efficacy, and exercise frequency (Cumming & Stanley, 2009; Giacobbi, 2007; Giacobbi, Hausenblas, Fallon, & Hall, 2003). Exercisers use imagery to increase energy, improve appearance, and improve exercise technique. It is also believed that imagery use increases self-efficacy, which in turn has a direct effect on exercise participation (Cumming, 2008).

Research also shows that self-determined motivation as discussed in chapter 3 (see figure 3.5)

FIGURE 17.3 | Perceived self-worth mediates the relationship between antecedents and long-term exercise adherence.

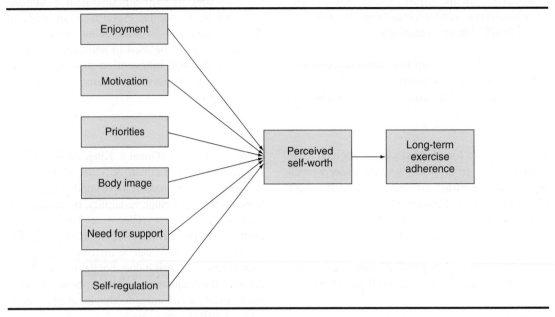

is important in facilitating exercise adherence (Edmunds, Ntoumanis, & Duda, 2007, 2008; Lonsdale, Sabiston, Raedeke, Ha, & Sum, 2009). Psychological need satisfaction in the form of perceived competence, autonomy, and relatedness are critical for developing intrinsic motivation necessary for adherence to an exercise program. An exercise program based on outcome goals such as weight loss, shape, appearance, and body shape are inherently controlling, and therefore may be difficult to be maintained for long periods of time.

An exercise program that results in an increase in positive mood will be perceived by the individual as enjoyable. People persist in doing the things they find to be enjoyable and have difficulty with things that are not perceived as enjoyable (Raedeke, 2007). This is why it is often important that we select physical activities that yield outcomes that are fun and enjoyable. Enjoyment is often associated with level of skill. If you look back to figure 8.7, you will recall that the psychological phenomenon of flow is best obtained under

conditions of high skill and high personal challenge. If a person chooses tennis as a sport to help him or her maintain a high level of physical fitness, it would help that person to develop a high level of skill in tennis. Based on research reported by Huberty et al. (2008), we are informed that *perceived self-worth* is a powerful predictor of long-term exercise adherence. Perceived self-worth is, in turn, predicted by a number of antecedents including enjoyment. Thus, as illustrated in figure 17.3, perceived self-worth mediates the relationship between antecedents such as enjoyment and long-term exercise adherence.

Transition from Dropout Status to Exercise Resumption (T₃)

As stated by Sallis and Hovell (1990), the transition from being an exercise dropout to resuming a vigorous exercise program has been largely ignored by researchers and theorists. This is an important part of the exercise psychology literature that must be addressed. Statistics are not available on the percentage of people who drop out of an exercise program and then get started again. Is it harder to resume an exercise program after once dropping out, or is it harder to start initially? Do people who resume their exercise programs after dropping out tend to be good adherers, or do they tend to drop out again? Are the determinants for exercise maintenance the same as those for exercise resumption, or is there a separate set of determinants? These questions and others need to be addressed by exercise psychologists.

Theories of Exercise Behavior

Psychological models of human behavior have been applied to the exercise setting in an attempt to explain why people don't exercise, why they start to exercise, why they do or do not continue to exercise, and why they start exercising again if they stop. These models include (a) the theory of reasoned action, (b) the theory of planned behavior, (c) the transtheoretical model of stages of change, (d) self-determination theory applied to exercise, (e) social cognitive theory, and (f) exercise self-schemata theory. Each of these theories will now be briefly discussed.

The Theory of Reasoned Action

Originated by Ajzen and Fishbein (1977), the **theory of reasoned action** proposes that the main precursor of a behavior such as exercise is the individual's *intention* to perform the behavior. The intention to perform the behavior is determined by the individual's *attitude* toward the behavior as well as *social norms* or social pressure to perform the behavior. Research by Estabrooks and Courneya (1997) has demonstrated the effectiveness of the theory of reasoned action in exercise settings. While the theory of reasoned action is a viable model for predicting exercise behavior, research has demonstrated that its predictive power is increased when personal control is added to the model (Yannis, 1994). This observation led to the development of the theory of planned behavior.

The Theory of Planned Behavior

Originated by Ajzen (1985), the **theory of planned behavior** is an extension of the theory of reasoned action (Godin, 1994). The *intention* to perform a behavior is fundamental to the theory. Intention is determined by the individual's *attitude* toward the behavior and *social norms*. The difference between the two theories is the addition of perceived *behavioral control* to the original model. An individual will maintain or initiate an exercise program if his intention is firm and he feels in control. Intention is in turn a function of his attitude toward exercise and perceived social norms.

The expanded theory of planned behavior (TPB) is illustrated in figure 17.4. In this figure, the original TPB is shown as solid-line boxes and solid-path arrows leading from one box to another. The box originally labeled *social norms* in the model is replaced by the box labeled *social support*. Researchers originally thought that these two terms were synonymous, but research reported by Rhodes, Jones, and Courneya (2002) demonstrated that social support is a stronger predictor of exercise intention than social norms. Therefore, in figure 17.4, social support instead of social norms leads to intention to exercise. In the model, intention to exercise completely mediates the effects of both exercise attitude and social support on exercise behavior. Self-efficacy and perceived behavioral control have both a direct and an indirect effect on exercise behavior. That is, intention to exercise is a partial mediator of the effects of self-efficacy and perceived control on exercise behavior. As you can see from the TPB model, a *mediator variable* mediates or conveys the effect of one variable on another.

In figure 17.4, self-efficacy is shown in a dashed-line box and with a dashed line leading to intention to exercise and exercise behavior. This is so because this variable was not originally included as part of the TPB, but is included here to reflect research reported by Hagger, Chatzisarantis, and Biddle (2002) and Gao and Kosma (2008).

Also included in figure 17.4, and shown with dashed lines is the effect of personality factors

FIGURE 17.4 | Schematic representation of the original theory of planned behavior (solid lines) and the expanded model of the theory (dashed lines).

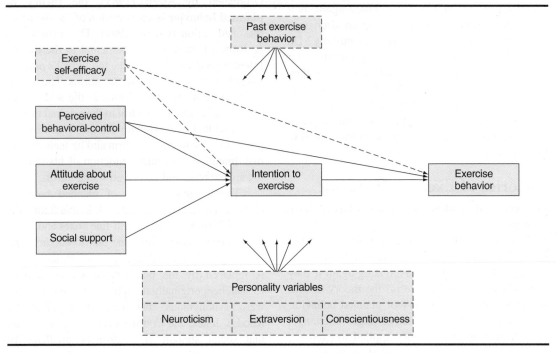

(neuroticism, extraversion, conscientiousness) on all aspects of the model. These effects come, in some cases, as direct effects on intention and exercise behavior, but also as moderators and mediators of various variables in the model (Conner, Rodgers, & Murray, 2007; de Bruijn, de Groot, van den Putte, & Rhodes, 2009; Hoyt, Rhodes, Hausenblas, & Giacobbi, 2009; Rhodes, Courneya, & Hayduk, 2001). For example, being highly conscientious will strengthen the effect of intention to exercise on exercise behavior. Finally, the dashed lines from *past exercise behavior* are based on numerous investigations which show that past exercise behavior has a direct and/or indirect effect on other variables in the model. As with personality, arrows are not shown between past exercise behavior and the other variables in order to avoid unnecessarily complicating the model (Hagger, Chatzisarantis, & Biddle, 2002; Hamilton & White, 2008; Norman & Conner, 2005).

In addition to the relationships shown in figure 17.4, researchers have studied and suggested a plethora of variables that could act as mediators and/or moderators in the model. The results of some of these investigations are summarized in the following two paragraphs.

Salient communication influences the effect that attitude and intention has upon other variables in the model (Chatzisarantis & Hagger, 2005). *Planning* moderates the strength of the relationship between exercise intention and exercise behavior (Norman & Conner, 2005), but research also shows that intention to exercise moderates (determines) the nature of the relationship between planning (action and coping) and exercise behavior (Scholz, Schuz, Ziegelmann, Lippke, & Schwarzer, 2008). Based on their research, Kiviniemi, Voss-Humke, and Seifert (2007) suggested that *feelings* about exercise could easily replace intentions in the model. *Incentive to exercise* is a predictor of both intention to exercise and exercise behavior and could be placed in the model along with self-efficacy (Gao & Kosma, 2008). Research reported by Hall Elias, et al. (2008) makes a strong case that cognitive function (IQ) should be placed in the TPB model as a moderator between intention to exercise and actual exercise behavior. Exercise *self-identity* is a strong predictor of both intention to exercise and exercise behavior and would make a good addition to the model (Hamilton & White, 2008).

Relative to the important mediating variable of intention in the TPB model, it has been shown that the intention to increase exercise behavior is strongest at the beginning of a 12-week exercise program whereas the intention to maintain is strongest near the end (Milne, Rodgers, Hall, & Wilson, 2008). Milne, Rodgers, et al. (2008) also showed that appearance imagery is a viable predictor of the intention and maintenance of exercise intention. In addition, the strongest relationship between intention to exercise and exercise behavior occurs when intention is stable over time and goal conflict is low (Li & Chan, 2008). Research shows that measured habit strength, for a particular exercise behavior, moderates the relationship between intention and the exercise behavior (de Bruijn, Kremers, Singh, van den Putte, & van Mechelen, 2009). This relationship is interesting because the strength of the relationship between intention and exercise behavior is strongest when habit strength is weak instead of high. When habit strength is high, intention to exercise becomes less relevant. Finally, research indicates that the TPB is a better predictor of *volitional* exercise behavior as

opposed to *constrained* daily physical training (Scott, Eves, Hoppe, & French, 2010).

Strong research support for the theory of planned behavior is provided by two meta-analyses (Hagger, Chatzisarantis, & Biddle, 2002; Hausenblas, Carron, & Mack, 1997). In addition to these two investigations, several studies have been reported that show both general support for the model as well as evidence that the model generalizes to African American children (Hagger & Chatzisarantis, 2005; Martin, Kulinna, et al., 2005), adolescent boys and girls (Downs, Graham, Yang, Bargainnier, & Vasil, 2006), both white and black college students (Blanchard, Kupperman, et al., 2007, 2008), Mexican American children (Martin, Oliver, & McCaughtry, 2007), and different cultures (Hagger, Chatzisarantis, Barkoukis, et al., 2007).

The Transtheoretical Model

The *transtheoretical model* was originally proposed as a stage theory of behavioral change by Prochaska and DiClemete (1986). Prochaska and Marcus (1994) provide an insightful explanation as to how the model is applied to exercise. According to the **transtheoretical model (TTM),** individuals pass through five dynamic stages in adopting healthy long-term exercise behavior. The stages are dynamic because individuals may move in and out of the several stages before reaching the final stage, which is also dynamic. The five stages of change, illustrated in figure 17.5, include

FIGURE 17.5 | The transtheoretical model, showing stages of change and processes of change that interact to bring about improved exercise behavior.

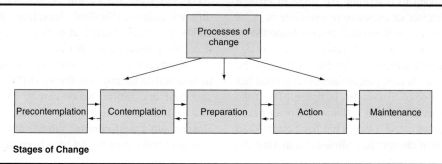

precontemplation, contemplation, preparation, action, and maintenance. Interventions called **processes of change** may be utilized to help exercisers move along the continuum from one stage to the next. It is important to know which stage an individual is in, because some interventions work better in one stage than in another. In applying the model, the exercise leader assesses the stage that the exerciser is in and then selectively applies a process of change intervention designed to help him move to the next level (Gorely & Gordon, 1995; Marcus & Simkin, 1994). Processes of change interact with the various stages of the transtheoretical model to bring about successful change in exercise behavior.

Marcus, Rossi, Selby, Niaura, and Abrams (1992) developed the 39-item Processes of Change Questionnaire (PCQ) to help behavioral psychologists to measure 10 different processes of change that may facilitate moving along the stages-of-change model. The 10 identified processes of change include five cognitive processes and five behavioral processes. Based on Marcus, Rossi, et al. (1992) it was hypothesized that cognitive processes are more effective in the pre-action phases (precontemplation, contemplation, and preparation), while the behavioral processes are most effective in the action and maintenance phases. Reading information about the values of exercise would be an example of a cognitive process to motivate a person to exercise. Utilizing social relationships to help people to exercise would be an example of a behavioral process to motivate a person to exercise.

Different approaches and inventories have been developed to determine the stage of change that an exerciser or prospective exerciser is in. A case in point is the Stage of Exercise Scale (SES) developed by Cardinal (1995) and illustrated in figure 17.6. In practice, the individual completes the SES, which allows the practitioner to categorize her as being in one of five stages. In figure 17.6, if the individual circled number 2, this would place her in the preparation phase. Once it has been established which stage of change the individual is in, then the

exercise leader applies interventions or processes of change to help the individual move to the next stage. For example, if an individual were in the contemplation phase, a discussion with the exercise leader about how exercise might fit into the contemplator's day might prove beneficial. If an individual were in the action phase, then seeking social support would be an intervention that might help move the exerciser into the maintenance phase.

The notion that cognitive processes of change should be most important for effecting change in the early stages of exercise change and that behavioral processes should be most important in the later stages is referred to as the *interaction hypothesis.* The testing and verification of the interaction hypothesis has been the object of several investigations, yielding generally supportive results (Lewis et al., 2006; Lowther, Mutrie, & Scott, 2007; Plotnikoff, Hotz, Birkett, & Courneya, 2001).

In the full transtheoretical model, in addition to stages of change and processes of change, other factors interact with the stages of change to bring about a change in exercise behavior. These include the familiar construct of exercise self-efficacy and *decisional balance.* Decisional balance has to do with the prospective exerciser considering the costs and/or benefits of making a behavioral change relative to exercise (Lowther et al., 2007).

In general, the research has supported the transtheoretical model as a means to enhance exercise behavior (Armstrong, Sallis, Hovell, & Hofstetter, 1993; Cardinal, 1997; Courneya, 1995; Marcus, Eaton, Rossi, & Harlow, 1994). Support for the transtheoretical model has extended to muscular fitness as well as aerobic fitness (Cardinal & Kosma, 2004; Van Vorst, Buckworth, & Mattern, 2002), to different cultures (Cardinal, Tuominen, & Rintala, 2004), and to adolescent as well as adult samples (Lee, Nigg, DiClemente, & Courneya, 2001).

A number of suggestions have been made as to how self-determination theory (SDT), the TPB, and goal orientation theory can be incorporated into the transtheoretical model (TTM). In addition, Rosenbaum's self-control model and Anshel's disconnected values model have been suggested as

FIGURE 17.6 │ Stage of exercise scale.

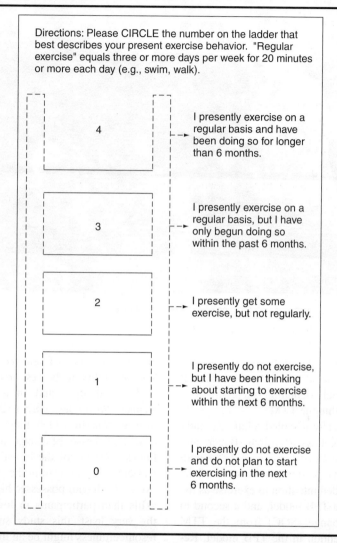

Directions: Please CIRCLE the number on the ladder that best describes your present exercise behavior. "Regular exercise" equals three or more days per week for 20 minutes or more each day (e.g., swim, walk).

4 — I presently exercise on a regular basis and have been doing so for longer than 6 months.

3 — I presently exercise on a regular basis, but I have only begun doing so within the past 6 months.

2 — I presently get some exercise, but not regularly.

1 — I presently do not exercise, but I have been thinking about starting to exercise within the next 6 months.

0 — I presently do not exercise and do not plan to start exercising in the next 6 months.

Source: Reproduced with permission from Cardinal, B. J. (1995). The stages of exercise scale and stages of exercise behavior in female adults. *Journal of Sports Medicine and Physical Fitness, 35,* 87–92.

possible alternatives to TTM. Self-determination theory will be treated in the next section as a freestanding theory of exercise behavior, while the application of the other theories will be briefly discussed here.

In the process of developing the Perceptions of Success of Questionnaire for Exercise (POSQ-E),

Zizi, Keeler, and Watson (2006) utilized the TTM and specifically stages of change to validate their new instrument. In the process, they discovered that task (mastery) goal orientation was positively correlated with stages of change such that as mastery goal orientation increased so did the stage of change on up to maintenance. Similarly, they

Tennis can be an excellent sport for maintaining physical fitness.

observed that ego (performance) goal orientation was negatively correlated with stages of change. This suggests that goal orientation is a predictor of stages of change within the TTM.

Utilizing physically disabled adults as study participants, Kosma, Ellis, Cardinal, Bauer, and McCubbin (2007) merged aspects of TTM with TPB. Specifically, they tested two versions of the TPB, one that included intention to exercise as the core mediator in the TPB model, and a second in which stages of change (SOC) from the TTM model replaced intention in the TPB model. Results of the investigation revealed that SOC is a stronger predictor of physical activity than intention. Because both versions of the TPB model were supported in the analyses, the authors concluded that both intention to exercise and stages of change should be considered in predicting exercise behavior.

Seemingly unrelated to the TTM, Rosenbaum (1990) proposed the *self-control model* of health behavior. The self-control model is based primarily on the construct of *learned resourcefulness* or learned ability to be resourceful in coping with health challenges and in adapting to change. Kennett, Worth, and Forbes (2009) reported on an investigation in which they measured stages of change, processes of change, and learned resourcefulness. Results of the investigation revealed that participants who were in the maintenance stage of exercise behavior possessed higher resourcefulness skills than participants in lower level stages. At the very least, this study suggests that learned resourcefulness might be an important predictor of exercise stage of change.

Finally, Anshel (2008), arguing that both the TPB and the TTM are ineffective in reducing sedentary behavior, proposed a new model of health behavior change named the **disconnected values model** (DVM). While currently untested, the DVM is based upon two main postulates. The first is that a person living an unhealthy sedentary lifestyle recognizes a basic disconnect (cognitive dissonance) between his deepest core values and his negative health habits. According to the DVM, the person either finds the cognitive dissonance to be acceptable or unacceptable. If it is determined that the disconnect is unacceptable, then he forms an action plan (second postulate) to adopt an active nonsedentary lifestyle. Contingent to the decision to adopt an active lifestyle, the goal is to (a) replace negative health habits with positive exercise rituals, and to (b) remove barriers to exercise.

Self-determination Theory Applied to Exercise

Self-determination as a theory of motivation was first introduced in chapter 3 and illustrated in figures 3.5 and 3.6. From figure 3.5, it is quite clear that SDT could logically be applied to exercise adoption, determination, and maintenance. The possession of high levels of competence, autonomy, and relatedness leads to a high level of intrinsic motivation which leads to desirable consequences (outcomes), such as exercise behavior. Many approaches to measuring psychological need satisfaction have been utilized in the motivation literature, among them is the Psychological Need Satisfaction in Exercise Scale (PNSE; Wilson, Rodgers, Rodgers, & Wild, 2006). Likewise, numerous approaches to measuring exercise behavior have been reported in the literature, among them is the Leisure-Time Exercise Questionnaire (LTEQ; Godin & Shephard, 1985). Several different inventories have also been developed for measuring self-determined motivation in exercise as illustrated in figure 3.6. These include the Behavioral Regulation Exercise Questionnaire (BREQ; Mullan, Markland, & Ingledew, 1997), the revised BREQ-2 (Markland & Tobin, 2004), and the Exercise Motivation Scale (EMS; Li, 1999; Wininger, 2007).

Wilson, Rodgers, Fraser, and Murray (2004) utilized the BREQ to study the relationship between self-determined motivation and exercise behavior. Results showed a strong predictive relationship between the BREQ subscales and actual exercise behavior. Consistent with expectations, identified regulation and intrinsic motivation were the strongest predictors of exercise behavior and exercise intention. In a similar fashion, Standage, Sebire, and Loney (2008) demonstrated that, after controlling for gender and a measure of obesity, autonomous but not controlling motivational regulation predicts exercise energy expenditure. These results suggest that the development of an autonomous form of motivation towards exercise is an effective way to encourage exercise adoption and maintenance.

Two other investigations studied the predictive relationship between self-determined motivation and stages of exercise change associated with the TTM. Utilizing college students, Buckworth, Lee, Regan, Schneider, and DiClemente (2007) demonstrated that the exercise maintenance stage of exercise was associated with greater intrinsic as opposed to extrinsic forms of motivation. Using a sample of African American women, Landry and Solmon (2004) studied the relationship between self-determination, as measured by the BREQ, and stage of change, as measured by a stage of change scale (see figure 17.6). Their results also showed that the autonomous forms of motivation are better predictors of stage of change than more controlling forms of motivation (external motivation). Important conclusions associated with this study are summarized as follows:

1. Strategies that rely on coercion are ineffective.

2. Reinforcing forms of motivation and autonomy are most effective in encouraging women to be physically active.

3. Rewards and threats are poor long-term motivators.

4. Strategies reinforcing higher levels of self-regulation (autonomous motivation) are more likely to foster long-term adherence to an exercise program.

Finally, Sebire, Standage, and Vansteenkiste (2009) reported on an ambitious investigation related to self-determination and exercise behavior.

CONCEPT The various theories of exercise behavior are useful in understanding human behavior and in designing interventions to help people adopt healthy exercise behaviors.

APPLICATION Rather than pitting one theory against another, it is best to bring elements of different theories together to understand the psychology of exercise adoption and adherence.

For example, the transtheoretical model can be very helpful in understanding where people are relative to exercise behavior. This information can then be integrated with concepts of self-efficacy, intentions, attitudes, social support, personal control, and self-determination to design interventions that can help individuals adopt and maintain exercise programs.

Dependent variables measured for the first phase of the study included exercise behavior, physical self-worth, exercise anxiety, psychological well-being, and psychological need satisfaction (competence, autonomy, relatedness). The independent variables for the first phase were (a) relative intrinsic goals (mean intrinsic goals minus mean extrinsic goals), and (b) self-determined motivation as summarized in a single relative autonomy index (RAI). Results showed that after controlling for gender, age, and relative intrinsic goals, RAI predicted each of the measured dependent variables including exercise behavior.

The results of the second phase of the Sebire et al. (2009) were equally impressive. The stated purpose of the second phase of the study was to determine if psychological need satisfaction (competence, autonomy, relatedness) mediates the relationship between relative intrinsic goals and three selected outcome variables (physical self-worth, psychological well-being, and exercise anxiety). The results of this phase of the investigation showed that (a) psychological need satisfaction is a partial mediator between relative intrinsic goals and the three outcome variables, (b) relative intrinsic goals have both an indirect and direct effect on the selected outcome measures, and (c) psychological need satisfaction predicts all three outcome variables in the expected direction.

Since its introduction in chapter 3, it has repeatedly been shown that self-determined motivation is a strong predictor of numerous outcomes associated with sport as well as exercise. In this section we have demonstrated the utility of STD as a means of predicting the adoption and maintenance of exercise behavior.

Social Cognitive Theory

As proposed by Bandura (1997), *social cognitive theory* provides a viable way to explain exercise behavior. Individuals who are dissatisfied with their current exercise behavior, who exhibit high levels of **exercise self-efficacy,** and who set exercise goals are generally able to achieve their goals. Exercise self-efficacy is a powerful predictor of exercise behavior. Individuals who believe in themselves and believe that they can be successful at maintaining an exercise program generally are successful (Maddison & Prapavessis, 2004; Rodgers, Wilson, Hall, Fraser, & Murray, 2008).

While social cognitive theory has been presented here as a stand-alone theory of exercise behavior, tenets of the theory are best incorporated into other theories. For example, self-efficacy is included as an important component of the theory of planned behavior and the transtheoretical model. Current theory suggests that best results may be obtained by applying components of several theories into the same strategies for improving exercise behavior in sedentary individuals. Instruments designed to measure exercise self-efficacy include the Self-Efficacy for Exercise Questionnaire (SEEQ; Garcia & King, 1991; Wilcox,

CONCEPT A person possessing an exercise self-schema is much more likely to maintain a chronic exercise program than a person who possesses a nonexercise self-schema.

APPLICATION The goal is to help individuals to develop exercise self-schemata. An exercise schema is really just a way of thinking about things. It is a cognitive generalization about how you want to live your life. As illustrated in figure 17.7, exercise must first be viewed as something you enjoy and want to try. In addition to wanting to exercise, you must take the next step by actually getting out and exercising. Trying to exercise and being successful lead to a commitment to continue and a belief in your own ability to exercise. Commitment and perceived ability lead to the development of the exercise self-schema.

Sharpe, Hutto, & Granner, 2005), and the Multidimensional Self-efficacy Scale (MSES; Rodgers et al., 2008).

Exercise Self-Schemata Theory

The notion of self-schemata to explain perception, inference, and memory was introduced by Markus (1977). According to Markus, **self-schemata** "are cognitive generalizations about the self, derived from past experience, that organize and guide the processing of self-related information contained in the individual's social experiences" (p. 64). Kendzierski (1988) was the first to apply the notion of self-schemata to behavior, and specifically to exercise behavior. Kendzierski (1988) developed specific questionnaire items that made it possible to categorize an individual as having an *exercise schema* or a *nonexercise schema*. By obtaining exercise intention and behavior information, it was possible to demonstrate that individuals with an exercise schema were much more likely to exercise than those who had a nonexercise schema.

Additional research with **exercise self-schemata** revealed that exercise-schematic individuals process exercise-related information more quickly and report more instances of past exercise behavior and future intent than nonexercise-schematic individuals (Kendzierski, 1990). Similarly, Kendzierski, Furr, Schiavoni (1998) found evidence of self-schemata in weightlifters and basketball players, showing that the self-schemata concept applies to physical activity generally, and not just to exercise. Exercise-schematic individuals tend to give unstable attributions to exercise lapses, whereas nonexercise-schematic individuals give more stable attributions (Kendzierski, Sheffield, & Morganstein, 2002). Research also shows that exercise self-schemata theory also applies to the exercise behaviors of older adults (Whaley & Schrider, 2005).

According to exercise self-schemata theory, the way to get people to exercise initially and to continue to exercise once they start (adherence) is to help them to develop the cognitive self-schemata for exercising. As explained by Kendzierski (2004), factors that are necessary for the development of an exercise self-schema include enjoyment of the exercise, wanting to exercise, trying to exercise, a commitment to exercise, and the ability to exercise. The relationships among the factors necessary for developing exercise self-schemata are illustrated in figure 17.7.

Research reported by Banting, Dimmock, and Lay (2009) add to our understanding of exercise self-schemata theory by differentiating between explicit and implicit exercise schemata. *Explicit* exercise self-schemata are based upon directly observed exercise behaviors and unambiguous feelings about the importance of regular exercise. Conversely, *implicit* exercise self-schemata are based on indirect assessment of an individual's commitment to regular exercise (e.g., the practice of wearing stylish athletic clothing). Both explicit

FIGURE 17.7 · | Structural model showing the relationships among factors that lead to development of exercise self-schemata.

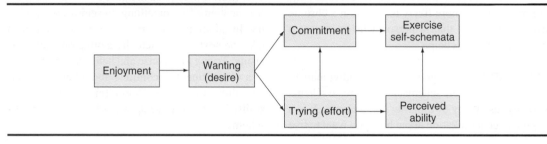

and implicit exercise schemata have a direct effect on exercise behavior, but explicit exercise schemata (EES) also have an indirect effect on exercise behavior through exercise intention.

EES → Exercise intention → Exercise behavior

Fitness as a Moderator of Life Stress

Given the positive relationship between exercise and improved mental health, it follows that physical fitness should serve as a buffer against life stress. The ability of individuals to insulate, protect, or inoculate themselves against the stresses of life through regular exercise is called **stress inoculation.** Research shows that the psychological benefits associated with regular exercise do not normally require an increase in physical fitness (Rejeski, Brawley, & Schumaker, 1996). Aerobic fitness, however, does appear to be a necessary precursor to the stress inoculation effect. Aerobically fit individuals appear to be inoculated against stress, illness, and the general hassles of life to a greater extent than less aerobically fit individuals. Children and adults who engage in healthy behavior that leads to physical fitness can insulate themselves from various physical and psychological health problems throughout their lives (Kubitz & Landers, 1993). While the exact mechanisms involved in stress inoculation are not known, it is believed that they may involve a complex pattern of central and autonomic nervous system adaptations.

Life stress represents an accumulation of the daily hassles and challenges of living out our lives. Individuals who exercise regularly and maintain a high level of physical fitness should be less susceptible to the negative effects of life stress. Evidence for this hypothesis has been provided by Brown (1991) and by others. The investigation by Brown is of special interest, because objective measures of physical fitness and illness were assessed. Brown studied the relationship between level of physical fitness, as measured by the bicycle ergometer; life stress, as measured by the Life Experience Survey; and number of visits to the university health center. As illustrated in figure 17.8, the results of the investigation show an interactive relationship between life stress, physical fitness, and number of visits to the health center (illness). Being physically fit serves to inoculate the individual against illness during periods of high stress. Conversely, physically unfit individuals appear to be unprotected against high stress.

Tangentially related to the life stress issue is the observation that exercise leading to physical fitness is an effective treatment to reduce high blood pressure. Martin and Calfas (1989) provided a review of 17 uncontrolled or partially controlled studies and 13 controlled studies. The results of this review suggest that exercise is an effective nonpharmacologic treatment for hypertension. Chronic aerobic exercise produces a reduction in blood pressure that is independent of weight loss or diet.

CONCEPT As a buffer of life stress, physical fitness, reduces hypertension and is associated with fewer visits to the doctor.

APPLICATION Time spent exercising is not wasted time. Because we live in a fast-paced, stressful world, steps must be taken to buffer daily stress. Individuals must be encouraged to place daily vigorous exercise at the top of their priority lists.

FIGURE 17.8 | Level of physical fitness moderates the relationship between life stress and illness.

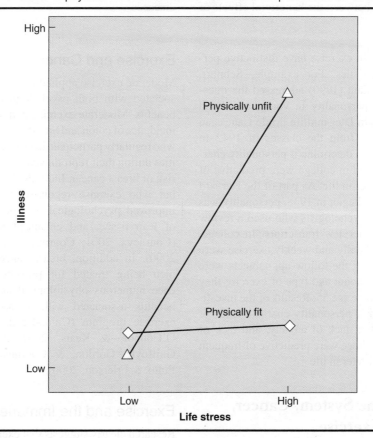

Source: Adapted with permission from Brown, J. D. (1991). Staying fit and staying well: Physical fitness as a moderator of life stress. *Journal of Personality and Social Psychology, 60,* 555–561. Copyright 1991 by the American Psychological Association.

Given the promising buffer effect that exercise has on life stress, one wonders why more people do not take advantage of it. One possible explanation could be lack of knowledge about the beneficial stress inoculation effects of exercise. Another partial explanation might be the personalities of individuals who either choose or do not choose to exercise. Research suggests that individuals who

CONCEPT Immune function is stimulated by moderate exercise but possibly suppressed by overly intense exercise. It appears that there exists an optimal level of regular physical activity conducive to the resistance to illness.

APPLICATION It is critical that coaches and exercise leaders recognize and understand the delicate balance between the beneficial effects of moderate exercise and the detrimental effects of overly intense exercise. When the integrity of the immune system is involved, the coach must be very sensitive to this balance. The most immediate concern is reduced immune system response and upper respiratory infection in the form of the cold virus and influenza. These illnesses weaken athletes and make them more susceptible to other diseases.

regularly engage in exercise have distinctive personality characteristics. For example, Schnurr, Vaillant, and Vaillant (1990) addressed the question of whether personality in young adulthood predicts exercise in later midlife. Male Caucasian Harvard graduates from the classes of 1942 to 1944 were traced to determine if personality characteristics measured in college were predictive of exercise habits later in life. As part of the Harvard longitudinal study begun in 1938, personality was assessed by two psychologists who used a review of 20 hours of interview transcripts. In college, hours and type of daily and weekly exercise were recorded. As part of the follow-up, subjects were asked about the amount and type of exercise they had engaged in since age 55. Results of the investigation showed that personality characteristics of vitality, integration, lack of anxiety, and lack of shyness during college were predictive of frequent exercise behavior later in life.

The Immune System, Cancer, HIV, and Exercise

In recent years research has linked two of the great plagues of our time (cancer and HIV) to exercise and its effect on the immune system. While exercise has generally been linked to benefits, in cases of excess it can have negative consequences. It is like a two-edged sword: it cuts both ways. If applied in moderation it can have beneficial effects, but if applied in excess it can have negative effects.

Exercise and Cancer

Moderate exercise applied on a regular basis is associated with both psychological and biological benefits. Moderate exercise is linked to a lowered incidence of colon and breast cancer. Young women who regularly participate in physical exercise activities during their reproductive years have a reduced risk of breast cancer. Individuals who have cancer, but who exercise regularly, may benefit from improved psychological well-being, preservation of lean tissue, and enhanced immune systems (Courneya, 2001; Courneya, Mackey, & Jones, 2000). In addition, breast cancer survivors and men being treated for prostate cancer experience numerous physiological and psychological benefits associated with a moderately intense exercise program (Culos-Reed, Robinson, Lau, O'Connor, & Keats, 2007; Milne, Wallman, Guilfoyle, Gordon, & Courneya, 2008; Rabin, Pinto, & Frierson, 2006).

Exercise and the Immune System

Research clearly suggests that exercising in moderation leads to improved psychological mood and enhanced **immune system functioning** (Mackinnon, 1994; Nieman, 2001; Shephard, Rhind, & Shek, 1995). Conversely, it is widely believed that chronic intense and stressful exercise may result in mood disturbance and in suppression of the immune system (Rowbottom & Green, 2000). Research indicates, however, that acute bouts of intense exercise

CONCEPT   The evidence suggests that asymptomatic HIV–positive individuals can enjoy the positive psychological and physiological benefits of chronic exercise without suppressing an already compromised immune system.

APPLICATION   Under the supervision of a physician, asymptomatic HIV–positive individuals should be encouraged to engage in an aerobic exercise program designed to improve cardiovascular fitness and reduce the debilitating effects of anxiety and depression.

are not associated with a reduction in immune system functioning as long as the exercise is within a range recommended by the American College of Sports Medicine (Rowbottom & Green, 2000). Chronic intense exercise and acute exercise that goes beyond recommended intensities may result in a reduction in immune system functioning (Mackinnon, 2000). There is growing evidence that for several hours following heavy sustained exertion, the immune system is suppressed (Nieman, Kernodle, Henson, Sonnenfeld, & Morton, 2000). Athletes who do experience transient or chronic immune system suppression seem to be most susceptible to upper respiratory tract infection. It is believed that the immune system is stimulated and strengthened by moderately intense exercise, but suppressed by overly intense exercise. It appears that there exists an optimal level of regular physical activity conducive to the resistance to illness.

Our current level of understanding about the positive effects of exercise on the immune system is summarized in an excellent position statement written by the President's Council on Physical Fitness and Sports (2001). As illustrated in figure 17.9, by far "the most important finding that has emerged from exercise immunology studies is that positive immune changes take place during each bout of moderate physical activity" (p. 6).

Exercise and the Human Immunodeficiency Virus

Magic Johnson's brief return to professional basketball and his participation in the 1992 Summer Olympics in Barcelona, Spain, after contracting the **human immunodeficiency virus (HIV)**, led to

FIGURE 17.9 | Illustration showing the effect of moderate and high exercise workloads on the integrity of the immune system.

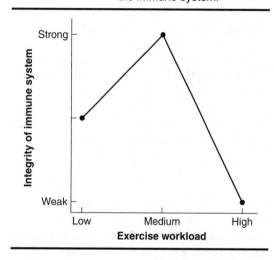

speculation as to the possible negative side effects of vigorous physical activity to his physical and psychological health. Since it is widely believed by the medical profession that the presence of the HIV ultimately leads to **acquired immune deficiency syndrome (AIDS)**, there was cause for concern (Cinelli, Sankaran, McConatha, & Carson, 1992). Evidence reported by Ironson et al. (1990) indicates that when asymptomatic gay males are informed of their *HIV-positive status,* they display a significant increase in anxiety and other distress scores. Furthermore, evidence has been accrued that links affective factors, such as depression and anxiety, with accelerated HIV infection (Ironson et al., 1990). Goodkin (1988) further suggests that

431

increased anxiety and depression should be viewed as risk factors facilitating the development of AIDS. Because exercise has been positively linked with decreased anxiety and depression, it follows that chronic exercise should be effective in retarding the negative progression and effects of HIV.

Since 1990, several investigations have been reported that have a bearing on the question of exercise among HIV-positive individuals. A study by LaPerriere et al. (1990) demonstrated the buffering or protective effect that aerobic exercise has on gay men who were informed of their HIV-positive status.

A study by Rigsby, Dishman, Jackson, MaClean, and Raven (1992) assigned HIV-positive men to either a 12-week aerobic exercise program or a counseling control group to see if exercise would further compromise an already weakened immune system. Results revealed that exercisers improved their strength and endurance without suppressing their immune systems, as evidenced by counting of leukocytes and lymphocytes.

While the previous two investigations focused on immune system response to aerobic exercise, a study by Lox, McAuley, and Tucker (1995) focused on psychological response to aerobic exercise on the part of HIV-infected men. Results of the research indicated that aerobic exercise and weight training enhanced physical self-efficacy, positive and negative mood, and satisfaction with life. These results suggest that moderate exercise is an effective complementary therapy for treating psychological manifestations associated with HIV infection.

An investigation by Stringer, Berezovskaya, O'Brian, Beck, and Casaburi (1998) demonstrated that a six-week exercise training program of moderate to high intensity would not compromise immune system indices of HIV-positive participants. Compared to a control group of HIV-positive men, the moderate exercise group improved aerobic functioning, improved on quality-of-life indices (hope, desire to live), and improved on one measure of immune system functioning.

A study by Wagner, Rabkin, and Rabkin (1998) demonstrated that 12 weeks of resistance exercise was an effective adjunct to testosterone treatment for slowing physical wasting symptoms in HIV-positive men with AIDS. Both exercisers and controls were given testosterone, but only the exercisers improved in psychological mood, lean body mass, strength, and nutritional status.

A study by Rojas, Schlicht, and Hautzinger (2003) confirms the findings of the previously cited investigations. In this study a sample of HIV-positive men and women were assigned to a 16-week moderate exercise group or a 16-week nonexercise control group. Results of the study revealed no differences between groups in terms of immune system functioning, but significant improvement in quality of life, psychological well-being, and cardiopulmonary fitness of the exercise participants.

Finally, a study reported by Robins et al. (2006) documents that a 10-week tai chi training class is effective in increasing the quality of life, emotional well-being, social well-being, and coping resources of 18 HIV-infected individuals. The participants also realized decreases in HIV-related psychological distress. HIV-infected individuals suffer from a great deal of uncertainty and psychological stress associated with the knowledge that possession of the virus can advance to the stage of being inflicted with AIDS. Well-organized, moderately intense exercise programs offer HIV-infected individuals numerous physiological and psychological benefits that they otherwise would not enjoy.

Social Physique Anxiety, Physical Self-Concept, and Body Image

Social physique anxiety, physical self-concept, and body image are all constructs that describe how an individual feels about her physical appearance. While these constructs are not identical to one another, they are correlated, and are predictive of exercise behavior. A high score on social physique anxiety and low scores on physical self-concept and body image are predictive of a low level of exercise behavior. Individuals who are anxious about their bodies, have low physical self-concepts, and have low body images have a hard time getting motivated to exercise. This is a sad situation, because it is these individuals who would benefit most from physical activity.

Social Physique Anxiety

Social physique anxiety is the anxiety that people experience when they perceive that other people evaluate their physiques negatively. They may feel that others evaluate them as too thin, or too heavy, or too fat, and so on. Because of our previous discussion about self-presentation concerns in sport (chap. 14), you will recognize social physique anxiety as a special case of self-presentation in exercise situations (Hausenblas, Brewer & Van Raalte, 2004). Recall that self-presentation was defined as all of the processes that people go through to try to control how they are perceived by other people. Individuals who perceive that they are ineffective in conveying the image that they are healthy, physically fit, and physically attractive experience an increase in social physique anxiety. Thus, in exercise situations negative self-presentational concerns and social physique anxiety are the same thing.

In the exercise and fitness environment, **exercise self-presentation efficacy** has been conceptualized as a person's confidence in his ability to create the public impression of himself as being physically fit, coordinated, and physically attractive (Fleming & Ginis, 2004). The Self-Presentation in Exercise Questionnaire (SPEQ) was developed by Conroy, Motl, and Hall (1998, 2000) to measure the exercise self-presentation efficacy construct. A

high score on the SPEQ subscales would indicate that the exerciser enjoys confidence in her ability to convey an image of fitness and attractiveness, while a low score would be highly correlated with social physique anxiety.

Female exercisers' perception of how well they convey an image of fitness and attractiveness to others is easily manipulated (Fleming & Ginis, 2004; Gammage, Ginis, & Hall, 2004; Raedeke, Focht, & Scales, 2009). A typical scenario is to place female exercisers in one or two exercise environments and measure their social physique anxiety and exercise self-presentation efficacy. An appearance-focused environment typically features form-fitting clothing, lots of mirrors and windows, a male instructor, and lots of appearance-related comments. Conversely, a health-focused environment features privacy, an instructor wearing loose-fitting exercise clothing, and lots of health-focused comments. Not surprisingly, social physique anxiety is higher and self-presentation efficacy is lower in the appearance-focused environment.

In an attempt to quantify the degree to which people experience social physique anxiety, Hart, Leary, and Rejeski (1989) developed the 12-item Social Physique Anxiety Scale (SPAS). Later, Martin, Rejeski, Leary, McAuley, and Bane (1997) refined the 9-item version of the same scale. Research with the SPAS has confirmed that women who score high on the SPAS may at times be reticent about starting an exercise program where other people will be present.

Appearance impression motivation (AIM) is the level of motivation that an individual has to present their appearance in a positive way.

Amorose and Hollembeak (2005) reported on an investigation in which they hypothesized that AIM moderates the predictive relationship between perceived physical attraction (PPA) and social physique anxiety (SPA). As you would expect, as PPA increases, SPA decreases, but AIM is only a weak moderator (determiner) of this effect. High levels of AIM and low levels of PPA yield high levels of SPA (an undesirable result), while low levels of AIM and high levels of PPA yield the lowest level of SPA (a desirable result). Thus, in order to reduce social physique anxiety, one must decrease appearance impression motivation and increase perceived physical attraction.

Social physique anxiety is a deterrent to individuals to be physically active in the presence of other people. Thus it is important to learn as much as possible about SPA so that we can find ways to reduce it. Brunet and Sabiston's (2009) linking of SPA to self-determination theory is helpful. In their research they measured social physique anxiety, psychological need satisfaction, self-determined motivation, and physical activity in college students. The results of their research revealed that increases in social physique anxiety are predictive of reductions in the three aspects of self-determination theory that lead to the development of intrinsic motivation (competence, autonomy, and relatedness). However, if SPA is low, this leads to increased psychological need satisfaction, increased intrinsic motivation, and ultimately increased exercise behavior.

As we have learned, aerobic exercise effectively reduces anxiety in most individuals. This effect, however, is not observed in high SPA women when they exercise in naturalistic settings with mirrors and other people watching (Focht & Hausenblas, 2004). Research by Russell and Cox (2003) show that body dissatisfaction and self-esteem are related to social physique anxiety in men as well as in women; and that weight discrepancy (actual weight minus ideal weight) is a precursor to social physique anxiety. For young women, more mature girls are more susceptible to SPA than the less mature. Physical activity also drops off in young women from the time they go from elementary school to high school (Niven, Fawkner, Knowles, Henretty, & Stephenson, 2009). Research also shows a correlation between social physique anxiety and the body mass index as calculated with height and weight measures (Gay, Monsma, & Torres-McGehee, 2009). It is well known that a high BMI score is indicative of obesity, but the Gay et al. research also clarifies that estimated height and weight as reported by participants is a reliable way to calculate BMI. The **body mass index** (BMI) is calculated by dividing weight in kilograms by height in meters squared (weight $(kg)/height^2(m)$).

Physical Self-Concept

Physical self-concept is the perception that people have about themselves relative to the physical self. Physical self-concept is closely tied to the notion that an individual's feeling of self-worth and self-esteem is related to how he perceives himself within his body. Physical self-concept is measured by the Physical Self-Perception Profile (PSPP; Fox & Corbin, 1989). The PSPP measures perceived body attractiveness, along with perceptions about physical competence, physical strength, and physical conditioning. The PSPP is the foundation of what has come to be referred to as the Fox (1990) Hierarchical Model of Physical Self-Concept. This model leads to the prediction that positive physical self-concept contributes to the development of global self-esteem. Individuals who enjoy a high level of positive physical self-concept are likely to enter into competitive situations and to feel good about exercising in the presence of other people (Crocker, Sabiston, Kowalski, McDonough, & Kowalski, 2006; Hayes, Crocker, & Kowalski, 1999). In an investigation reported by Kowalski, Crocker, and Kowalski (2001), it was shown that the physical conditioning component of the PSPP predicts physical activity.

The PSPP as developed by Fox and Corbin (1989) is not the only inventory designed to measure physical self-concept. Marsh, Richards, Johnson, Roche, and Tremayne (1994) developed the Physical Self-Description Questionnaire (PSDQ). Composed of 70 items, the PSDQ measures nine specific components of physical self-concept and two additional components of global physical self-concept (physical self-concept, self-esteem). A revised short version of the PSDQ (PSDQ-S) was developed and tested by Marsh, Martin, and Jackson (2010).

Body Image

Body image refers to the images or mental pictures that people have about their own bodies. These images can have a powerful influence on how people feel about themselves (e.g., self-esteem and physical self-concept). Body image can be measured using the Multidimensional Body-Self Relations Questionnaire (MBSRQ; Cash, 1994). The MBSRQ is a 69-item inventory that measures satisfaction with body appearance, fitness, and health, as well as orientation with body appearance, fitness, and health. Research shows that from 1973 to 1997, body dissatisfaction for women increased from 23 percent to 56 percent, and that for men it increased from 15 percent to 43 percent (Hausenblas & Downs, 2001). Despite this disappointing trend, body-image-disturbed women who participated in a 13-week program of weight training and fitness were able to significantly improve their body image, compared to a control group (Depcik & Williams, 2004).

For women, a trend towards thinness has been motivated by the media and popular culture. For female athletes, however, the trend appears to be moving away from thinness towards the goal of fitness and muscle tone in moderation (George, 2005). In regard to this new trend toward body image, four themes have emerged (Mosewich, Vangool, Kowalski, & McHugh, 2009). These themes include (a) muscularity holds a variety of meanings, (b) tension between muscularity and performance, (c) the sport culture is a culture of body comparison, and (d) for women, it is a journey towards self-acceptance. For many female athletes, increased muscle tone translates into greater self-confidence and improved performance.

The **drive for muscularity** (DFM) has been defined by Morrison, Morrison, and Hopkins (2003) as the "desire to achieve an idealized, muscular body type" (p. 113). The drive towards muscularity in both male and female athletes may be measured using the Drive for Muscularity Attitude Questionnaire (DMAQ; Morrison, Morrison, Hopkins, & Rowan, 2004).

Related to the notions of body image and the drive for muscularity are the concepts of ideal body size and the body mass index. Markland and Ingledew (2007) reported on an investigation that merged ideal body size and the BMI with the prediction of self-determined autonomous motivation. Measures of height and weight were taken to calculate BMI, and body size discrepancy (BSD) was calculated as the difference between perceived personal body size and idealized body size (BSD = ideal − perceived). A positive BSD indicates that ideal body size is greater than perceived personal body size (desire to increase body size), while a negative BSD indicates that ideal body size is smaller than perceived personal body size (desire to decrease). A relative autonomy index (RAI) was calculated from motivation scores obtained from the BREQ-2. Results of the investigation showed convincingly that greater intrinsic motivation is associated with moderate BMI scores (not excessively thin or obese), and with small body size discrepancy scores (ideal body size not greater or less than perceived).

Finally, Swami, Steadman, and Tovee (2009) studied the relationship between group membership and three measures related to body image. Female participants for the study were either (a) track athletes (emphasis upon leanness), (b) Tae Kwon Do participants (no emphasis on leanness), or (c) nonathletes. Measurements taken included body mass index, ideal body size, body dissatisfaction, and media bias towards thinness. After controlling for BMI (removing the effect) the three groups did not differ in terms of measured ideal body size indices, but did differ as a function of body dissatisfaction and media message influence. Specifically, the group with a leanness emphasis (track athletes) displayed the highest levels of body dissatisfaction and admitted to being influenced by the media the most.

Summary

A large body of literature has been amassed that supports the position that regular exercise leads to improved psychological affect. Improved psychological affect is manifested in the form of a reduction in negative affect and an increase in positive affect. These consistent findings have led many health care professionals to prescribe exercise as a treatment for selected mental health symptoms. Exercise in many cases is as effective as psychotherapy and antidepressant drugs in treating emotional disorders.

Factors such as exercise intensity, exercise mode, special populations, and other factors such as time of day, music, and social environment all have a moderating effect on positive benefits of exercise on mental health. Exercise intensity is of particular interest because of the new theories that have proposed to explain the relationship between exercise intensity and psychological benefits. These include the dual-mode hypothesis and the circumplex model. The dual-mode hypothesis hypothesizes two different mechanisms through which affective responses are generated. The circumplex model provides a simple and convenient way of simultaneously considering the effects of hedonic tone and felt arousal on psychological affect.

Sport psychologists have long believed that a positive relationship exists between physical activity and cognitive function. It is only recently that consistent evidence has accumulated in support of the relationship. One creative way to study cognitive function is to focus either on (a) information processing speed or (b) the executive function component of cognitive function. Of the two, executive function is believed to be the truest indicator of improved cognitive function, as it controls planning and selective attention. As confirmed by Ekkekakis, the prefrontal cortex of the brain has been identified as an important cortex structure associated with physical activity and its effects on cognitive functioning.

Six specific theoretical explanations for the beneficial effects of exercise on mental health were discussed. These included (a) the cognitive behavioral hypothesis, (b) the social interaction hypothesis, (c) the distraction hypothesis, (d) the cardiovascular fitness hypothesis, (e) the amine hypothesis, and (f) the endorphin hypothesis.

Exercise adherence and determinants were discussed within the framework of the natural history of exercise model. The important transitions in the model included (a) going from the sedentary state to adoption of exercise, (b) going from adoption to maintenance or dropout status, and (c) resumption of exercise following dropout. Most research has been conducted relative to the second transition, involving exercise maintenance or dropout. Factors that determine exercise adherence include available time, behavioral coping skills, equipment accessibility, self-efficacy, group cohesion, heart disease risk, intrinsic motivation, good health, and social support.

Several theories of behavior that explain why people don't exercise, why they start to exercise, why they do or do not continue to exercise, and why they start exercising again if they stop were discussed. Models included in this discussion were (a) the theory of reasoned action, (b) the theory of planned behavior, (c) the transtheoretical model of stages of change, (d) self-determination theory, (e) social cognitive theory, and (f) exercise self-schemata theory.

Fitness was discussed as a moderator of life stress. The ability of individuals to insulate, protect, or inoculate themselves against the stresses of life through regular exercise is called stress inoculation. Being physically fit serves to inoculate the individual against illness during periods of high stress. Conversely, physically unfit individuals appear to be less protected against high stress.

Important connections between exercise and the immune system, the human immunodeficiency virus, and cancer were discussed. While too much exercise can compromise the responsiveness of the immune system, moderate exercise is viewed as a possible moderator of HIV and cancer. In the final section of the chapter, the important concepts of social physique anxiety, physical self-concept, and body image were discussed. Social physique

anxiety is the anxiety that people experience when they perceive that other people evaluate their bodies negatively. Physical self-concept is the perception that people have about their physical bodies and their physical self. Finally, body image refers to the images that people have about their own bodies.

Critical Thought Questions

1. Are there alternative explanations for the positive effects of exercise on mental health? Discuss some of these explanations and their viability.

2. Following an acute bout of exercise, a decrease in anxiety below baseline does not occur until 30 minutes or even 60 minutes after the cessation of exercise. Can you think of plausible explanations for the delayed anxiolytic effect?

3. Relatively speaking, why do mentally ill individuals benefit more from exercise than mentally healthy individuals?

4. Provide some clarification of differences and similarities among the following terms: acute exercise, chronic exercise, aerobic exercise, anaerobic exercise, resistance exercise. Discuss these terms in terms of exercise intensity and the lactate threshold.

5. Discuss and explain the Ekkekakis dual-mode hypothesis as it relates to exercise intensity and psychological affect. How does this model help us understand exercise intensity and psychological affect?

6. Discuss and explain the application of the circumplex model to exercise and psychological affect. What are the strengths and weaknesses of this model?

7. What does the research tell us about the positive effects of exercise on cognitive function? What are some of the specific effects that exercise can have upon cognition? Include a

discussion of information processing speed, executive function, and cortex stimulation.

8. Six different explanations were given for why exercise has a positive effect on psychological well-being. Which explanation do you think is most viable and why? Compose your own eclectic theory based on these explanations.

9. Discuss exercise, adoption, adherence, and determinants as related to the natural history of exercise. Provide some summarizing concepts associated with transitions from the various phases involved in the history.

10. A number of theories have been proposed and tested to help explain why people do or do not adopt a physically active lifestyle (theories of exercise behavior). Identify and briefly explain these theories and include your own assessment of their explanatory power.

11. Based on the literature, would you recommend an exercise program for an individual who has the HIV virus? What sort of program would you recommend? How about if the person had AIDS symptoms?

12. What is the relationship between social physique anxiety and exercise self-presentation efficacy? How is social physique anxiety counterproductive to a physically active lifestyle?

13. Differentiate among the terms social physique anxiety, physical self-concept, and body image.

Glossary

acquired immune deficiency syndrome (AIDS) Caused by the human immunodeficiency virus, and the inability of the human immune system to combat disease.

acute exercise Short-duration, isolated bouts of exercise lasting approximately 30 minutes.

aerobic exercise Continuous and rhythmic exercise in which a sufficient supply of oxygen is available to the exerciser.

amine hypothesis The hypothesis that increased secretion of neurotransmitters associated with exercise is responsible for improved mental health.

anaerobic exercise High-intensity and short-duration exercise requiring a period of recovery to replenish stored energy.

anxiolytic Refers to the anxiety-reducing effect that exercise has on mental health.

appearance impression motivation The level of motivation possessed by an individual to present her physical appearance in a positive way to other people.

body image The image or picture that a person has about her body.

body mass index An index based on a person's body weight relative to his height (weight in kg divided by height-squared in meters). A high index suggests obesity.

cardiovascular fitness hypothesis The hypothesis that improved mental health associated with exercise is due to improved cardiovascular fitness.

chronic exercise A daily or regular exercise program across a long period of time.

circumplex model As applied to exercise, the model is a two-dimensional plane for simultaneously describing the hedonic tone and felt arousal effects of exercise, of various intensities, on an individual.

cognitive behavioral hypothesis The hypothesis that exercise encourages and generates positive thoughts and feelings that serve to counteract negative mood states.

delayed anxiolytic effect The phenomenon that beneficial reduction in anxiety does not manifest itself until sometime following an acute bout of exercise.

disconnected values model A model of exercise behavior which suggests that a person's decision to adopt an active lifestyle is based on a disconnect (cognitive dissonance) between the person's core values and her negative health habits, and how the disconnect is resolved.

distraction hypothesis The hypothesis that exercise affords the individual an opportunity to be distracted from worries and frustrations.

drive for muscularity Desire to achieve an idealized, muscular body type.

dual-mode hypothesis Based upon the observation that exercising above the lactate threshold may be perceived as unpleasant, while exercising below the threshold may be perceived as being pleasant. Two different mechanisms are hypothesized to explain these effects.

endorphin hypothesis The hypothesis that exercise is associated with brain production of chemicals that have a "morphine-like" effect on the exerciser.

executive function A higher-order cognitive ability that controls basic, underlying cognitive functions for purposeful, goal-directed behavior and that has been associated with frontal [cortical] lobe activity.

exercise adherence The process of adhering to or complying with a prescribed exercise program.

exercise determinants Factors that motivate a person to make a transition from a sedentary lifestyle to regular physical activity.

exercise self-efficacy Confidence that one can initiate and/or maintain a personal exercise program.

exercise self-presentation efficacy A person's confidence in his ability to create the public impression of himself as being physically fit, coordinated, and physically active.

exercise self-schemata Self-schemata that focus upon exercise and exercise-related experiences.

human immunodeficiency virus (HIV) A communicable virus that leads to the weakening of the human immune system.

immune system functioning The degree to which the immune system is working to fight off disease and illness.

lactate threshold The point at which the body's physiological metabolism begins to transition from exercising with oxygen (aerobic) to exercising without oxygen (anaerobic).

life stress Positive and negative stress associated with living.

mode of aerobic exercise Type or mode of aerobic exercise employed (e.g., running versus cycling).

natural history of exercise A framework for studying the determinants of exercise behavior.

physical self-concept The perception people have about themselves relative to the physical self.

processes of change Interventions used in the transtheoretical model to move from one stage of exercise to another.

resistance exercise Exercise such as weightlifting, in which resistance can be increased by adding weight.

self-schemata Cognitive generalizations about the self, derived from past experience, that organize and guide the processing of information contained in the individual's social experiences.

social interaction hypothesis The hypothesis that improved mental health associated with exercise is due to social interaction with friends and colleagues who are also exercising.

social physique anxiety Anxiety that people experience when they perceive that other people evaluate their physiques negatively.

stress inoculation The ability of individuals to insulate, protect, or inoculate themselves against the stresses of life through regular exercise.

theory of planned behavior A theory of exercise behavior that suggests that intention is caused by attitude, subjective norm, and perceived behavioral control, and that intention and perceived control leads to exercise behavior.

theory of reasoned action A theory of exercise behavior that suggests that intention is caused by attitude and subjective norm, and that intention leads to exercise behavior.

transtheoretical model A stage theory of behavioral change. When applied to exercise, the model proposes that individuals pass through five dynamic stages in adopting healthy long-term exercise behavior.

The Psychology of Athletic Injuries and Career Termination

KEY TERMS

Acute pain
Adherence to injury
   rehabilitation
Athletic identity
Behavioral response
Benign pain
Chronic pain
Cognitive appraisal
Conceptual model of career
   termination
Coping behavior
Distributed approach
Emotional disclosure paradigm
Emotional response
Harmful pain
Injury contagion
Injury pain
Injury rehabilitation
   interventions
Integrated sport injury model
Nonpharmacological
   pain-focusing techniques
Nonpharmacological
   pain-reduction techniques
Pain catastrophizing
Pain tolerance
Performance pain
Personal factors

Psychological response
   to injury
Rehabilitation rehearsal
Situational factors

Specialist approach
Stress and injury model
Stress response

My knee's shot. My knee's shot. There goes my career. It's over. I'm through.

(Keith Millard,
Minnesota Vikings' defensive tackle)

The above words by an injured National Football League player reveal the anguish and frustration associated with an athletic injury. As explained by sports writer Jill Lieber (1991, p. 37), Millard sustained his season-ending injury while rushing the Tampa Bay quarterback. Following his injury, and while agonizing over his misfortune, the 6-foot-5-inch, 265-pound football player put his head in his hands and sobbed.

Physical factors such as overtraining, equipment failure, poor playing conditions, and contact sports are believed to be the major factors contributing to athletic injuries. Evidence is mounting, however, to suggest that psychological factors play an important role in the incidence, prevention, and rehabilitation of athletic injuries. An athlete trains his body and mind for optimal athletic performance, only to have it all come to a halt with an injury. Athletes and athletic teams enter each season with high hopes. Oftentimes, season results are determined not by which team is the best at the beginning of the season, but by which team suffers the fewest injuries during the course of the season. For the athlete who has her self-image tied to her performance on the athletic field, a season-ending or partial-season-ending injury can leave the athlete emotionally crippled. It is at this point that the sport injury rehabilitation personnel take over and the journey to full recovery begins. To be successful, the rehabilitation process must take into consideration both physical and psychological training and preparation.

In addressing the important subject of the psychology of athletic injuries, three main chapter sections have been prepared. These include (a) psychological predictors of athletic injuries, (b) psychological response to injury and rehabilitation, (c) career termination due to injury and other causes, and (d) other considerations.

Psychological Predictors of Athletic Injury

It stands to reason that if researchers can identify psychological factors associated with the occurrence of injuries, steps can be taken to reduce the number and severity of those that do occur. A model for explaining the interactive relationship between athletic injury and such psychological factors as personality, life stress, coping resources, the stress response, and potential interventions was proposed by Andersen and Williams (1988) and revised by Williams and Andersen (1998). The Williams and Andersen (1998) **stress and injury model** is illustrated in figure 18.1. The key element of the model is the **stress response.** The stress response in this model is similar to the stress process illustrated in figure 7.2 of chapter 7. A potentially stressful athletic situation requires the athlete to complete a cognitive appraisal of the task's *associated demands,* the athlete's *coping resources,* and the *consequences.* If, in the athlete's judgment, the situational demands exceed the personal resources needed to address the situation, the stress response will be significant. Conversely, if the athlete's perceived resources outweigh the demands, the stress response will be minimal. The elicitation of the stress response represents a perceived imbalance between the athlete's resources to cope with the demands of the situation and the actual demands. The elicitation of the stress response evokes selected physiological and attentional changes in the athlete. These changes include *increased muscle tension, narrowing of the visual field,* and *increased distractibility.* Each change is believed to enhance the chances of the athlete's sustaining an athletic injury (Williams, Tonymon, & Andersen, 1991). In addition to an imbalance between demands and resources, perceived consequences of the athletic situation can lead to the elicitation of the stress response. In essence, any cognitive appraisal that leads to the stress response puts the athlete at risk for injury.

CONCEPT An athlete's perceived inability to respond to the demands of a potentially stressful athletic situation results in the stress response. The stress response in turn gives rise to increased muscle tension, narrowing of the visual field, and attentional distractibility.

APPLICATION Once the athlete experiences the stress response, she is in a situation of heightened risk for injury. Every effort must be used to prevent this situation from developing in the first place.

FIGURE 18.1 | Revised version of the stress and injury model.

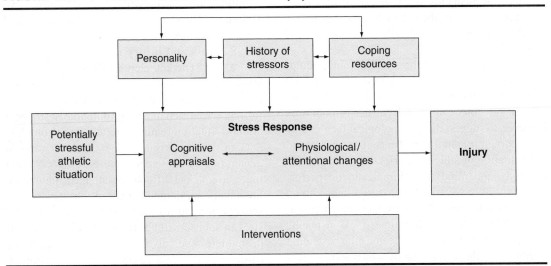

Source: Reproduced with permission from Williams, J. M., & Andersen, M. B. (1998). Psychosocial antecedents of sport injury: Review and critique of the stress and injury model. *Journal of Applied Sport Psychology, 10,* 5–25.

As illustrated in figure 18.1, factors that impact the stress response include personality of the athlete, history of stressors, coping resources, and potential planned interventions. Each of these four moderating variables will be discussed below. Research support for the overall stress and injury model has been forthcoming from Maddison and Prapavessis (2005) and Rogers and Landers (2005).

Personality Factors

An incomplete list of personality factors that might have an effect upon how the athlete responds to a stressful athletic situation include mental toughness, internal locus of control, mastery goal orientation, competitive trait anxiety, and intrinsic motivation. As can be observed in figure 18.1, personality factors affect the stress response directly, as well as indirectly, through the history of stressors and coping resources. They are not directly related to the incidence of athletic injuries, but are directly and indirectly related to how the athlete reacts to the stress response, which in turn directly predicts athletic injury (Deroche, Stephan, Brewer, & LeScanff, 2007; Galambos, Terry, Moyle, & Locke, 2005; Williams & Andersen, 1998).

History of Stressors

Factors incorporated under the category of history of stressors include stressful life events, daily hassles, and previous injuries. Taken together, these factors are believed to have an interactive effect upon the stress response leading to athletic injury.

Life Stress and Daily Hassles   As previously illustrated in figure 17.8, life stress is related to the incidence of illness. This relationship between stressful life events and increased illness is extended to the athletic domain. Life stress and daily hassles tend to undermine the ability of the athlete to effectively address the stress response and associated physiological and attentional consequences that may lead to injury vulnerability (Hanson, McCullagh, & Tonymon, 1992; Rogers & Landers, 2005). *Positive life stress* includes such events as studying for examinations, developing social relationships, and raising a family. *Negative life stress* includes such events as divorce, death in the family, and loss of job. The more life stress the athlete experiences, the greater is the incidence and severity of athletic injury (Patterson, Smith, Everett, & Ptacek, 1998; Rogers & Landers, 2005).

Previous Injury   How an athlete adjusts to a previous injury will determine its impact on the stress response to a potentially stressful athletic situation. Athletes who are worried about the recurrence of an injury, or about whether or not they have fully recovered from a previous injury, are vulnerable to further injury. This is the case because they will tend to be distracted and inappropriately focused during competition. As indicated in figure 18.1, negative appraisal may result if an athlete is psychologically unprepared to return to competition after sustaining an injury. Physical recovery from an athletic injury is only part of the equation. The other part is psychological recovery and the confidence that the athlete is completely healed and ready for full-speed competition.

Without this confidence, worry about a subsequent injury can result in a distraction that can contribute to the stress response and another injury (Appaneal, Perna, & Larkin, 2007).

Coping Resources

Coping resources available to the athlete include general coping behavior, social support, stress management techniques, attentional strategy, and prescribed or self-prescribed medication. Collectively, these factors are believed to have an interactive effect on whether or not the athlete will experience the stress response.

Coping Behaviors   Any behavior that assists an individual in dealing with a stressful situation is considered to be a **coping behavior.** The use of coping strategies or behaviors to address high-stress situations was discussed in detail in chapter 9. Coping behaviors are highly individualistic and varied in nature. Well-developed general coping behaviors have been linked with the reduced incidence of athletic injuries in several research investigations (Hanson et al., 1992; Rogers & Landers, 2005; Wiechman, Smith, Smoll, & Ptacek, 2000).

Social Support   Social support is one of the important coping resources available to athletes to reduce the debilitating effect of the stress response (Petrie, 1993). Individuals and groups that provide social support for the athlete include parents, friends, coaches, teammates, fraternity/sorority, clubs, and religious groups. In a study reported by Smith, Smoll, and Ptacek (1990), twenty different individuals or groups were identified that might provide social support to the athlete. Not only is social support an effective coping mechanism in its own right, it is also a powerful moderator between life stress and the incidence of athletic injury. When social support is either absent or negative, a strong association is observed between life stress and athletic injury. Conversely, when social support is present, the relationship between life

CONCEPT   Factors that determine whether or not an athlete will experience the stress response include the athlete's personality, history of stress, and coping resources.

APPLICATION   From a psychological perspective, knowledge about these three factors may be useful in helping the athlete reduce the probability of injury. Understanding the person's personality and stress history will help the coach identify at-risk individuals. Assisting the athlete in developing coping skills and supportive social relationships will help her deal effectively with a potentially stressful environment.

---

stress and athletic injury is negligible (Patterson et al., 1998; Rogers & Landers, 2005; Smith, Smoll, & Ptacek, 1990).

As we shall learn in this chapter, social support is important for both injury prevention and injury rehabilitation. Bianco (2001) and Bianco and Eklund (2001) provided researchers and practitioners with background information about the complexities of social support construct. For example, they clarified that social support is of three interrelated but different types: emotional, informational, and tangible. *Emotional support* involves such things as listening, emotional comfort, and emotional challenge. *Informational support* involves reality confirmation, task appreciation, and task challenge (e.g., expressing appreciation for hard work and challenging/motivating for even greater accomplishments). Finally, *tangible support* involves providing actual material and personal assistance. Social support may be measured using the Social Support Survey (SSS; Rees, Hardy, & Evans, 2007).

Stress Management   Many athletes utilize stress management and cognitive intervention techniques as coping strategies for controlling the stress response. Often these same techniques are used by the athletes as arousal control strategies to buffer the effects of the stress response once it has developed. Research has demonstrated that effective reduction in the stress response is associated with a reduction in the number and severity of injuries sustained by athletes (Davis, 1991; Kerr & Goss, 1996).

Attentional Strategy   A coping resource available to distance runners is attentional strategy. As we learned in chapter 6, distance runners use some combination of associative and dissociative strategies when they run. The associative strategy is related to internal monitoring of their body and greater effort. Runners who use the associative strategy are highly motivated, are driven, and seek high performance. Dissociative runners get more enjoyment out of their runs and are less motivated to high performance. Research shows that the dissociative strategy of running is related to lower incidence of injury (Masters & Ogles, 1998b). Greater reliance upon a dissociative strategy is a coping strategy that could protect the athlete from muscle and bone injury.

Medication   Drugs are used by athletes for various legitimate and illegitimate reasons, including performance enhancement, recreation, injury treatment, and pain management. Many drugs have the ability to influence the stress response, and thus the probability of injury. For example, animal and human research suggests that the side effects of anabolic steroids may include aggression, depression, anxiety, and social withdrawal. All these psychological effects have the potential to reduce the coping resources of the athlete (Gregg & Rejeski, 1990).

Interventions

Part 4 (chapters 9–12) of this book was dedicated to arousal control techniques and cognitive interventions that may be utilized to enhance athletic performance, as well as to inhibit the development of the stress response. As illustrated in figure 18.1, these interventions play an important role in determining whether or not a potentially stressful athletic situation will lead to conditions conducive to athletic injury. One set of interventions seeks to *change the cognitive appraisal* of potentially stressful events, while a second seeks to *modify the physiological/attentional aspects* of the stress response.

Cognitive appraisal might be changed by rethinking how one plans to address a particularly stressful situation. Physiological/attentional aspects might be modified through progressive relaxation and imagery (Williams & Andersen, 1998). Evidence supporting the position that pre- injury interventions can reduce the number and severity of athletic injuries has been documented by empirical studies (Johnson, Ekengren, & Andersen, 2005; Kerr & Goss, 1996; Schomer, 1990). The fundamental goal of pre-injury intervention is to identify the subjective cost of injury, while teaching and strengthening coping resources (Cupal, 1998).

Psychological Response to Injury and Rehabilitation

Factors associated with an athlete's **psychological response to injury** and follow-up rehabilitation occur after the injury has occurred. In order to understand the complexities of what occurs following injury, a comprehensive model is needed. In response to this need, an *integrated model of psychological response to injury and rehabilitation* was developed (Wiese-Bjornstal, Smith, & LaMott, 1995; Wiese-Bjornstal, Smith, Shaffer, & Morrey, 1998). A recent version of the integrated model is illustrated in figure 18.2. The top part of the integrated model is an abbreviated version of the stress and injury model (figure 18.1). The main panel of the **integrated sport injury model** focuses upon the athlete's response to sport injury and the rehabilitation process. In the integrated model, the moderators of the stress response are also moderators of the response to sport injury and the rehabilitation process (personality, history of stressors, coping resources, and interventions).

The main panel of the integrated model is composed of *cognitive appraisal, emotional response,* and *behavioral response.* These are the three main components of the integrated model that we will consider. Behavioral response relates primarily to the rehabilitation process. *Personal factors* and *situational factors* serve as a background to the entire response to the sport injury and rehabilitation process. Notice that these two factors have their initial impact upon cognitive appraisal of the sports injury.

The core of the model (arrows) illustrates the dynamic nature of the recovery process. The

FIGURE 18.2 | Integrated model of psychological response to the sport injury and rehabilitation process.

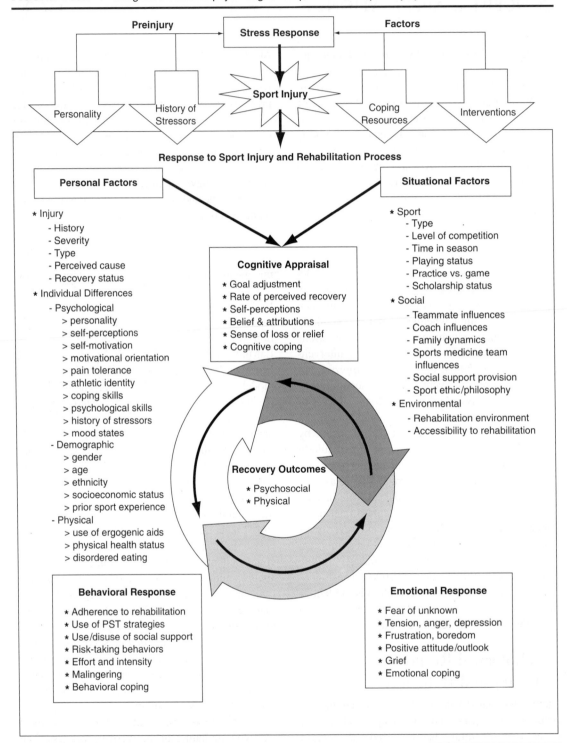

Source: Reproduced with permission from Wiese-Bjornstal, D. M., Smith, A. M., Shaffer, S. M., & Morrey, M. A. (1998). An integrated model of response to sport injury: Psychological and sociological dynamics. *Journal of Applied Sport Psychology, 10,* 46–70.

CONCEPT   Cognitive appraisal at the time of an athletic injury is a predictor of emotional response. Self-esteem, self-worth, self-confidence, and self-efficacy may be reduced as a result of an injury, but the reduction depends on the specific nature of the measure (e.g., self-efficacy for what?). Interventions designed to enhance self-esteem, self-worth, self-confidence, and self-efficacy following injury are effective.

APPLICATION   Cognitive appraisals made by the athlete influence his emotional responses, which in turn influence rehabilitation. For this reason, it is important that interventions be applied at the time of injury to bolster the injured athlete's self-esteem, self-worth, self-confidence, and self-efficacy.

predominant path followed is in a clockwise direction (wide arrows) to full recovery. In the full recovery path, cognitive appraisal affects emotional response, which in turn affects behavior, which in turn affects cognitive appraisal again. Slippage or nonadherence to the rehabilitation process is also possible, and is reflected by the narrower arrows moving in a counterclockwise direction. Research support for the integrated model has been forthcoming from three longitudinal investigations involving injured elite athletes from skiing, rugby, and other sports (Bianco, Malo, & Orlick, 1999; Carson & Polman, 2008; Quinn & Fallon, 1999).

Cognitive Appraisal

Factors associated with **cognitive appraisal** include (a) the need to adjust performance goals, (b) an estimate of recovery time, (c) evaluation of perceived self-worth and self-confidence, (d) appraisal of beliefs about attributions, (e) sense of loss, and (f) appraisal of coping skills. Cognitive appraisal of these factors helps determine the athlete's emotional response to injury, as well as her behavioral response. For example, Daly, Brewer, Van Raalte, Petitpas, and Sklar (1995) found that athletes' cognitive appraisals were correlated with total mood disturbance (emotional response). Most research in cognitive appraisal has focused upon the athlete's perception of self-esteem and self-worth following a serious sport injury. Perceptions

of self-worth and self-esteem tend to be lower in the injured athlete than in the noninjured athlete (Brewer, 1993; McGowan, Pierce, Williams, & Eastman, 1994).

Researchers have also studied self-confidence and self-efficacy in injured athletes. As would be expected, self-confidence and self-efficacy decline as a result of sports injury, but increase in response to intervention. Self-efficacy about adhering to a rehabilitation program is just as strong at the time of injury as it is during rehabilitation. Self-confidence about sport performance declines following an injury, but recovers by the end of the rehabilitation phase (Connelly, 1991; Flint, 1991; Quinn & Fallon, 1999).

Emotional Response

As illustrated in figure 18.2, factors associated with **emotional response** following injury include (a) fear of the unknown, (b) feelings of tension, anger, and depression, (c) frustration and boredom associated with being injured, (d) positive/negative attitude, (e) grief associated with an injury, and (f) emotional coping skills. These factors parallel very closely the stress and frustration expressed by 21 U.S. alpine and freestyle ski team members who suffered season-ending injuries (Gould, Udry, Bridges, & Beck, 1997). Frustrations expressed by these elite athletes included shattered hopes and dreams, fear of reinjury, isolation, others' recovery expectations, physical inactivity, concern about

CONCEPT   Athletic injury is associated with mild to severe mood disturbance. The degree of mood disturbance is believed to be associated with severity of injury as well as with cognitive appraisal.

APPLICATION   Psychological mood of injured athletes should be measured at the time of injury and monitored thereafter using the Profile of Mood States or some other short inventory. Psychological mood at the time of the injury will help the sport-injury rehabilitation personnel (SIRP) determine the degree of mood disturbance and to implement appropriate interventions to reduce the debilitating effect of negative affect. It is expected that negative mood will dissipate as the road to full recovery proceeds, but fluctuations should be anticipated.

future poor performance, uncertainty of medical diagnosis, instability of sponsorship, and missed non-skiing opportunities. Given this list of frustrations, it is understandable that mood disturbances accompany season- or career-ending injuries.

LaMott (1994) and Morrey (1997) monitored mood state across three and six months. Their research showed negative affect to be very high immediately following a knee injury, but to decrease gradually over time. Similarly, Quinn and Fallon (1999) observed linear decreases in negative mood across 4- to 99-week recovery periods of 136 elite athletes. However, they also observed significant quadratic and cubic trends, suggesting that patterns of change were not constant across time. From these investigations we learn that injury is associated with mood disturbance, and that mood improves with time across a successful recovery period. The mood improvements, however, are not necessarily smooth and consistent.

Wiese-Bjornstal, Smith, Shaffer, et al. (1998) summarized 19 studies associated with emotional responses of injured athletes. From this review we learn that while some athletes experience clinical levels of mood disturbance (professional care needed), most experience only normal to mild manifestations. Competitive athletes experience higher levels of negative affect associated with injury than do recreational athletes, but in turn competitive athletes recover more quickly. Perhaps the extreme frustration and associated mood disturbance in the competitive athlete motivate the athlete during the long and arduous rehabilitation process (Tracey, 2003).

Negative mood associated with a serious athletic injury is to be expected, but clinical depression is not. Research reported by Appaneal, Levine, Perna, and Roh (2009) suggests that between 9 to 30 percent of injured athletes may be classified as depressed. This same study showed that injury-related depression declines across time and is higher for women than for men.

In order to remain connected to their teams, injured athletes typically remain in close contact with their teammates by attending practices, traveling with the team, and staying involved. A study reported by Mankad, Gordon, and Wallman (2009a) described the team climate experienced by the injured athlete. In addition to the emotional trauma associated with a serious athletic injury, injured athletes typically describe the team emotional climate as one in which they must suppress their injury-related emotions in order to conform to the accepted positive, mentally tough, emotional climate of the team. While the injured athletes may have felt negative and discouraged, they typically reported "acting out" the accepted emotional climate of the team. Thus, with some difficulty, they controlled their outward emotions and only displayed emotions that seemed appropriate for the team climate.

Negative mood caused by an athletic injury is predicted by maladaptive methods of coping with injury-related stress and by avoidance coping strategies. Athletes who use maladaptive and avoidance methods of coping with an athletic injury may be expected to suffer from higher levels of negative mood. Examples of maladaptive methods of coping with injury-related stress include disconnection and rejection, impaired autonomy, impaired limits, other directedness, and inhibition (Gallagher & Gardner, 2007). In addition to maladaptive coping strategies, negative mood is also predicted by dissatisfaction with existing social support network (Green & Weinberg, 2001). One intervention for reducing negative mood associated with athletic injury is to use a journal and write down emotional thoughts and feelings that are experienced. Emotional disclosure through writing has been found to be effective in reducing mood disturbance and negative mood (Mankad, Gordon, & Wallman, 2009b).

Rehabilitation and the Behavioral Response to Injury

The third factor leading to injury recovery, and associated with cognitive and emotional response, is the **behavioral response** of the athlete to injury. Factors associated with behavioral response to injury include (a) adherence to rehabilitation, (b) use of psychological skill training strategies, (c) use of social support, (d) risk-taking behavior, (e) effort and intensity, (f) malingering, and (g) behavioral coping. The primary focus of research in the area of behavioral response to injury has been upon adherence to injury rehabilitation; coping, social support, and intervention; pain management; and return to competition. These four focus areas will be discussed in the following paragraphs.

Adherence to Injury Rehabilitation   Several theories have been proposed to explain **adherence to injury rehabilitation** (Brewer, 1998). According to *personal investment theory* (Maehr & Braskamp, 1986), motivation to adhere to rehabilitation is thought to be based upon personal incentives, beliefs about self, and perceived options. Another approach, *protection motivation theory* (Maddux & Rogers, 1983), posits that the motivation to adhere is thought to be related to a person's desire for a healthy recovery. Finally, *cognitive*

appraisal theory holds that adherence to rehabilitation is related to cognitive and emotional responses to injury, as illustrated in figure 18.2 (Wiese-Bjornstal, Smith, Shaffer, et al., 1998).

In order for an injury rehabilitation program to be successful, it is believed that the athlete must adhere to the program. Thus, adherence to sport injury rehabilitation programs has emerged as a very important area of study. Adherence to a rehabilitation program is often measured as a function of attendance or through the administration of the Sport Injury Rehabilitation Adherence Scale (SIRAS; Brewer, Van Raalte, Petitpas, et al., 2000). According to Brewer (1998), typical behaviors associated with adherence to injury rehabilitation include the following:

1. Compliance with instructions to restrict physical activity

2. Faithful completion of home rehabilitation exercises

3. Faithful completion of home cryotherapy or injury icing schedule

4. Compliance with medical prescriptions (e.g., painkillers)

5. Consistent and enthusiastic participation in clinic-based rehabilitation and exercise programs

Predictors of injury rehabilitation adherence are identified in figure 18.2 as personal factors and situational factors. *Personal factors* represent relatively stable characteristics of the injured athlete, while *situational factors* represent the social and physical environment. Various aspects of these two factors interact to influence the entire rehabilitation process, including adherence (Brewer, 1998).

Self-motivation is the personal factor most consistently related to adherence. Other **personal factors** related to adherence include pain tolerance, tough-mindedness (e.g., self-assurance, assertiveness, independence), and goal perspective. A task or mastery goal orientation is associated with better adherence, as is a mastery-oriented climate (Gilbourne & Taylor, 1998; Magyar &

Duda, 2000). Based on research, it is predicted that injured athletes who are self-motivated, are tolerant of pain, are tough-minded, and exhibit a mastery goal orientation will be good adherers to an injury rehabilitation program.

As indicated earlier in this chapter, protection motivation theory hypothesizes that the motivation to adhere is thought to be related to a person's desire for a healthy recovery. Brewer, Cornelius, Van Raalte, et al. (2003) reported the results of an investigation designed to test this theory. In so doing, they correlated adherence as measured by the SIRAS with beliefs about health behavior. Beliefs or perceptions about health behavior were measured using the Sports Injury Rehabilitation Beliefs Scale (SIRBS; Taylor & May, 1996). The SIRBS measures perceived *severity* of injury, perceived *susceptibility* to injury, perceived *treatment self-efficacy,* and perceived *self-efficacy* to perform prescribed health behaviors. Results of the investigation showed strong association between measures of adherence to rehabilitation and beliefs about performing health behaviors.

Another personal factor that influences the behavioral response to athletic injury is **athletic identity**. Brewer, Cornelius, Stephan, and Van Raalte (2010) reported on an investigation involving 108 men and women who underwent anterior cruciate ligament (ACL) surgery in which athletic identity was measured prior to surgery at 6, 12, and 24 months after surgery. In addition, measures of rehabilitation progress were taken at 6, 12, and 24 months postsurgery. Results showed that athletic identity dropped precipitously pre- to postsurgery, with the largest drops occurring between 6 and 12 months. Results also showed that the greatest decreases in athletic identity occurred in individuals who were struggling with rehabilitation. The precipitous drop in athletic identity, for individuals struggling with rehabilitation, may have occurred as a self-protective measure to protect the athlete's self-image. Athletic identity is typically measured using the Athletic Identity Measurement Scale (AIMS; Brewer, Van Raalte, & Linder, 1993).

Situational factors most closely related to adherence include (a) belief in the efficacy of treatment procedures, (b) comfort of the rehabilitation clinical environment, (c) convenience of rehabilitation program scheduling, (d) the exertion put forth during rehabilitation exercises, and (e) social support for the rehabilitation program (Brewer, 1998). Best results for adherence will occur when the athlete believes in the efficacy of the rehabilitation program, the rehabilitation program is comfortable and conveniently scheduled, the athlete works hard at the exercises, and the athlete receives positive social support from family, friends, and health care professionals.

As illustrated in figure 18.2, both personal and situational factors affect cognitive appraisal, which in turn influences adherence to an injury rehabilitation program. Within cognitive appraisal, goal setting and goal adjustment play a role in the injury rehabilitation process. This expectation, relative to goal setting, is supported by research reported by Evans and Hardy (2002a, 2002b). Seventy-seven injured athletes were randomly assigned to one of three rehabilitation treatment interventions: (a) goal setting, (b) social support, and (c) control. Results showed a superiority of the goal-setting intervention compared to those of the other two groups in terms of adherence to an injury rehabilitation program.

Coping, Social Support, and Interventions
Coping skills possessed by the athlete, availability of positive social support, and cognitive-behavioral interventions (applied by others or the athlete) are all effective in enhancing adherence to injury rehabilitation programs (Cupal, 1998; Udry, 1997). Injured U.S. ski team members who were able to recover to pre-injury rankings reported using the following coping strategies more than unsuccessful skiers: (a) management of emotions and thoughts, (b) use of visualization and mental skills, (c) being patient and "taking it slow" (Gould, Udry, et al., 1997).

Imagery has been used effectively by athletes to help them recover from an athletic injury

CONCEPT Personal factors and situational factors, as well as their interaction, are predictive of adherence to injury rehabilitation.

APPLICATION The ideal rehabilitation situation will involve athletes possessing desirable personality characteristics, and an environment that is both comfortable and convenient. The reality, however, is that most circumstances will not be ideal in terms of both personal and situational factors. It is the responsibility of the sport injury rehabilitation personnel to make the best of every situation and to be aware of both personal and situation factors. Where appropriate, cognitive-behavioral interventions should be implemented in order to improve the fit between personal and situational factors.

An injured athlete enjoys the encouragement and support of friends. Courtesy Ball State University Sports Information.

(Evans, Hare, & Mullen, 2006; Hare, Evans, & Callow, 2008). As defined by Russell (2000), **rehabilitation rehearsal** is "the conscious use of mental imagery for the purpose of effective coping with injury rehabilitation" (p. 43). Rehabilitation rehearsal and imagery can be used at any time during the rehabilitation process to help the athlete cope with the challenges of a grueling rehabilitation schedule. In one application, of rehabilitation rehearsal, the athlete introduces anticipated problems into a rehearsal scenario. The athlete imagines herself coping with a difficult adherence problem and visualizes herself producing a positive outcome.

Injury rehabilitation interventions typically include guided imagery, relaxation, stress inoculation, goal setting, and biofeedback. Cognitive-behavioral interventions that may be applied to injury rehabilitation and adherence were discussed in detail in part 4 of the text. The student is encouraged to review the chapters included in that part of the book.

As described by Pennebraker (2004), the **emotional disclosure paradigm** consists of using writing as a therapeutic catharsis to reduce emotional trauma. Mankad, Gordon, and Wallman (2009c) effectively used the emotional disclosure paradigm as a means to reduce emotional trauma in injured athletes going through a difficult rehabilitation process. Traumatized injured athletes initially inhibit negative thoughts and emotions as a coping mechanism against stress and trauma. Writing about suppressed thoughts and feelings has the effect of reducing pent-up frustration and emotion associated with the injury rehabilitation process.

Pain Management   Pain tolerance is a personality characteristic that has an important impact upon cognitive appraisal, emotional response, and adherence to rehabilitation. Individuals with a low tolerance to pain may have a more difficult time going through the stages of the sport injury recovery process. Pain is a subjective experience that cannot be directly measured or felt by another individual (hence the falseness of the cliché, "I feel your pain"). Additionally, research indicates that

mentally tough athletes are better able to cope with pain (Levy, Polman, Clough, Marchant, & Earle, 2006).

There are different ways of categorizing pain as it relates to the athletic experience (Taylor & Taylor, 1998). Performance pain can be differentiated from injury pain. **Performance pain** is controlled by the athlete and is associated with improved performance and a sense of accomplishment. Conversely, **injury pain** is not controlled by the athlete and may be of either the acute or the chronic variety. **Acute pain** is due to a trauma to the body and is intense and short in duration. Conversely, **chronic pain** is long lasting, is uncontrollable, continues long after the initial injury, and is very complex in its origin. Pain can also be categorized as benign or harmful. **Benign pain** is generally short in duration and is not associated with swelling and soreness. Conversely, **harmful pain** is present before and after exertion and is associated with swelling, tenderness, and prolonged soreness. The different ways of conceptualizing and categorizing pain are illustrated in figure 18.3.

The intensity and unpleasantness of pain experienced by an injured athlete can be ascertained using a scale that runs from 0 to 10, with 0 being no pain, and 10 being the highest level possible (Kenntner-Mabiala, Gorges, Alpers, Lehmann, &

FIGURE 18.3 | Two ways of categorizing pain in sport and exercise.

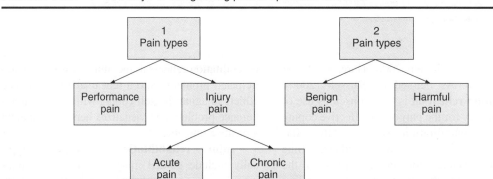

Pauli, 2007). In addition to ascertaining the intensity of pain, it is important to measure how different injured athletes respond psychologically when in pain. To accomplish this, Meyers, Bourgeois, Stewart, and LeUnes (1992) developed the 25-item Sports Inventory for Pain (SIP). The SIP measures five aspects of perceived pain, including (a) use of direct action coping strategies, (b) use of mental coping strategies such as imagery, (c) catastrophizing or degree of despair, (d) use of avoidance coping, and (e) degree of sensitivity to somatic stimuli. An abbreviated version of the Sports Inventory for Pain, the SIP-15, was later developed by Bourgeois, Meyers, and LeUnes, 2009.

Pain associated with an athletic injury may be managed through a combination of pharmacological (prescription drug) and nonpharmacological approaches. Pharmacological pain management strategies are often needed short term, but there is always a concern of dependency and masking of important body information. Nonpharmacological pain management strategies are classified as being of the pain-reduction or the pain-focusing variety.

Nonpharmacological pain-reduction techniques that can be applied during rehabilitation include deep breathing, muscle relaxation, meditation, and therapeutic massage (Taylor & Taylor, 1998). Most recently, listening to music has been included as an effective method to reduce the intensity of pain. As reported by Kenntner-Mabiala et al. (2007) listening to fast tempo music affects the perceived pain intensity and pain pleasantness differently in men than women. For men, increasing the tempo of music has no measurable effect upon perceived pain intensity or upon music valence (pleasantness). Conversely, for women, increasing the tempo of music has the effect of increasing the perceived intensity of the pain being experienced as well as the unpleasantness of the pain. For women, listening to low tempo as opposed to high tempo music should reduce the perceived intensity and unpleasantness of the pain being experienced.

Nonpharmacological pain-focusing techniques utilize association and dissociation attentional strategies to manage pain. Dissociation is used to direct the injured athlete's attention away from pain and is believed to be most effective in acute pain. In the case of association, the injured athlete's attention is internalized and focused on the pain. Focusing internally upon the emotional and informational aspects of pain seems to be most beneficial with chronic pain. Association heightens body awareness, cultivates a sense of emotional detachment, and increases the athlete's perception of control over the pain (Taylor & Taylor, 1998).

As introduced earlier, **pain catastrophizing** is the degree to which individuals focus on pain, exaggerate the threat of pain to their well-being, and perceive themselves as unable to cope effectively with pain (Sullivan, Tripp, Rodgers, & Stanish, 2000). Catastrophizing may be measured by the 13-item Pain Catastrophizing Scale (PCS; Sullivan, Bishop, & Pivik, 1995). Consistent with the general definition of catastrophizing, the PCS measures the three conceptually integrated subscales of *rumination, magnification,* and *helplessness.* High scores on the PCS subscales would indicate a psychological inability to cope well with pain. Using a sample of male and female collegiate athletes and sedentary nonathletes, Sullivan, Tripp, et al. (2000) studied the relationship between pain tolerance, catastrophizing, group membership, and sex. Pain tolerance was measured by immersing a participant's arm in a cold pressor apparatus for 60 seconds (2° to 4° Celsius) and obtaining a rating of pain on a scale from 0 to 10. Results showed that men tolerate pain better (had lower pain ratings) than women and athletes tolerate pain better than sedentary individuals.

Return to Competition   To a greater or lesser extent, return to competition is the ultimate goal of athletes who have been injured. This is also the goal of coaches and dedicated sport injury rehabilitation personnel. Research has shown that there is a great deal of worry, frustration, and psychological trepidation associated with enduring a grueling rehabilitation process and then taking the final step to return to competition. Athletes worry that they may not be ready for competition or that their injured limb or body part may not be strong enough to withstand the return to full-speed competition. In this regard, negative affect associated with injury is predictive of reduced confidence in a successful return to competition. In addition, fear of reinjury is predictive of a lower likelihood of resuming preinjury levels of competitive competence (Tripp, Stanish, Ebel-Lam, Brewer, & Birchard, 2007).

One review article (Podlog & Eklund, 2007a) and three research investigations (Podlog & Eklund, 2006, 2009; Podlog, Lochbaum, & Stevens, 2010) sought to study the psychology of return to competition after injury within a self-determination theory perspective. Consequently, results were discussed relative to the psychological needs of competence, autonomy, and relatedness. Athletes high in these three psychological constructs tend to enjoy high levels of intrinsic motivation and to meet their goals of full recovery from injury and successful return to competition. Specifically, the athlete who successfully returns to competition and a high level of performance experiences the following: (a) high motivation to return to competition, (b) both positive and negative emotions associated with return, (c) does not rush decision to return to competition, (d) resists pressure to return too early, (e) copes with adversity and injury flare-ups, (f) enjoys aspects of return to competition, and (g) recognizes positive consequences of injury and overcoming adversity.

Finally, Podlog and Eklund (2007b) reported on a study that focused on successful athlete return to competition from the perspective of professional coaches. In this study, 14 professional coaches of elite Australian and New Zealand injured athletes were interviewed. The result of this investigation revealed three main themes and several subthemes. Theme number *one* focused on coaches' recognition that the sport injury rehabilitation personnel have the final say on when an athlete returns to competition. Theme number *two* identified three stressors that the athlete must deal with in order to return to successful competition. These included *physical stressors* (reinjury fear, regain fitness, regain skill level), *social stressors*

(isolation, pressure to return early, negative social comparisons), and *performance stressors* (falling behind, losing spot on team, regaining preinjury level). Theme number *three* focused upon the coaches' role in assisting athlete to return to competition. Subthemes associated with the coaches' role included (a) individual training sessions for the injured athlete, (b) keeping the athlete involved in the team, and (c) providing social, emotional, tangible, and informational support.

Career Termination Due to Injury and Other Causes

> Athletic participation is characterized by glorious peaks and debilitating valleys. The range of events and emotions experienced by athletes seems to be extreme compared to the normal population. Perhaps the most significant and potentially traumatic experience encountered by athletes is career termination (Taylor & Olgilvie, 2001, p. 672).

In addition to career termination facilitated by a career-ending athletic injury, there are many other reasons why an athlete's career might come to an end. Consider the high school junior who plans on playing college basketball but is cut from the team before he even gets to the senior year. Consider the college quarterback who aspires to play professional football but is not drafted by any professional team. Consider the professional football player who plays three years and then sustains a career-ending injury. The list goes on. In many cases, even when retirement is planned, the athlete is unprepared for the sudden change in lifestyle. Because sport psychologists are not routinely employed by all collegiate athletic departments and professional sport teams, there is often no one available to help athletes face a sudden or even planned termination of the athletic experience.

While there has been much written about career termination and transition in sport, we owe much of our conceptual understanding of career termination and transition to Jim Taylor and Bruce Ogilvie (Ogilvie & Taylor, 1993; Taylor & Ogilvie,

Athlete contemplating career termination?
© Royalty-Free Corbis

1994, 2001). As illustrated in figure 18.4, Taylor and Ogilvie (1994) proposed the **conceptual model of career termination.** Taking a closer look at this figure, we see that the flow diagram begins at the top with the notion of multiple causes of career termination and then drops down to (a) factors related to adaptation to career termination, and (b) available resources, which interact with each other to determine the quality of adaptation to career termination. At the next level, if adaptation to career termination is not smooth, then career termination distress occurs with multiple possible negative consequences. If this occurs, then various interventions are required to help the former athlete cope with such things as psychological trauma and substance abuse. Most, but not all, of the research on career termination in athletes has focused on factors related to adaptation to career termination and available resources. In the paragraphs that follow we look at research associated with the various processes shown in figure 18.4.

There are various causes for career termination. Some of the causes for career termination are traumatic, such as a career-ending injury, but some are

equally traumatic, but without injury. Consider, for example, the elite female gymnast who starts her career at a very young age but also ends it at a very young age (Lavallee & Robinson, 2007; Warriner & Lavallee, 2008). These young women are still adolescents or young adults when their careers are terminated. A second example is young men selected to attend a three- to four-year soccer academy designed to prepare them to be professional soccer players. At the end of their four years, only 5 to 10 percent are offered professional contracts while the remainder must change their career goals and aspirations (Laurin, Nicolas, & Lavallee, 2008).

There are many important factors related to adaptation to career termination. Athletes who completely commit their self-identity and their social-identity to training for and competing in their sport have a particularly difficult time adapting to career termination. Young female elite gymnasts not only have their self-identity tied to their sport, but their lives are completely controlled by their practice schedules, competitions, and their drive to excel. When they do retire from competition due to an injury, age, or physical maturity, they are thrust into an environment of very little structure and control from others (Warriner & Lavallee, 2008). While it is a difficult prospect to consider, athletes must learn to proactively diminish their athletic identities prior to their actual retirement (Lally, 2007). Failure to do this can result in a poor adaptation to career termination.

Resources available to athletes to influence and bring to pass a smooth athletic career termination include coping skills, social support, and preretirement planning. While developing coping skills and receiving social support are tremendously important to adapting to career termination, research clearly shows the elevated importance of preretirement planning. Someone, if not the athlete, must help the athlete prepare for retirement before the event actually occurs. Ideally, every sport organization or athletic department would hire a full-time sport psychologist or consultant to do retirement planning for every athlete in their organization (Van Raalte & Andersen, 2007). It is

FIGURE 18.4 | The conceptual model of career termination as proposed by Taylor and Ogilvie (1994).

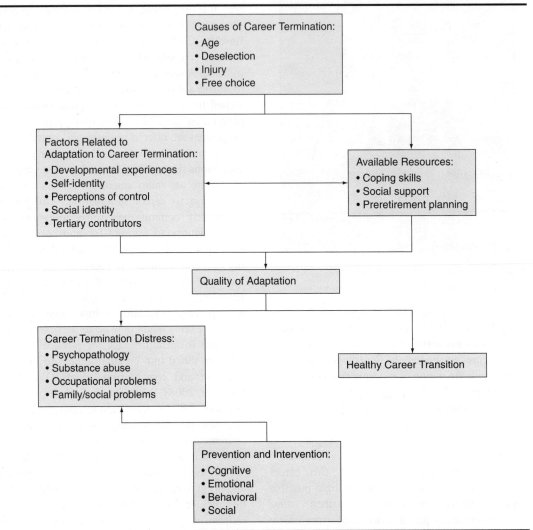

Source: From Taylor, J., & Ogilvie, B. (1994). A conceptual model of adaptation to retirement among athletes. *Journal of Applied Sport Psychology, 6,* 1–20. Reproduced with permission of the publisher (Taylor & Francis).

"athlete abuse" to use an athlete until he is of no use to the organization and then to "cut him loose" without any career termination planning. Numerous research investigations may be cited to support the effectiveness of and need for career termination planning for athletes (Laurin, et al., 2008; Lavallee, 2005; Stambulova, Stephan, & Japhag, 2007).

Failing a smooth career termination adaptation, career termination distress will be the resulting outcome (Wippert & Wippert, 2010). These distressful outcomes include but are not limited to

CONCEPT Athletes who suffer sudden career termination and have a strong athletic identification are particularly susceptible to personal adjustment problems.

APPLICATION Athletes who suffer sudden career termination should be provided with psychological

counseling to help them deal with the trauma of having their athletic careers ended so quickly and completely. This is particularly true for athletes who identify strongly with the athletic culture and environment. Athletic identity can easily be assessed with the Athletic Identity Measurement Scale (Brewer, Van Raalte, & Linder, 1993).

psychopathological disorders, substance abuse, occupational problems, and family/social problems. Professional German national ski team members who approached career termination with preretirement planning reported fewer cases of traumatic stress symptoms compared to those who did not (Wippert & Wippert, 2008). In another example, former French elite athletes who experienced body difficulties (e.g., weight gain, loss of muscle mass, body pain) following retirement also reported reduced physical self-worth and reduced self-esteem (Stephan, Torregrosa, & Sanchez, 2007).

Other Considerations

Other factors that will be briefly discussed include (a) providing sport injury rehabilitation personnel with psychological expertise, (b) benefits associated with sustaining and recovering from an athletic injury, and (c) effects of injury on teammates.

Providing Sport Injury Rehabilitation Personnel with Psychological Expertise

There are two basic approaches to providing sport injury rehabilitation personnel (SIRP) with knowledge and skill relative to the psychology of athletic injuries: the distributed approach and the specialist approach. In the **distributed approach,** the goal is to make sure that all SIRP receive training in sport psychology applications. SIRP who would require training in sport psychology would include (a) sport physiotherapists, (b) physical therapists, (c) athletic trainers, and (d) sport physicians.

According to Gordon, Potter, and Ford (1998), a prospective SIRP should do the following things in the course of a psychoeducational curriculum:

1. Learn to recognize the limitations of his own expertise

2. Listen to and be tested on lectures of psychological aspects of sport injuries

3. Attend lectures and workshops on applied psychological skills

4. Learn about coping behaviors, recognize psychological distress, and learn how to deal with poor psychological response to injury

5. Learn how to deal with athletes who experience long-term injury, career-ending injury, or permanent disability

6. Learn how to recognize if an athlete is malingering relative to rehabilitation

A second approach to providing a SIRP team with psychological expertise is to employ a full-time sport psychologist. In the **specialist approach,** the SIRP team hires a sport psychologist to work with injured athletes requiring psychological services. While this second approach seems ideal, it presents challenges (Petitpas, 1998). Only about 5 to 13 percent of injured athletes are expected to display psychological distress that requires the services of a psychologist. Unless a sports medicine clinic were very large, it would be difficult to keep a full-time psychologist busy. Therefore, in order to gain entrance into the typical sports medicine clinic, the sport psychologist would have to convince the clinic that her services

CONCEPT A truly successful rehabilitation from an athletic injury is associated with benefits related to personal growth, psychological skill, physical health, and skill improvement.

APPLICATION Experiencing an athletic injury is a traumatic experience for an athlete. Yet, once the decision is made to enter the rehabilitation process with optimism and determination, unexpected benefits may be realized. It is the responsibility of the sport injury rehabilitation personnel to provide the expertise and climate that will enhance the realization of positive personal growth benefits.

---

were cost effective and necessary. Possessing multiple skills and licensures (e.g., in athletic training, counseling, exercise physiology, research) is a good way to demonstrate added value.

Benefits Associated with Sustaining and Recovering from an Athletic Injury

While it is generally assumed that nothing good comes from an athletic injury, this may not be entirely true. Evidence suggests that successful recovery from an athletic injury is associated with several benefits. Twenty-one U.S. ski team members who sustained and recovered from season-ending injuries were asked to identify benefits associated with being injured (Udry, Gould, Bridges, & Beck, 1997). Seventeen of the athletes identified *personal growth* benefits associated with sustaining and recovering from an athletic injury. Relative to personal growth, athletes felt they had gained perspective, experienced personality development, developed non- skiing aspects of their lives, and learned better time management skills. Seventeen of the athletes identified *psychologically based performance enhancement* benefits. Relative to the enhancement of psychological skills, the athletes felt they had experienced an increase in self-efficacy, mental toughness, personal motivation, and had learned to be more realistic in their performance expectations. Finally, 10 of the athletes identified *physical and technical development* benefits associated with the injury/ recovery experience. They felt their general health was improved and that they had learned to ski technically better and more intelligently as a result of the injury and recovery process. In addition to the U.S. ski team investigation, other investigations have confirmed that positive benefits can come from successfully recovering from a serious athletic injury (Podlog & Eklund, 2006; Young, Pain, & Pearce, 2007).

Effects of Injury on Teammates Based on the research, we are well informed of how an athletic injury affects the athlete from a cognitive, emotional, and behavioral perspective. Much less is known, however, about how a serious injury inflicted on a member of a team might affect the injured athletes' team and teammates. According to O'Neill (2008), an emotional contagion or in this case **injury contagion** arises in teammates when they see someone on their own team sustain a serious injury. The emotional trauma associated with injury contagion may cause uninjured teammates to worry about an injury to them, which in turn may result in a change in performance tactics and in the stress response (figure 18.1). Research also suggests that collective team efficacy may suffer as a result of serious injury to a member of the team (Damato, Grove, Eklund, & Cresswell, 2008). The notion that a serious injury to a key member of a team could result in injury contagion and/or reduced collective team efficacy underscores the importance of planned interventions designed to help athletes cope with injury to a teammate. Such interventions could focus on maintaining appropriate attentional focus, regulating emotions and arousal, and trusting in team preparation.

Summary

In addressing the important subject of the psychology of athletic injuries, four main chapter sections were discussed. These were (a) psychological predictors of athletic injuries, (b) psychological response to injury and rehabilitation, (c) career termination, and (d) other considerations.

The discussion of psychological predictors of athletic injuries focused upon Williams and Andersen's (1998) stress and injury model. The elicitation of the stress response represents a perceived imbalance between the athlete's resources to cope with the demands of the situation and the actual demands. The stress response evokes physiological and attentional changes in the athlete that enhance chances of an athletic injury. Moderators of the stress response include personality factors, history of stressors, coping resources, and psychological interventions.

Factors associated with an athlete's psychological response to injury and follow-up rehabilitation occur after the injury has occurred. In order to understand the complexities of what occurs following injury, a comprehensive model is needed. In response to this need, the Wiese-Bjornstal, Smith, Shaffer, et al. (1998) integrated sport injury model was introduced and discussed. Response to sport injury and the rehabilitation process was discussed as a function of cognitive appraisal, emotional response, and behavioral response. Factors associated with behavioral response to injury include (a) adherence to rehabilitation, (b) use of psychological skill training strategies, (c) use of social support, (d) risk-taking behavior, (e) effort and intensity, (f) malingering, and (g) behavioral coping. Coping skills possessed by the athlete, availability of positive social support, and cognitive-behavioral interventions (applied by others or the athlete) are all effective in enhancing adherence to injury rehabilitation programs.

Predictors of cognitive appraisal, emotional response, and injury rehabilitation include personal and situational factors. Individuals with a low tolerance to pain may have a more difficult time going through the three stages of the sport injury recovery process. Pain associated with an athletic injury is managed through a combination of pharmacological (prescription drug) and non-pharmacological approaches. Once the athlete has completed the rehabilitation process, the psychology of a successful return to full competition becomes an important issue. Athletes who successfully return to competition are characterized by motivation, emotional control, patience, and an appreciation of personal growth.

Athletes who experience sudden career termination due to injury or some other cause should be provided with psychological counseling to help them deal with the psychological trauma of having their athletic careers ended so quickly and completely. This is particularly true for athletes who identify strongly with the athletic culture and environment.

Other factors that were discussed included providing sport injury personnel with psychological expertise, benefits associated with sustaining and recovering from an injury, and the effects of injury upon teammates.

Critical Thought Questions

1. Research links personality of the athlete, history of stressors, and coping mechanisms with athletic injury. The Williams and Andersen stress injury model provides one way of conceptualizing the actual mechanism, or connection between these factors and injury. See if you can think of an alternate plausible explanation as to how these connections can be made. Provide a written description of your model.

2. Now that you have studied the integrated sport injury rehabilitation model, do you think it provides an adequate explanation of the complexities of the rehabilitation process? How would you suggest that the model be revised?

3. Develop a detailed nonpharmacological plan for pain reduction in the injured athlete.

4. Why do you think different athletes have different tolerances to pain?

5. What is meant by pain catastrophizing? How does it relate to pain perception, sex, or whether a person is an athlete or not?

6. Once the injury rehabilitation process has run it course, the athlete's goal is a successful return to competition. Discuss the challenges associated with this ultimate goal.

7. Discuss the conceptual model of career termination and make suggestions for application and improvement in the model.

8. Is having a strong athletic identity good or bad relative to early retirement from sport? Justify your answer.

9. Differentiate between the distributed and specialist approaches to building a SIRP team. Which approach do you favor and why? Can you think of a third approach? Explain.

10. Discuss the potential benefits associated with suffering an athletic injury and making a full recovery from it.

11. How does an injury to a teammate affect the team? What can be done about it?

Glossary

acute pain Pain caused by a trauma to the body that is intense, but of short duration.

adherence to injury rehabilitation The degree to which an athlete follows an athletic rehabilitation program.

athletic identity Degree to which an individual identifies with the athletic culture and environment.

behavioral response The way an athlete behaves following cognitive and emotional response to injury. Generally interpreted to mean the way the athlete responds to rehabilitation.

benign pain Pain that is short in duration and not associated with swelling and soreness.

chronic pain Long-lasting, uncontrollable pain that continues long after the initial injury.

cognitive appraisal The way an athlete thinks about a demanding situation leading to the stress response, as well as about an actual injury. It is moderated by both personality and situational factors.

conceptual model of career termination Beginning with causes of career termination, the model describes (a) factors related to adaptation, (b) available resources for adapting, (c) termination distress associated with poor adaptation, and (d) prevention and intervention.

coping behavior A behavior that assists an individual in dealing with a stressful situation.

distributed approach Situation in which sport psychology knowledge and skill are distributed among the sport injury rehabilitation personnel.

emotional disclosure paradigm Using writing as a therapeutic catharsis to reduce emotional trauma.

emotional response The way an athlete responds in emotional ways to an athletic injury.

harmful pain Pain that occurs before and after exertion, and is associated with swelling, tenderness, and prolonged soreness.

injury contagion Like emotional contagion, it is a distraction that affects a team and causes them to worry about suffering an athletic injury. The distraction it causes may contribute to the stress response and athletic injury.

injury pain Pain that is not controlled by the athlete and that occurs as a result of an injury, as opposed to performance.

injury rehabilitation interventions Interventions, such as guided imagery, relaxation, stress inoculation, goal setting, and biofeedback, designed to facilitate the rehabilitation process.

integrated sport injury model A sport injury model that integrates antecedents of injury, cognitive appraisal of injury, emotional response to injury, and behavioral response to injury into a comprehensive injury rehabilitation model.

nonpharmacological pain-focusing techniques The use of either association or dissociation attentional strategies to manage pain.

nonpharmacological pain-reduction techniques Pain reduction techniques, such as deep breathing, muscle relaxation, meditation, and massage, applied during injury rehabilitation.

pain catastrophizing The degree to which individuals focus on pain, exaggerate the threat of pain to their well-being, and perceive themselves as unable to cope effectively with pain.

pain tolerance A personality characteristic to tolerate or endure pain.

performance pain Pain controlled by the athlete during performance.

personal factors Personality characteristics of the athlete that influence the rehabilitation process, beginning with cognitive appraisal.

psychological response to injury In the integrated sport injury model, an athlete's response to injury that comprises both cognitive appraisal and the emotional response.

rehabilitation rehearsal The conscious use of mental imagery for the purpose of effective rehabilitation.

situational factors Sport, social, and environmental factors that influence injury rehabilitation, beginning with cognitive appraisal.

specialist approach Situation in which a sports medicine clinic hires a sport psychologist to work with sport injury rehabilitation team personnel relative to psychological applications.

stress and injury model A model developed by Williams and Andersen (1998) to explain what causes the stress process, what moderates the stress process, and how it is related to athletic injury.

stress response The manifestation of distress or state anxiety in response to a demanding or threatening situation.

Negative Aspects of Sport and Exercise

KEY TERMS

Activity anorexia
Alternative identity
Anabolic effect
Anabolic steroids
Anabolic-androgenic steroids
Androgenic effect
Androstenedione
Anorexia analogue hypothesis
Anorexia athletica
Anorexia nervosa
Behavioral techniques
Body objectification theory
Bulimia nervosa
Burnout in sport and exercise
Cognitive techniques
Continuum model of obligatory
   exercise
Creatine
Deterrence theory
EDNOS
Empowerment model of
   burnout
Endogenous testosterone
Entrapment
Exercise addiction
Exercise dependence
Exogenous testosterone
Female triad

Investment model
   of burnout
Mood disturbance
Muscle dysmorphia
Obligatory runner
Overreaching
Overtraining
Phosphocreatine
Psychological
   expectancy effect
Reverse anorexia nervosa
Smith's cognitive-affective
   model of stress and burnout

Staleness
Subclinical eating disorders
Super-adherer

The focus of this textbook up to this point has been on the positive benefits associated with participating in sport and exercise. When practiced in moderation, sport and exercise offer many healthy psychological and physiological benefits. When not practiced in moderation, however, many negative aspects are connected to the sport and exercise culture. The most common negative aspects include using performance-enhancing drugs; being addicted to exercise; buying into the thinness craze as a means to enhance performance; an unhealthy fixation on building muscle mass; and burnout due to stress, entrapment, or a loss of autonomy. These are all familiar negative outcomes associated with an unhealthy obsession with sport and exercise. Topics addressed in this chapter on the negative aspects of sport and exercise include (a) drug abuse in sport and exercise, (b) exercise dependence. (c) eating disorders and physical activity, (d) muscle dysmorphia, and (e) burnout in sport and exercise.

Drug Abuse in Sport and Exercise

Drug abuse by athletes has become a national and international embarrassment for athletes and for organizations promoting ethical conduct in sport. While athletes have abused many types of drugs in an effort to gain an edge against competitors, by far the most publicized and commonly used drugs are called anabolic steroids. Many assume that the drug abuse problem is found only among professional and collegiate athletes, but evidence suggests that drug abuse has filtered down to adolescent and youth sport athletes as well (Denham, Hawkins, Jones, & Billings, 2007; Laure & Binsinger, 2007; Llosa & Wertheim, 2008; Schirlin et al., 2009). In this section we discuss drug abuse under the headings of (a) anabolic-androgenic steroids, (b) other banned drugs and unbanned supplements, and (c) combating drug abuse in sport.

Anabolic-Androgenic Steroids

While of little scientific value, anecdotal evidence of anabolic steroid abuse by high-profile athletes heightens our awareness of this problem. Ben Johnson, a Canadian world record holder in the 100 meters, tested positive for anabolic steroids following his gold medal race in the 1988 Seoul Olympics. He had set a new world record of 9.79 seconds, beating his old world record of 9.83 by 0.04 seconds. The International Olympic Committee (IOC) declared Johnson's race null and void, stripped him of his gold medal, and awarded it to Carl Lewis of the United States (Johnson & Moore, 1988).

Lyle Alzado, a former National Football League (NFL) star, admitted to using anabolic steroids for purposes of performance enhancement and blamed his drug abuse for a brain lymphoma (cancer) that a short time later resulted in his death (Alzado, 1991). Alzado gave personal testimony to the incredible mood swings that he said made him mean, aggressive, and violent both on and off the field of play. In his dying words, he exclaimed, "It was addicting, mentally addicting, I just didn't feel strong unless I was taking them" (p. 24).

High-profile baseball players Barry Bonds, Mark McGwire, and Sammy Sosa thrilled the nation with home run feats in 1998 and 2001. Mark McGwire and Sammy Sosa hit 70 and 66 home runs in 1998, to break Roger Maris's long-standing record of 61 home runs in the 1961 season. Shortly after that, Barry Bonds hit 73 home runs in the 2001 season. How can this be? Maris's record of 61 home runs held for 37 years, yet it was broken three times in a span of three years. Unfortunately, the accomplishments of these three great home run hitters have been tainted by the possibility of anabolic steroid use (Ballard, 2007; Dohrmann, 2004; Smith, 2005).

Related to the skepticism that has arisen as a result of these and other super-human batting feats, Major League Baseball (MLB) commissioner Bud Selig, authorized George Mitchell, former Senate Majority Leader, to write the Mitchell Report on MLB. Released on December 20, 2007, the Mitchell Report yielded the names of 89 alleged users of performance-enhancing drugs. In addition, the Mitchell Report recommended that MLB get out of the drug-testing business immediately and entirely, as they could not be trusted to run a transparent, state-of-the-art drug testing program (Roberts & Epstein, 2009; Verducci, 2007). While Barry Bonds and Sammy Sosa have not yet admitted to using performance-enhancing drugs, to his credit, Mark McGuire admitted on January 11, 2010, to using steroids and human growth harmone on and off from 1990 to 2000 and during the time he broke Roger Maris's home run record (Blum, 2010).

While it seems logical that taking anabolic steroids to increase muscle mass and strength might help a MLB player hit more home runs, many questioned if it could help a MLB pitcher throw a fastball to the plate at a faster rate. Addona and Roth (2010) reported on an investigation in which they compared average fastball pitching velocity of MLB pitchers who had been implicated in the Mitchell Report or suspended for suspected performance enhancing drug use (PED) with those who had not. Data were collected on any pitcher who threw at least 10 innings in a month between 2002 and 2008. Results showed that pitchers who allegedly used PED during that period of time increased average fastball velocity by 1.074 miles per hour overall.

While the Mitchell Report and Senate hearings about the use of PED by MLB players seem to have slowed the use of performance enhancing drugs, there may be an alarming trend that has athletes turning to genetic engineering as a means to enhance performance while at the same time avoiding detection. Genetic engineering has already been shown to double the normal muscle mass in mice without an exercise regime (Epstein, 2008). There is concern that advances in genetic engineering could be perverted to aid athletes in their quest for sports glory. Dick Pound, the current chairman of the World Anti-Doping Agency

made the following statement about doping in sport (Kaufman, 2006):

> Doping is the most serious problem we have in sport, and if we don't do something about it, sports will degenerate into an extreme and violent collection of mutant gladiators. Responsible parents and educators will not encourage children, or will not allow them, to participate if it requires becoming a chemical stockpile to be good.

Bad and unethical behavior by professional athletes and the accompanying consequences and publicity create a negative climate for competitive sports. As explained by Longman (2003) and Layden (2009), a corrosive atmosphere persists in sports from football to cycling and table tennis. High-profile athletes perform under constant suspicion, and parents wonder if their own children will have to use drugs to complete. Records are perceived as tainted and fans watch events wondering if the results are valid. It seems as if only a return to super-ethics can defeat the cheaters' insatiable drive to cheat in order to grab fame and fortune.

As explained by Anshel (2006), three fundamental problems are associated with the use of drugs to enhance athletic performance. The first is that it is fundamentally *unethical* to take drugs to obtain an unfair advantage over the opposition. Second, performance enhancing drugs are potentially psychologically and/or physiologically *addictive* leaving the athlete a "slave" to the drug. Finally, there are potentially *lethal health effects* associated with drug use. While it is often difficult to prove that the abuse of a drug led to the death or serious illness of an athlete, it is difficult to ignore the "gut-wrenching" testimonials of drug abusers such as Lyle Alzado.

What Are Anabolic-Androgenic Steroids?

Anabolic steroids are hormones that stimulate protein anabolism in the body. Athletes ingest anabolic steroids because they believe that they are responsible for alterations in body composition that result in greater size, strength, and power. What we call **anabolic steroids** are a group of

Chapter 19 Negative Aspects of Sport and Exercise **465**

synthetic derivatives of the male hormone testosterone that have been modified so that their presence in the bloodstream is prolonged. They have both an **anabolic effect** (increasing muscular strength and size) and an **androgenic effect** (masculinizing effect) on the user. Consequently, what we commonly refer to as anabolic steroids are really **anabolic-androgenic steroids** that are synthetically derived to increase muscle mass while at the same time minimizing the masculinizing, or androgenic, effect.

The term **exogenous testosterone** refers to the administration of an anabolic steroid to mimic the effects of testosterone in the body. Conversely, the term **endogenous testosterone** refers to the naturally occurring levels of testosterone in the body. The food supplement **androstenedione** (pronounced andro-steen-dee-own) is a direct precursor hormone to the production of endogenous testosterone in the body. (Bahrke, Yesalis, & Wright, 1996; McCallum, 2008; Wertheim & Epstein, 2008).

Biological Effects of Anabolic Steroid Use
Research clearly shows that anabolic steroid use is associated with increased body weight and mass, altered body composition, increased muscle size and strength, increased blood volume, and increased number of red blood cells (Stone, 1993). Suspected negative physiological consequences associated with anabolic steroid use include increased risk of heart disease, certain cancers, and undesirable sex-specific effects. For men, undesirable sex effects *may* include shrinking testes, hair loss, enlarged breasts, and possible sterility. For women, undesirable sex effects *may* include shrinking breasts and uterus, enlarged clitoris, irregular menstruation, increased facial and body hair, and a deepening voice (Is it safe, 2000).

Because males have 40 times more natural testosterone circulating in their bodies than females, the use of anabolic steroids by females may have a particularly strong anabolic (muscle building) and androgenic (masculinizing) effect. There

is good reason to be concerned that anabolic steroid use by females may exacerbate the female triad and associated health conditions. The **female triad** consists of disordered eating, amenorrhea (absence of menses), and osteoporosis (Denham et al., 2007).

Perhaps the most extreme example of the effect of anabolic steroids on women is the case of Heidi Krieger (Longman, 2004a). Heidi, a victim of a state-sponsored attempt to build a country of 16 million into a sports power rivaling the United States and the former Soviet Union, began taking the anabolic steroid Oral-Turinabol when she was 16 years of age. She was told by her East German coaches that the round blue pill that she was told to take was a vitamin pill that would increase strength. At age 16 she threw the shot put just over 46 feet; three years later, weighing 200 pounds, she threw the shot 65 feet, 6 inches at the 1986 European women's shot put championship. Confused as a teenager about her sexual identity, she later had a sex change operation and became known as Andreas.

Psychological Effects of Anabolic Steroid Use
From the standpoint of increased size and muscle mass, it is relatively clear what the biological effects of anabolic steroid use are, but it is far less clear what the psychological effects are. We do know that *endogenous testosterone levels* in animals and humans are linked to aggressive behavior. The higher the serum level of naturally occurring testosterone in the body, the higher the level of aggression. Ingesting moderate levels of *exogenous anabolic steroids* does not seem to result in overt aggressive behavior in humans, but ingestion of high levels does (Bahrke et al., 1996). Assuming that most users of anabolic steroids ingest them at moderate levels, there should be relatively few reported cases of deviant psychological behavior and aggression. Indeed, Bahrke et al. write that "it is interesting to note that with a million or more steroid users in the U.S., only a small percentage of users appear to experience mental disturbances which result in clinical treatment"

CONCEPT   Anabolic steroid use is associated with increased body weight and mass, altered body composition, increased muscle size and strength, increased blood volume, and an increased number of red blood cells.

APPLICATION   From purely a strength and muscle mass perspective, it seems clear that anabolic steroid use should lead to an unfair advantage in certain sport tasks involving strength and power. Examples might include weight lifting, body building, track and field, swimming, and American football. Despite the expected short-term performance enhancement benefits of anabolic steroid use, they are not worth the potential negative long-term health effects. Athletes seeking fame and fortune may come to believe that the risk is worth it, but coaches and sports medicine personnel must take extraordinary steps to teach athletes the dangers and risks associated with the use of anabolic steroids.

CONCEPT   While extremely high levels of anabolic steroid use are linked to aggressive behavior, the cause-and-effect link between moderate levels of anabolic steroid use and deviant psychological behavior has not been established. Even when links have been observed, they are obscured by confounding psychosocial factors.

APPLICATION   It is counterproductive to cry "wolf" when there is no "wolf." Trying to convince athletes that they should not use anabolic steroids because of negative psychological affect or negative feelings is in conflict with the literature and in conflict with what they hear from other athletes. A better approach is to appeal to the athlete's sense of fairness and desire to accomplish great things without the aid of drugs and supplements.

(p. 387). Bahrke et al. (1996) further lament that there may be many beneficial medical effects associated with anabolic steroid use, but they remain unstudied because of the paranoia of the media and hysterical unsubstantiated references.

The scientific link between anabolic steroid use and deviant psychological behavior is a weak one. Sharp and Collins (1998) note that there is a growing body of literature that links anabolic steroid use with aggressive behavior, but that the causal connections are weak. They point out that there are numerous psychosocial factors that likely interact with anabolic steroid use to bring about aggressive behavior. These psychosocial factors include (a) social mediation, (b) expectancy effects, and (c) the power of group conformity. Athletes read the newspapers and popular magazines. They know how they are supposed to behave in response to anabolic steroid use.

Olrich and Ewing (1999) conducted in-depth interviews of 10 body builders or weight lifters who were using or had used anabolic steroids. These athletes started using anabolic steroids out of curiosity and a desire to make strength improvements. Five lifters indicated that they started using steroids in the face of strong internal conflict, and one athlete did so even though he believed it would result in cancer. Nine of the ten athletes described their experience with anabolic steroids in a positive light, but did indicate a perception of psychological dependence. None reported horrific negative side effects associated with their use of the drug. The users reported enhanced physical functioning (energy, libido, muscle mass); enhanced psychological functioning (alertness, aggressiveness, confidence); enhanced social recognition and acceptance (peer recognition, sexual attraction); and enhanced vocational functioning (alertness, confidence, effectiveness). One lifter did complain of joint pains, fluid retention, a bloated feeling, muscle strains and tears, and *extreme guilt*. Overall, the researchers concluded that you cannot deter anabolic steroid use by claiming negative short-term benefits or feelings, although they noted that the long-term effects are unknown.

There seems to be no question that anabolic steroid use is associated with increased muscle mass and body size, but it is less clear that their use leads to an increase in performance. Stated another way, it may be that increases in performance may be due to the **psychological expectancy effect,** and only indirectly to anabolic steroid use. This possibility is reinforced by an investigation reported by Maganaris, Collins, and Sharp (2000). Eleven national-level power lifters (bench, dead lift, squat) took two pills immediately before an experimental trial in which they completed a one maximum repetition (1RM) on all three lifts. The lifters believed that the pills contained an anabolic steroid that would have an immediate action on their strength, when in fact the pills contained saccharin. All 11 lifters improved their lifts above baseline. They were given two more pills for the following week's training. Seven days later, they again completed a second 1RM lifting trial on all three lifts. Five of the lifters were informed in confidence, just before they made their lifts, that the pills they had been taking contained saccharine. The six lifters who thought they were taking pills containing an anabolic steroid again posted lifts above baseline. The other five lifters did not

perform above baseline, and in fact, dropped significantly below baseline. This is the psychological expectancy effect.

The psychological expectancy effect of drug use was recently studied by McClung and Collins (2007). In this investigation, not involving anabolic steroids, endurance runners were either given a performance enhancement drink containing sodium bicarbonate (SB) or a placebo containing no sodium bicarbonate prior to four counterbalanced 1,000 meter runs. As explained to the runners, sodium bicarbonate has the effect of increasing the pH acid-base balance in the blood and thereby reducing the blood lactate concentration, resulting in increased performance and reduced perceived effort. In addition to actually receiving or not receiving the performance enhancing drink, the runners were also either informed that they had received the performance enhancing drink or informed that they had not received the performance enhancing drink. This resulted in a 2 × 2 design containing the following four manipulated conditions: (a) received SB / told they received SB, (b) received SB / told they did not receive SB, (c) received no SB / told they received SB, and (d) received no SB / told they did not receive SB. Results showed that for both performance and perceived exertion measures, differences were only observed relative to what they believed (told) they received and not what they actually received. Runners ran faster and with less effort when they believed they took the performance enhancing drink compared to when they believed they had not taken the performance enhancing drink. Whether the runners did or did not actually take SB had no effect on performance or perceived effort.

The long-term effects of anabolic steroid use are unknown. Many sport psychologists believe that long-term use of this drug will lead to poor health. Organs that are particularly susceptible to negative consequences of anabolic steroid abuse are those, such as the kidneys and liver, that are responsible for the transport, metabolism, and detoxification of the drug. Since the liver serves a central role in the metabolism of drugs, it is not surprising

CONCEPT   Athletes who take anabolic steroids expect to be stronger, expect to perform better, and expect to be aggressive and more confident. Superior performance associated with anabolic steroid use may be due to the effects of taking the drug, but it also may be due to the psychological expectancy effect or some combination of the two, as well as other psychosocial factors.

APPLICATION   The relationship between anabolic steroid use and improved performance and mood is a very complex one. Coaches and sports medicine personnel must be completely honest and truthful with athletes regarding the use of anabolic steroids. The bottom line, however, is that their use is illegal, and athletes must not get mixed signals from their coaches in this regard.

that it is frequently damaged by drug use and abuse. If a drug has a negative effect upon even one part of the body, the function of the entire body can suffer.

Reversing the Trend towards Steroid Abuse

In 2003 the American College of Sports Medicine (ACSM) condemned the use of steroids to enhance body size and strength and further condemned the development and use of new *designer steroids* developed to avoid detection in drug tests (ACSM, 2003). The most recent designer drug is Tetra-hydrogestrinone (THG), pronounced "tetra-hydro-gest-re-own." In its news release, the ACSM also appealed to "clean" athletes to publicly deplore the use of steroids among their teammates and peers.

As a result of the outrage over the apparent use of anabolic steroids by such famous MLB players as Jose Canseco, Mark McGwire, Sammy Sosa, and Barry Bonds, MLB was forced to establish a tougher policy on steroid use (Kepner, 2005). The new rules require mandatory unannounced testing of all MLB players once a year and unlimited random testing throughout the season and off-season. As of November 15, 2005, MLB players and owners agreed to tougher penalties for steroid use (Blum & Fendrich, 2005). The penalty for the first failed test will be a 50 game suspension, 100 games for the second, while for the third it will be a lifetime ban. Hopefully, other professional sports and leagues will adopt these harsher penalties. To the baseball purist, Roger Maris's 61 home runs in a

single season look pretty good right now. Tellingly, the following statement was made by Jose Canseco on CBS's *60 Minutes* (Steroids made baseball career possible, 2005):

> I don't recommend steroids for everyone and I don't recommend growth hormones for everyone, but for certain individuals, I truly believe, because I've experimented with it for so many years, that it can make an average athlete a super athlete. It can make a super athlete incredible. Just legendary.

Later in this chapter we talk more about combating drug abuse, but for now it seems apparent that neither professional sports nor society as a whole is prepared to make the penalty for anabolic steroid use severe enough to prevent its use. If being caught using anabolic steroids meant that you were banned from professional sport for two years on the first infraction, as is the case with Olympic sports (Kepner, 2005), far fewer athletes would risk being caught.

Other Banned Drugs and Unbanned Substances

In addition to anabolic steroids there is a long list of other banned drugs and unbanned substances that are used by some athletes in hopes of improving athletic performance. Our purpose in this section is to highlight and discuss some of the more commonly used banned drugs and substances including stimulants, depressants, diuretics, hallucinogens, beta-blockers, creatine, and dietary supplements.

Stimulants Stimulants, such as amphetamines and cocaine, increase the rate and work capacity of the central nervous system, respiratory system, and heart. The neural-stimulating and cardiac-stimulating effects of these drugs can provide a physiological advantage to the athlete by inhibiting mental and physical fatigue. The illegal and unethical use of stimulants may result in performance enhancement, but not without some danger to the athlete. These drugs are physically and/or psychologically addicting and their use may lead to serious health problems.

The danger of stimulants is illustrated in the death of Steve Bechler, a former pitcher for the Baltimore Orioles professional baseball team (Olney, 2003). Belcher died of apparent heart failure during spring training in 2003. He had been taking the weight loss drug Xenadrine, which contains Ephedra, a stimulant banned by the NCAA and the NFL. As stated by Dr. John Lombardo, medical advisor for the National Football League, "The heart of someone in poor condition is forced to work hard, and if that person is taking a stimulant, there is additional stress on the heart."

Depressants Depressants, such as barbiturates, sedative-hypnotics, and alcohol, are designed to relieve tension, depression, and anxiety in the athlete. Theoretically, this could help the fearful and anxious athlete by providing a steadying effect. These drugs, however, do not always have the desired effect on the athlete. Depressants may actually have the effect of reducing inhibition, reducing judgment, and heightening risk-taking behavior, which may in turn result in poor as opposed to superior performance. These drugs are also highly addictive, making it difficult to quit using them without severe withdrawal symptoms. As with all drugs, their abuse may lead to serious health consequences due to damage to organs responsible for metabolizing them.

At the present time, alcohol consumption and marijuana use seem to be the drugs of choice on college campuses and in particular by college athletes. Research shows that (a) alcohol use is higher in the off-season compared to in-season, (b) competitiveness is a predictor of alcohol use among athletes, (c) alcohol consumption is greater among athletes than among nonathletes, (d) male athletes use both alcohol and marijuana to a greater extent than female athletes, (e) increased alcohol use by athletes is predicted by high attraction to team, (f) increased alcohol and marijuana use is predicted by normative beliefs about others' use, (g) approximately 37 percent of collegiate athletes report using marijuana at least once per year, and (h) reduced physical and cognitive performance are associated with alcohol and marijuana use (Grossbard, Hummer, LaBrie, Pederson, & Neighbors, 2009; LaBrie, Grossbard, & Hummer, 2009; Martens, Dams-O'Connor, & Duffy-Paiement, 2006; Serrao, Martens, & Rocha, 2008).

Diuretics, Hallucinogens, and Beta-Blockers Other drugs that have been banned by the International Olympic Committee (IOC) include diuretics, hallucinogens, and beta-adrenergic blockers. *Diuretics* are sometimes used by wrestlers, jockeys, and boxers to artificially induce an acute reduction in body weight through fluid elimination via the urine. Negative effects of diuretics may include nausea, heat stroke, blood clotting, reduced blood volume, and muscle cramps. The primary purpose of hallucinogens is to alter the perception of incoming stimuli. Because *hallucinogens* inhibit response and decision time as well as attentional focus, they tend to inhibit athletic performance instead of facilitating it. *Beta-adrenergic blockers* are used to steady and slow the heart rate, which may decrease anxiety/tension and indirectly enhance athletic performance.

Creatine Use by Athletes While creatine is not a substance currently banned by the International Olympic Committee, it is a food supplement extensively used by athletes seeking enhanced performance. Creatine use has been on the rise since the early 1990s; along with androstenedione, creatine gained some notoriety because of its alleged use by Sammy Sosa and Mark McGwire during the 1999 baseball season. **Creatine** is a naturally occurring energy-producing substance that is synthesized from amino acids in the human body. It is also consumed in the diet through the consumption of animal products. Creatine, in the form of **phosphocreatine,** serves as an energy buffer (shield) during periods of intense exercise. Creatine use is associated with an increase in body mass that is generally attributed to increased water retention.

The majority of the evidence indicates that creatine supplementation has a beneficial effect on acute, repetitive bursts of intense exercise, but little beneficial effect upon distance or aerobic exercise. Anecdotal evidence suggests that short-term adverse reactions to creatine use include gastrointestinal distress, nausea, and muscle cramping. Long-term negative effects on the liver, kidneys, and brain are only beginning to be investigated. Kreider et al. (2001) reported no negative side effects associated with 21 months of creatine use by collegiate football players. However, Keys et al. (2001) reported that 10 months of creatine supplementaion yielded evidence of liver damage and chronic hepatitis in mice. No negative psychological effects have been reported (Williams, Anderson, & Winett, 2004).

Dietary Supplements Dietary supplements are often recommended by various promoters as safe alternatives to drugs. Starting in high school, some of the drugs that athletes take are labeled dietary supplements, as if they are innocuous and beneficial for their health. To further confuse the issue, selected dietary supplements are banned by some professional organizations but not others. Tellingly, Frank Uryasz, President of the National Center for Drug Free Sport was quoted as making the following statement about dietary supplements and sport (Wertheim, 2003, p. 73):

> What kids—especially those health conscious and interested in sports—don't want to supplement their diet? But the notion is a joke. No one is

going to suffer because of an ephedra or creatine deficiency. We need to call these things what they are: drugs.

In 1994 Congress passed the Dietary Supplement Health and Education Act (DSHEA), which allowed supplements to be sold across the counter with no proof of effectiveness or safety. This act effectively opened the door for supplements to be sold, for purposes of improved health and performance, without the approval of the Food and Drug Administration (FDA). In the 1990's, ephedra was the golden herb of the supplement industry; but the dangers of ephedra became apparent in 2001 when the American Association of Poison Control Centers received 11,178 calls about adverse effects associated with supplements containing ephedra. Almost every energy and weight-loss drink on the market contains the stimulants yerba mate, green tea, yohimbine, and caffeine, which effectively speeds up the body's metabolism. In addition, many supplements promising increased energy and strength contain anabolic steroids that have or have not been added to the controlled substance list of the Drug Enforcement Administration (DEA). Without the protection of the FDA and DEA, consumers of food supplements do so at their own risk and in some cases the risks may be high (Epstein & Dohrmann, 2009).

Combating Drug Abuse in Sport

Better and more accurate research is needed relative to the use and abuse of drugs among scholastic, collegiate, and professional athletes. Underreporting is a serious limitation of research involving drug use among athletes. It is even more difficult to get accurate information from athletes about their coach's direct or indirect role in encouraging drug use for purposes of performance enhancement. Accurate data must be collected in a manner that would make it impossible to detect the name of the athlete reporting a result or the name of a coach associated with a particular athlete. This can only be accomplished if two conditions exist. First, data must be truly anonymous and untraceable, even in the face of a court subpoena. Second, the athletes filling out the questionnaires must *believe* that the data are truly anonymous and untraceable, even in the face of a court subpoena.

Two basic approaches to combating drug use in sport are mentioned by Anshel (2006). These are the use of cognitive techniques and the use of behavioral techniques. *Cognitive techniques* utilize intellectual and psychological methods to influence behavior and attitude. Conversely, *behavioral techniques* shape the athlete's environment in ways that will elicit desirable responses and behaviors from the athlete.

Using **cognitive techniques,** the coach utilizes support groups among the players to encourage drug abstinence. The coach shows concern for athletes, sets limits on unacceptable behavior, develops team policy, and teaches athletes specific coping skills to deal with the pressure to excel. The coach must be aware of each athlete's mental status, both in and out of the sport environment. Coaches can also help athletes by making them feel part of the team and by seeking their input on important team decisions (Lazuras, Barkoukis, Rodafinos, & Tzorbatzoudis, 2010).

As a cognitive strategy to reduce drug abuse among athletes, Strelan and Boeckmann (2003) proposed the Drugs in Sport Deterrence Model (DSDM) to study athlete decision making and to provide structure for research aimed at minimizing drug use by athletes. **Deterrence theory** is based on a cost-benefit approach to decision making relative to drug use. Instead of merely asking athletes to "just say no" to drugs, the athlete is asked to complete a cost-benefit analysis of reasons for using or not using drugs and then to make an informed decision. Costs associated with using drugs would include such things as legal sanctions, social sanctions, guilt and reduced self-esteem, and health concerns. Benefits associated with using drugs might include material gain (e.g., money, sponsorships, endorsements), social acknowledgment, and satisfaction for high achievement.

The vast majority of athletes take drugs for the purpose of performance enhancement. Therefore,

the focus of **behavioral techniques** should be upon teaching athletes alternative ways to enhance performance that do not include the use of drugs. These alternative methods to increased performance include teaching motor skills and strategies that lead to increased performance. Coaches do not always spend much time in practice helping individual athletes improve their personal skills. They may instead run scrimmages in which individual skills are largely overlooked and assumed to already exist. Other behavioral techniques that are effective include peer involvement in drug education and drug prevention efforts. Young athletes are much more likely to take advice from an admired peer than from an adult. In fact, many athletes get involved in the use of drugs because they have listened to an admired peer who was not setting a good example.

In addition to employing cognitive and behavioral techniques to combat drug use in sport, it may be necessary to adopt mandatory drug testing for all Olympic, collegiate, and professional sports with severe penalties for violators of the organization's drug use policy. Even with mandatory drug testing, severe penalties, and quality education, there will always be unsavory characters who will seek to "beat the system" and continue to exploit athletes and a public thirst for "bigger, faster, and better." Ultimately, the whole issue will come down to character, ethics, and a personal repugnance against cheating. Just think how Mark McGuire would feel right now if he had hit 70 home runs in a single season and could honestly say that he never used performance enhancing drugs to assist him.

Research on the topic of discouraging drug use by athletes provides additional insights that educators and coaches can use to help them in their personal "war against drugs." Research reported by Storch, Storch, Kovacs, Okun, and Welsh (2003) suggests that athletes who score high on religiosity or spirituality may be less prone to use alcohol, marijuana, or performance enhancing drugs. In addition, Donahue, Miquelon, et al. (2006) reported on research that

CONCEPT   Athletes are under tremendous pressure from coaches, parents, peers, and themselves to exhibit superior athletic performance. It does not seem to be enough to do your best anymore; you must be better than everyone else. Since this is an unrealistic expectation, it is not too surprising that some athletes turn to "performance-enhancing" drugs.

APPLICATION   It is the personal responsibility of all coaches and parents to make sure that no athlete they are associated with feels the pressure to excel to such a degree that she would resort to "performance-enhancing" drugs to accomplish this. Coaches, teachers, and athletes must "buy into" the notion of task, or mastery, goal orientation, as opposed to ego orientation. Athletics should be about becoming the best that you can become, but not necessarily about being better than everyone else. Mandatory drug testing can serve as a deterrent to athletes prone to using drugs for purposes of performance enhancement, but it cannot address the deeper issue of why an athlete would resort to such illegal behavior in the first place.

suggested that a motivational model could be used to combat drug use in sport. According to this model, based on self-determination theory, the *decreased* use of performance enhancing substances is predicted by (a) an increase in intrinsic motivation, (b) a decrease in extrinsic motivation, and (c) an increase in sportspersonship and prosocial behavior. Athletes who are primarily motivated by the prospect of notoriety, fame, and financial rewards may not be inclined to prosocial behavior, ethical behavior, and good sportsmanship. Consequently, concerted efforts must be made by coaches and parents to promote intrinsic motivation in athletes beginning in youth sports. Intrinsically motivated athletes will be inclined towards prosocial behavior and a strong bias against using performance enhancing drugs to gain an unfair advantage over competitors. As developed by Petroczi and Aidman (2009), the Performance Enhancement Attitude Scale (PEAS) may be helpful to coaches in identifying "doping attitudes" of athletes they are responsible for.

Exercise Dependence

In the literature, **exercise dependence** defines the individual who is psychologically dependent on a regular regimen of exercise. Other terms that have been used to describe exercise dependence include **exercise addiction** and the **obligatory runner**. The super-adherer is another term that describes an individual who may be addicted to exercise. The **super-adherer** is an exerciser who participates in and constantly trains for endurance events that require significant long-term effort and commitment. Often these super-endurance events range in distance from 50 to 100 miles.

The normal benefits associated with regular moderate exercise are lost for the exercise-addicted individual. Failure to exercise according to schedule results in a mood state disturbance and significant emotional trauma. From an attributional perspective, the addicted exerciser is controlled by the activity, as opposed to the activity being controlled by the exerciser. Compared to nonaddicted exercisers, addicted exercisers report being more restless and stressed-out prior to an exercise bout. They also experience a higher degree of depression, anxiety, and general discomfort when they miss a scheduled workout. An important characteristic of the exercise addict is that he will generally insist on exercising in the face of physical pain or injury. Fortunately, exercise dependence is fairly rare. Edmunds, Ntuomanis, and Duda (2006) tested 339 adult fitness participants and only found 11 or 3.4 percent who could be classified as exercise dependent. In order to be classified as being addicted to exercise, an individual must score high in three of seven exercise dependence characteristics which include the following (Hausenblas & Symons Downs, 2002a):

1. Tolerance—must continually increase exercise to obtain desired effect.

2. Withdrawal—experience symptoms of anxiety and fatigue when deprived of exercise.

3. Intention effects—typically exercise longer and with greater intensity than intended.

4. Loss of control—unsuccessful at reducing amount of exercise taken.

5. Time—spend excessive amounts of time exercising.

6. Conflict—occupational or social activities sacrificed in order to exercise.

7. Continuance—continue to exercise in face of illness or injury.

Exercise dependence can be measured using a variety of instruments including the Obligatory Exercise Questionnaire (OEQ; Passman & Thompson, 1988), the Running Addiction Scale (RAS; Chapman & Castro, 1990), the Exercise Dependence Questionnaire (EDQ; Ogden, Veale, & Summers, 1997), and the Exercise Dependence Scale (EDS; Hausenblas & Symons Downs, 2002b). The Exercise Dependence Scale allows exercisers to be categorized as exercise dependent, nondependent but symptomatic, or nondependent and asymptomatic.

Research indicates that exercise dependence can be predicted by perfectionism (Hall, Kerr, Kozub, & Finnie, 2007), the proclivity to use imagery for purposes of increased energy and appearance (Hausenblas & Symons Downs, 2002c), being male (Edmunds, Ntoumanis, et al., 2006; Hausenblas & Symons Downs, 2002c), and substance use and abuse (Ferreira, Perez-Diaz, &

Cohen-Salmon, 2009; Martin, Martens, Serrao, & Rocha, 2008). Using the animal model, Ferreira, Perez-Diaz, et al. (2009) found evidence to suggest that (a) intense physical activity may be addictive, (b) intense physical activity may be associated with increased vulnerability to substance use and abuse, and (c) moderate physical activity may be associated with reduced vulnerability to substance use and abuse.

Using a self-determination theory of motivation perspective, Edmunds, Ntoumanis, et al. (2006) categorized adult fitness participants as being either symptomatic or asymptomatic of exercise dependence characteristics. Once categorized, the two groups of exercisers were compared in terms of exercise behavior, motivational regulation, and psychological need satisfaction (competence, autonomy, and relatedness). Results showed that individuals categorized as symptomatic of exercise dependence characteristics (a) expressed greater exercise competence, (b) were higher on all forms of motivational regulation, and (c) exhibited higher levels of exercise behavior. In addition, it was demonstrated that identified motivational regulation mediates the relationship between exercise competence and strenuous exercise.

Finally, Elbourne and Chen (2007) found modest support for the continuum model of obligatory exercise. The **continuum model of obligatory exercise** conceptualizes exercise dependence as a continuum, running at one end from mildly obsessive-compulsive traits to the other end with significant obsessive-compulsive traits. This model also conceptualizes that at the far left of the model there is little indication of clinical eating disorders, while at the other extreme the risk for clinical eating disorders is high. While a cause-and-effect relationship has not been proven between eating disorders and obligatory exercise, a preoccupation with body weight and shape predicts both obligatory exercise and clinical eating disorders. Clinical and subclinical eating disorders are discussed in the next section.

CONCEPT Exercise addiction is associated with depression and anxiety in response to missing a regular exercise session. Additionally, individuals suffering from exercise addiction risk more serious injury or illness by refusing to take a day off in the face of sickness or an exercise-related injury.

APPLICATION It is not consistent with a wellness lifestyle to allow an exercise addiction to control a person's behavior. Steps should be taken to assist an individual who suffers from exercise addiction to take control of her own exercise behavior. Alternative forms of recreational activity should be used to replace addictive exercise behaviors when they become controlling.

Eating Disorders and Physical Activity

> The table is set, and I can smell the turkey cooking. My stomach turns in disgust. My family huddles around the television to watch Macy's Thanksgiving Day Parade. The day seems ideal. I wait in anticipation for my worst fear, the meal. I do not want to gain weight. I have anorexia.
> (Von Rein, 2001, p. 4)

Actual clinically diagnosed eating disorders are relatively rare among athletes and physical activity enthusiasts. Much more prevalent are a whole array of unhealthy subclinical eating disorders. We will discuss both in this section. Perhaps the most well-known example of a clinically diagnosed sport-related eating disorder was the case of former U.S. Olympic gymnast Christy Henrich (Beals, 2000). Christy died in 1994 at the age of 22 from an eight-year struggle with anorexia nervosa, effectively calling the nation's attention to the dangers of clinically diagnosed eating disorders. In a non-sport-related example, the following quotation by Samantha Skinner describes Erin Anderson's battle with bulimia nervosa. Growing up, Erin was called "skinny." As she grew up, her drive for perfection and size "0," influenced by Western culture and glamorous magazines, drove her into an eating disorder.

> Erin did not binge and purge as many bulimics do. She did not eat whole pizzas or tubs of ice cream and then throw up. Instead she would make herself sick after only a normal meal or snack. The number of times she threw up ranged from once a day or not at all to three or four times a day. Looking in the mirror or flipping through the newly delivered magazines might make her want to be sick, but stress or sadness could send her to the bathroom just as quickly. Sometimes, even if she wasn't hungry, she would eat just to throw up. Like a cigarette calms a smoker, vomiting calmed Erin. It made everything go away
> (Skinner, 2000, p. 9).

The balance of this section will be devoted to three areas of discussion. First, an explanation of the most severe cases of clinically diagnosed eating disorders will be presented. Second, clinical and subclinical eating disorders among athletes will be discussed. Finally, we will conclude with a discussion of eating disorders as they relate to exercise dependence.

Clinically Diagnosed Eating Disorders

> Nothing tastes as good as skinny feels. (British super model, Kate Moss, 2009).

The two most severe clinically diagnosed or pathogenic eating disorders are anorexia nervosa and bulimia nervosa. Individuals suffering from one of these two disorders are suffering from a clinically diagnosed mental illness as defined by the *Diagnostic and Statistical Manual of Mental Disorders* (DSM-IV; American Psychiatric Association, 1994). The Questionnaire for Eating Disorder Diagnosis (Q-EDD; Mintz, O'Holloran, Mulholland, &

Schneider, 1997) is an instrument that operationalizes the DSM-IV criteria for eating disorders.

Anorexia Nervosa   In order for individuals to be diagnosed with **anorexia nervosa,** they must exhibit the following symptoms: (a) severe weight loss, (b) refusal to maintain normal body weight, (c) intense fear of gaining weight or becoming fat, (d) severe body image disturbance, and (e) absence of three or more consecutive menstrual cycles (amenorrhea). Anorexics eat very little food, and when they do eat they tend to "play" with their food and take tiny bites, chewing each bite a given number of times. They are proud of their rigid control, fear others will force them to eat, and dress in loose, layered clothing to hide their thinness. To burn off fat and calories, anorexics often become hyperactive, exercising excessively. Mentally, anorexics display mood and attitude disturbance, low self-esteem, depression, and social anxiety (Tod & Andersen, 2010). Treatment and recovery from anorexia nervosa requires professional help. The diagnosed anorexic cannot overcome this mental illness herself.

Bulimia Nervosa   In order for individuals to be diagnosed with **bulimia nervosa,** they must exhibit the following symptoms: (a) binge eating followed by purging at least twice per week for three months, (b) loss of self-control, (c) severe body image disturbance. Bulimics are preoccupied with food and weight, fear getting fat, and exhibit chaotic eating behaviors. Mentally, bulimics display mood and attitude disturbance, low self-esteem, depression, and social anxiety (Tod & Andersen, 2010). Unlike anorexics, bulimics turn to food, rather than away from it, to cope with emotional problems. Purging may come in the form of laxatives, diuretics, enemas, and/or self-induced vomiting. Eating binges are followed by periods in which bulimics may fast, exercise too much, or turn to vomiting. Physical symptoms associated with vomiting may include finger calluses, sore throat, feeling of bloating, stomach alkalosis, and chemical imbalance. As with

anorexia nervosa, treatment and recovery from bulimia nervosa requires professional help.

Eating Disorders Not Otherwise Specified (EDNOS)   The DSM-IV also lists eating disorders that contain some but not all of the required criteria associated with anorexia and bulimia. For example, anorexia nervosa is diagnosed if four core features are present, but if only three of the four are present, the condition is labeled **EDNOS**. In the literature, eating disorders are often categorized as being clinical (including EDNOS), subclinical (symptomatic), or asymptomatic (Currie, 2007). Another category of eating disorder that is EDNOS in nature is the category of **anorexia athletica**,

Female athletes who participate in aesthetic sports may be susceptible to eating disorders.
PhotoLink/Getty Images.

which describes fear of obesity among female athletes. Because clinically diagnosed eating disorders, such as anorexia nervosa and bulimia nervosa, are relatively rare in the population generally and in athletes specifically, it is the subclinical disorders that are of greatest concern for female athletes who participate in sports that encourage low body weight and thinness. **Subclinical eating disorders** are more prevalent among female athletes than anorexia nervosa or bulimia nervosa. It should also be pointed out that the incidence of clinical eating disorders are more prevalent in females than in men, more prevalent in athletes than nonathletes, and more prevalent in sports such as dance and gymnastics that encourage low body weight and thinness compared to those that do not (Currie, 2007; Hausenblas & Carron, 1999; Martens-Sanford, Davidson, et al., 2005; Petrie, Greenleaf, Carter, & Reel, 2007; Petrie, Greenleaf, Reel, & Carter, 2009; Smolak, Muren, & Ruble, 2000; Sundgot-Borgen & Torstveit, 2004).

Subclinical and Clinical Eating Disorders among Athletes

Males and females involved in activities that link leanness to success are often pressured to be thin. This is especially true of female athletes involved in gymnastics, dancing, and modeling. In an effort to be thin and to meet their coaches' expectations, athletes may turn to a number of questionable eating and exercise behaviors that may compromise their health. In most cases, desire to be thin does not result in clinically diagnosed anorexia or bulimia. If left unchecked, however, subclinical eating disorders may result in dysfunctional social interaction, decreased physical performance, reduced physical health, and, in some cases, anorexia or bulimia. Ways in which athletes suffering from subclinical eating disorders attempt to lose weight and become thin include the following: fasting/starvation, diet pills, diuretics, laxatives/enemas, vomiting, fat-free diets, saunas, and excessive exercise. These pathogenic health weight control behaviors along with potential negative consequences are listed in table 19.1.

While it is believed that clinically diagnosed eating disorders among females in general and athletes in particular are relatively rare in North America, the actual percentages vary greatly from study to study. As relating to clinically diagnosed eating disorders among elite male and female athletes, a study reported by Sundgot-Bogen and Torstveit (2004) and commented upon by Currie (2007) is of great interest. This study examined the

TABLE 19.1 | Pathogenic Weight Control Behaviors and Health Consequences

Behavior	Health Consequence
Diet pills	Heightened anxiety, rapid heart rate, poor concentration, insomnia, dehydration
Diuretics	Dehydration, electrolyte imbalance, little fat loss, weight loss quickly regained
Excessive exercise	Menstrual dysfunction in females, fatigue, increased risk of overuse injuries, hunger following exercise
Fasting/starvation	Loss of lean body mass and bone density, poor physical and cognitive performance, poor nutrition
Fat-free diets	Difficulty of maintaining weight loss and possible lack in essential vitamins, nutrients, and fatty acids
Laxatives/enemas	Dehydration, electrolyte imbalance, constipation, cathartic colon
Saunas	Dehydration and electrolyte imbalance, no permanent weight loss
Self-induced vomiting	Dehydration, electrolyte imbalance, gastrointestinal problems, stomach ulcers, erosion of tooth enamel

Source: Adapted from Beals, K. A. (2000, September). Subclinical eating disorders in female athletes. *Journal of Physical Education, Recreation, and Dance, 71,* 23–29.

prevalence of anorexia nervosa, bulimia nervosa, and EDNOS in both male and female Norwegian elite athletes as well as a control group of healthy Norwegian individuals. The sample included the entire population of Norwegian male and female elite athletes (n = 1,620) and a sample of controls (1,696). The results corroborated earlier findings that show that the prevalence of eating disorders is higher in athletes than controls, higher in female than male athletes, and higher in sports that encourage low body weight, leanness, and thinness compared to those that do not.

More specifically, the data showed that 8 percent of elite male athletes and 20 percent of elite female athletes suffer from some form of clinically diagnosed eating disorder (including EDNOS). When the EDNOS athletes are excluded, the percentage of elite athlete suffering from anorexia or bulimia was only 2.5 percent for males and 8.2 percent for females. For controls, only 0.5 percent of the males and 9.1 percent of the females suffer from some form of clinically diagnosed eating disorder (including EDNOS). Relative to sport types, the data showed that for male athletes 21.6 percent of the antigravity (e.g., ski-jumping) athletes and 17.7 percent of the weight class (wrestling) athletes suffered from some form of clinically diagnosed eating disorder (including EDNOS). For female athletes, 42.3 percent of the aesthetic sport athletes and 30.2 percent of the weight class athletes suffered from some form of clinically diagnosed eating disorder (including EDNOS).

As pertaining to the psychological characteristics of female athletes categorized as being either (a) asymptomatic of eating disorders, (b) symptomatic/subclinical, or (c) having a clinically diagnosed eating disorder were studied by Petrie, Greenleaf, Reel, et al. (2009). Their investigation, involving 442 female collegiate athletes, showed that these three groups of athletes could be differentiated as a function of pressure to lose weight, negative mood state, internalization of desire to be thin, and body image concerns. As hypothesized, asymptomatic individuals, compared to other groups, were low in pressure to lose weight, low in negative mood state, low in internalization to be thin, and low on body image concerns.

Body Image and Eating Disorders   Body image, body self-esteem, and body satisfaction all predict or are predicted by eating disorders. **Body objectification theory** describes a thinness culture in which a female comes to view herself and her body as an object to be used, consumed, and evaluated by others, as opposed to being a person with feelings and specific functions (Fredrickson & Roberts, 1997). Women and girls who report receiving critical comments about their bodies also report higher incidence of disordered eating and lower body self-esteem (Muscat & Long, 2008). As body satisfaction decreases, symptoms of bulimia in female collegiate athletes increase. In addition, the predictive relationship between body satisfaction and bulimic symptoms is moderated by perfectionism and body self-esteem (Brannan, Petrie, Greenleaf, Reel, & Carter, 2009; Ferrand, Champely, & Filaire, 2009). Finally, individual sport athletes who are high in social physique anxiety (SPA) experience heightened levels of eating disorders compared to team sport female athletes (Haase, 2009).

The Female Triad   As introduced and defined earlier, female triad describes the athlete who suffers from disordered eating, menstrual dysfunction, and low bone mineral density. Low bone mineral density manifests itself in number and intensity of skeletal bone injuries. It is believed that menstrual dysfunction and low bone density are caused by a reduction in estrogen. While female athletes are not typically diagnosed with a clinical eating disorder, many are diagnosed as being symptomatic in terms of possessing characteristics that may lead to an eating disorder. Athletes who are at risk for an eating disorder are also at greater risk for menstrual irregularity and bone injuries. While few female athletes possess all three aspects of the female triad, many possess at least one or two aspects. Female athletes who participate in aesthetic individual sports that encourage thinness and low body weight are most at risk for the possession of the female triad (Beals & Hill, 2006; Beals & Manore, 2002; Reel, SooHoo, Doetsch, Carter, & Petrie, 2007).

Factors That Influence the Incidence of Eating Disorders   In addition to the gender of the participant, type of sport, and athletic involvement, there remain several factors that the literature suggests may predict the incidence of eating disorders. Possessing a mastery motivational orientation and enjoying the benefits of a mastery motivational climate is predictive of low levels of eating disorders among aesthetic female athletes (de Bruin, Bakker, & Oudejans, 2009). In order to minimize eating disorders, coaches should create a mastery climate that encourages self-improvement and self-referenced comparisons. Kerr, Berman, and DeSouza (2006) reported on a study contrasting perceptions of current and former (retired) female gymnasts. From the group, about 15 percent of the parents of these athletes reported that their child's coach advised the gymnasts to lose weight, while only 4 percent of the coaches admitted to this behavior. Contrasting the two groups of gymnasts, current athletes gave more positive descriptions of their weight control experiences than the former gymnasts. Furthermore, only 3 percent of the current gymnasts reported having an eating disorder, while 20 percent of the former athletes reported this. Only 18 percent of the current gymnasts reported experiencing subclinical disordered eating behaviors, while 73 percent of the former athletes did. In addition, many retired athletes cited an emphasis on thinness and the disparaging comments from coaches about the athletes' bodies as having led to an ongoing food and weight preoccupation. These results point to the sport culture and comments made by coaches and peers as to reasons why female athletes are at risk of experiencing subclinical and sometimes clinical eating disorders. Other factors that may predispose an athlete to being at risk of eating disorders include nationality (Hulley, Currie, Njenga, & Hill, 2007) and young girls' culturally biased attitudes about thinness (Mond & Marks, 2007).

Eating Disorders and Exercise Dependency

As pointed out by Cook and Hausenblas (2008), excessive exercise has been implicated in the development and maintenance of eating disorders such as anorexia and bulimia. This has led theorists such as Dess (2000) and Yates (1987, 1991) to hypothesize that obligatory runners and anorexic females share a common drive for thinness, common personality characteristics, similar family backgrounds, socioeconomic status, tolerance for pain, and quest for asceticism. Yates referred to this commonality as the **anorexia analogue hypothesis**, while Dess referred to it as **activity anorexia**. According to the anorexia analogue hypothesis, obligatory runners use running to control their body weight. As they continue to run and diet to reduce body fat, they are following the anorexia format. The need to have absolute control over the body is similar to that found in the anorexic.

Despite the observation that both the anorexic person and the exercise dependent person engage in excessive exercise and that excessive exercise burns fat and calories, the anorexia analogue hypothesis has not been fully supported. In order to fully support the anorexia analogue hypothesis it must be demonstrated that individuals diagnosed with anorexia nervosa and individuals diagnosed with exercise dependence share the same personality characteristics and the same psychological disturbances.

Blaydon, Linder, and Kerr (2004) reported on an investigation that used reversal theory as a means to test the anorexia analogue hypothesis. Participants of this study comprised 339 competitive amateur and recreational level athletes, of which 95 (28 percent) were diagnosed as possessing an eating disorder. Each of the participants completed the Eating Attitudes Test (EAT), the Exercise Dependency Questionnaire (EDQ), and the Motivational Style Profile for Sport and Exercise (MSP-SE). The MSP-SE is designed to measure reversal theory motivational pairs such as telic and paratelic personality modes. Each participant's

CONCEPT The incidence of anorexia nervosa and bulimia nervosa among female athletes and females generally is of serious concern. Of even greater concern, however, is the very high rate of eating disturbances among female athletes that are not diagnosed as pathogenic. These tend to go untreated and unnoticed.

APPLICATION Eating disturbances of any kind should be of concern to athletes, coaches, and professionals associated with women's sports. Unhealthy behaviors such as fasting, dieting, and the taking of weight-control drugs are particularly

dangerous to young women engaging in demanding training schedules. Athletes are under tremendous pressure to excel at their sports. When they come to believe that losing weight and becoming thin will help them perform better, they become particularly vulnerable to pathogenic eating disorders such as anorexia or bulimia. Extraordinary steps should be taken to educate female athletes about the danger of unhealthy eating behaviors. While we must be similarly concerned about eating disorders among boys and young men, they are far less prevalent in sport and in our society today.

EAT and EDQ scores were cluster analyzed to form four clusters as follows:

1. Low EAT, High EDQ—EDQ is primary
2. High EAT, High EDQ—While high, EDQ is secondary to EAT
3. High EAT, Low EDQ—EAT is primary
4. Low EAT, Low EDQ—Control

These four groups were statistically contrasted using eight MSP-SE motivational pairs as dependent variables. If the anorexia analogue hypothesis is true, the psychological characteristics of group one and two should be identical in terms of personality traits. However, if exercise dependence is only a symptom of anorexia nervosa then the two groups should not be the same but should differ in terms of personality traits. Results failed to support the anorexia analogue hypothesis in that group two was higher than group one in terms of telic dominance and arousal avoidance.

While not a direct test of the anorexia analogue hypothesis, an investigation reported by Cook and Hausenblas (2008) provide important information about the role that exercise dependence plays in the relationship between exercise behavior and eating pathology. Using the Internet, 335 collegiate undergraduates completed the Thinness subscale of the

Eating Disorder Inventory-2 (EDI-2), the Exercise Dependency Scale (EDS), and the Leisure-Time Exercise Questionnaire (LTEQ). The LTEQ measures exercise behavior or amount of exercise completed in one week in metabolic equivalents (METS). Multiple regression was used to determine if exercise dependence mediates or moderates the relationship between exercise behavior and eating disorder pathology. Results of tests showed that exercise dependence mediates but does not moderate the relationship between exercise behavior (EB) and eating disorder pathology (EDP) as illustrated below:

$$EB \rightarrow \text{Exercise Dependence} \rightarrow EDP$$

This relationship demonstrates that exercise behavior does not influence eating pathology directly, but does so through exercise dependence. This finding indicates that a person's motivation or compulsion to exercise is a key mechanism in the relationship between exercise behavior and eating pathology.

Muscle Dysmorphia

Male bodybuiders suffering from muscle dysmorphia differ from normal bodybuilders on many measures, including body dissatisfaction, eating disorders, anabolic steroid use, and mood disturbance.

Muscle dysmorphia is defined as an individual's preoccupation with the notion that he is insufficiently muscular. Because of its similarity to anorexia nervosa, this body image disorder has been called **reverse anorexia nervosa** (Kuennen & Waldren, 2007). The unrealistic pursuit of thinness in anorexics shows parallels to the unrealistic pursuit of "bigness" in muscle dysmorphics. As demonstrated by Olivardia and Pope (2000), individuals classified as being muscle dysmorphic think constantly about their muscularity and have little control over compulsive weightlifting and dietary regimens. Just as Western culture has created the image of the ideal female body, Western culture has also created the image of the ideal male body. The ideal male body, as aspired to by muscle dysmorphic individuals, is the V-shaped muscular male body (Ridgeway & Tylka, 2005).

Two basic inventories have evolved over time for the measurement of muscle dysmorphia. These include the Muscle Dysmorphic Inventory (MDI; Hildebrandt, Langenbucher, & Schlundt, 2004; Schlundt, Woodford, & Brownlee, 2000), and the Muscle Dysmorphia Inventory (MDI; Lantz, Rhea, & Cornelius, 2002). Note that the only difference in the names of these two inventories is that the former uses the word *Dysmorphic* in the title, while the latter uses the word *Dysmorphia*. Perhaps to distinguish between the two, the Muscle Dysmophic Inventory evolved into the Muscle Dysmorphic Disorder Inventory (MDDI; Hildebrandt, Schlundt, Langenbucher, & Chung (2006). Both the MDDI and the MDI are multidimensional in nature. The MDDI measures three muscle dysmorphia subscales (desire for size, appearance intolerance, and functional impairment), while the MDI measures six subscales (body size and symmetry, physique protection, exercise dependence, dietary behavior, supplements to diet, and pharmacological use).

In addition to the illogical drive for muscularity, it is hypothesized that men suffering from muscle dysmorphia share mood, personality, and psychological characteristics with women suffering from anorexia nervosa. Evidence shows a positive predictive relationship between muscle dysmorphia

and social physique anxiety (Ebbeck, Watkins, Concepcion, Cardinal, & Hammermeister, 2009; Grieve, Jackson, Reece, Marklin, & Delaney, 2008), depression (Ebbeck et al., 2009), and perfectionism (Kuennen & Waldren, 2007). Evidence also shows a negative predictive relationship between muscle dysmorphia and self-efficacy (Ebbeck et al., 2009; Kuennen & Waldren, 2007), and perceived body attractiveness (Ebbeck et al., 2009). In summary, high levels of muscle dysmorphia are linked to increased social physique anxiety, depression, and perfectionism; and decreased levels of self-efficacy and perceived body attractiveness.

In recent years, bullying in schools has taken a center place in the educational and psychological literature. A study reported by Wolke and Sapouna (2008) linked muscle dysmorphia with childhood bullying experiences. In this investigation, male bodybuilders completed inventories designed to measure muscle dysmorphia, childhood bully victimization, self-esteem, and measures of global psychopathology (depression, anxiety, obsessive, and obsessive compulsive symptoms). The results of this research showed a predictive relationship between bully victimization and global psychopathology, with muscle dysmorphia serving as both a moderator and mediator between the two. Thus, as illustrated in figure 19.1 (a), whether or not victimization causes a disturbance in global psychopathology is moderated by whether or not muscle dysmorphia is high or low. If muscle dysmorphia is high, childhood bully victimization predicts global psychopathology and reduced self-esteem. As illustrated in figure 19.1 (b), muscle dysmorphia also serves as a partial mediator between bully victimization and global psychopathology. This means that bully victimization has both a direct and indirect effect (through muscle dysmorphia) on global psychopathology and self-esteem.

Burnout in Sport and Exercise

Exercise and physical activity in moderation yeild powerful psychological and physiological benefits. However, too much exercise can result in a

FIGURE 19.1 | Muscle dysmorphia moderates (a) and mediates (b) the predictive relationship between childhood bully victimization and global psychopathology and reduced self-esteem.

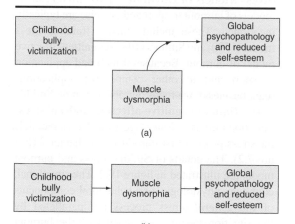

(a)

(b)

Source: Based on Wolke, D., & Sapouna, M. (2008). Big men feeling small: Childhood bullying experience, muscle dysmorphia and other mental health problems in bodybuilders. *Psychology of Sport and Exercise, 9,* 595–604.

reduction in the effectiveness of the immune system to fight disease and an increase in negative psychological mood. In a very practical way, exercise can be considered along a continuum from not enough exercise to too much exercise. Negative psychological and biological outcomes are associated with too little and too much exercise. Overtraining in athletes represents a paradox, because many of the benefits associated with exercise are reversed in the athlete who trains too much. For the athlete, the question of how much is too much is a complex one. Athletes are continually challenging the delicate balance between training and overtraining, as high levels of training are required for success in sport.

> When I was sixteen, I was swimming worse than when thirteen, and I felt like I was never going to come out of it. I really wasn't enjoying the sport anymore because I was doing so poorly, and that time was really tough. . . . I'd done it for over ten

years, and it's hard to give up something after that long. I kept thinking, 'Maybe it will turn around, maybe things will get better.' . . . I guess I realized that you have to make it fun. If you're so serious about it all the time and it starts going bad, then it's really going to destroy you.

> (Leslie Hoh, University of
> Missouri–Columbia swimmer)

As quoted by Quitmeir (2000, p. B1), the above statement reflects Leslie Hoh's struggle to remain in swimming and to be invited to compete in the year 2000 Olympic trials. Leslie's story of her love-hate relationship with swimming and near burnout is similar to those of many other young athletes.

Defining Burnout and Other Related Terms

As defined by Raedeke and Smith (2001, p. 283), **burnout in sport and exercise** is "a psychological syndrome of emotional/physical exhaustion, reduced sense of accomplishment, and sport devaluation." As can be observed, the focus of this particular definition of burnout is upon physical and mental exhaustion, reduced interest in sport, and reduced performance. In discussing burnout in sport, authors typically use words and terms that are believed to be precursors to burnout. Common terms include *overtraining, overreaching, staleness,* and *withdrawal.* (Cresswell & Eklund, 2006; Roose, de Vries, Schmikli, Backx, & Van Doornen, 2009).

Overtraining and Overreaching   Not to be confused with the physiological principle of *training overload,* **overtraining** implies that the athlete trains beyond the level that is ideal for maximum benefit. Overtraining is maladaptive behavior that may lead to staleness and burnout. **Overreaching** is a form of short-term overtraining that is a part of normal training. Overreaching, for short periods of time, is synonymous with training overload and progressive resistance. Overreaching that extends for long periods of time at high intensities eventually becomes overtraining (Roose et al., 2009).

Staleness In a stress model, staleness and overtraining are believed to work together to bring about the condition of athlete burnout. As a result of training, an athlete makes rapid gains in achieving specific training goals. Often, the athlete will experience a *plateau* in performance that is difficult to overcome. For example, a weight lifter might reach a plateau where he cannot get past five repetitions at 250 pounds (bench press). After remaining at this plateau for three weeks, the athlete begins to experience a feeling of **staleness,** which is the initial failure of the body to adapt to training. In an effort to break through the physical or psychological plateau, the athlete initiates a period of overtraining that could result in burnout. The same scenario may be applied to sports of all varieties.

Models of Burnout

Burnout is a multidimensional phenomenon that may have multiple causes. These causes are clarified through the presentation of the different models of burnout. In this section, we briefly consider three different explanations or models of the etiology of burnout: the stress model, the investment model, and the investment model.

Stress Models of Burnout Two different stress models of burnout in sport and exercise are typically mentioned. These include Silva's training stress model (1990) and Smith's (1986) cognitive-affective model of burnout. Because of its broad application to sport and to other competitive applications (e.g., business), we focus our discussion on Smith's model. **Smith's cognitive-affective model of stress and burnout** is a four-stage model that parallels the stress process first introduced in chapter 7 (figure 7.2). The details of Smith's stress and burnout model are illustrated in figure 19.2. The situational, cognitive, physiologic, and behavioral components of the *general* stress process are paralleled by the situation-specific components of the burnout process (moving from left to right).

FIGURE 19.2 | Smith's cognitive affective model of stress and burnout.

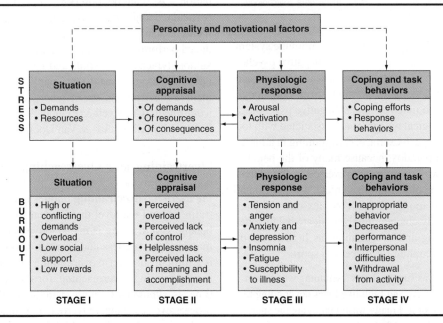

Source: Smith, R. E. (1986). Toward a negative-affective model of athletic burnout. *Journal of Sport Psychology, 8:* 40, fig. 1. Adapted with permission from Human Kinetics (Champaign, IL).

Age group swimming is a prime candidate for athlete burnout due to grueling nature of training schedule. PhotoLink/Getty Images

In the *first stage* of the model, the athlete is confronted with objective demands that are beyond her ability to address. These demands are presented in the form of pressure to win, excessive practice and training time, and perhaps a low return on her time investment (lack of playing time). In *stage two,* a cognitive appraisal is made of the objective demands being placed on the athlete. The cognitive appraisal results in a threat to the athlete in the form of perceived overload, lack of control, feelings of helplessness, and lack of meaning. In *stage three,* perceived threat, as a consequence of cognitive appraisal, results in a physiologic response manifested in the form of anxiety/tension, depression, insomnia, fatigue, and/or susceptibility to illness. Finally, in *stage four,* the athlete responds with some sort of coping behavior or response, such as inappropriate behavior, decreased performance, interpersonal difficulties, and/or withdrawal from activity. Thus, *burnout is viewed as a response to chronic stress.* It is characterized by psychological, emotional, and perhaps physical withdrawal from a sport or activity the athlete formerly pursued and enjoyed.

Smith's stress model of burnout also shows that the four stages of the stress process are influenced by personality and by motivational factors. This aspect of the model makes intuitive sense, but it is also borne out by research related to perfectionism and self-determined motivation. In terms of perfectionism, research shows that an adaptive form of perfectionism leads to a decrease in burnout and an increase in mastery goal orientation, which also leads to a decrease in burnout. Conversely, a maladaptive form of perfectionism leads to an increase in burnout and an increase in ego goal orientation, which leads to an increase in burnout (Appleton, Hall, & Hill, 2009; Hill, Hall, Appleton, & Kozub, 2008; Hill, Hall, Appleton, & Murray, 2010). Relative to motivation, research shows that autonomous motivation is associated with decreased susceptibility to burnout, while amotivation or a more controlling form of motivation is associated with increased susceptibility to burnout (Cresswell & Eklund, 2005; Lemyre, Treasure, & Roberts, 2006).

Investment Model of Burnout   Various versions of the **investment model of burnout** have been proposed for sport (Raedeke, 1997; Raedeke, Granzyk, & Warren, 2000; Schmidt & Stein, 1991; Weiss & Weiss, 2003). In its simplest form it can

CONCEPT According to Smith's affective-cognitive model, burnout parallels stress, in that burnout is viewed as a process resulting from the inability of the athlete to cope with high levels of stress.

APPLICATION The problem begins when the athlete perceives that the demands of the situation are greater than his ability to cope. The perception that he cannot cope with the demands of the situation leads to painful cognitive conclusions and physiological responses. Unresolved stress only becomes worse as the athlete becomes tired, depressed, and fatigued. Finally, in stage four, the athlete withdraws from sport as a way to reduce stress. In this sense, withdrawal from sport is a form of coping. To avoid burnout and sport withdrawal, the athlete must either change the objective situation, change the way he thinks about stress, or develop more effective coping skills.

---

be viewed as an imbalance between the costs and benefits associated with athletic participation. In its more complete form, it is conceptualized as being a function of five determinants of commitment to sport involvement (rewards, costs, satisfaction, investment, alternatives). How the athlete evaluates these five determinants will determine whether his commitment is based upon *enjoyment* or upon *entrapment*. If sport commitment is based upon enjoyment, the athlete will participate enthusiastically. If sport commitment is based upon **entrapment**, it is only a matter of time until burnout sets in and the athlete withdraws from sport.

If commitment is due to *enjoyment*, the rewards of participation are high and the costs are low. High investment is perceived as being worth it because of the favorable reward/cost ratio and because of the satisfaction that participation gives the athlete. Alternatives remain low because satisfaction is high and because the athlete has not felt the need to cultivate an interest in competing activities. In commitment due to *entrapment*, investment remains high but an unfavorable reward/cost ratio makes it seem dissatisfying. The athlete continues her involvement because of the time and energy already committed to the activity as well as the fact that alternatives seem low. Alternatives are low because the athlete has had little time to develop other viable interests. The unhealthy situation of sport commitment due to entrapment cannot last long, because burnout begins to set in. If the athlete is unable to cope with the onset of burnout and its symptoms, she will withdraw from sport in spite of high investment and low alternatives.

Empowerment Model of Burnout Coakley's (1992) **empowerment model of burnout** is based on the notion that burnout in sport is a social problem caused by an overly controlling and constraining social structure. Coakley does not deny the existence of stress in a young athlete's life, but asserts that it is only a symptom of burnout and not the cause. In Coakley's model, burnout is defined as

> a social phenomenon grounded in a set of social relations through which young athletes become disempowered to the point of realizing that sport participation has become a developmental dead-end for them and that they no longer have any meaningful control over important parts of their lives (pp. 272–73).

Coakley argues that stress models of burnout focus exclusively upon the individual and do not consider the possibility that the burnout could be caused by the social organization of sport. Under the stress model, when an athlete experiences burnout, one treatment is to teach him coping skills; this suggests that the problem lies within the athlete and not the social institution of sport.

Young athletes who participate in high-performance sports usually start at a young age

CONCEPT   The empowerment model of burnout provides a sociological explanation for burnout and withdrawal from sport. Burnout occurs as athletes seek to develop identities separate from sport and to have more personal control over their lives. Failure to realize these desires may cause an athlete to experience burnout and to withdraw from sport.

APPLICATION   The issues raised by Coakley in the empowerment model of burnout remind us of issues raised in chapter 5 about youth sports. If the sport experience is so constraining that an athlete cannot develop an alternate identity and feel control over her life, then the sport experience needs to be restructured. Coaches, parents, and organizers of youth sport programs must work hard to make the sport experience one that is not so constraining that athletes are forced to leave in order to realize fundamental needs of autonomy and self-identity.

---

and are expected to continue on to adulthood. During this period of time they are highly controlled by the social organization and are not given opportunities to develop identities separate from sport. Coakley's contention is that at some point a young person's desire for an **alternative identity** and personal control over his life (autonomy) forces him to leave sport. This is a painful experience involving stress-like symptoms that we have come to associate with burnout. In a sense, the athlete is "empowered," or liberated, by her decision to withdraw from sport. Burnout from sport could be eliminated by restructuring the social organization of high-performance sport.

The craving for an alternative identity and the craving for personal control are powerful needs in young people. If the sport experience restricts the athlete from realizing these needs, burnout may occur. The reader will recognize that personal control, autonomy, and self-determination are fundamental components of intrinsic motivation. When an athlete comes to believe that she no longer has control over an activity, she loses intrinsic motivation for the activity.

Burnout Attributions and Symptoms

In the previous section we introduced and discussed three models of burnout that provide theoretical explanations of why burnout occurs. Taking a pragmatic perspective, it is likely that the causes of burnout are complex and cut across the stress, commitment, and empowerment explanations of what causes burnout. In this section we examine some of the reasons (attributions) given by athletes as to why burnout occurs and some of the symptoms they have experienced (Cresswell & Eklund, 2006, 2007; Dubuc, Schinke, Eys, Battochio, & Zaichkowsky, 2010; Goodger, Gorely, Lavallee, & Harwood, 2007).

Attributions of Sport Burnout   Much of what we know about what causes burnout in sport was summarized in a review article by Goodger et al. (2007). In addition to this review article, athletes from various sports have revealed through in-depth interviews their perceptions of what leads to burnout in their particular sports. Studies involving the team sport of professional rugby (Cresswell & Eklund, 2006, 2007) and the individual sport of women's gymnastics (Dubuc et al., 2010) are particularly revealing. Women gymnasts who are experiencing symptoms of burnout complain that their sport is too physically demanding and that they can't balance their commitment to gymnastics with other important demands upon their time. Professional rugby players who experience symptoms of burnout complain of (a) heavy training and playing demands, (b) pressure to perform at a high level, (c) constant competitive transition demands, (d) nagging injuries, (e) media and fan expectations, (f) playing position insecurity, (g) intense competitive rugby environment, (h) anti-rest culture of rugby, and (i) poor management relationships.

Symptoms of Burnout   Symptoms of burnout identified in the literature (Cresswell & Eklund, 2006, 2007; Dubuc et al., 2010; Goodger et al., 2007) are consistent with the definition of burnout given at the beginning of this chapter. Specifically, burnout is associated with (a) emotional/physical exhaustion, (b) reduced sense of accomplishment, and (c) sport devaluation. An incomplete list of physiological and psychological symptoms associated with burnout is illustrated in table 19.2. As summarized in this table, the athlete experiences a reversal of many of the physiological benefits associated with exercise, suffers from a loss of appetite and libido, gets more colds and upper respiratory infections, loses weight, loses sleep, becomes irritable or depressed, experiences feelings of exhaustion, suffers a loss of self-esteem, and experiences a negative change in interpersonal interactions. While athletes experiencing burnout have many common characteristics, it is also true that individual athletes often experience very different symptoms.

Measurement of Burnout, Coping Strategies, and Psychological Mood

Burnout can be identified through symptoms listed in table 19.2 as well as through the administration of an instrument designed to measure burnout in athletes. Available instruments include the Maslach Burnout Inventory (MBI; Maslach & Jackson, 1986), the Eades Athletic Burnout Inventory (EABI; Eades, 1991; Gustafsson, Kentta, Hassmen, & Lundquist, 2007), and the Athlete Burnout Questionnaire (ABQ; Raedeke & Smith, 2001). The ABQ is composed of 15 items that measure the following three aspects of athlete burnout: (a) emotional and physical exhaustion, (b) reduced sense of accomplishment, and (c) sport devaluation.

When symptoms of burnout have been identified, steps must be taken to reverse the debilitating effects of the symptoms as soon as possible. Of

TABLE 19.2 | Physiological and Psychological Symptoms of Burnout

Physiological Symptoms

1. Increased resting and exercise heart rate
2. Increased resting systolic blood pressure
3. Increased muscle soreness and chronic muscle fatigue
4. Increased presence of biochemical indicators of stress in the blood
5. Increased sleep loss
6. Increased colds and respiratory infections
7. Decreased body weight
8. Decreased maximal aerobic power
9. Decreased muscle glycogen
10. Decreased libido and appetite

Psychological Symptoms

1. Increased mood disturbances
2. Increased perception of physical, mental, and emotional exhaustion
3. Decreased self-esteem
4. Negative change in the quality of personal interaction with others (cynicism, lack of feeling, impersonal relating)
5. Negative cumulative reaction to chronic everyday stress as opposed to acute doses of stress

CONCEPT   Many things, such as fatigue, performance decline, and proneness to infection, may signal overtraining in an athlete, but monitoring of mood states is one of the simplest and most effective ways to get an early warning of overtraining.

APPLICATION   Mood states can be easily measured and monitored using the Profile of Mood States (POMS) or some variation of it. The important thing is to establish a baseline from which to work. The baseline represents the athlete's normal healthy level of mood. It is from this baseline, which will differ for each athlete, that a determination of mood disturbance is made. A 50 percent increase in total mood is recommended as a criterion for concern. When using the POMS, total mood is determined by summing the five negative mood states and subtracting the score for vigor (see figure 7.8). Since this value may be less than zero, always add a constant of 100 to each total mood score.

CONCEPT   A completely linear relationship does not exist between increased training and enhanced strength, endurance, and performance.

APPLICATION   The mistaken belief that "more is better" when it comes to sports training may lead to staleness, overtraining, and burnout. Coaches and trainers must carefully monitor their training regimens to assure that their efforts actually result in increased performance and positive affect.

importance in heading off or reversing burnout are the coping strategies possessed by athletes. In this regard, the COPE instrument (Carver et al., 1989) and the modified COPE instrument (MCOPE; Crocker & Graham, 1995) were developed and tested (Eklund, Grove, & Heard, 1998) for the purpose of measuring coping strategies of athletes suffering from a performance slump (stale-ness). If coping strategies are found to be deficient, then steps can be taken to bolster the athlete's ability to cope with the demands of competitive sport.

Another technique for early detection of burnout symptoms is to routinely monitor an athlete's mood state throughout a competitive season. Research shows that **mood disturbance** is an indicator of overtraining in sport and for possible burnout if training adjustments are not made (Berglund & Safstrom, 1994; Goodger et al., 2007; Hooper & MacKinnon, 1995; Puffer & McShane, 1992). Introduced in chapter 7, the Profile of Mood States (POMS) is a simple and efficient method of monitoring psychological mood. A first step in utilizing the POMS is to determine an athlete's healthy normal baseline for psychological mood. If you don't know an athlete's ideal baseline, then you will not be able to determine if a mood disturbance has occurred or is occurring. The next step is to monitor mood throughout the competitive season and particularly before, during, and following intense training periods. While the POMS has been the instrument of choice for measuring mood disturbance in athletes, it is not the only inventory available. Developed by Kellman, Altenburg, Lormes, and Steinacker (2001), the Recovery-Stress Questionnaire for Sport (RESTQ-Sport; Kellman & Kallus, 2001; Maestu, Jurimae, Kreegipuu, &

Jurimae, 2006) is a viable alternative to the POMS. Composed of 77 items, the RESTQ-Sport measures 9 recovery-related subscales and 10 stress-related subscales.

Recommendations for Athletes, Coaches, and Parents

Few empirical studies of burnout have been conducted. An exception to this observation is a pair of studies reported by Gould, Udry, Tuffey, and Loehr (1996) and Gould, Tuffey, Udry, and Loehr (1996). These investigations involved the study of burnout in 30 junior tennis burnouts and 32 non-burnout comparison tennis players who were similar in age, playing experience, and sex. In the first study (Gould, Udry, et al., 1996), the burned-out and nonburned-out junior tennis players were compared on a number of quantitative measures. In the second study (Gould, Tuffey, et al., 1996), a qualitative analysis was conducted on 10 tennis players identified quantitatively in the first study as

being most burned out. While a number of interesting results came out of these studies, two were of great importance. The first was that from a demographic, psychological, personal, and behavioral perspective, it was possible to differentiate between the two groups of athletes. The burned-out tennis players, in contrast to comparison players, exhibited higher burnout scores, were lower in motivation, were more withdrawn, were less likely to use coping strategies, and differed on a variety of perfectionism subscales (e.g., showed greater concern over mistakes). The second result of import was that through the qualitative analyses, recommendations were given to players, coaches, and parents as to how to avoid burnout in junior tennis. These recommendations are shown in tabular form in table 19.3. These recommendations are of particular importance for parents and coaches, because evidence exists that these individuals are often perceived by the athlete as contributing to stress that leads to burnout (Udry, Gould, Bridges, & Tuffey, 1997).

TABLE 19.3 | Recommendations (Advice) Given to Players, Coaches, and Parents on How to Avoid Burnout in Junior Tennis Players

Target Population	Recommendations
Player	1. Play for your own reasons. 2. Balance tennis with other things in your life. 3. If it is not fun, then don't play. 4. Try to make practice and games fun. 5. Relax and take time off occasionally.
Coach	1. Cultivate personal involvement with player. 2. Establish two-way communication with athlete. 3. Solicit and utilize player input. 4. Work to understand player feelings and perspective.
Parent	1. Recognize the optimal amount of "pushing" needed. 2. Back off and lessen involvement. 3. Reduce importance of winning. 4. Show support and empathy for child's efforts. 5. Don't coach if not the coach, and separate roles if you are the coach. 6. Solicit child's input.

Source: Gould, D., Tuffey, S., Udry, E., & Loehr, J. (1996). Burnout in competitive junior tennis players: II. Qualitative analysis. *The Sport Psychologist, 10,* 341–366.

Summary

This chapter focused on negative aspects associated with sport and exercise. Topics addressed included (a) drug abuse in sport and exercise, (b) exercise dependence, (c) eating disorders and physical activity, (d) muscle dysmorpia, and (e) burnout in sport and exercise. Topics discussed relative to drug abuse included anabolic steroids, other banned drugs and unbanned supplements, and combating drug abuse in sport. The psychophysiological effects of anabolic steroids, stimulants, depressants, creatine, and other substances were discussed with a primary focus upon anabolic-androgenic steroid abuse. Both cognitive and behavioral approaches were discussed as ways of combating drug abuse.

The normal benefits associated with regular moderate exercise are lost for the exercise-addicted individual. Failure to exercise according to schedule results in a mood state disturbance and significant emotional trauma. From an attributional perspective, the addicted exerciser is controlled by the activity, as opposed to the activity being controlled by the exerciser. Compared to nonaddicted exercisers, addicted exercisers report being more restless and stressed-out prior to an exercise bout. They also experience a higher degree of depression, anxiety, and general discomfort when they miss a scheduled workout.

Clinically diagnosed eating disorders include anorexia nervosa, bulimia nervosa, and eating disorders not otherwise specified (EDNOS). Because clinically diagnosed eating disorders, such as anorexia nervosa and bulimia nervosa, are relatively rare in the population generally and in athletes specifically, it is the subclinical disorders that are of greatest concern for female athletes who participate in sports that encourage low body weight and thinness. The female triad describes the athlete who suffers from disordered eating, menstrual dysfunction, and low bone mineral density. While few female athletes possess all three aspects of the female triad, many possess at least one or two aspects. Female athletes who participate in aesthetic individual sports that encourage thinness and low body weight are most at risk for the possession of the female triad. Excessive exercise has been implicated in the development and maintenance of eating disorders such as anorexia and bulimia. This has led theorists to hypothesize that obligatory runners and anorexic females share a common drive for thinness, common personality characteristics, similar family backgrounds, similar socioeconomic status, tolerance for pain, and quest for asceticism. Yates referred to this commonality as the anorexia analogue hypothesis. Muscle dysmorphia is defined as an individual's preoccupation with the notion that he is insufficiently muscular. Because of its similarity to anorexia nervosa, this body image disorder has been called reverse anorexia nervosa.

Burnout in sport and exercise is defined as "a psychological syndrome of emotional/physical exhaustion, reduced sense of accomplishment, and sport devaluation." Models discussed that purport to explain the burnout phenomenon include the cognitive-affective stress model, the investment model, and the empowerment model. Physiological and psychological symptoms and recommendations to avoid burnout were discussed.

Critical Thought Questions

1. Discuss the psychology of illegal drug use by athletes. Why do they use illegal drugs when they know it is cheating and they know there are health risks?

2. What is the psychological expectancy effect? How much of this effect do you think is involved in drug use and performance?

3. Discuss the biological and psychological effects of anabolic steroid use.

4. Do you know anybody who is addicted to exercise? Describe this person's behavior when they are unable to exercise. Do you think exercise dependence is a serious abnormality? Why?

5. Why are subclinical eating disorders more of a threat to the athlete than actual clinical eating disorders? Discuss the relationship between type of sport and incidence of eating disorder.

6. Describe and discuss the anorexia analogue hypothesis. What evidence can you cite that exercise dependent men and anorexic women share similar global psychopathology?

7. Discuss muscle dysmorphia as it relates to anorexia symptoms. What is the relationship between being victimized by bullying, muscle dysmorphia, and global psychopathology?

8. Discuss the three theories of burnout discussed in this chapter? Which one do you relate to the most? Give examples and reasons.

9. In which kind of sports do you think burnout is most likely to occur and why?

10. Discuss physiological and psychological symptoms of burnout. How can burnout be avoided? What can athletes, coaches, and parents do to prevent burnout?

Glossary

activity anorexia Obligatory runners and anorexic females share a common drive for thinness, common personality characteristics, similar family backgrounds, and quest for asceticism (*see* anorexia analogue hypothesis).

alternative identity An identity that an athlete can establish separate from sport.

anabolic effect The effect of increasing muscle mass and body size. Used in reference to anabolic steroids.

anabolic steroids Synthetically derived hormones that have both an anabolic effect (increase in muscular size and strength) and an androgenic effect (masculinization). Same as anabolic-androgenic steroids (shortened for convenience).

anabolic-androgenic steroids Synthetically derived hormones that have both an anabolic effect (increase in muscle size and strength) and an androgenic effect (masculinization).

androgenic effect The effect of masculinization. Used in reference to anabolic-androgenic steroids.

androstenedione A precursor hormone to the production of endogenous testosterone in the body.

anorexia analogue hypothesis Obligatory runners and anorexic females share a common drive for thinness, common personality characteristics, similar family backgrounds, and quest for asceticism.

anorexia athletica Fear of obesity among female athletes.

anorexia nervosa A pathogenic eating disorder characterized by bizarre dieting behaviors and rapid weight loss.

behavioral techniques An approach used to combat drug use in sport that is based on teaching athletes alternative ways to maximize athletic performance.

body objectification theory A thinness culture in which a female person comes to view herself and her body as an object to be used, consumed, and evaluated by others, as opposed to being a person with feelings and specific functions.

bulimia nervosa A pathogenic eating disorder characterized by binge eating and vomiting to remain thin.

burnout in sport and exercise A syndrome of physical/emotional exhaustion, sport devaluation, and reduced athletic accomplishment.

cognitive techniques An approach used to combat drug use in sport that is based upon teaching athletes how to avoid drugs and to resist peer pressure.

continuum model of obligatory exercise Conceptualization of exercise dependence as a continuum, running at one end from mildly obsessive-compulsive traits to the other end with significant obsessive-compulsive traits.

creatine A naturally occurring energy-producing substance that is synthesized from amino acids in the human body.

deterrence theory A theory that helps explain cognitive decisions made by athletes relative to drug use.

EDNOS Eating disorders not otherwise specified.

empowerment model of burnout A model of burnout based on the notion that burnout in sport is a social problem caused by an overly controlling and constraining social structure.

endogenous testosterone Naturally occurring levels of testosterone in the body.

entrapment Condition in which an athlete's continuation of her sport involvement is based on the wrong reasons.

exercise addiction Psychological dependence (addiction) on a regular regimen of exercise (*see* exercise dependence).

exercise dependence Psychological dependence on a regular regimen of exercise (*see* exercise addiction).

exogenous testosterone An anabolic steroid that is administered to mimic the effects of testosterone in the body.

female triad The female athlete who suffers from disordered eating, menstrual dysfunction, and low bone mineral density.

investment model of burnout A model of burnout based on the notion that five determinants of sport commitment determine whether an athlete's sport involvement will be based upon enjoyment or entrapment. Personal investment is one of the determinants.

mood disturbance An indicator of overtraining in sport.

muscle dysmorphia An individual's preoccupation with the notion that he is not sufficiently muscular.

obligatory runner A runner who is addicted to exercise (*see* exercise addiction).

overreaching Short-term overtraining that is part of normal training.

overtraining Training beyond the level that is ideal for maximum benefit.

phosphocreatine A form of creatine that serves as an energy buffer (shield) during periods of intense exercise.

psychological expectancy effect The expectation of athletes that they will get stronger and more aggressive when they take anabolic steroids.

reverse anorexia nervosa Muscular dysmorphia is conceptualized as anorexia nervosa in reverse.

Smith's cognitive-affective model of stress and burnout A four-stage stress model of burnout that parallels the stress process.

staleness Initial failure of the body to adapt to training stress.

subclinical eating disorder Eating disorders that fail to meet the clinical standards required to be classified as anorexic or bulimic.

super-adherer An exerciser who participates in and constantly trains for endurance events that require significant long-term effort and commitment.

References

A

Abrahamsen, F. E., Roberts, G. C., & Pensgaard, A. M. (2008). Achievement goals and gender effects on multidimensional anxiety in national elite sport. *Psychology of Sport and Exercise, 9,* 494–464.

Adams, R. M. (1995). Momentum in the performance of professional tournament pocket billiards players. *International Journal of Sport Psychology, 26,* 580–587.

Addona, V., & Roth, J. (2010). Quantifying the effect of performance-enhancing drug use on fastball velocity in major league baseball. *Journal of Quantitative Analysis in Sports, 6,* Article 6.

Adie, J. W., Duda, J. L., & Ntoumanis, N. (2008). Achievement goals, competition appraisals, and the psychological and emotional welfare of sport participants. *Journal of Sport & Exercise Psychology, 30,* 302–322.

Adie, J. W., Duda, J. L., & Ntoumanis, N. (2010). Achievement goals, competition appraisal, and the well- and ill-being of elite youth soccer players over two competitive seasons. *Journal of Sport & Exercise Psychology, 32,* 555–579.

Agnew, G. A., & Carron, A. V. (1994). Crowd effects and the home advantage. *International Journal of Sport Psychology, 25,* 53–62.

Aiken, L. S., & West, S. G. (1991). *Multiple regression: Testing and interpreting interactions.* London: Sage Publications.

Ajzen, I. (1985). From intention to actions: A theory of planned behavior. In J. Kuhl & J. Beckman (Eds.), *Action-control: From cognition to behavior* (pp. 11–39). Heidelberg: Springer.

Ajzen, I., & Fishbein, M. (1977). Attitude-behavior relations: A theoretical analysis and review of empirical research. *Psychology Bulletin, 84,* 888–918.

Albrecht, R. R., & Feltz, D. L. (1987). Generality and specificity of attention related to competitive anxiety and sport performance. *Journal of Sport Psychology, 9,* 231–248.

Alexander, R. (July 5, 1999). Sampras overwhelms Agassi for the men's title. *Columbia Missourian,* 253, B1.

Alferman, D., & Stoll, O. (2000). Effects of physical exercise on self-concept and well being. *International Journal of Sport Psychology, 30,* 47–65.

Allen, J. (2003). Social motivation in youth sport. *Journal of Sport & Exercise Psychology, 25,* 551–567.

Allen, J. B., & Howe, B. L. (1998). Player ability, coach feedback, and female adolescent athletes' perceived competence and satisfaction. *Journal of Sport & Exercise Psychology, 20,* 280–299.

Allen, J. B., & Shaw, S. (2009). Women coaches' perceptions of their organizations' social environment: Supporting coaches' psychological needs? *The Sport Psychologist, 23,* 346–366.

Alzado, L. (1991, July 8). I'm sick and I'm scared. *Sports Illustrated, 75,* 21–24, 27.

American College of Sports Medicine. (2003, October 23). Steroids threaten health of athletes and integrity of sports performances. *American College of Sports Medicine News Release.*

American Heart Association. (1999). *2000 heart and stroke statistical update.* Dallas, TX: American Heart Association.

American Psychiatric Association. (1994). *Diagnostic and statistical manual of mental disorders* (4th ed.). Washington, DC: American Psychiatric Association.

American Psychiatric Association. (2000). *Diagnostic and statistical manual of mental disorders* (4th ed.). Washington, DC: Author.

Amiot, C. E., Gaudreau, P., & Blanchard, C. M. (2004). Self-determination, coping, and goal attainment in sport. *Journal of Sport and Exercise Psychology, 26,* 396–411.

Amorose, A. J. (2003). Reflected appraisals and perceived importance of significant others' appraisals as predictors of college athletes' self-perceptions of competence. *Research Quarterly for Exercise and Sport, 74,* 60–71.

Amorose, A. J., & Anderson-Butcher, D. (2007). Autonomy-supportive coaching and self-determined motivation in high school and college athletics: a test of self-determination theory. *Psychology of Sport and Exercise, 8,* 654–670.

Amorose, A. J., & Hollembeak, J. (2005). Examining the moderating effect of appearance impression motivation on the relationship between perceived physical appearance and social physique anxiety. *Research Quarterly for Exercise and Sport, 76,* 507–513.

Amorose, A. J., & Horn, T. S. (2000). Intrinsic motivation: Relationships with collegiate athletes' gender, scholarship status, and perceptions of their coaches' behavior. *Journal of Sport & Exercise Psychology, 22,* 63–84.

Amorose, A. J., & Horn, T. S. (2001). Pre- to post-season changes in the intrinsic motivation of first year college athletes: Relationships with coaching behavior and scholarship status. *Journal of Applied Sport Psychology, 13,* 355–373.

Amos, C. (1992). Achievement goals, motivational climate, and motivational processess. In G. C. Roberts (Ed.), *Motivation in sport and exercise* (pp. 161–176). Champaign, IL: Human Kinetics.

Anderson, C. A., Deuser, W. E., & DeNeve, K. M. (1995). Hot temperatures, hostile affect, hostile cognition, and arousal: Tests of a general model of affective aggression. *Personality and Social Psychological Bulletin, 21,* 434–448.

Anderson, C. B., Hughes, S. O., & Fuemmeler, B. F. (2009). Parent-child attitude congruence on type and intensity of physical activity: Testing multiple mediators of sedentary behavior in older children. *Health Psychology, 28,* 428–438.

Anderson, K. (2007, October 1). Let us now praise Kartch Kiraly. *Sports Illustrated, 107,* 58–60.

Andersen, M. B., & Williams, J. M. (1988). A model of stress and athletic injury: Prediction and prevention. *Journal of Sport and Exercise Psychology, 10*(3), 294–306.

Anderson, M. B., Williams, J. M., Aldridge, T., & Taylor, J. (1997). Tracking the training and careers of graduates of advanced degree programs in sport psychology, 1989–1994. *The Sport Psychologist, 11,* 326–344.

Andrew, D. P. S. (2009). The impact of leadership behavior on satisfaction of college tennis players: A test of the leadership behavior contingency hypothesis of the multidimensional model of leadership. *Journal of Sport Behavior, 32,* 261–277.

Annesi, J. J. (1997). Three-dimensional state anxiety recall: Implications for individual zone of optimal functioning research and application. *The Sport Psychologist, 11,* 43–52.

Annesi, J. J. (1998). Application of the individual zones of the optimal functioning model for the multimodal treatment of precompetitive anxiety. *The Sport Psychologist, 12,* 300–316.

Anshel, M. H. (2006). Drug abuse in sport: Causes and cures. In J. M. Williams (Ed.), *Applied Sport Psychology: Personal growth to peak performance* (pp. 505–540). St. Louis, MO: McGraw-Hill.

Anshel, M. H. (2008). The disconnected values model: International strategies for exercise behavior change. *Journal of Clinical Sport Psychology, 2,* 357–380.

Anshel, M. H., Jamieson, J., & Raviv, S. (2001). Cognitive appraisals and coping strategies following acute stress among skilled competitive male and female athletes. *Journal of Sport Behavior, 24,* 128–143.

Anshel, M. H., & Si, G. (2008). Coping styles following acute stress in sport among elite Chinese athletes: A test of trait and transactional coping theories. *Journal of Sport Behavior, 31,* 3–21.

Anshel, M. H., & Sutarso, T. (2007). Relationships between sources of acute stress and athletes' coping style in competitive sport as a function of gender. *Psychology of Sport and Exercise, 8,* 1–24.

Anshel, M. H., & Sutarso, T. (2010). Conceptualizing maladaptive sport perfectionism as a function of gender. *Journal of Clinical Sport Psychology, 4,* 263–281.

Anshel, M. H., Williams, L. R. T., & Hodge, K. (1997). Cross-cultural and gender differences on coping style in sport. *International Journal of Sport Psychology, 28,* 141–156.

Anton, S. D., Perri, M. G., Riley, J. III., Kanasky, W. F. Jr., Rodrigue, J. R., Sears, S. F., & Martin, A. D. (2005). Differential predictors of adherence in exercise programs with moderate versus higher levels of intensity and frequency. *Journal of Sport & Exercise Psychology,* 171–187.

Antonen, M. (2005, October 26). Astros first series team since 1953 without black players. *USA Today,* 5C.

Aoyagi, M. W., & Cox, R. H. (2009). The effects of scholarship status on intrinsic motivation. *Athletic Insight Journal, 1,* 63–74.

Aoyagi, M. W., Cox, R. H., McGuire, R. T. (2008). Organizational citizenship behavior in sport: Relationship with leadership, team cohesion, and athlete satisfaction. *Journal of Applied Sport Psychology, 20,* 25–41.

Appaneal, R. N., Levine, B. R., Perna, F. M., & Roh, J. L. (2009). Measuring postinjury depression among male and female competitive athletes. *Journal of Sport & Exercise Psychology, 31,* 60–76.

Appaneal, R. N., Perna, F. M., & Larkin, K. T. (2007). Psychophysiological response to severe sport injury among competitive male athletes: A preliminary investigation. *Journal of Counseling Sport Psychology, 1,* 68–88.

Appleton, P. R., Hall, H. K., & Hill, A. P. (2009). Relations between multidimensional perfectionism and burnout in junior–elite male athletes. *Psychology of Sport and Exercise, 10,* 457–465.

Appleton, P. R., Hall, H. K., & Hill, A. P. (2010). Family patterns of perfectionism: An examination of elite junior athletes and their parents. *Psychology of Sport and Exercise, 11,* 363–371.

Apter, M. J. (1982). *The experience of motivation: The theory of psychological reversals.* London, New York: Academic Press.

Apter, M. J. (1984). Reversal theory and personality: A review. *Journal of Research in Personality, 18,* 265–288.

Arathoon, S. M., & Malouff, J. M. (2004). The effectiveness of a brief cognitive intervention to help athletes cope with competitive loss. *Journal of Sport Behavior, 27,* 213–229.

Arent, S. M., Alderman, B. L., Short, E. J., & Landers, D. M. (2007). The impact of the testing environment on affective changes following acute resistance exercise. *Journal of Applied Sport Psychology, 19,* 364–378.

Arent, S. M., & Landers, D. M. (2003). Arousal, anxiety, and performance: A reexamination of the Inverted-U hypothesis. *Research Quarterly for Sport and Exercise, 74,* 436–444.

Arent, S. M., Landers, D. M., & Etnier, J. L. (2000). The effects of exercise on mood in older adults: A meta-analytic review. *Journal of Aging and Physical Activity, 8,* 407–430.

Arent, S. M., Landers, D. M., Matt, K. S., & Etnier, J. L. (2005). Dose-response and mechanistic-issues in the resistance training and affect relationship. *Journal of Sport & Exercise Psychology, 27,* 92–110.

Arms, R. L., & Russell, G. W. (1997). Impulsivity, fight history and camaraderie as predictors of a willingness to escalate a disturbance. *Current Psychology: Research & Reviews, 15,* 279–285.

Armstrong, C. A., Sallis, J. F., Hovell, M. F., & Hofstetter, C. R. (1993). Stages of change, self-efficacy, and the adoption of vigorous exercise: A prospective analysis. *Journal of Sport & Exercise Psychology, 15,* 390–402.

Arthur-Banning, S., Wells, M. S., Baker, B. L., & Hegreness, R. (2009). Parents behaving badly: The relationship between the sportsmanship behaviors of adults and athletes in youth basketball games. *Journal of Sport Behavior, 32,* 3–18.

Arvinen-Barrow, M., Weigand, D. A., Thomas, S., Hemmings, B., & Walley, M. (2007). Elite and novice athletes' imagery use in open and closed sports. *Journal of Applied Sport Psychology, 19,* 93–104.

Atkinson, J.W. (1964). *An introduction to motivation.* New York, NY: D. Van Nostrand Company.

B

Babyak, M., Blumenthal, J. A., Herman, S., Parinda, K., Doraiswamy, M., Moore, K., . . . Krishman, K. R. (1999). Effect of exercise training on older adults with major depression. *Archives of Internal Medicine, 159,* 2349–2356.

Babyak, M., Blumenthal, J. A., Herman, S., Parinda, K., Doraiswamy, M., Moore, K., Craighead, W. E., Baldewicz, T. T., & Krishman, K. R. (2000). Exercise treatment for major depression: Maintenance of therapeutic benefits at 10 months. *Psychosomatic Medicine, 62,* 633–638.

Bach, G. (2002, Fall). Recommendations for communities comes out of International Youth Sports Congress. *Missouri Parks and Recreation,* 10–11.

Backhouse, S. H., Bishop, N. C., Biddle, S. J. H., & Williams, C. (2005). Effect of carbohydrate and prolonged exercise on affect and perceived exertion. *Medicine and Science in Sports and Exercise, 37,* 1768–1773.

Backhouse, S. H., Ekkekakis, P., Biddle, S. J. H., Foskett, A., & Williams, C. (2007). Exercise makes people feel better but people are inactive: Paradox or artifact? *Journal of Sport & Exercise Psychology, 29,* 498–517.

Baer, L. (1980). Effect of a time-slowing suggestion on performance accuracy on a perceptual motor task. *Perceptual and Motor Skills, 51,* 167–176.

Bahrke, M. W., & Morgan, W. P. (1978). Anxiety reduction following exercise and medication. *Cognitive Therapy and Research, 2,* 323–333.

Bahrke, M. W., Yesalis, C., & Wright, J. (1996). Psychological behavioral effects of endogenous testosterone and anabolic-androgenic steroids: An update. *Sports Medicine, 22*(6), 367–390.

Baker, J., Coté, & Hawes, R. (2000). The relationship between coaching behaviors and sport anxiety in athletes. *Science and Medicine in Sport, 3,* 110–119.

Ballard, C. (2007, August 13). End of the chase. *Sports Illustrated, 107,* 44–53.

Bamberger, M. (1999, October 25). No backing down. *Sports Illustrated, 91,* 48–53.

Bandura, A. (1973). *Aggression: A social learning analysis.* Englewood Cliffs, NJ: Prentice Hall.

Bandura, A. (1977). Self-efficacy: Toward a unifying theory of behavioral change. *Psychological Review, 84,* 191–215.

Bandura, A. (1982). Self-efficacy mechanism in human agency. *American Psychologist, 37,* 122–147.

Bandura, A. (1986). *Social foundations of thought and action: A social cognitive theory.* Englewood Cliffs, NJ: Prentice Hall.

Bandura, A. (1997). *Self-efficacy: The exercise of control.* San Francisco, CA: Freeman.

Bandura, A., Barbaranelli, C., Caprara, G. V., & Pastorelli, C. (1996). Mechanisms of moral disengagement in the exercise of moral agency. *Journal of Personality and Social Psychology, 71,* 364–374.

Banting, L. K., Dimmock, J. A., & Lay, B. S. (2009). The role of implicit and explicit components of exerciser self-schema in the prediction of exercise behavior. *Psychology of Sport and Exercise, 10,* 80–86.

Bar-Eli, M., Hartman, I., Levy-Kolker, N. (1994). Using goal setting to improve physical performance of adolescents with behavior disorders: The effect of goal proximity. *Adapted Physical Activity Quarterly, 11,* 86–97.

Bar-Eli, M. B., Tenenbaum, G., Pie, J. S., Btesh, Y., & Almong, A. (1997). Effects of goal difficulty, goal specificity and duration of practice time intervals on muscular performance. *Journal of Sport Sciences, 15,* 125–135.

Barker, J. B., & Jones, M. V. (2006). Using hypnosis, technique refinement, and self-modeling to enhance self-efficacy: A case study in cricket. *The Sport Psychologist, 20,* 94–111.

Barker, J. B., & Jones, M. V. (2008). The effects of hypnosis on self-efficacy, affect, and soccer performance: A case study. *Journal of Clinical Sport Psychology, 2,* 127–147.

Barker, J. B., Jones, M. V., & Greenlees, I. (2010). Assessing the immediate and maintained effects of hypnosis on self-efficacy and soccer wall–volley performance. *Journal of Sport & Exercise Psychology, 32,* 243–252.

Barnett, N. P., Smoll, F. L., & Smith, R. E. (1992). Effects of enhancing coach-athlete relationships on youth sport attrition. *The Sport Psychologist, 6,* 111–127.

Baron, R. M., & Kenny, D. A. (1986). The moderator–mediator distinction in social psychological research: Conceptual, strategic, and statistical considerations. *Journal of Personality and Social Psychology, 51,* 1173–1182.

Barr, K., & Hall, C. (1992). The use of imagery by rowers. *International Journal of Sport Psychology, 23,* 243–261.

Bartholomew, J. B. (1999). The effect of resistance exercise on manipulated preexercise mood states for male exercisers. *Journal of Sport & Exercise Psychology, 21,* 39–51.

Bartholomew, J. B., Moore, J., Todd, J., Todd, T., & Elrod, C. C. (2001). Psychological states following resistant exercise of different workloads. *Journal of Applied Sport Psychology, 13,* 399–410.

Bartholomew, K. J., Ntoumanis, N., & Thogersen-Ntoumanis, C. (2010). The controlling interpersonal style in a coaching context: Development and initial validation of a psychometric scale. *Journal of Sport & Exercise Psychology, 32,* 193–216.

Bartone, P. T. Ursano, R. J., Wright, K. M., Ingraham, L. H. (1989). The impact of military air disaster on the health of assistance workers. *Journal of Nervous & Mental Disease, 177,* 317–328.

Bass, B. M., & Avolio, B. J. (2000). *MLQ Multifactor Leadership Questionnaire.* Red City: Mind Garden.

Baumeister, R. F., & Steinhilber, A. (1984). Paradoxical effects of supportive audiences on performance under pressure: The home field advantage in sports championships. *Journal of Personality and Psychology, 47,* 85–93.

Beals, K. A. (2000, September). Subclinical eating disorders in female athletes. *Journal of Physical Education, Recreation, and Dance, 71,* 23–29.

Beals, K. A., & Hill, A. K. (2006). The prevalence of disordered eating, menstrual dysfunction, and low bone mineral density among U.S. collegiate athletes. *International Journal of Sport Nutrition and Exercise Metabolism, 16,* 1–23.

Beals, K. A., & Manore, M. M. (2002). Disorders of the female athlete triad among collegiate athletes. *International Journal of Sport Nutrition and Exercise Metabolism, 12,* 281–293.

Beattie, S., Hardy, L., & Woodman, T. (2004). Pre-competition self-confidence: The role of the self. *Journal of Sport & Exercise Psychology, 26,* 427–441.

Beauchamp, M. R., Maclachlan, A., & Lothian, A. M. (2005). Communication with sport teams: Jungian preferences and group dynamics. *The Sport Psychologist, 19,* 203–220.

Becker, A. J., & Wrisberg, C. A. (2008). Effective coaching in action: Observations of legendary collegiate basketball coach Pat Summitt. *The Sport Psychologist, 22,* 197–211.

Beedie, C. J., Terry, P. C., & Lane, A. M. (2000). The profile of mood states and athletic performance: Two meta-analyses. *Journal of Applied Sport Psychology, 12,* 49–68.

Behling, O., & Schriesheim, C. (1976). *Organizational behavior: Theory, research, and application.* Boston, MA: Allyn and Bacon.

Beilock, S. L., Afremow, J. A., Rabe, A. L., & Carr, T. H. (2001). "Don't Miss!" The debilitating effects of suppressive imagery on golf putting performance. *Journal of Sport and Exercise Psychology, 23,* 200–221.

Beilock, S. L., Bertenthal, B. I., McCoy, A. M., & Carr, T. H. (2004). Haste does not always make waste: Expertise, direction of attention, and speed versus accuracy in performing sensorimotor skills. *Psychometric Bulletin & Review, 11,* 373–379.

Beilock, S. L., & Carr, T. H. (2001). On the fragility of skilled performance: What governs choking under pressure? *Journal of Experimental Psychology, 130,* 701–725.

Beilock, S. L., Carr, T. H., MacMahon, C., & Starkes, J. L. (2002). When paying attention becomes counterproductive: Impact of divided versus skill-focused attention on novice and experienced performance of sensorimotor skills. *Journal of Experimental Psychology: Applied, 8,* 6–16.

Beilock, S. L., & Sibley, B. A. (2007). Exercise and working memory: An individual differences investigation. *Journal of Sport & Exercise Psychology, 29,* 783–791.

Bell, J. J., & Hardy, J. (2009). Effects of attentional focus on skilled performance in golf. *Journal of Applied Sport Psychology, 21,* 163–177.

Bell, R. J., Skinner, C. H., & Fisher, L. A. (2009). Decreasing putting yips in accomplished golfers via solution–focused guided imagery: A single subject research design. *Journal of Applied Sport Psychology, 21,* 1–14.

Benson, H., Beary, J. F., & Carol, M. P. (1974). The relaxation response. *Psychiatry, 37,* 37–46.

Benson, P. L. (1997). *All kids are our kids: What communities must do to raise caring and responsible children and adolescents.* San Francisco, CA: Jossey-Bass.

Berger, B. G., & Motl, R. W. (2000). Exercise and mood: A selective review and synthesis of research employing the Profile of Mood States. *Journal of Applied Sport Psychology, 12,* 69–92.

Berglund, B., & Safstrom, H. (1994). Psychological monitoring and modulation of training load of world-class canoeists. *Medicine and Science in Sports and Medicine, 26,* 1036–1040.

Berkowitz, L. (1958). The expression and reduction of hostility. *Psychological Bulletin, 55,* 257–283.

Berkowitz, L. (1993). *Aggression: Its causes, consequences, and control.* Philadelphia: Temple University Press.

Betts, G. H. (1909). *The distribution and functions of mental imagery.* New York: Teachers College, Columbia University.

Beuter, A., & Duda, J. L. (1985). Analysis of the arousal/motor performance relationship in children using movement kinematics. *Journal of Sport Psychology, 7,* 229–243.

Bianco, T. (2001). Social support and recovery from sport injury: Elite skiers share their experiences. *Research Quarterly for Exercise and Sport, 72,* 376–388.

Bianco, T., & Eklund, R. C. (2001). Conceptual considerations for social support research in sport and exercise settings: The case of sport injury. *Journal of Sport and Exercise Psychology, 23,* 85–107.

Bianco, T., Malo, S., & Orlick, T. (1999). Sport injury and illness: Elite skiers describe their experiences. *Research Quarterly for Exercise and Sport, 70,* 157–169.

Biddle, S. J. H. (1995). Exercise and psychosocial health. *Research Quarterly for Exercise and Sport, 66*(4), 292–297.

Bidonde, M. J., Goodwin, D. L., & Drinkwater, D. T. (2009). Older women's experience of a fitness program: The importance of social networks. *Journal of Applied Sport Psychology, 21* (Supplement), S86–S101.

Binsch, O., Oudejans, R. R. D., Bakker, F. C., & Savelsbergh, G. J. P. (2009). Unwanted effects in aiming actions: The relationship between gaze behavior and performance in a golf putting task. *Psychology of Sport and Exercise, 10,* 628–635.

Bishop, D. T., Karageorghis, C. I., & Kinrade, N. P. (2009). Effects of musically induced emotions on choice reaction time performance. *The Sport Psychologist, 23,* 59–76.

Bishop, D. T., Karageorghis, C. I., & Loizou, G. (2007). A grounded theory of young tennis players' use of music to manipulate emotional state. *Journal of Sport & Exercise Psychology, 29,* 584–607.

Bivens, S., & Leonard, W. M. (1994). Race, centrality, and educational attainment: An NFL perspective. *Journal of Sport Behavior, 17,* 24–42.

Bixby, W. R., & Lochbaum, M. R. (2008). The effects of modality preference on the temporal dynamics of affective response associated with acute exercise in college aged females. *Journal of Sport Behavior, 31,* 299–311.

Bixby, W. R., Spalding, T. W., & Hatfield, B. D. (2000). The temporal dynamics of affect during and following exercise. *Medicine & Science in Sports & Exercise, 32,* Supplement, Abstract 1497, S301.

Blake, R. R., & Mouton, J. S. (1985). *The Managerial Grid III.* Houston: Gulf Publishing Company.

Blake, R. R., & Mouton, J. S. (1994). *The Managerial Grid.* Houston: Gulf Publishing Company.

Blanchard, C. M., Amiot, C. E., Perreault, S., Vallerand, R. J., & Provencher, P. (2009). Cohesiveness, coach's interpersonal style and psychological needs: Their effects on self-determination and athletes' subjective well–being. *Psychology of Sport and Exercise, 10,* 545–551.

Blanchard, C. M., Kupperman, J., Sparling, P., Nehl, E., Rhodes, R. E., Courneya, K. S., . . . Hunt, T. (2007). Ethnicity as a moderator of the theory of planned behavior and physical activity in college students. *Research Quarterly for Exercise and Sport, 78,* 531–541.

Blanchard, C. M., Kupperman, J., Sparling, P., Nehl, E., Rhodes, R. E., Courneya, K. S., . . . Rupp, J. C. (2008). Ethnicity and the theory of planned behavior in an exercise context: A mediation and moderation perspective. *Psychology of Sport and Exercise, 9,* 527–545.

Blaydon, M. J., Linder, K. J., & Kerr, J. H. (2004). Metamotivational characteristics of exercise dependence and eating disorders in highly active amateur sport participants. *Personality and Individual Differences, 36,* 1419–1432.

Bloom, G. A., Stevens, D. E., & Wickwire, T. L. (2003). Expert coaches' perceptions of team building. *Journal of Applied Sport Psychology, 15,* 129–143.

Blum, R. (2010, January 11). McGuire admits using steroids. Associated Press News Break.

Blum, R., & Fendrich, H. (2005, November 15). MLB, players strike deal on steroids testing policy. Retrieved from http://USAtoday.com/sports/baseball/2005-11-15-steroids-agreement_x.htm

Blumenstein, B., Bar-Eli, M., & Tenenbaum, G. (1995). The augmenting role of biofeedback: Effects of autogenic, imagery, and music training on physiological indices and athletic performance. *Journal of Sports Sciences, 13,* 343–354.

Boardley, I. A., & Kavussanu, M. (2010). Effects of goal orientation and perceived toughness on antisocial behavior in soccer: The mediating role of moral disengagement. *Journal of Sport & Exercise Psychology, 32,* 176–192.

Boardley, I. D., Kavussanu, M., & Ring, C. (2008). Athletes' perceptions of coaching effectiveness and athlete-related outcomes in Rugby Union: An investigation based on the coaching efficacy model. *The Sport Psychologist, 22,* 269–287.

Bodin, T., & Martinsen, E. W. (2004). Mood and self-efficacy during acute exercise in clinical depression. A randomized, controlled study. *Journal of Sport and Exercise Psychology, 26,* 623–633.

Bodner, T., & Langer, E. (2001). *Individual differences in mindfulness: The Langer Mindfulness Scale.* Poster presented at the annual meeting of the American Psychological Society, Toronto, Canada.

Boixados, M., Cruz, J., Torregrosa, M., & Valiente, L. (2004). Relationships among motivational climate, satisfaction, perceived ability, and fair play attitudes in young soccer players. *Journal of Applied Sport Psychology, 16,* 301–317.

Bolgar, M. R., Janelle, C., & Giacobbi, P. R., Jr. (2008). Trait anger, appraisal, and coping differences among adolescent tennis players. *Journal of Applied Sport Psychology, 20,* 73–87.

Boone, K. S., Beitel, P., & Kuhlman, J. (1997). The effects of the win/loss record on cohesion. *Journal of Sport Behavior, 20,* 125–134.

Botterill, C. (1983). Goal setting for athletes with examples from hockey. In G. L. Martin & D. Hrycaiko (Eds.), *Behavioral modification and coaching: Principles, procedures, and research* (pp. 67–85). Springfield, IL: Thomas.

Bourgeois, A. E., Meyers, M. C., & LeUnes, A. (2009). The sports inventory for pain: Empirical and confirmatory validity. *Journal of Sport Behavior, 32,* 19–35.

Bourgeois, A., LeUnes, A., & Myers, M. (2010). Full-scale and short-form of the Profil of Mood States: A factor analytic comparison. *Journal of Sport Behavior, 33,* 355–376.

Boutcher, S. H., & Rotella, R. J. (1987). A psychological skills education program for closed-skill performance enhancement. *The Sport Psychologist, 1,* 127–137.

Boutcher, S. H., & Trenske, M. (1990). The effects of sensory deprivation and music on perceived exertion and affect during exercise. *Journal of Sport & Exercise Psychology, 12,* 167–176.

Boutcher, S. H., & Zinsser, N. W. (1990). Cardiac deceleration of elite and beginning golfers during putting. *Journal of Sport & Exercise Psychology, 12,* 37–47.

Boyce, B. A., Gano-Overway, L. A., & Campbell, A. L. (2009). Perceived motivational climate's influence on goal orientations, perceived competence, and practice strategies across the athletic season. *Journal of Applied Sport Psychology, 21,* 381–394.

Brannan, M., Petrie, T. A., Greenleaf, C., Reel, J., & Carter, J. (2009). The relationship between body dissatisfaction and bulimic symptoms in female collegiate athletes. *Journal of Clinical Sport Psychology, 3,* 103–126.

Bray, C. D., & Whaley, D. E. (2001). Team cohesion, effort, and objective individual performance of high school basketball players. *The Sport Psychologist, 15,* 260–275.

Bray, S. R. (1999). The home advantage from an individual team perspective. *Journal of Applied Sport Psychology, 11,* 116–125.

Bray, S. R. (2007). Self-efficacy for coping with barriers help students stay physically active during transition to their first-year at a university. *Research Quarterly for Exercise and Sport, 78,* 61–70.

Bray, S. R., Beauchamp, M. R., Eys, M. A., & Carron, A. V. (2005). Does the need for role clarity moderate the relationship between role ambiguity and athlete satisfaction? *Journal of Applied Sport Psychology, 17,* 306–318.

Bray, S. R., & Carron, A. V. (1993). The home advantage in alpine skiing. *The Australian Journal of Science and Medicine in Sport, 25,* 76–81.

Bray, S. R., Law, J., & Foyle, J. (2003). Team quality and game location effects in English professional soccer. *Journal of Sport Behavior, 26,* 319–334.

Bray, S. R., & Widmeyer, W. N. (2000). Athletes' perceptions of the home advantage: An investigation of perceived causal factors. *Journal of Sport Behavior, 23,* 1–10.

Bredemeier, B. J. (1978). The assessment of reactive and instrumental athletic aggression. *Proceedings of the International Symposium on Psychological Assessment.* Neyanya, Israel: Wingate Institute for Physical Education and Sport.

Bredemeier, B. J. (1985). Moral reasoning and the perceived legitimacy of intentionally injurious sport acts. *Journal of Sport Psychology, 7,* 110–124.

Bredemeier, B. J. (1994). Children's moral reasoning and their assertive, aggressive, and submissive tendencies in sport and daily life. *Journal of Sport & Exercise Psychology, 16,* 1–14.

Brewer, B. W. (1993). Self-identity and specific vulnerability to depressed mood. *Journal of Personality, 61,* 343–364.

Brewer, B. W. (1998). Adherence to sport injury rehabilitation programs. *Journal of Applied Sport Psychology, 10,* 70–82.

Brewer, B. W., Cornelius, A. E., Stephan, Y., & Van Raalte, J. (2010). Self-protective changes in athletic identity following anterior cruciate ligament reconstruction. *Psychology of Sport and Exercise, 11,* 1–5.

Brewer, B. W., Cornelius, A. E., Van Raalte, J. L., Petitpas, A. J., Sklar, J. H., Pholman, M. H., . . . Ditmar, T. D. (2003). Protection motivation theory and adherence to sport injury rehabilitation revisited. *The Sport Psychologist, 17,* 95–103.

Brewer, B. W., Van Raalte, J. L., & Linder, D. E. (1993). Athletic identity: Hercules' muscles or achilles' heel? *International Journal of Sport Psychology, 24,* 237–254.

Brewer, B. W., Van Raalte, J. L., & Linder, D. E. (1996). Attentional focus and endurance performance. *Applied Research in Coaching and Athletics Annual, 11,* 1–14.

Brewer, B. W., Van Raalte, J. L., Petitpas, A. J., Sklar, J. H., Pohlman, M. H., Krushell, R. J., . . . Weinstock, J. (2000). Preliminary psychometric evaluation of a measure of adherence to clinic based sport injury rehabilitation. *Physical Therapy in Sport, 1,* 68–74.

Bringer, J. D., Brackenridge, C. H., & Johnston, L. H. (2002). Defining appropriateness in coach–athlete sexual relationships: The voice of coaches. *Journal of Sexual Aggression, 8,* 83–98.

Bringer, J. D., Brackenridge, C. H., & Johnston, L. H. (2006). A swimming coaches' perceptions of sexual exploitation in sport: A preliminary model of role conflict and role ambiguity. *The Sport Psychologist, 20,* 465–479.

British Supermodel's motto draws strong rebuke. (2009, November, 20). *Salt Lake City Deseret News,* D2.

Broadbent, D. E. (1957). Mechanical model for human attention and immediate memory. *Psychological Review, 64,* 205–215.

Broadbent, D. E. (1958). *Perception and communication.* London: Pergamon Press.

Broucek, M. W., Bartholomew, J. B., Landers, D. M., & Linder, D. E. (1993). The effects of relaxation with a warning cue on pain tolerance. *Journal of Sport Behavior, 16,* 239–254.

Brown, J. D. (1991). Staying fit and staying well: Physical fitness as a moderator of life stress. *Journal of Personality and Social Psychology, 60*(4), 555–561.

Brown, K. W., & Ryan, R. M. (2003). The benefits of being present: Mindfulness and its role in psychological well-being. *Journal of Personality and Social Psychology, 84,* 822–848.

Brown, T. D., Van Raalte, J. L., Brewer, B. W., Winter, C. R., Cornelius, A. E., & Andersen, M. (2002). World Cup soccer home advantage. *Journal of Sport Behavior, 25,* 135–144.

Brunelle, J. P., Janelle, C. M., & Tennant, L. K. (1999). Controlling competitive anger among male soccer players. *Journal of Applied Sport Psychology, 11,* 283–297.

Brunet, J., & Sabiston, C. M. (2009). Social physique anxiety and physical activity: A self-determination theory perspective. *Psychology of Sport and Exercise, 10,* 329–335.

Buck, J. N. (1948, October). The H-T-P technique: A qualitative and quantitative scoring manual. *Journal of Clinical Psychology* (Monog. Suppl. No. 5).

Buckworth, J., Lee, R. E., Regan, G., Schneider, L. K., & DiClemente (2007). Decomposing intrinsic and extrinsic motivation for exercise: Application to stages of motivational readiness. *Psychology of Sport and Exercise, 8,* 441–461.

Bueno, J., Weinberg, R. S., Fernández-Castro, J., & Capdevila, L. (2008). Emotional and motivational mechanisms mediating the influence of goal setting on endurance athletes' performance. *Psychology of Sport and Exercise, 9,* 786–799.

Bull, S. J., Shambrook, C. J., James, W., & Brooks, J. E. (2005). Towards an understanding of mental toughness in elite English cricketers. *Journal of Applied Sport Psychology, 17,* 209–227.

Buman, M. P., Omli, J. W., Giacobbi, P. R. Jr., & Brewer, B. W. (2008). Experiences and coping responses of "hitting the wall" for recreational marathon runners. *Journal of Applied Sport Psychology, 20,* 282–300.

Burke, K., Burke, M., & Joyner, M. (1999). Perceptions of momentum in college and high school basketball: An exploratory, case study investigation. *Journal of Sports Behavior, 22,* 303–309.

Burke, K. L., Edwards, T. C., Weigand, D. A., & Weinber, R. S. (1997). Momentum in sport: A real or illusionary phenomenon for spectators. *International Journal of Sport Psychology, 28,* 79–96.

Burke, K. L., & Houseworth, S. (1995). Structural charting and perceptions of momentum in intercollegiate volleyball. *Journal of Sport Behavior, 18,* 167–182.

Burke, S. M., Carron, A. V., Eys, M. A., Ntoumanis, N., & Estabrooks, P. A. (2006). Group versus individual approach? A meta–analysis of the effectiveness of interventions to promote physical activity. *Sport & Exercise Psychology Review, 2,* 13–29.

Burns, B. D. (2004). Heuristics as beliefs and behaviors: The adaptiveness of the "hot hand." *Cognitive Psychology, 48,* 295–331.

Burton, D. (1988). Do anxious swimmers swim slower?: Reexamining the elusive anxiety-performance relationship. *Journal of Sport and Exercise Psychology, 10,* 45–61.

Burton, D., Pickering, M., Weinberg, R., Yukelson, D., & Weigand, D. (2010). The competitiveness goal effectiveness paradox revisited: Examining the goal practices of prospective Olympic athletes. *Journal of Applied Sport Psychology, 22,* 72–86.

Burton, D., Weinberg, R., Yukelson, D., & Weigand, D. (1998). The goal effectiveness paradox in sport: Examining the goal practices of collegiate athletes. *The Sport Psychologist, 12,* 404–418.

Buss, A. H., & Perry, M. (1992). The aggression questionnaire. *Journal of Personality and Social Psychology, 63,* 452–459.

Butcher, J. N., Graham, J. R., Williams, C. L., & Ben-Porath, Y. S. (1990). *Development and use of the MMPI-2 content scales.* Minnesota: University of Minnesota Press.

Butcher, J., Linder, K. J., & Jones, D. P. (2002). Withdrawal from competitive youth sport: A retrospective ten year study. *Journal of Sport Behavior, 25,* 145–163.

Butler, J. L., Baumeister, R. F. (1998). The trouble with friendly faces: Skilled performance with a supportive audience. *Journal of Personality and Social Psychology, 75,* 1213–1230.

Butryn, T. M. (2002). Critically examining white racial identity and privilege in sport psychology consulting. *The Sport Psychologist, 16,* 316–336.

C

Caliari, P. (2008). Enhancing forehand acquisition in table tennis: The role of mental practice. *Journal of Applied Sport Psychology, 20,* 88–96.

Calmels, C., & Fournier, J. F. (2001). Duration of physical and mental execution of gymnastic routines. *The Sport Psychologist, 15,* 142–150.

Campen, C., & Roberts, D. C. (2001). Coping strategies of runners: Perceived effectiveness and match to precompetitive anxiety. *Journal of Sport Behavior, 24,* 144–161.

Cardinal, B. J. (1995). The stages of exercise scale and stages of exercise behavior in female adults. *Journal of Sports Medicine and Physical Fitness, 35,* 87–92.

Cardinal, B. J. (1997). Predicting exercise behavior using components of the transtheoretical model of behavior change. *Journal of Sport Behavior, 20,* 272–283.

Cardinal, B. J., & Kosma, M. (2004). Self-efficacy and the stages and processes of change associated with adopting and maintaining muscular fitness–promoting behavior. *Research Quarterly for Exercise and Sport, 75,* 186–196.

Cardinal, B. J., Tuominen, K. J., & Rintala, P. (2004). Cross-cultural comparison of American and Finnish college students' exercise behavior using transtheoretical model constructs. *Research Quarterly for Exercise and Sport, 75,* 92–101.

Carey, C. (1999, October 4). Psych job. *St. Louis Dispatch,* BP12.

Carlson, C. R., & Hoyle, R. H. (1993). Efficacy of abbreviated progressive muscle relaxation training: A quantitative review of behavioral medicine research. *Journal of Consulting and Clinical Psychology, 61,* 1059–1067.

Carpenter, P. J., & Yates, B. (1997). Relationship between achievement goals and the perceived purposes of soccer for semiprofessional and amateur players. *Journal of Sport & Exercise Psychology, 19,* 302–311.

Carr, C. (2004, November 28). Spectator-sport dynamics can turn frightening. *Indianapolis Star,* Retrieved from http://Indystar.com/2004/11/28

Carr, S. (2009). Adolescent–parent attachment characteristics and quality of youth sport friendship. *Psychology of Sport and Exercise, 10,* 653–661.

Carr, S., & Weigand, D. A. (2002). The influence of significant others on the goal orientations of youngsters in physical education. *Journal of Sport Behavior, 25,* 19–40.

Carron, A. V. (1980). *Social psychology of sport.* Ithaca, NY: Mouvement Publications.

Carron, A. V. (1982). Cohesiveness in sport groups: Interpretations and considerations. *Journal of Sport Psychology, 4,* 123–138.

Carron, A. V., Brawley, L. R., Bray, S. R., Eys, M. A., Dorsch, K. D., Estabrooks, P. A., . . . Hardy, J. (2004). Using consensus as a criterion for groupness. *Small Group Research, 35,* 466–491.

Carron, A. V., Burke, S. M., & Prapavessis, H. (2004). Self-presentation and group influence. *Journal of Applied Sport Psychology, 16,* 41–58.

Carron, A. V., Coleman, M. M., Wheeler, J., & Stevens, D. (2002). Cohesion and performance in sport: A meta-analysis. *Journal of Sport and Exercise Psychology, 24,* 168–188.

Carron, A. V., & Dennis, P. W. (1998). The sport team as an effective group. In J. M. Williams (Ed.), *Applied sport psychology: Personal growth to peak performance* (pp. 127–141). Mountain View, CA: Mayfield.

Carron, A. V., Hausenblas, H. A., & Mack, D. (1996). Social influence and exercise: A meta-analysis. *Journal of Sport & Exercise Psychology, 18,* 1–16.

Carron, A. V., Prapavessis, H., & Grove, J. R. (1994). Group effects and self-handicapping. *Journal of Sport & Exercise Psychology, 16,* 246–257.

Carron, A. V., Spink, K. S., & Prapavessis, H. (1997). Team building and cohesiveness in the sport and exercise setting: Use of interventions. *Journal of Applied Sport Psychology, 9,* 61–72.

Carson, F., & Polman, R. C. J. (2008). ACL injury rehabilitation: A psychological case study of a professional rugby union player. *Journal of Counseling Sport Psychology, 2,* 71–90.

Carver, C. S., Scheier, M. F., & Weintraub, J. K. (1989). Assessing coping strategies: A theoretically based approach. *Journal of Personality and Social Psychology, 56,* 267–283.

Case, R. (1998). Leader member exchange theory and sport: Possible applications. *Journal of Sport Behavior, 21,* 387–395.

Caserta, R. J., Young, J., & Janelle, C. M. (2007). Old dogs, new tricks: Training the perceptual skills of senior tennis players. *Journal of Sport & Exercise Psychology, 29,* 479–497.

Casey, S. (2008, August 25). We are all witnesses. *Sports Illustrated, 109,* 68–73.

Cash, T. F. (1994). *The Multidimensional Body-Self Relations Questionnaire user's manual.* Available from the author, Department of Psychology, Old Dominion University, Norfolk, VA.

Castaneda, B., & Gray, R. (2007). Effects of focus of attention on baseball batting performance in players of differing skill levels. *Journal of Sport & Exercise Psychology, 29,* 60–77.

Castelli, D. M., Hillman, C. H., Buck, S. M., & Erwin, H. E. (2007). Physical fitness and academic achievement in third- and fifth-grade students. *Journal of Sport & Exercise Psychology, 29,* 239–252.

Cattell, R. B. (1965). *The scientific analysis of personality.* Baltimore: Penguin.

Cattell, R. B. (1973, July). Personality pinned down. *Psychology Today,* 40–46.

Cerin, E., Szabo, A., Hunt, N., & Williams, C. (2000). Temporal patterning of competitive emotions: A critical review. *Journal of Sport Sciences, 18,* 605–626.

Chalabaev, A., Sarrazin, P., Stone, J., & Cury, F. (2008). Do achievement goals mediate stereotype threat? *Journal of Sport & Exercise Psychology, 30,* 143–158.

Chang, Y.-K., & Etnier, J. L. (2009). Exploring the dose-response relationship between resistance exercise intensity and cognition function. *Journal of Sport & Exercise Psychology, 31,* 640–656.

Chang, Y.-K., Etnier, J. L., & Barella, L. A. (2009). Exploring the relationship between exercise-induced arousal and cognition using fractionated response time. *Research Quarterly for Exercise and Sport, 80,* 78–88.

Chaouloff, F. (1997). Effects of acute physical exercise on central serotonergic systems. *Medicine & Science in Sports & Exercise, 29,* 58–62.

Chapman, C. L., & Castro, J. M. (1990). Running addiction: Measurement and associated psychological characteristics. *The Journal of Sports Medicine and Physical Fitness, 30,* 283–290.

Chartrand, J. M., Jowdy, D. P., & Danish, S. J. (1992). The psychological skills inventory for sports: Psychometric characteristics and applied implications. *Journal of Sport and Exercise Psychology, 14,* 405–413.

Chase, M. A. (2001). Children's self-efficacy, motivational intentions, and attributions in physical education and sport. *Research Quarterly for Sport and Exercise, 72,* 47–54.

Chass, M. (1994, November 9). Teams look behind plate for managers. *Kansas City Star,* sec. D, 1, 4.

Chatzisarantis, N. L. D., & Hagger, M. S. (2005). Effects of a brief intervention based on the theory of planned behavior on leisure-time physical activity participation. *Journal of Sport & Exercise Psychology, 27,* 470–487.

Chelladurai, P. (1978). *A multidimensional model of leadership.* Unpublished doctoral dissertation, University of Waterloo, Waterloo, Ontario.

Chelladurai, P. (1993). Leadership. In R. N. Singer, M. Murphey, & L. K. Tennant (Eds.), *Handbook on research on sport psychology* (p. 447). New York, NY: Macmillan.

Chelladurai, P., & Carron, A. V. (1977). A reanalysis of formal structure in sport. *Canadian Journal of Applied Sciences, 2,* 9–14.

Chelladurai, P., & Saleh, S. D. (1980). Dimensions of leader behavior in sports: Development of a leadership scale. *Journal of Sport Psychology, 2,* 34–35.

Chian, L. K. Z., & Wang, C. K. J. (2008). Motivational profiles of junior college athletes: A cluster analysis. *Journal of Applied Sport Psychology, 20,* 137–156.

Choquet, M., & Arvers, P. (2003). Sports practices and violent behaviors in 14–16 year olds: Analysis based on the ESPAD 99 survey data. *Annales de Medecine Interne, 154 (Spec No. 2),* S15–S22.

Chow, G. M., Murray, K. E., & Feltz, D. L. (2009). Individual, team, and coach predictors of players' likelihood to aggress in youth soccer. *Journal of Sport & Exercise Psychology, 31,* 425–443.

Church, T. S., & Blair, S. N. (2009). When will we treat physical activity as a legitimate medical therapy . . . even though it does not come in a pill? [Editorial]. *British Journal of Sports Medicine, 43,* 80–81.

Ciani, K. D., & Sheldon, K. M. (2010). Evaluating the mastery-avoidance goal construct: A study of elite college baseball players. *Psychology of Sport and Exercise, 11,* 127–132.

Cinelli, B., Sankaran, G., McConatha, D., & Carson, L. (1992). Knowledge and attitudes of pre-service education majors about AIDS: Implications for curriculum development. *Health Education, 23,* 204–208.

Clark, L. V. (1960). Effect of mental practice on the development of a certain motor skill. *Research Quarterly, 31,* 560–569.

Cleary, T. J., & Zimmerman, B. J. (2001). Self-regulation differences during athletic practice by experts, non-experts, and novices. *Journal of Applied Sport Psychology, 13,* 184–206.

Cleary, T. J., Zimmerman, B. J., & Keating, T. (2006). Training physical education students to self-regulate during basketball free throw practice. *Research Quarterly for Exercise and Sport, 77,* 251–262.

Clingman, J. M., & Hilliard, D. V. (1987). Some personality characteristics of the super-adherer: Following those who go beyond fitness. *Journal of Sport Behavior, 10,* 123–136.

Coakley, J. (1992). Burnout among adolescent athletes: A personal failure or social problem. *Sociology of Sport Journal, 9,* 271–285.

Coatsworth, J. D., & Conroy, D. E. (2009). The effects of autonomy-supportive coaching, need satisfaction, and self-perceptions on initiative and identity in youth swimmers. *Developmental Psychology, 45,* 320–328.

Cofer, C. N., & Johnson, W. R. (1960). Personality dynamics in relation to exercise and sports. In W. R. Johnson (Ed.), *Science and medicine of exercise and sport.* New York: Harper & Row.

Cohen, A., Pargman, D., & Tenenbaum, G. (2003). Critical elaboration and empirical investigation of the Cusp Catastrophe model: A lesson for practitioners. *Journal of Applied Sport Psychology, 15,* 144–159.

Cohen, A. B., Tenenbaum, G., & English, R. W. (2006). Emotions and golf performance: An IZOF–based applied sport psychology case study. *Behavior Modification, 30,* 259–280.

Cohen, J. (1992). A power primer. *Psychological Bulletin, 112,* 155–159.

Coleman, T. R. (1976). *A comparative study of certain behavioral, physiological, and phenomenological effects of hypnotic induction and two progressive relaxation procedures.* Ph.D. dissertation, Brigham Young University, Provo, UT.

Compas, B. E., Connor-Smith, J. K., Saltzman, H., Harding-Thompson, A., & Wadsworth, M. E. (2001). Coping with stress during childhood and adolescence: Problems, progress, and potential in theory and research. *Psychological Bulletin, 12,* 87–127.

Connaughton, D., & Hanton, S. (2010). The development and maintenance of mental toughness in the world's best performers. *The Sport Psychologist, 24,* 168–193.

Connelly, S. L. (1991). *Injury and self-esteem: A test of Sonstroem and Morgan's model.* Unpublished master's thesis, South Dakota State University, Brookings.

Conner, M., Rodgers, W., & Murray, T. (2007). Conscientousness and the intention–behavior relationship: Predicting exercise behavior. *Journal of Sport & Exercise Psychology, 29,* 518–533.

Connolly, C. T., & Janelle, C. M. (2003). Attentional strategies in rowing: Performance, perceived exertion, and gender considerations. *Journal of Applied Sport Psychology, 15,* 195–212.

Conroy, D. E., & Coatsworth, J. D. (2007). Assessing autonomy supportive coaching strategies in youth sport. *Psychology of Sport and Exercise, 8,* 671–684.

Conroy, D. E., Elliot, A. J., Hofner, S. M. (2003). A 2x2 achievement goals questionnaire for sport: Evidence for factorial invariance, temporal stability, and external validity. *Journal of Sport & Exercise Psychology, 25,* 456–476.

Conroy, D. E., Kaye, M. P., & Coatsworth, J. D. (2006). Coaching climates and the destructive effects of mastery-avoidance achievement goals on situational motivation. *Journal of Sport & Exercise Psychology, 28,* 69–92.

Conroy, D. E., & Metzler, J. N. (2004). Patterns of self-talk associated with different forms of competitive anxiety. *Journal of Sport and Exercise Psychology, 26,* 69–89.

Conroy, D. E., Motl, R. W., & Hall, E. G. (1998). Factorial validity of the Self-Presentation in Exercise Questionnaire. *Journal of Applied Sport Psychology, 10,* 270–280.

Conroy, D. E., Motl, R. W., & Hall, E. G. (2000). Progress toward construct validation of the Self-Presentation in Exercise Questionnaire (SPEQ). *Journal of Sport and Exercise Psychology, 23,* 21–38.

Cook, B. J., & Hausenblas, H. A. (2008). The role of exercise dependence for the relationship between exercise behavior and eating pathology. *Journal of Health Psychology, 13,* 495–502.

Cook, K., & Mravic, M. (1999, May 17). Scorecard—a purpose pitch. *Sports Illustrated, 90,* 24.

Cooper, L. (1969). Athletics, activity, and personality: A review of the literature. *Research Quarterly, 40,* 17–22.

Corbin, C. B. (1967a). The effects of covert practice on the development of a complex motor skill. *Journal of General Psychology, 76,* 143–150.

Corbin, C. B. (1967b). Effects of mental practice on skill development after controlled practice. *Research Quarterly, 38,* 534–538.

Corbin, C. B. (1977). The reliability and internal consistency of the motivation rating scale and the general trait rating scale. *Medicine and Science in Sports, 9,* 208–211.

Cornelius, A., Silva, J. M., Conroy, D. E., Peterson, G. (1997). The projected performance model: Relating cognitive and performance antecedents of psychological momentum. *Perceptual and Motor Skills, 84,* 475–485.

Corrion, K., Long, T., Smith, A. L., & d'Arripe-Longueville, F. (2009). "It's not my fault; it's not serious": Athlete accounts of moral disengagement in competitive sport. *The Sport Psychologist, 23,* 388–404.

Costa, A., Bonaccorsi, M., & Scrimali, T. (1984). Biofeedback and control of anxiety preceding athletic competition. *International Journal of Sport Psychology, 15,* 98–109.

Costa, P. T., Jr., & McCrae, R. R. (1992). Revised NEO Personality Inventory (NEO-PI-R) and NEO Five Factor Inventory (NEO-FFI) professional manual. Odessa, FL: Psychological Assessment Resources.

Côté, J., & Fraser-Thomas, J. (2007). Youth involvement in sport. In P. R. E. Crocher (Ed.), *Introduction to sport psychology: A Canadian perspective* (pp. 266–294). Toronto: Pearson Prentice Hall.

Cotterill, S. T., Sanders, R., & Collins, D. (2010). Developing effective pre-performance routines in golf: Why don't we ask the golfer? *Journal of Applied Sport Psychology, 22,* 51–64.

Cottyn, J., de Clercq, D., Pannier, J., Crombez, G., & Lenoir, M. (2006). The measurement of competitive anxiety during balance beam performance in gymnastics. *Journal of Sports Sciences, 24,* 157–164.

Cottyn, J., de Clercq, D., Crombez, G., & Lenoir, M. (2008). The role of preparatory heart rate deceleration on balance beam performance. *Journal of Sport & Exercise Psychology, 30,* 159–170.

Coudevylle, G. R., Ginis, K. A. M., Famose, J.-P., & Gernigon, C. (2008). Effects of self-handicapping strategies on anxiety before athletic performance. *The Sport Psychologist, 22,* 304–315.

Courneya, K. S. (1995). Perceived severity of the consequences of physical inactivity across the stages of change in older adults. *Journal of Sport & Exercise Psychology, 17,* 447–457.

Courneya, K. S. (2001). Exercise interventions during cancer treatment: Biopsychosocial outcomes. *Exercise and Sport Science Review, 29,* 60–64.

Courneya, K. S., & Carron, A. V. (1991). Effects of travel and length of home stand/road trip on the home advantage. *Journal of Sport & Exercise Psychology, 13,* 42–49.

Courneya, K. S., Mackey, J. R., & Jones, L. W. (2000, May). Coping with cancer: Can exercise help? *The Physician and Sports Medicine, 28,* 49–73.

Couture, R. T., Jerome, W., & Tihanyi, J. (1999). Can associative and dissociative strategies affect the swimming performance of recreational swimmers? *The Sport Psychologist, 13,* 334–343.

Cox, R. H. (1985). *Sport psychology: Concepts and applications.* Dubuque, IA: Wm. C. Brown Publishers.

Cox, R. H. (1987). *Relationship between psychological variables with player position and experience in women's volleyball.* Unpublished manuscript.

Cox, R. H. (1990). *Sport psychology: Concepts and applications* (2nd ed.). Dubuque, IA: Wm. C. Brown Publishers.

Cox, R. H. (1998). *Sport psychology: Concepts and applications.* Maidenhead, UK: McGraw-Hill.

Cox, R. H. (2007). *Sport psychology: Concepts and Applications* (6th ed.). Boston: McGraw-Hill.

Cox, R. H. (2000, September). *Confirmatory factor analysis of the Competitive State Anxiety Inventory–2.* Paper presented at the annual meeting of the Association for the Advancement of Applied Sport Psychology, Nashville, TN.

Cox, R. H., Martens, M. P., & Russell, W. D. (2003). Measuring anxiety in athletics: The Revised Competitive State Anxiety Inventory-2. *Journal of Sport and Exercise Psychology, 25,* 519–533.

Cox, R. H., Robb, M., & Russell, W. D. (2000). Concurrent validity of the Revised Anxiety Rating Scale. *Journal of Sport Behavior, 23,* 327–334.

Cox, R. H., Robb, M., & Russell, W. D. (2001). Construct validity of the revised Anxiety Rating Scale (ARS-2). *Journal of Sport Behavior, 24,* 10–18.

Cox, R. H., Shannon, J. K., McGuire, R. T., & McBride, A. (2010). Predicting subjective athletic performance from psychological skills after controlling for sex and sport. *Journal of Sport Behavior, 33,* 129–145.

Cox, R. H., Thomas, T. R., & Davis, J. E. (2000). Delayed anxiolytic effect associated with an acute bout of aerobic exercise. *Journal of Exercise Physiology Online, 3,* 59–66.

Cox, R. H., Thomas, T. R., Hinton, P. S., & Donahue, O. M. (2004). Effect of acute 60 and 80 percent of VO2 max bouts of aerobic exercise on state anxiety of women of different age groups across time. *Research Quarterly for Exercise and Sport, 75,* 165–175.

Cox, R. H., Thomas, T. R., Hinton, P. S., & Donahue, O. M. (2006). Effects of acute bouts of aerobic exercise of varied intensity on subjective mood experience in women of different age groups across time. *Journal of Sport Behavior, 29,* 40–59.

Crabbe, J. B., & Dishman, R. K. (2004). Brain electrocortical activity during and after exercise: A quantitative synthesis. *Psychophysiology, 41,* 563–574.

Craft, L. L., & Landers, D. M. (1998). The effect of exercise on clinical depression and depression resulting from mental illness: A meta-analysis. *Journal of Sport & Exercise Psychology, 20,* 339–357.

Craft, L. L., Magyar, T. M., Becker, B. J., & Feltz, D. L. (2003). The relationship between the Competitive State Anxiety Inventory-2 and sport performance: A meta-analysis. *Journal of Sport and Exercise Psychology, 25,* 444–465.

Craighead, D. J., Privette, F. V., & Byrkit, D. (1986). Personality characteristics of basketball players, starters, and nonstarters. International *Journal of Sport Psychology, 17,* 110–119.

Cratty, B. J., & Sage, J. N. (1964). The effects of primary and secondary group interaction upon improvement in a complex movement task. *Research Quarterly, 35,* 164–175.

Crawford, S., & Eklund, R. C. (1994). Social physique anxiety, reasons for exercise, and attitudes toward exercise settings. *Journal of Sport & Exercise Psychology, 16,* 70–82.

Creasy, J., Stratton, R., Maina, M., Rearick, M., & Reincke, K. (2008, April). Mental toughness in sports. *Scholastic Coach and Athletic Director Magazine, 9,* 30–35.

Cregg, M., Hall, C. R., & Nederhof, E. (2005). The imagery ability, imagery use, and performance relationship. *The Sport Psychologist, 19,* 93–99.

Cresswell, S. L., & Eklund, R. C. (2005). Motivation and burnout in professional rugby players. *Research Quarterly for Exercise and Sport, 76,* 370–376.

Cresswell, S. L., & Eklund, R. C. (2006). The nature of player burnout in rugby: Key characteristics and attributions. *Journal of Applied Sport Psychology, 18,* 219–239.

Cresswell, S. L., & Eklund, R. C. (2007). Athlete burnout: A longitudinal qualitative study. *The Sport Psychologist, 21,* 1–20.

Crocker, P. R. E. (1989). A follow-up of cognitive-affective stress management training. *Journal of Sport & Exercise Psychology, 11,* 236–242.

Crocker, P. R. E. (1992). Managing stress by competitive athletes: Ways of coping. *International Journal of Sport Psychology, 23,* 161–175.

Crocker, P. R. E., & Graham, T. R. (1995). Coping by competitive athletes with performance stress: Gender differences and relationships with affect. *The Sport Psychologist, 9,* 325–338.

Crocker, P. R. E., & Isaak, K. (1997). Coping during competition and training session: Are youth swimmers consistent? *International Journal of Sport Psychology, 28,* 355–369.

Crocker, P. R. E., Sabiston, C. M., Kowalski, K. C., McDonough, M. H., & Kowalski, N. (2006). Longitudinal assessment of the relationship between physical self-concept and health-related behavior and emotion in adolescent girls. *Journal of Applied Sport Psychology, 18,* 185–200.

Cromer, J., & Tenenbaum, G. (2009). Meta-motivational dominance and sensation seeking effects on motor performance and perceptions of challenge and pressure. *Psychology of Sport and Exercise, 10,* 552–558.

Csikszentmihalyi, M. (1990). *Flow: The psychology of optimal experience.* New York: Harper & Row.

Cullen, J. B., & Cullen, F. T. (1975). The structure and contextual conditions of group norm violations: Some implications from the game of ice hockey. *International Review of Sport Sociology, 10,* 69–77.

Culos-Reed, S. N., Robinson, J. L., Lau, H., O'Connor, K., & Keats, M. R. (2007). Benefits of a physical activity intervention for men with prostate cancer. *Journal of Sport & Exercise Psychology, 29,* 118–127.

Cumming, J. (2008). Investigating the relationship between exercise imagery, leisure time exercise behavior, and self-efficacy. *Journal of Applied Sport Psychology, 20,* 184–198.

Cummings, J., Clark, S. E., Ste-Marie, D. M., McCullagh, P., & Hall, C. (2005). The functions of observational learning questionnaire (FOLQ). *Psychology of Sport and Exercise, 6,* 517–537.

Cumming, J., & Hall, C.R. (2002). Athlete's us of imagery in the off season. *The Sport Psychologist, 16,* 160–172.

Cumming, J., Hall, C., & Starkes, J. L. (2005). Deliberate imagery practice: The reliabililty of using a retrospective recall methodology. *Research Quarterly for Exercise and Sport, 76,* 306–314.

Cumming, J., Nordin, S. M., Horton, R., & Reynolds, S. (2006). Examining the direction of imagery and self-talk on dart throwing performance and self-efficacy. *The Sport Psychologist, 20,* 257–274.

Cumming, J., Olphin, T., & Law, M. (2007). Self-reported psychological states and physiological responses to different types of motivational general imagery. *Journal of Sport & Exercise Psychology, 29,* 629–644.

Cumming, S. P., Smith, R. E., & Smoll, F. L. (2006). Athlete-perceived coaching behaviors: Relating two measurement traditions. *Journal of Sport & Exercise Psychology, 28,* 205–213.

Cumming, S. P., Smith, R. E., Smoll, F. L., Standage, M., & Grossbard, J. R. (2008). Development and validation of the achievement goal scale for youth sports. *Psychology of Sport and Exercise, 9,* 686–703.

Cumming, S. P., Smoll, F. L., Smith, R. E., & Grossbard, J. R. (2007). Is winning everything? The relative contributions of motivational climate and won–lost percentage in youth sports. *Journal of Applied Sport Psychology,* 322–336.

Cumming, J., & Stanley, D. M. (2009). Are images of exercising related to feeling states? *Journal of Imagery Research in Sport and Physical Activity, 4,* Article 5.

Cupal, D. D. (1998). Psychological interventions in sport injury prevention and rehabilitation. *Journal of Applied Sport Psychology, 10,* 103–123.

Currie, A. (2007). A psychiatric perspective on athletes with eating disorders. *Journal of Clinical Sport Psychology, 1,* 329–339.

Cutton, D. M., & Landin, D. (2007). The effects of self-talk and augmented feedback on learning the tennis forehand. *Journal of Applied Sport Psychology, 19,* 288–303.

Czech, D. R., Ploszay, A., & Burke, K. L. (2004). An examination of the maintenance of preshot routines in basketball free throw shooting. *Journal of Sport Behavior, 27,* 323–329.

D

Daly, J. M., Brewer, B. W., Van Raalte, J. L., Petitpas, A. J., & Sklar, J. H. (1995). Cognitive appraisal, emotional adjustment, and adherence to rehabilitation following knee surgery. *Journal of Sport Rehabilitation, 4,* 22–30.

Damato, G. C., Grove, J. R., Eklund, R. C., & Cresswell, S. (2008). An exploratory examination into the effects of absence due to hypothetical injury on collective efficacy. *The Sport Psychologist, 22,* 253–268.

Davis, C. L., Tomporowski, P. D., Boyle, C. A., Waller, J. L., Miller, P. H., Naglieri, J. A., & Gregoski, M. (2007). Effects of aerobic exercise on overweight children's cognitive functioning: A randomized controlled trial. *Research Quarterly for Exercise and Sport, 78,* 510–519.

Davis, C., & Mogk, J. P. (1994). Some personality correlates of interest and excellence in sport. *International Journal of Sport Psychology, 25,* 131–143.

Davis, H. (1991). Criterion validity of the athletic motivation inventory: Issues in professional sport. *Journal of Applied Sport Psychology, 3,* 176–182.

Davis, J. E., & Cox, R. H. (2002). Interpreting direction of anxiety within Hanin's individual zone of optimal functioning. *Journal of Applied Sport Psychology, 14,* 43–52.

Davis, M., Eshelman, E. R., & McKay, M. (1995). *The relaxation & stress reduction workbook* (4th ed.). Oakland, CA: New Harbinger Publications, Inc.

Davis, M. H., & Harvey, J. C. (1992). Declines in major league batting performance as a function of game pressure: A drive theory analysis. *Journal of Applied Social Psychology, 22,* 714–735.

Davis, S. F., Huss, M. T., & Becker, A. H. (1995). Norman Triplett and the dawning of sport psychology. *The Sport Psychologist, 9,* 366–375.

Davranche, K., Hall, B., & McMorris, T. (2009). Effect of acute exercise on cognitive control required during an Ericksen flanker task. *Journal of Sport & Exercise Psychology, 31,* 628–639.

de Bruijn, G.-J., de Groot, R., van den Putte, B., & Rhodes, R. (2009). Conscientiousness, extroversion, and action control: Comparing moderate and vigorous physical activity. *Journal of Sport & Exercise Psychology, 31,* 724–742.

de Bruijn, G.-J., Kremers, S. P., Singh, A., van den Putte, B., & van Mechelen, W. (2009). Adult active transportation: Adding habit strength to the theory of planned behavior. *American Journal of Preventive Medicine, 36,* 189–194.

de Bruin, A. P., Bakker, F. C., & Oudejans, R. R. D. (2009). Achievement goal theory and disordered eating: Relationships of disordered eating with goal orientations and motivational climate in female gymnasts and dancers. *Psychology of Sport and Exercise, 10,* 72–79.

de Bruin, A. B. H., Rikers, R. M. J. P., & Schmidt, H. G. (2007). The influence of achievement motivation and chess-specific motivation and chess-specific motivation on deliberate practice. *Journal of Sport & Exercise Psychology, 29,* 561–583.

DeCharms, R. C., & Carpenter, V. (1968). Measuring motivation in culturally disadvantaged school children. *Journal of Experimental Education, 37,* 31–41.

Deci, E. L., Koestner, R., & Ryan, R. M. (1999). A meta-analytic review of experiments examining the effects of extrinsic rewards on intrinsic motivations. *Psychological Bulletin, 125,* 627–668.

Deci, E. L., & Ryan, R. M. (1985). *Intrinsic motivation and self-determination in human behavior.* New York: Plenum.

Deci, E. L., & Ryan, R. M. (1991). A motivational approach to self: Integration in personality. In R. A. Dienstbier (Ed.), Nebraska Symposium on Motivation 1991: Vol 38. *Perspectives on motivation: Current theory and research in motivation* (pp. 237–288). Lincoln, NE: University of Nebraska Press.

Deci, E. L., Vallerand, R. J., Pelletier, L. G., & Ryan, R. M. (1991). Motivation and education: The self-determination perspective. *The Educational Psychologist, 26,* 325–346.

Deeny, S. P., Hillman, C. H., Janelle, C. M., & Hatfield, B. D. (2003). Cortico-cortical communication and superior performance in skilled marksmen: An EEG coherence analysis. *Journal of Sport and Exercise Psychology, 25,* 188–204.

Deford, F. (1999, May 10). The ring leader. *Sports Illustrated, 90,* 96–114.

DeFrancesco, C., & Burke, K. L. (1997). Performance enhancement strategies used in a professional tennis tournament. *International Journal of Sport Psychology, 28,* 185–195.

Denham, B. E., Hawkins, K. W., Jones, K. O., & Billings, A. C. (2007). Anabolic-androgenic steroid use as a complicating factor in the female athlete triad: Behavioral complications for sport psychology. *Journal of Applied Sport Psychology, 19,* 457–470.

Depcik, E., & Williams, L. (2004). Weight training and body satisfaction of body-image-disturbed college women. *Journal of Applied Sport Psychology, 16,* 287–299.

Deroche, T., Stephen, Y., Brewer, B., & LeScanff, C. (2007). Predictors of perceived susceptibility to sport-related injury. *Personality and Individual Differences, 43,* 2218–2228.

Desha, L. N., Ziviani, J. M., Nicholson, J. M., Martin, G., & Darnell, R. E. (2007). Physical activity and depression symptoms in American adolescents. *Journal of Sport & Exercise Psychology, 29,* 534–543.

Dess, N. K. (2000, May/June). Killer workout: The dark side of diet and exercise. *Psychology Today, 32,* 26.

Dimmock, J. A., & Grove, J. R. (2005). Relationships of fan identification to determinants of aggression. *Journal of Applied Sport Psychology, 17,* 37–47.

Dionigi, R. A. (2007). Resistance training and older adults' beliefs about psychological benefits: The importance of self-efficacy and social interaction. *Journal of Sport & Exercise Psychology, 29;* 723–746.

Dionigi, R. A., & Cannon, J. (2009). Older adults perceived changes in physical self-worth associated with resistance training. *Research Quarterly for Exercise and Sport, 80,* 269–280.

Dishman, R. K. (1987). Exercise adherence and habitual physical activity. In W. P. Morgan & S. E. Goldston (Eds.), *Exercise and Mental Health* (pp. 57–83). Washington, DC: Hemisphere Publishing Corporation.

Dishman, R. K. (2001). The problem of exercise adherence: Fighting sloth in nations with market economics. *Quest, 53,* 279–294.

Dohrmann, G. (2004, December 13). Babo blows up. *Sports Illustrated, 101,* 50–54.

Dollard, J., Miller, N., Doob, I., Mourer, O. H., & Sears, R. R. (1939). *Frustration and aggression.* New Haven, CT: Yale University Press.

Donahue, E. G., Miquelon, P., Valois, P., Goulet, C., Buist, A., & Vallerand, R. J. (2006). A motivational model of performance enhancing substance use in elite athletes. *Journal of Sport & Exercise Psychology, 28,* 511–520.

Donahue, E. G., Rip, B., & Vallerand, R. J. (2009). When winning is everything: On passion, identity, and aggression in sport. *Psychology of Sport and Exercise, 10,* 526–534.

Donaldson, A. (2010, February 18). Vonn wins gold. *Deseret News, 160* (249), A1, A8.

Donnelly, P., Carron, A. V., & Chelladurai, P. (1978). *Group cohesion and sport.* Ottawa, Ontario: Canadian Association for Health, Physical Education and Recreation.

Dorsch, T. E., Smith, A. L., & McDonough, M. H. (2009). Parents' perceptions of child-to-parent socialization in organized youth sports. *Journal of Sport & Exercise Psychology, 31,* 444–468.

Downs, D. S., Graham, G. M., Yang, S., Bargainnier, S., & Vasil, J. (2006). Youth exercise intention and past exercise behavior: Examining the moderating influences of sex and meeting exercise recommendations. *Research Quarterly for Exercise and Sport, 77,* 91–99.

Dubuc, N. G., Schinke, R. J., Eys, M. A., Battochio, R., & Zaichkowsky, L. (2010). Experiences of burnout among adolescent female gymnasts: Three case studies. *Journal of Clinical Sport Psychology, 4,* 1–18.

Duda, J. L. (1989). Relationship between task and ego orientation and the perceived purpose of sport among high school athletes. *Journal of Sport & Exercise Psychology, 11,* 318–335.

Duda, J. L. (1992). Motivation in sport settings: A goal perspective approach. In G. Roberts (Ed.), Motivation in Sport and Exercise (pp. 57–91). Champaign, IL: Human Kinetics.

Duffy, E. (1957). The psychological significance of the concept of arousal or activation. *Psychological Review, 64,* 265–275.

Dugdale, J. R., Eklund, R. C., & Gordon, S. (2002). Expected and unexpected stressors in major international competitions: Appraisal, coping, and performance. *The Sport Psychologist, 16,* 20–33.

Dunn, J. G. H. (1999). A theoretical framework for structuring the content of competitive worry in ice hockey. *Journal of Sport & Exercise Psychology, 21,* 259–279.

Dunn, J. G. H., Causgrove-Dunn, J., & Syrotuik, D. G. (2002). Relationship between multidimensional perfectionism and goal orientation in sport. *Journal of Sport & Exercise Psychology, 24,* 376–395.

Dunn, J. G. H., Causgrove-Dunn, J., Gotwals, J. K., Vallance, J. K. H., Craft, J. M., & Syrotuik, D. G. (2006). Establishing construct validity evidence for the Sport Multidimensional Perfectionism Scale. *Psychology of Sport and Exercise, 7,* 57–79.

Dunn, J. G. H., & Dunn, J. C. (1999). Goal orientation, perceptions of aggression, and sportspersonship in elite male youth ice hockey players. *The Sport Psychologist, 13,* 183–200.

Dunn, J. G. H., Dunn, J. D., & Syrotuik, D. G. (2002). Relationship between multidimensional perfectionism and goal orientations in sport. *Journal of Sport and Exercise Psychology, 24,* 376–395.

Dunn, J. G. H., & Holt, N. L. (2003). Collegiate ice hockey players' perceptions of the delivery of an applied sport psychology program. *The Sport Psychologist, 17,* 351–368.

Dunn, J. G. H., & Holt, N. L. (2004). A qualitative investigation of personal-disclosure mutual sharing team building activity. *The Sport Psychologist, 18,* 363–380.

Durand-Bush, N., Salmela, J. H., & Green-Demers, I. (2001). The Ottawa Mental Skills Assessment Tool (OMSAT-3). *The Sport Psychologist, 15,* 1–19.

Durand-Bush, N., & Salmela, J. H. (2002). The development and maintenance of expert athletic performances: Perception of world and Olympic champions. *Journal of Applied Sport Psychology, 14,* 154–171.

Durr, K. R. (1996). *Relationship between state anxiety and performance in high school divers.* Unpublished master's thesis, University of Missouri, Columbia.

Dweck, C. S. (1975). The role of expectations and attributions in the alleviation of learned helplessness. *Journal of Personality and Social Psychology, 31,* 674–685.

Dweck, C. S. (1980). Learned helplessness in sport. In C. H. Nadeau, W. R. Halliwell, K. M. Newell, & G. C. Roberts (Eds.). *Psychology of motor behavior and sport, 1979.* Champaign, IL: Human Kinetics.

E

Eades, A. (1991). *An investigation of burnout in intercollegiate athletes: The development of the Eades Athletic Burnout Inventory.* Paper presented at the North American Society for the Psychology of Sport and Physical Activity National Conference, Asilomar, CA.

Easterbrook, J. A. (1959). The effect of emotion on cue utilization and the organization of behavior. *Psychological Review, 66,* 183–201.

Ebbeck, V., & Gibbons, S. L. (1998). The effect of a team building program on the self-conceptions of grade 6 and 7 physical education students. *Journal of Sport & Exercise Psychology, 20,* 300–310.

Ebbeck, E., Watkins, P. L., Concepcion, R. Y., Cardinal, B. J., & Hammermeister, J. (2009). Muscle dysmorphia symptoms and their relationship to self-concept and negative affect among college recreational exercisers. *Journal of Applied Sport Psychology, 21,* 262–275.

Eccles, D. W., & Tenenbaum, G. (2004). Why an expert team is more than a team of experts: A social-cognitive conceptualization of team coordination and communication in sport. *The Journal of Sport and Exercise Psychology, 26,* 542–560.

Edmonds, W. A., Mann, D. T. Y., Tenenbaum, G. & Janelle, C. M. (2006). Analysis of affect-related performance zones: An idiographic method using physiological and introspective data. *The Sport Psychologist, 20,* 40–57.

Edmunds, J., Ntoumanis, N., & Duda, J. L. (2006). Examining exercise dependence symptomatology from a self-determination perspective. *Journal of Health Psychology, 11,* 887–903.

Edmunds, J., Ntoumanis, N., & Duda, J. L. (2007). Adherence and well-being in overweight and obese patients referred to an exercise on prescription scheme: A self-determination theory perspective. *Psychology of Sport and Exercise, 8,* 722–740.

Edmunds, J., Ntoumanis, N., & Duda, J. L. (2008). Testing a self-determination theory-based teaching style intervention in the exercise domain. *European Journal of Social Psychology, 38,* 375–388.

Edwards, T., Kingston, K., Hardy, L., & Gould, D. (2002). A qualitative analysis of catastrophic performances and the associated thoughts, feelings, and emotions. *The Sport Psychologist, 16,* 1–19.

Eisler, L., & Spink, K. S. (1998). Effects of scoring configuration and task cohesion on the perceptions of psychological momentum. *Journal of Sport & Exercise Psychology, 20,* 311–320.

Ekkekakis, P. (2003). Pleasure and displeasure from the body: Perspectives from exercise. *Cognition and Emotion, 17,* 213–239.

Ekkekakis, P. (2009). Illuminating the black box: Investigating prefrontal cortical hemodynamics during exercise with near-infared spectroscopy. *Journal of Sport & Exercise Psychology, 31,* 505–553.

Ekkekakis, P., & Petruzzello, S. J. (2002). Analysis of the affect measurement conundrum in exercise psychology: IV. A conceptual case for the affect circumplex. *Psychology of Sport and Exercise, 3,* 35–63.

Ekkekakis, P., Backhouse, S. H., Gray, C., & Lind, E. (2008). Walking is popular among adults but is it pleasant? A framework for clarifying the link between walking and affect as illustrated in two studies. *Psychology of Sport and Exercise, 9,* 246–264.

Ekkekakis, P., Hall, E. E., & Petruzzello, S. J. (2005). Some like it vigorous: Measuring individual differences in the preference for and tolerance of exercise intensity. *Journal of Sport & Exercise Psychology, 27,* 350–374.

Ekkekakis, P., Lind, E., & Joens-Matre, R. R. (2006). Can self-reported preference for exercise intensity predict physiologically defined self-selected exercise intensity? *Research Quarterly for Exercise and Sport, 77,* 81–90.

Eklund, R. C., Grove, J. R., & Heard, N. P. (1998). The measurement of slump-related coping: Factorial validity of the COPE and modified-COPE inventories. *Journal of Sport & Exercise Psychology, 20,* 157–175.

Elbourne, K. E., & Chen, J. (2007). The continuum model of obligatory exercise: A preliminary investigation. *Journal of Psychosomatic Research, 62,* 73–80.

Ellemberg, D., & St-Louis-Deschenes, M. (2010). The effect of acute physical exercise on cognitive function during development. *Psychology of Sport and Exercise, 11,* 122–126.

Elliot, A. J., & McGregor, H. A. (2001). A 2x2 achievement goal framework. *Journal of Personality and Social Psychology, 80,* 501–519.

Elliot, A. J., Cury, F., Fryer, J. W., & Huguet, P. (2006). Achievement goals, self-handicapping, and performance attainment: A meditational analysis. *Journal of Sport & Exercise Psychology, 28,* 344–361.

Ellison, C. W. (1983). Spiritual well-being: Conceptualization and measurement. *American Journal of Psychology and Theology, 11,* 330–340.

Elston, T., & Ginis, K. A. M. (2004). The effects of self-set versus assigned goals on exercises' self-efficacy for an unfamiliar task. *Journal of Sport and Exercise Psychology, 26,* 500–504.

Emery, C. F., & Blumenthal, J. A. (1988). Effects of exercise training on psychological functioning in healthy Type A men. *Psychology and Health, 2,* 367–379.

Endler, N. S. (1978). The interaction model of anxiety: Some possible implications. In D. M. Landers & R. W. Christina (Eds.), *Psychology of motor behavior and sport—1977* (pp. 332–351). Champaign, IL: Human Kinetics.

Endler, N. S. (1983). Interactionism: A personality model but not yet a theory. In M. M. Page (Ed.), *Nebraska Symposium on Motivation (1992): Personality–Current theory and research* (pp. 155– 200). Lincoln: University of Nebraska Press.

Endler, N. S., & Parker, J. D. A. (1990). *Coping Inventory for Stressful Situations (CISS): Manual.* Toronto, Ontario: Multihealth Systems, Inc.

Endler, N. S., Parker. J. D. A., Bagby, R. M, & Cox, B. J. (1991). Multidimensionality of state and trait anxiety: Factor structure of the Endler Multidimensional Anxiety Scales. *Journal of Personality and Social Psychology, 60,* 919–926.

Engelhardt, G. M. (1995). Fighting behavior and winning national hockey league games: A paradox. *Perceptual and Motor Skills, 80,* 416–418.

Epstein, D. (2008, March 17). Steroids in America Part 3: The future. *Sports Illustrated, 108,* 44–47.

Epstein, D., & Dohrmann, G. (2009, May 18). What you don't know might kill you—Supplements. *Sports Illustrated, 110,* 54–63.

Epstein, J. (1989). Family structures and student motivation: A developmental perspective. In C. Ames & R. Ames (Eds.), *Research on motivation in education* (Vol. 3, pp. 259–295). New York: Academic Press.

Ericksen, B. A., & Ericksen, C. W. (1974). Effects of noise letters upon the identification of a target in a nonsearch task. *Perception & Psychophysics, 16,* 143–149.

Estabrooks, P., & Courneya, K. S. (1997). Relationships among self-schema, intention, and exercise behavior. *Journal of Sport & Exercise Psychology, 19,* 156–168.

Estabrooks, P. A. (2000). Sustaining exercise participation through group cohesion. *Exercise and Sport Science Reviews, 28,* 63–67.

Etnier, J. L., & Chang, Y.-K. (2009). The effect of physical activity on executive function: A brief commentary on definitions, measurement issues, and the current state of the literature. *Journal of Sport & Exercise Psychology, 31,* 469–483.

Etnier, J. L., & Landers, D. M. (1996). The influence of procedural variables on the efficacy of mental practice. *The Sport Psychologist, 10,* 48–57.

Etnier, J. L., Salazar, W., Landers, D. M., Petruzzello, S. J., Han, M., & Nowell, P. (1997). The influence of physical fitness and exercise upon cognitive functioning: A meta-analysis. *Journal of Sport & Exercise Psychology, 19,* 249–277.

Etzel, E. F., Watson, J. C., II, & Zizzi, S. (2004). A web-based survey of AAASP members' ethical beliefs and behaviors in the new millennium. *Journal of Applied Sport Psychology, 16,* 236–250.

Eubank, M., Collins, D., & Smith, N. (2000). The influence of anxiety direction on processing bias. *Journal of Sport and Exercise Psychology, 22,* 292–306.

Evans, L., & Hardy, L. (2002a). Injury rehabilitation: A goal-setting intervention study. *Research Quarterly for Exercise and Sport, 73,* 310–319.

Evans, L., & Hardy, L. (2002b). Injury rehabilitation: A qualitative follow-up study. *Research Quarterly for Exercise and Sport, 73,* 320–329.

Evans, L., Hare, R., & Mullen, R. (2006). Imagery use during rehabilitation from injury. *Journal of Imagery Research in Sport and Physical Activity, 1,* 1–19.

Ewing, M. E., & Seefeldt, V. (1996). Patterns of participation and attrition in American agency-sponsored youth sports. In F. L. Smoll & R. E. Smith (Eds.), *Children and youth in sport: A biopsychosocial perspective* (pp. 31–45). Madison, WI: Brown & Benchmark.

Eys, M. A., Carron, A. V., Bray, S. R., & Brawley, L. R. (2007). Item wording and internal consistency of a measure of cohesion: The Group Environment Questionnaire. *Journal of Sport & Exercise Psychology, 29,* 395–402.

Eys, M. A., Hardy, J., Carron, A. V., & Beauchamp, M. R. (2003). The relationship between task cohesion and competitive state anxiety. *Journal of Sport and Exercise Psychology, 25,* 66–76.

Eys, M. A., Loughead, T. M., Bray, S. R., & Carron, A. V. (2009a). Perceptions of cohesion by youth sport participants. *The Sport Psychologist, 23,* 330–345.

Eys, M. A., Loughead, T. M., Bray, S. R., & Carron, A. V. (2009b). Development of a cohesion questionnaire for youth: The Youth Sport Environment Questionnaire. *Journal of Sport & Exercise Psychology, 31,* 390–408.

Eysenck, H. J., & Eysenck, S. B. G. (1968). *Eysenck personality inventory manual.* London: University of London Press.

F

Fairall, D. G., & Rodgers, W. M. (1997). The effects of goal-setting method on goal attributes in athletics: A field experiment. *Journal of Sport & Exercise Psychology, 19,* 1–16.

Fallstrom, R. B. (1993, February 7). Antlers rack up reputation with opponents. *Columbia Daily Tribune* (MO), 5B.

Farrell, P. A., Gustafson, A. B., Morgan, W. P., & Pert, C. B. (1987). Enkephalins, catecholamines, and psychological mood alternatives: Effects of prolonged exercise. *Medicine & Science in Sports & Exercise, 19,* 347–353.

Fasting, K., Brackenridge, C. H., & Sundgot-Borgen, J. (2003). Experiences of sexual harassment and abuse amongst Norwegian elite female athletes and non-athletes. *Research Quarterly for Exercise and Sport, 74,* 84–97.

Fasting, K., Brackenridge, C., & Walseth, K. (2007). Women athletes' personal responses to sexual harassment in sport. *Journal of Applied Sport Psychology, 19,* 419–433.

Faulkner, F., & Sparkes, S. (1999). Exercise as therapy for schizophrenia: An ethnographic study. *Journal of Sport & Exercise Psychology, 21,* 52–69.

Faulkner, G., & Biddle, S. J. H. (2004). Exercise and depression: Considering variability and contextuality. *Journal of Sport & Exercise Psychology, 26,* 3–18.

Fazey, J., & Hardy, L. (1988). *The inverted-U hypothesis: A catastrophe for sport psychology?* British Association of Sports Sciences Monograph No. 1. Leeds: The National Coaching Foundation.

Feltz, D. A., Hepler, T. J., & Roman, N. (2009). Coaching efficacy and volunteer youth sport coaches. *The Sport Psychologist, 23,* 24–41.

Feltz, D. L. (1982). A path analysis of the causal elements in Bandura's theory of self-efficacy and an anxiety based model of avoidance behavior. *Journal of Personality and Social Psychology, 42,* 764–781.

Feltz, D. L., & Chase, M. A. (1998). The measurement of self-efficacy and confidence in sport. In J. L. Duda (Ed.), *Advances in sport and exercise psychology measurement* (65–80). Morgantown, WV: FIT Press.

Feltz, D. L., Chase, M. A., Moritz, S., & Sullivan, P. (1999). Development of the multidimensional coaching efficacy scale. *Journal of Educational Psychology, 91,* 765–776.

Feltz, D. L., Chow, C. M., & Hepler, T. J. (2008). Path analysis of self-efficacy and diving performance revisited. *Journal of Sport and Exercise Psychology, 30,* 401–411.

Feltz, D. L., & Landers, D. M. (1983). The effects of mental practice on motor skill learning and performance: A meta-analysis. *Journal of Sport Psychology, 5,* 25–57.

Fenz, W. D. (1975). Coping mechanisms and performance under stress. In D. M. Landers (Ed.), *Psychology of sport and motor behavior,*

11 (pp. 3–24). Penn State HPER Series, No. 10. University Park: Pennsylvania State University Press.

FEPSAC (1996). Position statement of the European Federation of Sport Psychology (FEPSAC): I. Definition of sport psychology. *The Sport Psychologist, 10,* 221–223.

Ferrand, C., Champely, S., & Filaire, E. (2009). The role of body-esteem in predicting disordered eating symptoms: A comparison of French aesthetic and non-athletic females. *Psychology of Sport and Exercise, 10,* 373–380.

Ferrand, C., Tetard, S., & Fontayne, P. (2006). Self-handicapping in rock climbing: A qualitative approach. *Journal of Applied Sport Psychology, 18,* 271–280.

Ferreira, A., Cornilleau, F., Perez-Diaz, F., & Cohen-Salmon, C. (2008). Exercise dependence and morphine addiction: Evidence from animal models. *Journal of Clinical Sport Psychology, 2,* 17–24.

Ferreira, A., Perez-Diaz, F., & Cohen-Salmon, C. (2009). The relationship between physical activity and cocaine intake in mice. *Journal of Clinical Sport Psychology, 3,* 232–243.

Ferrell, M. D., Beach, R. L., Szeverenyi, N. M., Krch, M., & Fernhall, B. (2006). An fMRI analysis of neural activity during perceived zone-state performance. *Journal of Sport & Exercise Psychology, 28,* 421–433.

Fiedler, F. E. (1967). *A theory of leadership effectiveness.* New York: McGraw-Hill.

Fiedler, F. E., Chemers, M. M., & Mahar, L. (1977). *Improving leadership effectiveness—the leader match concept.* New York: John Wiley & Sons.

Fifer, A., Henschen, K., Gould, D., & Ravizza, K. (2008). What works when working with athletes. *The Sport Psychologist, 22,* 356–377.

Filby, W. C. D., Maynard, I. W., & Graydon, J. K. (1999). The effect of multiple-goal strategies on performance outcomes in training and competition. *Journal of Applied Sport Psychology, 11,* 230–246.

Fisher, A. C. (1976). *Psychology of sport.* Palo Alto, CA: Mayfield.

Fleming, J. C., & Ginis, K. A. M. (2004). The effects of commercial exercise video models on women's self-presentational efficacy and exercise task self-efficacy. *Journal of Applied Sport Psychology, 16,* 92–102.

Fletcher, D., & Hanton, S. (2003). Sources of organizational stress in elite sports performances. *The Sport Psychologist, 17,* 175–195.

Flett, G. L., & Hewitt, P. L. (2006). Positive versus negative perfectionism in psychopathology. *Behavior Modification, 30,* 472–495.

Flint, F. A. (1991). *The psychological effect of modeling in athletic injury rehabilitation.* Unpublished doctoral dissertation, University of Oregon, Eugene.

Focht, B. C. (2009). Brief walks in outdoor and laboratory environments: Effects on affective responses, enjoyment, and intentions to walk for exercise. *Research Quarterly for Exercise and Sport, 80,* 611–620.

Focht, B. C., & Hausenblas, H. A. (2004). Perceived evaluations threat and state anxiety during exercise in women with social physique anxiety. *Journal of Applied Sport Psychology, 16,* 361–368.

Focht, B. C., & Koltyn, K. F. (1999). Influence of resistance exercise of different intensities on state anxiety and blood pressure. *Medicine & Science in Sports & Exercise, 31,* 456–463.

Folkman, S., & Lazarus, R. S. (1985). If it changes it must be a process: Study of emotion and coping during three stages of a college examination. *Journal of Personality and Social Psychology, 48,* 150–170.

Fontana, F. E., Mazzardo, O., Mokgothu, C., Furtado, O. Jr., & Gallagher, J. D. (2009). Influence of exercise intensity on the decision-making performance of experienced and inexperienced

soccer players. *Journal of Sport & Exercise Psychology, 31,* 135–151.

Fortier, M. S., Vallerand, R. J., Briere, N. M., & Provencher, P. J. (1995). Competitive and recreational sport structures and gender: A test of their relationship with sport motivation. *International Journal of Sport Psychology, 26,* 24–39.

Foster, D. J., & Weigand, D. A. (2006). The effect of removing superstitious behavior and introducing a pre-performance routine on basketball free-throw performance. *Journal of Applied Sport Psychology, 18,* 167–171.

Fournier, J. F., Deremaux, S., & Bernier, M. (2008). Content, characteristics and function of mental images. *Psychology of Sport and Exercise, 9,* 734–748.

Fox, K. R. (1990). *The physical self-perception profile manual.* DeKalb, IL: Northern Illinois University, Office for Health Promotion.

Fox, K. R., & Corbin, C. B. (1989). The physical self-perception profile: Development and preliminary validation. *Journal of Sport & Exercise Psychology, 11,* 408–430.

Franken, R. E., Hill, R., & Kierstead, J. (1994). Sport interest as predicted by the personality measures of competitiveness, mastery, instrumentality, expressivity, and sensation seeking. *Personality and Individual Differences, 17*(4), 467–476.

Fraser-Thomas, J., & Côté, J. (2009). Understanding adolescents' positive and negative developmental experiences in sport. *The Sport Psychologist, 23,* 3–23.

Fraser-Thomas, J., Côté, J., & Deakin, J. (2008a). Understanding dropout and prolonged engagement in adolescent competitive sport. *Psychology of Sport and Exercise, 9,* 645–662.

Fraser-Thomas, J., Côté, J., & Deakin, J. (2008b). Examining adolescent sport dropout and prolonged engagement from a developmental perspective. *Journal of Applied Sport Psychology, 20,* 318–334.

Fredricks, J. A., & Eccles, J. (2004). Parental influences on youth involvement in sports. In M. R. Weiss (Ed.), *Developmental sport and exercise psychology: A lifespan perspective* (pp. 145–164). Morgantown, WV: Fitness Information Technology.

Fredrickson, B. L., & Roberts, T. (1997). Objectification theory. *Psychology of Women Quarterly, 21,* 173–206.

Freedson, P. S., Mihevic, P., Loucks, A., & Girandola, R. (1983). Physique, body composition, and psychological characteristics of competitive female bodybuilders. *The Physician and Sports Medicine, 11,* 85–90, 93.

Freeman, P., Rees, T., & Hardy, L. (2009). An intervention to increase social support and improve performance. *Journal of Applied Sport Psychology, 21,* 186–200.

Freud, S. (1933). *New introductory lectures on psychoanalysis.* New York: Norton.

Freud, S. (1950). Why war? In J. Strachey (Ed.), *Collected papers.* London: Hogarth.

Frost, R. O., Marten, P., Lahart, C., & Rosenblate, R. (1990). The dimensions of perfectionism. *Cognitive Therapy and Research, 14,* 449–468.

Frost, R. O., Marten, P., Lahart, C., & Rosenblate, R. (1990). The dimensions of perfectionism. *Cognitive Therapy and Research, 14,* 449–468.

Fry, M. D. (2000). A developmental analysis of children's and adolescents' understanding of luck and ability in the physical domain. *Journal of Sport & Exercise Psychology, 22,* 145–166.

Fry, M. D., & Duda, J. L. (1997). A developmental examination of children's understanding of effort and ability in the physical and academic domains. *Research Quarterly for Exercise and Sport, 68,* 331–444.

Fry, M. D., & Newton, M. (2003). Application of achievement goal theory in an urban youth tennis setting. *Journal of Applied Sport Psychology, 15,* 50–66.

G

Galambos, S. A., Terry, P. C., Moyle, G. M., & Locke, S. A. (2005). Psychological predictors of injury among elite athletes. *British Journal of Sports Medicine, 39,* 351–354.

Gallagher, B. V., & Gardner, F. L. (2007). An examination of the relationship between early maladaptive schemas, coping, and emotional response to athletic injury. *Journal of Clinical Sport Psychology, 1,* 47–67.

Galli, N., & Vealey, R. S. (2008). "Bouncing back" from adversity: Athletes' experiences of resilience. *The Sport Psychologist, 22,* 316–335.

Glaros, N. M., & Janelle, C. M. (2001). Varying the mode of cardiovascular exercise to increase adherence. *Journal of Sport Behavior, 24,* 42–62.

Gammage, K. L., Ginis, K. A. M., & Hall, C. R. (2004). Self-presentational efficacy: Its influence on social anxiety in an exercise context. *Journal of Sport and Exercise Psychology, 26,* 179–190.

Gano-Overway, L. A., & Ewing, M. E. (2004). A longitudinal perspective of the relationship between perceived motivational climate, goal orientations, and strategy use. *Research Quarterly for Exercise and Sport, 75,* 315–325.

Gano-Overway, L. A., Newton, M., Magyar, T. M., Fry, M. D., & Guivernau, M. R. (2009). Influence of caring youth sport contexts on efficacy-related beliefs and social behaviors. *Developmental Psychology, 45,* 329–340.

Gao, Z. & Kosma, M. (2008). Intention as a mediator of weight training behavior among college students: An integrative framework. *Journal of Applied Sport Psychology, 20,* 363–374.

Gao, Z., Kosmo, M., & Harrison, L., Jr. (2009). Ability beliefs, task value, and performance as a function of race in a dart-throwing task. *Research Quarterly for Exercise and Sport, 80,* 122–130.

Gao, Z., Xiang, P., Lee, A. M., & Harrison, L., Fr. (2008). Self-efficacy and outcome expectations in beginning weight training class: Their relations to students' behavioral intention and actual behavior. *Research Quarterly for Exercise and Sport, 79,* 92–100.

Garcia, A. W., & King, A. C. (1991). Predicting long-term adherence to aerobic exercise: A comparison of two models. *Journal of Sport & Exercise Psychology, 13,* 394–410.

Gardner, F. L. (2009). Efficacy, mechanisms of change, and the scientific development of sport psychology. *Journal of Clinical Sport Psychology, 3,* 139–155.

Gardner, F. L., & Moore, Z. E. (2004). The multilevel clarification system for sport psychology(MCS-SP). *The Sport Psychologist, 18,* 89–109.

Gardner, F. L., & Moore, Z. E. (2007). *The psychology of enhancing human performance: The mindfulness–acceptance–commitment (MAC) approach.* New York: Springer Publishing.

Gat, I., & McWhirter, B. (1998). Personality characteristics of competitive and recreational cyclists. *Journal of Sport Behavior, 21,* 408–420.

Gaudreau, P., & Antl, S. (2008). Athletes' broad dimensions of dispositional perfectionism: Examining changes in life satisfaction and the mediating role of sport-related motivation and coping. *Journal of Sport & Exercise Psychology, 30,* 356–382.

Gaudreau, P., & Blondin, J.-P. (2004). Different athletes cope differently during a sport competition: A cluster analysis of coping. *Personality and Individual Differences, 36,* 1865–1877.

Gaudreau, P., & Blondin, J.-P. (2002). Development of a questionnaire for the assessment of coping strategies employed by athletes in competitive sport settings. *Psychology of Sport and Exercise, 3,* 1–34.

Gaudreau, P., & Fecteau, M.-C. (2010). Individual self-determination and relationship satisfaction of athletes in dyadic sports: Examining the moderating role of dyadic self-determination. *Journal of Applied Sport Psychology, 22,* 34–50.

Gay, J., Monsma, E. V., & Torres-McGehee, T. (2009). Give or take a few? Comparing measured and self-reported height and weight as correlates of social physique anxiety. *Research Quarterly for Exercise and Sport, 80,* 656–663.

Gayton, W. F., Very, M., & Hearns, J. (1993). Psychological momentum in team sports. *Journal of Sport Behavior, 16,* 121–123.

George, M. (2005). Making sense of muscle: The body experiences of collegiate women athletes. *Sociological Inquiry, 75,* 317–345.

George, T. R., & Feltz, D. L. (1995). Motivation in sport from a collective efficacy perspective. *International Journal of Sport Psychology, 26,* 98–116.

Gernigon, C., d'Arripe-Longueville, F., Delignieres, D., & Ninot, G. (2004). A dynamic systems perspective on goal involvement states in sport. *Journal of Sport & Exercise Psychology, 26,* 572–596.

Gernigon, C., & Delloye, J. B. (2003). Self-efficacy, causal attribution, and track athlete performance following unexpected success or failure among elite sprinters. *The Sport Psychologist, 17,* 55–56.

Giacobbi, P., Jr., Foore, B., & Weinberg, R. S. (2004). Broken clubs and expletives: The sources of stress and coping responses of skilled and moderately skilled golfers. *Journal of Applied Sport Psychology, 16,* 166–182.

Giacobbi, P. R. Jr. (2007). Age and activity-level differences in the use of exercise imagery. *Journal of Applied Sport Psychology, 19,* 487–493.

Giacobbi, P. R., Hausenblas, H. A., Fallon, E. A., & Hall, C. A. (2003). Even more about exercise imagery: A grounded theory of exercise imagery. *Journal of Applied Sport Psychology, 15,* 160–175.

Giacobbi, P. R. Jr., Tuccitto, D. E., Buman, M. P., & Munroe-Chandler, K. (2010). A measurement and conceptual investigation of exercise imagery establishing construct validity. *Research Quarterly for Exercise and Sport, 81,* 485–493.

Giacobbi, P. R., & Weinberg, R. S. (2000). An examination of coping in sport: Individual trait anxiety differences and situational consistency. *The Sport Psychologist, 14,* 42–62.

Giges, B., Petitpas, A. J., & Vernacchia, R. A. (2004). Helping coaches meet their own needs: Challenges for the sport psychology consultant. *The Sport Psychologist, 18,* 430–444.

Gilbourne, D., & Taylor, A. H. (1998). From theory to practice: The integration of goal perspective theory and life development approaches within an injury-specific goal-setting program. *Journal of Applied Sport Psychology, 10,* 124–139.

Gill, D. L. (1995). Women's place in the history of sport psychology. *The Sport Psychologist, 9,* 418–433.

Gill, D. L. (1999). Gender issues: Making a difference in the real world of sport psychology. In G. G. Brannigan (Ed.), *The sport scientists: Research interests.* New York: Longman.

Gill, D. L. (2001). Feminist sport psychology: A guide for our journey. *The Sport Psychologist, 15,* 363–372.

Gill, D. L. (2009). Social psychology and physical activity: Back to the future. *Research Quarterly for Exercise and Sport, 80,* 685–695.

Gillet, N., Vallerand, R. J., Amoura, S., & Baldes, B. (2010). Influences of coaches' autonomy support on athletes' motivational and sport performance: A test of the hierarchical model of intrinsic and extrinsic motivation. *Psychology of Sport and Exercise, 11,* 155–161.

Gillison, F. B., Skevington, S. M., Sato, A., Standage, M., & Evangelidou, S. (2009). The effects of exercise interventions on quality of life in clinical and healthy populations: A meta-analysis. *Social Science & Medicine, 68,* 1700–1710.

Gilovich, T., Vallone, R., & Tversky, A. (1985). The hothand in basketball: On the misperception of random sequences. *Cognitive Psychology, 17,* 295–314.

Ginnis, K. A. M., & Leary, M. R. (2004). Self-presentational processes in health-damaging behavior. *Journal of Applied Sport Psychology, 16,* 59–74.

Gladue, B. A. (1991). Qualitative and quantitative sex differences in self-reported aggressive behavior characteristics. *Psychological Reports, 68,* 675–684.

Gladwell, M. (1999, August 2). The physical genius. *The New Yorker, 75,* 57–65.

Gladwell, M. (2000, August 21 and 28). The art of failure: Why some people choke and others panic. *The New Yorker,* 84–92.

Godin, G. (1994). Theories of reasoned action and planned behavior: Usefulness for exercise promotion. *Medicine and Science in Sports and Exercise, 26,* 1391–1394.

Godin, G., & Shephard, R. J. (1985). A simple method to assess exercise behavior in the community. *Canadian Journal of Applied Sciences, 10,* 141–146.

Goode, K. T., & Roth, D. L. (1993). Factor analysis of cognitions during running: Association with mood change. *Journal of Sport & Exercise Psychology, 15,* 375–389.

Goodger, K., Gorely, T., Lavallee, D., & Harwood, C. (2007). Burnout in sport: A systematic review. *The Sport Psychologist, 21,* 127–151.

Gooding, A., & Gardner, F. L. (2009). An investigation of the relationship between mindfulness, preshot routine, and basketball free throw percentage. *Journal of Clinical Sports Psychology, 3,* 303–319.

Goodkin, K. (1988). Psychiatric aspects of HIV infection. *Texas Medicine, 84,* 55–61.

Gordon, R. A. (2008). Attributional style and athletic performance: Strategic and defensive pessimism. *Psychology of Sport and Exercise, 9,* 336–350.

Gordon, S. (1990). A mental skills training program for the Western Australia cricket team. *The Sport Psychologist, 4,* 368–399.

Gordon, S., Potter, M., & Ford, I. W. (1998). Toward a psychoeducational curriculum for training sport-injury rehabilitation personnel. *Journal of Applied Sport Psychology, 10,* 140–156.

Gorely, T., & Gordon, S. (1995). An examination of the transtheoretical model and exercise behavior in older adults. *Journal of Sports & Exercise Psychology, 17,* 312–324.

Gosling, S. D., Rentfrow, P. J., & Swann, W. B., Jr. (2009). A very brief measure of the Big-Five personality domains. *Journal of Research in Personality, 37,* 504–528.

Goudas, M., Biddle, S., & Fox, K. (1994). Perceived locus of causality, goal orientations and perceived competence in school physical education classes. *British Journal of Educational Psychology, 64,* 453–463.

Gould, D. (2002a). Sport psychology in the new millennium: The psychology of athletic excellence and beyond. *Journal of Applied Sport Psychology,* 137–139.

Gould, D. (2002b). Moving beyond the psychology of athletic excellences. *Journal of Applied Sport Psychology, 14,* 247–298.

Gould, D. (2010). Goal setting for peak performance. In J. M. Willams (Ed.), *Applied sport psychology: Personal growth to peak performance.* Boston: McGraw-Hill.

Gould, D., Collins, K., Lauer, L., & Chung, Y. (2007). Coaching life skills through football: A study of award winning high school coaches. *Journal of Applied Sport Psychology, 19,* 16–37.

Gould, D., Dieffenbach, K., & Moffett, A. (2002). Psychological characteristics and their development in Olympic champions. *Journal of Applied Sport Psychology, 14,* 172–204.

Gould, D., Eklund, R. C., & Jackson, S. A. (1993). Coping strategies used by U.S. Olympic wrestlers. *Research Quarterly for Exercise and Sport, 64,* 83–93.

Gould, D., Finch, L. M., & Jackson, S. A. (1993). Coping strategies used by national champion figure skaters. *Research Quarterly for Exercise and Sport, 64,* 453–468.

Gould, D., Greenleaf, C., Chung, Y., & Guinan, D. (2002). A survey of U.S. Atlanta and Nagano Olympians: Variables perceived to influence performance. *Research Quarterly for Exercise and Sport, 73,* 175–186.

Gould, D., Greenleaf, C., Guinan, D., & Chung, Y. (2002). A survey of U.S. Olympic coaches: Variables perceived to have influenced athlete performances and coach effectiveness. *The Sport Psychologist, 16,* 229–250.

Gould, D., Lauer, L., Rolo, C., Jannes, C., & Pennise, N. (2008). The role of parents in tennis success: Focus group interviews with tennis coaches. *The Sport Psychologist, 22,* 18–37.

Gould, D., Petlichkoff, L., Simons, J., & Vevera, M. (1987). Relationship between competitive state anxiety inventory-2 subscales scores and pistol shooting performance. *Journal of Sport Psychology, 9,* 33–42.

Gould, D., & Pick, S. (1995). Sport psychology: The Griffith era. *The Sport Psychologist, 9,* 391–405.

Gould, D., Russell, M., Damarjian, N., & Lauer, L. (1999). A survey of mental skills training knowledge, opinions, and practices of junior tennis coaches. *Journal of Applied Sport Psychology, 11,* 28–50.

Gould, D., Tuffey, S., Udry, E., & Loehr, J. (1996). Burnout in competitive junior tennis players: II. Qualitative analysis. *The Sport Psychologist, 10,* 341–366.

Gould, D., Udry, E., Bridges, D., & Beck, L. (1997). Stress sources encountered when rehabilitating from season-ending ski injuries. *The Sport Psychologist, 11,* 361–378.

Gould, D., Udry, E., Tuffy, S., & Loehr, J. (1996). Burnout in competitive junior tennis players: I. A quantitative psychological assessment. *The Sport Psychologist, 10,* 322–340.

Gould, S. J. (2000, June 25). The brain of brawn. *The New York Times,* CXLIX, (#51, 430), section 4, p. 17.

Granito, V. J. (2002). Excellence is a journey, not a goal: The historical significance of Betty J. Wentz (1934–2001). *The Sport Psychologist, 16,* 291–295.

Gray, S. W., & Fernandez, S. J. (1990). Effects of visuo-motor behavior rehearsal with videotaped modeling on basketball shooting performance. *Psychology: A Journal of Human Behavior, 26,* 41–47.

Green, C. D. (2003). Psychology strikes out: Coleman R. Griffith and the Chicago Cubs. *History of Psychology, 6,* 267–283.

Green, S. L., & Weinberg, R. S. (2001). Relationships among athletic identity, coping skills, social support, and the psychological impact of injury in recreational participants. *Journal of Applied Sport Psychology, 13,* 40–59.

Greenberg, J. S. (2009). *Comprehensive stress management.* New York: McGraw-Hill.

Greenleaf, C., Gould, D., & Dieffenbach, K. (2001). Factors influencing Olympic performance: Interviews with Atlanta and Nagano U.S. Olympics. *Journal of Applied Sport Psychology, 13,* 154–184.

Greenspan, M. J., & Feltz, D. L. (1989). Psychological interventions with athletes in competitive situations: A review. *The Sport Psychologist, 3,* 219–236.

Greenwood, B. N., Foley, T. E., Burhans, D., Maier, S. F., & Fleshner, M. (2005). The consequences of uncontrollable stress are sensitive to duration of prior wheel running. *Brain Research, 1033,* 164–178.

Greer, D. L. (1983). Spectator booing and the home advantage: A study of social influence in the basketball arena. *Social Psychology Quarterly, 46,* 252–261.

Gregg, M., & Hall, C. (2006). The relationship of skill level and age to the use of imagery by golfers. *Journal of Sport Psychology, 18,* 363–375.

Gregg, M., Hall, C., & Nederhof, E. (2005). The imagery ability, imagery use, and performance relationship. *The Sport Psychologist, 19,* 93–99.

Gregg, E., & Rejeski, J. (1990). Social psychobiologic dysfunction associated with anabolic steroid abuse: A review. *The Sport Psychologist, 4,* 275–284.

Grieve, F. G., Jackson, L., Reece, T., Marklin, L., & Delaney, A. (2008). Correlates of social physique anxiety in men. *Journal of Sport Behavior, 31,* 329–337.

Grieve, F. G., Whelan, J. P., & Meyers, A. W. (2000). An experimental examination of the cohesion-performance relationship in an interactive team. *Journal of Applied Sport Psychology, 12,* 219–235.

Grindstaff, J. S., & Fisher, L. A. (2006). Sport psychology consultants' experience of using hypnosis in their practice: An exploratory investigation. *The Sport Psychologist, 20,* 368–386.

Groslambert, A., Candau, R., Grappe, F., Dugue, B., & Rouillon, J. D. (2003). Effects of autogenic and imagery training on the shooting performances in Biathlon. *Research Quarterly for Exercise and Sport, 74,* 337–341.

Grossbard, J., Hummer, J., LaBrie, J., Pederson, E., & Neighbors, C. (2009). Is substance abuse a team sport? Attraction to team, perceived norms, and alcohol and marijuana use among male and female intercollegiate athletes. *Journal of Applied Sport Psychology, 21,* 247–261.

Grossman, A., & Sutton, J. R. (1985). Endorphins: What are they? How are they measured? What is their role in exercise? *Medicine & Science in Sports & Exercise, 17,* 74–81.

Grouios, G. (1992). Mental practice: A review. *Journal of Sport Behavior, 15,* 42–59.

Grove, J. R., Fish, M., & Eklund, R. C. (2004). Changes in athletic identity following team selection: Self-protection versus self-enhancement. *Journal of Applied Sport Psychology, 16,* 75–81.

Grove, J. R., & Heard, N. P. (1997). Optimism and sport confidence as correlates of slump related coping among athletes. *The Sport Psychologist, 11,* 400–410.

Grove, J. R., Norton, P. J., Van Raalte, J. L., & Brewer, B. W. (1999). Stages of change as an outcome measure in the evaluation of mental skills training programs. *The Sport Psychologist, 13,* 107–116.

Grove, J. R., & Prapavessis, H. (1992). Preliminary evidence for the reliability and validity of an abbreviated profile of mood states. *International Journal of Sport Psychology, 23,* 93–109.

Gruber, J. J., & Gray, G. R. (1981). Factor patterns of variables influencing cohesiveness at various levels of basketball competition. *Research Quarterly for Exercise and Sport, 52,* 19–30.

Grusky, O. (1963). The effects of formal structure on managerial recruitment: A study of baseball organization. *Sociometry, 26,* 345–353.

Guay, F., Mageau, G. A., & Vallerand, R. J. (2003). On the hierarchical structure of self-determined motivation: A test of top-down, bottom-up, reciprocal, and horizontal effects. *Personality and Social Psychology Bulletin, 29,* 992–1004.

Gucciardi, D. F., & Dimmock, J. A. (2008). Choking under pressure in sensorimotor skills: Conscious processing or depleted attentional resources? *Psychology of Sport and Exercise, 9,* 45–59.

Gucciardi, D. F., & Gordan, S. (2009). Revisiting the performance profile technique: Theoretical underpinnings and application. *The Sport Psychologist, 23,* 93–117.

Gucciardi, D. F., Gordon, S., & Dimmock, J. A. (2008). Towards an understanding of mental toughness in Australian football. *Journal of Applied Sport Psychology, 20,* 261–281.

Gucciardi, D. F., Gordon, S., & Dimmock, J. A. (2009a). Evaluation of mental toughness training program for youth aged Australian footballers: I. A quantitative analysis. *Journal of Applied Sport Psychology, 21,* 307–323.

Gucciardi, D. F., Gordon, S., & Dimmock, J. A. (2009b). Evaluation of a mental toughness training program for youth-aged Australian footballers: II. A qualitative analysis. *Journal of Applied Sport Psychology, 21,* 324–339.

Gucciardi, D. F., Gordon, S., & Dimmock, J. A. (2009c). Development and preliminary validation of a mental toughness inventory for Australian football. *Psychology of Sport and Exercise, 10,* 201–209.

Gucciardi, D. F., Longbottom, J.-L., Jackson, B., & Dimmock, J. A. (2010). Experienced golfers' perspectives on choking under pressure. *Journal of Sport & Exercise Psychology, 32,* 61–83.

Guillot, A., & Collet, C. (2005). Duration of mentally simulated movement: A review. *Journal of Motor Behavior, 37,* 10–20.

Gula, B., & Raab, M. (2004). Hot hand belief and hot hand behavior: A comment on Koehler and Conley. *Journal of Sport & Exercise Psychology, 26,* 167–170.

Gustafsson, H., Kentta, G., Hassmen, P., & Lundquist, C. (2007). Pevalence of burnout in competitive adolescent athletes. *The Sport Psychologist, 21,* 21–37.

Guyton, A. C., & Hall, J. E. (2006). *Textbook of medical physiology* (11th ed.). Philadelphia, PA: Elsevier Saunders.

H

Haase, A. M. (2009). Physique anxiety and disordered eating correlates in female athletes: Differences in team and individual sports. *Journal of Clinical Sport Psychology, 3,* 218–231.

Haddad, K., & Tremayne, P. (2009). The effects of centering on the free-throw shooting performance of young athletes. *The Sport Psychologist, 23,* 118–136.

Hagemann, N., Strauss, B., & Canal-Bruland, R. (2006). Training perceptual skill by orienting visual attention. *Journal of Sport & Exercise Psychology, 28,* 143–158.

Hagger, M. S., Chatzisarantis, N. L. D., & Biddle, S. J. H. (2002). A meta-analytic review of the theories of reasoned action and planned behavior in physical activity: Predictive validity and the contribution of additional variables. *Journal of Sport and Exercise Psychology, 24,* 3–32.

Hagger, M. S., & Chatzisarantis, N. L. D. (2005). First- and higher-order models of attitudes, normative influence, and perceived behavioural control in the Theory of Planned Behavior. *British Journal of Social Psychology, 44,* 513–535.

Hagger, M. S., Chatzisarantis, N. L. D., Barkoukis, V., Wang, J. C. K., Hein, V., Pihu, M., . . . I., Karsai, I., et al. (2007). Cross-cultural generalizability of the theory of planned behavior among young people in a physical activity context. *Journal of Sport & Exercise Psychology, 29,* 2–20.

Hagger, M. S., Chatzisarantis, N. L. D., Hein, V., Pihu, M., Soós, I., & Karsai, I. (2007). The perceived autonomy support scale for exercise settings (PASSES): Development, validity, and cross-cultural invariance in young people. *Psychology of Sport and Exercise, 8,* 632–653.

Hagtvet, K. A., & Hanin, Y. L. (2007). Consistency of performance-related emotions in elite athletes: Generalizability theory applied to the IZOF model. *Psychology of Sport and Exercise, 8,* 47–72.

Halberstam, D. (1994). *October 1964.* New York: Villard Books.

Hale, B. S., Koch, K. R., & Raglin, J. S. (2000). State anxiety responses to 60-minutes of cross-training. *Medicine & Science in Sports & Exercise, 32,* Supplement, Abstract #497, S124.

Hall, C. R., Mack, D. E., Paivio, A., & Hausenblas, H. A. (1998). Imagery use by athletes: Development of the sport imagery questionnaire. *International Journal of Sport Psychology, 29,* 73–89.

Hall, C. R., & Martin, K. A. (1997). Measuring movement imagery abilities: A revision of the Movement Imagery Questionnaire. *Journal of Mental Imagery, 21,* 143–154.

Hall, C. R., Munroe-Chandler, K. J., Cumming, J., Law, B., & Murphy, L. (2009). Imagery and observational learning use and their relationship to sport confidence. *Journal of Sports Sciences, 27,* 327–337l.

Hall, C. R., & Pongrac, J. (1983). *Movement imagery questionnaire.* London, Ontario: University of Western Ontario.

Hall, C. R., Rodgers, W. M., & Barr, K. A. (1990). The use of imagery by athletes in selected sports. *The Sport Psychologist, 4,* 1–10.

Hall, E. E., Ekkekakis, P., & Petruzzello, S. J. (2007). Regional brain activity and strenuous exercise: Predicting affective response using EEG asymmetry. *Biological Psychology, 75,* 194–200.

Hall, E. G., & Hardy, C. J. (1991). Ready, aim, fire . . . relaxation strategies for enhancing pistol marksmanship. *Perceptual and Motor Skills, 72,* 775–786.

Hall, H. K., Kerr, A. W., & Matthews, J. (1998). Precompetitive anxiety in sport: The contribution of achievement goals and perfectionism. *Journal of Sport & Exercise Psychology, 20,* 194–217.

Hall, H. K., Kerr, A. W., Kozub, S. A., & Finnie, S. B. (2007). Motivational antecedents of obligatory exercise: The influence of achievement goals and multidimensional perfectionism. *Psychology of Sport and Exercise, 8,* 297–316.

Hall, P. A., Elias, L. J., Fong, G. T., Harrison, A. H., Borowsky, R., & Sarty, G. E. (2008). A social neuroscience perspective on physical activity. *Journal of Sport & Exercise Psychology, 30,* 392–410.

Hall, R. L. (2001). Shaking the foundation: Women of color in sport. *The Sport Psychologist, 15,* 386–400.

Halliburton, A. L., & Weiss, M. R. (2002). Sources of competence information and perceived motivational climate among adolescent female gymnasts varying in skill level. *Journal of Sport & Exercise Psychology, 24,* 396–419.

Hallinan, C. J. (1998). Dimensions of gender differentiation and centrality in the employment of university recreation centers. *Journal of Sport Behavior, 21,* 256–264.

Halpin, A. W. (1966). *Theory and research in administration.* London: Macmillan.

Hamer, M., Taylor, A., & Steptoe, A. (2006). The effect of acute aerobic exercise on stress related blood pressure responses: A systematic review and meta-analysis. *Biological Psychology, 71,* 183–190.

Hamilton, K., & White, K. M. (2008). Extending the theory of planned behavior: The role of self and social influences in predicting adolescent regular moderate-to-vigorous physical activity. *Journal of Sport & Exercise Psychology, 30,* 56–74.

Hamilton, S. A., & Fremouw, W. J. (1985). Cognitive behavioral training for college basketball free-throw performance. *Cognitive Therapy and Research, 9,* 479–483.

Hammereister, J., & Burton, D. (2001). Stress, appraisal, and coping revisited: Examining the antecedents of competitive state anxiety with endurance athletes. *The Sport Psychologist, 15,* 66–90.

Hammereister, J., & Burton, D. (2004). Gender differences in coping with endurance sport stress: Are men from Mars and women from Venus? *Journal of Sport Behavior, 27,* 148–164.

Hanin, Y. L. (1980). A study of anxiety in sports. In W. F. Straub (Ed.), *Sport psychology: An analysis of athlete behavior* (pp. 236–249). New York: Mouvement Publications.

Hanin, Y. L. (1986). State-trait anxiety research on sports in the USSR. In C. D. Speilberger & R. Dias-Guerrero (Eds.), *Cross-cultural anxiety* (pp. 45–64). Washington, DC: Hemisphere.

Hanin, Y. L. (1989). Interpersonal and intragroup anxiety: Conceptual and methodological issues. In D. Hackfort & C. D. Spielberger (Eds.), *Anxiety in sports: An international perspective* (pp. 19–28). Washington, DC: Hemisphere Publishing Corporation.

Hanlon, T. (1994). *SportParent.* Champaign, IL: Human Kinetics.

Hannon, J., Soohoo, S., Reel, J., & Ratliffe, T. (2009). Gender stereotyping and the influence of race in sport among adolescents. *Research Quarterly for Exercise and Sport, 80,* 676–884.

Hanson, S. J., McCullagh, P., & Tonymon, P. (1992). The relationship of personality characteristics, life stress, and coping resources to athletic injury. *Journal of Sport and Exercise Psychology, 14*(3), 262–272.

Hanson, T. W., & Gould, D. (1988). Factors affecting the ability of coaches to estimate their athlete's trait and state anxiety levels. *The Sport Psychologist, 2,* 298–313.

Hanton, S., & Connaughton, D. (2002). Perceived control of anxiety and its relationship to self-confidence. *Research Quarterly for Exercise and Sport, 73,* 87–97.

Hanton, S., & Jones, G. (1999a). The acquisition and development of cognitive skills and strategies: I. Making the butterflies fly in formation. *The Sport Psychologist, 13,* 1–21.

Hanton, S., & Jones, G. (1999b). The effects of a multimodal intervention program on performers: II. Training the butterflies to fly in formation. *The Sport Psychologist, 13,* 22–41.

Hanton, S., Wadey, R., & Mellalieu, S. D. (2008). Advanced psychological strategies and anxiety responses in sport. *The Sport Psychologist, 22,* 472–490.

Harber, V. J., & Sutton, J. R. (1984, March–April). Endorphins and exercise. *Sports Medicine, 1,* 154–171.

Hardman, K. (1973). A dual approach to the study of personality and performance in sport. In H. T. A. Whiting, K. Hardman, L. B. Hendry, & M. G. Jones (Eds.), *Personality and performance in physical education and sport.* London: Kimpton.

Hardy, C. J., & Rejeski, W. J. (1989). Not what, but how one feels: The measurement of affect during exercise. *Journal of Sport & Exercise Psychology, 11,* 304–317.

Hardy, J. (2006). Speakiing clearly: A critical review of self-talk literature. *Psychology of Sport and Exercise, 7,* 81–97.

Hardy, J., Gammage, K., & Hall, C. (2001). A descriptive study of athlete self-talk. *The Sport Psychologist 15,* 306–318.

Hardy, J., Hall, C. R., & Hardy, L. (2004). A note on athletes' use of self-talk. *Journal of Applied Sport Psychology, 16,* 251–257.

Hardy, L., & Callow, N. (1999). Efficacy of external and internal visual imagery perspectives for the enhancement of performance on tasks in which form is important. *Journal of Sport & Exercise Psychology, 21,* 95–112.

Hardy, J., Hall, C. R., & Hardy, L. (2005). Quantifying athlete self-talk. *Journal of Sport Sciences, 23,* 905–917.

Hardy, J., Roberts, R., & Hardy, L. (2009). Awareness and motivation to change negative self-talk. *The Sport Psychologist, 23,* 435–450.

Hardy, L. Beattie, S., & Woodman, T. (2007). Anxiety-induced performance catastrophes: Investigating effort required as an asymmetry factor. *British Journal of Psychology, 98,* 15–31.

Hardy, L., & Parfitt, G. (1991). A catastrophe model of anxiety and performance. *British Journal of Psychology, 82,* 163–178.

Hardy, L., Parfitt, G., & Pates, J. (1994). Performance catastrophes in sport: A test of the hysteresis hypothesis. *Journal of Sport Sciences, 12,* 327–334.

Hardy, L., Roberts, R., Thomas, P. R., Murphy, S. M. (2010). Test of Performance Strategies (TOPS): Instrument refinement using confirmatory factor analysis. *Psychology of Sport and Exercise, 11,* 27–35.

Hardy, L., Woodman, T., & Carrington, S. (2004). Is self-confidence a bias factor in higher-order catastrophe models? *Journal of Sport & Exercise Psychology, 26,* 359–368.

Hare, R., Evans, L., & Callow, N. (2008). Imagery use during rehabilitation from injury: A case study of an elite athlete. *The Sport Psychologist, 22,* 405–422.

Harger, G. J., & Raglin, J. S. (1994). Correspondence between actual and recalled precompetition anxiety in collegiate track and field athletes. *Journal of Sport & Exercise Psychology, 16,* 206–211.

Harlow, R. G. (1951). Masculine inadequacy and compensatory development of physique. *Journal of Personality, 19,* 312–323.

Harrell, W. A. (1980). Aggression by high school basketball players: An observational study of the effects of opponents' aggression and frustration-inducing factors. *International Journal of Sport Psychology, 11,* 290–298.

Harris, D. V., & Robinson, W. J. (1986). The effects of skill level on EMG activity during internal and external imagery. *Journal of Sport Psychology, 8,* 105–111.

Hart, E. A., Leary, M. R., & Rejeski, W. J. (1989). The measurement of social physique anxiety. *Journal of Sport & Exercise Psychology, 11,* 94–104.

Harter, S. (1978). Effectance motivation reconsidered: Towards a developmental model. *Human Development, 21,* 34–64.

Harwood, C., & Hardy, L. (2001). Persistence and effort in moving achievement goal research forward: A response to Treasure and colleagues. *Journal of Sport & Exercise Psychology, 23,* 330–345.

Harwood, C., Hardy, L., & Swain, A. (2000). Achievement goals in sport: A critique of conceptual and measurement issues. *Journal of Sport & Exercise Psychology, 22,* 235–255.

Harwood, C., & Knight, C. (2009). Stress in youth sport: A developmental investigation of tennis parents. *Psychology of Sport and Exercise, 10,* 447–456.

Harwood, C., & Swain, A. (2001). The development and activation of achievement goals in tennis: I. Understanding the underlying factors. *The Sport Psychologist, 15,* 319–341.

Harwood, C., & Swain, A. (2002). The development and activation of achievement goals in tennis: II. A player, parent, and coach intervention. *The Sport Psychologist, 16,* 138–159.

Harwood, C., Cummings, J., & Fletcher, D. (2004). Motivational profiles and psychological skills use within elite youth sport. *Journal of Applied Sport Psychology, 16,* 318–332.

Hathaway, S. R., & McKinley, J. C. (1940). A multiphasic personality schedule (Minnesota): I. Construction of the schedule. *Journal of Psychology, 10,* 249–254.

Hatzigeorgiadis, A., & Biddle, S. (1999). The effect of goal orientation and perceived competence on cognitive interference during tennis and snooker performance. *Journal of Sports Behavior, 22,* 479–501.

Hatzigeorgiadis, A., & Biddle, S. J. H. (2000). Assessing cognitive interference in sports: The development of the Thought Occurrence Questionnaire for Sport (TOQS). *Anxiety, Stress, and Coping, 13,* 65–86.

Hatzigeorgiadis, A., & Biddle, S. J. H. (2008). Negative self-talk during sports performance: Relationships with pre–competition anxiety and goal performance discrepancies. *Journal of Sport Behavior, 31,* 237–253.

Hatzigeorgiadis, A., Theodorakis, Y., & Zourbanos, N. (2004). Self-talk in the swimming pool: The effects of self-talk on thought content and performance on water-polo tasks. *Journal of Applied Sport Psychology, 16,* 138–150.

Hatzigeorgiadis, A., Zourbanos, N., & Theodorakis, Y. (2007). The moderating effects of self-talk content on self-talk functions. *Journal of Applied Sport Psychology, 19,* 240–251.

Hatzigeorgiadis, A., Zourbanos, N., Goltsios, C., & Theodorakis, Y. (2008). Investigating the functions of self-talk: The effects of motivational self-talk on self-efficacy and performance in young tennis players. *The Sport Psychologist, 22,* 458–471.

Hatzigeorgiadis, A., Zourbanos, N., Mpoumpaki, S., & Theodorakis, Y. (2009). Mechanics underlying the self-talk performance relationship: The effects of motivational self-talk on self-confidence and anxiety. *Psychology of Sport and Exercise, 10,* 186–192.

Hausenblas, H. A., Brewer, B. W., & Van Raalte, J. L. (2004). Self-presentation and exercise. *Journal of Applied Sport Psychology, 16,* 3–18.

Hausenblas, H. A., & Carron, A. V. (1996). Group cohesion and self-handicapping in female and male athletes. *Journal of Sport & Exercise Psychology, 18,* 132–143.

Hausenblas, H. A., & Carron, A. V. (1999). Eating disorder indices and athletes: An integration. *Journal of Sport & Exercise Psychology, 21,* 230–258.

Hausenblas, H. A., Carron, A. V., & Mack, D. E. (1997). Application of the theories of reasoned action and planned behavior to exercise behavior: A meta-analysis. *Journal of Sport & Exercise Psychology, 19,* 36–51.

Hausenblas, H. A., & Downs, D. S. (2001). Comparison of body image between athletes and nonathletes: A meta-analytic review. *Journal of Applied Sport Psychology, 13,* 323–339.

Hausenblaus, H. A., & Symons Downs, D. (2002a). Exercise dependence: A systematic review. *Psychology of Sport and Exercise, 3,* 89–123.

Hausenblaus, H. A., & Symons Downs, D. (2002b). How much is too much? The development and validation of the exercise dependence scale. *Psychology and Health, 17,* 387–404.

Hausenblaus, H. A., & Symons Downs, D. (2002c). Relationship among sex, imagery, and exercise dependence symptoms. *Psychology of Addictive Behaviors, 16,* 169–172.

Hawkley, L. C., Thisted, R. A., Cacioppo, J. T. (2009). Loneliness predicts reduced physical activity: Cross-sectional & longitudinal analyses. *Health Psychology, 28,* 354–363.

Hayes, S., Crocker, P., & Kowalski, K. (1999). Gender differences in physical self-perceptions, global self-esteem and physical activity: Evaluation of the physical self-perception profile model. *Journal of Sport Behavior, 22,* 1–14.

Hays, K. F. (2002). The enhancement of performance excellence among performing artists. *Journal of Applied Sport Psychology, 14,* 299–312.

Hays, K., Maynard, I. Thomas, O., & Bawden, M. (2007). Sources and types of confidence identified by world class sport performers. *Journal of Applied Sport Psychology, 19,* 434–456.

Hays, K., Thomas, O., Butt, J., & Maynard, I. (2010). The development of confidence profiling for sport. *The Sport Psychologist, 18,* 373–392.

Hayslip, B., Jr., Petrie, T. A., MacIntire, M. M., & Jones, G. M. (2010). The influence of skill level, anxiety, and psychological skills use on amateur golfers' performance. *Journal of Applied Sport Psychology, 22,* 123–133.

Heitkamp, H. C., Schulz, H., Rocker, K., & Dickhuth, H. H. (1998, May). Endurance training in females: Changes in beta-endorphin and ACTH. *International Journal of Sports Medicine, 19,* 260–264.

Henry, F. M. (1941). Personality differences in athletes, physical education, and aviation students. *Psychological Bulletin, 38,* 745.

Henley, R., Schweizer, I., de Gara, F., & Vetter, S. (2007). How psychosocial sport & play programs help youth manage diversity: A review of what we know & what we should research. *The International Journal of Psychosocial Rehabilitation, 12,* 51–58.

Hersey, P., & Blanchard, K. H. (1977). *Management of organizational behavior.* Englewood Cliffs, NJ: Prentice Hall.

Heuze, J. P., Sarrazin, P., Masiero, M., Raimbault, N., & Thomas, J. P. (2006). The relationships of perceived motivational climate to cohesion and collective efficacy in elite female teams. *Journal of Applied Sport Psychology, 18,* 201–218.

Heuze, J. P., & Thomas, J. (2007). Should the coaches of elite female handball teams focus on collective efficacy or group cohesion? *The Sport Psychologist, 21,* 375–382.

Hewitt, P. L., & Flett, G. L. (1991). Perfectionism in the self and social contexts: Conceptualization, assessment, and association with psychopathology. *Journal of Personality and Social Psychology, 60,* 456–470.

Hildebrandt, T., Langenbucher, J., & Schlundt, D. G. (2004). Mascularity concerns among men: Development of attitudinal and perceptual measures. *Body Image, 1,* 169–181.

Hildebrandt, T., Schlundt, D., Langenbucher, J., & Chung, T. (2006). Presence of muscle dysmorphia symtomology among male weightlifters. *Comprehensive Psychiatry, 47,* 127–135.

Hill, A. P., Hall, H. K., & Appleton, P. R. (2010). A comparative examination of the correlates of self-oriented perfectionism and conscientious achievement striving in male cricket academy players. *Psychology of Sport and Exercise, 11,* 162–168.

Hill, A. P., Hall, H. K., Appleton, P. R., & Kozub, S. A. (2008). Perfectionism and burnout in junior elite soccer players: The mediating influence of unconditional self-acceptance. *Psychology of Sport and Exercise, 9,* 630–644.

Hill, A. P., Hall, H. K., Appleton, P. R., & Murray, J. J. (2010). Perfectionism and burnout in canoe polo and kayak slalom athletes: The mediating influences of validation and growth seeking. *The Sport Psychologist, 24,* 16–34.

Hill, D. M., Hanton, S., Matthews, N., & Fleming, S. (2010). A qualitative exploration of choking in elite golf. *Journal of Clinical Sport Psychology, 4,* 221–240.

Hill, K. L., & Borden, F. (1995). The effect of attentional cueing scripts on competitive bowling performance. *International Journal of Sport Psychology, 26,* 503–512.

Hillman, C. H., Castelli, D. M., & Buck, S. M. (2005). Aerobic fitness and neurocognitive function in healthy preadolescent children. *Medicine & Science in Sports & Exercise, 37,* 1967–1974.

Hinshaw, K. E. (1991). The effects of mental practice on motor skill performance: Critical evaluation and meta-analysis. *Imagination, Cognition, and Personality, 11,* 3–35.

Hird, J. S., Landers, D. M., Thomas, J. R., & Horan, J. J. (1991). Physical practice is superior to mental practice in enhancing cognitive and motor task performance. *Journal of Sport & Exercise Performance, 13,* 281–293.

Hodge, K., Lonsdale, C., & Jackson, S. A. (2009). Athlete engagement in elite sport: An exploratory investigation of antecedents and consequences. *The Sport Psychologist, 23,* 186–202.

Hodge, K., & Petlichkoff, L. (2000). Goal profiles in sport motivation: A cluster analysis. *Journal of Sport & Exercise Psychology, 22,* 256–272.

Hollander, D. B., & Acevedo, E. O. (2000). Successful English Channel swimming: The peak experience. *The Sport Psychologist, 14,* 1–16.

Hollander, E. P. (1976). *Principles and methods of social psychology* (3rd ed.). New York, NY: Oxford University Press.

Holland, M. J. G., Woodcock, C., Cumming, J., & Duda, J. L. (2010). Mental qualities and employed mental techniques of young elite team sport athletes. *Journal of Clinical Sport Psychology, 4,* 19–38.

Hollembeak, J., & Amorose, A. J. (2005). Perceived coaching behaviors and college athletes' intrinsic motivation: A test of self-determination theory. *Journal of Applied Sport Psychology, 17,* 20–36.

Holliday, B., Burton, D., Sun, G., Hammermeister, J., Naylor, S., & Freigang, D. (2008). Building the better mental training mousetrap: Is periodization a more systematic approach to promoting performance excellence? *Journal of Applied Sport Psychology, 20,* 199–219.

Holmbeck, G. N. (1997). Toward terminological, conceptual, and statistical clarity in the study of mediators and moderators: Examples from the child-clinical and pediatric psychology literatures. *Journal of Counseling and Clinical Psychology, 65,* 599–610.

Holmes, P. S., & Collins, D. J. (2001). The PETTLEP approach to motor imagery: A functional equivalence model for sport psychologists. *Journal of Applied Sport Psychology, 13,* 60–83.

Holsopple, J. Q., & Miale, F. R. (1954). *Sentence completion.* Springfield, IL: Charles C. Thomas.

Holt, N. L., Berg, K.-J., & Tamminen, K. A. (2007). Tales of the unexpected: Coping among female collegiate volleyball players. *Research Quarterly, 78,* 117–132.

Holt, N. L., Black, D. E., Tamminen, K. A., Fox, K. R., & Mandigo, J. L. (2008). Levels of social complexity and dimensions of peer experiences in youth sport. *Journal of Sport & Exercise Psychology, 30,* 392–410.

Holt, N. L., & Dunn, G. H. (2006). Guidelines for delivering personal-disclosure mutual–sharing team building interventions. *The Sport Psychologist, 20,* 348–367.

Holt, N. L., & Hogg, J. M. (2002). Perceptions of stress and coping during preparations for the 1999 Women's Soccer World Cup finals. *The Sport Psychologist, 16,* 251–271.

Holt, N. L., Tamminen, K. A., Black, D. E., Mandigo, J. L., & Fox, K. R. (2009). Youth sport parenting styles and practices. *Journal of Sport & Exercise Psychology, 31,* 37–59.

Holt, N. L., Tamminen, K. A., Black, D. E., Sehn, Z. L., & Wall, M. P. (2008). Parental involvement in competitive youth sport settings. *Psychology of Sport and Exercise, 9,* 663–685.

hooks, b. (2000). *Feminism is for everybody: Passionate politics.* Cambridge, MA: South End Press.

Hooper, S. L., & MacKinnon, L. T. (1995). Monitoring overtraining in athletes: Recommendations. *Sports Medicine, 20,* 321–327.

Hopkins, T., & Magel, Rhonda, C. (2008). Slugging percentage in differing baseball counts. *Journal of Quantitative Analysis in Sports, 4,* Article 2.

Horn, T. S. (1984). Expectancy effects in the interscholastic athletic setting: Methodological considerations. *Journal of Sport Psychology, 6,* 60–76.

Horne, T., & Carron, A. V. (1985). Compatibility in coach-athlete relationships. *Journal of Sport Psychology, 7,* 137–149.

House, R. J., & Mitchell, T. R. (1974, Autumn). Path-goal theory of leadership. *Journal of Contemporary Business, 5,* 81–97.

Hoyt, A. L., Rhodes, R. E., Hausenblas, H. A., & Giacobbi, P. R., Jr. (2009). Integrating five-factor model facet-level traits with the theory of planned behavior and exercise. *Psychology of Sport and Exercise, 10,* 565–572.

Hrycaiko, D. W., & Martin, G. L. (1996). Applied research studies with single-subject designs: Why so few? *Journal of Applied Sport Psychology, 8,* 183–199.

Huberty, J. L., Ransdell, L. B., Sidman, C., Flohr, J. A., Shultz, B., Grosshans, O., & Durrant, L. (2008). Explaining long-term exercise adherence in women who complete a structured exercise program. *Research Quarterly for Exercise and Sport, 79,* 374–384.

Hudson, J., & Bates, M. D. (2000). Factors affecting reversals: A laboratory study. *Perceptual and Motion Skills, 91,* 373–384.

Hudson, J., & Walker, N. C. (2002). Metamotivational state reversals during matchplay golf: An idiographic approach. *The Sport Psychologist, 16,* 200–217.

Hughes, S. L., Case, H. S., Stuempfle, K. J., & Evans, D. S. (2003). Personality profiles of Iditasport Ultra-marathon participants. *Journal of Applied Sport Psychology, 15,* 256–261.

Hull, C. L. (1943). *Principles of behavior.* New York: Appleton-Century-Crofts, Inc.

Hull, C. L. (1951). *Essentials of behavior.* New Haven, CT: Yale University Press.

Hulley, A., Currie, A., Njenga, F., & Hill, A. (2007). Eating disorders in elite female distance runners: Effects of nationality and running environment. *Psychology of Sport and Exercise, 8,* 521–533.

Husak, W. S., & Hemenway, D. P. (1986). The influence of competition day practice on the activation and performance of collegiate swimmers. *Journal of Sport Behavior, 9,* 95–100.

Hutchinson, J. C., & Tenenbaum, G. (2007). Attentional focus during physical effort: The mediating role of task intensity. *Psychology of Sport and Exercise, 8,* 233–245.

I

Imlay, G. J., Carda, R. D., Stanbrough, M. E., Dreiling, A. M., & O'Connor, P. J. (1995). Anxiety and athletic performance: A test of Zone of Optimal Functioning theory. *International Journal of Sport Psychology, 26,* 295–306.

Ironson, G., LaPerriere, A., Antoni, M., Klimas, N., Fletcher, M. A., & Schneiderman, N. (1990). Changes in immunologic and psychological measures as a function of anticipation and reaction to news of HIV–1 antibody status. *Psychosomatic Medicine, 52,* 247–270.

Is it safe? (2000, December 19). Androstenedione (made famous by baseball's Mark McGuire)—Is it safe? *Columbia University's Health Education Fitness Nutrition Web-page* (www.goaskalice .columbia.edu/1385).

Isaac, A., Marks, D. F., & Russell, D. G. (1986). An instrument for assessing imagery of movement: The vividness of movement imagery questionnaire (VMIQ). *Journal of Mental Imagery, 10,* 23–30.

Isaacs, P. (1982). *Hypnotic responsiveness and dimensions of thinking style and imagery.* Unpublished doctoral dissertation, University of Waterloo, Waterloo, Ontario.

Ito, M. (1979). The differential effects of hypnosis and motivational suggestions on muscular strength. *Japanese Journal of Physical Education, 24,* 93–100.

J

Jackson, B., & Beauchamp, M. R. (2010). Self-efficacy as a meta-perception within coach–athlete and athlete–athlete relationships. *Psychology of Sport and Exercise, 11,* 188–196.

Jackson, B., Knapp, P., & Beauchamp, M. R. (2009). The coach–athlete relationship: A tripartite efficacy perspective. *The Sport Psychologist, 23,* 203–232.

Jackson, P., & Delehanty, H. (1995). *Sacred hoops.* New York: Hyperion.

Jackson, R. C., Ashford, K. J., & Norsworthy, G. (2006). Attentional focus, dispositional reinvestment, and skilled motor performance under pressure. *Journal of Sport & Exercise Psychology, 28,* 49–68.

Jackson, S. A. (1995). Factors influencing the occurrence of flow state in elite athletes. *Journal of Applied Sport Psychology, 7,* 138–166.

Jackson, S. A., & Eklund, R. C. (2002). Assessing flow in physical activity: The Flow State Scale-2 and Dispositional Flow Scale-2, *Journal of Sport and Educational Psychology, 24,* 133–150.

Jackson, S. A., Ford, S. K., Kimiecik, J. G., & Marsh, H. W. (1998). Psychological correlates of flow in sport. *Journal of Sport & Exercise Psychology, 20,* 358–378.

Jackson, S. A., Martin, A. J., & Eklund, R. C. (2008). Long and short measures of flow: The construct validity of the FSS–2, DFS–2, and new brief counterparts. *Journal of Sport & Exercise Psychology, 30,* 561–587.

Jacobi, J. (1973). *The psychology of C. J. Jung.* New Haven, CT: Yale University Press.

Jacobson, E. (1929). *Progressive relaxation* (1st ed.). Chicago, IL: University of Chicago Press.

Jacobson, E. (1938). *Progressive relaxation* (2d ed.). Chicago, IL: University of Chicago Press.

Jago, R. P., Brockman, J. R., Fox, K. R., Cartwright, K., Page, A. S., & Thompson, J. L. (2009). Friendship groups and physical activity: Qualitative findings on how physical activity is initiated and maintained among 10–11 year old children. *International Journal of Behavioral Nutrition and Physical Activity, 6* (Article 4, http://www.ijbnpa.org/).

Jakicic, J. M., Winters, C., Lang, W., & Wing, R. R. (1999, October 27). Effects of intermittent exercise and use of home exercise equipment on adherence, weight loss, and fitness in overweight women. *Journal of American Medical Association, 282,* 1554–1560.

James, W. (1890). *The principles of psychology* (Vol. 1). New York: Henry Holt and Company.

Janelle, C. M., Singer, R. N., & Williams, A. M. (1999). External distraction and attentional narrowing: Visual search evidence. *Journal of Sport & Exercise Psychology, 21,* 70–91.

Janssen, J. J., & Sheikh, A. A. (1994). Enhancing athletic performance through imagery: An overview. In A. A. Sheikh & E. R. Korn (Eds.), *Imagery in sports and physical performance.* Amityville, NY: Baywood.

Jeannerod, M. (1995). Mental imagery in the motor context. *Neuropsychologia, 33,* 1419–1432.

Jedlic, B., Hall, N., Munroe-Chandler, K., & Hall, C. (2007). Coaches' encouragement of athletes' imagery use. *Research Quarterly for Exercise and Sport, 78,* 351–363.

Jenkins, L. (2008, July 14). Jim Abbott one-handed wonder. *Sports Illustrated, 109,* 102–104.

Jerome, G. J., & Williams, J. M. (2000). Intensity and interpretation of competitive state anxiety: Relationship to performance and repressive coping. *Journal of Applied Sport Psychology, 12,* 236–250.

Johnson, J. J. M., Hrycaiko, D. W., Johnson, G. V., & Halas, J. M. (2004). Self-talk and female youth soccer performance. *The Sport Psychologist, 18,* 44–59.

Johnson, M. B., Edmonds, W. A., Kamato, A., & Tenenbaum, G. (2009). Determining individual affect-related performance zones (IAPZs): A tutorial. *Journal of Clinical Sport Psychology, 3,* 34–57.

Johnson, M. B., Edmonds, W. A., Moraes, L. C., Filho, E. S. M., & Tenenbaum, G. (2007). Affect and performance of an international level archer: Incorporating an idiosyncratic probabilistic method. *Psychology of Sport and Exercise, 8,* 317–335.

Johnson, M. B., Edmonds, W. A., Tenenbaum, G., & Kamata, A. (2007). The relationship between affect and performance in competitive collegiate tennis: A dynamic conceptualization and application. *Journal of Clinical Sport Psychology, 1,* 130–146.

Johnson, S. R., Ostrow, A. C., Perna, F. M., & Etzel, E. F. (1997). The effects of group versus individual goal setting on bowling performance. *The Sport Psychologist, 11,* 190–200.

Johnson, U., Ekengren, J., & Andersen, M. B. (2005). Injury prevention in Sweden: Helping soccer players at risk. *Journal of Sport & Exercise Psychology, 27,* 32–38.

Johnson, W. O., & Moore, K. (1988, October 3). The loser. *Sports Illustrated, 69,* 20–27.

Johnson, W. R. (1961). Hypnosis and muscular performance. *Journal of Sports Medicine and Physical Fitness, 1,* 71–79.

Jones, E. E., & Rhodewalt, F. (1982). *The Self-handicapping scale.* Unpublished manuscript, Department of Psychology, Princeton Press.

Jones, G. (1991). Recent developments and current issues in competitive state anxiety research. *The Psychologist: Bulletin of the British Psychological Society, 4,* 152–155.

Jones, G. (2002). Performance excellence: A personal perspective on the link between sport and business. *Journal of Applied Sport Psychology, 14,* 268–281.

Jones, G., & Cale, A. (1989). Precompetition temporal patterning of anxiety and self-confidence in males and females. *Journal of Sport Behavior, 12,* 183–195.

Jones, G., & Hanton, S. (1996). Interpretation of competitive anxiety symptoms and goal attainment expectancies. *Journal of Sport & Exercise Psychology, 18,* 144–157.

Jones, G., Hanton, S., & Connaughton, D. (2002). What is this thing called mental toughness? An investigation of elite sport performers. *Journal of Applied Sport Psychology, 14,* 205–218.

Jones, G., Hanton, S., & Connaughton, D. (2007). A framework of mental toughness in the world's best performers. *The Sport Psychologist, 21,* 243–264.

Jones, G., Hanton, S., & Swain, A. (1994). Intensity and interpretation of anxiety symptoms in elite and non-elite sports performers. *Personality & Individual Differences, 17,* 657–663.

Jones, M. I., & Harwood, C. (2008). Psychological momentum within competitive soccer: Players' perspectives. *Journal of Applied Sport Psychology, 20,* 57–72.

Jones, G., Swain, A., & Cale, A. (1991). Gender differences in precompetition temporal patterning and antecedents of anxiety and self-confidence. *Journal of Sport & Exercise Psychology, 13,* 1–15.

Jones, G., & Swain, A. B. J. (1992). Intensity and direction dimensions of competitive state anxiety and relationships with competitiveness. *Perceptual and Motor Skills, 74,* 467–472.

Jones, G., & Swain, A. (1995). Predispositions to experience debilitative and facilitative anxiety in elite and nonelite performers. *The Sport Psychologist, 9,* 201–211.

Jones, M. V. (2003). Controlling emotions in sport. *The Sport Psychologist, 17,* 471–486.

Jones, M. V., Lane, A. M., Bray, S. R., Uphill, M., & Catlin, J. (2005). Development and validation of the Sport Emotion Questionnaire. *Journal of Sport & Exercise Psychology, 27,* 407–431.

Jordan, M. (1994). *I can't accept not trying.* New York: Harper Collins Publishers.

Jordet, G. (2005). Perceptual training in soccer: An imagery intervention study with elite players. *Journal of Applied Sport Psychology, 17,* 140–156.

Jordet, G. (2009). When superstars flop: Public status and choking under pressure in international soccer penalty shootouts. *Journal of Applied Sport Psychology, 21,* 125–130.

Jowdy, D. P., & Harris, D. V. (1990). Muscular responses during mental imagery as a function of motor skill level. *Journal of Sport & Exercise Psychology, 12,* 191–201.

Jowett, S. (2003). When the "honeymoon" is over: A case study of a coach-athlete dyad in crisis. *The Sport Psychologist, 17,* 444–460.

Jowett, S. (2006). Interpersonal and structural features of Greek coach-athlete dyads performing in individual sports. *Journal of Applied Sport Psychology, 18,* 69–81.

Jowett, S., & Ntoumanis, N. (2003). The Greek Coach–Athlete Relationship Questionnaire (GrCART–Q): Scale development and validation. *International Journal of Sport Psychology, 34,* 101–124.

Jowett, S., & Ntoumanis, N. (2004). The Coach–Athlete Relationship Questionnaire (CART–Q): Development and initial validation. *Scandinavian Journal of Medicine & Science in Sports, 14,* 245–257.

Jowett, S., & Timson-Katches, M. (2005). Social networks in sport: Parental influence on the coach-athlete relationship. *The Sport Psychologist, 19,* 267–287.

K

Kahn, R. I., & Katz, D. (1960). Leadership practices in relation to productivity and morale. In D. Cartwright & A.T. Zander (Eds.), *Group dynamics.* Evanston, IL: Row, Peterson and Company.

Kalat, J. W. (1999). *Introduction to psychology.* Pacific Grove, CA: Brooks/Cole Wadsworth.

Kamata, A., Tenenbaum, G., & Hanin, Y. L. (2002). Individual zone of optimal functioning (IZOF): A probabilistic estimation. *Journal of Sport and Exercise Psychology, 24,* 189–208.

Kamm, R. L. (2008). Diagnosing emotional disorders in athletes: A sport psychologist's perspective. *Journal of Clinical Sport Psychology, 2,* 178–201.

Kamphoff, C. S., Gill, D. L., & Huddleston, S. (2005). Jealousy in sport: Exploring jealousy's relationship to cohesion. *Journal of Applied Sport Psychology, 17,* 290–305.

Kane, J. E. (1970). Personality and physical abilities. In G. S. Kenyon (Ed.), *Contemporary psychology of sport: Second International Congress of Sports Psychology.* Chicago: The Athletic Institute.

Kanters, M. A., & Casper, J. (2008). Supported or pressure? An examination of agreement among parents and children on parents' role in youth sport. *Journal of Sport Behavior, 31,* 64–68.

Karageorghis, C. I., Moujourides, D. A., Priest, D.-L., Sasso, T. A., Morrish, D. J., & Walley, C. L. (2009). Psychophysical and ergogenic effects of synchronous music during treadmill walking. *Journal of Sport & Exercise Psychology, 31,* 3–17.

Karteroliotis, C., & Gill, D. L. (1987). Temporal changes in psychological and physiological components of state anxiety. *Journal of Sport Psychology, 9,* 261–274.

Kaufman, K. A., Glass, C. R., & Arnkoff, D. B. (2009). Evaluation of mindfulness sport performance enhancement (MSPE): A new approach to promote flow in athletes. *Journal of Clinical Sport Psychology, 3,* 334–356.

Kaufman, M. (2006, October 1). Pound's goal: Curtail cheating. *The Miami Herald*, 2D.

Kavussanu, M., & Boardley, I. D. (2009). The prosocial and antisocial behavior in sport scale. *Journal of Sport & Exercise Psychology, 31*, 97–117.

Kavussanu, M., Boardley, I. D., Jutkiewicz, N., Vincent, S., & Ring, C. (2008). Coaching efficacy and coaching effectiveness: Examining their predictors and comparing coaches' and athletes' reports. *The Sport Psychologist, 22*, 383–404.

Kavussanu, M., & Ntoumanis, N. (2003). Participation in sport and moral functioning: Does ego orientation mediate their relationship? *Journal of Sport & Exercise Psychology, 25*, 501–518.

Kavussanu, M., & Roberts, G. C. (2001). Moral functioning in sport: An achievement goal perspective. *Journal of Sport & Exercise Psychology, 23*, 37–54.

Kavussanu, M., Roberts, G. C., & Ntoumanis, N. (2002). Contextual influences on moral functioning of college basketball players. *The Sport Psychologist, 16*, 347–367.

Kavussanu, M., Stamp, R., Slade, G., & Ring, C. (2009). Observed prosocial and antisocial behaviors in male and female soccer players. *Journal of Applied Sport Psychology, 21 (Supp. 1)*, S62–S76.

Kawabata, M., Mallett, C. J., & Jackson, S. A. (2008). The Flow State-2 and Dispositional Flow Scale-2: Examination of factorial validity and reliability for Japanese adults. *Psychology of Sport and Exercise, 9*, 465–485.

Kay, J. (1988, June 30). Trouble in river city: Players can't cite reason for Red's poor play. *Muncie Evening Press*, 15.

Kee, Y. A., & Wang, C. K. J. (2008). Relationship between mindfulness, flow dispositions, and mental skill adoption: A cluster analytic approach. *Psychology of Sport and Exercise, 9*, 393–411.

Keegan, R., Spray, C., Harwood, C., & Lavallee, D. (2010). The motivational atmosphere in youth sport: Coach, parent, and peer influences on motivation in specializing sport participants. *Journal of Applied Sport Psychology, 22*, 87–105.

Keele, S. W. (1973). *Attention and human performance*. Pacific Palisades, CA: Goodyear Publishing Company.

Keele, S. W., & Hawkins, H. (1982). Exploration of individual differences relevant to high level skill. *Journal of Motor Behavior, 14*, 3–23.

Kellman, M., Altenburg, D., Lormes, W., & Steinacker, J. M. (2001). Assessing stress and recovery during preparation for the world championships in rowing. *The Sport Psychologist. 15*, 151–167.

Kellman, M., & Kallus, K. W. (2001). *The Recovery-Stress Questionnaire for Athletes: User Manual*. Champaign, IL: Human Kinetics.

Kendzierski, D. (1988). Self-schemata and exercise. *Basic and Applied Social Psychology, 9*, 45–61.

Kendzierski, D. (1990). Exercise self-schemata: Cognitive and behavioral correlates. *Health Psychology, 9*, 69–82.

Kendzierski, D. (October 2004). *Physical activity self-definitions: Research, issues, and implications*. Keynote address presented at the annual convention of the Association for the Advancement of Applied Sport Psychology, Minneapolis, MN, October, 2004.

Kendzierski, D., Furr, R. M., Jr., & Schiavoni, J. (1998). Physical activity self-definitions: Correlates and perceived criteria. *Journal of Sport and Exercise Psychology, 20*, 176–193.

Kendzierski, D., & Sheffield, A. (2000). Self-schema and attributions for an exercise laps. *Basic and Applied Social Psychology, 22*, 1–8.

Kendzierski, D., Sheffield, A., & Morganstein, M. S. (2002). The role of self-schema in attributions for own versus other's exercise laps. *Basic and Applied Social Psychology, 24*, 251–260.

Kennett, D. J., Worth, N. C., & Forbes, C. A. (2009). The contributions of Rosenbaum's model of self-control and the trans-theoretical model to the understanding of exercise behavior. *Psychology of Sport and Exercise, 10*, 602–608.

Kenntner-Mabiala, R., Gorges, S., Alpers, G. W., Lehmann, A. C., & Pauli, P. (2007). Musically induced arousal affects pain perception in females but not males: A psychological examination. *Biological Psychology, 75*, 19–23.

Kenow, L. J., & Williams, J. M. (1992). Relationship between anxiety, self-confidence, and the evaluation of coaching behaviors. *The Sport Psychologist, 6*, 344–357.

Kenow, L. J., & Williams, J. M. (1999). Coach-athlete compatibility and athlete's perception of coaching behaviors. *Journal of Sport Behavior, 22*, 251–259.

Kepner, T. (2003, October 7). If pitching is the key Yankees like chances. *The New York Times*, Retrieved from http://www .nytimes.com/2003/10/7

Kepner, T. (2004, October 19). Even longer: Red Sox win game 5 in 14 innings. *The New York Times*, Retrieved from http://www.nytimes.com/2004/10/19/sports/baseball/19yankees.html?

Kepner, T. (2005, January 14). Baseball players and owners set though policy on steroid use. *The New York Times*, Retrieved from http://www.nytimes.com/2005/1/14/sports/baseball

Kerick, S. E., Iso-Ahola, S. E., & Hatfield, B. D. (2000). Psychological momentum in target shooting: Cortical, cognitive-affective, and behavioral responses. *Journal of Sport & Exercise Psychology, 22*, 1–20.

Kerr, G., & Goss, J. (1996). The effects of a stress management program on injuries and stress levels. *Journal of Applied Sport Psychology, 8*, 109–117.

Kerr, G., & Leith, L. (1993). Stress management and athletic performance. *The Sport Psychologist, 7*, 221–231.

Kerr, G., Berman, E., DeSouza, M. J. (2006). Disordered eating in women's gymnastics: Perspectives of athletes, coaches, parents, and judges. *Journal of Applied Sport Psychology, 18*, 28–43.

Kerr, J. H. (1997). *Motivation and emotion in sport: Reversal theory*. East Sussex, United Kingdom: Psychology Press Ltd.

Kerr, J. H. (2007). Sudden withdrawal from sky diving: A case study informed by reversal theory's protective frames. *Journal of Applied Sport Psychology, 19*, 337–351.

Kerr, J. H., & Vlaswinkel, E. H. (1995). Sports participation at work: An aid to stress management. *International Journal of Stress Management, 2*, 87–96.

Kerr, J., Norman, G. J., Sallis, J. F., & Patrick, K. (2008). Exercise aids neighborhood safety, and physical activity in adolescents and parents. *Medicine and Science in Sports and Exercise, 40*, 1244–1248.

Keys, S., Tyminski, M., Davis, J., Bacon, C., Bengiovanni, J., & Hossain, A. (2001, May). The effects of long-term creatine supplementation on liver architecture in mice. *Medicine & Science in Sports & Exercise, 33*, S206, Abstract 1162.

Khawaja, N. G., Armstrong, K. A. (2005). Factor structure and psychometric properties of the Frost Multidimensional Perfectionism Scale: Developing shorter versions using an Australian sample. *Australian Journal of Psychology, 57*, 129–138.

Kilpatrick, M., Bartholomew, J., & Reimer, H. (2003). The measurement of goal orientations in exercise. *Journal of Sport Behavior, 26*, 121–136.

Kim, M. S., & Duda, J. L. (2003). The coping process: Cognitive appraisals of stress, coping strategies, and coping effectiveness. *The Sport Psychologist, 17*, 406–425.

Kim, M. Y., & Sugiyama, Y. (1992). The relation of performance norms and cohesiveness for Japanese school athletic teams. *Perceptual and Motor Skills, 74,* 1096–1098.

Kimiecik, J. C., & Horn, T. S. (1998). Parental beliefs and children's moderate-to-vigorous physical activity. *Research Quarterly for Exercise and Sport, 69,* 163–175.

King, L. A., & Williams, T. A. (1997). Goal orientation and performance in martial arts. *Journal of Sport Behavior, 20,* 297–411.

King, P. (2002, August 5). Inside the NFL. *Sports Illustrated, 97,* 68–69.

Kingston, K., Lane, A., & Thomas, O. (2010). A temporal examination of elite performers sources of sport confidence. *The Sport Psychologist, 18,* 313–332.

Kingston, K. M., & Hardy, L. (1997). Effects of different types of goals on processes that support performance. *The Sport Psychologist, 11,* 277–293.

Kirker, B., Tenenbaum, G., & Mattson, J. (2000). An investigation of the dynamics of aggression: Direct observation in ice hockey and basketball. *Research Quarterly for Exercise and Sport, 71,* 373–386.

Kirsch, I., & Lynn, S. J. (1995). The altered state of hypnosis. *American Psychologist, 50,* 846–858.

Kirsch, I., & Lynn, S. J. (1998). Dissociation theories of hypnosis. *Psychological Bulletin, 123,* 100–115.

Kiviniemi, M. T., Voss-Humke, A. M., & Seifert, A. L. (2007). How do I feel about the behavior? The interplay of affective associations with behaviors and cognitive beliefs as influences on physical behavior. *Health Psychology, 26,* 152–158.

Klavora, P. (1978). An attempt to derive inverted-U curves based on the relationship between anxiety and athletic performance. In D. M. Landers & R. W. Christina (Eds.), *Psychology of motor behavior and sport—1977* (pp. 369–377). Champaign, IL: Human Kinetics Publishers.

Kleiber, D., & Brock, S. (1992). The effect of career-ending injuries on the subsequent well-being of elite college athletes. *Sociology of Sport Journal, 9,* 70–75.

Knight, J. L., & Giuliano, T. A. (2003). Blood, sweat and jeers: The impact of the media's heterosexist portrayals on perceptions of male and female athletes. *Journal of Sport Behavior, 26,* 272–384.

Knott, P. D., & Drost, B. A. (1972). Effects of varying intensity of attack and fear arousal on the intensity of counteraggression. *Journal of Personality, 4,* 27–37.

Koehler, J. J., & Conley, C. A. (2003). The "hot hand" myth in professional basketball. *Journal of Sport & Exercise Psychology, 25,* 253–259.

Koka, A., & Hagger, M. S. (2010). Perceived teaching behaviors and self-determined motivation in physical education: A test of self-determined theory. *Research Quarterly for Exercise and Sport, 81,* 74–86.

Kolonay, B. J. (1977). *The effects of visuo-motor behavior rehearsal on athletic performance.* Unpublished master's thesis, Hunter College, New York.

Kontos, A. P., & Breland-Noble, A. M. (2002). Racial/ethnic diversity in applied sport psychology: A multicultural introduction to working with athletes of color. *The Sport Psychologist, 16,* 296–315.

Kornspan, A. S. (2007). The early years of sport psychology: The work and influence of Pierre de Coubertin. *Journal of Sport Behavior, 30,* 77–93.

Kosma, M., Ellis, R., Cardinal, B. J., Bauer, J. J., & McCubbin, J. A. (2007). The mediating role of intention and stages of change in physical activity among adults with disabilities: An integrative framework. *Journal of Sport & Exercise Psychology, 29,* 21–38.

Kowal, J., & Fortier, M. S. (2000). Testing relationships from the hierarchical model of intrinsic and extrinsic motivation using flow as a motivational consequence. *Research Quarterly for Exercise and Sport, 71,* 171–181.

Kowalski, K. C., & Crocker, P. R. E. (2001). Development and validation of the coping function questionnaire for adolescents in sport. *Journal of Sport and Exercise Psychology, 23,* 136–155.

Kowalski, N. P., Crocker, P. R. E., & Kowalski, K. C. (2001). Physical self and physical activity relationships in college women: Does social physique anxiety moderate effects? *Research Quarterly for Exercise and Sport, 72,* 55–62.

Kozub, S. A., & Button, C. J. (2000). The influence of a competitive outcome on perceptions of cohesion in rugby and swimming teams. *International Journal of Sport Psychology, 31,* 82–95.

Kozub, S. B., & McDonnell, J. F. (2000). Exploring the relationship between cohesion and collective efficacy in rugby teams. *Journal of Sport Behavior, 23,* 120–129.

Kramer, J. (1970). *Lombardi: Winning is the only thing.* New York: The World Publishing Company.

Krane, V. (2001). One lesbian feminist epistemology: Integrating feminist standpoint, queer theory, and feminist cultural studies. *The Sport Psychologist, 15,* 401–411.

Krane, V., & Barber, H. (2005). Identity tensions in lesbian intercollegiate coaches. *Research Quarterly for Exercise and Sport, 76,* 67–81.

Krane, V., Joyce, D., & Rafeld, J. (1994). Competitive anxiety, situation criticality, and softball performance. *The Sport Psychologist, 8,* 58–72.

Krane, V., & Whaley, D. E. (2010). Quiet competence: Writing women into the history of U.S. sport and exercise psychology. *The Sport Psychologist, 18,* 349–372.

Krane, V., & Williams, J. M. (2010). Psychological characteristics of peak performance. In J. M. Williams (Ed.), *Applied sport psychology: Personal growth to peak performance* (pp. 169–220). Boston: McGraw-Hill.

Kreider, R., Melton, C., Rasmussen, C., Greenwood, M., Cantler, E., Milnor, P., & Almanda, A. (2001, May). Effects of long-term creatine supplementation on renal function and muscle liver enzyme efflux. *Medicine & Science in Sports & Exercise, 33,* S207, Abstract 1163.

Kroll, W. (1967). Sixteen personality factor profiles of collegiate wrestlers. *Research Quarterly, 38,* 49–57.

Kroll, W., & Carlson, R. B. (1967). Discriminant function and hierarchical grouping analysis of karate participants' personality profiles. *Research Quarterly, 38,* 405–411.

Kroll, W., & Crenshaw, W. (1970). Multivariate personality profile analysis of four athletic groups. In G. S. Kenyon (Ed.), *Contemporary psychology of sport: Second International Congress of Sport Psychology* (pp. 97–106). Chicago: The Athletic Institute.

Kubitz, K. A., & Landers, D. M. (1993). The effects of aerobic training on cardiovascular responses to mental stress: An examination of underlying mechanisms. *Journal of Sport & Exercise Psychology, 15,* 326–337.

Kuennen, M. R., & Waldren, J. J. (2007). Relationships between specific personality traits, fat free mass indices, and the Muscle Dysmorphia Inventory. *Journal of Sport Behavior, 30,* 453–470.

Kunzell, S., & Muller, J. (2008). The use of bigfoots reduces state anxiety in novice skiers. *Journal of Applied Sport Psychology, 20,* 253–260.

Kyllo, L. B., & Landers, D. M. (1995). Goal setting in sport and exercise: A research synthesis to resolve the controversy. *Journal of Sport & Excerise Psychology, 17,* 117–137.

L

LaBrie, J. W., Grossbard, J. R., & Hummer, J. F. (2009). Normative misperceptions and marijuana use among male and female college athletes. *Journal of Applied Sport Psychology, 21,* S77–S85.

Lacy, A. C., & Darst, P. W. (1984). Evolution of systematic observation instrument: The ASU observation instrument. *Journal of Teaching Physical Education, 3,* 59–66.

LaFontaine, T. P., DiLorenzo, T. M., Frensch, P. A., Stucky-Ropp, R. C., Bargman, E. P., & McDonald, D. G. (1992). Aerobic exercise and mood: A brief review, 1985–1990. *Sports Medicine, 13*(3), 160–170.

Lafreniere, M.-A. K., Jowett, S., Vallerand, R. J., Donahue, E. G., & Lorimer, R. (2008). Passion in sport: On the quality of the coach–athlete relationship. *Journal of Sport & Exercise Psychology, 30,* 541–560.

Lally, P. (2007). Identity and athletic retirement: A prospective study. *Psychology of Sport and Exercise, 8,* 85–99.

Lam, W. K., Maxwell, J. P., & Masters, R. (2009). Analogy learning and the performance of motor skills under pressure. *Journal of Sport & Exercise Psychology, 31,* 337–357.

Lambert, S. M., Moore, D. W., & Dixon, R. S. (1999). Gymnasts in training: The differential effects of self- and coach-set goals as a function of locus of control. *Journal of Applied Sport Psychology, 11,* 72–82.

LaMott, E. E. (1994). *The anterior cruciate ligament injured athlete: The psychological process.* Unpublished doctoral dissertation, University of Minnesota, Minneapolis.

Lampinen, P., Heikkinen, R. L., & Ruoppila, I. (2000). Changes in intensity of physical exercise as predictors of depressive symptoms among older adults: An eight-year follow-up. *Preventive Medicine, 30,* 371–380.

Landers, D. M. (1980). The arousal-performance relationship revisited. *Research Quarterly for Exercise and Sport, 51,* 77–90.

Landers, D. M. (1988, April). *Cognitive states of elite performers: Psychological studies of attention.* Paper presented at the meeting of the American Alliance for Health, Physical Education, Recreation and Dance (Research Consortium Scholar Lecture). Kansas City, MO.

Landers, D. M. (1991). Optimizing individual performance. In D. Druckman & R. A. Bjork (Eds.), *In the mind's eye: Enhancing human performance* (pp. 193–246). Washington, DC: National Academy Press.

Landers, D. M. (1995). Sport psychology: The formative years, 1950–1980. *The Sport Psychologist, 9,* 406–417.

Landers, D. M., & Arent, S. M. (2010). Arousal performance relationships. In J. M. Williams (Ed.), *Applied sport psychology: Personal growth to peak performance* (pp. 221–246). Boston: McGraw-Hill.

Landin, D., & Herbert, E. P. (1999). The influence of self-talk on the performance of skilled female tennis players. *Journal of Applied Sport Psychology, 11,* 263–282.

Landry, J. B., & Solmon, M. A. (2004). African American women's self-determination across the changes of change for exercise. *Journal of Sport and Exercise Psychology, 26,* 457–469.

Lane, A. M., Harwood, C., Terry, P. C., & Karageorghis, C. I. (2004). Confirmatory factor analysis of the Test of Performance Strategies (TOPS) among adolescent athletes. *Journal of Sport Sciences, 22,* 803–812.

Lane, A. M., Nevill, A. M., Bowes, N., & Fox, K. R. (2005). Test–retest stability of the task and ego orientation questionnaire. *Research Quarterly for Exercise and Sport, 76,* 339–346.

Lane, A. M., Sewell, D. F., Terry, P. C., Bertram, D., & Nesti, M. S. (1999). Confirmatory factor analysis of the Competitive State Anxiety Inventory-2. *Journal of Sport Sciences, 17,* 505–512.

Lane, A. M., & Terry, P. C. (2000). The nature of mood: Development of a conceptual model with a focus on depression. *Journal of Applied Sport Psychology, 12,* 16–33.

Lane, A. M., Terry, P. C., Beedie, C. J., Curry, D. A., & Clark, N. (2002). Mood and performance: Test of a conceptual model with focus on depressed mood. *Psychology of Sport & Exercise, 2,* 157–172.

Lansing, R. W., Schwartz, E., & Lindsley, D. B. (1956). Reaction time and EEG activation. *American Psychologist, 11,* 433.

Lantz, C. D., Rhea, D. J., & Cornelius, A. E. (2002). Muscle dysmorphia in elite-level power lifters and body builders: A test of differences within a conceptual model. *Journal of Strength and Conditioning Research, 16,* 649–655.

LaPerriere, A. R., Antonio, M. H., Schneiderman, N., Ironson, G., Klimas, N., Caralis, P., & Fletcher, M. A. (1990). Exercise intervention attenuates emotional distress and natural killer cell decrements following notification of positive serologic status for HIV-1. *Biofeedback and Self-Regulation, 15,* 229–242.

Latham, G. P., & Locke, E. A. (2007). New developments in and directions for goal-setting research. *European Psychologist, 12,* 290–300.

Lauer, L., Gould, D., Roman, N., & Pierce, M. (2010). How parents influence junior tennis players' development: Qualitative narratives. *Journal of Clinical Sport Psychology, 4,* 69–92.

Laure, P., & Binsinger, C. (2007). Doping prevalence among preadolescent athletes: A 4-year follow-up. *British Journal of Sports Medicine, 41,* 660–663.

Laurin, R., Nicolas, M., & Lavallee, D. (2008). Personal goal management intervention and mood states in soccer academics. *Journal of Clinical Sport Psychology, 2,* 57–70.

Lausic, C., Tenebaum, G., Eccles, D., Jeong, A., & Johnson, T. (2009). Intrateam communication and performance in doubles tennis. *Research Quarterly for Exercise and Sport, 80,* 281–290.

Lavallee, D. (2005). The effect of a life development intervention on sports career transition adjustment. *The Sport Psychologist, 19,* 193–202.

Lavallee, D., & Robinson, H. K. (2007). In pursuit of an identity: A qualitative exploration of retirement form women's artistic gymnastics. *Psychology of Sport and Exercise, 8,* 119–141.

Law, B., & Hall, C. (2009). The relationship among skill level, age, and golfers' observational learning use. *The Sport Psychologist, 23,* 42–58.

Law, J., Masters, R., Bray, S. R., Eves, F., & Bardswell, I. (2003). Motor performance as a function of audience affability and metaknowledge. *Journal of Sport and Exercise Psychology, 25,* 484–500.

Lawther, J. D. (1951). *Psychology of coaching.* Englewood Cliffs, NJ: Prentice Hall.

Layden, T. (2009, August 31). Bolt strikes twice. *Sports Illustrated, 111,* 36–39.

Lazuras, L., Barkoukis, V., Rodafinos, A., & Tzorbatzoudis, H. (2010). Predictors of doping intentions in elite-level athletes: A social cognition approach. *Journal of Sport & Exercise Psychology, 32,* 694–710.

Lazarus, R. S. (2000a). How emotions influence performance in competitive sports. *The Sport Psychologist, 14,* 229–252.

Lazarus, R. S. (2000b). Cognitive-motivational-relational theory of emotion. In Y. L. Hanin (Ed.), *Emotions in sport* (39–63). Champaign, IL: Human Kinetics.

Lazarus, R. S., & Folkman, S. (1984). *Stress appraisal and coping.* New York: Springer.

Leary, M. R., & Kowalski, R. M. (1990). Impression management: A literature review and two-component model. *Psychological Bulletin, 107,* 34–47.

Leary, M. R. (1992). Self-presentation processes in exercise and sport. *Journal of Sport and Exercise Psychology, 14,* 339–351.

Lee, M. J., Whitehead, J., & Balchin, N. (2000). The measurement of values in youth sport: Development of the Youth Sport Values Questionnaire. *Journal of Sport & Exercise Psychology, 22,* 307–326.

Lee, M. J., Whitehead, J., Ntoumanis, N., & Hatzigeorgiadis, A. (2008). Relationships among values, achievement orientations, and attitudes in youth sport. *Journal of Sport & Exercise Psychology, 30,* 588–610.

Lee, R. E., Nigg, C. R., DiClemente, C. C., & Courneya, K. S. (2001). Validating motivational readiness for exercise behavior with adolescents. *Research Quarterly for Exercise and Sport, 72,* 401–410.

Lefebvre, L. M., & Passer, M. W. (1974). The effects of game location and importance on aggression in team sport. *International Journal of Sport Psychology, 5*(2), 102–110.

Leffingwell, T. R., Rider, S. P., & Williams, J. M. (2001). Application of the transtheoretical model to psychological skills training. *The Sport Psychologist, 15,* 168–187.

Legrand, F., & Heuze, J. P. (2008). Antidepressant effects associated with trial exercise conditions in participants with depression: A pilot study. *Journal of Sport & Exercise Psychology, 29,* 348–364.

Leith, L. M., & Taylor, A. H. (1990). Psychological aspects of exercise: A decade literature review. *Journal of Sport Behavior, 13*(4), 219–239.

Lemyre, F., Trudel, P., & Durand-Bush, N. (2007). How youth-sport coaches learn to coach. *The Sport Psychologist, 21,* 191–209.

Lemyre, P. N., Roberts, G. C., & Ommundsen, Y. (2002). Achievement goal orientations, perceived ability, and sportspersonship in youth soccer. *Journal of Applied Sport Psychology, 14,* 120–136.

Lemyre, P.-N., Treasure, D. C., & Roberts, G. C. (2006). Influence of variability in motivation and affect on elite athlete burnout susceptibility. *Journal of Sport & Exercise Psychology, 28,* 32–48.

Lenney, E. (1977). Women's self-confidence in achievement situations. *Psychological Bulletin, 84,* 1–13.

Leonard, W. M. III (1989). The "home advantage": The case of the modern Olympics. *Journal of Sport Behavior, 12,* 227–241.

Lerner, R. M., Fisher, C. B., & Weinberg, R. A. (2000). Toward a science for and of the people: Promoting civil society through the application of developmental science. *Child Development, 71,* 11–20.

LeScanff, C., & Taugis, J. (2002). Stress management for police special forces. *Journal of Applied Sport Psychology, 14,* 330–343.

Leslie-Toogood, A., & Martin, G. L., (2003). Do coaches know the mental skills of their athletes? Assessments for volleyball and track. *Journal of Sport Behavior, 26,* 56–68.

LeUnes, A., & Burger, J. (1998). Bibliography of the Profile of Mood States in sport and exercise research, 1971–1998. *Journal of Sport Behavior, 21,* 53–70.

LeUnes, A., & Burger, J. (2000). Profile of mood states research in sport and exercise psychology: Past, present, and future. *Journal of Applied Sport Psychology, 12,* 5–15.

Levy, A. R., Polman, R. C. J., Clough, P. J., Marchant, D. C., & Earle, K. (2006). Mental toughness as a determinant of beliefs, pain, and adherence in sport injury rehabilitation. *Journal of Sport Rehabilitation, 15,* 246–254.

Lewis, B. A., Forsyth, L. H., Pinto, B. M., Bock, B. C., Roberts, M., & Marcus, B. H. (2006). Psychosocial mediators of physical activity in a randomized controlled intervention trial. *Journal of Sport & Exercise Psychology, 28,* 193–204.

Li, F. (1999). The Exercise Motivation Scale: Its multifaceted structure and construct validity. *Journal of Applied Sport Psychology, 11,* 97–115.

Li, K.-K., & Chan, D. K.-S. (2008). Goal conflict and the moderating effects of intention stability in intention-behavior relations: Physical activity among Hong Kong Chinese. *Journal of Sport & Exercise Psychology, 30,* 39–55.

Lidor, R., Blumenstein, B., & Tenenbaum, G. (2007). Psychological aspects of training programs in European basketball: Conceptualization, periodization, and planning. *The Sport Psychologist, 21,* 353–367.

Lidor, R., & Mayan, Z. (2005). Can beginning learners benefit from preperformance routines when serving volleyball? *The Sport Psychologist, 19,* 343–363.

Lidor, R., & Singer, R. N. (2000, September). Teaching performance routines to beginners. *Journal of Physical Education, Recreation & Dance, 71,* 34–36, 52.

Lieber, J. (1991, July 29). Deep scars. *Sports Illustrated, 75*(5), 36–44.

Lind, E., Ekkekakis, P., & Vazou, S. (2008). The affective impact of exercise intention that slightly exceeds the preferred level: "Pain" for no additional "gain." *Journal of Health Psychology, 13,* 464–468.

Lind, E., Joens-Matre, R. R., Ekkekakis, P. (2005). What intensity of physical activity do previously sedentary middle-aged women select? Evidence of a coherent pattern from physiological, perceptual, and affective markers. *Preventive Medicine, 40,* 407–419.

Linsdey, P., Maynard, I., & Thomas, O. (2005). Effects of hypnosis on flow states and cycling performance. *The Sport Psychologist, 19,* 164–177.

Lirgg, C. D. (1991). Gender differences in self-confidence in physical activity: A meta-analysis of recent studies. *Journal of Sport & Exercise Psychology, 13,* 294–310.

Lirgg, C. D., George, T. R., Chase, M. A., & Ferguson, R. H. (1996). Impact of conception of ability and sex-type of task on male and female self-efficacy. *Journal of Sport & Exercise Psychology, 18,* 426–434.

Llobet, J. M. (1999). *Correlation between WPAI scores and coaches' ratings.* Unpublished manuscript. PsyMetrics, Inc., Ft. Lauderdale, FL.

Llosa, L. F., & Wertheim, J. (2008, January 21). Sins of a father. *Sports Illustrated, 108,* 30–34.

Lochbaum, M. R., Karoly, P., & Landers, D. M. (2004). Affect responses to acute bouts of aerobic exercise: A test of opponent-process theory. *Journal of Sport Behavior, 27,* 330–348.

Locke, E. A. (1991). Problems with goal-setting research in sports—and their solution. *Journal of Sport & Exercise Psychology, 8,* 311–316.

Locke, E. A., & Latham, G. P. (1985). The application of goal setting to sports. *Journal of Sports Psychology, 7,* 205–222.

Locke, E. A., & Latham, G. P. (1990). *A theory of goal setting and task performance.* Englewood Cliffs, NJ: Prentice Hall.

Locke, E. A., Shaw, K. M., Saari, L. M., & Latham, G. P. (1981). Goal setting and task performance: 1969–1980. *Psychological Bulletin, 90,* 125–152.

Long, B. C., & Van Stavel, R. (1995). Effects of exercise training on anxiety: A meta-analysis. *Journal of Applied Sport Psychology, 7,* 167–189.

Long, T., Pantaleon, N., Bruant, G., & d'Arripe-Longueville, F. (2006). A qualitative study of moral reasoning of young elite athletes. *The Sport Psychologist, 20,* 330–347.

Longman, J. (2003, November 18). Drugs in sports creating games of illusion. *New York Times,* Retrieved from http://www.nytimes.com/2003/11/18

Longman, J. (2004a, January 26). East German steroids toll: They killed Heidi. *The New York Times,* Retrieved from http://www.nytimes.com

Longman, J. (2004b, December 8). Like Jordan and Ruth, Hamm has a home in sports lore. *The New York Times,* C11, C14.

Lonsdale, C., Hodge, K., & Jackson, S. (2007). Athlete engagement: II. Development and initial validation of the Athlete Engagement Questionnaire. *International Journal of Sport Psychology, 38,* 471–492.

Lonsdale, C., Hodge, K., & Rose, E. A. (2008). The behavioral regulation in sport questionnaire (BRSQ): Instrument development and initial validity evidence. *Journal of Sport & Exercise Psychology, 30,* 323–355.

Lonsdale, C., Sabiston, C. M., Raedeke, T. D., Ha, A. S. C., & Sum, R. K. W. (2009). Self-determined motivation and students' physical activity during structured physical education lessons and free choice periods. *Preventive Medicine, 48,* 69–73.

Lorimer, R., & Jowett, S. (2009a). Empathetic accuracy in coach–athlete dyads who participated in team and individual sports. *Psychology of Sport and Exercise, 10,* 152–158.

Lorimer, R., & Jowett, S. (2009b). Empathetic accuracy, meta-perspective, and satisfaction in the coach–athlete relationship. *Journal of Applied Sport Psychology, 21,* 201–212.

Lorr, M., & McNair, D. M. (1988). *Manual for the Profile of Mood States—Bipolar form.* San Diego, CA: Educational and Industrial Testing Service.

Louvet, B., Gaudreau, P., Menaut, A., Gentry, J., & Deneuve, P. (2007). Longitudinal patterns of stability and change in coping across three competitions: A latent class growth analysis. *Journal of Sport & Exercise Psychology, 29,* 100–117.

Lowe, R. (1973). *Stress, arousal, and task performance of Little League baseball players.* Unpublished doctoral dissertation, University of Illinois, Urbana-Champaign.

Lown, D. A., & Braunschweig, C. L. (2008). Determinants of physical activity in low-income, overweight African American girls. *American Journal of Health Behavior, 32,* 253–259.

Lowther, J., & Lane, A. (2002). Relationship between mood, cohesion and satisfaction with performance among soccer players. *Athletic Insight* (online *Journal of Sport Psychology*), *4,* Retrieved from http://www.athleticinsight.com.vol4Iss3.

Lowther, M., Mutrie, N., & Scott, E. M. (2007). Identifying key processes of exercise behavior change associated with movement through the stages of exercise behavior change. *Journal of Health Psychology, 12,* 261–272.

Lox, C. L., McAuley, E., & Tucker, R. S. (1995). Exercise as an intervention for enhancing subjective well-being in an HIV-1 population. *Journal of Sport & Exercise Psychology, 17,* 345–362.

Loy, J. W., & Sage, J. N. (1970). The effects of formal structure on organizational leadership: An investigation of interscholastic baseball teams. In G. S. Kenyon (Ed.), *Contemporary psychology of sport.* Chicago, IL: The Athletic Institute.

Lubker, J. R., Watson, II, J. C., Visek, A. J., & Geer, J. R. (2005). Physical appearance and the perceived effectiveness of performance enhancement consultants. *The Sport Psychologist, 19,* 446–458.

M

Mace, R. D., & Carroll, D. (1985). The control of anxiety in sport: Stress inoculation training prior to abseiling. *International Journal of Sport Psychology, 16,* 165–175.

Mace, R. D., & Carroll, D. (1986). Stress inoculation training to control anxiety in sport: Two case studies in squash. *British Journal of Sports Medicine, 16,* 115–117.

MacIntyre, T., & Moran, A. P. (2007). A qualitative investigation of meta-imagery processes and imagery direction among elite athletes. *Journal of Imagery Research in Physical Activity, 2,* Article 4.

Mack, M. G., & Stephens, D. E. (2000). An empirical test of Taylor and Demick's multidimensional model of momentum in sport. *Journal of Sport Behavior, 23,* 349–363.

Mack, M. G., Miller, C., Smith, B., Monaghan, B., & German, A. (2008). The development of momentum in a basketball shooting task. *Journal of Sport Behavior, 31,* 254–263.

Mackay, G. J., & Neill, J. T. (2010). The effect of "green exercise" on state anxiety and the role of exercise duration, intensity, and greenness: A quasi-experimental study. *Psychology of Sport and Exercise, 11,* 238–245.

Mackinnon, L. T. (1994). Current challenges and future expectations in exercise immunology: Back to the future. *Medicine and Science in Sports and Exercise, 26,* 191–194.

Mackinnon, L. T. (2000, July). Chronic exercise training effects on immune function. *Medicine & Science in Sports & Exercise, 32,* S369–S376.

MacNamara, A., Button, A., & Collins, D. (2010a). The role of psychological characteristics in facilitating the pathway to elite performance Part 1: Identifying the mental skills and behaviors. *The Sport Psychologist, 24,* 52–73.

MacNamara, A., Button, A., & Collins, D. (2010b). The role of psychological characteristics in facilitating the pathway to elite performance Part 2: Examining environmental and stage related differences in skills and behaviors. *The Sport Psychologist, 24,* 74–96.

Maddison, R., & Prapavessis, H. (2004). Using self-efficacy and intention to predict exercise compliance among patients with ischemic heart disease. *Journal of Sport & Exercise Psychology, 26,* 511–524.

Maddison, R., & Prapavessis, H. (2005). A psychological approach to the prediction and prevention of athletic injury. *Journal of Sport & Exercise Psychology, 27,* 289–310.

Maddux, J. E., & Rogers, R. W. (1983). Protection motivation and self-efficacy: A revised theory of fear appeals and attitude change. *Journal of Experimental Social Psychology, 19,* 469–479.

Madrigal, R., & James, J. (1999). Team quality and the home advantage. *Journal of Sport Behavior, 22,* 381–398.

Maehr, M., & Braskamp, L. (1986). *The motivational factor: A theory of personal investment.* Lexington, MA: Lexington Books.

Maestu, J., Jurimae, J., Kreegipuu, K., & Jurimae, T. (2006). Changes in perceived stress and recovery during heavy training in highly trained male rowers. *The Sport Psychologist, 20,* 1–23.

Maganaris, C. N., Collins, D., & Sharp, M. (2000). Expectancy effects and strength training: Do steroids make a difference? *The Sport Psychologist, 14,* 272–278.

Mageau, G. A., & Vallerand, R. J. (2003). The coach–athlete relationship: A motivational model. *Journal of Sport Sciences, 21,* 883–904.

Magyar, T. M., & Duda, J. L. (2000). Confidence restoration following athletic injury. *The Sport Psychologist, 14,* 372–390.

Magyar, T. M., Feltz, D. L., & Simpson, I. P. (2004). Individual and crew level determinants of collective efficacy in rowing. *Journal of Sport & Exercise Psychology, 26,* 136–153.

Mahoney, M. J., Gabriel, T. J., & Perkins, T. S. (1987). Psychological skills and exceptional athletic performance. *The Sport Psychologist, 1,* 181–199.

Males, J. R., & Kerr, J. H. (1996). Stress, emotion, and performance in elite slalom canoeists. *The Sport Psychologist, 10,* 17–36.

Males, J. R., Kerr, J. H., & Gerkovich, M. M. (1998). Metamotivational states during canoe slalom competition: A qualitative analysis using reversal theory. *Journal of Applied Sport Psychology, 10,* 185–200.

Malete, L., & Feltz, D. L. (2000). The effect of a coaching education program on coaching efficacy. *The Sport Psychologist, 14,* 410–417.

Mallett, C. J. (2005). Self-determination theory: A case study of evidence-based coaching. *The Sport Psychologist, 19,* 417–429.

Mallett, C., Kawabata, M., & Newcombe, P. (2007). Progressing measurement in sport motivation with the SMS–6: A response to Pelletier, Vallerand, and Sarrazin. *Psychology of Sport and Exercise, 8,* 622–631.

Mallett, C., Kawabata, M., Newcombe, P., Otero-Forero, A., & Jackson, S. (2007). Sport motivation scale-6 (SMS-6): A revised six-factor sport motivation scale. *Psychology of Sport and Exercise, 8,* 600–614.

Malmo, R. B. (1959). Activation: A neuropsychological dimension. *Psychological Review, 66,* 367–386.

Malouff, J. M., McGee, J. A., Halford, H. T., & Rooke, S. E. (2008). Effects of pre-competition positive imagery and self-instruction on accuracy of serving in tennis. *Journal of Sport Behavior, 31,* 264–275.

Mamassis, G., & Doganis, G. (2004). The effects of mental training program on juniors' pre-competitive anxiety, self-confidence, and tennis performance. *Journal of Applied Sport Psychology, 16,* 118–137.

Maniar, S. D., Curry, L. A., Sommers-Flanagan, J., Walsh, J. A. (2001). Student-athlete performances in seeking help when confronted with sport performance problems. *The Sport Psychologist, 15,* 205–223.

Mankad, A., Gordon, S., & Wallman, K. (2009a). Perceptions of emotional climate among injured athletes. *Journal of Counseling Sport Psychology, 3,* 1–14.

Mankad, A., Gordon, S., & Wallman, K. (2009b). Psycholinguistic analysis of emotional disclosure: A case study in sport injury. *Journal of Clinical Sport Psychology, 3,* 182–196.

Mankad, A., Gordon, S., & Wallman, K. (2009c). Psycho-immunological effects of written emotional disclosure during long-term injury rehabilitation. *Journal of Clinical Sport Psychology, 3,* 205–217.

Mann, D. T. Y., Williams, A. M., Ward, P., & Janelle, C. M. (2007). Perceptual expertise in sport: A meta-analysis. *Journal of Sport & Exercise Pyschology, 29,* 457–478.

Maraniss, D. (2001, September/October). An elephant ate my baseball. *Modern Maturity, 44W,* 86.

Marcus, B. H., Eaton, C. A., Rossi, J. S., & Harlow, L. L. (1994). Self-efficacy, decision making, and stages of change: An integrative model of physical exercise. *Journal of Applied Social Psychology, 24,* 489–508.

Marcus, B. H., Rossi, J. S., Selby, V. C., Niaura, R. S., & Abrams, D. B. (1992). The stages and processes of exercise adoption and maintenance in a worksite sample. *Health Psychology, 11,* 386–395.

Marcus, B. H., & Simkin, L. R. (1994). The transtheoretical model: Applications to exercise behavior. *Medicine and Science in Sports and Exercise, 26,* 1400–1404.

Markland, D., & Ingledew, D. K. (2007). The relationships between body mass and body image and relative autonomy for exercise among adolescent males and females. *Psychology of Sport and Exercise, 8,* 836–853.

Markland, D., & Tobin, V. (2004). A modification to the Behavioral Regulation in Exercise Questionnaire to include an assessment of amotivation. *Journal of Sport & Exercise Psychology, 26,* 191–196.

Marks, D. F. (1973). Visual imagery differences in recall of pictures. *British Journal of Psychology, 64,* 17–24.

Marks, D. R. (2008). The Buddha's extra scoop: Neural correlates of mindfulness and clinical sport psychology. *Journal of Clinical Sport Psychology, 2,* 216–241.

Markus, H. (1977). Self-schemata and processing information about the self. *Journal of Personality and Social Psychology, 35,* 63–78.

Marsh, H. W., Martin, A. J., & Jackson, S. (2010). Introducing a short version of the Physical Self-Description Questionnaire: New strategies, short-form evaluative criteria, and application of factor analyses. *Journal of Sport & Exercise Psychology, 32,* 438–482.

Marsh, H. W., & Perry, C. (2005). Self-concept contributes to winning gold medals: Causal ordering of self-concept and elite swimming performance. *Journal of Sport & Exercise Psychology, 27,* 71–91.

Marsh, H. W., Richards, G. E., Johnson, S., Roche, L., & Tremayne, P. (1994). Physical Self-Description Questionnaire: Psychometric properties and a multitrait–multimethod analysis of relations to existing instruments. *Journal of Sport & Exercise Psychology, 16,* 270–305.

Martens, M. P., Mobley, M., & Zizzi, S. J. (2000). Multicultural training in applied sport psychology. *The Sport Psychologist, 14,* 81–97.

Martens, M. P., & Webber, S. N. (2002). Psychometric properties of the Sport Motivation Scale: An evaluation with college varsity athletes from the U.S. *Journal of Sport & Exercise Psychology, 24,* 254–270.

Martens, M. P., Dams-O'Connor, K., & Duffy-Paiement, C. (2006). Comparing off-season with in-season alcohol consumption among intercollegiate athletes. *Journal of Sport & Exercise Psychology, 28,* 502–510.

Martens, R. (1975). *Social psychology and physical activity.* New York, NY: Harper & Row.

Martens, R. (1977). *Sport competition anxiety test.* Champaign, IL: Human Kinetics.

Martens, R. (1982). *Sport competition anxiety test.* Champaign, IL: Human Kinetics.

Martens, R. (1987). *American coaching effectiveness program: Level 1 instructor's guide.* Champaign, IL: Human Kinetics.

Martens, R., Burton, D., Vealey, R. S., Bump, L. A., & Smith, D. (1990). Development and validation of the competitive state anxiety inventory-2. In R. Martens, R. S. Vealey, & D. Burton (Eds.), *Competitive anxiety in sport* (pp. 117–190). Champaign, IL: Human Kinetics.

Martens, R., & Landers, D. M. (1970). Motor performance under stress: A test of the inverted-U hypothesis, *Journal of Personality and Social Research, 16,* 29–37.

Martens, R., & Peterson, J. A. (1971). Group cohesiveness as a determinant of success and member satisfaction in team performance. *International Review of Sport Sociology, 6,* 49–61.

Martens, R., Vealey, R. S., & Burton, D. (1990). *Competitive anxiety in sport.* Champaign, IL: Human Kinetics.

Martens-Sanford, T. C., Davidson, M. M., Yakushko, O. F., Martens, M. P., Hinton, P., & Beck, N. (2005). Clinical and subclinical eating disorders: An examination of collegiate athletes. *Journal of Applied Sport Psychology, 17,* 79–86.

Martin, A. J., & Jackson, S. A. (2008). Brief approaches to assessing task absorption and enhanced subjective experience: Examining "short" and "core" flow in diverse performance domains. *Motivation and Emotion, 32,* 141–157.

Martin, J. E., & Calfas, K. J. (1989). Is it possible to lower blood pressure with exercise? Efficacy and adherence issues. *Journal of Applied Sport Psychology, 1*(2), 109–131.

Martin, J. J., & Cutler, K. (2002). An exploratory study of flow and motivation in theater actors. *Journal of Applied Sport Psychology, 14,* 344–352.

Martin, J. J., & McCaughtry, N. (2008). Using social cognitive theory to predict physical activity in inner-city African American school children. *Journal of Sport & Exercise Psychology, 30,* 378–391.

Martin, J. J., Kulinna, P. H., McCaughtry, N., Cothran, D., Dake, J., & Fahoome, G. (2005). The theory of planned behavior: Predicting physical activity and cardiorespiratory fitness in African American children. *Journal of Sport & Exercise Psychology, 27,* 456–469.

Martin, J. J., Oliver, K., & McCaughtry, N. (2007). The theory of planned behavior: Predicting physical activity in Mexican American children. *Journal of Sport & Exercise Psychology, 29,* 225–238.

Martin, J. J., Waldron, J. J., McCabe, A., & Choi, Y. S. (2009). The impact of "girls on the run" on self-concept and fat attitudes. *Journal of Clinical Sport Psychology, 3,* 127–138.

Martin, J. L., Martens, M. P., Serrao, H. F., & Rocha, T. L. (2008). Alcohol use and exercise dependence: Co-occuring behaviors among college students? *Journal of Clinical Sport Psychology, 2,* 381–392.

Martin, K. A., Moritz, S. E., & Hall, C. R. (1999). Imagery use in sport: A literature review and applied model. *The Sport Psychologist, 13,* 245–268.

Martin, K. A., Rejeski, W. J., Leary, M. R., McAuley, E., & Bane, S. (1997). Is the Social Physique Anxiety Scale really multidimensional? Conceptual and statistical arguments for a undimensional model. *Journal of Sport & Exercise Psychology, 19,* 359–367.

Martin, L. A. (1976). Effects of competition upon the aggressive responses of college basketball players and wrestlers. *Research Quarterly, 47,* 388–393.

Martin, M. M., Rocca, K. A., Cayanus, J. L., & Weber, K. (2009). Relationship between coaches' use of behavior alteration techniques and verbal aggression on athletes' motivation and affect. *Journal of Sport Behavior, 32,* 227–241.

Martin, S. B., Jackson, A. W., Richardson, P. A., & Weiller, K. H. (1999). Coaching preferences of adolescent youths and their parents. *Journal of Applied Sport Psychology, 11,* 247–262.

Martinent, G., Ferrand, C., Guillet, E., & Gautheur, S. (2010). Validation of the French version of the Competitive State Anxiety Inventory-2 revised (CSAI-2R) including frequency and direction scales. *Psychology of Sport and Exercise, 11,* 51–57.

Martinent, G., & Ferrand, C. (2009). A naturalistic study of the directional interpretation process of discrete emotions during high-stakes table tennis matches. *Journal of Sport & Exercise Psychology, 31,* 318–336.

Martinsen, E. W., Raglin, J. S., Hoffart, A., & Friis, S. (1998). Tolerance to intensive exercise and high levels of lactate in panic disorder. *Journal of Anxiety Disorders, 12,* 333–342.

Maslach, C., & Jackson, S. (1986). *Maslach Burnout Inventory* (2nd ed.). Palo Alto, CA: Consulting Psychologists Press.

Maslow, A. H. (1970). *Motivation and personality.* New York, NY: Harper & Row.

Maslow, A. H. (1987). *Motivation and personality* (3rd ed.). New York, NY: Harper & Row.

Masters, K. S., & Ogles, B. M. (1998a). Associative and dissociative cognitive strategies in exercise and running: 20 years later, what do we know? *The Sport Psychologist, 12,* 253–270.

Masters, K. S., & Ogles, B. M. (1998b). The relations of cognitive strategies with injury, motivation, and performance among marathon runners: Results from two studies. *Journal of Applied Sport Psychology, 10,* 281–296.

Masters, R. S. W., Polman, R. C. J., & Hammond, N. V. (1993). "Reinvestment": A dimension of personality implicated in skill breakdown under pressure. *Personality and Individual Differences, 14,* 655–666.

Matheson, H., Mathes, S., & Murray, M. (1997). The effect of winning and losing on female interactive and coactive team cohesion. *Journal of Sport Behavior, 20,* 284–298.

Matter, D. (2000, December 17). Sold on Pinkel. *Columbia Daily Tribune,* B1.

Maxwell, J. P., & Moores, E. (2007). The development of a short scale measuring aggressiveness and anger in competitive athletes. *Psychology of Sport and Exercise, 8,* 179–193.

Maxwell, J. P., & Moores, E. (2008). Measuring aggressiveness and anger, but not aggression? A response to the CAAS critique. *Psychology of Sport and Exercise, 9,* 729–733.

Maxwell, J. P., Masters, R. S. W., & Poolton, J. M. (2006). Performance breakdown in sport: The roles of reinvestment and verbal knowledge. *Research Quarterly for Exercise and Sport, 77,* 271–276.

May, J. R. (1986, Summer). Sport psychology: Should psychologists become involved? *The Clinical Psychologist, 39,* 77–81.

Mayer, J. D., & Salovey, P. (1997). What is emotional intelligence? In P. Salovey, & D. Sluyter (Eds.), *Emotional development and emotional intelligence: Implications for educators* (pp. 3–31). New York, NY: Basic Books.

Mayer, J. D., Salovey, P., & Caruso, D. R. (2002). *Mayer-Salovey-Caruso Emotional Intelligence Test (MSCEIT): User's manual.* Toronto, Ontario, Canada: Multi-Health Systems.

McAuley, E., & Blissmer, B. (2000). Self-efficacy determinants and consequences of physical activity. *Exercise and Sport Sciences Review, 28,* 85–88.

McAuley, E., Blissmer, B., Katula, J., Duncan, T. E., & Mihalko, S. L. (2000). Physical activity, self-esteem, and self-efficacy relationships in older adults: A randomized controlled trial. *Annals of Behavioral Medicine, 22,* 131–139.

McAuley, E., Blissmer, B., Marquez, D. X., Jerome, G. J., Kramer, A. F., & Katula, J. (2000). Social relations, physical activity, and well-being in older adults. *Preventive Medicine, 31,* 608–617.

McCallum, J. (1991, November 11). For whom the Bulls toil. *Sports Illustrated, 75,* 106–118.

McCallum, J. (1994, March 28). Radical stupidity. *Sports Illustrated, 80,* 8.

McCallum, J. (2008, March 17). Steroids in America Part 1: The real dope. *Sports Illustrated, 108,* 28–37.

McCarthy, P. J., & Jones, M. V. (2007). A qualitative study of sport enjoyment in the sampling years. *The Sport Psychologist, 21,* 400–416.

McCarthy, P. J., Jones, M. V., & Clark-Carter, D. (2008). Understanding enjoyment in youth sport: A developmental perspective. *Psychology of Sport and Exercise, 9,* 142–156.

McCarthy, P. J., Jones, M. V., Harwood, C. G., & Davenport, L. (2010). Using goal setting to enhance positive affect among junior multi-event athletes. *Journal of Clinical Sport Psychology, 4,* 53–68.

McClelland, D. C., Atkinson, J. W., Clark, R. W., & Lowell, E. L. (1953). *The achievement motive.* New York, NY: Appleton-Century-Crofts.

McClung, M., & Collins, D. (2007). "Because I know it well!": Placebo effects of an ergogenic aid on athletic performance. *Journal of Sport & Exercise Psychology, 29,* 382–394.

McDonell, T. (2008, August 25) A small world after all. *Sports Illustrated, 109,* 17.

McDonough, M. H., & Crocker, P. R. E. (2005). Sport participation motivation in young adolescent girls: The role of friendship quality and self-concept. *Research Quarterly for Exercise and Sport, 76,* 456–467.

McDonough, M., & Crocker, P. R. E. (2007). Testing self-determined motivation as a mediator of the relationship between psychological needs and affective and behavioral outcomes. *Journal of Sport & Exercise Psychology, 29,* 645–663.

McGhie, A., & Chapman, J. (1961). Disorders of attention and perception in early schizophrenia. *British Journal of Medical Psychology, 34,* 103–116.

McGill, J. C., Hall, J. R., Ratliff, W. R., & Moss, R. F. (1986). Personality characteristics of professional rodeo cowboys. *Journal of Sport Behavior, 9,* 143–151.

McGowan, E., Prapavessis, H., & Wesch, N. (2008). Self-presentational concerns and competitive anxiety. *Journal of Sport & Exercise Psychology, 30,* 383–400.

McGowan, R. W., Pierce, E. F., Williams, M., & Eastman, N. W. (1994). Athletic injury and self-diminution. *The Journal of Sports Medicine and Physical Fitness, 34,* 299–304.

McInman, A. D., & Grove, J. R. (1991). Peak moments in sport: A literature review. *Quest, 43,* 333–351.

McKay, J., Niven, A. G., Lavallee, D., & White, A. (2008). Sources of strain among elite UK track athletes. *The Sport Psychologist, 22,* 143–163.

McLafferty, C. L., Jr., Hunter, G. R., Wetzstein, C. J., & Bamman, M. M. (2000). Does resistance exercise training relate to mood in older adults? *Medicine & Science in Sport & Exercise, 32,* Supplement, Abstract #494, S124.

McNair, D. M., Heuchert, J. P., & Shilony, E. (2003). *Profile of Mood States: Bibliography 1964–2002.* Toronto, Ontario, Canada: Multi-Health System.

McNair, D. M., Lorr, M., & Droppleman, L. F. (1971, 1981, 1992). *Profile of Mood States manual.* San Diego, CA: Educational and Industrial Testing Service.

Meeus, M. S. P., Serpa, S., & DeCuyper, B. (2010). The effects of video feedback on coaches' behavior and the coach-athlete relationship. *Journal of Clinical Sport Psychology, 4,* 323–340.

Meichenbaum, D. (1977). *Cognitive behavior modification.* New York, NY: Plenum Press.

Meichenbaum, D. (1985). *Stress inoculation training.* New York, NY: Pergamon Press.

Mellalieu, S. D. (2003). Mood matters: But how much? A comment on Lane and Terry (2000). *Journal of Applied Sport Psychology, 15,* 99–114.

Mellalieu, S. D., Neil, R., & Hanton, S. (2006). Self-confidence as a mediator of the relationship between competitive anxiety intensity and interpretation. *Research Quarterly for Exercise Psychology, 77,* 263–270.

Memmert, D., & Furley, P. (2007). "I spy with my little eye!": Breadth of attention, inattentional blindness, and tactical decision making in team sports. *Journal of Sport & Exercise Psychology, 29,* 365–381.

Menez, G. (2003, October 6). Special report: The American athlete age 10. *Sports Illustrated, 99,* 59–75.

Merten, M. J. (2008). Acceptability of dating violence among late adolescents: The role of sports participation, competitive attitudes, and selected dynamics of relationship violence. *Adolescence, 43,* 31–56.

Mesagno, C., Marchant, D., & Morris, T. (2008). A pre-performance routine to alleviate choking in "choking susceptible" athletes. *The Sport Psychologist, 22,* 439–457.

Mesagno, C., Marchant, D., & Morris, T. (2009). Alleviating choking: The sounds of distraction. *Journal of Applied Sport Psychology, 21,* 131–147.

Metcalf, H. C., & Urwick, L. (Eds.). (1963). *Dynamic administration: The collected papers of Mary Parker Follett,* (p. 277). London, England: Harper & Brothers.

Meyer, B. B., & Fletcher, T. B. (2007). Emotional intelligence: A theoretical overview and implications for research and professional practice in sport psychology. *Journal of Applied Sport Psychology, 19,* 1–15.

Meyers, M. C., Bourgeois, A. E., Stewart, S., & LeUnes, A. (1992). Predicting pain response in athletes: Development and assessment of the Sports Inventory for Pain. *Journal of Sport & Exercise Psychology, 14,* 249–261.

Miller, B. M., Bartholomew, J. B., & Springer, B. A. (2005). Postexercise affect: The effect of mode preference. *Journal of Applied Sport Psychology, 17,* 263–272.

Miller, A., & Donohue, B. (2003). The development and controlled evaluation of athletic mental preparation strategies in high school distance runners. *Journal of Applied Sport Psychology, 15,* 321–334.

Miller, N. E. (1941). The frustration–aggression hypothesis. *Psychological Review, 48,* 337–342.

Miller, P. S., & Kerr, G. A. (2002). Conceptualizing excellence: Past, present, and future. *Journal of Applied Sport Psychology, 14,* 140–153.

Miller, T. W. (1982). Assertiveness training for coaches: The issue of healthy communication between coaches and players. *Journal of Sport Psychology, 4,* 107–114.

Milne, H. M., Wallman, K. E., Guilfoyle, A., Gordon, S., & Courneya, K. S. (2008). Self-determination theory and physical activity among breast cancer survivors. *Journal of Sport & Exercise Psychology, 30,* 23–38.

Milne, M. I., Rodgers, W. M., Hall, C. R., & Wilson, P. M. (2008). Starting up or starting over: The role of intentions to increase and maintain the behavior of exercise initiates. *Journal of Sport & Exercise Psychology, 30,* 285–302.

Minnix, D. (2010). *Mental toughness in the classical martial arts.* Unpublished dissertation, Virginia Tech University.

Mintz, L. B., O'Halloran, M. S., Mulholland, A. M., & Schneider, P. A. (1997). Questionnaire for eating disorders: Reliability and validity of operationalizing DSM-IV into a self-report format. *Journal of Counseling Psychology, 44,* 63–79.

Mischel, W. (1986). *Introduction to personality.* New York, NY: Holt, Rinehart and Winston.

Mischel, W., & Shoda, Y. (1995). A cognitive-affective system theory of personality: Reconceptualizing situations, dispositions, dynamics, and invariance in personality structure. *Psychological Review, 102,* 246–268.

Mond, J., & Marks, P. (2007). Beliefs of adolescent girls concerning the severity and prevalence of bulimia nervosa. *Australian Journal of Psychology, 59,* 87–93.

Moore, D. L. (2000, May 17). All eyes on Tom at volleyball tryouts. *USA Today,* 8C.

Moore, J. C., & Brylinski, J. (1995). Facility familiarity and the home advantage. *Journal of Sport Behavior, 18,* 302–310.

Moore, Z. E. (2007). Critical thinking and the evidence-based practice of sport psychology. *Journal of Clinical Sport Psychology, 1,* 9–22.

Moore, Z. E. (2009). Theoretical and empirical developments of the mindfulness-acceptance-commitment (MAC) approach to performance enhancement. *Journal of Clinical Sports Psychology, 3,* 291–302.

Moore, Z. E., & Gardner, F. L. (2001, October). *Taking applied sport psychology from research to practice: Integrating empirically supported interventions into a self-regulatory model of athletic performance.* Workshop presented at the meeting of the Annual Conference of the Association for the Advancement of Applied Sport Psychology, Orlando, FL.

Morgan, W. P. (1972). Hypnosis and muscular performance. In W. P. Morgan (Ed.), *Ergogenic aids in muscular performance* (pp. 193–233). New York, NY: Academic Press.

Morgan, W. P. (1978, April). The mind of the marathoner. *Psychology Today,* 38–49.

Morgan, W. P. (1979). Prediction of performance in athletics. In P. Klavora & J. V. Daniel (Eds.), *Coach, athlete, and the sport psychologist* (pp. 172–186). Champaign, IL: Human Kinetics.

Morgan, W. P. (1980a). Sport personology: The credulous-skeptical argument in perspective. In W. F. Straub (Ed.), *Sport psychology: An analysis of athlete behavior* (2nd ed.) (pp. 330–339). Ithaca, NY: Mouvement Publications.

Morgan, W. P. (1980b). The trait psychology controversy. *Research Quarterly for Exercise and Sport, 51,* 50–76.

Morgan, W. P., & Brown, D. R. (1983). Hypnosis. In M. H. Williams (Ed.), *Ergogenic aids in sport* (pp. 223–252). Champaign, IL: Human Kinetics.

Moritz, S. E., Feltz, D. L., Fahrbach, K. R., & Mack, D. E. (2000). The relation of self-efficacy measures to sports performance: A meta-analytic review. *Research Quarterly for Exercise and Sport, 71,* 280–294.

Morrey, M. A. (1997). *A longitudinal examination of emotional response, cognitive coping, and physical recovery among athletes undergoing anterior cruciate ligament reconstructive surgery.* Unpublished doctoral dissertation, University of Minnesota, Minneapolis.

Morris, R. L., & Kavussanu, M. (2008). Antecedents of approach-avoidance goals in sport. *Journal of Sports Sciences, 26,* 465–476.

Morrison, T. G., Morrison, M. A., & Hopkins, C. (2003). Striving for bodily perfection? An exploration of the drive for muscularity in Canadian men. *Psychology of Men and Muscularity, 4,* 111–120.

Morrison, T. G., Morrison, M. A., Hopkins, C., & Rowan, E. T. (2004). Muscle mania: Development of a new scale examining the drive for muscularity in Canadian males. *Psychology of Men and Masculinity, 5,* 30–39.

Morrow, R. G., & Gill, D. L. (2003). Perceptions of homophobia and heterosexism in physical education. *Research Quarterly for Exercise and Sport, 74,* 205–214.

Morse, E. D. (2008). What a sport psychiatrist does. *Journal of Clinical Sport Psychology, 2,* 202–203.

Morse, E. D. (2009). The divide between sport psychologists and sport scientists: A sport psychologist's view. *Journal of Clinical Sport Psychology, 3,* 396–397.

Mosewich, A. D., Vangool, A. B., Kowalski, K. C., & McHugh, T.-L. F. (2009). Exploring women track and field athletes' meanings of muscularity. *Journal of Applied Sport Psychology, 21,* 99–115.

Mouratidis, A., Lens, W., & Vansteenkiste, M. (2010). How you provide corrective feedback makes a difference: The motivating role of communicating in an autonomony-supporting way. *Journal of Sport & Exercise Psychology, 32,* 619–637.

Moyna, N. M., Robertson, R. J., Meckes, G. L., Peoples, J. A., Millich, N. B., & Thompson, P. D. (2001). Intermodal comparisons of energy expenditure and exercise intensities corresponding to the perceptual preferences range. *Medicine and Science in Sport and Exercise, 33,* 1404–1410.

Mullan, E., Markland, D., & Ingledew, D. K. (1997). A graded conceptualization of self-determination in the regulation of exercise behavior: Development of a measure using confirmatory factor analytic procedures. *Personality and Individual Differences, 23,* 745–752.

Mullen, B., & Cooper, C. (1994). The relationship between group cohesiveness and performance: An integration. *Psychological Bulletin, 115,* 210–227.

Mullen, R., & Hardy, L. (2010). Conscious processing and the process goal paradox. *Journal of Sport & Exercise Psychology, 32,* 275–297.

Mullen, R., Hardy, L., & Tattersall, A. (2005). The effect of the conscious processing hypothesis. *Journal of Sport & Exercise Psychology, 27,* 212–225.

Müller, N. (1997, August–September). The Olympic Congresses in Lausanne. *Olympic Review, 16,* 49–51, 53–59.

Munroe, K. J., Giacobbi, P. R., Jr., Hall, C. R., & Weinberg, R. (2000). The four Ws of imagery use: Where, when, why, and what. *The Sport Psychologist, 14,* 119–137.

Munroe-Chandler, K. J., Hall, C. R., Fishburne, G. J., & Strachan, L. (2007). Where, when, and why young athletes use imagery: An examination of developmental differences. *Research Quarterly for Exercise and Sport, 78,* 103–116.

Munroe-Chandler, K. J., Hall, C. R., & Weinberg, R. S. (2004). A qualitative analysis of the types of goals athletes set in training and competition. *Journal of Sport Behavior, 27,* 58–74.

Murphy, A. (2004, August 2). The joy of six. *Sports Illustrated, 101,* 40–46.

Murphy, S. M., Greenspan, M., Jowdy, D., & Tammen, V. (1989, October). *Development of a brief rating instrument of competitive anxiety. Comparisons with the CSAI-2.* Paper presented at the meeting of the Association for the Advancement of Applied Sport Psychology, Seattle, WA.

Muscat, A. C., & Long, B. C. (2008). Critical comments about body shape and weight: Disordered eating of female athletes and sport participants. *Journal of Applied Sport Psychology, 20,* 1–24.

Mutrie, N. (2000). The relationship between physical activity and clinically defined depression. In S. J. H. Biddle, K. R. Fox, & S. H. Boutcher, (Eds.), *Physical activity and psychological well-being* (pp. 46–62). London, England: Routledge.

Myers, I. B. (1962). *Manual: The Myers-Briggs Type Indicator.* Princeton, NJ: Educational Testing Service.

Myers, I. B., McCaulley, M. H., Quenk, N. L., & Hammer, A. L. (1998). *MBTI manual: A guide to the development and use of the Myers-Briggs Type Indicator.* Palo Alto, CA: Consulting Psychologists Press.

Myers, N. D., Feltz, D. L., Maier, J. S., Wolfe, E. W., & Reckase, M. D. (2006). Athletes' evaluations of their head coach's coaching competency. *Research Quarterly for Exercise and Sport, 77,* 111–121.

Myers, N. D., Wolfe, E. W., Maier, K. S., Feltz, D. L., & Reckase, M. D. (2006). Extending validity evidence for multidimensional measures of coaching competency. *Research Quarterly for Exercise and Sport, 77,* 451–463.

N

Nack, W. (2001, May 7). The wrecking yard. *Sport Journal, 94,* 60–75.

Neupert, S. D., Lachman, M. E., & Whitbourne, S. B. (2009). Exercise self-efficacy and control beliefs: Effects on exercise behavior after an exercise intervention for older adults. *Journal of Aging and Physical Activity, 17,* 1–17.

Newberg, D., Kimiecik, J., Durand-Bush, N., & Doell, K. (2002). The role of resonance in performance excellence and life engagement. *Journal of Applied Sport Psychology, 14,* 249–267.

Newin, J., Bloom, G. A., & Loughead, T. M. (2008). Youth ice hockey coaches' perceptions of a team-building intervention program. *The Sport Psychologist, 22,* 54–72.

Newman, B. (1984). Expediency as a benefactor: How team building saves time and gets the job done. *Training and Development Journal, 38,* 26–30.

Newton, M. (1994, October). *The relationship between perceived motivational climate and dispositional goal orientation on selected indices of intrinsic motivation.* Paper presented at the Association for the Advancement of Applied Sport Psychology, Tahoe, NV.

Newton, M., & Duda, J. L. (1999). The interaction of motivational climate, dispositional goal orientation, and perceived ability in predicting indices of motivation. *International Journal of Sport Psychology, 30,* 63–82.

Newton, M., Duda, J. L., & Yin, Z. (2000). Examination of the psychometric properties of the Perceived Motivational Climate in Sport Questionnaire-2 in a sample of female athletes. *Journal of Sports Sciences, 18,* 275–290.

Nicholls, A. R., Holt, N. L., & Polman, R. C. J. (2005). A phenomenological analysis of coping effectiveness in golf. *The Sport Psychologist, 19,* 111–130.

Nicholls, A. R., Holt, N. L., Polman, R. C. J., & Bloomfield, J. (2006). Stressors, coping, and coping effectiveness among professional ruby union players. *The Sport Psychologist, 20,* 314–329.

Nicholls, A. R., Holt, N. L., Polman, R. C. J., & James, D. W. G. (2005). Stress and coping among international adolescent golfers. *Journal of Applied Sport Psychology, 17,* 333–340.

Nicholls, A. R., Polman, R. C. J., Morley, D., & Taylor, N. J. (2009). Coping and coping effectiveness in relation to a competitive sport event: Pubertal status, chronological age, and gender among adolescent athletes. *Journal of Sport & Exercise Psychology, 31,* 299–317.

Nicholls, J. G. (1984). Conceptions of ability and achievement motivation. In R. Ames & C. Ames (Eds.), *Research on motivation in education: Student motivation* (Vol. I). New York, NY: Academic Press.

Nicholls, J. G. (1989). *The competitive ethos and democratic education.* Cambridge, MA: Harvard University Press.

Nicklaus, J. (1974). *Golf my way.* New York, NY: Simon & Schuster.

Nicoloff, G., & Schwenk, T. L. (1995). Using exercise to ward off depression. *The Physician and Sportsmedicine, 23,* 44–56.

Nideffer, R. M. (1976). Test of attentional and interpersonal style. *Journal of Personality and Social Psychology, 34,* 394–404.

Nideffer, R. M., & Sagal, M. S. (2006). Concentration and attention control training. In J. M. Williams (Ed.), *Applied sport psychology: Personal growth to peak performance* (pp. 382–403). St. Louis, MO: McGraw-Hill.

Nieman, D. C. (2001, June). Cold facts on exercise and immunity. Paper presented at the annual convention of the American College of Sports Medicine, Baltimore, MD.

Nieman, D. C., Kernodle, M. W., Henson, D. R., Sonnenfeld, G., & Morton, D. S. (2000). The acute response of the immune system to tennis drills in adolescent athletes. *Research Quarterly for Exercise and Sport, 71,* 403–408.

Nien, C.-L., & Duda, J. L. (2008). Antecedents and consequences of approach and avoidance achievement goals: A test of gender invariance. *Psychology of Sport and Exercise, 9,* 352–372.

Nietfeld, J. L. (2003). An examination of metacognitive strategy use and monitoring skills by competitive middle distance runners. *Journal of Applied Sport Psychology, 15,* 307–320.

Nieuwenhuys, A., Pijpers, J. R., Oudejans, R. R. D., & Bakker, F. C. (2008). The influence of anxiety on visual attention in climbing. *Journal of Sport & Exercise Psychology, 30,* 171–185.

Niven, A., Fawkner, S., Knowles, A., Henretty, J., & Stephenson, C. (2009). Social physique anxiety and physical activity in early adolescent girls: The influence of maturation and physical activity motives. *Journal of Sports Sciences, 27,* 299–305.

Noel, R. C. (1980). The effect of visuo-motor behavior rehearsal on tennis performance. *Journal of Sport Psychology, 2,* 221–226.

Nordin, S. M., & Cumming, J. (2005a). Professional dancers describe their imagery: Where, when, what, why, and how. *The Sport Psychologist, 19,* 395–416.

Nordin, S. M., & Cumming, J. (2005b). More than meets the eye: Investigating imagery type, direction, and outcome. *The Sport Psychologist, 19,* 1–17.

Nordin, S. M., & Cumming, J. (2007). Where, when, and how: A quantitative account of dance imagery. *Research Quarterly for Exercise and Sport, 78,* 390–395.

Nordin, S. M., Cumming, J., Vincent, J., & McGrory, S. (2006). Mental practice or spontaneous play? Examining which types of imagery constitute deliberate practice in sport. *Journal of Applied Sport Psychology, 18,* 345–362.

Norman, D. A. (1968). Toward a theory of memory and attention. *Psychological Review, 75,* 522–536.

Norman, P., & Conner, M. (2005). The theory of planned behavior and exercise: Evidence for the mediating and moderating roles of planning on intention-behavior relationships. *Journal of Sport & Exercise Psychology, 27,* 488–504.

Norris, J., & Jones, R. L. (1998). Towards a clearer definition and application of the centrality hypothesis in English Professional Association Football. *Journal of Sport Behavior, 21,* 181–195.

North, T. C., McCullagh, P., & Tran, Z. V. (1990). Effect of exercise on depression. In K. B. Pandolf & J. O. Holloszy (Eds.), *Exercise and sport science reviews, 18,* 379–415. Baltimore, MD: William & Wilkins.

Ntoumanis, N., & Standage, M. (2009). Morality in sport: A self-determination theory perspective. *Journal of Applied Sport Psychology, 21,* 365–380.

Ntoumanis, N., & Vazou, S. (2005). Peer motivational climate in youth sport: Measurement development and validation. *Journal of Sport & Exercise Psychology, 27,* 432–455.

Ntoumanis, N., Pensgaard, A. M., Martin, C., & Pipe, K. (2004). An idiographic analysis of amotivation in compulsory school physical education. *Journal of Sport & Exercise Psychology, 26,* 197–214.

O

O, J., & Hall, C. (2009). A quantitative analysis of athletes' voluntary use of slow motion, real time, and fast motion images. *Journal of Applied Sport Psychology, 21,* 15–30.

O, J., & Munroe-Chandler, K. J. (2008). The effects of image speed on the performance of a soccer task. *The Sport Psychologist, 22,* 1–17.

O'Brian, D., & Sloan, R. (1999, September). *Physical and mental preparation of the world's greatest athlete.* Paper presented at the meeting of the Association for the Advancement of Applied Sport Psychology, Banff, Alberta, Canada.

O'Brien, M., Mellalieu, S., & Hanton, S. (2009). Goal-setting effects in elite and nonelite boxers. *Journal of Applied Sport Psychology, 21,* 293–306.

O'Neill, D. F. (2008). Injury contagion in alpine ski racing: The effect of injury on teammates' performance. *Journal of Clinical Sport Psychology, 2,* 278–292.

Ogden, J., Veale, D., & Summers, Z. (1997). The development and validation of the Exercise Dependence Questionnaire. *Addiction Research, 5,* 343–356.

Ogilvie, B., & Taylor, J. (1993). Career termination issues among elite athletes. In R. N. Singer, M. Murphy, and L. K. Tennant (Eds.), *Handbook of Research on Sport Psychology* (pp. 761–778). New York, NY: Macmillan.

Ogilvie, B. C. (1968). Psychological consistencies within the personality of high-level competitors. *Journal of the American Medical Association, 205,* 780–786.

Ogilvie, B. C. (1976). Psychological consistencies within the personality of high-level competitors. In A. C. Fisher (Ed.), *Psychology of sport.* Palo Alto, CA: Mayfield.

Ogilvie, B. C., Johnsgard, K., & Tutko, T. A. (1971). Personality: Effects of activity. In L. A. Larson (Ed.), *Encyclopedia of sport sciences and medicine.* New York, NY: Macmillan.

Ogilvie, B. C., & Tutko, T. A. (1966). *Problem athletes and how to handle them.* London, England: Palham Books.

Oglesby, C. A. (2001). To unearth the legacy. *The Sport Psychologist, 15,* 373–385.

Olivardia, R., & Pope, H. G. (2000). Muscle dysmorphia in male weightlifters: A case-control study. *American Journal of Psychiatry, 157,* 1291–1296.

Olney, B. (2003, February 19). Players seek every edge in modern training culture. *The New York Times,* Retrieved from http://www.nytimes.com/2001/2/19

Olrich, T. W., & Ewing, M. E. (1999). Life on steroids: Bodybuilders describe their perceptions of the anabolic-androgenic steroid use period. *The Sport Psychologist, 13,* 299–312.

Olympiou, A., Jowett, S., & Duda, J. L. (2008). The psychological interface between the coach-created motivational climate and the coach–athlete relationship in team sports. *The Sport Psychologist, 22,* 423–438.

Oman, R. F., & King, A. C. (2000). The effect of life events and exercise program format on the adoption and maintenance of exercise behavior. *Health Psychology, 19,* 605–612.

Ommundsen, Y. (2001). Self-handicapping strategies in physical education classes. The ability and achievement goal orientation. *Psychology of Sport and Exercise, 2,* 139–156.

Ommundsen, Y. (2004). Self-handicapping related to task and performance-approach and avoidance goals in physical education. *Journal of Applied Sport Psychology, 16,* 183–197.

Orlick, T. (1986). *Psyching for sport: Mental training for athletes.* Champaign, IL: Leisure Press.

Orlick, T., & Partington, J. (1988). Mental links to excellence. *The Sport Psychologist, 2,* 105–130.

Osborn, R. N., & Hunt, J. G. (1975). An adaptive-reactive theory of leadership: The role of macro variables in leadership research. In J. G. Hunt & L. L. Larson (Eds.), *Leadership frontiers.* Kent, OH: Kent State University Press.

Otten, M. (2009). Choking vs. clutch performance: A study of sport performance under pressure. *Journal of Sport & Exercise Psychology, 31,* 583–601.

Oudejans, R. R. D., & Pijpers, J. R. (2010). Training with mild anxiety may prevent choking under higher levels of anxiety. *Psychology of Sport and Exercise, 11,* 44–50.

Oxendine, J. B. (1968). *Psychology of motor learning.* New York, NY: Appleton-Century-Crofts.

P

Paa, H. K., Sime, W. E., & Llobet, J. (1999, September). *An examination of sport-specific psychological characteristics among high school, collegiate, and professional athletes.* Poster session presented at the annual meeting of the Association for the Advancement of Applied Sport Psychology, Banff, Alberta, Canada.

Paffenbarger, R. S. (1994). 40 years of progress: Physical activity, health and fitness. In *40th anniversary lectures* (pp. 93–109). Indianapolis, IN: American College of Sports Medicine.

Page, S. J., Sime, W., & Nordell, K. (1999). The effects of imagery on female college swimmers' perceptions of anxiety. *The Sport Psychologist, 13,* 458–469.

Pain, M., & Harwood, C. (2009). Team building through mutual sharing and open discussion of team functioning. *The Sport Psychologist, 23,* 523–542.

Paivio, A. (1971). *Imagery and verbal processes.* New York, NY: Holt, Rinehart and Winston.

Paivio, A. (1985). Cognitive and motivational functions of imagery in human performance. *Canadian Journal of Applied Sport Sciences, 10,* 225–285.

Papaioannou, A. G., Milosis, D., Kosmidou, E., & Tsigilis, N. (2007). Motivational climate and achievement goals at the situational level of generality. *Journal of Applied Sport Psychology, 19,* 38–66.

Papaioannou, A. G., Simou, T., Kosmidou, E., Milosis, D., & Tsigilis, N. (2009). Goal orientation at the global level of generality and in physical education: Their association with self-regulation, affect, beliefs and behaviors. *Psychology of Sport and Exercise, 10,* 466–480.

Papaioannou, A., Marsh, H. W., & Theordorakis, Y. (2004). *Journal of Sport & Exercise Psychology, 26,* 90–118.

Parfitt, G., Hardy, L., & Pates, J. (1995). Somatic anxiety and physiological arousal: Their effects upon a high anaerobic, low memory demand task. *International Journal of Sport Psychology, 26,* 196–213.

Park, J. K. (2000). Coping strategies used by Korean national athletes. *The Sport Psychologist, 14,* 63–80.

Parker, J. K., & Lovell, G. (2009). Characteristics affecting the use of imagery: A youth sports academy study. *Journal of Imagery Research in Sport and Physical Activity, 4,* Article 8.

Partington, J. T., & Shangi, G. M. (1992). Developing an understanding of team psychology. *International Journal of Sport Psychology, 23,* 28–47.

Partington, S., Partington, E., & Olivier, S. (2009). The dark side of flow: A qualitative study of dependence in big wave surfing. *The Sport Psychologist, 23,* 170–185.

Passman, L., & Thompson, J. K. (1988). Body image and eating disturbance in obligatory runners, obligatory weight lifters, and sedentary individuals. *International Journal of Eating Disorders, 7,* 759–769.

Pate, R. R., Pratt, M., Blair, S. N., Haskell, W. L., Macera, C. A., Bouchard, C., . . . King, A. C., et al. (1995). Physical activity and public health. *Journal of the American Medical Association, 273,* 402–407.

Pates, J., Cummings, A., & Maynard, I. (2002). The effects of hypnosis on flow states and three-point shooting performance in basketball players. *The Sport Psychologist, 16,* 34–45.

Pates, J., Cummings, A., Maynard, I., & Westbury, T. (2000, October). *The effects of hypnosis upon three point shooting performance in basketball players.* Paper presented at the meeting of the Association for the Advancement of Applied Sport Psychology, Nashville, TN.

Pates, J., Maynard, I., & Westbury, T. (2001). An investigation into the effects of hypnosis on basketball performance. *Journal of Applied Sport Psychology, 13,* 84–102.

Pates, J., Oliver, R., & Maynard, I. (2001). The effects of hypnosis on flow states and golf-putting performance. *Journal of Applied Sport Psychology, 13,* 341–354.

Patrick, D. (2009, August 3). Just my type. *Sports Illustrated, 111,* 28.

Patterson, E. L., Smith, R. E., Everett, J. J., & Ptacek, J. T. (1998). Psychosocial factors as predictors of ballet injuries. *Journal of Sport Behavior, 21,* 101–112.

Pelletier, L. G., Fortier, M. S., Vallerand, R. J., Tuson, K. M., Briere, N. M., & Blais, M. R. (1995). Toward a new measure of intrinsic motivation, extrinsic motivation, and amotivation in sports: The sport motivation scale (SMS). *Journal of Sport & Exercise Psychology, 17,* 35–53.

Pelletier, L. G., Vallerand, R. J., & Sarrazin, P. (2007). The revised six-factor sport motivation scale (Mallett, Kawabata, Newcombe, Otero-Forero, Jackson, 2007): Something old, something new, and something borrowed. *Psychology of Sport and Exercise, 8,* 615–621.

Pennebraker, J. W. (2004). Theories, therapies, and taxpayers: On the complexities of the expressive writing paradigm. *Clinical Psychology: Science and Practice, 11,* 138–142.

Perkins, D., Wilson, G. V., & Kerr, J. H. (2001). The effects of elevated arousal and mood on maximal strength performance in athletes. *Journal of Applied Sport Psychology, 13,* 239–259.

Perkos, S., Theodorakis, Y., & Chroni, S. (2002). Enhancing performance and skill acquisition in novice basketball players with instructional self-talk. *The Sport Psychologist, 16,* 368–383.

Perreault, S., Vallerand, R. J., Montgomery, D., & Provencher, P. (1998). Coming from behind: On the effect of psychological momentum on sport performance. *Journal of Sport & Exercise Psychology, 20,* 421–436.

Perri, M. G., Anton, S. D., Durning, P. E., Ketterson, T. W., Sydeman, S. J., Berlant, N. E., . . . Martin, A. D. (2002). Adherence to exercise prescriptions: Effects of prescribing moderate versus higher levels of intensity and frequency. *Health Psychology, 21,* 452–458.

Perry, J. D., & Williams, J. M. (1998). Relationship of intensity and direction of competitive trait anxiety to skill level and gender in tennis. *The Sport Psychologist, 12,* 169–179.

Pesce, C., Cereatti, L., Casella, R., Baldari, C., & Capranica, L. (2007). Preservation of visual attention in older expert orienteers at rest and under physical effort. *Journal of Sport & Exercise Psychology, 29,* 78–99.

Peters, H. J., & Williams, J. M. (2006). Moving cultural background to the foreground: An investigation of self-talk, performance, and persistence following feedback. *Journal of Applied Sport Psychology, 18,* 240–253.

Petitpas, A. J. (1998). Practical considerations in providing psychological services to sports medicine clinic patients. *Journal of Applied Sport Psychology, 10,* 157–167.

Petitpas, A. J., Cornelius, A. E., Van Raalte, J. L., & Jones, T. (2005). A framework for planning youth sport programs that foster psychological development. *The Sport Psychologist, 19,* 63–80.

Petrides, K. V., & Furnham, A. (2000). On the dimensional structure of emotional intelligence. *Personality and Individual Differences, 29,* 313–320.

Petrie, T. A. (1993). Coping skills, competitive trait anxiety, and playing status: Moderating effects on the life stress-injury relationship. *Journal of Sport & Exercise Psychology, 15,* 261–274.

Petrie, T. A., Greenleaf, C., Carter, J. E., & Reel, J. J. (2007). Psychological correlates of disordered eating among male collegiate athletes. *Journal of Clinical Sport Psychology, 1,* 340–357.

Petrie, T. A., Greenleaf, C., Reel, J. J., & Carter, J. E. (2009). An examination of psychosocial correlates of eating disorders. *Research Quarterly for Exercise and Sport, 80,* 621–633.

Petroczi, A., & Aidman, E. (2009). Measuring explicit attitude toward doping: Review of the psychometric properties of the Performance and Enhancement Attitude Scale. *Psychology of Sport and Exercise, 10,* 390–396.

Petruzzello, S. J., Landers, D. M., Hatfield, B. D., Kubitz, K. A., & Salazar, W. (1991). A meta-analysis on the anxiety-reducing effects of acute and chronic exercise. *Sports Medicine, 11*(3), 143–182.

Pierce, B. E., & Burton, D. (1998). Scoring the perfect 10: Investigating the impact of goal-setting styles on a goal-setting program for female gymnasts. *The Sport Psychologist, 12,* 156–168.

Pierce, S. D. (2009, November 13). Go figure—ESPN suddenly loves MWC. *Deseret News,* D7.

Plotnikoff, R. C., Hotz, S. B., Birkett, N. J., & Courneya, K. S. (2001). Exercise and the transtheoretical model: A longitudinal test of a population sample. *Preventive Medicine, 33,* 441–452.

Poczwardowski, A., Sherman, C. P., & Ravizza, K. (2004). Professional philosophy in the sport psychology service delivery: Building on theory and practice. *The Sport Psychologist, 18,* 445–463.

Podlog, L., & Eklund, R. C. (2006). A longitudinal investigation of competitive athletes' return to sport following serious injury. *Journal of Applied Sport Psychology, 18,* 44–68.

Podlog, L., & Eklund, R. C. (2007a). The psychosocial aspects of a return to sport following serious injury: A review of the literature from a self-determination perspective. *Psychology of Sport and Exercise, 8,* 535–566.

Podlog, L., & Eklund, R. C. (2007b). Professional coaches' perspectives on the return to sport following serious injury. *Journal of Applied Sport Psychology, 19,* 207–225.

Podlog, L., & Eklund, R. C. (2009). High-level athletes' perceptions of success in returning to sport following injury. *Psychology of Sport and Exercise, 10,* 535–544.

Podlog, L., Lochbaum, M., & Stevens, T. (2010). Need satisfaction, well-being, and perceived return to sport outcomes among injured athletes. *Journal of Applied Sport Psychology, 22,* 167–182.

Pollard, R. (2006). Home advantage in soccer: Variations in its magnitude and a literature review of the interrelated factors associated with its existence. *Journal of Sport Behavior, 29,* 169–189.

Pontifex, M. B., Hillman, C. H., Fernhall, B., Thompson, K. M., & Valentini, T. A. (2009). The effect of acute aerobic and resistance exercise on working memory. *Medicine & Science in Sport & Exercise, 41,* 927–934.

Poolton, J. M., Maxwell, J. P., Masters, R. S. W., & Raab, M. (2006). Benefits of an external focus of attention: Common coding or conscious processing? *Journal of Sports Sciences, 24,* 89–99.

Posnanski, J. (1998, January 9). Seconds can tick so loudly. *The Kansas City Star,* D1, D9.

Posner, M. I., & Raichle, M. E. (1997). *Images of mind.* New York, NY: Scientific American Library.

Post, P. G., Wrisberg, C. A., & Mullins, S. (2010). A field test of the influence of pre-game imagery on basketball free throw shooting. *Journal of Imagery Research in Sport and Physical Activity, 5,* Article 2.

Prapavessis, H. (2000). The POMS and sports performance: A review. *Journal of Applied Sport Psychology, 12,* 34–48.

Prapavessis, H., & Grove, J. R. (1991). Precompetitive emotions and shooting performance: The mental health and zone of optimal function models. *The Sport Psychologist, 5,* 223–234.

Prapavessis, H., Grove, J. R., & Eklund, R. C. (2004). Self-presentational issues in competition and sport. *Journal of Applied Sport Psychology, 16,* 19–40.

President's Council on Physical Fitness and Sports (2001, June). Does exercise alter minimum function and respiratory infections? *Research Digest,* series 3, no. 13.

Price, S. L. (2003, April 28). When fans attack. *Sports Illustrated, 98,* 48–53.

Price, S. L. (2004, June 28). Lance in France (part 6). *Sports Illustrated, 100,* 46–53.

Prochaska, J. O., & DiClemente, C. C. (1986). Toward a comprehensive model of change. In W. E. Miller & N. Heather (Eds.), *Treating addictive behaviors* (pp. 3–27). London, England: Plenum Press.

Prochaska, J. O., & Marcus, B. H. (1994). The transtheoretical model: The applications to exercise. In R. K. Dishman (Ed.), *Advances in exercise adherence* (pp. 161–180). Champaign, IL: Human Kinetics.

Puffer, J. C., & McShane, J. M. (1992). Depression and chronic fatigue in athletes. *Clinics in Sports Medicine, 11,* 327–338.

Purcell, I. (1999). Verbal protocols and structured interviews for motives, plans, and decisions in golf. In J. H. Kerr (Ed.), *Experiencing sport: Reversal Theory* (pp. 69–100). Chichester, England: John Wiley & Sons.

Q

Quinn, A. M., & Fallon, B. J. (1999). The changes in psychological characteristics and reactions of elite athletes from injury onset until full recovery. *Journal of Applied Sport Psychology, 11,* 194–209.

Quitmeir, L. (2000, November 16). Olympic trial and error. *Columbia Missourian,* B1, B3.

R

Rabin, C., Pinto, B. M., & Frierson, G. M. (2006). Mediators of a randomized controlled physical activity intervention for breast cancer survivors. *Journal of Sport & Exercise Psychology, 28,* 269–284.

Radel, R., Sarrazin, P., & Pelletier. (2009). Evidence of subliminally primed motivational orientations: The effects of unconscious motivational processes on the performance of a new motor task. *Journal of Sport & Exercise Psychology, 31,* 657–674.

Raedeke, T. D. (1997). Is athlete burnout more than just stress? A sport commitment perspective. *Journal of Sport & Exercise Psychology, 19,* 396–417.

Raedeke, T. D. (2007). The relationship between enjoyment and affective response to exercise. *Journal of Applied Sport Psychology, 19,* 105–115.

Raedeke, T. D., Focht, B. C., & Scales, D. (2009). Mediators of affective responses to acute exercise among women with high social physique anxiety. *Psychology of Sport and Exercise, 10,* 573–578.

Raedeke, T. D., Granzyk, T. L., & Warren, A. (2000). Why coaches experience burnout: A commitment perspective. *Journal of Sport & Exercise Psychology, 22,* 85–105.

Raedeke, T. D., & Smith, A. L. (2001). Development and preliminary validation of an athlete burnout measure. *Journal of Sport & Exercise Psychology, 23,* 281–306.

Raedeke, T. D., & Stein, G. L. (1994). Felt arousal, thoughts/feelings, and ski performance. *The Sport Psychologist, 8,* 360–375.

Raglin, J. S., & Hanin, Y. L. (2000). Competitive anxiety. In Y. L. Hanin (Ed.), *Emotions in sport* (93–112). Champaign, IL: Human Kinetics.

Raglin, J. S., & Morris, M. J. (1994). Precompetition anxiety in women volleyball players: A test of ZOF theory in a team sport. *British Journal of Sports Medicine, 28,* 47–51.

Raglin, J. S., & Turner, P. E. (1993). Anxiety and performance in track and field athletes: A comparison of the inverted-U hypothesis with zone of optimal functioning theory. *Personality and Individual Differences, 14,* 163–171.

Ram, N., Stareck, J., & Johnson, J. (2004). Race, ethnicity, and sexual orientation: Still a void in sport and exercise psychology? *Journal of Sport & Exercise Psychology, 26,* 250–268.

Rand, J. (2000, February 27). The profiler. *The Kansas City Star,* C4.

Ransford, C. P. (1982). A role for amines in the antidepressant effect of exercise: A review. *Medicine & Science in Sports & Exercise, 14,* 1–10.

Rascle, O., Coulomb-Cabagno, G., & Delsarte, A. (2005). Perceived motivational climate and observed aggression as a function of competitive level in youth male French handball. *Journal of Sport Behavior, 28,* 51–67.

Rascle, O., Traclet, A., Souchon, N., Coulomb-Cabagno, G., & Petrucci, C. (2010). Aggressor-victim dissent in perceived legitimacy of aggression in soccer: The moderating role of situational background. *Research Quarterly for Exercise and Sport, 81,* 340–348.

Reddy, J. K., Bai, A. J. L., & Rao, V. R. (1976). The effects of the transcendental meditation program on athletic performance. In D. J. Orme-Johnson & I. Farrow (Eds.), *Scientific research on the transcendental meditation program* (Collected papers, Vol. 1). Weggis, Switzerland: MERU Press.

Reed, C. E., & Cox, R. H. (2007). Motives and regulatory style underlying senior athletes' participation in sport. *Journal of Sport Behavior, 30,* 307–329.

Reed, J., & Buck, S. (2009). The effect of regular aerobic exercise on positive-activated affect: A meta-analysis. *Psychology of Sport and Exercise, 10,* 581–594.

Reel, J. J., SooHoo, S., Doetsch, H., Carter, J. E., & Petrie, T. A. (2007). The female athlete triad: Is the triad a problem among Division I female athletes? *Journal of Clinical Sport Psychology, 1,* 358–370.

Rees, T., Hardy, L., & Evans, L. (2007). Construct validity of the social support survey in sport. *Psychology of Sport and Exercise, 8,* 355–368.

Reeves, C. W., Nicholls, A. R., & McKenna, J. (2009). Stressors and coping strategies among early and middle adolescent premier league academy soccer players: Differences according to age. *Journal of Applied Sport Psychology, 21,* 31–48.

Reifman, A. S., Larrick, R. P., & Fein, S. (1991). Temper and temperature on the diamond: The heat-aggression relationship in major league baseball. *Personality and Social Psychology Bulletin, 17,* 580–585.

Reilly, R. (1996, April 22). Master strokes. *Sports Illustrated, 84,* 24–31.

Reilly, R. (2000, February 28). Bringing parents up to code. *Sports Illustrated, 92,* 88.

Rejeski, W. J., Brawley, L. R., & Schumaker, S. A. (1996). Physical activity and health-related quality of life. In J. O. Holloszy (Ed.), *Exercise and Sport Science Reviews, 24,* 71–108.

Rendi, M., Szabo, A., & Szabo, T. (2008). Performance enhancement with music in rowing sprint. *The Sport Psychologist, 22,* 175–182.

Reynolds, W. M. (1982). Development of reliable and valid short forms of the Marlowe-Crowne Social Desirability Scale. *Journal of Clinical Psychology, 38,* 119–125.

Rhind, D. J. A., & Jowett, S. (2010). Relationship maintenance strategies in the coach–athlete relationship: The development of the COMPASS model. *Journal of Applied Sport Psychology, 22,* 106–121.

Rhodes, R. E., Courneya, K. S., & Hayduk, I. A. (2001). Does personality moderate the theory of planned behavior in the exercise domain? *Journal of Sport & Exercise Psychology, 24,* 120–132.

Rhodes, R. E., Jones, L. W., & Courneya, K. S. (2002). Extending the theory of planned behavior in the exercise domain: A comparison of social support and subjective norm. *Research Quarterly for Exercise and Sport, 73,* 193–199.

Richardson, A. (1969). *Mental imagery.* New York, NY: Springer.

Richardson, G. E. (2002). The meta theory of resilience and resiliency. *Journal of Clinical Psychology, 58,* 307–321.

Ridgeway, R. T., & Tylka, T. L. (2005). College men's perceptions of ideal composition and shape. *Psychology of Men and Masculinity, 6,* 209–220.

Ridnour, H., & Hammermeister, J. (2008). Spiritual well-being and its influence on athletic coping profiles. *Journal of Sport Behavior, 31,* 81–92.

Riemer, B. A., & Visio, M. E. (2003). Gender typing of sports: An investigation of Metheny's classification. *Research Quarterly for Exercise and Sport, 74,* 193–205.

Riemer, H. A., & Chelladurai, P. (1995). Leadership and satisfaction in athletics. *Journal of Sport & Exercise Psychology, 17,* 276–293.

Riemer, H. A., & Chelladurai, P. (1998). Development of the Athlete Satisfaction Questionnaire (ASQ). *Journal of Sport & Exercise Psychology, 20,* 127–156.

Riemer, H. A., & Toon, K. (2001). Leadership and satisfaction in tennis: Examination of congruence, gender, and ability. *Research Quarterly for Exercise and Sport, 72,* 243–256.

Reinboth, M., & Duda, J. L. (2004). The motivational climate, perceived ability, and athletes' psychological and physical well-being. *The Sport Psychologist, 18,* 237–251.

Rigsby, L. W., Dishman, R. K., Jackson, A. W., MaClean, G. S., & Raven, P. B. (1992). Effects of exercise training on men seropositive for human immunodeficiency virus-1. *Medicine and Science in Sports and Exercise, 24*(1), 6–12.

Robazza, C., Bortoli, L., & Hanin, Y. (2006). Perceived effects of emotion intensity on athletic performance: A contingency-based individualized approach. *Research Quarterly for Exercise and Sport, 77,* 372–385.

Roberts, G. C. (1993). Motivation in sport: Understanding and enhancing the motivation and achievement of children. In R. N. Singer, M. Murphey, & L. K. Tennant (Eds.), *Handbook of research on sport psychology* (pp. 405–420). New York, NY: Macmillan.

Roberts, G. C., & Treasure, D. C. (1995). Achievement goals, motivation climate and achievement strategies and behaviors in sport. *International Journal of Sport Psychology, 26,* 64–80.

Roberts, G. C., Treasure, D. C., & Balague, G. (1998). Achievement goals in sport: The development and validation of the perception of success questionnaire. *Journal of Sport Sciences, 16,* 337–347.

Roberts, R., Callow, N., Hardy, L., Markland, D., & Bringer, J. (2008). Movement imagery ability: Development and assessment of a revised version of the Vividness of Movement Imagery Questionnaire. *Journal of Sport & Exercise Psychology, 30,* 200–221.

Roberts, R., Callow, N., Hardy, L., Woodman, T., & Thomas, L. (2010). Interactive effects of different visual imagery perspectives and narcissism on motor performance. *Journal of Sport & Exercise Psychology, 32,* 499–517.

Roberts, S. A., & Epstein, D. (2009, February 16). Confronting A-Rod. *Sports Illustrated, 110,* 28–31.

Robertson, O. (2004, December 19). From the past, a new game emerges. *The New York Times,* Retrieved from http//www .nytimes.com/2004/12/19/sports/basketball.

Robins, J. L. W., McCain, N. L., Gray, D. P., Elswick, R. K., Walter, J. M., & McDade, E. (2006). Research on psychoneuroimmunology: Tai chi as a stress management approach for individuals with HIV disease. *Applied Nursing Research, 19,* 2–9.

Robinson, D. W. (1985). Stress seeking: Selected behavioral characteristics of elite rock climbers. *Journal of Sport Psychology, 7,* 400–404.

Rodgers, W. M., Wilson, P. M., Hall, C. R., Fraser, S. N., & Murray, T. C. (2008). Evidence for a multidimensional self-efficacy for exercise scale. *Research Quarterly for Exercise and Sport, 79,* 222–234.

Rogers, T. J., & Landers, D. M. (2005). Mediating effects of peripheral vision in the life event stress/athletic injury relationship. *Journal of Sport & Exercise Psychology, 27,* 271–288.

Rogerson, L. J., & Hrycaiko, D. W. (2002). Enhancing competitive performance of ice hockey goaltenders using centering and self-talk. *Journal of Applied Sport Psychology, 14,* 14–26.

Rojas, R., Schlicht, W., & Hautzinger, M. (2003). Effects of exercise training on quality of life, psychological well-being, immune status, and cardiopulmonary fitness in HIV-1 positive populations. *Journal of Sport & Exercise Psychology, 25,* 440–455.

Ronglan, L. T. (2007). Building and communicating collective efficacy: A season-long in-depth study of an elite sport team. *The Sport Psychologist, 21,* 78–93.

Roose, J., de Vries, W. R., Schmikli, S. L., Backx, F. J. G., & van Doornen, L. J. P. (2009). Evaluation and opportunities in overtraining approaches. *Research Quarterly for Exercise and Sport, 80,* 756–764.

Roper, E. A. (2002). Women working in the applied domain: Examining the gender bias in applied sport psychology. *Journal of Applied Sport Psychology, 14,* 53–66.

Rose, E. A., & Parfitt, G. (2007). A quantitative analysis and qualitative exploration of the individual differences in affective responses to prescribed and self-selected exercise intensities. *Journal of Sport & Exercise Psychology, 28,* 281–311.

Rosenbaum, M. (1990). The role of learned resourcefulness in the self-control of health behavior. In M. Rosenbaum (Ed.), *Learned resourcefulness: On coping skills, self-control, and adaptive behavior* (pp. 3–30). New York, NY: Springer.

Ross-Stewart, L., & Short, S. E. (2009). The frequency and perceived effectiveness of images used to build, maintain, and regain confidence. *Journal of Applied Sport Psychology, 21,* S34–S47.

Rowbottom, D. G., & Green, K. J. (2000, July). Acute exercise effects on the immune system. *Medicine & Science in Sport & Exercise, 32,* S396–S405.

Rowley, A., Landers, D. M., Kyllo, L., & Etnier, J. (1995). Does the iceberg profile discriminate between successful and less successful athletes? A meta-analysis. *Journal of Sport & Exercise Psychology, 17,* 185–199.

Rowold, J. (2006). Transformational and transactional leadership in martial arts. *Journal of Applied Sport Psychology, 18,* 312–325.

Ruffer, W. A. (1975). Personality traits of athletes. *The Physical Educator, 32*(1), 105–109.

Ruffer, W. A. (1976a). Personality traits of athletes. *The Physical Educator, 33*(1), 50–55.

Ruffer, W. A. (1976b). Personality traits of athletes. *The Physical Educator, 33*(4), 211–214.

Rushall, B. S. (1970). An evaluation of the relationship between personality and physical performance categories. In G. S. Kenyon (Ed.), *Contemporary psychology of sport: Second International Congress of Sports Psychology.* Chicago, IL: The Athletic Institute.

Rushall, B. S. (1972). Three studies relating personality variables to football performance. *International Journal of Sport Psychology, 3,* 12–24.

Rushall, B. S. (1973). The status of personality research and application in sports and physical education. *Journal of Sports Medicine and Physical Fitness, 13,* 281–290.

Rushall, B. S., & Lippman, L. G. (1998). The role of imagery in physical performance. *International Journal of Sport Psychology, 29,* 57–72.

Rushin, S. (2000, July 31). Grand stand. *Sports Illustrated, 93,* 52–61.

Russell, G. W. (1995). Personalities in the crowd: Those who would escalate a sports riot. *Aggressive Behavior, 21,* 91–100.

Russell, G. W. (1999). Spectators, hostility, and riots. In G. G. Brannigan (Ed.), *The sport scientists: Research interests.* New York, NY: Longman.

Russell, G. W., & Arms, R. L. (1995). False consensus effect, physical aggression, anger, and a willingness to escalate a disturbance. *Aggressive Behavior, 21,* 381–386.

Russell, G. W., & Arms, R. L. (1998). Toward a social psychological profile of would-be rioters. *Aggressive Behavior, 24,* 219–226.

Russell, G. W., & Drewery, B. P. (1976). Crowd size and competitive aspects of aggression in ice hockey: An archival study. *Human Relations, 29,* 723–735.

Russell, G. W., & Mustonen, A. (1998). Peacemakers: Those who would intervene to quell a sports riot. *Personality and Individual Differences, 24,* 335–339.

Russell, J. A. (1980). A circumplex model of affect. *Journal of Personality and Social Psychology, 39,* 1161–1178.

Russell, J. A. (2003). Core affect and the psychological construction of emotion. *Psychological Review, 110,* 145–172.

Russell, J. A., Weiss, A., & Mendelsohn, G. A. (1989). Affect Grid: A single-item scale of pleasure and arousal. *Journal of Personality and Social Psychology, 57,* 493–502.

Russell, M. T., & Karol, D. L. (1994). *The 16 PF fifth edition administrator's manual.* Champaign, IL: Institute for Personality and Ability Testing.

Russell, W. D. (2000, September). Coping with injuries in scholastic athletics. *Journal of Physical Education, Recreation, and Dance, 71,* 41–46.

Russell, W. D., & Cox, R. H. (2000). A laboratory investigation of positive and negative affect within individual zones of optimal functioning theory. *Journal of Sport Behavior, 23,* 164–180.

Russell, W. D., & Cox, R. H. (2003). Social physique anxiety, body dissatisfaction, and self-esteem in college females differing in exercise frequency, perceived weight discrepancy and race. *Journal of Sport Behavior, 26,* 298–318.

Ryan, E. D. (1977). Attribution, intrinsic motivation, and athletics. In L. I. Gedvilas & M. E., Kneer (Eds.), *Proceedings of the NCPEAM/NAPECW National Conference, 1977.* Chicago, IL: University of Illinois at Chicago Circle.

Ryan, E. D. (1980). Attribution, intrinsic motivation and athletics: A replication and extension. In C. H. Nadeau (Ed.), *Psychology of motor behavior and sport, 1979.* Champaign, IL: Human Kinetics.

Ryan, E. D., & Simons, J. (1981). Cognitive demand, imagery, and frequency of mental rehearsal as factors influencing acquisition of motor skills. *Journal of Sport Psychology, 1,* 35–45.

Ryan, R. M. (2000, October). *Vital research: Intrinsic and extrinsic motivation for sport, exercise, and other health-related behaviors.* Paper presented at the meeting of the Association for the Advancement of Applied Sport Psychology, Nashville, TN.

Ryba, T. V., Stambulova, N. B., Wrisberg, C. A. (2005). The Russian origins of sport psychology: A translation of an earlier work. *Journal of Applied Sport Psychology, 17,* 157–169.

Rymal, A. M., & Ste-Marie, D. M. (2009). Does self-modeling affect imagery ability or vividness? *Journal of Imagery Research in Sport and Physical Activity, 4,* Article 6.

Ryska, T., Zenong, Y., & Boyd, M. (1999). The role of dispositional and goal orientation and team climate on situational self-handicapping among young athletes. *Journal of Sport Behavior, 22,* 410–425.

S

Sage, G. H. (1975). An occupational analysis of the college coach. In D. W. Ball & J. W. Loy (Eds.), *Sport and social order* (pp. 408–455). Reading, MA: Addison-Wesley.

Sage, L., & Kavussanu, M. (2007a). The effects of goal involvement on moral behaviors in experimentally manipulated competitive setting. *Journal of Sport & Exercise Psychology, 29,* 190–207.

Sage, L., & Kavussanu, M. (2007b). Multiple goal orientations as predictors of moral behavior in youth soccer. *The Sport Psychologist, 21,* 417–437.

Sager, S. S., & Lavallee, D. (2010). The developmental origins of fear of failure in adolescent athletes: Examining parental practices. *Psychology of Sport and Exercise, 11,* 177–187.

Sager, S. S., & Stoeber, J. (2009). Perfectionism, fear of failure, and affective responses to success and failure: The central role of fear of experiencing shame and embarrassment. *Journal of Sport & Exercise Psychology, 31,* 602–627.

Sager, S. S., Lavallee, D., & Spray, C. M. (2009). Coping with the effects of fear of failure: A preliminary investigation of young athletes. *Journal of Clinical Sport Psychology, 3,* 73–98.

Sallis, J. F., Haskell, W. L., Fortmann, S. P., Vranizan, K. M., Taylor, C. B., & Solomon, D. S. (1986). Predictors of adoption and maintenance of physical activity in a community sample. *Preventive Medicine, 15,* 331–341.

Sallis, J. F., & Hovell, M. F. (1990). Determinants of exercise behavior. In K. B. Pandolf & J. O. Holloszy (Eds.), *Exercise and sport science reviews,* (Vol. 18, pp. 307–330). Baltimore, MD: Williams & Wilkins.

Salmon, J., Hall, C. R., & Haslam, I. (1994). The use of imagery by soccer players. *Journal of Applied Sport Psychology, 6,* 116–133.

Salmon, J., Owen, N., Crawford, B. Bauman, A., & Sallis, J. F. (2003). Physical activity and sedentary behavior: A population-based study of barriers, enjoyment, and preference. *Health Psychology, 22,* 178–188.

Salmon, P., Hannenman, S., & Harwood, B. (2010). Associative/dissociative cognitive strategies in sustained physical activity: Literature review and a proposal for a mindfulness-based conceptual model. *The Sport Psychologist, 24,* 127–156.

Sarason, S. B. (1954). *The clinical interaction with special reference to Rorschach.* New York, NY: Harper & Brothers.

Scanlan, T. K., Russell, D. G., Magyar, T. M., & Scanlan, L. A. (2009). Project on elite athlete commitment (PEAK): III. An examination of the external validity across gender, and the expansion and clarification of the sport commitment model. *Journal of Sport & Exercise Psychology, 31,* 685–705.

Schedlowski, M., & Tewes, U. (1992). Physiological arousal and perception of bodily state during parachute jumping. *Psychophysiology, 29,* 95–103.

Scheer, J. K., & Ansorge, C. J. (1979). Influence due to expectations of judges: A function of internal-external locus of control. *Journal of Sport Psychology, 1,* 53–58.

Schilling, T. A., & Hayashi, C. T. (2001). Achievement motivation among high school basketball and cross-country athletes: A personal investment perspective. *Journal of Applied Sport Psychology, 13,* 103–127.

Schirlin, O., Rey, G., Jouvent, R., Dubal, S., Komano, O., Perez-Diaz, F., & Soussignan, R. (2009). Attentional bias for doping words and its relation with physical self-esteem in young adolescents. *Psychology of Sport and Exercise, 10,* 615–620.

Schlundt, D. G., Woodford, H., & Brownlee, A. (2000). *Muscle dysmorphia in male weightlifters: Psychological characteristics and practices.* Unpublished manuscript.

Schmid, A., & Peper, E. (1998). Training strategies for concentration. In J. M. Williams (Ed.), *Applied sport psychology: Personal growth to peak performance* (pp. 316–328). Mountain View, CA: Mayfield.

Schmidt, G. W., & Stein, G. L. (1991). Sport commitment: A model integrating enjoyment, dropout, and burnout. *Journal of Sport & Exercise Psychology, 13,* 254–265.

Schneider, M. L., & Graham, D. J. (2009). Personality, physical fitness, and affective response to exercise among adolescents. *Medicine & Science in Sports & Exercise, 41,* 947–955.

Schnurr, P. P., Vaillant, C. O., & Vaillant, G. E. (1990). Predicting exercise in later midlife from young adult personality characteristics. *International Journal of Aging and Human Development, 30,* 153–160.

Scholz, U., Schuz, B., Ziegelmann, J. P., Lippke, S., & Schwarzer, R. (2008). Beyond behavioural intentions: Planning mediates between intentions and physical activity. *British Journal of Health Psychology, 13,* 479–494.

Schomer, H. H. (1990). A cognitive strategy training programme for marathon runners: Ten case studies. *South African Journal for Research in Sport, Physical Education and Recreation, 13,* 47–78.

Schultz, J. H., & Luthe, W. (1959). *Autogenic training: A psychophysiological approach to psychotherapy.* New York, NY: Grune and Stratton.

Schurr, K. T., Ashley, M. A., & Joy, K. L. (1977). A multivariate analysis of male athlete characteristics: Sport type and success. *Multivariate Experimental Clinical Research, 3,* 53–68.

Schurr, K. T., Ruble, V. E., Nisbet, J., & Wallace, D. (1984). Myers-Briggs type inventory characteristics of more and less successful players on an American football team. *Journal of Sport Behavior, 7,* 47–57.

Schutte, N. S., Malouff, J. M., Hall, L. E., Haggerty, D. J., Cooper, J. T., Golden, C. J., & Dornheim, L. (1998). Development and validation of a measure of emotional intelligence. *Personality and Individual Differences, 25,* 167–177.

Schutte, N. S., Malouff, J. M., Simunek, M., McKenley, J., & Hollander, S. (2002). Characteristic emotional intelligence and emotional well-being. *Cognition and Emotion, 16,* 769–785.

Schutz, R. W., Eom, H. J., Smoll, F. L., & Smith, R. E. (1994). Examination of the factorial validity of the Group Environment Questionnaire. *Research Quarterly for Exercise and Sport, 65,* 226–236.

Schutz, W. C. (1966). *The interpersonal underworld.* Palo Alto, CA: Science and Behavior Books.

Schwartz, B., & Barsky, S. F. (1977). The home advantage. *Social Forces, 55,* 641–661.

Schwartz, G. E., Davidson, R. J., & Goleman, D. J. (1978). Patterning of cognitive and somatic processes in the self-regulation of anxiety: Effects of meditation vs. exercise. *Psychosomatic Medicine, 40,* 321–328.

Schwartz, L., & Kinderman, W. (1992). Changes in beta-endorphin levels in response to aerobic and anaerobic exercise. *Sports Medicine, 13,* 25–36.

Schwartz, L., & Kindermann, W. (1989, October). Beta-endorphin, catecholamines, and cortisol during exhaustive endurance exercise. *International Journal of Sports Medicine, 10,* 324–328.

Schwarz, L., & Kindermann, W. (1990). Beta-endorphin, adrenocorticotropic hormone, cortisol and catecholamines during aerobic and anaerobic exercise. *Journal of Applied Physiology and Occupational Physiology, 61,* 165–171.

Scott, E. J., Eves, F. F., Hoppe, R., & French, D. P. (2010). Dancing to a different tune: The predictive utility of the theory of planned behavior when the behavior is constrained. *Psychology of Sport and Exercise, 11,* 250–257.

Seabourne, T. G., Weinberg, R. S., & Jackson, A. (1984). The effect of individualized practice and training of visuo-motor behavior rehearsal in enhancing karate performance. *Journal of Sport Behavior, 7,* 58–67.

Search Institute. (2004). *Developmental assets profile preliminary user manual.* Minneapolis, MN: Author.

Sebire, S. J., Standage, M., & Vansteenkiste, M. (2009). Examining intrinsic versus extrinsic exercise goals: Cognitive, affective, and behavioral outcomes. *Journal of Sport & Exercise Psychology, 31,* 189–210.

Seefeldt, V., & Brown, E. W. (Eds.). (1992). *Program for athletic coaches' education.* Dubuque, IA: Brown & Benchmark.

Seifriz, J. J., Duda, J. L., & Chi, L. (1992). The relationship of perceived motivational climate to intrinsic motivation and beliefs about success in basketball. *Journal of Sport & Exercise Psychology, 14,* 375–391.

Seijts, G. H., Latham, G. P., Tasa, K., & Latham, B. W. (2004). Goal setting and goal orientation: An integration of two different yet related literatures. *Academy of Management Journal, 47,* 227–239.

Seiler, R., & Wylleman, P. (2009). FEFSAC's role and position in the past and in the future of sport psychology in Europe. *Psychology of Sport and Exercise, 10,* 403–409.

Seligman, M. E. P., & Csikszentmihalyi, M. (2000). Positive psychology: An introduction. *American Psychologist, 55,* 5–14.

Selye, H. (1983). The stress concept: Past, present, and future. In C. L. Cooper (Ed.), *Stress research* (pp. 1–20). New York, NY: John Wiley & Sons.

Senecal, J., Loughead, T. M., & Bloom, G. A. (2008). A season-long team building intervention: Examining the effect of team goal setting on cohesion. *Journal of Sport & Exercise Psychology, 30,* 186–199.

Serrao, H. F., Martens, M. P., Martin, J. L., & Rocha, T. L. (2008). Competitiveness and alcohol use among recreational and elite collegiate athletes. *Journal of Clinical Sport Psychology, 2,* 205–215.

Seve, C., Ria, L., Poizat, G., Saury, J., & Durand, M. (2007). Performance-induced emotions experienced during high-stakes table tennis matches. *Psychology of Sport and Exercise, 8,* 25–46.

Shacham, S. (1983). A shortened version of the Profile of Mood States. *Journal of Personality Assessment, 47,* 305–306.

Sharp, M., & Collins, D. (1998). Exploring the "inevitability" of the relationship between anabolic-androgenic steroid use and aggression in human males. *Journal of Sport & Exercise Psychology, 20,* 379–394.

Shaw, J. M., Dzewaltowski, D. A., & McElroy, M. (1992). Self-efficacy and causal attributions as mediators of perceptions of psychological momentum. *Journal of Sport & Exercise Psychology, 14,* 134–147.

Shay, K. A., & Roth, D. L. (1992). Association between aerobic fitness and visuospatial performance in healthy older adults. *Psychology of Aging, 7,* 15–24.

Sheehan, P. W. (1967). A shortened version of Betts' questionnaire on mental imagery. *Journal of Clinical Psychology, 23,* 386–389.

Sheldon, J. P., & Aimor, C. M. (2001). The role aggression plays in successful and unsuccessful ice hockey behavior. *Research Quarterly for Exercise and Sport, 72,* 304–309.

Sheldon, J. P., & Eccles, J. S. (2005). Physical and psychological predictors of perceived ability in adult male and female tennis players. *Journal of Applied Sport Psychology, 17,* 48–63.

Sheldon, K. M., & Elliot, A. J. (1999). Goal striving, need satisfaction, and longitudinal well-being: The self-concordance model. *Journal of Personality and Social Psychology, 76,* 482–497.

Shephard, R. J., Rhind, S., & Shek, P. N. (1995). The impact of exercise on the immune system: NK cells, interleukins 1 and 2, and related responses. *Exercises and Sport Science Reviews, 23,* 215–241.

Shields, D. L., & Bredemeier, B. J. (2007). Advances in sport morality research. In G. Tenenbaum, & R. C. Eklund (Eds.), *Handbook of sport psychology* (pp. 662–684). New York, NY: Wiley.

Shields, D. L., LaVoi, N. M., Bredemeier, B. L., & Power, F. C. (2007). Predictors of poor sportspersonship in youth sports: Personal attitudes and social influences. *Journal of Sport & Exercise Psychology, 29,* 747–762.

Short, S. E., & Short, M. W. (2005). Differences between high- and low-confident football players on imagery functions: A consideration of the athletes' perceptions. *Journal of Applied Sport Psychology, 17,* 197–208.

Short, S. E., Bruggeman, J. M., Enel, S. G., Marback, T. L., Wang, L. J., Willadsen, A., & Short, M. W. (2002). The effect of imagery function and imagery direction on self-efficacy and performance on a golf-putting task. *The Sport Psychologist, 16,* 48–67.

Short, S. E., Monsma, E. V., & Short, M. W. (2004). Is what you see really what you get? Athletes' perceptions of imagery's functions. *The Sport Psychologist, 18,* 341–349.

Short, S. E., Smiley, M., & Ross-Stewart, L. (2005). The relationship between efficacy beliefs and imagery use in coaches. *The Sport Psychologist, 19,* 380–394.

Short, S. E., Sullivan, P., & Feltz, D. L. (2005). Development and preliminary validation of the Collective Efficacy Questionnaire for Sports. *Measurement in Physical Education & Exercise Science, 9,* 181–202.

Sibley, B. A., & Etnier, J. L. (2003). The relationship between physical activity and cognition in children: A meta-analysis. Pediatric Exercise Science, 15, 243–256.

Sibley, B. A., & Etnier, J. L., & Le Masurier, G. C. (2006). Effects of an acute bout of exercise on cognitive aspects of Stroop performance. *Journal of Sport & Exercise Psychology, 28,* 285–299.

Siedentop, D., & Ramey, G. (1977). Extrinsic rewards and intrinsic motivation. *Motor Skills: Theory into Practice, 2,* 49–62.

Silva, J. M., III (1984). Personality and sport performance: Controversy and challenge. In J. M. Silva & R. S. Weinberg (Eds.), *Psychological foundations of sport* (pp. 59–69). Champaign, IL: Human Kinetics Publishers.

Silva, J. M., III. (1989). The evolution of AAASP and JASP. *Journal of Applied Sport Psychology, 1,* 1–3.

Silva, J. M., III, & Andrew, J. A. (1987). An analysis of game location and basketball performance in the Atlantic coast conference. *International Journal of Sport Psychology, 18,* 188–204.

Silva, J. M., III., & Appelbaum, M. I. (1989). Association-dissociation patterns of United States Olympic Marathon Trial contestants. *Cognitive Therapy and Research, 13,* 185–192.

Silva, J. M., III, Conroy, D. E., & Zizzi, S. J. (1999). Critical issues confronting the advancement of applied sport psychology. *Journal of Applied Sport Psychology, 11,* 298–320.

Silva, J. M., III, Hardy, C. J., & Grace, R. K. (1998). Analysis of psychological momentum in intercollegiate tennis. *Journal of Sport & Excercise Psychology, 10,* 346–354.

Singer, R. N. (1968). *Motor learning and human performance: An application to motor skills and movement behaviors.* New York, NY: Macmillan.

Singer, R. N. (1969). Personality differences between and within baseball and tennis players. *Research Quarterly, 40,* 582–587.

Singer, R. N. (2002). Preperformance state, routines, and automaticity: What does it take to realize expertise in self-paced events? *Journal of Sport & Exercise Psychology, 24,* 359–375.

Sit, C. H. P., & Lindner, K. J. (2006). Situational state balance and participation motivation in youth sport: A reversal theory perspective. *British Journal of Educational Psychology, 76,* 369–384.

Skinner, B. F. (1938). *The behavior of organisms: An experimental analysis.* New York, NY: Appleton-Century-Crofts.

Skinner, B. F. (1953). *Science and human behavior.* New York, NY: Macmillan.

Skinner, S. (2000, June 8). Striving for perfection. *Columbia Missourian Voxmagazine,* 8–13.

Slade, J. M., Landers, D. M., & Martin, P. E. (2002). Muscular activity during real and imagined movements: A test of inflow explanations. *Journal of Sport & Exercise Psychology,* 151–167.

Smith, A. L. (1999). Perceptions of peer relationships and physical activity participation in early adolescence. *Journal of Sport & Exercise Psychology, 21,* 329–350.

Smith, A. L., Ullrich-French, S., Walker, E. II, & Hurley, K. S. (2006). Peer relationship profiles and motivation in youth sport. *Journal of Sport & Exercise Psychology, 28,* 362–382.

Smith, A. M. (1996). Psychological impact of injuries in athletes. *Sports Medicine, 22,* 391–405.

Smith, A., Ntoumanis, N., & Duda, J. (2007). Goal striving, goal attainment, and well-being: Adapting and testing the self-concordance model. *Journal of Sport & Exercise Psychology, 29,* 763–782.

Smith, A., Ntoumanis, N., & Duda, J. (2010). An investigation of coach behaviors, goal motives, and implementation intentions as predictors of well-being in sport. *Journal of Applied Sport Psychology, 22,* 17–23.

Smith, D. (1992). The coach as sport psychologist: An alternate view. *Journal of Applied Sport Psychology, 4,* 56–62.

Smith, D. (2005, Winter). Golden rules. *Mizzou, 93,* 32–37.

Smith, D., & Collins, D. (2004). Mental practice, motor performance, and the late CNV. *Journal of Sport & Exercise Psychology, 26,* 412–426.

Smith, D., & Stewart, S. (2003). Sexual aggression and sports participation. *Journal of Sport Behavior, 26,* 384–395.

Smith, D., Wright, C. J., & Cantwell, C. (2008). Beating the bunker: The effect of PETTLEP imagery on golf bunker shot performance. *Research Quarterly for Exercise and Sport, 79,* 385–391.

Smith, D., Wright, C., Allsopp, A., & Westhead, H. (2007). It's all in the mind: PETTLEP-based imagery and sports performance. *Journal of Applied Sport Psychology, 19,* 80–92.

Smith, G. (2004, May 3). Pat Tillman 1976–2004: Code of honor. *Sports Illustrated, 100,* 40–46.

Smith, G. (2005, March 28). Steroids and baseball: What do we do now? *Sports Illustrated, 102,* 40–50.

Smith, G. (2008, June 23). Alive and kicking. *Sports Illustrated, 108,* 58–68.

Smith, M. D. (1980). Hockey violence: Interring some myths. In W. F. Straub (Ed.), *Sport psychology: An analysis of athlete behavior* (2nd ed.). Ithaca, NY: Mouvement Publications.

Smith, R. E. (1980). A cognitive-affective approach to stress management training for athletes. In C. H. Nadeau (Ed.), *Psychology of motor behavior and sport, 1979.* Champaign, IL: Human Kinetics.

Smith, R. E. (1986). Toward a cognitive-affective model of athletic burnout. *Journal of Sport Psychology, 8,* 36–50.

Smith, R. E. (1996). Performance anxiety, cognitive interference, and concentration enhancement strategies in sports. In I. G. Sarason, G. R. Pierce, & B. R. Sarason (Eds.), *Cognitive interference: Theories, methods, and findings* (pp. 261–283). Mahwah, NJ: Erlbaum.

Smith, R. E. (1999). Generalization effects in coping skills training. *Journal of Sport & Exercise Psychology, 21,* 189–204.

Smith, R. E. (2006). Understanding sport behavior: A cognitive-affective approach. *Journal of Applied Sport Psychology, 18,* 1–27.

Smith, R. E., & Christensen, D. S. (1995). Psychological skills as predictors of performance and survival in professional baseball. *Journal of Sport & Exercise Psychology, 17,* 399–415.

Smith, R. E., Cumming, S. P., & Smoll, F. (2008). Development and validation of the motivational climate scale for youth sports. *Journal of Applied Sport Psychology, 20,* 116–136.

Smith, R. E., & Johnson, J. (1990). An organizational empowerment approach to consultation in professional baseball. *The Sport Psychologist, 4,* 347–357.

Smith, R. E., Schutz, R. W., Smoll, F. L., & Ptacek, J. T. (1995). Development and validation of a multidimensional measure of sport-specific psychological skills: The athletic coping skills inventory-28. *Journal of Sport & Exercise Psychology, 17,* 379–398.

Smith, R. E., Shoda, Y., Cumming, S. P., & Smoll, F. L. (2009). Behavioral signatures at the ballpark: Intra individual consistency of adults' situation-behavioral patterns and their interpersonal consequences. *Journal of Research in Personality, 43,* 187–195.

Smith, R. E., Smoll, F. L., & Barnett, N. P. (1995). Reduction of children's sport performance anxiety through social support and stress-reduction training for coaches. *Journal of Applied Developmental Psychology, 16,* 125–142.

Smith, R. E., & Smoll, F. L. (1996). Way to go coach! A scientifically-proven approach to coaching effectiveness. Portola Valley, CA: Warde.

Smith, R. E., & Smoll, F. L. (1997a). Coach-mediated team building in youth sports. *Journal of Applied Sport Psychology, 9,* 114–132.

Smith, R. E., & Smoll, F. L. (1997b, February). Coaching the coaches: Youth sports as a scientific and applied behaviorial setting. *Current Directions in Psychological Science, 6,* 16–21.

Smith, R. E., Smoll, F. L., & Cumming, S. P. (2007). Effects of a motivational climate interpretation for coaches on young athletes' sport performance anxiety. *Journal of Sport & Exercise Psychology, 29,* 39–59.

Smith, R. E., Smoll, F. L., & Curtis, B. (1978). Coaching behaviors in Little League Baseball. In F. L. Smoll, & R. E. Smith (Eds.), *Psychological perspectives in youth sports* (pp. 173–201). Washington, DC: Hemisphere.

Smith, R. E., Smoll, F. L., & Curtis, B. (1979). Coach effectiveness training: A cognitive-behavioral approach to enhancing relationship skills in youth sport coaches. *Journal of Sport Psychology, 1,* 59–75.

Smith, R. E., Smoll, F. L., & Hunt, E. (1977). A system for the behavioral assessment of athletic coaches. *Research Quarterly, 48,* 401–407.

Smith, R. E., Smoll, F. L., & Ptacek, J. T. (1990). Conjunctive moderatory variables in vulnerability and resiliency research: Life stress, social support and coping skills, and adolescent sport injuries. *Journal of Personality and Social Psychology, 58*(2), 560–570.

Smith, R. E., Smoll, F. L., & Schutz, R. W. (1990). Measurement correlates of sport-specific cognitive and somatic trait anxiety: The sport anxiety scale. *Anxiety Research, 2,* 263–280.

Smith, R. E., Smoll, F. L., Cumming, S. P., & Grossbard, J. R. (2006). Measurement of multidimensional sport performance anxiety in children and adults: The Sport Anxiety Scale-2. *Journal of Sport & Exercise Psychology, 28,* 479–501.

Smith, S. L., Fry, M. D., Ethington, C. A., & Li, Y. (2005). The effect of female athletes, perceptions of their coaches' behaviors on their perceptions of the motivational climate. *Journal of Applied Sport Psychology, 17,* 170–177.

Smolak, L., Muren, S. K., & Ruble, A. E. (2000). Female athletes and eating problems: A meta-analysis. *International Journal of Eating Disorders, 27,* 371–380.

Smoll, F. L. (1998). Improving the quality of coach-parent relationships in youth sports. In J. M. Williams (Ed.), *Applied sport psychology: Personal growth to peak performance* (pp. 63–73). Mountain View, CA: Mayfield.

Smoll, F. L., & Cumming, S. P. (2006). Enhancing coach-parent relationships in youth sports: Increasing harmony and minimizing hassle. In J. M. Williams (Ed.), *Applied sport psychology: Personal growth to peak performance* (pp. 192–204). New York, NY: McGraw-Hill.

Smoll, F. L., & Smith, R. E. (1989). Leadership behaviors in sport: A theoretical model and research paradigm. *Journal of Applied Social Psychology, 19,* 1522–1551.

Smoll, F. L., & Smith, R. E. (1998). Conducting psychologically oriented coach-training programs: Cognitive-behavioral principles and techniques. In J. M. Williams (Ed.), *Applied sport psychology: Personal growth to peak performance* (pp. 41–62). Mountain View, CA: Mayfield.

Smoll, F. L., & Smith, R. E. (1999). Coaching behavior research in youth sports: Sport psychology goes to the ballpark. In G. G. Brannigan (Ed.), *The sport scientists: Research interests* (pp. 113–132). New York, NY: Longman.

Smoll, F. L., & Smith, R. E. (2010). Conducting psychologically oriented coach-training programs: A social-cognitive approach. In J. M. Williams (Ed.), *Applied sport psychology: Personal growth to peak performance* (pp. 392–515). Boston, MA: McGraw-Hill.

Smoll, F. L., Smith, R. E., & Cumming, S. P. (2007). Effects of a motivational climate intervention for coaches on changes in young athletes' achievement goal orientations. *Journal of Clinical Sport Psychology, 1,* 23–46.

Smoll, F. L., Smith, R. E., Curtis, B., & Hunt, E. (1978). Toward a mediational model of coach-player relationships. *Research Quarterly, 49,* 528–541.

Sonstroem, R. J., & Bermardo, P. (1982). Intraindividual pregame state anxiety and basketball performance: A reexamination of the inverted-U curve. *Journal of Sport Psychology, 4,* 235–245.

Sordoni, C., Hall, C., & Forwell, L. (2000). The use of imagery by athletes during rehabilitation. *Journal of Applied Sport Psychology, 3,* 329–338.

Sousa, C., Smith, R. E., & Cruz, J. (2008). An individualized behavioral goal-setting program for coaches. *Journal of Clinical Sport Psychology, 2,* 258–277.

Spence, J. C., McGannon, K. R., & Poon, P. (2005). The effect of exercise on global self-esteem: A quantitative review. *Journal of Sport & Exercise Psychology, 27,* 311–334.

Spence, K. W. (1956). *Behavior theory and conditioning.* New Haven, CT: Yale University Press.

Spielberger, C. D. (1971). Trait-state anxiety and motor behavior. *Journal of Motor Behavior, 3,* 265–279.

Spielberger, C. D. (1983). *Manual for the state-trait anxiety inventory* (Form Y). Palo Alto, CA: Consulting Psychologists Press.

Spigolon, L., & Annalisa, D. (1985). Autogenic training in frogmen. *International Journal of Sport Psychology, 16,* 312–320.

Spink, K. S. (1992). Group cohesion and starting status in successful and less successful elite volleyball teams. *Journal of Sport Sciences, 10,* 379–388.

Spink, K. S. (1995). Cohesion and intention to participate of female sport team athletes. *Journal of Sport & Exercise Psychology, 17,* 416–427.

Spink, K. S., Wilson, K. S., & Odnokon, P. (2010). Examining the relationship between cohesion and return to team in elite athletes. *Psychology of Sport and Exercise, 11,* 6–11.

Spirduso, W. W. (1975). Reaction and movement time as a function of age and physical activity level. *Journal of Gerontology, 30,* 435–440.

Sprecher, S., Felmlee, D., Orbuch, T. L., & Willets, M. C. (2002). Social networks and change in personal relationships. In A. Vagelistsi, H. Reis, & M. A. Fitzpatrick (Eds.), *Stability and change in relationships* (pp. 257–284). Cambridge, UK: Cambridge University Press.

Stadulis, R. E., Eidson, T. A., & MacCracken, M. J. (1994). A children's form of the competitive state anxiety inventory (CSAI-2C). *Journal of Sport & Exercise Psychology, 16,* S109.

Staff. (1992, September/October). AHA declares regular exercise to be a major factor in cardiovascular health. *President's Council on Physical Fitness and Sports Newsletter, 92*(5), 1, 5.

Stambulova, N. B., Wrisberg, C. A., & Ryba, T. V. (2006). A tale of two traditions in applied sport psychology: The heyday of Soviet Sport and wake-up calls for North American. *Journal of Applied Sport Psychology, 18,* 173–184.

Stambulova, N., Stephan, Y., & Japhag, U. (2007). Athletic retirement: A cross-national comparison of elite French and Swedish athletes. *Psychology of Sport and Exercise, 8,* 101–118.

Standage, M., Duda, J. L., & Ntoumanis, N. (2006). Students' motivational processes and their relationship to teacher ratings in school physical education: A self-determination theory approach. *Research Quarterly for Exercise and Sport Psychology, 77,* 100–110.

Standage, M., Sebire, S. J., & Loney, T. (2008). Does exercise motivation predict engagement in objectively assessed bouts of moderate-intensity exercise?: A self-determination theory perspective. *Journal of Sport & Exercise Psychology, 30,* 337–352.

Stanley, C. T., Pargman, D., & Tenenbaum, G. (2007). The effect of attentional coping strategies on perceived exertion in a cycling task. *Journal of Applied Sport Psychology, 19,* 352–363.

Stavrou, N. A., Jackson, S. A., Zervas, Y. & Karteroliotis, K. (2007). Flow experience and athletes' performance with reference to the orthogonal model of flow. *The Sport Psychologist, 21,* 438–457.

Steers, D. (1982, November). Trapped in Peru, U.S. women shouted down. *Volleyball Monthly,* 15–21.

Stein, J. (1999, October 4). The oldest rookie. *Time, 154,* 6.

Steinberg, G. M. B., Singer, R. N., & Murphy, M. (2000). The benefits to sport achievement when a multiple goal orientation is emphasized. *Journal of Sport Behavior, 23,* 407–422.

Stennet, R. C. (1957). The relationship of performance level to level of arousal. *Journal of Experimental Psychology, 54,* 54–61.

Stephan, Y., Torregrosa, M., & Sanchez, X. (2007). The body matters: Psychophysical impact of retiring from elite sport. *Psychology of Sport and Exercise, 8,* 73–83.

Stephen, D. E., & Bredemeier, B. J. L. (1996). Moral atmosphere and judgments about aggression in girls' soccer: Relationships among moral and motivational variables. *Journal of Sport & Exercise Psychology, 18,* 158–173.

Stephens, D. E. (2000). Predictors of likelihood to aggress in youth soccer: An examination of coed and all-girls teams. *Journal of Sport Behavior, 23,* 311–325.

Stephens, D. E. (2001). Predictors of aggressive tendencies in girls' basketball: An examination of beginning and advanced participants in a summer skills camp. *Research Quarterly for Exercise Sport, 72,* 257–266.

Stephens, D. E., Bredemeier, B. J., & Shields, D. L. (1997). Construction of a measure designed to assess players' descriptions of moral behavior in youth sport soccer. *International Journal of Sport Psychology, 28,* 370–390.

Steptoe, A., & Cox, S. (1988). Acute effects of aerobic exercise on mood. *Health Psychology, 7,* 329–340.

Steroids made baseball career possible (2005, February 13). Canseco: Steroids made baseball career possible, Retrieved from http://www.USAtoday.com/2005/2/13/

Stevens, T. A., To, Y., Stevenson, S. J., & Lochbaum, M. R. (2008). The importance of physical activity in the prediction of academic achievement. *Journal of Sport Behavior, 31,* 368–389.

Stevinson, C. D., & Biddle, S. J. H. (1999). Cognitive strategies in running: A response to Masters and Ogles (1998). *The Sport Psychologist, 13,* 234–236.

Stoeber, J., & Becker, C. (2009). Perfectionism, achievement motives, and attribution of success and failure in female soccer players. *International Journal of Psychology, 43,* 980–987.

Stoeber, J., Otto, K., & Stoll, O. (2004). Mehrdimensionales Inventar zu Perfektionismus im Sport (MIPS) [Multidimensional Inventory of Perfectionism in Sport (MIPS)]. In C. Dalbert (Ed.), *Hallesche Berichte zur Padagogischen Psychologie* (No. 7, pp. 4–13). Halle/Saale, Germany: Martin Luther University of Halle.

Stoeber, J., Otto, K., Pescheck, E., Becker, C., & Stoll, O. (2007). Perfectionism and competitive anxiety in athletes: Differentiating striving for perfection and negative reactions to imperfection. *Personality and Individual Differences, 42,* 959–969.

Stoeber, J., Stoll, O., Pescheck, E., & Otto, K. (2008). Perfectionism and goal orientations in athletes: Relations with approach and avoidance orientations in mastery and performance goals. *Psychology of Sport and Exercise, 9,* 102–121.

Stoeber, J., Uphill, M. A., & Hotham, S. (2009). Predicting race performance in triathlon: The role of perfectionism, achievement goals, and personal goal setting. *Journal of Sport & Exercise Psychology, 31,* 211–245.

Stogdill, R. M. (1948). Personal factors associated with leadership: Survey of literature. *Journal of Psychology, 25,* 35–71.

Stoll, O., Lau, A., & Stoeber, J. (2008). Perfectionism and performance in a new basketball task: Does striving for perfection enhance or undermine performance? *Psychology of Sport and Exercise, 9,* 620–629.

Stone, J., & McWhinnie, C. (2008). Evidence that blatant versus subtle stereotype threat cues impact performance through dual processes. *Journal of Experimental Social Psychology, 44,* 273–280.

Stone, M. H. (1993). Literature review: Anabolic-androgenic steroid use by athletes. *National Strength and Conditioning Association Journal, 15,* 10–28.

Storch, E. A., Storch, J. B., Kovacs, A. H., Okun, A., & Welsh, E. (2003). Intrinsic religiosity and substance use in intercollegiate athletes. *Journal of Sports & Exercise Psychology, 25,* 248–252.

Storch, E. A., Werner, N. E., & Storch, J. B. (2003). Relational aggression and psychosocial adjustment in intercollegiate athletes. *Journal of Sport Behavior, 26,* 155–167.

Strachan, L., Côté, J., & Deakin, J. (2009a). "Specializers" versus "samplers" in youth sport: Comparing experiences and outcomes. *The Sport Psychologist, 23,* 77–92.

Strachan, L., Côté, J., & Deakin, J. (2009b). An evaluation of personal and contextual factors in competitive youth sport. *Journal of Applied Sport Psychology, 21,* 340–355.

Strelan, P., & Boeckmann, R. J. (2003). A new model for understanding performance-enhancing drug use by elite athletes. *Journal of Applied Sport Psychology, 15,* 176–183.

Stringer, W. W., Berezovskaya, M., O'Brian, W. A., Beck, C. K., & Casaburi, R. (1998). The effect of exercise training on aerobic fitness, immune indices, and quality of life in HIV-positive patients. *Medicine & Science in Sports & Exercise, 30,* 11–16.

Stroop, J. R. (1935). Studies of interference in serial verbal reactions. *Journal of Experimental Psychology, 18,* 643–662.

Stuntz, C. P., & Weiss, M. R. (2003). Influence of social goal orientation and peers on unsportsman-like play. *Research Quarterly for Exercise and Sport, 74,* 421–435.

Stuntz, C. P., & Weiss, M. R. (2009). Achievement goal orientations and motivational outcomes in youth sport: The role of social orientations. *Psychology of Sport and Exercise, 10,* 255–262.

Sue, D., & Sue, D. W. (1999). *Counseling the culturally different: Theory and practice* (3rd ed.). New York, NY: Wiley.

Suinn, R. (2000, October). *Psychological interventions with heart disease, cancer, and pain management.* Paper presented at the meeting of the Association for the Advancement of Applied Sport Psychology, Nashville, TN.

Suinn, R. M. (1972). Removing emotional obstacles to learning and performance by visuo-motor behavior rehearsal. *Behavioral Therapy, 31,* 308–310.

Suinn, R. M. (1994). Visualization in sports. In A. A. Sheikh & E. R. Korn (Eds.), *Imagery in sports and physical performance* (pp. 23–42). Amityville, NY: Baywood.

Sullivan, M. I. L., Bishop, S., & Pivik, J. (1995). The Pain Catastrophizing Scale: Development and validation. *Psychological Assessment, 7,* 524–532.

Sullivan, M. I. L., Tripp, D. A., Rodgers, W. M., & Stanish, W. (2000). Catrastrophizing and pain perception in sport participants. *Journal of Applied Sport Psychology, 12,* 151–167.

Sullivan, P. J., & Kent, A. (2003). Coaching efficacy as a predictor of leadership style in intercollegiate athletics. *Journal of Applied Sport Psychology, 15,* 1–11.

Sundgot-Borgen, J., & Torstveit, M. K. (2004). Prevalence of eating disorders in elite athletes is higher than in the general population. *Clinical Journal of Sport Medicine, 14,* 25–32.

Svebak, S., & Murgatroyd, S. (1985). Metamotivational dominance: A multimethod validation of reversal theory constructs. *Journal of Personality and Social Psychology, 48,* 107–116.

Swain, A., & Jones, G. (1992). Relationship between sport achievement orientation and competitive state anxiety. *The Sport Psychologist, 6,* 42–54.

Swain, A. B. J., & Jones, G. (1993). Intensity and frequency dimensions of competitive state anxiety. *Journal of Sports Sciences, 11,* 533–542.

Swami, V., Steadman, L., & Tovee, M. J. (2009). A comparison of body size ideals, body dissatisfaction, and media influence between female track athletes, martial artists, and non-athletes. *Psychology of Sport and Exercise, 10,* 609–614.

Swift, E. M. (2004, August 30). How the fallen was mighty. *Sports Illustrated, 101,* 44–47.

Szameitat, A. J., Shen, S., & Sterr, A. (2007). Motor imagery of complex every day movements: An fMRI study. *NeuroImage, 34,* 702–713.

T

Tang, Y.-Y., Ma, Y., Fan, Y., Feng, H., Wang, J., Feng, S., . . . Fan, M., et al. (2009, June 2). Central and autonomic nervous system interaction is altered by short-term meditation. *Proceedings of the National Academy of Sciences, USA, 106,* 8865–8870.

Tang, Y.-Y., Ma, Y., Wang, J., Fan, Y., Feng, S., Lu, Q., . . . Posner, M. I., et al. (2007, October 23). Short term meditation training improves attention and self-regulation. *Proceedings of the National Academy of Sciences, 104,* 17152–17156.

Tang, Y.-Y., & Posner, M. I. (2009). Attention training and attention state training. *Trends in Cognitive Sciences, 13,* 222–227.

Tattersfield, C. R. (1971). *Competitive sport and personality development.* Unpublished doctoral dissertation, University of Durham, NC.

Tauer, J. M., Guenther, C. L., & Rozek, C. (2009). Is there a home choke in decisive playoff basketball games? *Journal of Applied Sport Psychology, 21,* 148–162.

Taylor, A. J., & May, S. (1996). Threat and coping appraisal as determinants of compliance to sports injury rehabilitation: An application of protection motivation theory. *Journal of Sports Sciences, 14,* 471–482.

Taylor, I. M., & Ntoumanis, N., & Standage, M. (2008). A self-determination theory approach to understanding the antecedents of teachers' motivational strategies in physical education. *Journal of Sport & Exercise Psychology, 30,* 75–94.

Taylor, J. (1994). Examining the boundaries of sport science and psychology trained practitioners in applied sport psychology: Title usage and area of competence. *The Sport Psychologist, 6,* 185–195.

Taylor, J. (2008). Prepare to succeed: Private consulting in applied sport psychology. *Journal of Clinical Sport Psychology, 2,* 160–177.

Taylor, J., & Demick, A. (1994). A multidimensional model of momentum in sports. *Journal of Applied Sport Psychology, 6,* 51–70.

Taylor, J., & Ogilvie, B. (1994). A conceptual model of adaptation to retirement among athletes. *Journal of Applied Sport Psychology, 6,* 1–20.

Taylor, J., & Ogilvie, B. C. (2001). Career termination among athletes. In R. N. Singer, H. A. Hausenblas, & M. C. M. Janelle (Eds.), *Handbook of Sport Psychology* (pp. 672–694). New York, NY: John Wiley & Sons.

Taylor, J., & Taylor, S. (1998). Pain education and management in the rehabilitation from sports injury. *The Sport Psychologist, 12,* 68–88.

Taylor, P. (1997, December 15). Center of the storm. *Sports Illustrated, 87,* 60–67.

Tenenbaum, G. (1984). A note on the measurement and relationships of physiological and psychological components of anxiety. *International Journal of Sport Psychology, 15,* 88–97.

Tenenbaum, G. (2001). A social-cognitive perspective of perceived exertion and exertion tolerance. In R. N. Singer, H. Hausenblas, & C. Janelle (Eds.), *Handbook of sport psychology* (pp. 810–820). New York, NY: Wiley.

Tenenbaum, G. (2002). The study of perceived and sustained effort: Concepts, research findings and new directions. In D. Hackfort,

J. S. Duda, & R. Lidor (Eds.), *Handbook on research in applied sport psychology.* Morgantown, WV: Fitness Information Technology.

Tenenbaum, G., & Connolly, C. T. (2008). Attention allocation under varied workload and effort perceptions in rowers. *Psychology of Sport and Exercise, 9,* 704–717.

Tenenbaum, G., Bar-Eli, M., & Yaaron, M. (1999). The dynamics of goal setting: Interactive effects of goal difficulty, goal specificity and duration of practice time intervals. *International Journal of Sport Psychology, 30,* 325–338.

Tenenbaum, G., Corbett, M., & Kitsantas, A. (2002). Biofeedback: Applications and methodological concerns. In B. Blumenstein, M. Bar-Eli, & G. Tenenbaum (Eds.). *Brain and body in sport and exercise: Biofeedback applications in performance enhancement* (pp. 101–122). John Wiley & Sons.

Tenenbaum, G., & Elran, E. (2003). Congruence between actual and retrospective reports of emotions for pre- and postcompetition states. *Journal of Sport & Exercise Psychology, 25,* 323–340.

Tenenbaum, G., Lloyd, M., Pretty, G., & Hanin, Y. L. (2002). Congruence of actual and retrospective reports of pre-competition emotions in equestrians. *Journal of Sport & Exercise Psychology, 24,* 271–288.

Tenenbaum, G., Stewart, E., Singer, R. N., & Duda, J. (1997). Aggression and violence in sport: An ISSP position stand. *The Sport Psychologist, 11,* 1–7.

Terry, P. C. (1995). The efficacy of mood state profiling with elite performers: A review and synthesis. *The Sport Psychologist, 9,* 309–324.

Terry, P. C., Keohane, L., & Lane, H. (1996). Development and validation of a shortened version of the profile of mood states suitable for use with young athletes. *Journal of Sports Sciences, 14,* 49.

Terry, P. C., & Lane, A. M. (2000). Normative values for the profile of mood states for use with athletic samples. *Journal of Applied Sport Psychology, 12,* 93–109.

Terry, P. C., Mayer, J. L., & Howe, B. L. (1998). Effectiveness of a mental training program for novice scuba divers. *Journal of Applied Sport Psychology, 10,* 251–267.

Thamel, P. (2003, May 5). Mavericks avoid meltdown. *The New York Times,* Retrieved from http://www.nytimes.com/2003/5/5/ sports/basketball/

Thatcher, J., & Day, M. C. (2008). Re-appraising stress appraisals: The underlying properties of stress in sport. *Psychology of Sport and Exercise, 9,* 318–335.

Thayer, R. E. (1986). Activation-Deactivation Check List: Current overview and structural analysis. *Psychological Reports, 58,* 607–614.

Thelwell, R. C., & Greenlees, I. A. (2001). The effects of a mental skills training package on gymnasium triathlon performances. *The Sport Psychologist, 15,* 127–141.

Thelwell, R. C., & Greenlees, I. A. (2003). Developing competitive endurance performance using mental skills training. *The Sport Psychologist, 17,* 318–337.

Thelwell, R. C., Greenlees, I. A., & Weston, N. J. V. (2006). Using psychological skills training to develop soccer performance. *Journal of Applied Sport Psychology, 18,* 254–270.

Thelwell, R. C., Greenlees, I. A., & Weston, N. J. V. (2010). Examining the use of psychological skills throughout soccer performances. *Journal of Sport Behavior, 33,* 109–127.

Thelwell, R. C., Weston, N. J. V., Greenlees, I. A., & Hutchings, N. V. (2008). A qualitative exploration of psychological-skills use in coaches. *The Sport Psychologist, 22,* 38–53.

Thelwell, R. C., Weston, N., & Greenlees, I. A. (2005). Defining and understanding mental toughness within soccer. *Journal of Applied Sport Psychology, 17,* 326–332.

Theodorakis, Y. (1996). The influence of goals, commitment, self-efficacy and self-satisfaction on motor performance. *Journal of Applied Sport Psychology, 8,* 171–182.

Theodorakis, Y., Chroni, S., & Laparidis, K., Bebetos, V., & Duoma, I. (2001). Self-talk in a basketball shooting task. *Perceptual and Motor Skills, 92,* 309–315.

Theodorakis, Y., Hatzigeorgiadis, A., & Chroni, S. (2008). Self-talk: It works, but how? Development and preliminary validation of the Functions of Self-Talk Questionnaire. *Measurement in Physical Education and Exercise Science, 12,* 10–30.

Theodorakis, Y., Weinberg, R., Natsis, P., Douma, I., & Kazakas, P. (2000). The effects of motivational versus instructional self-talk on improving motor performance. *The Sport Psychologist, 14,* 253–271.

Thirer, J., & Greer, D. L. (1981). Personality characteristics associated with beginning, intermediate, and competitive bodybuilders. *Journal of Sport Behavior, 4,* 3–11.

Thomas, O., Hanton, S., & Jones, G. (2002). An alternative approach to short-form self-report assessment of competitive anxiety: A research note. *International Journal of Sport Psychology, 33,* 325–336.

Thomas, O., Hanton, S., & Maynard, I. (2007). Anxiety responses and psychological skill use during the time leading up to competition: Theory to practice I. *Journal of Applied Sport Psychology, 19,* 379–397.

Thomas, O., Maynard, I., & Hanton, S. (2004). Temporal aspects of competitive anxiety and self-confidence as a function of anxiety perception. *The Sport Psychologist, 18,* 172–187.

Thomas, O., Maynard, I., & Hanton, S. (2007). Intervening with athletes during the time leading up to competition: Theory to practice II. *Journal of Applied Sport Psychology, 19,* 398–418.

Thomas, P. R., Murphy, S. M., & Hardy, L. (1999). Test of Performance Strategies: Development and preliminary validation of a comprehensive measure of athletes' psychological skills. *Journal of Sport Sciences, 17,* 697–713.

Thompson, B. (2002, March 20). Homecoming kings. *Columbia Daily Tribune,* B.

Thorn, P., Floras, J. S., Hoffman, P., & Seals, D. R. (1990). Endorphins and exercise: Physiological mechanisms and clinical implications. *Medicine & Science in Sports & Exercise, 22,* 417–428.

Thune, A. R. (1949). Personality of weight lifters. *Research Quarterly, 20,* 296–306.

Thuot, S., Kavouras, S., & Kenefick, R. (1998). Effect of perceived ability, game location, and state anxiety on basketball performance. *Journal of Sport Behavior, 21,* 311–321.

Tod, D., & Andersen, M. B. (2010). When to refer athletes for counseling or psychotherapy. In J. M. Williams (Ed.), *Applied sport psychology: Personal growth to peak performance* (pp. 443–462). Boston, MA: McGraw-Hill.

Tolson, J. (2000, July 3). Into the zone. *U.S. News & World Report, 129,* 38–45.

Tompkins, S. S. (1947). *The Thematic Apperception Test: The theory and technique of interpretation.* New York, NY: Grune and Stratton.

Tomporowski, P. D., Ellis, N. R. (1986). Effects of exercise on cognitive processes: A review. *Psychological Bulletin, 99,* 338–346.

Tomporowski, P. D. (2003). Effects of acute bouts of exercise on cognition. *Acta Psychologica, 112,* 297–324.

Tracey, J. (2003). The emotional response to the injury and rehabilitation process. *Journal of Applied Sport Psychology, 15,* 279–293.

Traclet, A., Rascle, O., Souchon, N., Coulomb-Cabagno, G., Petrucci, C., & Ohbuchi, K.-I. (2009). Aggression in soccer: An exploratory study of accounts preference. *Research Quarterly for Exercise and Sport, 80,* 398–402.

Treasure, D. C., Duda, J. L., Hall, H. K., Roberts, G. C., Ames, C., & Maehr, M. L. (2001). Clarifying misconceptions and misrepresentations in achievement goal research in sport: A response to Haywood, Hardy, and Swain. *Journal of Sport & Exercise Psychology, 23,* 317–329.

Treasure, D. C., Lox, C. L., & Lawton, B. R. (1998). Determinants of physical activity in a sedentary obese female population. *Journal of Sport & Exercise Psychology, 20,* 218–224.

Treasure, D. C., & Roberts, G. C. (1995). Application of achievement goal theory to physical education: Implications for enhancing motivation. *Quest, 47,* 475–489.

Treasure, D. C., & Roberts, G. C. (1998). Relationship between female adolescents' achievement goal orientations, perceptions of the motivational climate, belief about success and sources of satisfaction in basketball. *International Journal of Sport Psychology, 29,* 211–230.

Treisman, A. M. (1965). Our limited attention. *The Advancement of Science, 22,* 600–611.

Triplett, N. (1897). The dynamogenic factors in pacemaking and competition. *American Journal of Psychology, 9,* 507–553.

Tripp, D. A., Stanish,W., Ebel-Lam, A., Brewer, B. W., & Birchard, J. (2007). Fear of reinjury, negative affect, and catastrophizing predicting return to sport in recreational athletes with anterior cruciate ligament injuries. *Rehabilitation Psychology, 52,* 74–81.

Tucker, L. W., & Parks, J. B. (2001). Effects of gender and sport type on intercollegiate athletes' perceptions of the legitimacy of aggressive behavior in sport. *Sociology of Sport Journal, 18,* 403–413.

Tuckman, B. W. (1965). Developmental sequences in small groups. *Psychological Bulletin, 63,* 384–399.

Turner, E. E., Rejeski, W. J., & Brawley, L. R. (1997). Psychological benefits of physical activity are influenced by the social environment. *Journal of Sport & Exercise Psychology, 19,* 119–130.

Turner, P. E., & Raglin, J. S. (1996). Variability in precompetition anxiety and performance in college track and field athletes. *Medicine & Science in Sports & Exercise, 28,* 378–385.

Tutko, T. A., & Richards, J. W. (1971). *Psychology of coaching.* Boston, MA: Allyn and Bacon.

Tutko, T. A., & Richards, J. W. (1972). *Coaches' practical guide to athletic motivation.* Boston, MA: Allyn and Bacon.

U

Udry, E. (1997). Coping and social support among injured athletes following surgery. *Journal of Sport & Exercise Psychology, 19,* 71–90.

Udry, E., Gould, D., Bridges, D., & Beck, L. (1997). Down but not out: Athlete responses to season-ending injuries. *Journal of Sport & Exercise Psychology, 19,* 229–248.

Udry, E., Gould, D., Bridges, D., & Tuffey, S. (1997). People helping people? Examining the social ties of athletes coping with burnout and injury stress. *Journal of Sport & Exercise Psychology, 19,* 368–395.

Ulett, G. A., & Peterson, D. B. (1965). *Applied hypnosis and positive suggestion.* St. Louis, MO: C. V. Mosby.

Ullrich-French, S., & Cox, A. (2009). Using cluster analysis to examine the combination of motivation regulations of physical education students. *Journal of Sport & Exercise Psychology, 31,* 358–379.

Ulrich, R. P. (1973). *The effect of hypnotic and non-hypnotic suggestions on archery performance.* Unpublished doctoral dissertation, University of Utah, Salt Lake City.

United States Olympic Committee. (1983). US Olympic Committee establishes guidelines for sport psychology services. *Journal of Sport Psychology, 5,* 4–7

Unkelbach, C., & Memmert, D. (2010). Crowd noise as a cue in referee decisions contributes to the home advantage. *Journal of Sport & Exercise Psychology, 32,* 483–498.

Uphill, M. A., & Jones, M. V. (2007). Antecedents of emotions in elite athletes: A cognitive motivational relational theory perspective. *Research Quarterly for Exercise and Sport, 78,* 79–89.

Utah's Drca Suspended. (2008, December 16). Utah's Drca suspended for 2 games by coach for tripping Oklahoma star. *Deseret News,* D2.

V

Vallance, J. K. H., Dunn, J. G. H., & Dunn, J. L. C. (2006). Perfectionism, anger, and situation criticality in competitive youth ice hockey. *Journal of Sport & Exercise Psychology, 28,* 383–406.

Vallerand, R. J. (1997). Toward a hierarchical model of intrinsic and extrinsic motivation. In M. P. Zanna (Ed.), *Advances in experimental and social psychology,* Vol. 29 (pp. 271–360). New York: Academic Press.

Vallerand, R. J., & Blanchard, C. M. (2000). The study of emotion in sport and exercise. In Y. L. Hanin (Ed.), *Emotions in sport* (pp. 3–38). Champaign, IL: Human Kinetics.

Vallerand, R. J., Blanchard, C. M., Mageau, G. A., Kostner, R., Ratelle, C., Le'onard, M., . . . Marsolais, J. (2003). Les passions de l'ame: On obsessive and harmonious passion. *Journal of Personality and Social Psychology, 85,* 756–767.

Vallerand, R. J., Colavecchio, P. G., & Pelletier, L. G. (1988). Psychological momentum and performance: A preliminary test of the antecedents-consequences psychological momentum model. *Journal of Sport & Exercise Psychology, 10,* 92–108.

Vallerand, R. J., & Losier, G. F. (1999). An integrative analysis of intrinsic and extrinsic motivation in sport. *Journal of Applied Sport Psychology, 11,* 142–169.

Vallerand, R. J., Mageau, G. A., Elliot, A. J., Dumais, A., Demers, M-A., & Rousseau, F. (2008). Passion and performance attainment in sport. *Psychology of Sport and Exercise, 9,* 373–392.

Vallerand, R. J., Rousseau, F. L., Grouzet, F. M. E., Dumais, A., Grenier, S., & Blanchard, C. M. (2006). Passion in sport: A look at determinants and affective experiences. *Journal of Sport & Exercise Psychology, 28,* 454–478.

Van Landuyt, L. M., Ekkekakis, P., Hall, E. E., & Petruzzello, S. J. (2000). Throwing the mountains into the lakes: On the perils of nomothetic conceptions of the exercise-affect relationship. *Journal of Sport & Exercise Psychology, 22,* 208–234.

Van Raalte, J. L., & Andersen, M. B. (2007). When sport psychology consulting is a means to an end(ing): Roles and agendas when helping athletes leave their sports. *The Sport Psychologist, 21,* 227–242.

Van Raalte, J. L., Brewer, B. W., Rivera, P. M., & Petitpas, A. S. (1994). The relationship between observable self-talk and competitive junior tennis players' match performances. *Journal of Sport & Exercise Psychology, 16,* 400–415.

Van Raalte, J. L., Cornelius, A. E., Brewer, B. W., & Hatten, S. J. (2000). The antecedents and consequences of self-talk in competitive tennis. *Journal of Sport & Exercise Psychology, 22,* 345–356.

Van Raalte, J. L., Cornelius, A. E., Linder, D. E., & Brewer, B. W. (2007). The relationship between hazing and team cohesion. *Journal of Sport Behavior, 30,* 491–507.

Van Raalte, J. L., Brown, T. D., Brewer, B. W., Avondoglio, J. B., Scherzer, C. B., & Hartmann W. M. (2000). An on-line survey of graduate course offerings satisfying AAASP certification criteria. *The Sport Psychologist, 14,* 98–104.

Van Yperen, N. W. (2009). Why some make it and others do not: Identifying psychological factors that predict career success in professional adult soccer. *The Sport Psychologist, 23,* 317–329.

Vandenberg, S., & Kuse, A. R. (1978). Mental rotations: A group of three-dimensional spatial visualization. *Perceptual and Motor Skills, 47,* 599–604.

Vansteenkiste, M., Simons, J., Soenens, B., & Lens, W. (2004). How to become a persevering exerciser? Providing a clear future intrinsic goal in an autonomy-supportive way. *Journal of Sport & Exercise Psychology, 26,* 232–249.

Van Vorst, J. G., Buckworth, J., & Mattern, C. (2002). Physical self-concept and strength changes in college weight training classes. *Research Quarterly for Exercise and Sport, 73,* 113–117.

Vanek, M., & Cratty, B. J. (1970). *Psychology and the superior athlete.* London: Macmillan.

Varca, P. E. (1980). An analysis of home and away game performance of male college basketball teams. *Journal of Sport Psychology, 2,* 245–257.

Vargas-Tonsing, T. M., Myers, N. D., & Feltz, D. L. (2004). Coaches' and athletes' perceptions of efficacy-enhancing techniques. *The Sport Psychologist, 18,* 397–414.

Vazou, S. (2010). Variations in the perceptions of peer and coach motivational climate. *Research Quarterly for Exercise and Sport, 81,* 199–211.

Vealey, R. S. (1986). Conceptualization of sport-confidence and competitive orientation: Preliminary investigation and instrument development. *Journal of Sport Psychology, 8,* 221–246.

Vealey, R. S. (1988). Sport-confidence and competitive orientation: An addendum on scoring procedures and gender differences. *Journal of Sport & Exercise Psychology, 10,* 471–478.

Vealey, R. S. (1994). Current status and prominent issues in sport psychology interventions. *Medicine and Science in Sport and Exercise, 26,* 495–502.

Vealey, R. S., Armstrong, L., Comar, W., & Greenleaf, C. A. (1998). Influence of perceived coaching behaviors on burnout and competitive anxiety in female collegiate athletes. *Journal of Applied Sport Psychology, 10,* 297–318.

Vealey, R. S., & Greenleaf, C. A. (2010). Seeing is believing: Understanding and using imagery in sport. In J. M. Williams (Ed.), *Applied sport psychology: Personal growth to peak performance* (pp. 267–304). Boston: McGraw-Hill.

Vealey, R. S., Hayashi, S. W., Garner-Holman, M., & Giacobbi, P. (1998). Sources of sports confidence: Conceptualization and instrument development. *Journal of Sport & Exercise Psychology, 20,* 54–80.

Vealey, R. S., Knight, B. J., & Pappas, G. (2002, November 2). *Self-confidence in sport: Conceptual and psychological advancement.* Paper presented at the annual convention of the Association for the Advancement of Applied Sport Psychology, Tucson, AZ.

Vecsey, G. (2004, March 11). Must crack down on threats. *The New York Times,* Retrieved from http://www.nytimes.com/2004/3/11/sports

Verducci, T. (2001, June 18). High-wire act. *Sports Illustrated, 94,* 82–96.

Verducci, T. (2003, March 31). The ultimate gamer. *Sports Illustrated, 98,* 70–81.

Verducci, T. (2007, December 24). Now what? *Sports Illustrated, 107,* 28–32.

Viseck, A., & Watson, J. (2008). Ice hockey players' legitimacy of aggression and professionalization of attitudes. *The Sport Psychologist, 19,* 178–192.

Visek, A. J., Maxwell, J. P., Watson, J. C., II., & Hurst, J. R. (2010). A cross-cultural evaluation of the factorial invariance of the Competitive Aggressiveness and Anger Scale. *Journal of Sport Behavior, 33,* 218–237.

Vlachopoulos, S., & Biddle, S. J. H. (1999). Modeling the relation of goal orientation to achievement-related affect in physical education: Does perceived ability matter? *Journal of Sport & Exercise Psychology, 19,* 169–187.

Voight, M., & Callaghan, J. (2001). The use of sport psychology services at NCAA Division I Universities from 1998–1999. *The Sport Psychologist, 15,* 91–102.

Volek, J. S. (1999, May/June). What we now know about creatine. *American College of Sport Medicine Health & Fitness Journal, 3,* 27–33.

Volkamer, N. (1972). Investigations into the aggressiveness in competitive social systems. *Sportwissenschaft, 1,* 33–64.

von Guenthner, S., Hammermeister, J., Burton, D., & Keller, L. (2010). Smoke and mirrors or wave of the future? Evaluating a mental skills training program for elite cross country skiers. *Journal of Sport Behavior, 33,* 3–24.

Von Rein, Patricia (2001, November 22). Weighing the issue. *Vocmagazine,* p. 4.

Vroom, V. H., & Yetton, P. W. (1973). *Leadership and decision making.* Pittsburgh: University of Pittsburgh Press.

W

Wadey, R., & Hanton, S. (2008). Basic psychological skills usage and competitive anxiety responses: Perceived underlying mechanisms. *Research Quarterly for Exercise and Sport, 79,* 363–373.

Wagman, D., & Khelifa, M. (1996). Psychological issues in sport injury rehabilitation: Current knowledge and practice. *Journal of Athletic Training, 13,* 257–261.

Wagner, G., Rabkin, J., & Rabkin, R. (1998). Exercise as a mediator of psychological and nutritional effects of testosterone therapy in HIV-positive men. *Medicine & Science in Sports & Exercise, 30,* 811–817.

Wahl, G. (2006, July 17). Surreal world. *Sports Illustrated, 105,* 48–50.

Wahl, G., Wertheim, L. J., & Dohrmann, G. (2001, September 10). Special report: Passion. *Sports Illustrated, 95,* 59–68.

Wakefield, C. J., & Smith, D. (2009). Impact of differing frequencies of PETTLEP imagery on netball shooting performance. *Journal of Imagery Research in Sport and Physical Activity, 4,* Article 7.

Waldron, J. J. (2007). Influence of involvement in the girls' self-perceptions. *Research Quarterly for Exercise and Sport, 78,* 520–530.

Walker, B. (1996, October 23). Yanks win on road. *Columbia Missourian,* p. B1.

Wallace, H. M., Baumeister, R. F., & Vohs, K. D. (2005). Audience support and choking under pressure: A home disadvantage? *Journal of Sports Sciences, 23,* 429–438.

Walling, M. D., Duda, J. L., & Chi, L. (1993). The perceived motivational climate in sport questionnaire: Construct and predictive validity. *Journal of Sport & Exercise Psychology, 15,* 172–183.

Walljasper, J. (2006, May 28). More than a one-track mind. *Columbia Daily Tribune,* 4B.

Walton, B. (2000, May 29). Basketball's tarnished Knight. *Time, 155*(22), 96.

Wang, C. K. J., & Biddle, S. J. H. (2001). Young people's motivational profiles in physical activity: A cluster analysis. *Journal of Sport & Exercise Psychology, 23,* 1–22.

Wang, C. K. J., Biddle, S. J. H., & Elliot, A. J. (2007). The 2×2 achievement goal framework in a physical education context. *Psychology of Sport & Exercise, 8,* 147–168.

Wang, C. K. J., Hagger, M., & Liu, W. C. (2009). A cross-cultural validation of perceived locus of causality scale in physical education context. *Research Quarterly for Exercise and Sport, 80,* 313–325.

Wang, J. C. K., Liu, W. C., Chatzisarantis, N. L. D., & Lim, C. B. S. (2010). Influence of perceived motivational climate achievement goals in physical education: A structural equation mixed modeling analysis. *Journal of Sport & Exercise Psychology, 32,* 324–338.

Wang, C. K. J., Lui, W. C., Lochbaum, M. R., & Stevenson, S. J. (2009). Sport ability beliefs, 2×2 achievement goals, and intrinsic motivation: The moderating role of perceived competence in sport and exercise. *Research Quarterly for Exercise and Sport, 80,* 303–312.

Wankel, L. M. (1972). An examination of illegal aggression in intercollegiate hockey. In I. D. Williams & L. M. Wankel (Eds.), *Proceedings of the Fourth Canadian Psychomotor Learning and Sport Psychology Symposium* (pp. 531–542). Waterloo, Ontario: University of Waterloo.

Wanlin, C. M., Hrycaiko, D. W., Martin, G. L., & Mahon, M. (1997). The effects of a goal setting package on the performance of speed skaters. *Journal of Applied Sport Psychology, 9,* 212–228.

Ward, D. G., & Cox, R. H. (2004). The Sport Grid-Revised as a measure of felt arousal and cognitive anxiety. *Journal of Sport Behavior, 27,* 93–113.

Ward, D. G., Sandstedt, S. D., Cox, R. H., & Beck, N. C. (2005). Athlete-counseling competencies for U.S. psychologists working with athletes. *The Sport Psychologists, 19,* 318–334.

Warriner, K., & Lavallee, D. (2008). The retirement experiences of elite female gymnasts: Self-identity and the physical self. *Journal of Applied Sport Psychology, 20,* 301–317.

Watson, D., Clark, L. A., & Tellegen, A. (1988). Development and validation of brief measures of positive and negative affect: The PANAS scales. *Journal of Personality and Social Psychology, 54,* 1063–1070.

Watson, N. J., & Nesti, M. (2005). The role of spirituality in sport psychology consulting: An analysis and integrative review of literature. *Journal of Applied Sport Psychology, 17,* 228–239.

Watt, A. P., Spittle, M., Jaakkola, T., & Morris, T. (2008). Adoptiing Paivio's general analytical framework to examine imagery use in sport. *Journal of Imagery Research in Sport and Physical Activity, 3,* Article 4.

Wegner, D. M. (1994). Ironic processes of mental control. *Psychological Review, 101,* 34–52.

Wegner, D. M. (1997). When the antidote is the poison: Ironic mental control processes. *Psychological Science, 8,* 148–150.

Wegner, D. M., Ansfield, M., & Pilloff, D. (1998). The putt and the pendulum: Ironic effects of the mental control of action. *Psychological Science, 9,* 196–199.

Weigand, D. A., & Broadhurst, C. J. (1998). The relationship among perceived competence, intrinsic motivation, and control perceptions in youth soccer. *International Journal of Sport Psychology, 29,* 324–338.

Weigand, D. A., & Burton, S. (2002). Manipulating achievement motivation in physical education by manipulating the motivational climate. *European Journal of Sport Science, 2*(1), 1–14.

Weinberg, R. (2008). Does imagery work? Effects on performance and mental skills. *Journal of Imagery Research in Sport and Physical Activity, 3,* 1–21.

Weinberg, R. S., Burke, K., & Jackson, A. (1997). Coaches and players' perceptions of goal setting in junior tennis: An exploratory investigation. *The Sport Psychologist, 11,* 426–439.

Weinberg, R. S., Burton, D., Yukelson, D., & Weigand, D. (1993). Goal setting in competitive sport: An exploratory investigation of practices of collegiate athletes. *The Sport Psychologist, 7,* 275–289.

Weinberg, R. S., Burton, D., Yukelson, D., & Weigand, D. (2000). Perceived goal setting practices of Olympic athletes: An exploratory investigation. *The Sport Psychologist, 14,* 279–295.

Weinberg, R. S., Butt, J., & Knight, B. (2001). High school coaches' perceptions of the process of goal setting. *The Sport Psychologist, 15,* 20–47.

Weinberg, R. S., Butt, J., Knight, B., & Perritt, N. (2001). Collegiate coaches' perceptions of their goal-setting practices: A qualitative investigation. *Journal of Applied Sport Psychology, 13,* 374–398.

Weinberg, R. S., & Comar, W. (1994). The effectiveness of psychological interventions in competitive sport. *Sports Medicine Journal, 18,* 406–418.

Weinberg, R. S., & Gould, D. (1999). *Foundations of sport and exercise psychology.* Champaign, IL: Human Kinetics.

Weinberg, R. S., & McDermott, M. (2002). A comparative analysis of sport and business organizations: Factors perceived critical for organizational stress. *Journal of Applied Sport Psychology, 14,* 282–298.

Weinberg, R. S., & Williams, J. M. (2010). Integrating and implementing a psychological skills training program. In J. M. Williams (Ed.), *Applied sport psychology: Personal growth to peak performance* (pp. 361–391). Boston: McGraw-Hill.

Weiss, M. R. (2008). "Field of dreams": Sport as a context for youth development. *Research Quarterly for Exercise and Sport, 79* 434–449.

Weiss, M. R., & Amorose, A. J. (2005). Children's self-perceptions in the physical domain: Between- and -within-age variability in level, accuracy, and sources of perceived competence. *Journal of Sport & Exercise Psychology, 27,* 226–244.

Weiss, M. R., & Fretwell, S. D. (2005). The parent–coach/child–athlete relationship in youth sport: Cordial, contentious, or conundrum? *Research Quarterly for Exercise and Sport, 76,* 286–305.

Weiss, M. R., & Horn, T. S. (1990). The relationship between children's accuracy estimates of their physical competence and achievement-related characteristics. *Research Quarterly for Exercise and Sport, 61,* 250–258.

Weiss, M. R., & Smith, A. L. (1999). Quality of youth sport friendships: Measurement development and validation. *Journal of Sport & Exercise Psychology, 21,* 145–166.

Weiss, W. M., & Weiss, M. R. (2003). Attraction- and entrapment-based commitment among competitive female gymnasts. *Journal of Sport & Exercise Psychology, 25,* 229–247.

Weiss, W. M., & Weiss, M. R. (2007). Sport commitment among competitive female gymnasts: A developmental perspective. *Research Quarterly for Exercise and Sport, 78,* 90–102.

Weitzenhoffer, A. M. (2000). *The practice of hypnotism.* New York: John Wiley & Sons.

Welch, A. S., Hulley, A., Beauchamp, M. (2010). Affect and self-efficacy responses during moderate intensity exercise among low-active women: The effect of cognitive appraisal. *Journal of Sport & Exercise Psychology, 32,* 154–175.

Welch, A. S., Hulley, A., Ferguson, C., & Beauchamp, M. R. (2007). Affective responses of inactive women to a maximal incremental exercise test: A test of the dual-mode model. *Psychology of Sport and Exercise, 8,* 401–423.

Welford, A. T. (1962). Arousal, channel-capacity, and decision. *Nature, 194,* 365–366.

Welford, A. T. (1965). Stress and achievement. *Australian Journal of Psychology, 17,* 1–9.

Welford, A. T. (1973). Stress and performance. *Ergonomics, 16,* 567–580.

Wertheim, L. J. (2003, April 7). Jolt of reality. *Sports Illustrated, 98,* 68–78.

Wertheim, L. J., & Epstein, D. (2008, March 17). Steroids in America Part 2: The Godfather. *Sports Illustrated, 108,* 38–43.

Whaley, D. E., & Haley, P. P. (2008). Creating community, assessing need: Preparing for a community physical activity intervention. *Research Quarterly for Exercise and Sport, 79,* 245–255.

Whaley, D. E., & Schrider, A. F. (2005). The process of adult exercise adherence: Self-perceptions and competence. *The Sport Psychologist, 19,* 148–163.

Whelan, J. P., & Meyers, A. W. (1998). An efficient measure of immediate mood state: The brief assessment of mood. Unpublished manuscript, University of Memphis.

White, R. (1959). Motivation reconsidered. The concept of competence. *Psychological Review, 66,* 297–323.

White, S., Duda, J., & Keller, M. (1998). The relationship between goal orientation and perceived purposes of sport among youth sport participants. *Journal of Sport Behavior, 21,* 474–483.

White, S. A., & Duda, J. L. (1994). The relationship of gender, level of sport involvement, and participation motivation to task and ego orientation. *International Journal of Sport Psychology, 25,* 4–18.

Whitmarsh, B. G., & Alderman, R. B. (1993). Role of psychological skills training in increasing pain tolerance. *The Sport Psychologist, 7,* 388–399.

Wickwire, T. L., Bloom, G. A., & Loughead, T. M. (2004). The environmental structure, and interaction process of elite same-sex dyadic sport teams. *The Sport Psychologist, 18,* 381–396.

Widman, G. (2005, February 25). Temple coach Cheney to take seat for rest of regular season. Retrieved from http://www.usatoday.com/2005/2/25

Widmeyer, W. N., Brawley, L. R., & Carron, A. V. (1985). *The measurement of cohesion in sport teams: The group environment questionnaire.* London, Ontario: Sports Dynamics.

Widmeyer, W. N., Brawley, L. R., & Carron, A. V. (1990). The effects of group size in sport. *Journal of Sport & Exercise Psychology, 12,* 177–190.

Widmeyer, W. N., Carron, A. V., & Brawley, L. R. (1993). Group cohesion in sport and exercise. In J. M. Williams (Ed.), *Applied sport psychology: Personal growth to peak performance* (pp. 672–692). Mountain View, CA: Mayfield.

Widmeyer, W. N., & McGuire, E. J. (1997). Frequency of competion and aggression in professional ice hockey. *International Journal of Sport Psychology, 28,* 57–66.

Widmeyer, W. N., & Williams, J. M. (1991). Predicting cohesion in coaching sport. *Small Group Research, 22,* 548–570.

Wiebush, J. (1971). *Lombardi.* Chicago: Follett Publishing Company, A National Football League Book.

Wiechman, S. A., Smith, R. E., Small, F. L., & Ptacek, J. T. (2000). Masking effects of social desirability response set on relations between psychosocial factors and sport injuries: A methodological note: *Journal of Science and Medicine in Sport, 3,* 194–202.

Wiersma, L. D. (2001). Conceptualization and development of the sources of enjoyment in youth sport questionnaire. *Measurement in Physical Education and Exercise Science, 5,* 153–177.

Wiersma, L. D., & Sherman, C. P. (2005). Volunteer youth sport coaches' perspectives of coaching education/certification and parental codes of conduct. *Research Quarterly for Exercise and Sport, 76,* 324–338.

Wiese-Bjornstal, D. M., Smith, A. M., & LaMott, E. E. (1995). A model of psychologic response to athletic injury and rehabilitation. *Athletic Training: Sports Health Care Perspectives, 1,* 17–30.

Wiese-Bjornstal, D. M., Smith, A. M., Shaffer, S. M., & Morrey, M. A. (1998). An integrated model of response to sport injury: Psychological and sociological dynamics. *Journal of Applied Sports Psychology, 10,* 46–70.

Wiggins, D. K. (1996). A history of highly competitive sport for American children. In F. L. Smoll & R. E. Smith (Eds.), *Children and youth in sport: A biopsychosocial perspective* (pp. 15–30). Madison, WI: Brown & Benchmark.

Wiggins, M. S. (1998). Anxiety intensity and direction: Preperformance temporal patterns and expectations in athletes. *Journal of Applied Sport Psychology, 10,* 201–211.

Wilcox, S., Sharpe, P. A., Hutto, B., & Granner, M. L. (2005). Psychometric properties of the Self-Efficacy for Exercise Questionnaire in a diverse sample of men and women. *Journal of Physical Activity and Health, 3,* 285–297.

Wilkinson, T., Pollard, R. (2006). A temporary decline in home advantage when moving to a new stadium. *Journal of Sport Behavior, 29,* 190–197.

Williams, A. M., & Elliot, D. (1999). Anxiety, expertise, and visual search strategy in karate. *Journal of Sport & Exercise Psychology, 21,* 362–375.

Williams, D. M. (2008). Exercise, affect, and adherence: An integrated model and a case for self-paced exercise. *Journal of Sport & Exercise Psychology, 30,* 471–496.

Williams, D. M., Anderson, E. S., & Winett, R. (2004). Social cognitive predictors of creative use versus non-use among male, undergraduate, recreational resistance trainers. *Journal of Sport Behavior, 27,* 170–183.

Williams, D. M., Dunsiger, S., Ciccolo, J. T., Lewis, B. A., Albrecht, A. E., & Marcus, B. H. (2008). Acute affective response to a moderate-intensity exercise stimulus predicts activity participation 6 and 12 months later. *Psychology of Sport and Exercise, 9,* 231–245.

Williams, J. M. (1980). Personality characteristics of the successful female athlete. In W. F. Straub (Ed.), *Sport psychology: An analysis of athlete behavior* (2nd ed., pp. 353–359). Ithaca, NY: Mouvement Publications.

Williams, J. M., & Andersen, M. B. (1998). Psychosocial antecedents of sport injury: Review and critique of the stress and injury model. *Journal of Applied Sport Psychology, 10,* 5–25.

Williams, J. M., Nideffer, R. M., & Wilson, V. E. (2010). Concentration and strategies for controlling it. In J. M. Williams (Ed.), *Applied sport psychology: Personal growth to peak performance.* Boston: McGraw-Hill.

Williams, J. M., & Scherzer, C. B. (2003). Tracking the training and careers of graduates of advanced degree programs in sport psychology, 1994 to 1999. *Journal of Applied Sport Psychology, 15,* 335–353.

Williams, J. M., Tonymon, P., & Andersen, M. B. (1991). The effects of stressors and coping resources on anxiety and peripheral narrowing. *Journal of Applied Sport Psychology, 3*(2), 126–141.

Williams, J. M., Zinsser, N., & Bunker, L. (2010). Cognitive techniques for building confidence and enhancing performance. In J. M. Williams (Ed.), *Applied sport psychology: Personal growth to peak performance* (pp. 305–335). Boston: McGraw-Hill.

Williams, L. (1998). Contextual influences and goal perspectives among female youth sport participants. *Research Quarterly for Sport and Exercise, 69,* 47–57.

Williams, L., & Desteno, D. (2008). Pride and perseverance: The motivational role of pride. *Journal of Personality and Social Psychology, 94,* 1007–1017.

Williams, L. R. T., & Parkin, W. A. (1980). Personality profiles of three hockey groups. *International Journal of Sport Psychology, 11,* 113–120.

Williams, M. H. (1998). *The ergogenics edge: Pushing the limits of sports performance.* Champaign, IL: Human Kinetics.

Williams, S. E., Cumming, J., & Balanos, G. M. (2010). The use of imagery to manipulate challenge and threat appraisal states in athletes. *Journal of Sport & Exercise Psychology, 32,* 339–358.

Wilson, K. A., Gilbert, J. N., Gilbert, W. D., & Sailor, S. R. (2009). College athletic directors' perceptions of sport psychology consulting. *The Sport Psychologist, 23,* 405–424.

Wilson, K. M., Hardy, L., & Harwood, C. G. (2006). Investigating the relationship between achievement goals and process goals in rugby Union players. *Journal of Applied Sport Psychology, 18,* 297–311.

Wilson, K. S., & Spink, K. S. (2009). Social influence and physical activity in older females: Does activity preference matter? *Psychology of Sport and Exercise, 10,* 481–488.

Wilson, M., Chattington, M., Marple-Horvat, D. E., & Smith, N. C. (2007). A comparison of self-focus versus attentional explanations of choking. *Journal of Sport & Exercise Psychology, 29,* 439–456.

Wilson, M., Smith, N. C., & Holmes, P. S. (2007). The role of effort in influencing the effect of anxiety on performance: Testing the conflicting prediction of processing efficacy theory and the conscious processing hypothesis. *British Journal of Psychology, 98,* 411–428.

Wilson, M., Vine, S. J., & Wood, G. (2009). The influence of anxiety on visual attention control in basketball free throw shooting. *Journal of Sport & Exercise Psychology, 31,* 152–168.

Wilson, M., Wood, G., & Vine, S. J. (2009). Anxiety, attentional control, and performance impairment in penalty kicks. *Journal of Sport & Exercise Psychology, 31,* 761–775.

Wilson, P. M., Rodgers, W. M., Fraser, S. N., & Murray, T. C. (2004). Relationships between exercise regulations and motivational consequences in university students. *Research Quarterly for Exercise and Sport, 75,* 81–91.

Wilson, P. M., Rodgers, W. T., Rodgers, W. M., & Wild, T. C. (2006). The Psychological Need Satisfaction in Exercise Scale. *Journal of Sport & Exercise Psychology, 28,* 231–251.

Wilson, P., & Eklund, R. C. (1998). The relationship between competitive anxiety and self-presentational concerns. *Journal of Sport & Exercise Psychology, 20,* 81–97.

Wilstein, S. (2004, November 21). Ugly sign of violent times. *Columbia Daily Tribune,* 10B.

Wininger, S. R. (2007). Self-determination theory and exercise behavior: An examination of the psychometric properties of the Exercise Motivation Scale. *Journal of Applied Sport Psychology, 19,* 471–486.

Wipfli, B. M., Rethorst, C. D., & Landers, D. M. (2008). The anxiolytic effects of exercise: A meta-analysis of randomized trials and dose-response analysis. *Journal of Sport & Exercise Psychology, 30,* 392–410.

Wippert, P.-M., & Wippert, J. (2008). Perceived stress and prevalence of traumatic stress symptoms following athletic career termination. *Journal of Clinical Sport Psychology, 2,* 1–16.

Wippert, P.-M., & Wippert, J. (2010). The effects of involuntary athletic career termination on psychological distress. *Journal of Clinical Sport Psychology, 4,* 133–149.

Wise, J. B. (2007). Testing a theory that explains how self-efficacy beliefs are formed: Predicting self-efficacy appraisals across recreational activities. *Journal of Social and Clinical Psychology, 26,* 841–848.

Wolke, D., & Sapouna, M. (2008). Big men feeling small: Childhood bullying experience, muscle dysmorphia and other mental health problems in bodybuilders. *Psychology of Sport and Exercise, 9,* 595–604.

Wolpe, J. (1958). *Psychotherapy by reciprocal inhibition.* Stanford, CA: Stanford University Press.

Woo, M., Kim, S., Kim, J., Petruzzello, S. J., & Hatfield, B. D. (2010). The influence of exercise intensity on frontal electroencephalographic asymmetry and self-reported affect. *Research Quarterly for Exercise and Sport, 81,* 349–359.

Woodman, T., & Davis, P. A. (2008). The role of repression in the incidence of ironic errors. *The Sport Psychologist, 22,* 183–196.

Woodman, T., & Hardy, L. (2003). The relative impact of cognitive anxiety and self-confidence upon sport performances: A meta-analysis. *Journal of Sport Sciences, 21,* 443–457.

Woodman, T., Cazenave, N., & Le Scanff, C. (2008). Skydiving as emotion regulation: The rise and fall of anxiety is moderated by alexithymia. *Journal of Sport & Exercise Psychology, 30,* 424–433.

Woodman, T., Davis, P. A., Hardy, L., Callow, N., Glasscock, I., Yuill-Proctor, J. (2009). Emotions and sport performance: An exploration of happiness, hope and anger. *Journal of Sport & Exercise Psychology, 31,* 169–188.

Wrisberg, C. A. (1990). An interview with Pat Head Summitt. *The Sport Psychologist, 4,* 180–191.

Wrisberg, C. A., & Anshel, M. H. (1989). The effect of cognitive strategies on the free throw shooting performance of young athletes. *The Sport Psychologist, 3,* 95–104.

Wrisberg, C. A., & Pein, R. L. (1992). The preshot interval and free throw shooting accuracy: An exploratory investigation. *The Sport Psychologist, 6,* 14–23.

Wrisberg, C. A., Simpson, D., Loberg, L. A., Withycombe, J. L., & Reed, A. (2009). NCAA Division-I student-athletes' receptivity to mental skills training by sport psychology consultants. *The Sport Psychologist, 23,* 470–486.

Wulf, G. (2008). Attentional focus effects in balance acrobats. *Research Quarterly for Exercise and Sport, 79,* 319–325.

Wulf, G., & Prinz, W. (2001). Directing attention to movement effects enhances learning: A review. *Psychometric Bulletin & Review, 8,* 648–660.

Wulf, G., & Su, J. (2007). An external focus of attention enhances golf shot accuracy in beginners and experts. *Research Quarterly for Exercise and Sport, 78,* 384–389.

Wulf, G., Tollner, T., & Shea, C. H. (2007). Attentional focus effects as a function of task difficulty. *Research Quarterly for Exercise and Sport, 78,* 257–264.

Y

Yannis, T. (1994). Planned behavior, attitude strength, role identity, and the prediction of exercise behavior. *The Sport Psychologist, 8,* 149–165.

Yates, A. (1987). Eating disorders and long distance running: The ascetic condition. *Integrated Psychiatry, 5,* 201–204.

Yates, A. (1991). *Compulsive exercise and eating disorders: Toward an integrated theory of activity.* New York: Brunner/Mazel.

Yerkes, R. M., & Dodson, J. D. (1908). The relationship of strength of stimulus to rapidity of habit formation. *Journal of Comparative Neurology and Psychology, 18,* 459–482.

Young, J. A., Pain, M. D., & Pearce, A. J. (2007). Experiences of Australian professional female tennis players returning to competition from injury. *British Journal of Sports Medicine, 41,* 806–811.

Yukelson, D. (1997). Principles of effective team building interventions in sport: A direct services approach at Penn State University. *Journal of Applied Sport Psychology, 9,* 73–96.

Yukelson, D. P. (2010). Communicating effectively. In J. M. Williams (Ed.), *Applied sport psychology: Personal growth to peak performance* (pp. 149–165). Boston: McGraw-Hill.

Yukelson, D., Weinberg, R., & Jackson, A. (1984). A multidimenisional group cohesion instrument for intercollegiate basketball teams. *Journal of Sport Psychology, 6,* 103–117.

Z

Zaichkowsky, L. D, & Fuchs, C. (1988). Biofeedback applications in exercise and athletic performance. *Exercise and Sport Science Reviews, 16,* 381–421.

Zajonc, R. B. (1965). Social facilitation. *Science, 149,* 269–274.

Zentgraf, K., & Munzert, J. (2009). Effects of attentional-focus instructions on movement mechanics. *Psychology of Sport and Exercise, 10,* 520–525.

Zervas, Y., & Kakkos, V. (1995). The effect of visuomotor behavior rehearsal on shooting performance of beginning archers. *International Journal of Sport Psychology, 26,* 337–347.

Zervas, Y., Stavrou, N. A., & Psychountaki, M. (2007). Development and validation of the Self-Talk Questionnaire (S–TQ) for sports. *Journal of Applied Sport Psychology, 19,* 142–159.

Zhang, J., Jensen, B. E., & Mann, B. L. (1997). Modification and revision of the leadership scale for sport. *Journal of Sport Behavior, 20,* 105–122.

Ziegler, S. G., Klinzing, J., & Williamson, K. (1982). The effects of two stress management training programs on cardiorespiratory efficiency. *Journal of Sport Psychology, 4,* 280–289.

Zimmer, C. (2010, March). The brain. *Discover Magazine,* 28–29.

Zinsser, N., Bunker, L., & Williams, J. M. (2010). Cognitive techniques for building confidence and enhancing performance. In J. M. Williams (Ed.), *Applied sport psychology personal growth to peak performance* (pp. 305–335). Champaign, IL: Human Kinetics.

Zizi, S. J., Keeler, L. A., & Watson, J. C., II. (2006). The interaction of goal orientation and stage of change on exercise behavior in college students. *Journal of Sport Behavior, 29,* 96–110.

Zizzi, S. J., Deaner, H. R., & Hirschhorn, D. K. (2003). The relationship between emotional intelligence and performance. *Journal of Applied Sport Psychology, 15,* 262–269.

Zourbanos, N., Hatzigeorgiadis, A., Chroni, S., Theodorakis, Y., & Papaioannou, A. (2009). Automatic Self-Talk Questionnaire for Sports (ASTQS): Development and preliminary validation of a measure identifying the structure of athletes' self-talk. *The Sport Psychologist, 23,* 233–251.

Photo Credits

CO 1: Royalty-Free/Corbis;

CO 2: © David Pu'u/Corbis;

CO 3: age fotostock;

CO 4: Courtesy Kansas State University Sports Information;

CO 5: Ryan McVay/Getty Images;

CO 6: Rubberball/Getty Images;

CO 7: Eyewire/Getty Images;

CO 8: Jeff Maloney/Getty Images;

CO 9: Courtesy University of Missouri-Columbia Sports Information;

CO 10: PhotoLink/Getty Images;

CO 11: Ryan McVay/Getty Images;

CO 12: © Royalty-Free/Corbis;

CO 13: Digital Vision/Getty Images;

CO 14: PhotoLink/Getty Images;

CO 15: Courtesy University of Missouri-Columbia Sports Information;

CO 16: Corbis Premium RF/Alamy;

CO 17: Royalty-Free/Corbis;

CO 18: Russel Illig/Getty Images;

CO 19: Steve Cole/Getty Images.

Subject Index

A

Abdominal breathing, 228
Accreditation, 12–13
Acculturation, 14
Achievement goal orientation, 81
Achievement Goal Scale (AGS), 84
Achievement Goal Scale for Youth Sport (AGSYS), 85
Achievement Goals Questionnaire for Sport (AGQ-S), 84
Achievement motivation, 80
Achievement situation, 60
Acquired immune deficiency syndrome, 431–432
Action-focused coping strategies, 216
Action-oriented goals, 252
Activation-Deactivation Checklist (AD-ACL), 162
Active coping, 159
Activity anorexia, 478
Actual leader behavior, 383
Acute exercise, 404–405
Acute pain, 452
Adaptive cluster, 114
Adaptive motivational patterns, 89
Addiction to exercise, 472
Additive principle, 72
Adherence to injury rehabilitation, 449
Aerobic exercise, 404–406
Affect, 155
Affect Grid, 162, 193
Affirmation statements, 225
Aggression, 324–340. *See also* Violence
  versus assertiveness, 327–328
  catharsis effect, 333
  defined, 326–328
  effect on performance, 335
  frustration-aggression theory, 330
  hostile, 327–328
  instinct theory, 329
  instrumental, 327–328
  kinds of, 327
  measurement of, 333–334
  moral reasoning theory, 330–333
  readiness for, 330
  reducing, 337–338
  situational factors, 335–337
  social learning theory, 25, 329–330
  theories of, 328–333
  in youth sports, 105–106

Aggression Inventory, 333
Aggression Questionnaire, 333
AIDS, 431–432
Alexithymia, 163
Alternative identity, 485
American Alliance for Health, Physical Education, Recreation, and Dance (AAHPERD), 9
American College of Sports Medicine (ACSM), 10, 430, 468
American Heart Association, 403
American Psychological Association (APA), 10
American Sport Education Program (ASEP), 109
Amine hypothesis, 413
Amotivation, 66
Anabolic-androgenic steroids, 463–468
Anabolic effect, 465
Anaerobic exercise, 404
Androgenic effect, 465
Androstenedione, 465
Anorexia analogue hypothesis, 478
Anorexia athletica, 475–476
Anorexia nervosa, 475
Antecedents, 159–160
Antecedents-consequences model, 57
Anticipatory skill, 135
Antisocial behavior, 89
Anxiety, 154–182. *See also* Stress
  antecedents, 159–160
  arousal (*See* Arousal)
  catastrophe theory, 185–189
  cognitive, 157, 185–189, 200
  competitive state, 159
  defined, 155
  directionality theory, 198–202
  effects of, 155
  IZOF theory, 189–200
  measurement of, 160–162
  mood state (*See* Mood state)
  multidimensional nature of, 156–157
  multidimensional theory, 157, 161–162, 184–185
  perfectionism and, 164–166
  precompetitive state, 159, 162–163, 200
  psychological pressure, 141–143
  reversal theory, 202–206
  signs of, 160–161

social physique, 416–417, 432–434
somatic, 157, 185, 188
state, 157–160, 167, 189–191
versus stress/emotion/mood, 155–156
trait, 157
in youth sports, 53, 104–105
Anxiety management training (AMT), 282
Anxiety Rating Scale, 162
Anxiety/stress spiral, 227
Anxiolytic, 404
Appearance impression motivation (AIM), 433
Applied attention, 125
Applied model of imagery in sport, 278
Applied sport psychology, 6, 13
Approach style of coping, 216–217
Apter's reversal theory, 202–206
Archival data, 345
Arizona State University Observation Instrument, 387
Arousal. *See also* Anxiety
  attention and, 145
  catastrophe theory, 185–189
  directionality theory, 198–202
  drive theory, 167, 172–173, 342
  emotional, 51
  flow, 195–198, 302
  inverted-U theory, 167–172
  performance and, 167–173
  physiological, 51, 185–189
Arousal energizing strategies, 236–241
Assertiveness, 327–328
Assertiveness training, 393
Association for Applied Sport Psychology (AASP), 9, 11, 12–13, 307–308, 311
Association for the Advancement of Applied Sport Psychology (AAASP), 9
Associators, 147–148
Athlete Burnout Questionnaire, 486
Athlete-centered sport model, 302
Athletes, *versus* nonathletes, 33–34
Athletic Aggression Inventory, 333
Athletic Coping Skills Inventory (ACSI-28), 306
Athletic engagement, 198
Athletic identity, 450
Athletic Identity Measurement Scale (AIMS), 450
Athletic Motivation Inventory (AMI), 7, 30–31, 299
Athletic pyramid, 37–38